DELHI

DEVELOPMENT REPORT

सत्यमेव जयते

PLANNING COMMISSION

GOVERNMENT OF INDIA

Delhi Development Report

सत्यमेव जयते

PLANNING COMMISSION
GOVERNMENT OF INDIA
NEW DELHI

Published by

ACADEMIC FOUNDATION
NEW DELHI

First Published in 2009 by
Academic Foundation
4772-73 / 23 Bharat Ram Road, (23 Ansari Road), Darya Ganj, New Delhi - 110 002 (India).
Phones : 23245001 / 02 / 03 / 04. Fax : +91-11-23245005. E-mail : academic@vsnl.com
www.academicfoundation.com

Published under arrangement with :
Planning Commission,
Government of India,
New Delhi.

Cataloging in Publication Data--DK
Courtesy: D.K. Agencies (P) Ltd. <docinfo@dkagencies.com>

Delhi development report / Planning Commission,
Government of India.
p. cm.
Includes bibliographical references.
ISBN 13: 9788171887194
ISBN 10: 8171887198

1. Human services--India--Delhi. 2. Economic development--India--Delhi. 3. Delhi (India)--Economic policy. 4. Infrastructure (Economics)--India--Delhi. 5. Urbanization--India--Delhi. I. India. Planning Commission.

DDC 338.954 22

Designed and typeset by Italics India, New Delhi
Printed and bound in India.

Core Committee

Prof. V.L. Chopra — **Chairman**
Member
Planning Commission

Shri A.N.P. Sinha — **Member**
Principal Adviser (SP/PC/ Education)
Planning Commission

Shri Rakesh Mehta — **Member**
Chief Secretary, Govt. of NCT Delhi

Dr. Sharad Pant — **Member Secretary**
Dy. Adviser (SP)
Planning Commission

Representative of Partner Institutions

1. M/s. MG School of Communications Management, New Delhi (Coordinator)
2. Institute of Human Development, New Delhi
3. Indian Council of Agriculture Research, New Delhi
4. Institute of Applied Manpower Research, New Delhi
5. Indian Council of Forestry Research & Education, Dehradun
6. Wildlife Institute of India, Dehradun
7. National Council of Applied Economic Research, New Delhi
8. Water & Power Consultancy Services (India) Ltd., New Delhi
9. Voluntary Health Association of India, New Delhi

Partner Agencies and Project Team

M.G. School of Communications Management

Mr. Vinay Shankar (Project Leader and Editor)
Mr. Neeraj Daftuar
Mr. Baikunth Behari
Mr. T.N. Srivastava
Dr. Dilip Biswas
Mr. Jagdish Sagar
Mr. K.P. Singh
Dr. Ashok Jain
Mr. P.S. Saran
Mr. R.P. Sharma
Mr. J. Sanyal

Water and Power Consultancy Services Ltd.

Mr. R.K. Aggarwal
Mr. V.K. Mathur
Mr. M.A. Khan

Indian Council of Forest Research and Education, Dehradun

Mr. S.S. Negi
Mr. A.S. Rawat

Wildlife Institute of India, Dehradun

Dr. V.B. Mathur
Dr. Ashish David

Institute of Human Development

Dr. Vandana Parashar
Dr. Anuradha De
Dr. Preet Rastogi
Dr. T. Ravi

Voluntary Health Association of India

Dr. P.C. Bhatnagar

Institute of Applied Manpower Research

Ms. Madhu Srivastava
Mr. M.C. Verma

एम. एस. आहलुवालिया
MONTEK SINGH AHLUWALIA

सत्यमेव जयते

उपाध्यक्ष
योजना आयोग
भारत
DEPUTY CHAIRMAN
PLANNING COMMISSION
INDIA

MESSAGE

An important Tenth Plan initiative of the Planning Commission was to sponsor preparation of the State Development Reports. Much of the work done for this assignment was given to national level institutes. This exercise was undertaken in recognition of the fact that economic circumstances and performance of individual States varied and it was necessary to examine development challenges for individual states in the light of State specific constraints. The basic idea is to produce quality reference documents on development profiles of individual States and the possible strategies for accelerating growth, and reducing poverty and inequality.

The Delhi Development Report reviews the experience of NCT Delhi and highlights issues critical for the State's development in the years ahead. I hope its publication will stimulate debate on the growth strategies appropriate for NCT Delhi. I am sure the roadmap indicated in the report will stimulate broader awareness of the critical policy issues facing the State, and assist the State to move to a higher growth path and achieve all round human and economic development.

The Planning Commission's endeavour will be rewarded if the report helps the State to achieve a higher rate of growth with an equitable distribution of the resulting benefits to the people of NCT Delhi.

(M.S. AHLUWALIA)

योजना भवन, संसद मार्ग, नई दिल्ली–110001 दूरभाष : 23096677, 23096688 फैक्स : 23096699
Yojana Bhawan, Parliament Street, New Delhi : 110001 Phones: 23096677, 23096688 Fax : 23096699, E-mail : dch@yojana.nic.in

SHEILA DIKSHIT
CHIEF MINISTER

GOVT. OF NATIONAL CAPITAL TERRITORY OF DELHI
DELHI SECRETARIAT, I.P. ESTATE, NEW DELHI-110002

FOREWORD

Delhi Development Report is the latest in their series of SDRs prepared by Planning Commission. It gives me great pleasure to acknowledge the role of Planning Commission as philosopher, friend and guide on developmental issues. I hope the Delhi Development Report will help to enhance this relationship.

Government of Delhi is committed towards making Delhi a world-class city having development with a human face. While bringing out Delhi's first Human Development Report, a set of Delhi Development Goals were drawn up, implementation of which, we believe, will facilitate inclusive growth in Delhi. Towards this end, we will also use the Delhi Development Report.

The Government of Delhi's association with the Planning Commission towards preparation of Delhi Development Report was in the form of a Core Committee wherein Delhi was a member. I understand that the workshop held last year, to give final touches to the Delhi Development Report, was a fruitful one where officials of Government of Delhi participated in large numbers and also gave qualitative inputs.

We, in the Government of Delhi look forward to this Delhi Development Report for helping all concerned in understanding the status of different sectors of development and taking up follow up action for all round development of Delhi.

(SHEILA DIKSHIT)

PHONE: OFF. 23392020, 23392030 • FAX: 23392111

प्रो. वी. एल. चोपड़ा
PROF. V. L. CHOPRA

सत्यमेव जयते

सदस्य
योजना आयोग
योजना भवन
नई दिल्ली–११० ००१
MEMBER
PLANNING COMMISSION
YOJANA BHAWAN
NEW DELHI-110 001

MESSAGE

To meet the requirements of the Central Plan Scheme "50th Year Initiative for Planning", the Planning Commission has launched preparation of Development Report of each State of the Indian Union. These SDRs attempt to compile quality reference documents on the profile and strategy of the State for accelerating the pace of development. These reports will be helpful to both the Centre and State machineries engaged in steering the plan process of the State on a higher and equitable growth path.

The NCT Delhi Development Report has been prepared by the Planning Commission with the assistance of M.G. School of Communications Management (MGSCM), New Delhi. A core committee identified and reviewed the dimensions of various developmental issues and helped to chart out the scope and coverage of State Development Report for NCT Delhi. The efforts made by MGSCM in coordinating and preparing the final report deserve to be specially noted.

This report will be an important value document and will impart value for development practitioners interested in the State and act as a road map for accelerated growth in the future.

I am thankful to the Govt. of NCT Delhi for their sustained support and cooperation to the team members in preparing this report. The efforts invested by the State Plan Adviser, and the officers of the State Plan Division in liaising with the State Government agencies are appreciated.

(V. L. CHOPRA)

दूरभाष : 23096708 टेलीफैक्स : 23096586
Phone: 23096708 Telefax : 23096586, e-mail : vl.chopra@yojana.nic.in

ए.एन.पी. सिन्हा, भा.प्र.से.
A.N.P. SINHA, IAS

प्रधान सलाहकार
भारत सरकार
योजना आयोग
Principal Adviser
Government of India
Planning Commission
New Delhi-110 001
Telphone: 011-23096610
Fax: 23096584
E-mail: anp.sinha@nic.in

INTRODUCTION

The State Development Report has to be seen in the context of planning process. The Eleventh Plan for Delhi is of special significance since Commonwealth Games to be held in 2010 provides an opportunity for making Delhi a World Class City. The Challenge is greater since multiplicity of agencies are responsible for its development. These agencies have to evolve a common vision and harmonious plan of action for sensitive convergence and synergy in efforts so that the identified plans and projects are synchronised and completed in time. Moreover, developmental efforts should benefit all citizens, rich or poor, and make Delhi an inclusive city.

2. In this context, the City Development Plan (CDP) of Delhi also deserves a mention. The CDP facilitates identification of projects within the framework of Master Plan for Delhi 2021. It contains a vision for development and strategies focused on Growth and Management of Urban Infrastructure and Basic Services for the Urban Poor, Reliable and Affordable Transport, Safeguarding of City Environment, Protection of Heritage Areas, Preservation of Water Bodies, Redevelopment of Inner City Areas, etc. Projects worth Rs.53,166 crore have been identified which include short term (2007-12) Rs.24,140 crore, medium term (2012-17) Rs.15,721 crore and long term (2017-21) Rs. I3,305 crore.

3. Resources are no longer a problem for the State. Its Annual Plan size has increased from Rs. 5200 cr in 2006-07 to Rs. 9000 cr in 2007-08 and further to Rs. 10,000 cr in 2008-09. The 11th Plan outlay is projected at about Rs. 55,000 cr as against the 10th Plan expenditure of about Rs. 23,000 cr. In fact, its resource potential permits a more ambitious Plan. Further, the scope for PPP in leveraging private investments in Delhi is very large. However, the administrative machinery has to be geared and procedures streamlined for absorption of such magnitude of resources.

4. The Development Plan of Delhi has to focus on Development of Yamuna River Front to global excellence including Rejuvenation of River, Expeditious completion of Renuka Dam in HP for drinking water and self-cleaning velocity of water in Yamuna, Ensuring Adequate Power, Efficient and Integrated Multi Modal Transport System, Treatment and Recycling of Waste Water, Cleaning & Greening of drains, Developing Delhi as a Knowledge Hub etc. Modern Land and Property

management using GIS, earmarking adequate land for public purposes/projects also need urgent attention. Implementation of reforms identified under JNNURM is an imperative which would make the city sustainable and competitive.

5. We need to put in place the Yamuna Development Authority which is autonomous, creative and empowered and can engage internationally reputed professional to prepare a Master Plan to build modern Delhi around the Yamuna which is ecologically and financially viable and sustainable.

6. Attaining the monitorable targets identified for the 11th Plan such as Infant Mortality Rate, Maternal Mortality Rate, Malnutrition among Children, Anaemia among Women, Sex ratio, Dropout Rate in Elementary Education, etc. would need gearing up Government machinery and focused strategies.

7. Much concern has been expressed about the low sex ratio: 838 for Delhi in the age group of 0-6 as against the National Average of 927. Delhi Government has already launched some major initiatives. But Delhi needs to take bigger measures in a Mission Mode, so that the target of 890 for the Eleventh Plan is exceeded. In fact Delhi should become a model for other States with low sex ratio.

8. Delhi is a historical city whose remnants are spread right from Mehrauli to Shahjahanabad. Accordingly, policies, strategies and appropriate action plans need to be prepared by all agencies to conserve and develop the civic and urban heritage, architecturally significant landmarks, living monuments, memorials and historical gardens, city wall, gates, bridges, vistas, public places, edicts and the ridge.

9. For making Delhi, the Nation Capital, an inclusive city, where people from all over the country are drawn, suitable policy and plans are required. The chronic issue of unauthorised colonies also need to be addressed in a sustainable manner.

10. The NCR Planning Board has played a significant role in development of infrastructure in the National Capital Region by promoting projects of regional importance covering a wide spectrum—roads, water supply, power, sewerage, solid waste disposal; land development etc. The Board, however, has to play a much bigger and vital role in the development of NCR as a Region of a global excellence since Delhi & NCR are inter-dependant and need to be developed as an integrated organic entity. Early completion of East and West Expressways, Integrated Multi Model Transport System (covering Road, Rail, Metro), planned development of townships and facilities etc. need urgent attention.

11. Lastly, Mughals built Old Delhi and Britishers built Lutyen's Delhi. Let us build a Delhi of 21st Century.

A.N.P. Sinha
Pr. Adviser,
Planning Commission

Acknowledgements

Preparation of State Development Report for the States of India in line with World Development Report is a unique idea which was not only conceived by the Planning Commission but also given concrete shape by them through liberal funding. This report analyses the status of various sectors of the economy, the trend of development, resource endowment and presents a detailed profile of the leading sectors of the economy. On the basis of the identified goals the Report also attempts to set out policy actions and a vision to achieve the desired outcomes.

We are extremely grateful to Dr. V.L. Chopra, Member, Planning Commission and Chairman of the Core Committee for providing valuable suggestions at every review meeting. We sincerely record our deep sense of gratitude to Shri A.N.P. Sinha, Principal Adviser, Planning Commission for his support, valuable guidance and suggestions.

The report has also greatly benefited from the comments of the Chief Secretary and Principal Secretary /Secretaries of the respective departments of the Government of NCT of Delhi during the final workshop organised on July 11, 2007 in Delhi. We are thankful to Shri Harish Chandra, Dr. Sharad Pant and a number of officers from the Planning Commission for organising the workshop and enabling us to benefit from the valuable discussions. We are also grateful for the comments and feedback obtained from the numerous participants including academicians, professionals and government officials at the workshop.

We are also thankful to the members of partner institutions who have been very cooperative in coordination of this study and provided rich information and valuable recommendation in their respective chapters.

We also take this opportunity to thank Shri Harish Chandra, Adviser, Shri J.P. Vijay, Director and various officials of Planning Commission, Dr. B.K. Sharma, Director, Shri Deepak Sen Gupta, Joint Director, and various officials of Government of NCT of Delhi for their unstinted help and cooperation.

In the course of preparation of the report generous help and assistance were rendered by a large number of people, both at official and non-official level, and we thank all of them for their help.

Vinay Shankar

(Project Leader)

Contents

List of Tables, Figures and Annexures

Tables

Figures

Annexures

DELHI DEVELOPMENT REPORT
PLANNING COMMISSION
GOVERNMENT OF INDIA

Executive Summary

1. Profile of Delhi

Delhi, located in an area which is agriculturally very fertile, has developed, in the northern part of the country, as the biggest market for agricultural as well as other goods. It is a historical city and has numerous architectural monuments of ages down its history. Its service sector has grown very fast. It is the capital of the largest democracy of the world. People from all parts of the country reside here and it has an international community in the foreign missions. It is thus a very cosmopolitan place where people may feel comfortable irrespective of their background—religious, social, cultural, and economic.

1.1 Rapid Growth

Delhi attracts people for work, trade and commerce, tourism, education etc., from all over the country, especially from the neighbouring states. Delhi has become the most densely populated city with a population density of 9224 per sq. km. compared to an average all-India density of 324. The area under agriculture has been reducing at a very high rate because of rapidly growing population caused by huge immigration from all over the country, especially the states to the east of Delhi and even from Bangladesh. As the discussion in Chapters 1 and 2, dealing with Profile of the State and Economy and Fiscal Management shows, the growth of the economy of Delhi has been rapid and places Delhi in the category of the developed states. But it must not be forgotten that wide disparities are reflected in the social and economic status of the population with many layers having differential access to facilities in the areas of health, education, housing, transport etc. There is scope for improvement in almost every sector. Simultaneously, the high rate of immigration and the rapid economic growth seem to have led Delhi to the limits of the "Carrying Capacity" when viewed from the point of view of resources such as land and infrastructure.

1.2 Status of Delhi

Because of its unique position and the requirements of the various roles that it has to perform, Delhi has been given the status of a Union Territory. In order to satisfy the democratic aspiration of self governance, striking a balance, it has been provided with an elected legislature and a government headed by a Chief Minister. Thus, while National Capital Territory of Delhi (NCTD) has very many features of a State it is not a State and its powers are curtailed, in relation to a normal State, as mentioned below:

1.2.1 "Law and Order" and "land" are within the jurisdiction of the Government of India. Accordingly, NCTD has no power to make laws relating to public order, police and offences and those relating to land.

1.2.2 Even in respect of other subjects the Parliament has overriding powers to make laws.

1.2.3 The Lt. Governor is a powerful institution and ensures that the governance runs smoothly.

1.2.4 The advice of the Council of Ministers to the Lieutenant Governor is not binding.

1.2.5 A Bill of Amendment relating to financial matters shall not be introduced in the Assembly except on the recommendations of the Lt. Governor.

1.2.6 The annual budget is to be laid before the Legislative Assembly by the Lt. Governor with the previous sanction of the President.

1.3 Multiplicity of Public Agencies

The MCD covers a very large proportion of the area of Delhi. It is an elected and a very powerful body and performs all civic functions. The area where the Government of India is housed is covered by the NDMC. Cantonment Board is responsible for the remainder. Delhi Development Authority is responsible for the planned development of Delhi and exercises influential voice in land use and development of housing. Apart from DDA, Central Government Departments too perform a number of functions. Thus there is the Government of India, the Government of NCTD, the Municipal Corporation of Delhi, the New Delhi Municipal Committee, the Cantonment Board, the Delhi Development Authority and other agencies under the Government of India and the Government of NCTD all working within the same geographical area. They are all very powerful legal entities. Frequently, situations arise in which, it seems, a function/ task is to be performed by more than one agency. Moreover, developmental activities need inputs from many of these bodies that are independent. The public agencies operating in the NCTD find themselves seriously constrained in implementing their programmes/projects as consultation with and concurrence of a large number of bodies becomes unavoidable. The citizen is confused about the agency that should be approached for a particular service or grievance. It also enables the agencies to pass the buck to other agencies for failure or inefficient or ineffective implementation of programmes.

1.4 Delhi: One of the Finest Cities of the Country

Despite the unique character of Delhi and limitations as mentioned above in this chapter, Delhi has been developing in to one of the finest cities in the country. The parameters briefly discussed below corroborate this view.

1.4.1 It is a cosmopolitan city and provides equality of opportunity to people irrespective of social, regional and religious differences and, therefore, attracts people from all over the country because of the opportunities that this city offers in the field of education, health, employment and enterprise etc.

1.4.2 The growth of population is so rapid that despite the availability of land, which appeared plentiful soon after Independence when the expansion phase began, looks too inadequate now and the city's infrastructure is unable to keep pace with its expanding population.

1.4.3 Delhi has a developed economy with services sector being dominant, the secondary sector way behind and agricultural being negligible. It had the second highest per capita NSDP at Rs. 48974 in 2001-02 and a very low poverty ratio. However, wide disparities are reflected in the social and economic status of the population with many layers having differential access to various facilities.

1.4.4 In the sphere of education it has a high literacy rate and the standards of higher education are believed by many to be the best in the country. It ranks not higher than fourth among the States in the matter of literacy mainly because of continuous migration of the poor in search of employment from all parts of the country.

1.4.5 Of the metropolitan towns, Delhi has the least percentage of its population living in slums.

1.4.6 Delhi has initiated measures to deal with the problem of transport and the Metro Rail project has started making its impact felt.

1.4.7 The over all birth rate in Delhi is substantially lower than the national average and the life expectancy at birth is 68.6 years against the national average of 60.7 years.

1.4.8 It is a green city having 12.5 trees per ha, as against the national average of 12.

1.4.9 Being a service industry centric city, the labour relations in Delhi are harmonious.

2. Fiscal and Financial Management

2.1 Areas of concern are the rising debt burden and the consequent fiscal deficit. Tax-GSDP ratio has to be improved. For this, mounting tax arrears have to be reduced, and it has to be ensured that there is no further addition to these arrears in future.

2.2 Despite the Union Government and local bodies taking the responsibilities of activities on which other states are required to spend their resources, the revenue expenditure of NCT has been steadily increasing in recent years.

2.3 The NCT of Delhi has been consistently having surplus on revenue account. But, its fiscal deficit has also been consistently going up, being 2.91 per cent of GSDP in 2003-04 against a low of 1.39 per cent in 1997-98.

2.4 Public debt of the NCT has been growing—from 2.42 per cent at the end of March 1995 to 17.08 per cent of the GSDP at the end of March 2004. The NCT borrows from the Central government and gives loans to its own public sector undertakings and other bodies. It is a net creditor, unlike many states.

2.5 The various bodies getting funds are defaulting on repayment. Since some of these are providing essential social and economic services, these cannot be closed down but have to be supported until some viable alternative is found. This is a matter of concern.

3. Urban Development

3.1 A number of features of the National Capital Territory of Delhi are unique in that it is almost entirely urbanised. Substantial population lives in the unplanned clusters, and unauthorised colonies. The majority of Delhi population is immigrant and employment in the primary sector including agriculture and mining has dwindled to negligible levels.

3.2 In 2004 only 23.6 per cent of the population was living in planned colonies, 64.5 per cent in *Jhuggi* and *Jhopri* (JJ) clusters, slum designated areas and unauthorised colonies and the remaining 11.9 per cent in rural and urban villages. The contribution to housing stock through institutional agencies was only 53 per cent (this excludes squatter housing) in 1991. DDA, the nodal agency for providing housing units, till March 2003, had allotted a total of 0.33 million flats. The component of housing through non institutional sources *viz.*, unauthorised colonies, squatter/JJ clusters, etc. is significant.

3.3 Slums/Informal Sector Housing: The slum population in Delhi was about 26.0 per cent in 2001, least of the metropolitan cities. Greater Mumbai (34.3 per cent) was followed by Kolkata (32.90 per cent) and Chennai (28.1 per cent). In JJ clusters/squatter settlements a population of 30 lakh was living in about 6 lakh house holds (1997).

The Municipal Corporation of Delhi (MCD) initiated the process of relocating the slum dwellers in early 1991. The relocation sites are generally located at the peripheries of Delhi. These sites have been selected with a vision of having a density of 200 dwelling units per acre with a plot size of 18.00 sq.m for each eligible family and 12.5 sq.m for each ineligible family.

3.4 Housing

3.4.1 The dwellings have been categorised as independent houses, flats, *Basti* and under "others".

3.4.2 An analysis of housing data for 1991 indicates that in Delhi 68.1 per cent of the houses are owned by the residents and 28.61 are rented. Status of 3.29 per cent of the houses was not known.

3.4.3 About 44 per cent of the dwelling units have only one room, 27 per cent two rooms and 15.5 per cent three rooms each. Larger accommodation accounts for only 12.4 per cent of the total dwelling units.

3.4.4 In 2001 Delhi's backlog of dwelling units stood at 4 lakh comprising 1 lakh net shortage and the rest by way of dilapidated and *Kutchha* structures requiring replacement.

3.4.5 An analysis of data on housing indicates that 58 per cent of the houses are in good condition, 36.65 per cent are livable and 5.35 per cent are in dilapidated condition.

3.5 Land Availability

3.5.1 According to the MPD 2021 the land that can be urbanised in the NCT Delhi is 97190.90 ha or 65.54 per cent of its total geographical area of 148,300 ha. The population holding capacity of the existing urban areas of Delhi is 122 lakh which is adequate to accommodate the (2001) population. However, further urban extension in about 27,000 hectares will be required to accommodate the population in the future.

3.6 Housing Policy

The long term goal of the NHP is to eradicate houselessness, improve the housing conditions of the inadequately housed and provide a minimum level of basic services and amenities to all; for this purpose provide land and legal and infrastructure support to enable the private sector to make heavy investments. No fresh encroachments are to be permitted on public land, and past encroachments which had been in existence prior to 31 January 1990 will not be removed without providing alternatives.

3.7 Master Plan 2021

3.7.1 The Delhi Master Plan 2021 has adopted the following vision:

> "Vision-2021 is to make Delhi a global metropolis and a world-class city, where all the people would be engaged in productive work with a better quality of life, living in a sustainable environment."

3.7.2 This will, amongst other things, necessitate planning and action to meet the challenge of population growth and in-migration into Delhi; provision of adequate housing, particularly for the weaker sections of the society; addressing the problems of small enterprises, particularly in the unorganised informal sector; dealing with the issue of slums, upgradation of old and dilapidated areas of the city; provision of adequate infrastructure services; conservation of the environment; preservation of Delhi's heritage and blending it with the new and complex modern patterns of development; and doing all this within a framework of sustainable development, public-private and community participation and a spirit of ownership and a sense of belonging among its citizens.

3.8 Data Base Development and Management

Data on housing in Delhi by agencies involved remains uncoordinated. The process of data collection is not within any regulatory framework. Such a framework needs to be developed for India and, until it is developed, the broad guidelines provided by the United Nations Human Settlements Programme may be adopted.

3.9 National Capital Region

3.9.1 The present National Capital Region (NCR) comprises of a total area of 33,578 sq. km. including areas of Delhi (1483 sq. kms), Haryana (13413 sq. kms.), Uttar Pradesh (10853 sq. kms.), and Rajasthan (7829 sq. kms).

3.9.2 The National Capital Region (NCR) Planning Board prepared draft Regional Plan-2021 for NCR. After inviting objections/suggestions from public under Section 12 of the NCR Planning Board Act, 1985 on draft Regional Plan-2021, final Plan was approved in 28th meeting of the Board held on 9th July 2005 and was notified on 17th September 2005.

3.9.3 The Plan aims to promote growth and balanced development of the whole region through providing economic base in the identified major settlements (Metro Centres/Regional Centres) for absorbing economic development impulse of Delhi, efficient transport network, development of physical infrastructure, rational land use pattern, improved environment and quality of life.

3.9.4 NCR has been divided in to "policy zones" on the bases of needs of cities that have developed in the areas near Delhi, highways planned and/or implemented and development of infrastructure.

There will be a hierarchy of settlements such as 5 Metro Centres (Ghaziabad-Loni complex, Gurgaon-Manesar complex, Sonepat-Kundli complex, Faridabad-Ballabhgarh complex and Noida) and one Regional Centre (Bahadurgarh). The settlements will be categorised on the basis of their population size starting with a village having population of less than five thousand and ending with metro centres having a million plus population.

3.9.5 **Economic Activity and Fiscal Policy in the NCR**

The fiscal policy in the NCR have the following objectives:

i) Facilitate value-added high-tech service sector in Delhi in the context of its emergence as a global city in the world economy.
ii) Adopt investment strategies to restrict less desirable economic activities by not allowing new industrial areas, wholesale trade areas and office spaces in NCT-Delhi.
iii) Allow only hi-tech industries in NCT-Delhi.
iv) Restrict the number and size of the government offices/PSUs in NCT-Delhi.
v) Shift space extensive/hazardous wholesale trades outside NCT-Delhi.
vi) Develop model industrial Estates/Special Economic Zones (SEZs) outside NCT-Delhi.
vii) Achieve uniformity in the tax regime, i.e., Sales Tax, VAT etc.

Plans have been prepared in the all the relevant sectors for integrated development, namely transport, power, water, sewerage, solid waste management, drainage and irrigation, telecommunication, shelter, social infrastructure, tourism & heritage, environment and disaster management. rural development, and land use.

3.9.6 **Development Strategies, Management Structure and Resource Mobilisation**

i) Plan of action for implementation of policies and proposals prepared along with its phasing and dovetailing the costs with five-year plans.
ii) Agencies to implement the policies and proposals of Regional Plan-2021 identified in the Plan.
iii) Strengthening of NCR Planning Board proposed to expedite the implementation, efficient coordination and creation of appropriate data base and its regular updations.
iv) Public, private partnership proposed to be promoted.

3.9.7 **Recommendation**

a) The powers of the NCR Board relate to preparation and implementation of plans. The State Government have a vital role as most of the items are within their jurisdiction. There is a pressing need for unified or coordinated administrative structure to deal effectively with problems of implementation of the plans and decisions of the NCR Planning Board relating to the economic and fiscal policy and governance including maintenance of public order, policing and judicial administration, and
b) There is need to give high priority to the housing sector.

4. Infrastructure

4.1 Transport

4.1.1 Roads

a) Limitations: The main limitations relating to roads include inadequate design, absence of clearly defined road hierarchy and lack of access control, inadequate provision of land to take care of, haphazard growth, poor maintenance, encroachments and hawking on carriage way, poor traffic management, inadequate integration of rail and road services and the environmental degradation resulting from the same, lack of road user discipline, huge amount of traffic using Delhi road system for passing through and absence of bye passes, satellite towns have instead of easing pressure added to it and poor project implementation.

b) State of Maintenance of Roads: It is stated that there are difficulties in keeping the roads in good condition such as:

i) Heavy traffic movement on roads all through the day and night leaving no time for maintenance.

ii) Unsatisfactory quality of bitumen.

iii) Unsatisfactory quality of stones extracted from quarries.

c) The Main Features of Road Improvement Plan:

- Providing an institutional framework for development, management and operation of an integrated multi-modal transport system.
- Measures to deal with identified deficiencies.
- Using improvements in technology for road surfaces such as improved wearing coats and plastic roads, fiber reinforced concrete surface and concrete roads depending on the circumstances.
- A separate Road Maintenance Corporation is to be set up generating its own resources.
- Road safety education should be provided in schools.
- Preparation and implementation of strategic action plans for special areas.
- Implementation of urban transport information system which will proivde updated inputs of actual traffic flows to enable proper planning.
- Providing special attention to slow green modes of transport namely, cycles and pedestrians.

4.1.2 Railways

The Railway services to Delhi primarily consist of national network services to all major cities of India, commuter services to surrounding towns and local services for the citizens of Delhi. All these services are unable to cope with the traffic offered and extensive capacity generation and inputs are essential. The upgradation and expansion plans of the railways include additional passenger terminals, upgradation of stations at New Delhi, Delhi main and Hazrat Nizamuddin, construction of separate freight corridors from Delhi to Kolkata/Mumbai, strengthening of rail corridors to neighbouring towns. Revitalisation of Ring Railway is an essential component of Delhi's transport scenario by augmenting capacity, increasing EMU services to suit commuter timings and coordinating feeder bus linkages at ring railway stations

4.1.3 Vision of Transport Facilities

The vision is to provide safe, eco-friendly, cost-effective and efficient modes of transportation through a well-integrated multi-modal transport system for a well-managed, clean and dynamic model capital city.

The policy action required would include, among other measures, upgradation and strengthening of road system, provision of metro system to cater for demand upto 2021, an integrated rail bus transit to neighbouring towns, augmentation of bus system, high capacity bus system on selected corridors (100 kms), introduction of electric trolley bus, and provision of LRT in walled city.

4.1.4 Even though schemes are being planned and implemented, the travelling time is going on increasing. This is because of a very rapid growth of population and even greater rate of increase of vehicles on Delhi roads. Both of these causes need to be addressed.

4.2 Power

4.2.1 Current Issues

Delhi faces considerable power shortage. It is necessary to enhance Delhi's core generation capacity and the government's inability to either do or facilitate this in over five years since the unbundling. Questions arise about further heavy public investment from Plan funds when the principal buyers are now the privately managed Discoms and some degree of market risk is involved. Alternatives to bring in private investment need to be considered. The Government's current policy is understood to be on these lines, and action in respect of Bawana site is reportedly being initiated, but time has slipped by.

4.2.2 Quality of Service

Delhi has consistently ranked high in the CRISIL/ICRA ratings of state-wise power sector performance commissioned by the Ministry of Power. There has been some genuine improvement but there is still a long way to go, and a need to introduce SAIDI and SAIFI measurement with effective third-party monitoring.

4.2.3 AT&C Loss Reduction

On this fundamental parameter, reforms are on track.

4.2.4 Tariff Orders and Issues Arising

DERC stated that repayment of the initial loan and of transitional assistance would not be recoverable from the ARRs. However, the Discoms were able to refinance and prepay the former and the government converted the latter in to equity, rescuing Transco's balance sheet.

DERC has also departed from the Transfer Scheme and Policy Directions in other ways, including notably its appropriation of the Holding Company's arrears to Transco's ARR. In addition, though they won appellate success on the issue of depreciation rate, the Discom investors had a legitimate issue in DERC's disregard for their stated requirements of compliance with accounting standards obligatory under Company law.

The reform package was thus impacted by the tariff issue, which led DERC to leave a large uncovered 'regulatory asset', though since amortised on the strength of loss reduction. But such 'back loading' increases, rather than reducing, the burden on the consumer in the long term.

4.2.5 Strengths

Successful restructuring has created scope for private sector investment not only in the distribution sector itself but also in generation. There is every prospect of the sector becoming substantially self-sustaining.

4.2.6 Weaknesses

The two main weaknesses are the failure to create strong feelings of consumer satisfaction, and the continuing tariff issue.

Nevertheless, all three Discoms have generally met the committed loss reduction targets and two of them have exceeded their targets; they and Transco are entitled to their legitimate costs. They should not be left grounds to allege that they have not been able actually to get the fixed return.

4.2.7 Interventions Required

DERC should complete its exercise of finalising a multi-year tariff expeditiously. The consumer mix data provided by Discoms after unbundling seems to require further regulatory scrutiny. It should also focus effectively on consumer satisfaction, and impose and monitor objective performance criteria like SAIDI and SAIFI. Steps to promote local generation should be expedited.

4.3 Drinking Water

4.3.1 The main features in this sector are given below:

i) Nearly 31 per cent of the population living in JJ clusters, unauthorised colonies and villages of various categories and does not have access to the piped water supply and sewerage system.

ii) The Delhi Jal Board (DJB) has adopted the norm of water supply as 275 lpcd at the source of production.

iii) South and Southwest zones suffer on account of water shortage.

iv) A significant portion of the water supply network of 9000 kms is 40-50 years old and the total distribution losses are about 40 per cent of the total water supplied. DJB has the target to bring down the leakage losses to 20 per cent.

v) There are about 1 million connections where the supply is to be metered. DJB proposes to involve consumers as well as private players to ensure that the work of installation of all the 0.53 million meters is completed by May 2006.

vi) The water tariff, which was heavily subsidised, has been revised and still continues to be subsidised.

vii) Rapid urbanisation of Delhi has put tremendous pressure on the groundwater table. DJB has initiated a scheme of rainwater harvesting in Delhi under which DJB provides financial assistance up to 50 per cent of the total cost of structures.

viii) Under Bhagidari Scheme in the water sector, RWAs and various associations are actively participating with DJB in a number of activities.

ix) DJB is planning to switchover to 24 hours supply system in phases through private firms and utility operators.

x) DJB has adopted universally proven state-of-art technologies at its WTPs. It is one of the few public utilities to undertake extensive work of GIS mapping of its various utilities. DJB has also initiated action to obtain ISO-9002 certification.

4.3.2 Policy Interventions and Recommendations (Drinking Water)

i) Measures including water conservation, loss reduction, dual plumbing, water recycling need to be strengthened and implemented rigorously.

ii) There is significant reduction in river-flows during the lean periods. The proposals for construction of the reservoirs on Yamuna river need to be considered urgently and implemented.

iii) The Ministry of Water Resources should intervene and resolve the matter of availability of raw water for Sonia Vihar Water Treatment Plant.

iv) The withdrawal of ground water should be regulated. Central Ground Water Authority may consider delegating necessary powers to bring the management and development of groundwater under DJB.

v) A decentralised approach for treating sewage may be more economic. The treated water from such STPs may be used for horticulture, parks and greening of Delhi.

vi) All the works and other measures in hand to augment and conserve water should be completed on priority.

vii) On the lines of Mumbai, wastewater from the high rise building should be treated *insitu* to the prescribed standards and reused for air conditioning and other industrial applications.

viii) Public awareness and education through the Bhagidari Scheme should be encouraged for conserving and managing potable water optimally.

ix) Delhi may have to depend on Yamuna only to meet the demand projected in the Master Plan Document-2021. An additional quantity of 350 cusec needs to be made available by the Upper Yamuna River Board (UYRB) during the lean period.

x) There is need to construct dams to minimise the shortfall during the lean periods. UYRB should be persuaded to treat the allocation of Yamuna water for consumptive use only.

4.4 Telecommunication

4.4.1 Telecommunication has made commendable progress in all services. The number of Telephone subscribers (Fixed + Mobile) has increased from 3.17 million in March 2002 to 7.98 million in March 2005 in Delhi representing a growth rate of more than 35 per cent. This leads to a Telephone Density of more than 50 per 100 population. The major growth has come from mobile telephones. There is a good competition with 6 service providers for mobile telephones in Delhi. There are about 100,000 PCOs (Public Call Office or Payphone) in Delhi. Internet service is also quite popular with a number of Service providers giving this service.

4.4.2 Broadband service is a recent phenomenon in India and Delhi. Government has recently announced a Broadband Policy. Broadband service provides "Triple Play" i.e., voice (telephony), data, and video which may include TV and video-on-demand. Broadband service will lead to great opportunity in tele-education, e-health, e-governance, entertainment, tele-working (home working) etc. Tele-working leads to less strain on transport system and is eco-friendly.

4.4.3 Telecom technology is fast changing and it is difficult to assess resource requirement on long term basis. There is likely to be no problem on this score since the capital required (a few thousand crore Rupees per year) are arranged by service providers out of their revenue earnings and market borrowings.

4.4.4 Introduction of private sector has led to good competition in telecom sector. This has led to a) faster growth, b) lower tariff c) improved quality of service and d) new types of applications and service. TRAI (Telecom Regulatory Authority of India) and TDSAT (Telecom Dispute Settlement and Appellate Tribunal) have been set up under the TRAI Act 1997 to fix tariff, regulate the telecom sector and provide for dispute settlement mechanism.

4.4.5 Vision should include broadband to all households and mobile phone to all who need it.

4.4.6 Central government is the main policymaking authority for telecom but state government must make policies to facilitate proper and fast growth of telecom infrastructure.

5. Environment

5.1 Pollution

a) The unprecedented growth of Delhi has an adverse impact on the environment. Motor vehicles are the biggest source of air pollution. The number of registered working factories has doubled between 1981 and 2000; so has the industrial production. The industrial census of 1988 gives a figure of 76559 industrial units in Delhi—many in residential or non-conforming areas.

b) The problem of toxic gases and discharge of liquid wastes has been a problem leading to air and water pollution. The standards prescribed by the regulatory agencies have not always been enforced. Recent interventions by the Supreme Court have led to some improvement but these would continue to be problem areas.

5.2 *Depletion of Flora and Fauna*

The flora and fauna of Delhi have depleted to a very great extent. The ridge, which used to be the habitat of many species of plant and animal life, has had unprecedented human intrusions in the last century. The technological changes as also the exposure to foreign countries have brought tremendous changes in the lifestyles of people, working to the degradation of the environment.

5.3 *Changing Land Use*

Till 1990-91, agricultural lands represented 49 per cent of the total area while non-agricultural land constituted 50 per cent of the total. However, by 2000-01, agricultural lands had fallen to 32 per cent of total area while non-agricultural land had risen to 68 per cent of the total. Diversion of agricultural land has serious environmental impact for the environment and ecology and needs to be curbed.

5.4 *Pollution of River Yamuna*

i) The increasing population has resulted in increased demand for water and the entire water of Yamuna is diverted to supply water to Delhi. But that is not sufficient and there is heavy extraction of ground water with the result that the ground water level has been falling. In the chapter dealing with the subject of drinking water, measures to address these problems have been discussed. As if this was not bad enough, the ground water is getting polluted. Strict control and enforcement of the relevant laws and rules for protecting ground water are necessary.

ii) Many localities are not connected to the sewers that carry waste water to the Sewage Treatment Plants (STPs). This is reflected in the form of gap between the waste water generated and that treated in STPs. Such waste water is being discharged into the river Yamuna, which in dry months carries negligible fresh water. Yamuna is, therefore, highly polluted. There is need to ensure that all the wastewater including sewage is taken to the STPs where there should be enough capacity to treat before the water is discharged in to the river.

iii) Among the measures needed are rational pricing of water, rainwater harvesting, participatory and integrated water resource and waste water management.

iv) The Hon'ble Supreme Court, in its order dated 4 August 2004, expressed concern regarding deteriorating water quality in the river Yamuna and inadequacy of various measures so far taken to improve the situation. Pursuant to the Court order, a High Powered Committee was constituted to determine the quantum of water/waste water generation, sources of pollution and to suggest the mode and manner of improving the quality in the river. The Committee has drawn up an Action Plan, the components of which include the following.

For improvement in water quality, the discharge of water in the river should be adequate and continuous. To this end, the riparian states need to contribute their share for maintaining a minimum flow in the river stretch. Based on the recommendation of a minimum flow of 10 cumecs earlier made, the Committee has determined the shares of different states in the raw water to be released in the river:

- 4.54 cumecs should continue to be released by the Government of Haryana at Tajewala.
- More than 10 cumecs should continue to be released by the Government of Haryana through Munak escape.
- 4 cumecs being released by the Government of Haryana at Najafgarh drain outfall should be continued.
- Adequate water and waste water handling capacities including refurbishment of trunk sewerage and treatment system.
- Laying of sewer lines in the unsewered areas of Delhi.
- Removal of slum clusters on the river bed.
- Treatment of industrial effluents.
- Utilisation of treated effluents, and
- Removal of coliform in the sewage treatment plants.

The Action Plan needs to be implemented effectively.

5.5 *Solid Waste Management*

The need to plan properly for Solid Waste Management—domestic, industrial and biomedical—and implement those plans is realised. Plans are being prepared. Action points include waste inventorisation, waste minimisation, private sector participation and public participation. It is also important to choose the right technological option for disposal of waste. MPD-2021 also makes provision for the land required for the Waste water and solid waste management. There is need to implement them efficiently.

5.6 Air Quality

Air quality is of particular concern during winter as ground-based temperature inversions are a regular feature that restricts mixing height to low levels. Lower temperatures, calm conditions, lower mixing height, and temperature inversions during winter restrict and confine pollutant dispersion and dispersal. Winter evenings have higher pollution build-up because of frequent calm conditions with temperature inversions resulting in poor natural ventilation and high emission loads due to evening traffic peaks.

Amongst the various types of industries that mushroomed in the city, the most polluting ones were stone crushers, hot mix plants, potteries, induction furnaces etc., besides the above important industrial air pollution sources, coal-fired boilers, foundries, forging units, etc., also contributed significantly to air pollution. In addition, significant pollution was also caused by a large number of Diesel Generating (DG) sets, which were installed in various commercial and industrial establishments. The erratic power supply caused phenomenal increase in the number and use of DG sets. In addition to these industries, emission from thermal power plants located in the heart of the city also adds to air pollution.

The main concern in the domestic sector is the use of inefficient and highly polluting fuels in the poorer households/urban slums, leading to deterioration in the indoor air quality and health.

The CO, CO_2, SPM emissions from fuel use are fairly significant and are inadequately dispersed. This brings about high exposure and risk to the slum dwellers. Pollutants from slow combustion of miscellaneous combustible materials by domestic and commercial sources account for eight per cent of the total pollution. Sulphur dioxide is the major pollutant emitted. Moreover, since these emissions take place at low heights, the problems due to domestic burning need proper attention in order to avoid any undesirable health effects.

Steps required to deal with pollution from vehicles, small industries and other sources have been detailed in the chapter.

6. Public Distribution System

The salient features of the Public Distribution Scheme and the measures taken by the government of the NCTD have been stated in the chapter on PDS. Here it will be sufficient to deal with the grievances and the remedial measures that may be considered.

6.1 Grievances Related to PDS

i) One of the significant objectives of PDS was to ensure Micro Level Food Security. The CAG report revealed that inefficient targeting has affected targeted PDS.

ii) Low availability of food grains through PDS assumes importance in the face of acute nutritional inadequacy in diet and very low per capita calorie intake of BPL population in the country.

iii) One of the major problems with the functioning of PDS is the problem of identification of the right target group. There is no availability of authentic data for classification of population in APL, BPL and other relevant categories. There still exists a gap between the targeted number of beneficiaries *vis-à-vis* actual beneficiaries. Approximately only about 57 per cent of the BPL households are covered by it TPDS.

iv) Due to callous attitude and low profit associated with PDS, FPS owners resort to illegal and inappropriate means and ways like:

- Excess issuances of ration cards to increase margins.
- Many FPSs have large number of ghost cards in order to get more quantity of food grains and earn huge profit by selling them in the open market.

v) As a result of low annual turnover some of FPS owners indulge in leakage of commodities and diversion of subsidised grains available with them.

vi) Irregularities in opening and closing of FPS.

vii) Harassment to the card holders.

viii) Entries of the commodity sold to the beneficiary is not made.

ix) Commodities sold are not weighed properly.

x) Over charging from consumers.

xi) Good quality commodities replaced by poor quality food grains/kerosene.

xii) Lacunae in the licensing and selection of FPS. Marked irregularities have been found in allotment of license to FPS.

xiii) Inaccessible location of FPS from the BPL or Antyodaya beneficiaries.

xiv) A significant portion of subsidised food grains and other essential commodities do not reach the beneficiaries due to their diversion.

xv) Mechanism of allotment of FPS license has also been made more stringent. The Chairman of Selection Committee is D.C. (Revenue) who is from the other department and hence selection is more transparent and based on merit.

xvi) Attempts are made to address these grievances from time to time, but the problems remain. Measures such as awareness generation, involvement of the people and the civil society at large, transparency in PDS, vigilance committees, and improved governance are some of the methods that have been tried.

6.2 Suggestions

6.2.1 Reward/Recognition

- Reward for the meritorious and honest officers who are vigilant and care for people's needs.
- Recognition or annual award for the FSPs so that more and more shop owners would try to follow the system.

6.2.2 Legalised Ways to Make Profit

- As there are low margins in the running of FPS, there should be legalised and genuine ways to earn profit for an honest business.
- There can be a provision for the supply of other essential items like tea, soap, matchbox etc., be made available through FPS.
- There can be various Tax exemption provisions in procurement and distribution of other essential commodities to encourage the concept of providing complete service to people.

6.2.3 Quantity/Quality/Timeliness of Food Grains

- A timely arrival of food grains at FPS can ensure timely distribution of essential commodities. It is interesting to note that most of the people get their wages/salaries in first seven days of the month so the system should be such that it ensures the supply of food grains during that period. Failing which people will buy from the commercial outfits leading to non-lifting of the quota and diversion of supply to blank marketers.
- The supply should be in adequate quantity keeping in mind the number of consumers registered with the FPS owners. Inadequate quantity of food grains leads to shaking of the trust of the consumer in the FPS owner and hence the whole Public Distribution System.

6.2.4 Licence to FPS

- The mechanism of allotment of FPS licence should be made more stringent. People from economically weaker section should be given opportunity.
- Last but not the least, people's participation should be sought for successful functioning of PDS. Voluntary organisations should also actively be involved for better functioning of the system. A vigilant and cooperative public will go a long way in making this system more viable and effective.
- The department is considering these proposals for reward/recognition to the honest officials, and the FPS licensees who adopt fair practices and legalised way to make profit.
- Strict instruction/monitoring is done on quantity/quality/timeliness of food grains.

7. Forest, Tree Crop Management, Greening, etc.

7.1 Current Status

NCT of Delhi has three main physiographical segments, *viz.*, Flood Plains of Yamuna, about the Ridge, and the Plains. Agriculture is practised extensively along the stretch of river. Most of the native vegetation has been cleared for the purpose of farming and the areas, which are not fit for agriculture, are used as grazing grounds when the floodwater recedes. The riverine ecosystem is under major threat.

On Delhi Ridge, planting was confined initially to indigenous species and *Prosopis juliflora* was introduced later, which showed good drought resistance and gradually the ridge has been covered with this species.

Although the capital has more trees per ha, than the national average the tree cover is unevenly distributed and is progressively declining. Delhi has 121 sq. km of forest cover and 40 sq. km of tree cover, which constitutes only 10.2 per cent of geographical area under green cover much less than 33 per cent as envisaged by National Forest Policy, 1988. More than 70 per cent of the forest cover is in south and southwest Delhi alone. The rest of

Delhi has very little green cover and enormous biodiversity has been lost.

7.2 Initiatives Taken

The following initiatives have been taken in the past to manage hotspots impacting Delhi's dwindling flora.

- A large portion of the ridge was declared a protected zone. Subsequently, large chunks of land on the ridge have also been notified Reserve Forest. Another development was the establishment of Asola Wildlife Sanctuary in 1991 to enhance the protection and conservation of the city's floral and faunal diversity.
- Delhi Tree Preservation Act 1994 laid down heavy penalties on individuals, institutions and organisations for tree felling.
- Greening Delhi Action Plan is launched every year to undertake additional plantation. A task force under the chairmanship of the Conservator of Forests, Government of NCT, Delhi was constituted. The plantation scales in the recent past have increased from around one-lakh seedlings per year in mid-90s to about 11 lakh presently.

7.3 Impediments

- Forests and tree cover in Delhi have always remained vulnerable to developmental activities.
- Inadequate coordination among agencies like forest department, CPWD, DDA and MCD further aggravates the existing threats.

7.4 Agencies—Their Role in Plantation

i) An area of 8,422 hectares, marked as green, is managed by a large number of government and non-government agencies.

ii) The Forest Department is carrying out a number of activities for the development of forests including enrichment planting in ridge area to augment the natural regeneration. It has identified about 1,400 acres in different zones to develop into mini forests in addition to the ridge.

iii) DDA has a greening project. It is working in collaboration with the Department of Botany, Delhi University to develop a biodiversity park along the Yamuna river-bed in North Delhi. It has fixed a target of planting 1.68 lakhs trees during 2004-05.

iv) The Municipal Corporation of Delhi (MCD) undertakes plantation in various areas such as schools, parks, bus stands and along roadsides. It has also set a target of planting 1.6 lakhs saplings in the current year.

v) The New Delhi Municipal Committee (NDMC) undertakes tree plantation along the wide roads, residential areas, parks etc. It has proposed to plant 10,000 trees during 2004-05.

vi) Other agencies also are involved in plantation work. Residents Welfare Associations (RWAs), Market Traders Associations (MTAs), Non-governmental organisations and schools have planted 90 lakhs seedlings in the last four years. Apart from this, 1500 Eco-clubs have been established in various schools/colleges of Delhi.

7.5 Greening of Delhi—Vision 2015

Delhi should be one of the green and clean capitals of the world with high aesthetic value, providing its people a safe and healthy environment and setting up an example of a modern metropolis. The following strategic actions should be taken up in this regard:

7.5.1 Expanding Green area—Afforestation of all available areas should be undertaken. The feasibility of acquiring a two km wide area on both sides of Yamuna and a 2 km wide strip of available land along the border of the state of Haryana for developing it into a green belt should be examined. It would serve the dual purpose of protecting the flood plains from further encroachment and degradation as well as help in recharge of ground water.

7.5.2 To protect Delhi from desertification from southwest direction, massive afforestation on private and public lands needs to be undertaken.

7.5.3 The existing tree cover should be protected and maintained by strictly enforcing the provisions of The Delhi Preservation of Tree Act, 1994.

7.5.4 Delhi Ridge should be preserved by adopting suitable combinations in which trees, shrubs and herbs co-exist as multi-layered vegetation. Assisted natural regeneration cum enrichment planting can be useful in conserving and protecting the biodiversity of this region.

7.5.5 Information of green cover and forests should be maintained in Geographical Information System format for which a suitably equipped Cell may be set up.

8. Wild Life Management

The fast pace of urbanisation leaves very little scope for wild life to thrive and it has been dwindling rapidly.

However, efforts must be made to conserve whatever is possible under the circumstances. Efforts at increasing awareness about the importance of wild life conservation need to be made. Delhi is being used as a transit point for the illegal trade in wildlife products. There is need for increased vigil and action on part of the concerned authorities. A multi-pronged approach is required to manage the problematic species *Macaca mulatta* and captive elephants.

9. Education

9.1 Elementary Education

The literacy rate in Delhi is 82 per cent, male having 87.4 per cent and their female counterpart has a literacy rate of 75 per cent. The share of illiterate people in urban Delhi is 13.7 per cent which is much better compared to the urban India average (20.2 per cent). It has been estimated that 25 per cent of Delhi population lives in slums (2000). These people mainly belong to minority groups, scheduled castes and are mostly casual labourers. The educational attainment rate for these people is very poor. More than 20 per cent of those enrolled at primary stage belong to the disadvantaged communities, but at the secondary stage this proportion is reduced to 14 per cent. The enrolment figures over last 25 years has seen an increasing trend.

The private schools play a significant role in managing school education. The share of private sector in schooling in Delhi increases sharply at the secondary and higher secondary stages while the government school is dominant in primary and middle stages.

The number of out of school children has been significant—6.39 per cent of total 6-10 children and 7.12 per cent of total 11-14 children were out of school in 2003. Compared with private schools, the government school performance is poor. There also exists slight gender discrimination in the percentage share of boys and girls appearing for class X examination, as girls comprised around 46 per cent of the students who appeared for class X exam. This bias is reduced slightly at the class XII level, with their share improving to 47 per cent of the total. It is perhaps not fair to compare results of government and private schools.

Another important aspect related to education is that emergence of unrecognised sector. In addition, taking private tuition, some from schoolteachers but largely from the educated unemployed, has become a common phenomenon among all income groups. These are the available alternatives for the parents to support their children's education.

9.2 Causes behind Poor Achievement

A major reason for so many children still being out of school is shortage in schooling facilities. This includes shortage of schools, of infrastructural facilities in existing schools and of teachers.

The schools are often very crowded. Not only are primary schools not enough to enrol all children, the facilities for upper primary education are insufficient. There is one more issue that needs to be addressed at primary level that is of fees.

The availability of teachers at Delhi schools varies according to the administration. The teacher-pupil ratio at the primary stage at MCD schools is 1:52 while it is much better at 1:34 for DOE (Directorate of Education), Govt. of Delhi schools. A major problem in improving quality of teaching was the absence of indicators of teaching quality. Poor teaching and poor achievement at earlier levels is often the main reason for poor retention. To introduce teacher accountability, continuous and comprehensive evaluation of students is carried out three to four times in a year and performance of students is linked to teachers who are teaching them different subjects.

The secondary schools sometimes run in tin sheds or tents (21 schools function from tents and 94 from SPS/ tents). Other basic facilities like toilets, drinking water, electricity supply are also often in short supply for all schools. Buildings are poorly maintained; piles of paper, broken desks and chairs are common occurrences. The basic facilities reported by the average government school student were very poor. It must be noted that the poorest facilities were found in east, north east and north west Delhi schools. Here the pressure on school facilities from a rapidly increasing slum population appears most acute. Facilities are also generally poorer the lower the level of schooling, i.e., upper primary was worse off than secondary and the latter was worse off than senior secondary schools.

For dealing with the major problems of poor retention and poor learning achievements higher budgetary allocations are necessary, but are not enough. Solving these problems is much more complicated.

9.3 Initiatives Taken in Delhi

About 3000 learning centres run by various NGOs bring out an appropriate level of competancy among the out-of-school children by putting them through condensed courses and then get them admitted into appropriate grades in formal schools. Nearly a lakh of out of school children are in these centres. A major problem faced by these learning centres is that sufficient schools or classrooms have not come up. So the problem of mainstreaming remains. The government is also experimenting with the concept of mobile learning centres.

Delhi government has also sought cooperation from private sector as well in its attempt to improve school availability. The private unaided schools in Delhi are also non-profit organisations. Delhi High Court had ordered that they are to reserve 20 per cent of the seats for the economically disadvantaged children—and grant them freeship.

Other measures include continuous and comprehensive evaluation of schools, computerising information system (web based MIS), improvement of retention and learning achievements by implementing different projects which make the schools enjoyable to the children, community participation, sports and other activities. Efforts has also be taken for provision of education for disabled children.

Several projects are being implemented in the government schools to make schools enjoyable and meaningful. YUVA has been introduced in government schools with twin objectives—to make sure that the school is a safer and happier place for the students and that they are taught to be responsible adults. So it would give basic education on all subjects like HIV-AIDS, career counseling etc. Project RAKSHA was launched to teach self defense skills to the girl students. In primary schools a hot cooked midday meal is served in all schools.

Initiatives have been taken to encourage the community to participate in developmental activities such as *Dakhila Abhiyan*, awareness programmes related to Polio, Dengue, participation in bhagidari *melas* and workshop, maintenance of schools through Vidyalaya Kalyan Samiti (VKS).

9.4 Strategies, Choices and Issues

9.4.1 Vocational Education

Under the Revised National Policy on Education, the priority has been assigned to vocational education. Presently 16 Vocational courses are being taught in 197 Government and 7 Government Aided Senior Secondary Schools scattered over Delhi. The enrolment under vocational education programme is nearly 10657 students in Government-aided Schools. However in percentage term the figure is very low. Government is, now, conducting several studies to evaluate vocational courses. Attempt has made to train the teachers after 10 years. Vocationalisation also lacks planning for selection of courses and training. It needs proper continuous and comprehensive research.

9.4.2 Higher Education

The government has encouraged and promoted private initiative in the field of higher education through affiliation to GGSIP. Eighty five per cent seats are reserved for students of Delhi in the institutes under GGSIP located in NCT of Delhi. It is proposed to initiate courses in emerging disciplines like Biotechnology, Genetics Plant Molecular Biology, Environment studies etc in the colleges fully funded by Delhi Government. The University of Delhi has included in its curriculum a good number of vocational courses.

The directorate of higher education has prepared a comprehensive policy for higher education for next five years which includes opening of new Degree Colleges in various localities of Delhi, and it also proposes to open Indira Gandhi Institute of Technology under GGSIP seeing the regional balance in north west India—only seven per cent intake facilities in north-west region comprising Chandigarh, Haryana, HP, Delhi, Rajasthan, and J&K in total technical intake of the country.

The issues related to better management of higher education such as strengthening of the Directorate of Higher education, directing colleges for proper utilisation of funds, financial audits for their proper uses, acquisition of new sites for opening of various colleges, opening of more new hostels for girls are addressed in new policy. In addition to these, to encourage meritorious students studying in Government colleges and to motivate intelligent and serious students of general stream education i.e., Science, Commerce, and Arts, in a three years Degree Course with two segments *viz.*, Honours and General Pass courses a cash award of Rs. 5000 each is proposed.

9.4.3 Technical Education

The efforts in the direction of expansion of technical colleges are reflected in the shape of upcoming new colleges. Aspects such as upkeep and maintenance of buildings, equipment, furniture, environment etc., of the institute, restructuring of the curriculum in coordination with the industry are also being addressed. There should be provision to arrange for industrial visits/industrial training for the trainees/students, to generate revenue for the institute by obtaining job works, services, consultancy etc., from industry/market, to explore the possibilities of more gainful employment for the students/trainees, to conduct short-term courses/seminars/workshops for the employees of industry and the entrepreneurs to associate the alumni/ex students in getting constructive feedback for the improvement of training standard.

9.5 Issues in Delhi

Some of the suggestions to improve Delhi education scenario in general are :

i) In the coming years, the economy of Delhi would be dominated by the services. Therefore, the steps should be initiated to introduce more and more courses as per the demand of job market, as the education directly and through its multiplier effect, is a dominant player in the economic activities and thereby growth of the state as well as the country.

ii) It is time that government gave appropriate weightage to both the general as well as vocational education as per the requirement of emerging industries.

iii) The privatisation as well as internationalisation of education is increasing at all levels starting from pre-school. The state should remain the pioneer and prime mover and should hold the responsibility of monitoring and controlling of quality magnitude and degree of commercialisation.

iv) Uncovered areas and irregular settlements, especially of migrants, without a neighbourhood school need to be provided with schooling facilities on priority.

v) In an attempt to reach the hitherto unreached groups of children, particularly those at construction sites, the government is experimenting with the concept of mobile learning centres.

vi) The government has sought cooperation from private sector in its attempt to improve school availability. The private unaided schools in Delhi are required to reserve 20 per cent of the seats for the economically disadvantaged children – and grant them freeship.

vii) So far the Boards results were the only accountability measure for teachers, and gave a performance appraisal for teachers who taught in class X or XII. Learning level and teaching quality in other classes have no similar measures. For this purpose the directorate took a major step to reform the examination system. In addition to the 3 terminal tests, 4 additional tests were introduced for students of class 3 to class 12.

viii) Web based MIS has been developed to store data on schools, students and teachers. Information is easily accessible not only for the planners but also the other stakeholders. All postings and transfers are carried out electronically. Budgetary allocations and sanctions are also issued electronically.

ix) Initiatives taken to invite the community to participate in activities such as *Dakhila Abhiyan*, awareness programmes related to polio, dengue, participation in bhagidari *melas* and workshop, maintenance of schools through Vidyalaya Kalyan Samiti (VKS) need to be strengthened.

x) Programmes aimed at improving quality of education include covering all government schools with computer education, setting up special schools for the talented children need to be intensified.

xi) There are also correspondence courses at school level and special programmes for the benefit of the school drop-outs, housewives, etc. They need to be expanded.

xii) At the post senior-secondary level, there are several technical institutions providing degree or diploma or even shorter courses with a certificate.

xiii) The private sector contribution in various forms of training and skill development is not fully documented. However, some private institutions are run by fly-by-night operators, which give a bad name to all others. Though long-term courses (Degree/Diploma) are regulated by the AICTE, there is no law like the Delhi School Education Act for full reporting of new technical training institutions, for short or medium term courses.

xiv) There is need for a comprehensive survey of training providers. The training providers need some regulatory framework which has legal backing so as to ensure high standards of training and protect the trainees from exploitation.

xv) Under the Revised National Policy on Education, the priority has been assigned to vocational education. But, the enrolment under vocational education programme is very low. Vocational education needs proper, continuous and comprehensive research including the aspect of its integration with training and hands on experience on the job itself.

xvi) For higher education Delhi is considered to be the most preferred destination. The city is home to several renowned universities, which attract students from all parts of the globe. Still Delhi government has taken initiative to establish a new university and it included Guru Govind Singh Indraprastha University (GGSIP) in the list of universities. The government has encouraged and promoted the private initiative in the field of higher education through affiliation to GGSIP. In order to keep pace with the changing industry environment the government propose to initiate courses like Biotechnology, Plant genetics and Molecular Biology, Environment studies etc., in the colleges fully funded by Delhi Government. To keep pace with the growing demands of the present day situation, the university of Delhi has included in its curriculum vocational courses.

xvii) The Directorate of Higher Education has prepared a comprehensive policy for higher education for next five years which includes opening of new Degree Colleges in various localities of Delhi and of Indira Gandhi Institute of Technology under GGSIP.

xviii) The issues related to better management of higher education such as strengthening of the Directorate of Higher Education, directing colleges for proper utilisation of funds, financial audits for their proper uses, acquisition of new sites for opening of various colleges, opening of more new hostels for girls are addressed in new policy. In addition to these to encourage meritorious students studying in Government colleges and to motivate intelligent and serious students of general stream education i.e., Science, Commerce, and Arts, in a three years Degree Course with two segments *viz.*, Honours and General Pass courses a cash award of Rs. 5000 each is proposed.

10. Health

10.1 Current Status

i) Delhi has done well in family welfare with birth rate being 18.1 against the national average of 25.4.

ii) Sex ratio at birth i.e., 820 females birth/1000 male births suggests the prevalence of sex selective abortion. This needs to be probed.

iii) Communicable diseases are still a major cause of morbidity. However, this trend is rapidly changing and is expected to reverse within the new next few years.

iv) Delhi represents a widely varying populace and correspondingly a widely varying disease pattern ranging from lifestyle diseases on the one hand to the infective and malnutrition related diseases on the other.

v) Many urbanised villages lack basic infrastructure and proper planning of the residential areas leading to unhealthy overcrowding with unhealthy surroundings.

vi) The life expectancy at birth for Delhi's population is 68.6 years compared to an all India average of 60.7 years.

vii) Delhi has a fairly well established healthcare infrastructure for its people with one of the highest bed capacity (1.98 beds/1000 persons) compared to the national average of about 0.7 beds per 1000 persons. The per capita public expenditure at Rs. 436 in 2001-02 is more than double of the all-India average of Rs. 180. But this is inadequate since most people depend on the government hospitals and dispensaries.

viii) Delhi has a fairly well established representation of the private entrepreneurs in health sector. Their range of practice varies from individual practice and small nursing homes to large charitable and corporate hospitals. However, these excellent medical facilities are beyond the reach of the common man.

ix) The state has constantly allocated more than 7 per cent of the Plan outlay to the health sector and has utilised more than 80 per cent of the outlay.

x) Infant mortality rate has significantly come down from 45 per 1000 to 29 per 1000 between 1990 and 2001.

xi) Tuberculosis is still a major public health problem in Delhi.

xii) Cholera and gastro-enteritis occurrence is not uncommon.

xiii) Delhi is prone to malaria and dengue.

xiv) As far as immunisation of children is concerned, as per NFHS-33, 63.2 per cent children received complete immunisation.

xv) Delhi falls under low prevalence state for HIV/AIDS. However, 42,000 HIV positive cases are estimated till January 2006, a total of 2759 cases were reported till August 2006 while 322 deaths were reported till January 2006.

xvi) Incidence of cancer, diabetes and fatal traffic accidents etc., are also seen more in the urban population. Delhi with 93 per cent urban population is more vulnerable to such diseases.

xvii) There is a multiplicity of agencies operating their healthcare outlets in different areas or for defined subset of populations in different areas like Delhi Government, MCD, NDMC, CGHS, DGHS, ESI, and Army etc., leading to some overlaps/duplications of services with wastage of efforts and resources on one-hand and deficient services on the other.

10.2 Recommendations

i) There are multiple agencies operating the health care outlets leading to duplication of services, wastage of efforts and resources and deficient services. Exercise to optimise the use of available resources needs to be taken.

ii) Qualified hospital administrators need to be posted in government hospitals to improve their services.

iii) Integration of the local area family practitioners with the government hospitals and dispensaries in the area for two-way referrals needs to be promoted.

iv) Development of high-class healthcare infrastructure in NCR towns should be encouraged.

v) In the localities deficient in potable water supply system, sewerage/sanitation system and electric supply infrastructure, their improvement will minimise incidence of morbidity and mortality.

vi) Greater attention needs to be given to health education of public with emphasis on preventive aspects.

vii) Health related topics should be included in school and college curricula.

viii) Strict enforcement of laws for control of food/ water borne infections and adulterations is necessary.

ix) Health Insurance sector base and corporate support to their employees for medical check ups and treatments need to be widened.

x) Well-equipped and dedicated trauma centers along the main highways entering Delhi need to be set up.

xi) Industries need to be shifted to outskirts to reduce health hazards, accidents, pollution and traffic congestion.

xii) The hazard caused by stray dogs and animals needs to be addressed to minimise traffic hazards/accidents and need for anti-rabies vaccine.

xiii) The values for various parameters like the gender, educational levels, residence type, region, religion, caste, community, socioeconomic status, occupation, etc., are not available and studies need to be undertaken accordingly.

xiv) Policies and programmes should be oriented to the realisation of the 'Vision' of the Chief Minister to make Delhi as a 'role model' for healthcare infrastructure.

11. Tourism

11.1 A Brief Picture of the Delhi Tourism Scene

(a) Tourist Traffic Trends

Global trends indicate an annual growth of 4.5 per cent for international tourism in the 2002-2012 period. In India the growth trend is higher at 9.7 per cent in the next ten years. Growth in domestic tourism is likely to be at a higher rate and will impact future growth. In Delhi the Commonwealth games 2010 provides a special opportunity to development as a destination.

Delhi accounts for 30.8 per cent of international arrivals. It accounts for 51 per cent (1.35 million) of total arrivals of international tourists. This has been showing a downward trend (it was 62 per cent earlier). It accounts for only 0.5 per cent of domestic tourists (most of them are pilgrim tourists).

(b) Hotel Rooms

i) Delhi has 9841 classified rooms—nearly half in the five star category.

ii) Almost an equal number are in the unclassified category.

iii) There is an obvious imbalance in the categories and classification spread in the tourist accomodation.

iv) Growth in demand has led to recent scarcity of hotel rooms to the tune of 3,000 rooms.

(c) Tourist Transport

i) Tourist transport needs to be strengthened by improving tourist transport facilities.

ii) Existing infrastructure can be improved by better traffic movement, flyovers, etc.

iii) Improved services—Radio taxis, Volvo buses, easier interstate movement.

iv) Metro will improve overall connectivity but have limited, impact on tourist movement.

(d) Tourist Traffic Providers

Travel agents, tour operators, guides, need to improve their quality of service and reliability.

(e) Role of Department of Tourism, DTTDC

However, Delhi Tourism Department has a very limited role in creating an impact on tourism in the state. Funds and resources are disproportionately low for the objectives indentified. DTTDC's role as an implementing agency is diluted by other activities eg., liquor trade, flyover construction.

11.2 Policy Since the Tenth Plan

The Tenth Five Year Plan provided a significant shift in policy by giving higher priority to this sector and offered increased opportunity for private investment and participation in tourism development. The new policy is based on "Tourism for All" and is covered under 'Bhagidari'. It is a government led, private sector driven community welfare approach. It seeks to promote Delhi as a World Class Heritage City for which special initiatives are proposed in developing Tourism in the following areas:

i) Cultural/Heritage Tourism

ii) Business Tourism

iii) Convention and Conference Tourism (MICE)

iv) Ethnic handicrafts, fashion, cuisine

v) Leisure Tourism—shopping, golf, adventure

vi) Medical/Health Tourism

vii) Develop Delhi as a hub for Tourism in North India.

11.3 Human Resource Development

Efforts are being made to enlarge training facilities to produce the needed skilled manpower for the jobs that get created with the growth of tourism.

11.4 Suggestions—Way Forward for Delhi Tourism

a) A new mindset for Tourism Development is needed. It means that–

i) Tourism must be seen as "the industry of industry" to fully realise the socioeconomic benefits.

ii) A statutory Tourism Board will make for more effective implementation and management of Tourism in the state.

iii) An empowered body such as a Tourism Board can effect better "Convergence" with important state agencies such as NDMC, DMC, DDA, Police, Transport etc.

iv) It can also coordinate more effectively with Airport Authority, Railway, ASI etc.

b) Delhi can become a world class Heritage City by developing "integrated tourism zones"—keeping tourism needs in mind and creating a unique tourism experience at each location as identified:

i) Red Fort/Chandni Chowk.

ii) Purana Quila/Pragati Maidan/Humayun's Tomb.

iii) Rajiv Chowk, India Gate, Rashtrapati Bhawan.

iv) Qutub Minar, Mehrauli heritage area, Garden of Five Senses.

v) Create tourism-friendly transport and other services linking them to Airport, Hotels, Railway stations, and Road transport.

c) Create a world class convention facility with all the related infrastructure and systems including administrative and manpower support.

d) Develop Delhi as a destination for Medical Tourism—Task Force recommendations or "Chemical Establishment Act", medical visa, health insurance and linkages with tourism marketing need to be acted on.

e) Develop leisure and entertainment facilities at selected locations:

i) Shopping—handicrafts, fashion goods, jewellery.

ii) Parks, gardens, water bodies, golf courses.

iii) Food and ethnic cuisine.

iv) Festivals and special events.

f) Create effective linkages with NCR and nearby destinations particularly Agra so as to prolong stay by tourists.

12. Employment, Rural Development and Poverty Alleviation

a) Main Features of the employment situation are:

i) The employment base in Delhi is almost entirely composed of services of various kinds and manufacturing.

ii) It has a low workforce participation rate of 33.5 per cent as against 39.2 per cent at the national level.

iii) Males account for 86 per cent of labour force as a whole with urban areas indicating as high as 91 per cent share of the males. Majority workforce is in the regular/wage-employed category for females the figure is over 77 per cent.

iv) The largest sector of activity on the basis of workforce numbers is the service group, trade and hotels etc., followed by public administration. Services are followed by manufacturing.

v) The construction sector accounts for less than 6 per cent of total workforce.

vi) Delhi has an overall unemployment rate of 12.5 per cent, higher than the national level with very high unemployment rates for females in the age group 20-24 and 25-29 years.

vii) The male unemployment rates are very high for the age groups 15-19 and 20-24 years. These are much higher than the countrywide picture.

viii) In Delhi, the phenomenon of 'discouraged workers' could possibly reduce the workforce participation rate and ultimately the rate of migration into Delhi itself.

ix) Educated unemployed form a large proportion of the unemployed.

x) The simple rate of growth of the registered unemployed persons has been 2.5 per cent a year—majority of them is increasingly from the educated category.

b) Suggestions: The above deficiencies in the employment situation need to be carefully examined and a plan prepared to take effective remedial measures. The employment situation reflects the state of health of the economy of the area and if the aspiration is to have Delhi as a capital which may be counted among the best capitals in the world, the situation will have to be addressed on priority.

13. Science and Technology

13.1 Categories of Activities

The activities in this sector can be divided into three categories:

a) Category 1: Science & Technology (S&T)-Information Technology (IT) and Biotechnology (BT) Education including technical training. It includes School level Science (including IT), vocational training in high technology (including IT related CAD/ CAM), popularisation of IT and lately also higher education in Science, IT and Biotechnology.

b) Category 2: Research and Development in S&T-IT&BT.

c) Category 3: Use of S&T-IT&BT in socio-economic sectors

It includes use of Information Technology (IT) in governance and health delivery, software industry and promotion of IT and Biotechnology related enterprise. S&T component is also reflected in programmes for development of rural areas, in energy supply, small-scale industry development and environmental protection.

13.2 Channels of Activities

Activities are channeled through three main agencies; the departments and institutions under the GNCTD (Government of Delhi), laboratories of Central Government agencies including Universities and IIT and private sector including NGO.

- Government of the National Capital Territory of Delhi (GNCTD), MCD and NDMC are active in Category 1 and Category 3 programmes. Category 2, namely R&D is mainly performed by the laboratories of the Central Government and Universities and IIT located in the NCTD. The thrust of S&T activities supported by the State Government is on IT and science education in schools, IT in governance, IT and BT embedded in its industrial and rural development programmes.
- Private sector is active in IT and Biotechnology marketing and consultancy as also lately in software industry through the IT Park being set up by the Delhi Metro Rail Corporation and in Biotechnology R&D Centre at South Campus of the University of Delhi.

- NGO participation is in science education, environment awareness, and water conservation and in rural development through Bhagidari is also note worthy.

13.3 Recommendations

a) The vision from the point of Science and Technology should be to make the economy of National Capital Region of Delhi a knowledge intensive economy.

b) One of the areas of thrust is to upgrade the technical competence of human resource in the use of modern techniques such as CAD/CAM and IT enabling them to work in industrial complexes.

c) Manufacturing units being private sector ventures, the technical training and facilities need to be matched with the demand profiles of the manufacturing units. It would be appropriate to associate the companies with the training programmes

d) Improvement of rural parts of Delhi by applying so called rural technologies developed in laboratories is another development goal receiving attention in the development plans of Delhi

e) The maximum concentration of villages is in the Mehrauli sub-division of Delhi (28 villages). Linking technology suppliers/sources and the rural populations is critical for such programmes. Some business and management schools are located in and around rural areas and can become effective link institutions. Business and management schools need to be utilised for coordinated implementation including the activities of NGOs.

f) It is recognised that knowledge industries are highly competitive and market niche of these units will have to be carefully developed. Exercise in this direction through industry involvement is necessary.

g) Substantive investment is envisaged for introduction of IT in government departments. There is a desire in the plan to strengthen government-citizen interface. The Delhi Government has made progress towards computerisation of its administration.

h) The next critical issue is the easy accessibility of information to the citizens. It is necessary to establish effective and sustainable network of access centres. These can be set up as micro enterprises. The example of the entrepreneurial model of AISECT (All India Society for Electronics and Computer Technology) that has already spread all over the country with maximum concentration in semi urban and rural areas of Madhya Pradesh and Chhattisgarh is worth emulating. AISECT model has been recognised by the Indian Innovation Award as the largest network with potential of wider applicability. This model can be effectively used in the National Capital Region.

i) Setting up of IT and Biotechnology industrial units in Delhi are important new initiatives towards knowledge based industries. These are best established through industry–academic linkages making full use of Delhi's strong conglomeration of post graduate science and engineering education (including Biotechnology and IT) and of R&D laboratories supported by the state and the Centre.

14. Labour

14.1 Labour Situation

The main features of the labour situation in Delhi are:

a) The proportion of employment in the organised sector is much higher than the national average.

b) Most activities are still in the unorganised sector without proper reporting.

c) The employment exchanges have failed to satisfy both the employers and potential employees. The organised sector has its own recruitment mechanisms.

d) Both the employees and the training providers are more and more in the private sector.

e) The job opportunities in Delhi have not only continued to grow, they have also changed and become more complex.

f) Requirement of any skill or education level is met by outsiders coming to Delhi in search of employment.

g) The casual workers in Delhi's small industries/enterprises came from outside without much of skills and learned the crafts on-the-job.

14.2 Skill Development and Training

a) In an open economy like Delhi, the classical

methods of manpower balancing as part of manpower planning are not practical. It is also not practical to decide the length of the course, subject matter, the skill sets and the teachers at the government level in a centralised fashion.

b) Delhi's economy lies mainly in the service sector whose needs are not known in advance. The government institutes have found it difficult to change courses/curricula to meet such short-term needs of potential employers.

c) In the case of Information Technology enabled services private training providers did the job under some kind of supervision of the Ministry of IT and the government accepted a variety of courses with different lengths, different quality/levels and different subject matters in the private unorganised sector. Likewise, there is enormous scope for innovation and participation by private sector to develop and organise a variety of courses.

d) The providers of the training in the private sector are in a position to develop some skills of use to the employers; they need to be encouraged.

e) In this regard ideas like Skill Development Fund have been mooted but none has come into existence so far.

f) However, government must ensure proper supervision over such training providers so that fresh migrants or weaker sections of society are protected against potential exploitation.

14.3 Labour Management

a) Labour management especially that of skilled/educated labour force or those engaged in services outside the government has not been a problem in the city.

b) The behaviour of trade unions in large manufacturing enterprises, i.e., blue-collar workers has been always different from that in the service sector and educated people. Formal Trade Unions have not had much impact on workers in Delhi after a large number of manufacturing enterprises, especially the bigger ones shifted out of Delhi.

c) The unorganised sector manufacturing, by definition, is not unionised but such workers face potential exploitation such as low wages and long hours of work.

d) The scheme of the NDA government for providing social security to unorganised sector workers became a non-starter.

e) The government needs to provide some form of social security to such workers.

15. Women and Vulnerable Groups

15.1 Sources of Vulnerability

Vulnerabilities are derived from a host of parameters including social, physical, gender related, economic, financial, infrastructural, health-related, legal, political or institutional. Powerlessness, income and structural poverty, and social exclusion are the characteristics associated with vulnerabilities.

15.2 Categories of Vulnerable Groups

Ten different segments are categorised as vulnerable groups that include women, socially disadvantaged groups, child labour and street children, the disabled and challenged, migrants, shelterless, those affected by the inadequacy of public transportation, unorganised workers (such as street vendors, sex and domestic workers), the elderly, and children facing violence and abuse.

15.2.1 Socially Deprived Sections

The socially deprived sections belonging to Scheduled Castes and Other Backward Castes face social discrimination and educational differentiation in terms of access and retention. There are a number of socioeconomic reasons. The initial unequal resource position perpetuates imbalance and disparity in their access to other infrastructure. In the labour market, they tend to find place in the lower echelons of the job hierarchies.

15.2.2 Children

a) Substantial numbers of children in the capital work as service providers, helpers, assistants, vendors and so on.

b) The poor, slum dwellers, pavement dwellers, shelterless, orphans, and street children are all vulnerable, easily exploitable and voiceless.

c) The concerns of many of these workers are akin to the plight of the unorganised workers who are unprotected by legal provisions and have no security as workers.

d) These children are deprived of childhood and avenues to develop themselves.

e) The girl child is often left in charge of the younger siblings in order to relieve her mother for labour market participation at the cost of her own all round growth.

f) The street children are exposed to and unprotected from abuse of various kinds, with the girls susceptible to finding themselves as part of trafficking and sex worker chains.

15.2.3 The Disabled

a) The challenges posed by disability, both physical and mental, render persons vulnerable.

b) The lack of understanding regarding these adds to the difficulties of the challenged in negotiating the institutional and infrastructural constraints present.

c) The incorporation of the disabled in the 2001 Census was a landmark that provided one crucial tool to make their presence and needs visible.

15.2.4 Migrants

a) Migration into the capital-state from various parts has assumed a problem of tremendous magnitude.

b) The migrants are able to find some paid employment, howsoever low paying and insecure.

c) There are however, no provisions for them by the state administrative authorities in terms of housing, water, toilets, electricity and so on, leave alone the needs of their families.

d) Commonly housed in some slum squatter settlement, these families have to face many difficulties.

e) The attempt to clean the city and remove the slums by relocation and rehabilitation without adequate transportation facilities curtails the workers from negotiating between their residences and workplaces.

f) There is need to reexamine the demand pattern for bus routes after resettlement of large slums as well as industrial complexes subsequent to closure of polluting industries.

15.2.5 Unorganised Sector Workers

a) The vulnerability of the unorganised sector workers arises out of the ambiguity in their legal status as no overt recognition of their work/ activity exists.

b) These workers go through undue suffering.

c) The lack of recognition as sex workers and the taboo attached to the service provider while the demander is often unaffected, makes the women/ sex worker vulnerable. The recognition of the sex worker to some extent has occurred in the context of the drive for protection against HIV/ AIDS.

15.2.6 Vulnerable Groups Not Covered Above

a) The elderly and the aged who are left alone in the city after children have gone for greener pastures or due to the death of the other family members, are vulnerable on account of the insecurity stemming from their loneliness and their health needs.

b) Abuse and violence forms another deplorable dimension of vulnerability faced by children in the capital. From heinous crimes like rape and murder to kidnapping and abduction, there seems to be a growing incidence of crimes against children.

c) The pedestrian in the wake of the flyovers and high speed roads that have come up faces great difficulty and feels unsafe while wanting to cross the road.

d) In the context of transportation, the shrinking spaces for the manually driven handcarts, cycle rickshaws and bicycles make things difficult for the class.

15.3 Women's Issues

The issues pertaining to women in Delhi in the context of vulnerability go beyond the poor and the needy and cover even the prosperous and better-off populations. There are various indicators to establish women's vulnerability. Declining sex ratio highlights the lower significance given to the girl child.

16. Industrial Development

16.1 Contribution of Primary, Secondary and Tertiary Sectors to Economy of NCTD

a) The contribution of the primary sector has rapidly declined and has become negligible. The share of manufacturing in the 80s and the first half of the 90s has declined from about 20 per cent to about 12 per cent. However, the contribution of Tertiary Sector has been rapidly rising and is dominant in the economy of NCTD.

b) The share of registered sub-sector (39.8 per cent) in total manufacturing in 2002-03 was well below its share for the nation as a whole at 66.1 per cent.

16.2 Contribution by Industry Groups

a) The top two industry groups alone (Electricity and Textile Products) contribute more than one-half to net value added. The composition of the industrial base of Delhi, evaluated in terms of share in employment, suggests a similar pattern of greater concentration.

b) In 2002-03 Delhi was heavily over-represented in publishing, printing, wearing apparel, radio, TV, communication equipment etc., and furniture and manufacturing etc.

c) Industry groups that are gravely under-represented include coke, refined petroleum products etc., tobacco products, other non-metallic mineral products, textile products, basic metals, and wood and wood products except furniture.

d) Delhi has the most specialised industrial structure as compared with the 14 major states. The specialisation index estimated for Delhi suggests an increasing degree of specialisation

e) The highest contributor to net value added was textile products (17.5 per cent) followed by machinery and equipment (12.0 per cent), paper and paper products (6.7), food products (6.4), and basic chemicals (4.4 per cent).

f) The concentration ratios derived in respect of both the top 3 and 5 industry groups suggest that there was clearly an increase in concentration, with the top two industry groups alone (Electricity and Textile Products) contributing more than one-half to net value added.

g) The Hirschman-Herfindahl indices derived for both the reference years also clearly indicate greater concentration in terms of share in NVA.

16.3 Industrial Structure

a) The industry-mix and competitive effects operated very differently in the 90s. Out of the 22 industry groups only nine had a positive industry mix effect and even more significantly, only 3 groups experienced a positive competitive effect.

b) Examination of some of the ratios and technical coefficients underlying the overall industrial (factory) structure indicates that the region does not seem to be suffering from locational disadvantages (relative to the country at large) associated with high levels capital use.

c) In 2002-03, the capital intensity for the region (average for all industries factory sector) was lower than the national average.

d) Decomposing employment growth indicates that in the 1980s nine industry groups experienced industry-mix and competitive effects that were both positive. These were beverages, tobacco and related products, textile products, leather and leather products, basic chemicals and chemical products, rubber and plastic products, machinery and equipment, repair of capital goods, generation and distribution of gas, steam etc., and storage and warehousing services.

e) The industry-mix and competitive effects operated very differently after the 1980s. Out of the 22 industry groups, only nine—NIC codes 24, 26, 30, 31, 34, 38, 39, 41-43, and 74—had a positive industry mix effect and even more significantly, only 3 groups—NIC codes 26, 40, and 41-43—experienced a positive competitive effect. Only two groups—textile products, and generation and distribution of gas, steam etc.—had both effects as positive.

f) Examination of some of the ratios and technical coefficients underlying the overall industrial (factory) structure indicates that the region does not seem to be suffering from locational disadvantages (relative to the country at large) associated with high levels capital use.

g) The capital intensity for the region (average for all industries factory sector) was lower than the national average.

h) The capital-output ratio was also lower within the region, being only slightly above half of the national ratio. Not more than five industry groups—NIC codes 16, 17, 19, 28, and 29—had capital-output ratios higher than the respective groups at the national level and of these only the last two were among the major industries within the region.

i) The average wage rate of labour went up in absolute terms. This increase, however, was commensurate with that for the entire industrial system (factory sector) of the country at large.

j) Labour productivity also increased for Delhi during this period as it did at the all-India level.

k) Delhi's industries utilised a greater amount of input per unit of output relative to the industries at the all India level. Only industry groups—NIC code 15, 19, 23, 29, 32, 34, 35, 36, and 'Others'—all had input use levels lower than their counter parts at the national level. Of these, industry groups food products and beverages, and machinery and equipment n.e.c. were among the more important in Delhi's industrial sector.

l) There was less generation of value added per unit of output by the regional industrial system as compared to the nation. Industry groups—NIC code 17, 19, 23, 24, 26, 29, 32, 33, 34, 36, and 'Others'—had higher value added per unit of output values than that for all-India.

m) The profitability of Delhi's industrial system, measured as profits per unit of value of output, was below that of the three industrialised states—Maharashtra, Gujarat, and Tamil Nadu—for most of the eighties and then, though fluctuating, became comparable with them. The profit ratio for Delhi was actually the highest for about half of the remaining period.

n) The movement of the Index of total factor productivity was broadly similar between the nation and the region over the decade of the eighties but became differentiated from the beginning of the nineties. From the mid-90s, total factor productivity of Delhi's industries grew at rates faster than that of the nation and even that experienced by the three developed industrial states. Delhi's industrial system seems to be becoming relatively more efficient than the rest of the country in terms of factor use.

o) There are 2.30 lakhs (NSSO 56 round) enterprises engaged in activities pertaining to unorganised manufacturing and 2.2 lakhs enterprises in unorganised service sector together making 4.5 lakh enterprises in unorganised manufacturing and service sector in Delhi.

16.4 Productivity and Other Indicators

a) The capital-output ratio was also lower within the region, being only slightly above half of the national ratio. Not more than five industry groups had capital-output ratios higher than the respective groups at the national level and of these only the last two were among the major groups within the region.

b) The average wage rate of labour went up in absolute terms over the period 1980-81 to 2001-02, this increase being commensurate with that for the entire industrial system (factory sector) of the country at large.

c) Labour productivity also increased for Delhi during this period as it did at the all-India level.

d) Delhi's industries utilised a greater amount of input per unit of output relative to the industries at the all India level. In 2002-03, only 8 industry groups had input use levels lower than their counter parts at the national level. Of these, industry groups food products and beverages, and machinery and equipment were among the more important groups in Delhi's industrial sector.

e) There was less generation of value added per unit of output by the regional industrial system as compared to the nation. In 2002-03, 10 industry groups had higher value added per unit of output values than that for all-India.

f) The profitability of Delhi's industrial (factory) sector was below that of the nation for much of the decade of the eighties but moved up above all-India levels for the remainder of the period, except for 1995-96 and 1996-97.

16.5 Priorities

a) Though manufacturing accounts for about 12 per cent of Delhi's GSDP and about 40 per cent of the total work force, the priority given to the industrial sector in the Five Year Plans is extremely low. In the Tenth Plan, the share of industry in the outlay decreased by nearly half to a mere 0.43 per cent of total outlays as compared to its expenditure share in the Ninth Plan.

b) In terms of expenditure priorities, industry dropped to rank 19 out of a total of 31 sectors. The all-States average outlay on industry for the Tenth Plan is 3.2 per cent—nearly eight times that for Delhi.

16.6 Environmental Factors Impact on Industry

a) The closure of many polluting and hazardous industrial units and the Relocation Scheme for non-conforming units, though reducing environmental pollution levels, may be expected to have had an adverse impact on industrial growth and employment within Delhi.

b) The contribution of industrial sources of pollution (including Thermal Power Plants) to ambient air has come down from 56 per cent in 1970-71 to 20 per cent in 2000-01, and with the coming into operation of all the 15 CETPs the contribution of this sector to both air and water pollution levels would be heavily reduced.

c) Under these circumstances there is some justification for the ongoing effort for regularisation of other industries situated in residential/non-conforming areas.

d) Corrective measures incorporating a system of suitable incentives and disincentives are required in relation to such industries in order to ensure shifting and relocation of industries failing to meet the broadened parameters in terms of environmental and other norms.

e) The Master Plan for Delhi rules out large and heavy industries. The share of manufacturing in GSDP has come down from 20 per cent in the mid-90s to around 12 per cent.

16.7 Problems and Policies

The major problems faced by small and tiny enterprises are power cuts, and shortage of capital. Another problem is perceived competition from larger units.

16.8 Policy Intervention Required

Policy Intervention is required to achieve the following ends:

a) Delhi does not become structurally disadvantaged in that its industries loose out in competition with other similar industries in other states.

b) The industrial base of Delhi broadens and becomes more diversified thus ensuring a higher level of resilience of the regional economy.

c) Strengthening of inter-regional and inter-industry linkages.

d) Delhi specialises in 'growth' industries that will result in higher overall growth

e) Delhi does not specialise in cyclically sensitive industries that are particularly sensitive to cyclical swings.

f) To the extent possible, that the prevalent terms of trade do not become detrimental to its current exports and imports.

16.9 Measures Proposed

a) Ad hoc licensing of industrial units should be avoided and policy measures introduced to ensure the dispersal of existing industries as well as their modernisation and technological upgradation.

b) The importance of unorganised sector in small-scale industry should be recognised so that proper policies as per their need could be designed.

c) There is need to review the credit policies for small scale units falling into the unorganised sector and to resolve the issue of power cuts.

d) There is necessity to save the small-scale sector from competition from larger units by providing them facilities for technical upgradation and marketing.

e) Corrective measures incorporating a system of suitable incentives and disincentives are required to ensure shifting and relocation of industries failing to meet the broadened parameters in terms of environmental and other norms.

f) The ongoing effort for regularisation of other industries situated in residential/non-conforming areas should ensure that they are non-polluting and non-hazardous. Regularisation would avoid loss of output, employment, under-utilisation of capacity, entrepreneurial confidence and productivity.

17. Institutional Reforms and Governance

17.1 Evolution of Institutions of Governance

a. The Institutions of Governance of NCTD have evolved in the context of the conflicts inherent in the situation of Delhi and the need to reconcile them. On the one hand, Delhi being the capital of the country, its governance cannot be left at the mercy of the Government of NCTD which, if given the status of a normal State Government, would be prone to be swayed by narrow state interests rather than the broad national interests. On the other hand, democratic aspirations of millions of people residing in Delhi for self governance cannot be ignored. Hence initially a strong MCD came into being. MCD did not perform all the functions of the state government and there was the institution of the Lt. Governor. In due course an elected assembly was introduced. It had a cabinet headed by Chief Minister and it comprised other ministers. Law and order and the subject of land are with the

Union Government. MCD enjoys very considerable autonomy and many of the functions normally performed by state governments are assigned to the MCD. Since NCTD is a UT with features of a State, the Lt. Governor is a very powerful institution. This arrangement has certain consequences. First, there are authorities and institutions, working under the control of different constitutional and legal authorities. Many of these authorities have overlapping functions and are dependent for inputs and help from others for discharging their responsibilities. Any issue cutting across a number of authorities would need enormous coordination and consequently time and human resources. For example, responsibility of education is of the state government, but the schools are run by the MCD, land is with the DDA, Sarva Shiksha Abhiyan would be with the state government. Similar would be the situation in the matter of housing, slums, road construction and maintenance, transport and so on. The situation gives rise to conflicts between and among institutions and affords them the opportunity to shirk responsibility for deficient performance.

17.2 Pursuit of Excellence in Governance—A Vision

The Government of Delhi has adopted a vision to facilitate the pursuit of excellence in governance through improvements in Government structures and processes.

17.2.1 Means Used

a) The means used to achieve the improvements consist of:

   i) Promote role of civil society, people's participation and decentralisation through the introduction of Bhagidari Scheme within the government departments and its agencies including those under the Union Government

   ii) Institute Preventive Vigilance

   iii) Introduction of:

   - E-governance for the citizens of Delhi and creation of a dynamic websites of Departments/Agencies.
   - Right of the citizen to information.
   - Mechanism to redress public grievances of which establishment of Public Grievances Commission are the main elements.

   iv) Civil Servicc Reforms

   v) Procedural Reform

   vi) Synergy and Coordination

   vii) Empowerment of the weak

b) Bhagidari Scheme

The Bhagidari Programme envisages voluntary participation of the citizens. Efforts have been made to make it well structured and sustainable. Nine organisations and 64 of their activities have been covered. A 'Bhagidari Cell' has been created in the Chief Minister's office. A detailed plan of 'Citizen-Government Interface' has been prepared. It has been decentralised at the Revenue District level.

In consultation with the Asian Centre for Organisation Research and Development, (ACORD), the 'Large Group Interactive Events' (LGIE) a model was developed to train citizen-groups and government officials to agree on solutions and their implementation.

The programme has shown encouraging results leading to the formation of more than 1200 citizen groups that have not only been successful in addressing their day-to-day problems, but have also been providing help to public utility departments in maintenance and upgradation of services.

c) Decentralisation

Administrative Decentralisation

With a view to making the access of the citizen to the government easier, in 1996 the exercise of decentralising the DC office was done by setting up 27 SDM offices and 9 DC offices.

d) Vigilance

The Central Vigilance Commissioner has jurisdiction over personnel of the NCTD.

The Delhi Lokayukta & Upalokayukta Act, 1995 provides a forum for attending to complaints against public functionaries to eradicate the vice of corruption, favouritism, abuse of position and power and present cleaner image. The Act takes within its ambit the Ministers including the Chief Minister, Members of Legislative Assembly, Members of Municipal Corporation etc.

e) Preventive Vigilance—Openness and Transparency

The Government of NCT of Delhi has initiated the following actions with emphasis on "preventive vigilance".

- **E-governance for the Citizens of Delhi:** The government has set up a dynamic website of Departments/Agencies to provide on line services including services on e-applications and making on line complaint. The citizen can also check the status of the complaint, send a reminder and send suggestions.

  However, introduction of e-governance requires the re-engineering of the processes in the government and its agencies and of the structure of the system of keeping and maintaining the record. A plan needs to be prepared after detailed study of the working of the various departments to take e-governance to its logical consequence of easy interaction between the citizen and the government.

- **Right to Information:** The Delhi Right to Information Act, 2001 makes provision for securing information as a matter of right. It provides for right to appeal in Public Grievances Commission.

- **Public Grievances Commission:** The Government has set up a Public Grievance Commission, which attends to complaints received against the departments of Government of Delhi, its local bodies, undertakings, autonomous institutions/ undertakings etc.

- **Citizen's Charter:** The citizens' charter programme has been adopted in the NCTD. These charters are required to spell out the standards of services and time limits within which the public can reasonably expect the disposal of the requests made by them to the government. Delhi Government has brought out 73 such citizens' charters. Coupled with the enactment of the Right to Information and putting in to place the mechanism of dealing with public grievances, the framework of providing the basic information to the public and to open the vistas of transparency and accountability in the systems has been created.

17.3 *Measures to Improve Governance in Municipal Corporation of Delhi*

a) The Municipal Corporation of Delhi provides civic services to some of the most densely populated areas in the world covering both rural and urban areas. The measures initiated are briefly mentioned below:

b) The entire MCD area is divided into 12 zones to make access easier.

c) Citizen Service Bureau:

The concept behind establishing Citizen Service Bureau is to provide all municipal services under one roof. MCD has started a unique and path breaking IT initiative with the objective to deliver electronically its services to citizens of Delhi through a Citizen Service Bureau set up, one in each Zone and one at Town Hall.

17.4 *New Delhi Municipal Council (NDMC)*

a) NDMC is a municipality with a difference and also performs the role of a mini-government. It is perhaps the only municipality in the country that supplies electricity and water and its discretionary functions encompass promotion of sports, art, music and culture, maintenance of libraries, and care for the old, mentally and hearing impaired.

The area of NDMC includes the seat of Central Government, Rashtrapati Bhawan, the Prime Minister's office and residence, Central Government office, Foreign Missions, residences of Ministers, Members of Parliament, Diplomats and Central Government employees.

b) Measures taken to improve governance include:

- **Citizens' Charter:** The NDMC had issued the first charter in 1997 and has issued the new one in February 2005. It is a measure towards transparency and efficient and timely provision of services.

- **Information and Facilitation Centre:** NDMC has set up an Information and Facilitation Centre and opened two Palika Suvidha Kendras where citizens can pay their taxes, fees etc., obtain birth/death certificates, book Barat Ghars and register their complaints relating to civic services.

- **Annual Administrative Report:** The NDMC publishes an Annual Administrative Report enabling those interested in getting to know the work done in the year gone by and the programme for the coming year.

17.5 *Delhi Development Authority*

a) Delhi Development Authority was constituted by promulgating the Delhi Development Act, 1957 with the primary objective of ensuring the development of Delhi in accordance with a plan. The planned development of Delhi is the main function of DDA. The Master Plan for Delhi-2021 has been prepared and brought in to force. It addresses the issues related to the use of land and property. It is hoped that the Master Plan will enable the realisation of the vision of a world class capital for Delhi.

b) Despite very impressive achievements of DDA, it has an image of being an organisation that needs to improve its sensitivity to the needs of its clients, efficiency and public perception about integrity of the organisation. The organisation is actively engaged in taking a host of measures among which transparency and automation are basic which if successful can make a qualitative impact.

17.6 Transparency and Automation in DDA

To minimise downtime, it has introduced systemic automation in the following departments:

- Land Disposal.
- Housing.
- Launching of a Website. This is dynamic and provides information on various aspects like housing, land, master plan, environment etc. The results of housing and land and tender notices are displayed. Senior officers are reachable through e-mail. Different forms are available on the website which can be down loaded.
- Land Record.
- Normal administrative functions such as payroll, receipt and dispatch, legal cases monitoring system etc. A training programme for computer literacy seeks to train the staffing in the use of computers.
- Vigilance department takes action to see that there are no unwarranted irregularities and also handle complaints that could tarnish the image of the DDA.

17.7 Conclusion

Any fast expanding city has to struggle on a continuing basis to find solutions to new problems that keep on arising, some of them totally unforeseen. In the case of Delhi, the growth of the city could already have reached the limits of "carrying capacity". Many of the resultant problems are known and some unanticipated problems may arise.

The experience in Delhi has been that the authorities have been unable to anticipate many major problems and have reacted only after they have arisen. This is indicative of serious deficiency in the institutional arrangement prevalent in Delhi. The deficiencies have been pointed out in the report. However, proposing a well studied, analysed solution is outside the scope of this study. It must be stated, however, that developing a more effective and efficient institutional arrangement in the very complex situation of Delhi is an extremely difficult task. But an effort at the highest levels by the government must be made. The Union Government and the Planning Commission in cooperation with the GNCTD need to have this issue studied in all its dimensions and make suitable changes.

Another issue is that of uncontrolled growth of the population of the city by immigration. Migration coupled with high rates of growth of Delhi's economy may already have taken the NCTD to the limits of its growth consistent with a good quality of life for its residents. India is a country where the Constitution guarantees the fundamental rights of movement and residence to every citizen and this right cannot be denied. Hence the issue of migration needs to be handled with the greatest sensitivity. However, it cannot brook any delay and needs attention of the Union Government, the Government of the NCTD and the State Governments involved in the National Capital Region.

If these two issues can be resolved satisfactorily, the vision of Delhi being a "global metropolis and world class city" is realisable.

Chapter 1

Profile of the State

Dilli jo ek shahar tha alam me intikhab
Rahte the jahan muntakhib hi rozgar ke
Jisko falak ne loot ke barbad kar diya
Ham rahne wale hain usi ujade dayar ke

Mir "taqi'Mir

1.1 History

Development and devastation has been the destiny of Delhi[1] during the best part of the last millennium. Many a time, it was re-built and re-christened with a new magnificence and many a time, it was depredated and destroyed by invaders. The anguish expressed by Mir in the cited couplet was only one such occasion when he fled from Delhi and had to introduce himself to a new audience in another seat of culture—Lucknow—in the middle of eighteenth century following the invasion of Nadir Shah. But it was not the last time that this happened to Delhi. There were a few more occasions soon thereafter. But what is astonishing is that despite the fate suffered by this splendid city, it had been the chosen capital of most empire builders who ruled from northern India. The last two great empires—the Mughal and the British—established their rule, not from Delhi, but from Agra and Calcutta respectively. But the magnetic charm, as also its location, was such that they shifted their capital to Delhi. The Mughals ruled from Agra for almost hundred years; so did the British from Calcutta for almost a century and a half. But as soon as conditions stabilised and they felt secure, the capital was shifted to Delhi. A new city was built with a new grandeur and magnificence, unseen and unheard of at any earlier time. It is a different story that the Mughals lost their empire building capacity and their glory soon after or that the British packed off from India in a short span of less than four decades. But the charm of the city continues, and brings millions of people to it from the country and from all over the world, some for temporary sojourn, and others for permanent abode in search of employment or personal glory.

Delhi has a unique history, seldom experienced by any other national capital in modern times. For long intervals, it was abandoned and existed as any other town, though an important one. Between the period of Delhi Sultanate and the Mughal rule, it was not a capital town for a long period. Even during the period of Sultanate, the site shifted within the area presently demarcated and known as Delhi. Thus Delhi of the period of Slave Dynasty was not the same place as the Delhi of the Tughlaqs. Shahjahan selected a new site for his Delhi and gave it the name of Shahjahanbad. Even though it remained the capital of the Mughals and the principal seat of their empire for almost one hundred and fifty years, after the demise of Aurangzeb, it gradually lost its importance as new centres of power developed. New *satrapies* developed new townships, though none of them could come anywhere near the splendour of Delhi even during the years of its decline. This splendour was not merely the many buildings of magnificence built by Shahjahan, or the township, but in the unique culture that blossomed in a multi-religious and multi-racial society which survives. And then, after the events of 1857, it formally ceased to be the capital of the empire or a country. As if this was not enough, it was reduced to the status of a provincial town. Though the extent of destruction was not as much as it used to be during the times of invasions from the north-west, the local population suffered a great deal—psychologically as also due to loss of wealth, status, and trade.

1. The name of the city still continues to be "Dilli" in Hindi. However, it got changed to Dehli and then to Delhi sometimes in the later part of the 19th century. How did it happen is difficult to say.

1.2 Phases in Development of Modern Delhi

Broadly, there are three distinct phases in the development of modern Delhi. The first phase may be taken to start from the time the Mughal rule formally ended in Delhi after the events of 1857, and the British became the masters. This was also the phase in which Delhi became the provincial town of the Punjab. The second phase commenced from the time of the building of Lutyens' New Delhi, after it was declared the capital of India. Development was confined to the construction of a new township for the rulers, and those who supported them. The area north of Delhi Gate soon came to be known as old Delhi, and still continues to be so called. The third phase commenced with Independence when New Delhi became the national capital. This has been a period of rapid expansion all around, so much so that a number of towns in the nearby area have also expanded to provide living space for the ever-growing population, and to accommodate the ever increasing government and non-government offices. The concept of a National Capital Region has evolved to meet the various needs of the growing metropolis. Some of the towns of the nearby states have been included in the national capital region as a strategy to relieve the pressure on the limited resources and infrastructure facilities available in Delhi.

The political set-up necessary for the administration of national capitals has been a subject of great deliberation in democracies. How much power should be given to the local or regional administrations and how much of it to be retained at the national level to ensure the smooth functioning of the national government has engaged the attention of the political functionaries, irrespective of the ideologies or the political shape of the national government. Some countries have special arrangements for the administration of their national capitals—Washington in the U.S.A., Canberra in Australia, Brasilia in Brazil, to mention a few. The sub-national governments do not have any say or control on their administrative affairs. The national government exercises control and supervision over the administration of the capital town; the administrative machinery—political and bureaucratic—is accountable, directly or indirectly, to it. The local government, whether municipal or otherwise, manages day-to-day affairs; important policy issues require directions, and even approval from the national government. Such an arrangement has been dictated by a variety of factors, not the least being a situation of confrontation when different political parties rule at the national level and in the representative political institutions of the national capital towns. These towns have the offices and residences of the functionaries of various international organisations, embassies, presidents, prime ministers and a host of other government functionaries; their functioning can be paralysed by deliberate or apathetic actions of the local government. The decision to shift the national capital from Calcutta to Delhi in the early twentieth century was also prompted by the need to have an administration independent of the provincial control. Delhi was separated from the province of the Punjab, and was given the status of the Chief Commissioner's province. A new site was selected for the development of the national capital on Raisina hills, away from Shahjahanabad, as also from other townships developed by earlier rulers of Delhi. The planning and development of the new township took nearly two decades, and was given the name of New Delhi to distinguish it from the earlier towns. After Independence, Delhi has seen many experiments of political governance, and though the present set-up has been in operation for more than a decade, there is already a clamour for change, and a demand for full statehood at par with other states. During this period the two major political parties which have wielded power at the local and the national level have not been able to find an acceptable solution to the problem of governance of the national capital. The dual control has continued with certain subjects coming exclusively in the domain of the national government.

The Constitution of India had then four broad categories of states when it came in force on 26 January 1950. The erstwhile princely states, after their merger in the Indian Union were placed in two categories—Part B and Part C; the Provinces of the British Indian Empire were given the status of Part A States while centrally administered areas were included in the category of Part D States. Delhi, even though, it was not a princely state, was placed in the category of Part C State and was governed under the provisions of Government of Part C States Act, 1951. Even among the Part C States, it had a special status. It did not enjoy the same legislative and executive powers envisaged under this enactment as did the other Part C States. Thus, while the Legislative Assemblies of other Part C States had the legislative powers mentioned in the State and Concurrent list of the Seventh Schedule of the Constitution, the Legislative Assembly of Delhi was deprived of the powers to legislate on matters relating to public order; police including railway police; the constitution and powers of municipal corporations and other local authorities; improvement trusts; water supply, drainage, electricity, transport and other public utility authorities in Delhi or New Delhi; land and buildings vested or in possession of the Union in Delhi or in New Delhi with all powers appurtenant thereto including the powers to collect rents, transfer and alienation; offences against laws with respect to any of the matters reserved for the Union; jurisdiction and powers of all courts in these matters ; and fees in respect of any of these matters except fees taken in a court.

Apart from the curtailment in the legislative powers of the Legislative Assembly of Delhi in the matter of legislation, there are a few other aspects, common to the governance of all Part C States. Firstly, the Chief Commissioner, appointed by the President, could preside over the meetings of the Council of Ministers headed by the Chief minister. Secondly, while the bills passed by the Legislative Assembly required the assent of the President who had the powers to refuse assent, annual financial statement or the budget, as it is commonly known, was required to have prior approval of the President, before it could be introduced in the Legislative Assembly. Thirdly, in case of difference of opinion between the Chief Commissioner and any of his Ministers, the matter had to be referred to the President for his decision. If the matter, in the opinion of the Chief Commissioner required urgent action, he was authorised to take such action or give necessary directions. Fourthly, every decision taken by a Minister or the Council of Ministers on any matter relating to New Delhi required concurrence of the Chief Commissioner. In any case of difference of opinion, the Chief Commissioner was authorised to take action in respect of administration of New Delhi as he deemed fit.

The sum and substance of this arrangement was that the Union government had overriding control in the governance of Delhi. The democratic institutions created by the Act and the Constitution had very limited powers in certain specific areas; matters of substance were directly administered by the Union government. This anomalous position of Delhi, even among Part C States, continued till 1 November 1956, when the second phase in the constitutional development of Delhi started with the implementation of the recommendations of the State Reorganisation Commission (SRC).

The SRC had in view only two types of arrangements for the governance of the vast areas of the country—States, and the centrally administered areas. It was contended before the SRC that the development of the capital was 'hampered by the division of responsibility between the Centre and the State Government.' There was a 'marked deterioration in the administrative standards in Delhi since dual control was introduced in 1951.' The State government also complained about the inadequacy of powers vested in it. In the memorandum submitted to the SRC, the State government stated that the existing arrangements for Delhi being a Part C State cannot last long as there was no future for Part C States. The SRC also noted that the existing arrangements of dual control over the administration of the federal capital did not work smoothly. However, the Commission's recommendations on the administrative arrangements for Delhi were guided by two considerations—it was the seat of the Union government, and that it was basically a city unit with an urban population of more than 82 per cent. After considering the arrangements for the administration of the national capitals in France and England, the Commission observed:

> Apart from reasons which are peculiar to each country or city, there are some general considerations necessitating special arrangements in respect of national capitals. Capital cities possess, or come to possess, some degree of political and social predominance. They are seats of national governments, with considerable property belonging to these governments. Foreign diplomatic missions and international agencies are located in these capitals. They also become centers of national culture and art. So far as federal capitals are concerned, there is also an additional consideration. Any constitutional division of powers, if it is applicable to units functioning in the seats of national governments, is bound to give rise to embarrassing situations. Practice in other countries, administrative necessity and the desirability of avoiding conflicting jurisdictions, all point to the need for effective control by national governments over federal capitals.
>
> (Government of India: Report of the State Reorganisation Commission, 1955, p.158)

While taking a view on the administrative set-up for Delhi, SRC relied on the reasons which prompted the shifting of capital from Calcutta to Delhi in 1912. It further observed:

> It may be recalled that the desirability of excluding the seat of the Central Government from the jurisdiction of a provincial government was one of the main considerations which led to the transfer of the Imperial capital from Calcutta in 1912. It was then considered essential that the Supreme Government should not be associated with any particular Provincial Government and it was also felt that the removal of the Central government from Calcutta would materially facilitate the growth of local-self government on sound and safe lines.
>
> (*Ibid.* pp. 158-9)

The SRC recommended that the national capital should be centrally administered area under the effective control of the Union government. Separation of New Delhi from old Delhi was ruled out. It stated that, " From the point of view of the law and order, the social life of the people, trade and commerce and common public utility services, old Delhi and New Delhi now constitute one integrated unit and it will be wholly unrealistic to draw a line between the two." (*Ibid* p.160) Recommendations of the SRC were accepted by the Union government, and Delhi was declared a Union Territory to be administered by the Chief Commissioner. It ceased to have a Legislative Assembly, but a Municipal Corporation was constituted under the Delhi Municipal Corporation Act, 1957, which partially fulfilled the democratic aspirations of people. Democratic governance was sought to be restored through the Constitution (Fourteenth) Amendment Act, 1962, in some of the Union Territories by insertion of Article 239A but Delhi was not included in it. The Government of Union Territories Act, 1963 provided for the setting up of Legislative Assemblies and the Council of Ministers for the Union Territories of Himachal Pradesh, Manipur, Tripura, Goa, Daman and Diu, and Pondicherry, and giving them more or less the same status and powers which were earlier given to Part C States. But for people of Delhi, the only representative body was the Municipal Corporation of Delhi. They did have representation in both the Houses of Parliament, unlike the residents of Washington D.C. who were disenfranchised for a long time and did not have any representation in the federal legislature.

The status of Delhi as a Union Territory without any popular representation continued till 1966, when an entirely new arrangement was introduced through the Delhi Administration Act, 1966. This marks the third phase in the constitutional development of Delhi. The position of Delhi did not change as a Union Territory, but a provision was made for a Metropolitan Council with 56 elected members and five nominated members. The nomination was to be done by the Central government but persons in the service of the Government were barred from the nomination. This Council did not have any legislative functions. Its sole job was to discuss, and to make recommendations on the following matters:

a. Proposals for undertaking legislation on any matter enumerated in the State list and Concurrent list of the Seventh Schedule of the Constitution, in so far as it was applicable to the Union Territory of Delhi.

b. Proposals for extension to Delhi of any enactment in force in a State relatable to any matter enumerated in the State or Concurrent list.

c. Proposals for legislation referred to it by the Administrator.

d. The estimated receipt and expenditure pertaining to Delhi to be credited to or debited from the Consolidated Fund of India, as also the receipt and expenditure of the Delhi Development Authority.

e. Matters of administration involving general policy and development of Delhi.

f. Any other matter referred to it by the Administrator.

It was contemplated as a deliberative forum where the popular view on any matter pertaining to Delhi could find expression. Political aspects of any policy could be gauged before these could be considered for adoption and implementation.

In addition to Metropolitan Council, provisions were also made for the constitution of an Executive Council with four members, one of whom was to be designated as the Chief Executive Councilor. The function of the Executive Council was to assist and advise the Administrator on matters related to the State and Concurrent list. As in the case of the abolished Part C State, the control of the Administrator in running the affairs of Delhi was ensured through a number of provisions. The Administrator was to preside over the meetings of the Council. In case of any difference of opinion with any Councilor or the Council, the matter was to be referred for a decision to the President of India. In urgent matters, the Administrator had the authority to act at his own discretion. What constituted 'urgent matters' was again left to the discretion of the Administrator to decide, and his decision on this was final. In addition, the Administrator was made responsible for the maintenance of law and order, including the organisation and discipline of the police force. The Administrator could act at his discretion 'with respect to such other matters' as may be specified by the President from time to time. In regard to matters relating to New Delhi, the concurrence of the Administrator was mandatory. Again, matters which related to New Delhi were left to the Administrator to decide at his discretion. Virtually it was a return to the position of a Part C State without any legislative powers, and a separate Consolidated Fund for the Union Territory. Popular representatives were provided a forum but had little say in the governance of Delhi.

This position continued for nearly a quarter of a century. During this period, a number of Union territories, much smaller in terms of area, population and resources, were granted statehood. To start with,

Manipur, Tripura, and Himachal Pradesh were made states in the early 70s. Another set of Union Territories—Goa, Mizoram, and Arunachal Pradesh—attained statehood in the mid-80s. The question of granting full statehood for Delhi again surfaced. The Union government constituted the Sarkaria (later Balkrishna) Committee to go into this issue. An amendment to the Constitution—the 69th amendment—was made in 1991and a new Article 239AA was inserted to make special provisions with respect to Delhi. The position obtaining in the erstwhile Part C States was more or less restored, except that now some provisions were incorporated in the Constitution itself. Thus:

a. The Union Territory of Delhi was renamed as the National Capital Territory of Delhi.

b. The Administrator was formally designated as the Lieutenant Governor.

c. Entries 1 (public order), 2 (police), and 18 (land) of List II—State List—were specifically excluded from the purview of the Legislative Assembly of the NCT, as also Entries 64, 65, and 66 in so far as these related to the excluded Entries.

d. Laws made by the Union Parliament on subjects included in the State List have supremacy, except in cases where a law has been passing by the Legislative Assembly subsequent to the passing by the Parliament, and has received the assent by the President. Parliament also has the powers to pass any law on matters included in the State List

e. Lieutenant Governor has been given the powers to promulgate ordinance, when the Legislative assembly is not in session.

f. President has the power to take action in case of failure of constitutional machinery.

g. The size of the Council of Ministers has been restricted to 10 per cent of the total membership of the House.

h. The Chief Minister and other Ministers are appointed by the President.

Delhi Administration Act, 1991 lays down the detailed provisions for the governance of Delhi based on the 69th amendment to the Constitution. The Assembly has 70 members, and thus can have seven Ministers including the Chief Minister. A significant feature of the Act is that the annual financial statement or the budget, as it is popularly known, requires the previous sanction of the President before it is presented to the Assembly. Lieutenant Governor can reserve any bill, passed by the Assembly, for the assent of the President. In any case, he has been prohibited from giving assent to bills relating to certain matters and has to reserve them for the consideration of the President. These relate to salaries and allowances of the Members, Deputy Speaker and Speaker of the Assembly, the salaries and allowances of the Ministers, official language of the NCT of Delhi, and matters relating to the High Court, apart from any other matters which the President may by order, direct to be reserved for his consideration.

The present arrangement has been in operation for more than a decade and a half. During this period, three general elections have taken place to elect members to Delhi Legislative Assembly. The two major political parties had the opportunity to head the administration during this period. The demand for full statehood surfaces from time to time, as the present arrangements put lot of constraint on the efficient functioning of the local administration. It is certainly better than what obtained between 1951 and 1956, when even as a Part C State, the working of the major utilities like power, water and transport were controlled and managed by the Union government, despite the existence of an elected Legislative Assembly and a Council of Ministers. Delhi Administration now controls the public utilities on which it did not have any control till 1991.

1.3 Geography

The NCTD is situated in the north of India (Latitude 28'35'N, Longitude 77'12'E) 160 km south of the Himalayas at an elevation of 216 m above mean sea level. The River Yamuna, a tributary of the Ganges forms the eastern boundary of the city. Delhi is situated between the Great Indian Desert (Thar Desert) of Rajasthan to the west, the central hot plains to the south, and the cooler, hilly region to the north and east.

1.4 Climate

The region has a tropical steppe climate. The general prevalence of Continental air leads to relatively dry conditions with extremely hot summers. Monthly mean temperatures range from 14.3°C in January (minimum 3°C) to 34.5°C in June (maximum 47°C). The annual mean temperature is 25.3°C (WMO, 1971). The main seasonal climatic influence is the monsoon, typically from June to October. The mean annual rainfall total is 715 mm. Maximum rainfall occurs in July (211 mm). The heavy rains of the monsoon act as a "scrubber". North-westerly winds usually prevail; however, in June and July south-easterly predominates. Wind speeds are typically higher in the summer and monsoon periods; in winter, calms are frequent (20 per cent of the time).

A regular pre-monsoon feature is the *andhi* (dust storm) where westerly winds from the Great Indian Desert deposit large concentrations of suspended particulate matter (SPM) into Delhi's atmosphere. Alliteratively, pre-monsoon calms often lead to increased pollution loads due to lack of mixing/dilution. Ground-based temperature inversions are a regular feature. These restrict mixing height to low levels thus limiting pollutant dispersal.

1.5 Area of NCTD

Delhi had a much larger area during the time of the Mughals. At the time of acquisition of Delhi Territory from the Marathas by the East India Company in 1803 under the Treaty of Arjungaon, it consisted of the Delhi and Hissar divisions. Shahjahanabad (area around Red Fort) was the chief city. It was divided into the districts of Haryana, Rohtak, Panipat, Gurgaon, and Delhi. Later, in 1848 and 1853, 193 miles from Meerut and Bulandshahar were added to the territory on the eastern side of the river Yamuna. These were also known as Eastern Parganah.[2] After the events of 1857, Delhi was merged with the province of the Punjab. It was only in 1912, when Delhi was declared as national capital, that it was separated from the Punjab, and became an Imperial enclave. According to one account[3], it had an area of 1240 sq. miles. How this area got reduced, one does not know, but presently it has an area of 1483 sq. kms.

Delhi was a single district Union Territory till the mid-90s. After the constitutional changes of the early 90s, the NCT was divided into nine districts. These districts are North, South, East, West, New Delhi, Central, North-west, South-west, and North-east. All districts, except New Delhi and Central Delhi, have rural areas in their administrative jurisdiction. Districts have been further sub-divided into sub-divisions. Presently, there are 27 sub-divisions and an equal number of *tehsils*. The number of *tehsils* was only two in 1991. The number of villages in Delhi are 165, according to 2001 census, while the number of deserted villages is 10. There has been a steady decline in the number of villages as also the rural area during the last half a century. In 1951, the number of inhabited villages was 304, and in 1991, these were 199. Consequently, the rural area has also declined from 797.66 sq. kms. in 1991 to 558.32 sq. kms. according to estimates of the Delhi Directorate of Census Operations. Rural areas of Delhi are divided in five community development blocks for development purposes. These are: Alipur, Kanjhiwala (Nangloi), Najafgarh, Mehrauli, and Shahdara. Despite the shrinking rural area, Delhi has been able to increase its forest cover from 26 sq. kms, which was almost constant till 1999-2000, to 88 sq. kms. in 2000-01, as reported by the Forest Survey of India.

1.6 Civic Administrative Division

For civic administration, Delhi is divided in three distinct areas, each working independently of the other. These are Delhi Municipal Corporation (known as MCD), New Delhi Municipal Committee (NDMC), and the Delhi Cantonment Board (DCB). The area falling within the jurisdiction of DCB and the NDMC is 43 and 42.73 sq. kms. respectively. The rest of the NCT is covered by the MCD, which includes the rural areas. There are no *panchayats* in the NCT of Delhi. Civic functions include construction, maintenance and improvement of streets; sanitation and public health; maintenance of vital statistics; suppression of public nuisances; public safety; regulation of slaughter houses, trade and occupations; regulation of construction of buildings; and framing of improvement schemes. These civic functions are common to MCD and NDMC, though provided in two different legislations enacted separately for the two civic bodies, and termed as obligatory functions. In addition, the obligatory functions of the NDMC also include the establishment, maintenance and aid to primary schools; maintenance, expansion and upgradation of existing hospitals; laying out or maintenance of parks, gardens or recreation grounds, and maintenance of monuments vested in the local authority. These local bodies may also perform certain other functions termed as 'discretionary', subject to any general or special orders of the Central or NCT government. These are: establishment and maintenance of (and aid to) libraries, museums, art galleries, botanical or zoological collections, stadia, gymanasia, *akharas*, and places of sports and games; relief to destitute and disabled persons; construction and maintenance of poor houses, rest houses, infirmaries, children's home; houses for the deaf and dumb and for disabled and handicapped persons; shelter for destitutes and dumb persons, and asylum for persons of unsound mind. There are a host of other functions like construction and maintenance of warehouses and godowns; establishment and maintenance of veterinary

2. This account is based on Narayani Gupta. *Delhi Between Two Empires 1803-1931*. Oxford. p.13.

3. Jain, A.K. *Delhi-Governance, Planning and Development*, mimeograph, p.2. He does not give any information, how and when the area of Delhi got reduced in subsequent years.

hospitals; management of cottage industries, handicraft centers and sales emporia etc. included in this list, which are not strictly municipal functions. The Central government has greater direct control over the NDMC than on MCD because of the spatial importance of the area due to its immediate proximity to the seat of governance.

The MCD is basically an elected body; the minimum number of elected councilors could be 80 and the maximum could be 134. Revision in the number of seats has to be done after every decennial census. In addition, there is a provision for nominated and ex-officio members. All members of the Lok Sabha elected from Delhi are members of the Corporation. Persons elected as members of Rajya Sabha and registered as voters in Delhi are also members of the MCD. One-fifth of the members of the Delhi Legislative Assembly, as nominated by the Speaker of the Assembly, are also members of the MCD. However, their tenure is only for one year and the Speaker has to ensure that every member of the Assembly is nominated as a member of the Corporation at least once in a period of five years. There is a provision for the nomination of ten other members by the Administrator (the Lt. Governor) as members of the Corporation, but they do not have any right to vote in the meetings of the Corporation. Chairpersons of the Rural Areas Committee, Special and adhoc Committees, and Standing Committees are also members of the Corporation if they are not councilors. In contrast, the NDMC is a body of eleven members, all nominated by the Central government. The Chairperson is a serving officer of the Government having the rank of Joint Secretary of the Government of India or above. It has three members of the Legislative Assembly of Delhi representing constituencies falling partly or wholly in the New Delhi area. Five members are to be nominated from the officers of the Central government or the Government or their undertakings. The remaining two members are nominated by the Central government in consultation with the Chief Minister from amongst the professionals and social scientists. The management of the civic affairs in the New Delhi area, which has the Ministries and the principal offices and residences of the Ministers, Members of Parliament, diplomats, and officers of the Central Government has been kept outside the domain of the Delhi Government. The idea is to avoid any conflict in the day-to-day functioning.

The two civic bodies have also been given the powers to raise revenue by imposing property tax; taxes on vehicles and animals; theatre tax; taxes on advertisements other than those published in the newspapers; and duty on transfer of property. The Commissioner of the MCD is appointed by the Central government, while other functionaries may be appointed by the MCD itself. The two democratic bodies—Delhi Government and MCD, barring the area coming under the domain of NDMC and Cantonment Board—have more or less the same jurisdiction, as MCD covers the rural areas also. While efforts have been made to avoid any overlapping of areas of responsibilities by delineation of functions and powers of taxation at the two levels by Central government legislation, it is not unusual for the differences and conflicts to crop up, especially when the two bodies are under the control of different political parties. Providing civic services in a large area—urban and rural even though small—serving a population of more than 15 millions is a stupendous task. Decentralisation, and dispersal of MCD offices in different parts of the city has helped the local population significantly, as they do not have to travel long distances. But the problem of management and supervision at the local level still remains; as many issues have to be decided by the Council itself. Local specific issues get meshed up with larger issues, and search for a uniform approach for the entire area sometimes leads to unintended neglect of local problems. Municipal administration needs effective democratic decentralisation, so that civic services can be efficiently managed. The other two civic bodies—the Delhi Cantonment Board and NDMC—cater to the needs of smaller areas and therefore are more effective and efficient.

1.7 Demography

There has been a phenomenal growth in the population of Delhi during the last century (Annex A-1.1). There was a setback, after the happenings of 1857, when a large segment of population had to leave Delhi following the repressive measures taken by the British, and closure and disruption of economic activities. Delhi was reduced to the position of a provincial town as the new capital was Calcutta. It took sometime to recover, and it was only in the last quarter of the eighteenth century that the population started showing the tendencies of natural growth. Even then the Census of 1901 registered a population of a little over four lakhs with an urban component of 52.76 per cent. (Annex A-1.1) The next decade only saw a marginal decennial growth of 2 per cent. It was only after the Delhi Durbar in 1911, which announced the shifting of national capital from Calcutta that significant increase in the population of Delhi started. From a mere two per cent decennial growth, it became more than 27 per cent in the next decade, and when the seat of Government shifted to Raisina hills in 1931, the decennial growth recorded was around 47 per cent. The partition, and Independence further accelerated the growth, and the population crossed a million. In fact, the rate of growth recorded by the Census of 1951 was more than 90 per cent over the previous decade, largely due to large-scale migration from what now constitutes Pakistan. Since then the decennial rate of growth has been hovering between 46 per cent and 61 per cent. The last census recorded a total population of more than 13.7 million, as against a figure of little over 4 lakhs, exactly a hundred years ago.

Such a large growth has not been entirely due to natural reasons. Large migrations have been responsible for such a phenomenal increase. Apart from sudden influx in the late 40s due to partition of the country, the immigration now is perennial. A study conducted by Singh[4] in the 60s showed that the immigration accounted for nearly 33 per cent increase in the population of Delhi during the previous decade. More than 85 per cent migrants came from the states of Rajasthan, Punjab, and Uttar Pradesh. And if Rajasthan is excluded, the two states of Punjab and U.P. would account for about 75 per cent. More than 60 per cent people came from the rural areas. Delhi Government has started collecting and compiling information about immigration. According to this data, the natural increase accounts for a little over 2 per cent per annum; the bulk of increase is due to immigration, and it is increasing every year. Most people come for better social and economic opportunities. The educational standards at the school and college level have been declining for quite some time in some states, and this brings thousands of students to the national capital every year. The declining employment opportunities in the organised and unorganised sectors in the neighbouring states have also contributed to the persistent flow of jobseekers in and around Delhi, as these areas have witnessed the highest rate of economic growth.

The high rate of growth of population, largely due to migration, is accompanied with one of the lowest sex ratio—the ratio of female population to per one thousand of male population. It is 821 for Delhi as against the all-India figure of 933 reported in the 2001 census, itself a cause of concern. Even though it has shown considerable improvements over the position obtaining in the pre-Independence period, it bears out the impact that continuous influx of people has made in the demographic profile of the capital. The male population has grown at a much faster pace than the female population throughout the previous century. Men come for jobs alone, and once they have a foothold, the womenfolk move in, and since this has been happening continuously, this accounts for the wide variance in the relative rate of growth.

Delhi has the highest density of population in India at 9340 per square kilometer, compared to the average all-India density of 324.[5] What is more important is that the density has gone up by almost 50 per cent during the last decade. The urban population constitutes 93 per cent of the total population of Delhi, but the urban area is only 60 per cent. This means that the density in the urban areas would be much higher, even after the increase in the urban area by 300 square kilometer during the last decade. The urban density works out to 14630 per square kilometer. The density in the rural areas at around 1630 per square kilometer is not small. The North-east, Central, East, and West districts have a very high density, and there has been a phenomenal increase in the density of North-east, East and West districts. Density has been increasing despite the growth of satellite towns around Delhi; this should be a cause of concern for the city planners.

1.8 Economy of NCTD

Delhi presents the picture of a developed economy, compared to one found in a developed country. The gross state domestic product (GSDP) has recorded a growth of 8.8 per cent since 1993-94 and 2004-05 at 1993-94 prices.[6] This is significantly higher than the growth of gross domestic product (GDP) at 6.8 per cent during the same period at the same price level. The annual compound growth rate in the per capita income has been at the rate of 4.29 per cent per annum, compared to all-India growth rate of 3.97 per cent during the same period. The per capita net state domestic product (NSDP) of Delhi at Rs.53976 in 2004-05 at current prices is only marginally lower than that of Goa, and the Union Territories of Chandigarh and Pondicherry. In fact, Pondicherry has recorded a higher per capita NSDP than Delhi only in 2004-05. It would rank as a lower middle-income state from the World Bank standards, even without adjustments for the purchasing power parity. There are quite a few states in India which have a per capita NSDP of 25 per cent or less than that of Delhi; Bihar being the lowest in the ladder with a per capita NSDP of a little over 10 per cent of what has already been achieved in Delhi. In fact, the per capita NSDP of Bihar, compared to some other states, shows the huge gap in

4. Singh, A.M. *Neighbourhood and Social Networks in Urban India*, p.31.
5. Government of NCT of Delhi. *Economic Survey of Delhi, 2001-02*.
6. Government of NCT of Delhi. *Economic Survey of Delhi, 2001-02*.

the levels of development of different regions in the country.

The high per capita NSDP is accompanied with a very low poverty ratio in Delhi as reported in the 1999-2000 survey conducted by the Planning Commission (Annex A-1.2). There has been a steady decline in the number of persons living below the poverty line since 1973-74; the earliest year for which the data on the extent of prevalence of poverty in the rural and urban areas was compiled state-wise, including the Union Territories. In 1973-74, the number of persons living below the poverty line was 24.44 per cent in rural areas of Delhi. More than half the population—52.23 per cent—in the urban areas was living below poverty line. As the rural component of the population has always been very small, nearly fifty per cent of the population has been poor. There has been a drastic change in the position since then. Every survey, conducted usually after every five years, shows a gradual decline. Persons living below the poverty line are now only 8.23 per cent of the population—0.4 per cent in rural areas and 9.42 per cent in urban areas, according to 1999-2000 survey conducted by NSSO. It is in sharp contrast to the position obtaining in other states, where the percentage of those living below poverty line is much higher in rural areas. This is largely due to the fact that Delhi has a small rural area and a small rural population, and secondly, the migration from other states is concentrated in urban areas. This has to be seen against the backdrop of an all-India poverty level of 26.10 per cent. In 1973-74, the all-India poverty level was 54.88 per cent, only five per cent higher than the level prevailing in Delhi at that time. Only Goa, Chandigarh, Punjab, Himachal Pradesh, and Jammu and Kashmir presently have a lower poverty ratio. Of these, the latter two are special category states while Chandigarh is a Union Territory, and all of them, except Punjab, have a much smaller population than Delhi.

The developed nature of the economy is also manifest in the changes that have taken place in the sectoral composition of NSDP. The primary sector has been shrinking; its contribution to GSDP, at current prices, has come down from 3.85 per cent in 1993-94 to 1 per cent in 2004-05. It provided employment to 1.54 per cent of the workers in 1900-2000, according to NSSO 55th Round Survey. The tertiary sector has grown in importance, contributing about 80 per cent of the GSDP. It also provides employment to nearly 70 per cent of the workers. The contribution of the secondary sector has also come down from over 25 per cent in 1993-94 to about 19 per cent in 2004-05 and provides employment to nearly 29 per cent of the workers. It is likely to go down, as Supreme Court has ordered the shifting of industrial units from some areas. The dependence of the national capital territory for supplies of essential commodities emanating from the agriculture and industry will continue to increase. In years to come, the economic activity will be supported by the service sector with a minuscule contribution made by the primary sector, and a very low contribution from the secondary sector.

1.9 Development Disparities

Development has many aspects. High rate of economic growth or per capita income do not tell the whole story. Averages are dubious and conceal the abysmally low level at which people are forced to live. The low level of poverty, based on certain level of per capita expenditure, does not indicate the deprivations to which a large segment of the population in Delhi, not to speak of country as a whole, is subjected. Nearly half the population of urban Delhi lives in slums, *jhuggi-jhopdi* clusters, or in unauthorised colonies. The persistent influx of population into Delhi makes it difficult for the planners to provide safe and developed habitations with all the basic facilities. Delhi presents a picture of extra-ordinary affluence at some places and utter deprivation in some other areas, with more of the latter. Theories of a dual economy or dual society with rural-urban divide or two different social or economic strata do not hold good here. There are many layers and levels of development, and social opportunities in terms of education, health, housing, etc. have developed to suit them.

1.10 Education

Elementary and higher education provide opportunities for upward mobility for those who have the capability. The per capita expenditure on education was Rs.1148, considerably higher than the all-India figure of Rs.705 in 2004-05. The literacy rate has gone up from 38.4 per cent in 1951 to 81.8 per cent in 2001. About 75 per cent of women and 87 per cent of men are literate, according to the 2001 census. Yet Delhi ranks fourth among the States in this area; Kerala, Mizoram, and Goa, registering a higher rate. But literacy by itself is no indication of the enhancement of capability. Delhi is still far behind in terms of 12-year schooling for every child, though it may be ahead of most states, and the all-India average. Product differentiation is high and starts manifesting itself from the pre-primary level; prices reflect, though not always, what is available in the schools in terms of quality. There are international public schools, and primary and middle schools run by the MCD and NDMC, and in between a host of private schools with varying degree of quality and prices. Majority of the population has to depend on the municipal schools, which are poorly equipped due to lack of adequate budgetary support. Delhi attracts the best pupils in schools and colleges from all over the country. Competition for an entry in the schools and colleges is stiff, and those who find a place are not many, compared to the over all student population. Vast majority of students at school level pass out from the government system, and form the backbone of the society. The gap in the quality of education imparted has been increasing over the years, and unless something is done and resources are diverted to improve it, Delhi will have a different set of problems of managing and administering people who have no contributions to make to the society in any sphere of life.

1.11 Medical Facilities

Delhi compares well with the best in the country in the matter of medical facilities. It has also started attracting foreigners, including some from developed countries, for surgical operations and medical care. The cost of care is much less than what obtains in some of the developed countries, and waiting time is small. But what is affordable to the better-off sections of society in Delhi or the foreigners is out of reach for the vast majority of the population, which depends on the health and medical infrastructure of the government hospitals and dispensaries. The per capita public expenditure at Rs.568 in 2004-05 is more than double of the all-India average of around Rs.164. But this highlights the inadequacy at both levels, and is no cause for satisfaction. Delhi has about 33030 hospital beds. Of these, more than one-third are in the private nursing homes, well out of the reach of the common man. There are more than 560 private nursing homes as against 86 government hospitals and nearly 1200 dispensaries, which include the maternity homes, maternity and child welfare centers, primary health centres, polyclinic and sub-centres. In recent years, Delhi Government has taken steps to improve the health infrastructure by adding new hospital blocks to existing hospitals, constructing new hospitals well dispersed in different parts of the capital, opening new centers for treatment of some diseases, and super speciality and research centers.

1.12 Physical Infrastructure

Development of physical infrastructure has not kept pace with the economic opulence and the excessive influx of population, since Delhi became the capital of the country. For a casual visitor—native or foreigner—it is immediately visible in the chaotic urban transport services. But for the bullock cart, Delhi has all sorts of transport vehicles—horse driven carts, carts pulled by men, cycle-rickshaws, three wheeler and four wheeler tempos, cars and buses—all driving on the same roads. The mix of fast driving mechanical vehicles, and the slow animal or men pulled vehicles, creates traffic hazards on the ever-shrinking road space. The numbers of motor vehicles have more than doubled since 1990-91, but the road space has increased by a mere 50 per cent during this period. There are nearly a million and a half cars and jeeps, three million scooters and motor cycles, and 25,000 buses. The number of motor vehicles has gone up from 192 per thousand populations in 1990-91 to 282 in 2004-2005. The man and animal driven vehicles have also doubled during the same period. The number of light commercial vehicles—cars and jeeps—as also the buses have gone up by two and half times. These have added to the ever increasing traffic congestion in almost all the cross-sections of Delhi and adjoining areas. It is not unusual to find the road space between one red light and another red light on the same road occupied by the buses leaving little space for the movement of other mechanical and non-mechanical transport. In fact, the daily use of Delhi roads is not confined to residents of Delhi alone. There is regular commuting between Delhi and the neighbouring towns in a big way adding further to the congestion of roads. All these vehicles are not reflected in the vehicle population of Delhi, as these are registered in the towns of adjoining states.

While the problem of congestion and shrinking road space has been there for the last many years, it was handled as a peak hour traffic management problem. It is only in recent years that concrete steps have been taken to look into the supply bottlenecks. This has been done, firstly, by constructing a series of flyovers on those inter-sections of the roads where traffic intensity is high. This has not only added to the road space, but has given relief to cross-section traffic and reduced congestion and waiting time at these places. Construction of the metro is the second step expected to reduce the pressure on the roads. This would divert the traffic, to a great extent, from the scooters/motor cycles and buses and, to a smaller extent from the cars, to the under-ground rail system. However, there will be a need to integrate it with the passenger road system of Delhi so that it is more efficient, economical and convenient for the Delhi commuters. Linking of the metro and bus schedules with a common time-table, and a combined fare and ticketing system for regular commuters would help them in changing over from the personalised or public transport system to the new arrangements. This would necessitate the creation of a single authority for planning and management. It may require a new set of rules and regulations, either by amending the existing legislation or by a new enactment.

The problem of road congestion is aggravated by the unauthorised parking of the motor vehicles on roads. While the numbers of vehicles have been increasing every year, very little space has been allocated for the parking of vehicles. Commercial and business areas are cluttered with vehicles; open space for movement of men and material has completely disappeared. Even the roads in market areas like Karol Bagh, Lajpat Nagar, Yusuf Sarai, etc. have little space for movement of traffic. What is disconcerting is that the use of road space for parking is officially recognised by diverting the traffic to other lanes or by converting the two way traffic into one way.[7] Underground and multi-storey parking facilities need to be developed for decongestion of road space. It is as important as building of flyovers on intersections. Even the roads and lanes in the residential areas are not free from this menace. As land is expensive, more and more area is used for provision of the living space. Road space is free and is therefore used for parking.

1.13 Energy

A persistent problem faced by the Delhites is the availability of energy—in terms of quantity and quality—for domestic, commercial, industrial, agricultural and other uses. Scheduled and unscheduled disruptions are an everyday affair, and it is not unusual to see residents and commercial establishments using generators and inverters to supplement energy supply during the period of non-availability. While the expenditure on the energy sector has been, on an average, more than 20 per cent of the total plan outlay of Delhi during the last 25 years, there has not been any visible relief to the population. One reason has been the increasing demand for energy with the expansion in population, economic activity, and affluence. Fans and ordinary coolers have given way to air conditioners and central cooling and heating systems, not only in commercial and industrial establishments, but also in a growing number of residential accommodations. But the mismatch in the supply and demand has been accentuated by mismanagement. The institutional changes made in the management by converting a municipal unit—Delhi State Electricity Undertaking—into a State unit, the Delhi Vidyut Board (DVB), did not make any impact. Low plant load factor, where generation was done by DVB, and high transmission and distribution losses continued. In fact, transmission and distribution losses continued to go up from 22.6 per cent in 1991-92 to around 44 per cent in 2001-02. Financial performance of the DVB, like other State Electricity Boards, continued to deteriorate, affecting its ability to make fresh investments and meet new challenges.

Reforms in the power sector have been initiated by the Delhi government on the same pattern as recommended for other states. In essence, it involved the setting up of a regulatory commission at the state level, the separation of the generation, transmission and distribution functions, and their eventual privatisation. The industry should pay for itself. Subsidies, if any, for any sector should be transparent and should be quantified, and where the state decides to subsidise any group of consumers, it should pay for it. Tariff has to be periodically revised by the regulatory commission, so that the interest of the consumer is protected from the mismanagement and inefficiency of the generators, transmitters and distributors. At the same time, the economic interest of power producers and service providers should be protected. Delhi has already started implementing the recommended reforms. Delhi Electricity Reforms Act was passed and the Delhi Vidyut Board was dissolved with effect from 1st July 2002. Its place has been taken by six companies—one each for generation and transmission, three for power distribution and a holding company. The generation and transmission of power is still in the public sector while distribution has been privatised. An electricity regulatory commission has been set up. A number of companies are now distributing power in Delhi, each responsible for a specified area in Delhi. A time schedule has been worked out for reducing the transmission and distribution losses, and the tariffs and subsidies have accordingly been fixed by the regulatory commission. However, the transmission and distribution losses still continue to be quite high, though some improvement has been visible during the last couple of years.

1.14 Water

Water is an essential requirement for the sustenance of any people in any area. Shortage of water like that of food is not immediately felt as people share voluntarily the available quantity, or they abide by the restrictions imposed on the quantum of supply through the public distribution system. However, shortage of water does have

7. Thus, Arya Samaj Road near the Ajmal Khan Road inter section in the Karol Bagh area used to have two way traffic, but a section of it has now been converted to one way traffic leading to diversion to nearby narrow lanes. Three-fourth of the road in this inter-section is officially used for car parking.

an impact on personal hygiene, cleanliness and sanitation, public and private. And, in turn, it affects the public health system as reflected in the spread of water borne diseases. The population of Delhi has been increasing every year, but not the sources of water supply. The per capita supply decrease with the addition of new persons every day. The existing sources are not adequate to meet the increasing requirements. The sub-surface or ground water is tapped but the availability here is also limited. While 96 per cent of the households have access to safe drinking water, the quantum will continue to be a matter for concern. At present, the average per capita supply of water is only 70 per cent of the prescribed norm. Even this supply is not evenly distributed throughout Delhi. Cantonment and NDMC areas get a very high level of supply, while Mehrauli, Najafgarh, and Narela get a very low level of supply. New sources of water supply need to be identified to augment the supply in the deficit areas as also to meet the growing requirements.

1.15 Environment

The unplanned and unprecedented growth of Delhi has its impact on the environment. The quality of life has deteriorated to an abysmally low level during the last few decades, due to water and air pollution and ever increasing and uncontrolled noise level. In addition, there is the problem of solid waste management and garbage disposal which also affects the immediate physical environment of the residents. Persistent campaigning by the non-governmental organisations and the intervention of the Supreme Court from time to time has helped in improving the environment. The mandatory switch from diesel and petrol to the use of gas as fuel by the buses and other commercial vehicles for locomotion alone has contributed to improvement in the quality of air in Delhi. Industries have been another major source of water and air pollution. Some of these are located in residential area. On orders of the Supreme Court, Delhi government has started taking action and relocating them. These measures would go a long way in the betterment of the quality of life in Delhi.

1.16 Industrial Effluent

The liquid waste discharged by the industrial units is another area of great concern. The 48 kilometre stretch of the Yamuna in Delhi is highly polluted—largely by the industrial waste water discharged by producing industrial units. The Central Pollution Board has prescribed standards for each industry in terms of neutralisation of acidity, removal of oil and grease and total suspended particles. The units are required to install Effluent Treatment Plants to ensure that the specified standards are maintained and that water is treated before it is discharged into water bodies or percolates down to the ground water. However, small units have found it difficult to adhere to it, and the problem persists. It also affects the sources of drinking water supply in Delhi.

Delhi has a small geographical area of 1483 square kilometres. It has had a long history, and unlike the many new capitals around the world which have come up after the formation of the nation, Delhi has been in existence even before the concept of nationhood took shape. During the pre-British times it had a larger expanse. Motor vehicles and modern industrial units were unknown. Now scientific and technological developments leading to development of modern transport, industry, and communication systems have altered the scene. At the same time, the area has got reduced from what it was earlier. The boundaries are water-tight and can not be altered by an executive fiat. Modern industrial units had started getting established during the British times leading to rapid expansion in the post-Independence period. Like in any other state, the emphasis has been on development, and development meant largely the setting up of industrial units. No thought was given, or perhaps, it did not occur to anyone that Delhi, being the seat of national government, would have a process of natural expansion unmatched by other provincial towns. Industrial units have occupied valuable scarce space, and have created problems of congestion, pollution, crime and a host of other avoidable problems. They have also been partially responsible for the on-going influx of people looking for economic opportunities. This has become the bane of Delhi. Even now, there is a need for rethinking in this sphere. If Delhi has to be preserved, many activities will have to be stopped, and over a period of time, they have to be shifted out of Delhi. The process has to be as painless as possible so that there is least resistance from the local population

1.17 National Capital Region (NCR)

The development of satellite towns around Delhi have created administrative problems which are outside the purview of the NCR Planning Board. Ghaziabad, Noida, Gurgaon, Sahibabad, Faridabad, Ballabhgarh, Palwal, and even Sonipat have become contiguous towns, or an extension of Delhi. Traffic, land-use, civic services, policing, and law and order, crimes in these areas are common problems; but these are the concerns of the participating states. There is no common administrative unit for all these towns. It is not unusual for a participating state to have a view different from that of

Delhi or another participating state. This has tremendous impact on policing, crime control and investigation, law and order, traffic control, judicial administration, etc. The problems become further compounded when the participating states are ruled by different political parties as is happening now. Perceptions change, with each one moving in different directions. Consultations take time, and valuable time is lost in the process. There is a need to have a common administrative unit for all these contiguous towns so that administrative machinery is made responsible to one administrative set up at the bureaucratic and political level.

1.18 Flora and Fauna

Economic development and prosperity are not unmixed blessings. The last century has been a saga of destructive creation. The flora and fauna of Delhi has, more or less, disappeared. The ridge and the surrounding areas, till the time of Independence, had been abode of a rich variety of wild animals. *Nilgais, chinkara,* and blackbuck roamed in the dry scrub jungles of Delhi. The forest areas were avoided because of the presence of hyenas, wolves and leopards. It was not unusual to find wild boar, hares and foxes around. But there has been a sea change in the scenario during last half a century. And this has not been entirely due to changing climatic conditions. As Ranjit Lal[8] observes, "More dangerous perhaps than summer's wrath and monsoon's infections, has been the city's own assault on its own green areas and woodlands in the last half of the twentieth century. As the city expanded explosively and land prices rocketed, the green areas were the first to be sacrificed. Both by the authorities and the residents. Officially sacrosanct green zones have been destroyed by road widening schemes, construction, encroachments, wood poaching and castle grazing."

1.19 Culture

The cultural life of Delhi has also undergone a complete transformation. Delhi is no more a haven for Mir, Zauq or Ghalib. *Mushairas* are rare. Persian and Urdu have made way for Punjabi and Hindi, as also English among the elite of the city. Evenings are spent around television or cinema halls, or performances organised in the many auditoria that have come up in Delhi. There is theatre, classical dance, and classical music—Hindustani and Carnatic. Not to speak of the performances organised by foreign troupes visiting the country. There are art galleries; variety of artists display their creations. A whole lot of professionalism has developed around these activities; for some this is a major source of livelihood. And yet there is something which has not changed. As Dalrymple states:

> Indraprastha had fallen; six hundred years of Muslim domination had come and gone; a brief interruption by the British was almost forgotten. But Shive, the oldest living God in the world, was still worshipped; Sanskrit—which predates any other living tongue by a millennia—was still read, still spoken. Moreover, the *sadhus* and *rishis*—familiar figures from the Mahabharat –remained today, still following the rigorous laws of India's most ancient vocation; giving up everything to wander the face of earth in search of enlightenment, renouncing the profane in the hope of a brief glimpse of the sacred. In these wet and disheveled figures sitting cross-legged under the neem and banyan trees of the river bank lay what most certainly be the most remarkable Delhi's survival of all.
>
> (William Dalrymple: *City of Djinns,* p.338)

During the course of last hundred years, tremendous changes have taken place all over the world. Science and technology have transformed the world we live in. In many countries, the signs of utter poverty and squalor are no more visible. Delhi has also been a part of this process of change. For once during the last one hundred and fifty years, there has been an era of peace. Delhi has been free from foreign invasions and internal trouble. There has been no destruction or loot from the marauders. The process of development started has gone on unhindered. But development has some pernicious aspects. Some prosper; many are thrown to the periphery. Something like that has been happening; and it is this which has to be corrected and avoided in the coming years.

8. Ranjit Lal. "The Flora and The Fauna", in B.P. Singh and P. Varma (eds.) *The Millenium Book on Delhi.*

ANNEX A-1.1

Decennial Changes in the Population of Delhi: 1901-2001

Year	Rural	Urban	Total	Decennial Growth %	Sex Ratio Delhi	Sex Ratio India
		in lakhs			Female per 1000 Male	
1901	1.92	2.1	4.06	—— (47.24) (57.26)	862	972
1911	1.76	2.38	4.14	1.98 (42.51) (57.49)	793	964
1921	1.84	3.05	4.89	18.03 (37.68) (62.32)	733	955
1931	1.89	4.47	6.36	30.26 (29.27) (70.33)	722	950
1941	2.22	6.96	9.18	44.27 (24.21) (75.79)	715	945
1951	3.07	14.37	17.44	90 (17.60) (82.40)	768	946
1961	2.99	23.6	26.59	52.44 (11.25) (88.75)	785	941
1971	4.19	36.47	40.66	52.93 (10.30) (89.70)	801	930
1981	4.52	57.68	62.2	53 (7.27) (92.73)	808	934
1991	9.49	84.72	94.21	51.45 (10.07) (89.93)	827	927
2001	9.63	128.2	137.83	46.31 (6.99) (93.01)	821	933

Notes : Figures in brackets show percentages of total population.

Source : Census of India

ANNEX A-1.2

Percentage of Population Below Poverty Line for Some States (1973-74 and 1999-2000)

States	1973-74			1999-00		
	R	U	C	R	U	C
Andhra Pradesh	48.41	50.61	48.86	11.05	26.63	15.77
Bihar	62.99	52.96	61.91	44.3	32.91	42.6
Goa	46.85	37.69	44.26	1.35	7.52	4.4
Gujarat	46.35	52.57	48.15	13.17	15.59	14.07
Haryana	34.23	40.18	35.36	8.27	9.99	8.74
Karnataka	55.14	52.53	54.47	17.38	25.75	20.04
Kerala	59.19	62.74	59.79	9.38	20.27	12.72
M.P.	62.66	57.65	61.78	37.06	38.44	37.43
Maharastra	57.71	43.87	53.24	23.72	28.81	25.02
Orissa	67.28	55.62	66.18	48.01	42.83	47.15
Punjab	28.21	27.96	28.15	6.35	5.75	6.16
Rajasthan	44.76	52.13	46.14	13.74	19.85	15.28
Tamil Nadu	57.43	49.4	54.94	20.55	22.11	21.12
U.P.	56.33	60.09	57.07	31.22	30.89	31.15
West Bengal	73.16	34.67	63.46	31.85	14.86	27.02
Delhi	24.44	52.23	49.61	0.4	9.42	8.23
All India	56.34	49.01	54.88	27.09	23.62	26.10

Notes : 1. R= Rural; U= Urban: C= Combined

2. Data on poverty for 1999-00 is based on 30-Day recall period.

Source : Planning Commission

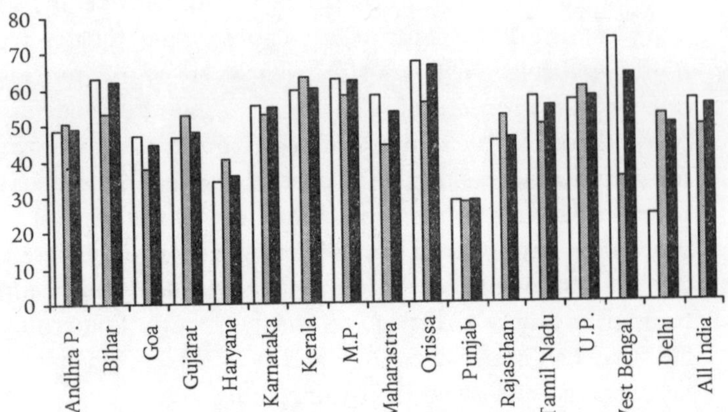

1973-74

□ Rural ▨ Urban ■ Combined

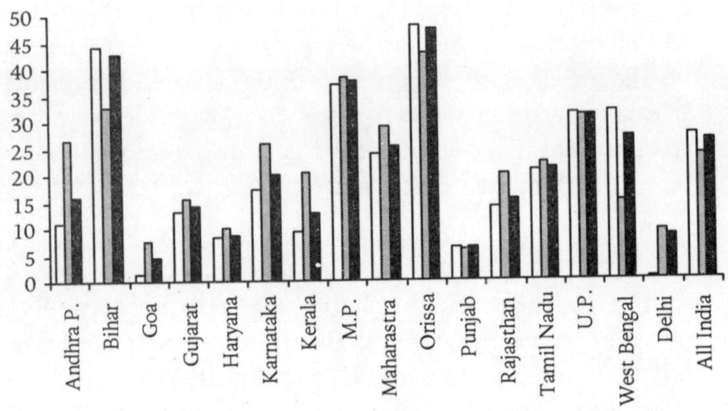

1999-2000

□ Rural ▨ Urban ■ Combined

References

Dalrymple, William. *The City of Djinns.*

Government of India. *Report of the State Reorganisation Commission.*

Kumar, Sudhir. "Towards Local Sustainable Development for Delhi: Review of Policies and Actions for Implementing Agenda 21", in M.C. Gupta *et al.* (ed.), *Governance and Poverty—Policy Reforms for India.*

Chapter 2

Economy and Fiscal Management

2.1 General

National capitals are the centres of economic activities in most countries. Formulation, adoption, and execution of economic policies are, by and large, the prerogative of the national governments in federations. Investors are attracted to them as they generally have a well-developed infrastructure, essential for any development activity. Proximity to the seat of the national government ensures smooth sailing in matters where government clearances and authorisations are essential. A national capital, with few exceptions, is the largest city in terms of area and population. These provide a ready market for any type of goods and services. Unless otherwise restricted, sheer presence of a large population, and an elite class, enhances the economic activity which leads to a rate of growth, not experienced in other parts of the country even with better endowment of resources, natural and others.

ECONOMY

2.2 Rate of Economic Growth

Delhi has been among some of the fastest growing states in the country. The net state domestic product grew at the rate of 5.1 per cent during the decade of the 60s. It was much higher than the all-India rate of growth of 3 per cent during the same period. Only four states recorded a higher rate of growth during this decade—Punjab (5.6), Haryana (5.5), Himachal Pradesh (5.6), and Orissa (9.7). In the decade of 70s, there was a further improvement in economic performance; the rate of growth, at 6.2 per cent, was not only the highest among states, but was much higher than the all-India trend growth rate of 3.6 per cent. This trend continued in the 80s; the average annual rate of growth of gross state domestic product (GSDP) reached was 7.6 per cent compared to the all-India rate of growth of 5.6 per cent. It continued to maintain, on an average, the same rate of growth in the decade of the 90s, though there have been wide fluctuations from year to year. In the first five years of the present century, the average rate of growth has been around 8.8 per cent, as against an average growth of 6 per cent in the GDP. The rate of growth has been one of the highest among states and union territories (Annex A-2.1).

2.3 Per Capita NSDP

High rate of economic growth over the years is reflected in a disproportionately high share of Delhi in the GDP. In 2000-01, the share of Delhi was 4.8 per cent in the GDP at factor cost. It has, however, declined to 3.18 per cent in 2004-05. Delhi accounted for a mere 1.34 per cent of the total population of the country, despite the phenomenal rate of growth recorded during the last half of the century, largely due to migration from other states. The per capita NSDP was Rs. 53976 in 2004-05, a little less than two and a half times the average per capita GDP for the country at factor cost and at current prices. It was more than nine times that of Bihar, four times that of Jharkhand, U.P, Chattisgarh, and M.P. (Annex A-2.2). In the first five years of the present decade, the average annual rate of growth in the per capita NSDP was 7.9 per cent. Among the states, only Goa had a higher per capita NSDP, and among the Union Territories, only Chandigarh and Pondicherry had a higher per capita NSDP in 2004-05. If Delhi had witnessed only the natural growth in population, its per capita NSDP could have been much higher than any state or Union Territory in the country.

2.4 Structure of the Economy

Sectoral composition of NSDP reflects the structural changes that characterise the economy of Delhi. The State has a small geographical area; rural area has been shrinking over the years with growing urbanisation. As a result, the primary sector never had a dominant position in Delhi's economy, as it has in the economy of other states or other Union territories. By itself, Delhi would find place among the highly developed economies of the world. Table 2.1 shows the composition of the three major sectors in the NSDP in terms of percentages.

TABLE 2.1

Sectoral Composition of NSDP of NCT of Delhi 1960-61 to 2004-05 at Current Prices

(in Percentages)

Sector	*1960-61*	*1970-71*	*1980-81*	*1990-91*	*1993-94*	*2000-01*	*2004-05*
Primary	7.01	6.82	3.05	2.04	4.22	1.35	1.06
Second	32.21	25.83	29.23	28.02	25.39	21.18	19.02
Services	60.79	67.35	67.72	69.94	70.39	77.47	79.92

Note: 1. Primary sector includes agriculture, forestry and logging, and fishing, quarrying and mining.

2. Secondary includes manufacturing, electricity, gas, water, water supply, and construction.

3. Services include the remaining sectors included in the NSDP.

Source: EPW Research Foundation. *Domestic Product of States of India 1960-61 to 2000-01*, and Central Statistical Organisation (CSO).

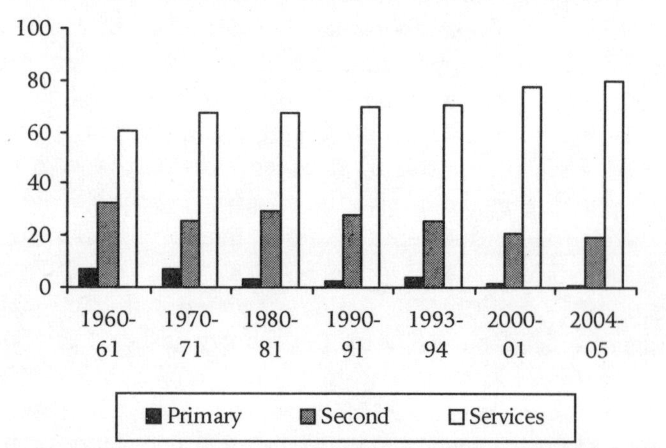

Some features in the growth and sectoral composition of NSDP of Delhi need to be highlighted here. Firstly, the general trend has been for the primary sector to decline at the state and national levels, and the share of the secondary sector to increase over the decades. But Delhi gives a different picture. Here, the share of the secondary sector in the NSDP has also been consistently declining but for some odd years and is now a little over a half of what it was four decades back. Secondly, services at around 80 per cent or four-fifth of the NSDP, form the back bone of the economy. This is in contrast to the structure of the economy in many states where the primary and the secondary sector continue to be important, contributing, together, more than 50 per cent of the NSDP. These provide the base for a growing services sector, which has now a bigger share in the NSDP of states, compared to primary or the secondary sector. During the last two decades, the services sector has become a major contributor to the GDP; its share in the GDP is more than 53 per cent (Table 2.2). If the present trend in the decline of secondary sector continues, as it is bound to, due to environment and space reasons, Delhi's economy will be solely dependent on the various types of tertiary activities for its sustenance. The incremental NSDP, by and large, will be accounted for by this sector.

TABLE 2.2

Sectoral Composition of GDP: 1960-61 to 2004-05 (at Current Prices)

(in Percentages)

Sector	*1960-61*	*1970-71*	*1980-81*	*1990-91*	*1993-94*	*2000-01*	*2004-05*
Primary	46.7	46.1	38.6	31.3	31	24.9	22.4
Second	19.6	20.7	24.4	27.5	26.3	26.9	23.9
Services	34.3	33.7	36.4	41.1	42.8	48.2	53.7

Note: As in Table 2.1.

Source: EPW Research Foundation. *National Accounts Statistics of India 1950-51 to 2000-01.*

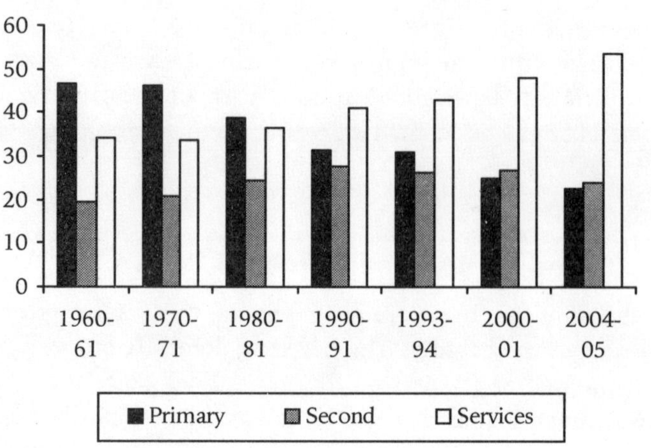

2.5 Primary Sector

Decline in the primary sector has been continuous as reflected in its percentage share of the NSDP in the different decadal series prepared by the CSO since 1960-1961. However, comparison is difficult, as back series of the NSDP/GSDP have not been worked out on any common base. Jitender Kumar and Chakresh Chandra have worked out the back series of GSDP and NSDP at current and constant prices up to 1980-81 with 1993-94 base at which the present national accounts statistics are now prepared, but these do not give the shares of different sectors even by major heads of economic activity. However, one thing is certain. The share of agriculture has declined, not merely as a percentage of NSDP, but also in terms of absolute values over the years. The 1980-81 series shows a continuous decline, while the 1993-94 series depicts a steep decline in the first year (1994-95) with mild fluctuations, though towards the end of the decade it has shown an increasing trend. This trend continued in the present decade also with mild fluctuations. The other two components—forestry and logging, and fishing—have also shown decline in absolute terms.

Diverse uses to which the available land can be put acts as a basic constraint on the development of the primary sector. Over the years, more and more land is required for other economic and non-economic activities in the National Capital Territory. For the first time in 2001, the census shows that the urban area of Delhi is much larger than the rural area. The number of villages has gone down from 209 in 1991 to 165 in 2001, and there has been an increase in the number of census towns from 29 to 59 during the same period. This has naturally resulted in the reduction of area for primary economic activities. The net area sown has come down to a mere 26971 hectares in 2004-05; so also the gross cropped area. As land gets diverted to non-agricultural uses, primary sector may record further decline, and Delhi may soon become totally urban. In fact, its contribution to NSDP has come down to bare 1.06 per cent from 1.35 per cent in 2000-01, and 4.22 per cent in 1993-94.

2.6 Secondary Sector

In sharp contrast, the secondary sector, though declining in its contribution to NSDP in terms of percentage, continued to grow. Industrial production, both in the organised and unorganised sector, has been increasing. But Delhi is among those few states in which the unorganised sector in the manufacturing is bigger than the organised sector. Mostly, it is the small states, especially the special category, with the notable exceptions of Himachal Pradesh and Assam, which have a big and growing unorganised sector. Among the major states, only in Bihar and West Bengal, the contribution of unorganised sector to industrial production, far exceeds that of the organised sector. Construction is another economic activity in this sector, which has recorded a high rate of growth with significant contribution to the NSDP. In fact, all over the country, development activities have given tremendous boost to this industry, which in turn has given boost to the industrial production (Annex A-2.3).

2.7 Services Sector

It is the services sector, or what has come to be known as the tertiary sector, which puts Delhi apart from the rest of the country. It gives Delhi the status of a mature economy, not dependent on the vagaries of weather, or the industrial fluctuations to which other developed economies are periodically subject. And as Delhi is the national capital, and the capital of National Capital Territory, an impression gets created that public administration would be a significant contributor to NSDP. But this is not so. As in most other states, the share of public administration hovers around 5 per cent. It is two groups—banking and insurance, and trade, hotels and restaurants—which accounted for nearly 50 per cent of the NSDP of Delhi in 2000-01. Of these, banking and insurance alone contributed 22 per cent in 2004-05 followed by trades, hotels and restaurants at 23 per cent. However, there has been a decline in the share of banking and insurance, as a group, in their contribution to NSDP in the present decade. Each of these groups, on its own, has a share in the NSDP larger than the combined share of primary and secondary sectors. In major states, agriculture and manufacturing continue to have prime position followed by trades, hotels and restaurants. Banking and insurance are also important but only after these economic activities. These differences in the composition of the tertiary sector, as also the other two sectors in comparison to other states, make Delhi a very different place from rest of the country.

2.8 Labour Supply and Employment

Economic structure that has emerged in Delhi has long-term implications for the economy and society. Firstly, the contribution of the primary sector, especially agriculture, to the NSDP will continue to decline. This has an impact on the employment generated in this sector. In fact, employment opportunities have been continuously declining in agriculture and related economic activities. According to the 48th round of the National Sample Survey Organisation (NSSO), primary sector provided employment to only 0.92 lakh workers or 2.82 per cent of the total work force in 1992. It declined to 0.60 lakh workers or 1.54 per cent of the work force in the survey conducted by NSSO in 1999-2000. Secondly, the rural area of around 40 per cent spread over 165 villages has only 7 per cent of the total population of Delhi. The NSDP generated in this area is much less; so is the employment. The incremental income and employment for supporting this population has to come from non-primary sectors. Thirdly, with decline in the secondary sector, the bulk of employment has to be generated in the tertiary sector, and that too in the unorganised sector. According to the 55th round of NSSO survey, the number of workers in employment was 39 lakh, of which two-thirds were in the tertiary sector, and another 11 lakh were employed in the secondary sector. The employment in the organised sector has been declining slowly. It was 8.45 lakh in March 1998 or nearly 20 per cent of the total employment. It has come down to 8.39 lakh in March 2004. Even though the decline has not been statistically significant, it only reflects the trend. Around 75 per cent of the employment is in the public sector, while the remaining 25 per cent is generated in the private sector. Employment opportunities in the organised sector have more or less remained constant even though Delhi's economy has been recording a very high rate of economic growth. Fourthly, the percentage of persons employed has declined from 33.04 per cent in the 48th round NSSO survey to 29.3 per cent in the 55th round survey in 1999-2000. The subsequent survey (59th Round Jan. 2003 to Dec. 2003) shows only marginal improvement by one per cent. During the same period, the number of unemployed person in the labour force increased from 5.67 per cent in 1992 to 12.57 per cent in 1999-2000 according to these two NSSO surveys. However, in the 2003 survey, the number of unemployed persons has declined to 4.63 per cent. The percentage of total labour force to estimated total population has also declined from 35 per cent in 1992 to 32 per cent in 2003. Fifthly, the damocles sword hanging on some of the existing industrial units required to either shift to some other area or close down would further affect the employment scenario, and also the income-generation from this sector in Delhi. During the decade of the nineties, the annual addition to the register of educated unemployed has been more than 2 per cent. There were around a million persons registered as unemployed with more than 75 per cent falling in the category of educated unemployed with educational qualifications of matriculation and above. However, there was a sudden and drastic change in the position of unemployed persons in Delhi. There was a decline of more than 42 per cent in the number of persons in the register of unemployed in Delhi in 2004. If this trend continues, Delhi would soon become, if not already one, a full employment economy.

FISCAL MANAGEMENT

2.9 Special Provisions for Delhi

The National Capital Territory of Delhi did not have any legislature before the fiscal year 1991-92. The revenue and expenditure formed part of the Consolidated Fund of India. The Metropolitan Council constituted under section 3 of the Delhi Administration Act, 1966, had the right to discuss and make recommendations to Central government on the estimated receipts and expenditure of the Union Territory of Delhi to be made from the Consolidated Fund of India. The legislative powers including the powers to consider and pass the budget of Delhi vested in the Parliament. The responsibility for fiscal management rested with the Union Government, and not on the Union Territory. The sixty-ninth amendment to the Constitution, which became effective from 1st February 1992, made a provision for a Legislative Assembly for Delhi. The Government of National Capital Territory of Delhi Act, 1991, passed, in pursuance to the constitutional amendment, made some fundamental changes in the financial arrangement. The state legislature has been given the same powers in financial matters, as have been enshrined in the Constitution, for the states, except for land, law and order, and police which rest with the Government of India. However, unlike the position obtaining in the states, the annual financial statement or the budget of Delhi requires prior approval of not only the Lt. Governor but also the President of India before it can be presented to the State legislature for consideration and passing. Provisions for setting up of a Consolidated Fund and a Contingency Fund of the Capital have been made. The receipts are now credited to the Consolidated Fund, and expenditure is made from it. Effective responsibility for fiscal management is now with the Government of the NCT. However, financial powers of the Delhi Government are not analogous to that of the states. The NCT finances have to function under the over all control of the Central government; and even though it places some restrictions on the freedom of action, it has also helped the NCT to emerge as a fiscally strong entity.

Special provisions made in the Constitution for the National Capital Territory of Delhi has given it a special status distinct from the states and other Union Territories. One such provision, already mentioned, is that prior approval of the President of India, which means the Union Ministry of Home, is mandatory before the budget of the NCT could be introduced in the legislature. In the case of states, the approval of the Governor is sufficient before it is placed before the State legislature for consideration and passing. Secondly, Parliament has overriding powers of legislation, in terms of article 239AB (3)(b) and (c) of the Constitution, with respect to any matter for the NCT as a whole or part thereof. The law enacted by Parliament has supremacy over any law passed by the NCT legislature. However, if on any subject, the NCT passes a legislation, which is subsequent to one passed by the Parliament on the same subject and has been assented to by the President, it prevails even if there is some variance. Thus, even in financial matters, the Parliament can amend and alter any fiscal measures taken by the Government of NCT. Not so, in the case of states, where Parliament can legislate only in the exceptional situations mentioned in articles 249 or 250 of the Constitution on any matter contained in the State List of the Seventh Schedule. Thirdly, the Government of NCT does not have any powers to borrow from the open market. It can borrow from the Central government only. It cannot stand guarantee to a loan raised by any of its public sector undertakings or local bodies working under its domain. It does not have any separate Public Account. It also does not have any separate account of cash balance, with the Reserve Bank, from that of Government of India. It does have some advantages in the sense that the NCT does not have to bother too much for its ways and means position, but it also deprives the NCT from getting the interest on surplus cash balance. An amendment was made in the NCT of Delhi Act, 1991, in 2001 to rectify this situation, and to authorise Delhi Government to borrow from the open market, to have separate Public Account as also cash balance with the Reserve Bank, and to stand guarantee to loans sanctioned to its various institutions and local bodies, subjects to over all limit fixed by the Government of India, but the date for its coming into force of this enactment has not yet been notified.

TABLE 2.3

Revenue Receipts of Delhi: 1994-95 to 2004-05

(in Crore of Rupees)

Items	*1994-95*	*1999-2000*	*2000-01*	*2001-02*	*2002-03*	*2003-04*	*2004-05*
Tax	1787 (90. 25)	3430 (80.26)	4401 (80.84)	4897 (78.30)	5324 (79.87)	5884 (80.08)	7106 (82.99)
Non-tax	100	398	548	876	830	950	921
Revenue	(5.05)	(9.31)	(10.07)	(14.01)	(12.45)	(12.93)	(10.75)
Central	93	446	495	481	512	514	535
Transfer	(4.70)	(10.43)	(9.09)	(7.69)	(7.68)	(6.99)	(6.25)
Total Revenue Receipts	1980	4274	5444	6254	6666	7348	8562
Growth over Previous year (%)	16.78	27.36	14.87	6.59	10.24	16.52	
As % of GSDP	8.06	8.68	9.2	8.91	9.25	9.12	

Note: 1. Figures rounded to the nearest whole number.
2. Figures in brackets indicate the % share in total revenue receipts.

Source: *Report of the CAG for various years, Economic Survey of Delhi 2003-04*, and Budgets.

2.10 Revenue Receipts

Revenues of the NCT compare well with some of the large states. Even though it has a small area, and a small population, as compared to non-special category States, it is in a comfortable financial position. Table 2.3 gives the position of revenue receipts of Delhi.

Revenue receipts have been consistently growing though not at a uniform or near uniform pace. During the last decade—1994-95 to 2004-05—it had a high growth of 27.28 per cent in 2000-01 and a low growth of 5.14 per cent in 1998-99. But for 1998-99, and 2002-03, when the growth was only 6.59 per cent, the revenue receipts consistently recorded a growth of more than 10 per cent.

2.11 Tax Receipts

The fluctuations in the revenue receipts have been due to changes in the annual growth rate of tax receipts, which form bulk of the revenue receipts of Delhi, as also in all major states. Sales tax, now value added tax (VAT) continues to be a major source of tax revenue contributing between 68 to 77 per cent during this period. State Excise is the next major contributor, though its share in the tax revenue has come down from 19 per cent in 1993-94 to around 12 per cent in 2004-05. The growth in the revenue from state excise has been only two and a half times as against a near four times growth in the revenue from sales tax and taxes on vehicles, and more than six and a half times in the recovery from stamp duty. In fact, the share of revenue from stamp duty has gone up from 4.63 per cent to 9.4 per cent in 2004-05, more than double of what it was in 1993-94. Delhi conforms to the usual pattern of collection of tax revenue under different heads obtaining in major states; sales tax has the prime place followed by state excise, stamp duty, motor vehicles related taxes, etc., except that in large states motor vehicles related taxes generate higher revenue than stamp duty. The land revenue, which used to be a major source of revenue at the time of Independence, has ceased to be a revenue earner in the NCT of Delhi.

The tax-GSDP ratio has hovered around 7 per cent during the decade, though it did reach a peak of 8.04 per cent in 1996-97, and a low of 6.48 per cent in 1999-2000 (Annex A-2.4). There are quite a few, among major states, which have a higher tax-GSDP ratio—Karnataka, Kerala, Tamil Nadu, Andhra Pradesh, Maharashtra, and Gujarat (Annex A-2.6). In terms of per capita income, Delhi ranks the fourth highest among the states and the Union Territories taken together; only Chandigarh and

Pondicherry among the Union Territories and Goa among the states have a higher per capita income. But these are very small units, in terms of population and area. Delhi, which should compare well with major states than any Union Territory, has a comparatively low tax-GSDP ratio, if one keeps in view the basic structure of its economy. There are two other points, apart from the high per capita income, which distinguish it from major states. Delhi has a very high urban population, nearly 93 per cent, in comparison to other states. Rural areas are indistinguishable from the urban areas and are as monetised as urban areas. They form part of the tax net. This is not so in the case of even large states where rural population forms a high component of the total population and primary sector, mainly agriculture, continues to be a very significant contributor to the GSDP. Part of the GSDP generated can, therefore, legitimately escape from the tax net. Secondly, Delhi has a much lower poverty ratio—persons living below the poverty line—compared to other states, suggesting a pattern of distribution of income in which a higher percentage of population has the purchasing power and therefore can contribute to tax revenue. If these factors are taken into account, Delhi has a much lower tax burden than some of the low- income states.

Tax-buoyancy is another indicator of the fiscal performance of a state (Annex A-2.4). During the decade of 1993-94 to 2002-03, the tax buoyancy of Delhi has been in the range of 0.9 to 1.09. The highest—1.09—was achieved in 1995-96, while the lowest of 0.9 occurred three years later in 1998-99. However, there has been tremendous improvement in the collection of taxes in 2004-05, largely due to reduction in the arrears, and this has resulted in higher tax buoyancy. For a fiscal administrator, this could be a matter of satisfaction that the collection of taxes is keeping pace with the incremental income, or not lagging far behind. But there are many states in India, where tax buoyancy is much higher even with lower per capita income. In terms of structure of economy or employment in the organised sector, these states are no better, when compared with Delhi. A part of the explanation can be had from the mounting arrears of tax revenue. (Annex A-2.7) These stood at 9364.77 crore in 2003-04; a staggering 159.15 per cent of the total tax revenue collected in that year. However, in 2004-05, as stated earlier, the arrears of tax revenue were 121.54 per cent of the taxes collected that year. All these arrears are on account of sales tax alone. In 2003-04, the collection of the sales tax was Rs. 4435.17 crore, while the arrears for the same year were 1036.17 crore or 23.38 per cent of the sales tax collected in that year. In the previous year i.e., 2002-03, the arrears on account of sales tax were 34.2 per cent of the total amounted collected in that year. This has been the highest arrear in comparison to demand during the last five years. However, there was no addition to arrears in 2004-05; the increase in the revenue of the sales tax (VAT) was mainly on account of the recovery of the past arrears. It shows that if the arrears alone are not allowed to mount, there would be tremendous improvement in the tax buoyancy and tax-GSDP ratio.

2.12 Own Non-Tax Revenue

Non-tax revenue has two components; own non-tax revenue, and transfers from the Central Government, other than share in Central taxes (Annex A-2.5) However, in the case of Delhi, the share of Delhi in Central taxes is transferred to it in the form of grants-in-aid, and is therefore clubbed with non-tax revenue. Own non-tax revenue generally comprises of interest, dividends, revenue from forestry and wild life, royalty on mineral resources, irrigation dues, included in a host of other state activities classified as general, economic and social services. In Delhi, there is a very small area under forests; it is not a source of revenue. There are hardly any minerals or irrigation sources, which could be tapped as a source of revenue.

2.12.1 Interest Receipts

The major source of non-tax revenue is the receipts from interest on loans given to local bodies and state public sector undertakings. These constituted 89.21 per cent of the total non-tax revenue in 2004-05. Interest receipts were only Rs. 5.52 crore in 1996-97, and constituted less than 10 per cent of the total non-tax receipts. The phenomenal increase in the receipts on account of interest has been, firstly, due to increasing budgetary support to local bodies, statutory corporations and local bodies by granting them loans. Secondly, in most cases, the receipts are mainly in the form of book entry where interest receipts are converted into loan to the same institution at specified rate of interest prevailing at that time. The conversion of interest due into loan every year notionally increases the interest receipts. This process started from 1997-98; interest receipts stood at Rs. 822 crore out of a total non-tax revenue of Rs. 921 crore in 2004-05.

2.12.2 Receipts from General Services

General services are the other important group from which a significant amount of non-tax revenue is collected. It used to be the most important among group of services, which contributed nearly 64 per cent of the non-tax revenue in 1995-96. Its share was only 5.23 per cent of the non-tax revenue in 2004-05. There have been year-to-year fluctuations in the amount collected; and it has not been able to attain the peak of Rs.53 crore recorded in 1999-2000. General services comprise police, jails, printing and stationery, and various other administrative services. The scope of any significant revenue from these services is always very limited. Most states get revenue from lotteries, but it also has a very high expenditure component in the form of prizes. In any case, Delhi has no lottery.

2.12.3 Receipts from Social Services

In the social service group, education, medical and public health, housing, urban development, labour and employment, water supply, and sanitation etc., are included. These are basically expenditure items, but some revenue is also collected from some of the services provided under these heads, but this is quite insignificant. It was only Rs. 27.73 crore in 2004-05 and accounted for 3.01 per cent of own non-tax receipts. The bulk of the revenue under this group is collected from public health, education, and labour and employment. Even though there is a clamour for collection of, at least, the maintenance cost of the social services, there is little possibility as most of these services cater to the basic needs of low-income families. Health, housing, elementary education, sanitation and water supply are, in any case, a part of the national programmes, and these have to be provided even to those who can not afford to pay for them.

2.12.4 Receipts from Economic Services

Revenue from economic services was Rs. 19.77 crore or 2.14 per cent of the own non-tax revenue in 2004-05. It has never been an important source of revenue, as most heads on which revenue is collected in other states are virtually non-existent in Delhi. In most states, economic services make a significant contribution to non-tax revenues. Royalty from minerals, sale of minor forest produce and timber, irrigation dues etc., are the important source of revenue. Small amounts are generated from animal husbandry, fisheries, dairy development etc. There is hardly any revenue earning forest area in Delhi. Nor are there any minerals. The small revenue generated under this group is from small and village industries, as it includes mining and quarrying activities. Major and minor irrigation projects also contribute a small amount to the state exchequer. Even though the share of economic services in the non-tax revenue has come down to 1.24 per cent, these two sectors have continued to contribute a major portion of the revenue under this group. However, looking to over all revenue receipts from other heads, these will continue to pale into insignificance.

2.13 Central Transfers

The 69th amendment to the Constitution has given a special status to Delhi, but this special status is among the Union Territories. Delhi is not a state; as such central transfers to Delhi are in the form of grants-in-aid to the revenues of the NCT administration. Basically there are three types of grants given to the government of NCT. These are: grants for the state plan schemes; grants for the centrally sponsored and central sector schemes; and statutory grants. While grants for the first two heads vary from year to year depending on the size of the plan, and the need and ability of the NCT to draw funds under various centrally sponsored and central sector schemes, statutory grants are, more or less, fixed for a period as would be discernible from the devolution during the last few years. These may be based on the NCT's share on the shareable tax revenue of the Central government accruing from the state, but instead of the share being fixed in terms of percentages, as is done by the Finance Commission for allocating shares vertically between the Centre and the states on the one hand, and horizontally between the states, the quantum has been fixed. This has deprived the NCT of the buoyancy, that is generally available in the Central taxes The Finance Commission makes recommendations for the states for a period of five years; Union Territories are not covered by it as administration of Union territories, including management of their finances, is basically the responsibility of the Central government.

A consequence of the approach adopted by the Central government on statutory grants is that there has been only marginal increase in the Central transfers during the last few years. In the decade of the nineties, grants were fixed afresh every year, and therefore it was possible to add on to the figures of the previous years. Thus, there was an increase of 31.02 per cent in 1995-96, 67.85 per cent in 1996-97, 91.84 per cent in 1997-98, and 32.42 per cent in 1999-2000 over the previous years. In comparison to trends recorded in the nineties, there was a growth of only 10.97 per cent in 2000-01 and a decline of 2.86 per cent in 2001-02. However, in 2002-03, there has been an increase of 6.5 per cent, but these are almost at the same level in 2003-04. There was a marginal increase in the central transfers from Rs. 514.02 crore to Rs. 535.11 crore in 2004-05. As stated, the growth in the level of grants has been on account of a marginally higher support to state plan schemes, and centrally sponsored schemes.

2.14 Expenditure

While the GNCT has the same sources of revenue receipts as a state, it has some advantages in the matter of expenditure, not available to any other state or Union Territory. Police, public order, management of land, and pension are the direct responsibility of the Central government. The GNCT does not have to spend any funds, nor does it contribute to the Central government for expenditure incurred on this account. Delhi has another unique feature, not to be found in any other state or Union Territory, which has an impact on its finances. Barring the area covered by the New Delhi Municipal Committee (NDMC), and the Delhi Cantonment Board (DCB), the entire area of Delhi, including the rural area comprising 165 villages, comes under the jurisdiction of Municipal Corporation of Delhi (MCD). MCD is responsible for the civic services in Delhi and shares responsibility with the NCT government for some social services, including public health and elementary education. The expenditure on these services is incurred by the civic bodies from their own resources, and from the grants received from the GNCT government. The grants-in-aid to local bodies are based on the recommendations of the State Finance Commission. To the extent that some of these functions, ordinarily performed in other states by the government, are shared by the civic bodies, the burden on the state exchequer is less. The Government of the NCT is fortuitously placed in this happier situation.

The expenditure of the GNCT of Delhi remained below 11 per cent of GSDP in the nineties (Table 2.4). It is only at the close of the century that it crossed the threshold of 11 per cent and since then it has been going up as a percentage of the GSDP. It is now more than 14 per cent. A significant feature is that the revenue expenditure has all along, during this period, been below 60 per cent of the total expenditure, hovering along 55 per cent mark. Since 2002-03, it has been around 45 per cent of the total expenditure. In most major states, the revenue expenditure is anywhere between 75 to 80 per cent of the total expenditure. This has been remarkable achievement, and has made possible higher capital expenditure, directly or indirectly, through various other bodies operating under its control by giving loans and advances. The capital expenditure at more than 4 per cent of the GSDP in the nineties, and to around 7 per cent since 2002-03 is one of the highest in recent years. No state government or Union Territory has been able to achieve this level. And this capital expenditure has been mainly on account of increase in the capital outlay, and in the form of loans and advances to various bodies, including local bodies. In recent years, the obligations of the NCT on account of repayment of loans have been going up on account of increasing debt burden. In the last three years, the amount, on account of repayment of loans, has gone up from Rs. 186 crore in 2001-02 to Rs. 944 crore in 2002-2003 and to 2302 crore in 2004-05. Till 1997-98, the NCT did not have any liability on account of repayment of loans (Annex A-2.9). If loans and advances made by the GNCT to various public bodies are made to finance expenditure of capital nature, as it should be, this would be an ideal composition of the expenditure for any state, which cherishes higher rates of economic growth. However, it has been made possible by the Central

TABLE 2.4

Expenditure of the GNCT of Delhi: 1994-95 to 2004-05

(in Crore of Rs.)

Items	*1994-95*	*1996-97*	*1997-98*	*1998-99*	*1999-00*	*2000-01*	*2001-02*	*2002-03*	*2003-04*	*2004-05*
Revenue	1431 (59.4)	2032 (57.8)	2322 (55.1)	2840 (57.5)	3523 (59.6)	3696 (51.3)	4963 (56.4)	4598 (45.0)	5087 (43.4)	5827 (45.26)
As% of GSDP Growth over	5.53	6.01	5.63	5.98	6.65	5.89	7.30	6.38	6.32	6.42
Previous year %	—	8.25	14.27	22.30	24.05	4.91	34.29	-7.36	10.63	14.55
Capital	976 (40.6)	1484 (38.2)	1889 (44.9)	2102 (42.5)	2389 (40.4)	3503 (48.7)	3830 (43.6)	5615 (55.0)	6633 (56.6)	7048 (54.74)
As % of GSDP Growth over	3.77	4.39	4.58	4.43	4.51	5.58	5.63	7.59	8241	7.77
Previous year (%)	—	52.04	27.29	11.27	13.65	46.63	9.33	46.60	18.13	6.26
Total Expenditure	2407	3516	4211	4942	5912	7200	8793	10213	11720	12875
Expenditure as % of GSDP	9.31	10.53	10.21	10.41	11.15	11.48	12.93	14.17	14.55	14.19
Previous year (%)	—	46.07	19.77	17.36	19.62	21.78	22.12	18.33	16.14	9.85

Notes: 1. Figures in brackets show percentage share in the total expenditure.

2. Figures rounded to nearest crore or percentage point.

Source: RBI. *State Finances of various years; Economic Survey of Delhi, 2001-02 & 2003-04*; National Accounts Statistics.

Government, which has undertaken the responsibility for plan and non-plan expenditure on police, public order, land, and pensions. In the budget of most state governments, a significant percentage of their non-plan revenue expenditure is devoted to these items.

2.15 Plan Expenditure

There are two notable features in the plan expenditure (Table 2.5) of the NCT, not to be found in any other state or Union Territory. Firstly, the plan expenditure, except for the year 1999-2000, has been more than 40 per cent of the total expenditure of the NCT, and on one occasion (1996-97) it has been more than 60 per cent till 2002-03. However, it has been less than 40 per cent since then. In most states, it has been around 20-25 per cent of the total expenditure of the state. Secondly, capital expenditure, but for the year 2001-02, forms more than 60 per cent, and occasionally more than 66 per cent, of the plan expenditure. In other words, revenue expenditure has been around manageable limits, and did not act as a constraint on the size of the next plan as a committed expenditure. Most states have nearly 57 to 65 per cent of the plan expenditure on revenue account leaving little for investment on infrastructure and other works of capital nature. The ability of these states to have a higher level of investment in succeeding plans gets adversely affected. A consequence of low plan revenue expenditure is that Delhi has been able to build capital assets during this period in a big way, unlike many states, where the pace of development has been slow. However, year to year growth in the plan expenditure has been quite uneven. There have been years when the plan expenditure went up by as much as 30 per cent over the previous years, while there were some years when it recorded a growth of less than six per cent. In the last three years there has not been much of an increase, and in fact in 2004-05, it has been less than the previous year.

2.16 Non-Plan Expenditure

The non-plan expenditure has generally been below 60 per cent of the total expenditure, except in 1999-2000 and 2003-04, when it marginally exceeded this threshold (Table 2.6). It was as low as 46.1 per cent in 1996-97, but this was mainly due to a sudden increase in the plan expenditure, as also due to a sudden decline in the non-plan capital expenditure. The non-plan expenditure has a

TABLE 2.5

Plan Expenditure: 1994-95 to 2004-05

(in Crore of Rs.)

Items	*1994-95*	*1996-97*	*1997-98*	*1998-99*	*1999-00*	*2000-01*	*2001-02*	*2002-03*	*2003-04*	*2004-05*
Revenue	391 (33.5)	659 (17.3)	636 (32.0)	795 (38.8)	883 (38.9)	968 (31.0)	1955 (49.1)	1218 (27.6)	1322 (28.91)	1392 (32.61)
Capital	776 (66.5)	1236 (61.4)	1352 (68.0)	1254 (61.2)	1386 (61.1)	2154 (69.0)	2030 (50.9)	3194 (72.4)	3251 (71.09)	2876 (67.39)
Total Plan Expenditure	1167	1895	1988	2049	2269	3122	3985	4412	4573	4268
As % of Total of GSDP	48.48	53.90	47.20	47.44	38.38	43.3	45.32	43.20	39.02	33.15
Growth over Previous year (%)	—	42.69	4.90	3.06	10.69	37.65	27.64	10.71	3.65	-6.67

Source: Reserve Bank of India. *State Finances of relevant years, Budgets of the GNCT*, and *CAG Reports*.

TABLE 2.6

Non-Plan Expenditure: 1994-95 to 2004-05

(in Crore of Rs.)

Items	*1994-95*	*1996-97*	*1997-98*	*1998-99*	*1999-00*	*2000-01*	*2001-02*	*2002-03*	*2003-04*	*2004-05*
Revenue	1040 (83.9)	1373 (84.7)	1686 (75.9)	2045 (70.6)	2640 (72.5)	2729 (66.9)	3008 (62.6)	3380 (58.3)	3765 (52.68)	4435 (51.52)
Capital	200 (16.1)	247 (15.3)	537 (24.1)	849 (29.4)	1003 (27.5)	1349 (33.1)	1800 (37.4)	2421 (41.7)	3382 (41.32)	4172 (48.48)
Total Plan Expenditure	1240	1620	2223	2894	3643	4078	4808	5801	7147	8607
As % of Total of GSDP	51.52	46.10	52.80	58.56	61.62	56.64	54.68	56.80	60.98	66.85
Growth over Previous year (%)	—	-0.19	37.22	30.1	25.88	11.94	17.90	20.65	23.20	20.43

Source: Reserve Bank of India. *State Finances of relevant years, Budgets of GNCT*, and *CAG Reports*.

very high component of revenue expenditure, usually more than 85 per cent in most states. But NCT of Delhi is an exception. The non-plan capital expenditure has been steadily increasing over the years; its share in the non-plan expenditure has been more than 30 per cent during the last five years, and more than 40 per cent since 2004-05. The increase has been mainly due to repayment of loans to Central government, and higher loans and advances to various bodies under its control.

2.17 Expenditure on General Services

General services include organs of the state, administrative services and payment of interest on borrowings. These account for nearly 97 to 98 per cent of the expenditure on the non-plan side. Nearly 75 per cent of the expenditure is payment of interest on borrowings, in this case to the Central government, as GNCT is not allowed to borrow from the market. Administrative services account for another 16 per cent. Expenditure on secretariat, district administration, police, etc., comes under this group. But in the case of Delhi expenditure on police is not included as it is met directly by the Central government from its own budget. Organs of the state i.e., Lt. Governor's establishment, State legislature, High Court, etc., account for nearly 5 per cent of the expenditure on this head. Expenditure on pensions, though a part of the group on general services, is not included here, as Central government have undertaken the responsibility in this area. Even after the exclusion of two major areas of state revenue expenditure on police and pensions, the revenue expenditure of the GNCT on general services has been continuously increasing, largely on account of increasing interest burden.

2.17.1 Payment of Interest

Payment of interest on borrowings is an important item of revenue expenditure on the non-plan side. This has been steadily going up; from a small amount of Rs.94 crore in 1995-96, it has gone up to Rs. 1569 crore in 2004-05. It constituted about 27 per cent of the total revenue expenditure in 2004-05. A significant feature of Delhi's finances has been that it has been lending more than its borrowings by deployment of the surplus in its revenue budgets. It receives interest, at least theoretically, from the various bodies to which lending is done. Receipts from interest have also been steadily going up, *albeit* on paper, except in 2004-05, when there was a decline in the receipts from this head (Table 2.7). If the

TABLE 2.7

Interest Receipts and Payments: 1995-96 to 2004-05

(in Crore of Rs.)

Items	*1995-96*	*1996-97*	*1997-98*	*1998-99*	*1999-00*	*2000-01*	*2001-02*	*2002-03*	*2003-04*	*2004-05*
Interest Paid	94	190	314	432	531	717	934	1115	1367	1569
As % of RE Interest	5.0	9.35	13.52	15.21	15.07	19.40	18.81	21.92	26.87	26.93
Receipts	7	5	133	139	301	477	790	741	869	822
Net Interest Paid	87	185	181	293	230	240	121	410	498	747
As % of RE	4.63	9.10	7.79	10.31	6.52	6.49	2.40	8.92	9.79	12.82

Source: Reserve Bank of India. *State Finances of relevant years, State Budgets,* and *Report of the CAG* for various years.

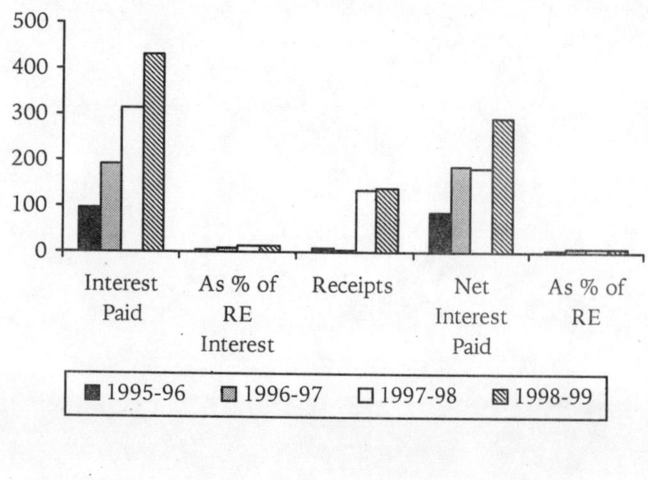

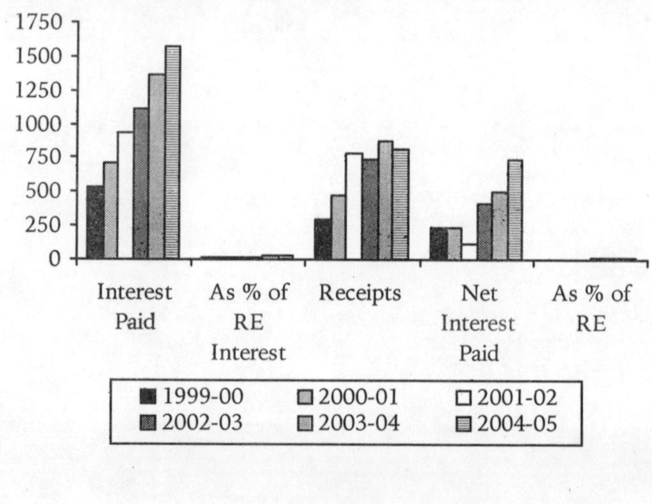

receipts from interest are compared with the amount of interest paid by the Delhi, the picture changes. Delhi has been getting much less amount, by way of interest on its loans and advances, than what it has been paying on its own borrowed funds. The loans and advances made by the GNCT are much more, as these include the surplus generated on revenue account. However, after taking into account the interest receipts of GNCT, the net interest paid by Delhi on its borrowings was only 12.82 per cent of the revenue expenditure in 2004-05.

2.18 Expenditure on Social and Economic Services

Expenditure in social services constitutes 30-35 per cent of the revenue expenditure in most states (Annex 2.8). In Delhi, it was more than 60 per cent in the 90s, and but has since then come down in the last four years. It has, on an average, been around 58 per cent during this period. Education gets a major share, as GNCT has the primary responsibility in this area. Public health and urban development are the other two major areas of importance, next to education, in which the GNCT of Delhi is directly involved in providing facilities, and maintaining them. Delhi runs a number of hospitals and dispensaries, primary health centres and maternity homes. Continuous migration of people from nearby and other states has always been a problem for Delhi. Basic living amenities have to be provided to migrants. GNCT of Delhi spends a very small percentage, usually less than 10 per cent, of its revenue expenditure on its economic services, compared to major states where it is around 15 to 20 per cent. Bulk of this expenditure is done on maintenance of roads and bridges, of which Delhi has large network, though not adequate for its sprawling population and urban area. The other areas of expenditure are flood control and drainage, village and small industries, and agriculture and allied activities. But these together account for much less than what is spent on roads and bridges.

2.19 Assignment to Local Bodies

Assignment to local bodies is now a responsibility imposed on the state government and the Union Territory administrations under the Constitution. The recommendations of the State Finance Commission constituted, at the expiration of every fifth year, form the basis of the devolution to local bodies. In the case of Delhi, the recipients are the two local bodies—NDMC, and MCD. MCD covers the entire rural area of the NCT as also those urban areas, which do not fall in the domain of NDMC and DCB. Present scheme of transfer of financial resources is based on the recommendations of the Second State Finance Commission and is effective from 2001-02. The fiscal transfers made to the local bodies are 10.5 per cent of the tax revenues—5.5 by way of sharing of tax revenue and 5 per cent by way of grants-in-aid—of the GNCT. These form part of the revenue expenditure.

2.20 Revenue Surplus

GNCT of Delhi has been consistently generating revenue surplus from the time it started having a separate budget. Its tax revenues alone have been adequate to meet the non-plan as well as the plan component of the revenue expenditure. The position of revenue surplus is given in Table 2.8. Such a high level of revenue surplus has been possible largely due to Central government undertaking direct responsibility for administering certain

TABLE 2.8

Revenue Surplus/Fiscal Deficit of Delhi: 1995-96 to 2004-05

(in Crore of Rs.)

Year	*Revenue Surplus*	*As % of GSDP*	*Fiscal Deficit*	*As % of GSDP*
1995-96	419.35	1.47	555.94	1.95
1996-97	764.18	2.26	689.98	2.04
1997-98	1158.72	2.81	575.93	1.39
1998-99	820.00	1.72	959.93	1.39
1999-00	751.34	1.42	1381.58	2.61
2000-01	1747.51	2.79	1609.66	2.57
2001-02	1209.57	1.90	1756.59	2.58
2002-03	2067.74	2.87	2396.43	3.32
2003-04	2261.44	2.81	2438.72	3.03
2004-05	2735.15	3.01	1483.18	1.63

Source: Reserve Bank of India. *State Finances of relevant years, and Report of the Comptroller & Auditor General of India on NCT* from various years.

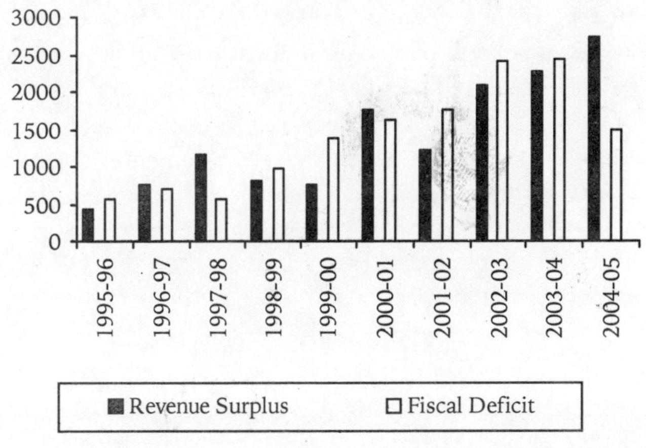

subjects, which are in the State List of the Seventh Schedule of the Constitution. Expenditure on these functions finds place in the Union budget; a mention of these subjects has already been made earlier. The peculiar nature of the administrative set up in which the jurisdiction of the urban local bodies, mainly the MCD, is co-terminus with that of the Government of the NCT also helps to an extent. The urban local bodies get only 10.5 of the GNCT's own tax revenue by way of share in taxes and grants-in-aid under the dispensation of the Second State Finance Commission, but these do share the responsibility with the GNCT in the provision of certain essential social services.

2.21 Fiscal Deficit and Debt

Despite the huge revenue surplus generated by the Government of the NCT every year, the fiscal deficit has been increasing every year as a percentage of GSDP. It crossed the 3 per cent mark in 2002-03, a limit set up by the European Economic Community for its members, and considered tolerable. It has marginally come down to 3.03 per cent in 2003-04. However, it came down drastically in 2004-05 to 1.63 per cent of the GSDP. This has been made possible by better tax collection and reduction in public expenditure. This resulted in reduced level of borrowings in 2004-05. Under the existing financial arrangements, the Government of the NCT can borrow only from the Union Government. It also does not have any Public Account; so all its receipts on account of provident funds, and other receipts are credited to the Public Account of the Union Government. The debt position of the NCT of Delhi is given in Table 2.9. There are some notable features, which need to be mentioned. Firstly, the debt-GSDP ratio has been rising; it has gone up from 2.42 per cent at the end of March, 1995 to 17.66 per cent at the end of March, 2005. However, it is still much less than the debt-GSDP ratio of some of the non-special category states. A problem faced by the Delhi government is that the National Savings organisation releases Delhi's share of collections on account of small savings despite their request to stop it, as they do not need it. These releases get reflected in the borrowings and fiscal deficits and thus does not give a correct picture. Secondly, the entire borrowings, supplemented by part of the surplus generated on revenue account, are re-lent to various bodies. It is not so with the states where part of the debt contracted during the year is used to finance revenue expenditure, plan and non-plan. Thirdly, the amount of loans and advances made by the GNCT are increasing every year. The outstanding amount due to Delhi has also been increasing every year. The amount lent by the Delhi government stood at Rs. 25144.02 crore at the end of March, 2005, neaarl six times of what it was a decade back. It was 27.71 per cent of the GSDP in March, 2005. While repayments are shown to be taking place, there has been a very high level of re-lending in the social and economic sectors, which means that installments due for repayment are adjusted in the fresh loans granted to various institutions. Fourthly, the sectors getting the major portion of the loans and advances made by Government of NCT are power, road transport, water supply and sanitation, and urban development. However, loans and advance are also given under the head 'miscellaneous' every year. These account for nearly 35 to 40 per cent of the loans and advances given every year,

TABLE 2.9

Debt Position of Delhi: 1995-2005
(As on 31 March of each year)

(in Crore of Rs.)

Year Advances From the Central Govt.	*Loans & GSDP*	*As % of Advances Made by GNCT*	*Loans & GSDP*	*As % of*	*Net Debt*
1995	627.33	2.42	4260.86	16.48	-3633.53
1996	1353.71	4.76	4967.42	17.49	-3613.71
1997	2204.91	6.52	6004.59	17.76	-3799.68
1998	3080.94	7.47	7074.11	17.15	-3993.17
1999	3788.17	7.97	8512.51	17.92	-4724.34
2000	5183.01	9.79	10134.95	19.15	-4951.94
2001	6759.00	10.81	12622.68	20.19	-5863.10
2002	8635.52	12.87	18503.78	24.84	-6970.99
2003	11329.57	15.24	18503.78	24.84	-6970.99
2004	14316.86	17.08	22351.21	26.66	-8034.05
2005	16026.86	17.66	25144.02	27.71	-9117.16

Source: Report of the Comptroller and Auditor General of India on Government of NCT for various years.

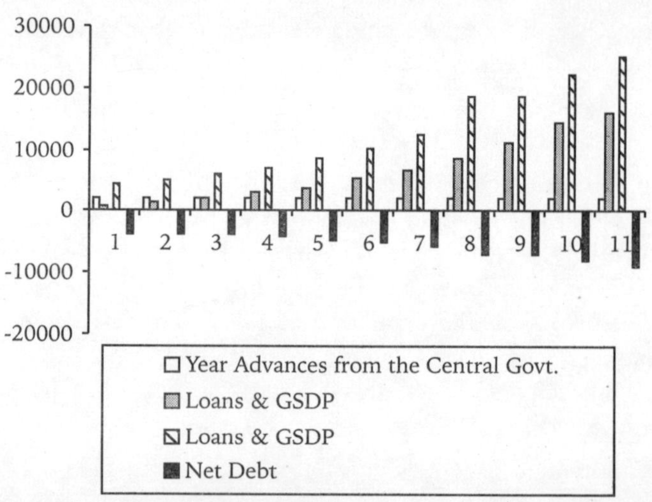

according to budget documents, but the details are not, however, in the budget documents. These could not be the loans to local bodies—MCD and NDMC—as the amount lent to them has not been more than 2 per cent of the total loans and advances, as indicated in the State Finance Commission Reports.

The institutions, which have been getting loans from the GNCT have the responsibility to provide certain essential services—electricity, water, transport, and other civic services—to public. These institutions have not been able to generate adequate revenue to cover the cost of services and generate surplus for meeting the repayment obligations. According to a report of the CAG for the year 2003-04, the overdue amounts, as of 31 March 2004 were Rs. 6588.52. Some of the institutions which had defaulted were: Delhi Vidyut Board Rs. 402.12 crore, Delhi Jal Board Rs. 1635.82 crore, MCD Rs. 563.05 crore, Delhi Transport Corporation Rs. 311.98 crore, NDMC Rs. 21.91 crore etc. The CAG Report for 2004-05 also states that an amount of Rs. 40,499.92 crore were also due these bodies. Unless there is a drastic improvement in their performance in the coming years, there is little hope that these public bodies will be able to live on their own and repay the loans received from the Government of NCT. If past trends are any guide, these institutions will continue to get financial support from the Government of NCT of Delhi, as they are providing essential services. The debt-GSDP ratio of the NCT will continue to rise which will have an impact on the fiscal deficit.

2.22 Concluding Remarks

Delhi has a very sound economy. It has maintained a consistently high rate of economic growth over the last many decades. The per capita income is one of the highest in the country. Service sector contributes more than 80 per cent of the GSDP; the primary sector, with contribution of one per cent is paling into insignificance. Even the secondary sector is declining in Delhi. A little less than half the area of Delhi is rural, but it has barely 7 per cent of population. Bulk of the economic activity is concentrated in urban Delhi; it supports not only the urban population but also the population of the nearby towns, as also its own rural population. As primary sector is disappearing, Delhi would become wholly urban economy, even though a large area may be officially recorded as rural.

The biggest challenge for Delhi in the coming years, apart from provision of social services and basic infrastructure facilities, has been the generation of employment opportunities for its growing population. Apart from the natural growth, Delhi gets around two per cent of the population from other states in search of jobs and better educational facilities. Significant progress was made in 2004-05. For the first time there has been a drastic reduction in the number of persons registered for employment. If this trend continues for a couple of years, Delhi would become a near full employment economy. However, employment opportunities in the organised sector have, more or less, dried up. It is the unorganised and informal sectors, which have been absorbing the growing labour force.

Financial position of Delhi has, so far, been quite sound. It has been generating huge revenue surplus. Its debt burden has been entirely on account of its loans and advances to its own public agencies. But this debt burden has been rising every year; both in absolute terms and as percentage to GSDP. There has been a significant decline in the fiscal deficit—below 1.63 per cent—in 2004-05, but it should not make the GNCT complacent. Most of the borrowing agencies are now at default, and the overdue amount is more than 25 per cent of loans advanced. Since most of these agencies are providing one or the other essential services, there is very little chance of recoveries in the near future. Some alternative has to be found, may be some of these services could be outsourced, or privatised.

The tax-GSDP ratio of Delhi needs improvement looking to the structure of its economy, which is almost fully urban. A beginning has been made in 2004-05 largely due to reduction in mounting arrears The effort made has to continue for some years to realise the full potential. For this, it is necessary that current dues are realised in full. Tax evasion and avoidance is another area requiring scrutiny and action. Many states with a big primary sector have a much higher tax-GSDP ratio. This would help in reducing the debt burden and fiscal deficit.

Present healthy financial position of Delhi is partially due to the fact that a significant amount of revenue expenditure—on police, law and order, land, and pensions—continues to be met by the Central government from its own budget, which does not get reflected in the budgetary position of the NCT under the present arrangement. Once Delhi is granted the status of a full state, these would directly become the responsibility of the NCT, and will reduce, if not eliminate, the revenue surplus. This, in turn, would add to the fiscal deficit of the NCT, as a part of the loans given to the local bodies and institutions is presently financed from the revenue surplus. The financial position will need close monitoring in the coming years.

ANNEX A-2.1

GSDP of Some States at 1993-94 Prices

(in Crore of Rs.)

States	*1993-94*	*1994-95*	*1995-96*	*1996-97*	*1997-98*	*1998-99*	*1999-00*	*2000-01*	*2001-02*	*2002-03*	*2003-04*
Andhra Pradesh	57867	61114 (5.6)	64279 (5.9)	68809 (6.3)	67866 (-1.4)	76116 (12.2)	79605 (4.6)	86513 (8.7)	90494 (4.6)	92835 (2.6)	99932 (7.6)
Goa	2397	2515 (4.9)	2706 (7.6)	3119 (15.3)	3207 (2.8)	3932 (22.6)	4015 (2.1)	4287 (7.0)	4472 (4.1)	4647 (3.9)	N.A
Gujarat	49194	58058 (18.0)	61246 (5.5)	69966 (14.2)	71442 (2.1)	76571 (7.2)	77354 (1.0)	75954 (-1.8)	81829 (7.7)	90068 (10.1)	103951 (15.4)
Haryana	22131	23692 (7.1)	24276 (2.5)	27095 (11.6)	27483 (1.4)	29011 (5.6)	31230 (7.6)	33313 (6.7)	35081 (5.3)	36834 (5.0)	39992 (8.36)
Karnataka	41079	43387 (5.6)	46167 (6.4)	50302 (9.0)	53778 (6.9)	60620 (12.7)	63851 (5.3)	70295 (10.1)	72053 (2.5)	75841 (5.3)	80550 (6.2)
Kerala	26326	28501 (8.3)	29788 (4.5)	30890 (3.7)	31783 (2.9)	34064 (7.2)	36516 (7.2)	37670 (3.2)	38235 (1.5)	40771 (6.6)	43344 (6.3)
M.P.	37971	39070 (2.9)	41464 (6.1)	44170 (6.5)	46380 (5.0)	49424 (6.6)	54614 (10.5)	49294 (-9.7)	53553 (8.6)	50570 (-5.6)	59960 (18.6)
Maharashtra	113320	116213 (2.6)	129567 (11.5)	136149 (5.1)	143723 (5.6)	147963 (3.0)	162287 (9.7)	156406 (-3.6)	164356 (5.1)	177138 (7.8)	190151 (7.3)
Orissa	18537	19528 (5.3)	20539 (5.2)	19566 (-4.7)	22136 (13.1)	22678 (2.4)	23821 (5.0)	23643 (-0.7)	25091 (6.1)	25071 (-0.08)	28686 (14.4)
Punjab	30248	31139 (2.9)	32433 (4.2)	34819 (7.4)	35865 (3.0)	37870 (5.6)	40003 (3.4)	41346 (3.4)	42028 (1.6)	42606 (1.6)	44862 (5.3)
Rajasthan	32970	38648 (17.2)	40225 (4.1)	44755 (11.3)	49821 (11.3)	51825 (4.0)	52920 (2.1)	52155 (-1.4)	56626 (8.6)	52950 (-6.5)	60738 (14.7)
Tamil Nadu	57549	64784 (12.6)	67021 (3.5)	70336 (4.9)	76105 (8.2)	79703 (4.7)	84656 (6.2)	91089 (7.6)	89157 (-2.1)	91703 (3.0)	94960 (3.6)
U.P.	80451	85106 (5.8)	88244 (3.7)	97719 (10.7)	97634 (-0.1)	105833 (2.8)	100321 (5.5)	107038 (1.1)	111673 (4.3)	111830 (0.1)	116828 (4.5)
West Bengal	53424	57060 (6.8)	61290 (7.4)	65562 (7.0)	70971 (8.3)	75483 (6.4)	80676 (6.9)	85832 (6.4)	92001 (7.2)	98374 (6.9)	105806 (7.6)
Delhi	20992	23503 (12.0)	24110 (2.6)	27268 (13.1)	31499 (15.5)	33022 (4.8)	34605 (4.8)	39444 (13.9)	41007 (4.0)	42920 (4.7)	47133 (9.8)

Notes: 1. Figures of M.P. and U.P. do not include Chhattisgarh and Uttaranchal.

2. Figures in brackets give percentage growth over previous year.

Source: Central Statistical Organisation. *National Accounts Statistics*.

ANNEX A-2.2

Per Capita NSDP of Some States at 1993-94 Prices

(in Rupees)

States	*1993-94*	*1994-95*	*1995-96*	*1996-97*	*1997-98*	*1998-99*	*1999-00*	*2000-01*	*2001-02*	*2002-03*	*2003-04*	*2004-05*
Andhra Pradesh	7416	7711	8071	8514	8191	9144	9445	10195	10639	10876	11756	12352
		(4.0)	(4.7)	(5.5)	(-3.8)	(11.6)	(3.3)	(7.9)	(4.4)	(2.2)	(8.1)	(5.1)
Goa	16558	16997	17929	20686	20595	25364	25371	25710	27603	31665	23586	24797
		(2.5)	(5.6)	(15.4)	(-0.4)	(23.2)	(0.0)	(1.3)	(7.4)	(14.7)	(-25.5)	
Gujarat	9796	11535	11649	13206	13018	13735	13298	12489	13321	14194	16302	16878
		(17.8)	(1.0)	(13.4)	(-1.4)	(5.5)	(-3.2)	(-6.1)	(5.9)	(9.9)	(15.4)	(3.5)
Haryana	11079	11598	11545	12591	12389	12728	13308	13848	14228	14712	15752	16872
		(4.7)	(-0.5)	(9.1)	(-1.6)	(2.7)	(4.6)	(3.9)	(2.6)	(3.6)	(7.0)	(7.1)
Karnataka	7838	8097	8368	8990	9416	10549	10912	11854	11857	12212	12634	13820
		(3.3)	(3.3)	(7.4)	(4.7)	(12.0)	(3.4)	(8.6)	(0.0)	(3.0)	(3.5)	(9.4)
Kerala	7938	8516	8748	8987	9079	9619	10430	10714	10762	11605	12328	13321
		(7.3)	(2.7)	(2.7)	(1.0)	(5.9)	(6.2)	(2.7)	(0.4)	(7.8)	(6.2)	(8.1)
M.P.	6584	6550	6790	7089	7301	7621	8248	7195	77.08	7062	8149	8238
		(-0.5)	(3.7)	(4.4)	(3.0)	(4.4)	(8.2)	(-12.8)	(7.1)	(-7.4)	(15.4)	(1.1)
Maharashtra	12183	12158	13221	13464	13925	14136	15257	14233	14656	15764	16765	17864
		(-0.2)	(8.7)	(1.8)	(3.4)	(1.5)	(7.5)	(-6.7)	(3.0)	(7.6)	(6.3)	(6.6)
Orissa	4896	5054	5204	4773	5382	5471	5742	5549	5803	5747	6640	7176
		(3.2)	(3.0)	(-8.3)	(12.8)	(1.7)	(5.0)	(-3.4)	(4.6)	(-1.0)	(15.5)	(8.1)
Punjab	12710	12784	13008	13705	13812	14333	14809	15071	15308	15407	16199	16756
		(0.6)	(1.8)	(5.4)	(0.8)	(3.8)	(3.3)	(1.8)	(1.6)	(0.6)	(4.6)	(4.0)
Rajasthan	6182	7134	7216	7862	8601	8754	8555	8175	8763	7903	10010	9853
		(15.4)	(1.1)	(9.0)	(9.4)	(1.8)	(-2.3)	(-4.4)	(7.2)	(-9.8)	(26.7)	(-1.6)
Tamil Nadu	8955	9932	10147	10451	11260	11592	12181	12994	12484	12696	12976	1399
		(10.9)	(2.2)	(3.0)	(7.7)	(2.9)	(5.0)	(6.8)	(-3.9)	(1.7)	(2.2)	(7.9)
U.P.	5066	5209	5256	5706	5518	5432	5675	5575	5603	5838	5975	6138
		(2.8)	(0.9)	(8.6)	(-3.3)	(-1-6)	(4.5)	(-1.8)	(0.5)	(4.1)	(2.5)	(2.7)
West Bengal	6756	7094	7492	7880	8408	8814	9320	9796	10380	10987	11608	12271
		(5.0)	(5.6)	(5.2)	(6.7)	(4.8)	(5.7)	(5.1)	(5.9)	(5.6)	(6.0)	
Delhi	18166	19575	19162	20983	23482	23762	24003	26523	26516	26969	28824	31345
		(7.8)	(-2.1)	(9.5)	(11.9)	(1.2)	(1.0)	(10.5)	(-0.0)	(1.7)	(6.9)	(8.7)

Source: As in Annex A-2.1

ANNEX A-2.3

Sectoral Composition of NSDP of Some States: 1960-61 to 2000-01 At Current Prices

(*in Percentages*)

States		*1960-61*	*1970-71*	*1980-81*	*1990-91*	*1993-94*	*2000-01*
Andhra Pradesh	A	58.18	56.58	45.59	33.76	35.95	31.53
	I	13.41	14.02	17.64	23.13	20.84	22.48
	S	28.41	29.40	36.77	43.11	43.21	45.99
Goa	A		30.91	23.02	13.66	15.88	10.61
	I		26.50	35.19	37.58	37.44	36.57
	S		42.59	41.79	48375	46.68	52.82
Gujarat	A	41.59	47.96	39.93	26.98	24.25	14.81
	I	25.96	21.77	28.12	35.25	35.92	38.74
	S	32.45	30.26	31.95	37.77	39.83	46.45
Haryana	A	62.71	64.54	54.23	46.59	42.61	31.09
	I	16.35	15.35	19.35	23.60	25.59	28.75
	S	20.94	20.01	26.42	30.81	31.79	40.15
Karnataka	A	60.41	54.20	45.41	34.59	37.48	28.89
	I	16.01	23.63	21.41	24.02	24.61	22.76
	S	28.78	22.17	33.18	41.39	37.90	48.35
Kerala	A	55.63	49.36	39.11	35.74	32.02	25.24
	I	15.59	16.40	24.49	24.17	20.53	21.36
	S	28.78	34.24	36.40	40.09	47.45	53.40
M.P.	A	62.11	59.70	52.12	45.32	42.93	28.75
	I	15.90	17.19	21.87	24.05	21.37	28.53
	S	21.99	23.11	26.01	30.62	35.70	42.72
Maharashtra	A	41.58	28.41	27.75	22.23	20.70	13.84
	I	26.88	34.40	35.45	35.37	31.68	30.71
	S	34.04	37.19	36.80	42.40	47.62	55.45
Orissa	A		65.46	53.14	39.12	45.17	37.99
	I		12.21	17.64	23.29	20.86	18.19
	S		22.34	29.22	37.58	33.96	44.12
Punjab	A	54.00	58.33	49.48	48.31	48.22	40.60
	I	15.63	15.35	18.49	22.57	19.83	22.63
	S	30.37	26.32	32.02	29.13	31.96	36.77
Rajasthan	A	56.21	60.98	50.34	47.26	35.19	27.83
	I	16.58	13.49	19.95	19.85	25.29	28.35
	S	27.21	25.53	32.89	32.89	39.53	43.82
Tamil Nadu	A	51.88	39.32	25.43	22.88	25.68	16.51
	I	17.69	26.66	33.97	33.63	32.78	30.68
	S	30.42	34.02	40.50	43.48	41.50	52.81
U.P.	A	59.04	58.40	52.01	42.73	41.11	33.96
	I	7.83	8.91	15.63	20.35	19.82	21.20
	S	33.12	32.69	32.36	36.92	39.07	44.84
West Bengal	A	40.51	43.51	31.63	30.90	34.70	29.32
	I	26.32	24.27	30.26	27.71	22.51	21.04
	S	33.17	32.22	38.12	41.39	42.79	49.65

Notes: 1. Figures for 1960-61 are based on 1960-61 series except for Andhra Pradesh, M.P., and U.P.

2. Figures for 1970-71 are based on 1970-71 series.

3. Figures for 1980-81 and 1990-91 are based on 1980-81 series.

4. Figures for 1993-94 and 2000-01 are based on 1993-94 series.

5. A = Agriculture; it covers agriculture, forestry, logging and fishing.

6. I = Industry; it covers mining and quarrying, manufacturing, electricity, gas, and water supply, and construction.

7. S= Services; it covers all other sectors in the GDP by economic activity.

Source: EPW Research Foundation. *Domestic Products of States of India 1960-61 to 2000-01*.

ANNEX A-2.4

Tax Revenue of GNCT of Delhi: 1993-94 to 2004-05

(in Crore of Rs.)

Taxes	*1993-94*	*1994-95*	*1995-96*	*1996-97*	*1997-98*	*1998-99*	*1999-00*	*2000-01*	*2001-02*	*2002-03*	*2003-04*	*2004-05*
Sales Tax	1001 (70.29)	1272 (71.81)	1539 (72.91)	1814 (71.60)	2029 (68.96)	2113 (68.41)	2347 (68.41)	3388 (76.99)	3704 (75.64)	3883 (72.94)	4435 (75.37)	5201 (73.19)
State Excise	284 (19.94)	306 (17.12)	336 (15.91)	447 (17.62)	515 (17.50)	526 (17.00)	566 (16.51)	557 (12.66)	606 (12.38)	726 (13.63)	710 (12.07)	844 (11.88)
Stamp Duty	66 (4.63)	112 (6.27)	127 (6.04)	115 (4.52)	117 (3.99)	151 (4.89)	190 (5.56)	192 (4.36)	283 (5.78)	437 (8.20)	435 (7.40)	668 (9.40)
Taxes on Vehicles	47 (3.30)	66 (3.69)	71 (3.34)	78 (3.08)	105 (3.57)	125 (4.06)	161 (4.68)	142 (3.23)	167 (3.41)	160 (3.01)	175 (2.98)	196 (2.76)
Others	26 (1.73)	31 (1.80)	38 (3.18)	81 (5.98)	176 (5.61)	173 (4.84)	166 (2.76)	122 (2.79)	136 (118.14)	118 (2.18)	129 (2.77)	197 (1.83)
Total Tax Revenue	1424	1787	2111	2535	2943	3088	3430	4401	4897	5324	5884	7106
Tax Revenue As % GSDP	6.83	6.96	7.73	8.04	7.13	6.50	6.47	7.01	7.20	7.39	7.31	7.83
% Growth over the previous year		25.49	18.10	20.08	16.08	5.0	11.06	28.28	11.27	8.73	10.52	20.77
Tax buoyancy		1.02	1.09	1.00	0.94	0.90	0.94	1.08	1.04	0.97	—	—
Tax Revenue As % of own Revenue	95.96	94.70	97.10	97.84	94.54	94.26	89.60	88.92	84.82	86.51	86.10	88.53

Notes: 1. Estimates for NSDP for the year 2001-02 and 2002-03 are Advance and Quick estimates respectively.

2. Figures in the brackets give the percentage share of each tax in the total tax revenue.

3. Figures of tax revenue including the total has been rounded to nearest whole number.

Source: *Economic Survey of Delhi 2001-02 and 2003-04; Reports of the Comptroller & Auditor General* for various years; and Reserve Bank of India. *State Finances* of relevant years.

ANNEX A-2.5

Non-Tax Revenue of the GNCT of Delhi 1994-95 to 2004-05

(in Crore of Rs.)

Heads	*1994-95*	*1995-96*	*1996-97*	*1997-98*	*1998-99*	*1999-00*	*2000-01*	*2001-02*	*2002-03*	*2003-04*	*2004-05*
A. Own Non-Tax Revenue of which	99.63	63.13	55.74	169.52	187.96	397.85	548.35	876.06	829.56	950.34	921.39
Interest	N.A.	7.88 (12.48)	5.52 (9.90)	132.85 (78.37)	139.01 (73.96)	300.77 (75.60)	477.28 (87.04)	789 (90.16)	741.42 (89.38)	868.83 (91.42)	821.96 (89.20)
General Service	N.A.	40.40 (63.99)	25.90 (46.46)	13.07 (6.91)	26.64 (14.17)	53.40 (13.42)	35.38 (6.45)	40.07 (4.57)	45.18 (5.44)	41.45 (4.36)	48.18 (5.23)
Social Service	N.A.	8.23 (13.03)	8.28 (14.85)	6.91 (4.08)	9.84 (5.24)	24.87 (6.25)	11.88 (2.17)	19.04 (2.17)	22.63 (2.73)	22.30 (2.35)	27.73 (3.00)
Economic Services	N.A.	6.62 (10.49)	9.10 (16.33)	3.15 (1.86)	7.65 (4.07)	14.40 (3.62)	15.11 (2.76)	19.95 (2.28)	13.14 (1.58)	11.73 (1.24)	19.77 (2.15)
B.Central Transfers	93.36	122.32	205.38	369.62	383.38	446.07	495.02	480.90	512.19	514.02	535.11
Total Non-Tax Revenue	192.99	185.45	261.12	539.14	571.34	843.92	1043.37	1356.96	1341.75	1464.36	1456.50

Source: As in Annex A-2.4.

ANNEX A-2.6

Tax-GSDP Ratio of Some States: 1994-95 to 2004-05

(in Percentages)

States	1994-95	1995-96	1996-97	1997-98	1998-99	1999-00	2000-01	2001-02	2002-03	2003-04	2004-05
Andhra Pradesh	6.14	5.16	5.42	7.43	6.93	7.19	7.53	8.30	7.77	7.64	8.55
Goa	7.96	8.19	7.64	7.42	5.88	6.77	6.83	7.29	7.13	7.51	8.74
Gujarat	7.47	7.40	7.06	7.23	7.23	7.49	8.34	7.64	6.75	6.68	7.21
Haryana	7.19	7.28	6.01	6.13	7.15	7.19	7.84	8.22	8.35	8.47	8.92
Karnataka	8.95	9.38	8.85	8.78	7.90	8.15	8.65	9.32	9.16	9.49	10.82
Kerala	8.78	8.73	8.77	9.10	8.27	8.30	8.41	8.19	9.03	9.04	9.34
Maharashtra	7.27	6.93	6.53	7.03	6.77	7.09	8.26	7.98	7.77	7.55	8.23
Orissa	4.15	4.16	5.06	4.41	5.22	4.41	5.63	6.52	6.43	6.13	6.33
Punjab	7.59	6.86	6.18	6.25	5.85	6.46	7.42	6.85	7.95	7.87	7.80
Rajasthan	5.56	5.77	5.43	5.63	5.01	5.76	6.68	6.41	7.32	6.94	7.66
Tamil Nadu	8.50	9.14	8.45	8.39	8.14	8.63	8.70	9.06	9.28	9.47	9.82
W. Bengal	6.01	5.59	5.19	4.61	4.13	4.02	4.23	4.15	4.21	4.62	5.17

Source: Central Statistical Organisation, and Reserve Bank of India. *State Finances* of relevant years.

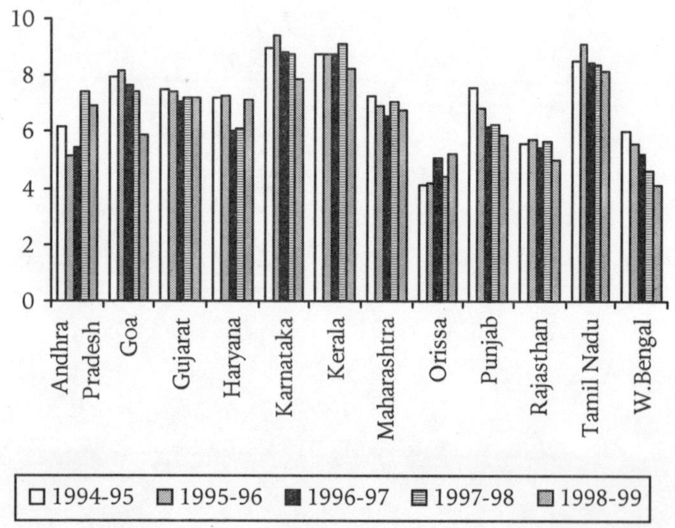

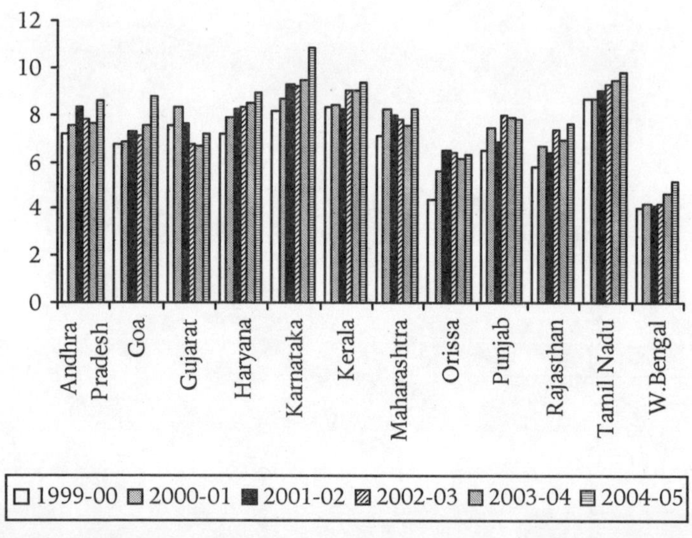

ANNEX A-2.7

Arrears of Tax Revenue: 1995-96 to 2004-05

(in Crore of Rs.)

Year	Amount	As % of collections	Increase over previous year	Percentage Increase
1995-96	3432.87	162.61	379.69	—
1996-97	3643.18	143.72	210.31	6.13
1997-98	4185.97	142.30	542.79	14.89
1998-99	4718.04	152.75	532.07	12.71
1999-00	5527.56	161.13	809.52	17.16
2000-01	6616.58	149.69	1089.02	19.81
2001-02	6999.37	142.94	382.79	5.78
2002-03	8327.83	156.41	1328.46	18.98
2003-04	9364.77	159.15	1036.94	12.45
2004-05	8636.53	121.54	-728.24	-7.78

Source: *Report of the Comptroller and Auditor General of India* for various years.

ANNEX A-2.8

Components of Revenue Expenditure: 1994-95 to 2004-05

(*in Crore of Rs.*)

Items	*1994-95*	*1996-97*	*1997-98*	*1998-99*	*1999-00*	*2000-01*	*2001-02*	*2002-03*	*2003-04*	*2004-05*
General Services	386	47423.33	52322.52	69724.54	82123.30	104928.38	126125.00	152133.08	180535.48	207435.59
of which Interest	—	190	314	432	531	717	911	1151	1367	1569
Social Service	822	123060.53	151465.20	183464.58	204157.94	212157.38	229745.54	245453.37	251049.34	301751.78
of which Education and Sport	—	569	783	952	1033	1043	1081	1153	1158	1566
Public Health	—	217	267	315	391	439	595	523	577	667
Urban Development	—	264	278	380	391	399	461	485	491	510
Social Security	—	110	76	69	83	79	95	107	128	127
Economic Services	222*	1989.74	1918.22	2388.38	2647.49	2897.82	122724.32	3166.87	4629.08	3726.38
of which Roads & Bridges	—	105	104	127	154	151	136	152	158	185
Assignment to Local Bodies	—	**1296.35**	**944.05**	**712.50**	**39611.24**	**2386.44**	**2595.13**	**3076.68**	**3096.07**	**3636.23**
Total Revenue Expenditure	1431	2032	2322	2840	3523	3696	4963	4598	5087	5827

Notes: * Includes other services also.

Sources: Reserve Bank of India. *State Finances* of relevant years.

ANNEX A-2.9

Components of Capital Expenditure: 1994-95 to 2003-04

(*in Crore of Rs.*)

Items	*1994-95*	*1996-97*	*1997-98*	*1998-99*	*1999-00*	*2000-01*	*2001-02*	*2002-03*	*2003-04*	*2004-05*
Capital Outlay	213	417	665	341	510	869	612	914	852	1425
Loans & Advances	763	1067	1224	1493	1873	2609	2789	3756	4103	3321
Repayment of Loans	—	—	—	268	5	188	186	944	1677	2302
Total Capital Expenditure	976	1484	1889	2102	2389	3503	3830	5615	6633	7048

Source: Reserve Bank of India. *State Finances* of Relevant years.

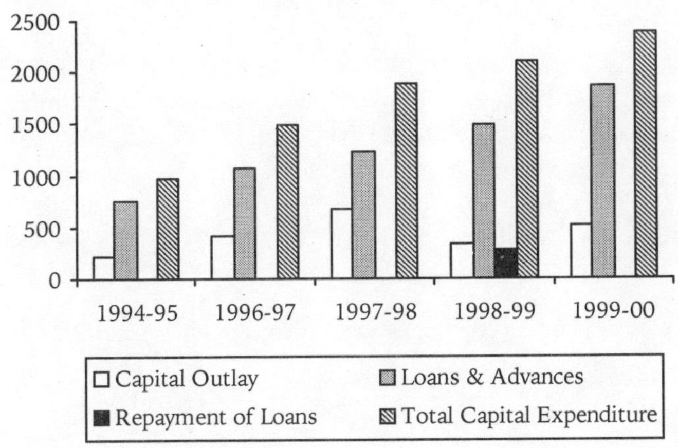

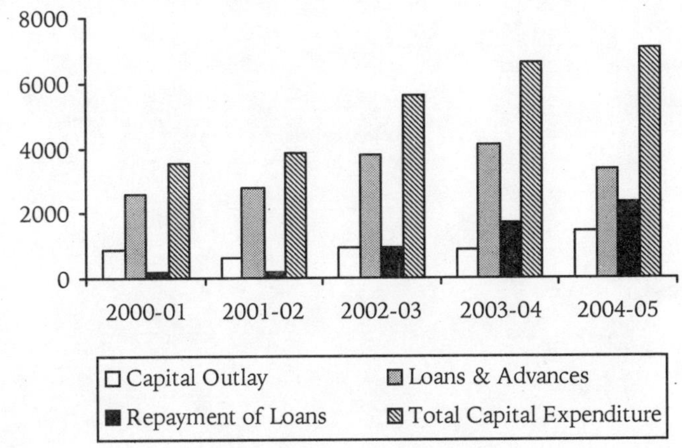

References

Central Statistical Organisation (various issues). *National Accounts Statistics*.

Comptroller & Auditor General of India (various years). *Reports of the Comptroller & Auditor General of India on the NCT of Delhi*.

EPW Research Foundation (n.d.). *Domestic Product of States of India: 1960-61 to 2000-01*.

Government of India (various years). *Economic Survey*.

Government of NCT of Delhi (various years). *Economic Survey of Delhi for 2002 and 2004*. Planning Department

———. (various years). *Budgets*.

Kumar, Jitender and Chakresh Chandra (n.d.). *Back Series of SDP Estimates in EPW Foundation: Domestic Products of States of India 1960-61 to 2001-02*.

Reserve Bank of India (various years). *State Finances*.

Chapter 3

Urban Development

3.1 Housing

3.1.1 *Introduction*

As per the 2001 Census, Delhi's population is 13.85 million against about 9.40 million in 1991. The rapid pace of urbanisation and the alarming trend of migration from different parts of the country, has distorted the housing scenario in the city. This has necessitated revision of the 1981-2001 Master Plan prepared by DDA.

The city's population in 2004 was estimated as 15.5 million and was projected to be 23 million by the year 2021 as shown below in the Table 3.1.

TABLE 3.1

Settlement-Wise Projected Population Upto the Year 2021

Type of Settlements	*Population in millions*				
	2004	*2005*	*2006*	*2011*	*2021*
JJ Clusters	2.300	2.374	2.448	2.819	3.413
Slum Designated Areas	2.957	3.052	3.148	3.625	4.338
Unauthorised Colonies	0.821	0.848	0.874	1.007	1.219
Resettlement Colonies	1.971	2.035	2.099	2.416	2.925
Rural Villages	0.821	0.848	0.874	1.007	1.219
Regularised Unauthorised Colonies	1.971	2.035	2.099	2.416	2.925
Urban Villages	0.986	1.107	1.049	1.208	1.463
Planned Colonies	3.672	3.790	3.909	4.501	5.4449
Total Population, millions	**15.5**	**16.0**	**16.5**	**19.0**	**23.0**

Source: Delhi Water Supply and Sewerage Project Preparation Study Report.

It is estimated that only 23.6 per cent of the projected population of 2004 was living in planned colonies, 64.5 per cent in *Jhuggi-Jhopri* (JJ) clusters, slum designated areas and unauthorised colonies and the remaining 11.9 per cent in rural and urban villages. As per the 1981-2001 Master Plan, the requirement of new housing under different categories assessed by the Delhi Development Authority upto 2001 was 1.61 million (Annex A-3.1). Bulk of this requirement, 0.7 million, was to be met through partially or fully built cooperative housing. Housing on individual plots was to provide 0.27 million dwelling units while 0.4 million sites were reserved for "Sites and Services". Based on the current status and future demand projections, the requirement for employer housing was assessed as 65,000. Realising the growing requirement for the slum dwellers, 49,000 dwelling units were envisaged as the bare minimum. It was expected that inspite of various preventative and corrective measures, about 0.13 million unauthorised dwelling units would still come up to fill part of the demand supply gap.

3.1.2 *Present Housing Scenario*

As per the Census 2001, Delhi has 24.5 lakh Census houses under the category of residence and residence-cum-other uses in which 25.5 lakh households are residing. This reflects a net housing shortage of about 1 lakh houses/dwelling units. The houses are accommodated in a variety of housing typologies including different categories of planned built housing, squatter settlements, unauthorised colonies, traditional areas and villages. A review of the housing stock up to the year 1991 indicates that the contribution through institutional agencies was only 53 per cent (this excludes squatter housing). DDA has been the nodal agency for providing bulk of the housing units under its various schemes. Till March 2003, it had allotted a total of 0.33 million flats under 33 schemes. Therefore, the component of housing through non-institutional sources *viz.*, unauthorised colonies, squatter/JJ clusters, etc., is quite significant. This trend has continued in the current decade as well and has to be kept in view while determining the plan and strategy for housing/shelter in future.

Based on the projected population of 230 lakh by 2021, the estimated additional housing stock required will be around 24 lakh dwelling units. This includes an estimated housing requirement of 20 lakh Dwelling Units (DUs) for additional population added during 2001 to 2021 and backlog of about 4 lakh units. The 4 lakh backlog comprises 1 lakh net shortage and the rest by way of dilapidated and Kutcha structures requiring replacement. It has also been assessed that around 20 and 40 per cent of housing needs can be satisfied by the development of accommodation in the adjacent National Capital Region (NCR) cities and through redevelopment/ upgradation of existing areas of Delhi. The study on holding capacity also supports that 40 per cent of additional housing needs may be met in the present urban limits and in the sub cities of Dwarka, Rohini, and Narela. This implies that the remaining 40 per cent of the requirement would have to be met through 10 lakh new housing units that will have to be provided in new areas to be developed.

For development of new housing, a major aspect would pertain to housing for the urban poor. Keeping in view the socioeconomic composition of the population, it is estimated that around 50-55 per cent of the housing requirement would be for the urban poor and the economically weaker sections in the form of houses of two rooms or less.

3.1.3 Slums/Informal Sector Housing

Because of acute shortage of affordable shelter, many of the migrants tend to encroach city space and squat on all forms of land, be they reserved for public utilities and services, commercial and office complexes, play grounds, parks etc. Such un-authorised squatter settlements, bereft of basic amenities, are not only over-crowded and unhygienic but also prone to various environment hazards.

An attempt has been made for the first time during the Census of India, 2001 to collect detailed data about slum areas of the country particularly in cities/towns having 50,000 population or more.

For the purpose of Census of India 2001, slum areas broadly constitute:

i) All specified areas notified as "Slum" by State/ Local Government and UT Administration under any Act.

ii) All areas recognised as "Slum" by State/Local Government and UT Administration, which may not have been formally notified as Slum under any Act;

iii) A compact area of at least 300 population or about 60-70 households of poorly built congested tenements, in unhygienic environment usually with inadequate infrastructure and lacking in proper sanitary and drinking water facilities.

The slum population in Delhi was about 23.55 per cent in 2006, which in percentage terms is the lowest among the four metropolitan cities. Greater Mumbai (35.50 per cent) has the highest slum population followed by Kolkata (32.55 per cent), Chennai (17.80 per cent), and Bangalore (8.40 per cent).

Delhi continues to face the problem of mushrooming growth of JJ Clusters on land pockets belonging to various land owning agencies i.e., DDA, MCD, NDMC, Delhi Cantonment Board, Railways, Government Departments, CPWD, Departments of Delhi Government and other Autonomous Organisations (Annex A-3.2).

The migrants come to Delhi in search of gainful employment opportunities, which are easily available in unorganised and informal segments of the metropolitan economy. Delhi stared witnessing the problem of JJ Clusters from the early sixties onwards. The huge influx of population from all parts of the country resulted in proliferation of JJ clusters/squatter settlements as given under in the Table 3.2.

TABLE 3.2

JJ Clusters and Households in NCT Delhi

Year	*JJ clusters*	*Jhuggi Households*	*Population*
1951	199	12,749	-
1973	-	98,483	-
1977	-	20,000	-
1983	534	1,13,000	-
1985	-	1,50,000	-
1990	929	2,59,000	12,000
1994	1080	4,81,000	24,00,000
1997	1100	6,00,000	30,00,000
2005	1080	NA	30,00,000

Source: Interim Status Report Delhi 2021, Delhi Urban Environment & Infrastructure Improvement Project (DUEIIP), May 2000.

It would be seen from the above Table that the slum population in 1997 was 30 lakh According to the recent estimates of the slum & JJ Department of MCD, the present *Jhuggi* population is still the same. However, according to them the census figure of 2001 is nowhere near this figure. The problem of different population figures estimated by different agencies is not new. For example, according to the 1981 census, the population in notified slum areas was about 18 lakh, where as according to the estimates of the Town & Planning Section of Delhi Government the population had dwindled to only 9.51 lakh because of the massive commercialisation of the walled city and its extensions. This problem of different population figures again came in sharp focus in the early nineties. The door-to-door survey of 1990 by the Food & Supply Department of Delhi Government came up with a figure of about 12 lakh where as the 1994 survey by the slum & JJ department put the figure at 24 lakh There is therefore an apparent need to estimate the slum population on more scientific basis. Most migrants are unskilled construction workers, low wage earners in small scale industrial activities, petty traders and community service personnel etc., who may not be able to move out to any far-away location, where they do not have any assured source of earning. They are often reluctant of shift from their more convenient central locations within the city to the outlying areas away from their places of employment due to the distance involved and the extra transportation expense, etc. Since these migrants have their roots somewhere else, either at the place of their last residence or at place of birth, they are very often reluctant to invest in formal housing and thus resort to squatting. In this situation, there is a need to provide them with sites with bare minimum facilities within their affordability limits. The facilities at such sites could be gradually upgraded on incremental basis.

Studies have revealed that settlers in these JJ clusters are pursuing various informal economic activities making significant contribution to the city's economy and over a period, have established an interdependent relationship with the formal commercial, industrial and manufacturing functions in the city. From domestic help and unskilled factory jobs to semi-skilled and manual work, they are now an essential requirement of the city's daily life. The cheap labour that they provide, the large numbers of domestic help and service personnel that they consist of, and the sizeable informal functions they perform, make them significant partners in Delhi's life and existence. Facilities provided in slums and JJ clusters are given in Table 3.3.

A significant feature of the dynamics of JJ clusters is that the number of large clusters is steadily increasing and smaller ones are decreasing in number. For example the number of settlements with 300 to 1500 or more households each had increased by 50 to 100 per cent during the four year period from 1990 to 1994, while that of smaller ones with 50 to 200 households each had decreased by about 30 to more than 50 per cent during the same period (Annex A-3.4). This is due to the large clusters attracting people from smaller ones, and clusters spread over a relatively small area getting merged over time. Areas that have potential for cheap employment generation for unskilled and semi-skilled labour are the main attractions for the migratory labour. Availability of public transport to and from work place, better amenities like drinking water supply, electricity, and cheap shopping areas are among the other drivers of this trend. Propensity of the government agencies to regularise from time to time, large and long established JJ clusters is also one of the various factors responsible for un-regulated growth of JJ clusters in the city as indeed elsewhere in the country.

TABLE 3.3

Facilities in Slum and JJ Clusters in Delhi

S. No.	*Item*	*Position as on 28.02.06*
1.	No. of JJ Cluster	1,080
2.	No. of Basti Vikas Kendras	327+32 Addl Addl. Floors
3.	No. of Shishu Vatikas	367
4.	No. of Jan Suvidha complexes	
	i. Pucca	429
	ii. Prefab	183
	iii. Mobile Toilet Vans	220
	Total	832
5.	W.C. seats of JSCs	
	i Pucca	14,700
	ii Prefab	4,461
	iii Mobile Toilet Vans	3,080
	Total	22,241
6.	No. of plots developed for relocation of JJ squatters	55,915
7.	No. of plots allotted to JJ squatters	54,830
8.	No. of Night Shelters	• 12 NS (Permanent) • 5 temporary NS C. Hall • 1 temporary NS for women at C. Hall • porta cabin NS
9.	No. of Katras	1,899
10.	No. of plots developed under in-situ-upgradation of JJ Clusters	5,583

Source: Socio Economic Profile of Delhi 2001-02. Planning Department and GNCT of Delhi

Relocation of Slum Population

The Municipal Corporation of Delhi (MCD) initiated the process of relocating the slum dwellers in early 1991. The relocation sites are generally located at the peripheries of Delhi in following areas:

i) Sahyog Vihar
ii) Rohini Sector 23, 24, 25
iii) Papankalan Pocket I, II, III
iv) Bidnapur Pocket I, II
v) Samaipur Badli
vi) Tikri Khurd
vii) Narela
viii) Bhalaswa
ix) Molarbund
x) Bakorwala
xi) Houlumbikalan

These sites have been selected with a vision of having a density of 200 dwelling units per acre with a plot size of 18.00 sq.m for each eligible family and 12.5 sq.m for each ineligible family. District map of Delhi showing selected resettlement sites is given in (Figure 3.1).

The situation obtaining for the four largest metropolitan cities is shown in the Table 3.3.

TABLE 3.3

Slum Population
(In Four Largest Metropolitan Cities of India, 2001)

Name of City	*Total Population*	*Slum Population*	*% of Population in slums*
Greater Mumbai	11,914,398	5,823,510	48.88
Delhi Municipal Corporation (Urban)	9,817,439	1,854,685	18.89
Kolkata	4,580,544	1,490,811	32.55
Bangalore	4,292,223	345,200	8.40
Chennai	42,16,000	7,45,000	17.80

Note: Data pertains to Municipal Corporation.

3.1.4 Quality of Housing

The quality of housing depends, *inter alia*, on the availability of facilities like piped water supply, electricity and toilets. In Delhi, inspite of steep rise in the number of households from 1.86 million in 1991 to 2.55 million in 2001, the coverage under these facilities both in urban and rural households has increased by 38.49 per cent during this period (Annex – III). While the increase of 36 per cent in coverage by piped water supply has kept pace with the increase in the number of households, the improvement in coverage by electricity and sanitation was more impressive with increase of 60.3 per cent and 68.78 per cent respectively. In rural areas toilet facilities registered a healthy growth of 119.64 per cent, which in percentage terms was better than that in urban areas. Urban areas however registered higher growth rates over rural areas in electricity and water supply coverage.

Reliable data on these facilities for slum and JJ clusters in the urban areas are not available. However, these figures give a fair indication that major part of the deficit could be attributed to these unregulated human settlements.

Type of Houses

As per census 2001, data for Delhi indicates that 35.40 per cent of dwellings are independent houses, 24.90 per cent are flats and 15.4 per cent are *Chawl/Basti*. About 24.3 per cent of the dwellings fall under "others" category.

Considering that *Chawls/Bastis* are low category of dwellings, Maharashtra (41.30 per cent), Goa (32.70 per cent), Dadra & Nagar Haveli (23.10 per cent), and Daman & Diu (23.40 per cent) have the dubionus distinction of having large sections of their population living in poor conditions. In Delhi, with only 70 per cent of the dwellings under the category of independent houses and flats and 15.4 per cent under *Chawl/Basti* the situation is non-too-happy.

Ownership of Houses

An analysis of housing data for 1991 indicates that in Delhi 68.1 per cent of houses are owned by the residents and 28.61 are rented. Status of 3.29 per cent of the houses is not known. Bihar and Kerala have high percentages of house ownerships of 95 per cent and 93.61 per cent respectively followed by Manipur (92.55 per cent), and Madhya Pradesh (88.29 per cent), Chandigarh and Mizoram have high percentages of rented houses with figures of 52.05 per cent and 39.48 per cent respectively. However, the National Sample Survey 50th Round (July 1993-June 1994) data gives a very different picture, which is as Table 3.4.

FIGURE 3.1

District Map of Delhi Showing Selected Resettlement Sites

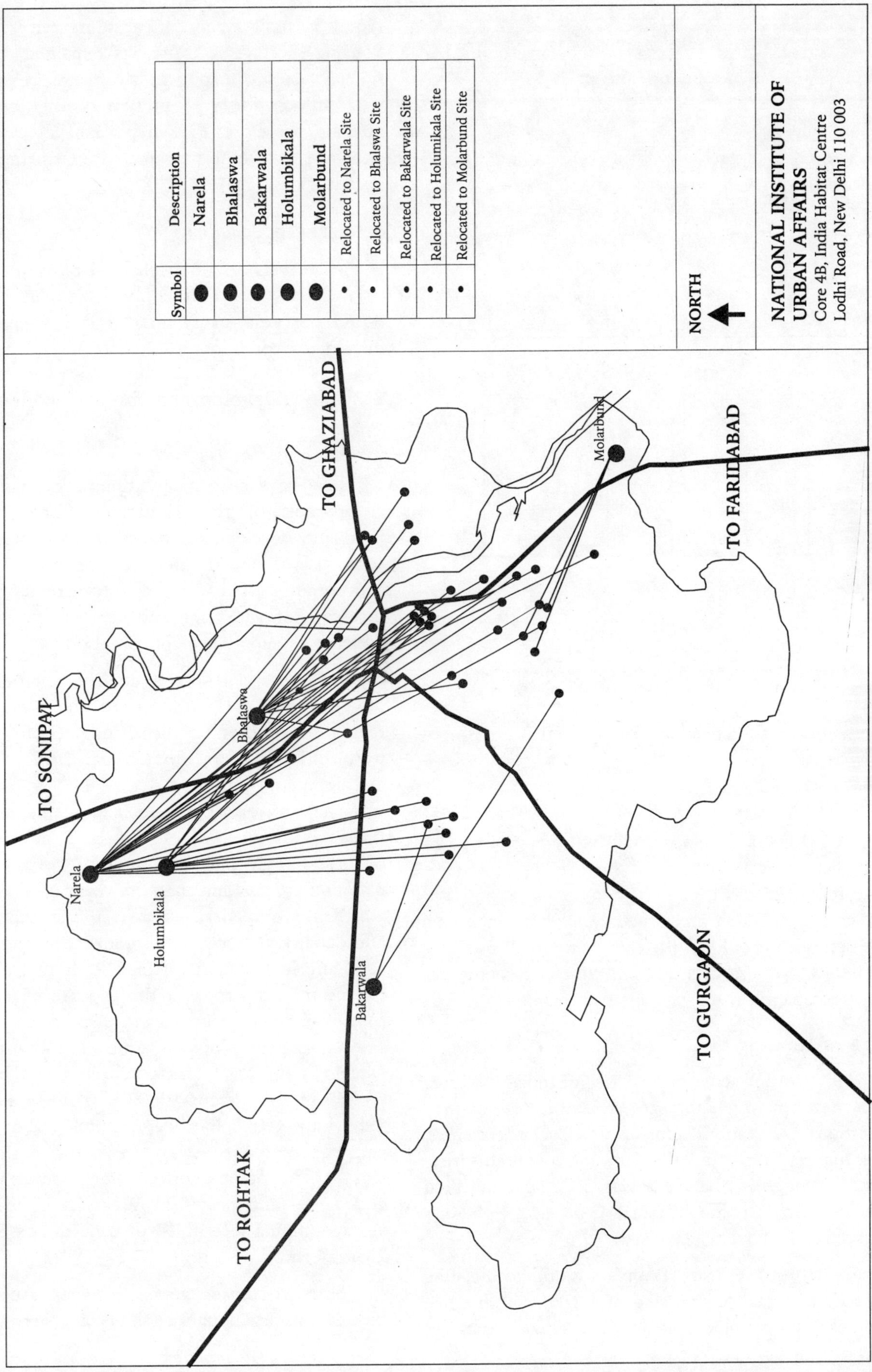

TABLE 3.4

Ownership of Houses

State	Owned	Rented	Others/ Unknown
Delhi	40.40	30.30	29.20
Bihar	58.50	32.60	8.70
Kerala	80.90	15.50	3.60
Manipur	86.00	14.00	2.90
Madhya Pradesh	59.00	34.60	6.40
Chandigarh	26.50	46.50	27.10
Mizoram	81.40	16.80	1.80

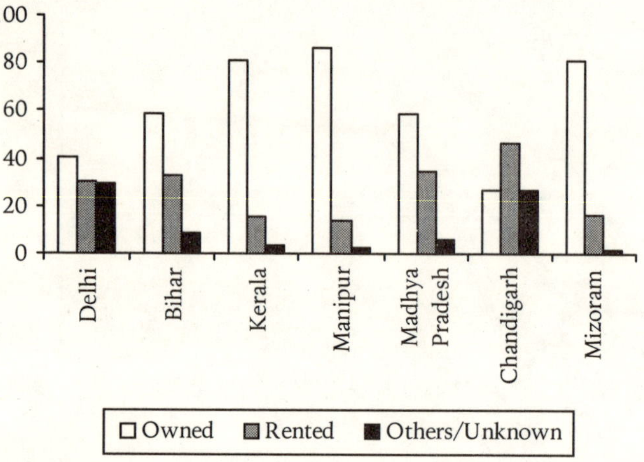

There is obviously a need for data collection on a more scientific basis.

Size of Houses

The 2001 data for occupied 25,54,149 houses in Delhi indicates that about 38 per cent of the dwelling units have only one room, 27 per cent two rooms and 18 per cent three rooms each. Larger accommodation with four rooms or more account for only 16 per cent of the total dwelling units. The average size of a dwelling unit is 2 rooms per unit with occupancy of 4.2 persons per room.

Shortage of Housing

The 1991 data for some major cities of India, indicates that the net housing shortage in Delhi, taking into consideration "Congestion factor" and "Obsolence factor", was the highest among all the four metropolitan cities. The total shortage in that year was 3.77 lakh dwelling units followed by Greater Mumbai (3.18 lakh), Kolkata (2.45 lakh), and Chennai (2.24 lakh).

As per the 2001 Census, Delhi's backlog of dwelling units stands at 4 lakh comprising of 1 lakh net shortage and the rest by way of dilapidated and *kutcha* structures requiring replacement. In absolute terms, therefore, the housing shortage in Delhi has remained the same during the last decade inspite of steep rise in population from 9.42 million to 13.85 million during this period. It is obvious, therefore, that in percentage terms the housing shortage in Delhi has decreased during the last one decade (1991-2001).

3.1.5 Living Conditions

An analysis of 2001 Census data on housing, indicates that 58 per cent of the houses are in good condition, 36.65 per cent are livable and 5.35 per cent are in dilapidated condition.

3.2 Land Development and Management

3.2.1 Delivery of Urban Land in Delhi

There have been many attempts in India to formulate an appropriate Urban Land Policy. The objectives of the first land development policy in 1937 were: (i) optimal social use of land (ii) moderate pricing (iii) prevention of concentration of land in single ownership to safeguard the interests of the poor and (iv) encourage cooperative housing to supplement public efforts.

Over the years, the guiding principles of land development have remained the same though the regulatory process has been modified from time-to-time with changing circumstances. In Delhi, the Delhi Development Authority Act of 1957 provides the DDA with powers for large-scale land acquisition. One of the under lying weaknesses of land development plan, however is the lack of community participation in the planning process and the outgrowth of planning standards which are unrealistic *vis-à-vis* the impact on costs and affordability. A second consequence is the impact of the revolving fund concept, which leads to land development for income generation at the expense of land delivery for the low-income groups. Land distribution is substantially skewed due to plots auctioned to high-income groups. Development and release of plots has been slow and erratic. In 1982 about 10300 plots were allotted while in 1989 only 4700 plots were allotted. The demand-supply gap has increased over the years, which has led to spiraling up of land prices. For example between 1980 and 1989 land prices in West Delhi increased on an average annual rate of 14 percent and in South Delhi by 23 per cent.

Equity in land delivery is a major issue that needs to be addressed. Though DDA as a government agency is committed to social equity in land distribution, there are large variations in reservation of plots for Economically Weaker Sections (EWS) and Low Income Groups (LIG) in different localities. For example, Rohini has about 83 per cent of total residential land reserved for EWS and LIG, Dwarka has only 22 per cent reserved plots. The private licensed colonisers are forced by legislation to reserve 20 per cent of residential plots for EWS/LIG and another 25 per cent for "no profit no loss" category. Such plots are cross-subsidised by large plots and commercial sites so that the prices are kept below the market rates. This leads to profiteering by the allotters. The plots are further sold for profit by one buyer to another thereby defeating the very concept of equity.

Delhi has a limited geographical area of 1483 sq. km. out of which about half of the area is already urbanised. For the remaining area, optimum utilisation has to be planned with due regard to the protection and preservation of natural features like the Ridge, water bodies, major green areas and other areas of ecological importance. In view of this, it has been suggested that:

- Only such central government offices be located in Delhi, which directly serve the Ministries of the Government of India.
- Existing offices of public sector undertakings within Delhi should be encouraged to shift, where as new offices of PSUs, to the extent possible within their operational areas should be set up outside Delhi.
- Industrial growth in Delhi should be restricted to small scale with emphasis on units, which require skill, less manpower and energy and do not create nuisance.
- Large and fiscal measures should be adopted to restrict employment in industries and distributive trade.
- Major regional transport corridor and communication network should be strengthened to enhance economic development within the region together with decentralisation of distributive trade.
- Natural features such as forests, the Ridge, the river Yamuna and other water bodies should be conserved and kept free from unrestricted and unplanned development.

As per the draft NCR Plan 2021, proposed availability of urbanisable land in the NCT Delhi is 65.54 per cent of its total geographical area as shown under (Table 3.5).

TABLE 3.5

Availability of Urbanisable Land in NCT-Delhi

Sl. No.	*Land Use*	*Area (Ha.)*	*Percentage to total Area*
1.	Total Geographical Area - NCTD	1,48,300	100
2.	Built-up Area (As per IRS IC LISS III satellite data 1999)	70,162	47.31
3.	Natural Features (Forest, Wild Life Sanctuary, Ridge, River Yamuna and other Water Bodies/Drains)	19,509	13.16
	Sub-Total (2+3)	**89,671**	**60.47**
	Land area available in NCT – Delhi (1-(2+3))	58,629	39.53
4.	Land requirement for disposal of 50 per cent of solid waste which will be generated up to 2051.	11,100	
5.	Land requirement for Metro Centres/Services/Utilities i.e. power plant, water and sewerage treatment plat, grid station etc.	10,000	
6.	Green belt along NCT boundary wherever available	5,000	
7.	Land requirements for diary colonies	3,500	
8.	Total (4 to 7)	29,600	21.31
9.	Land not available for urbanisation	51,109	34.46
10.	Actual land available for urban development	27,029	18.23
11.	Total urbanisable 2+8	99,762	65.54

12. Population which can be accommodated in 97,190 ha. @ 225 PPH = 218.68 lakh, say 220 lakh.

Source: Draft NCR Plan (2004).

Population Holding Capacity of Delhi

The area within the existing unbanisable limits of Delhi Urban Area–2001 consists of the sub city planning zones A to H and the Dwarka, Rohini, Narela projects. Population holding capacity of A to H zones is to be enhanced through a redevelopment strategy and modified development norms.

Studies based on redevelopment potential of existing residential areas and the actual population as per census 2001 have revealed that the present urban limits i.e., DUA-2001 would be able to accommodate about 153 lakh population ultimately i.e., 114 lakh in A to H and 39 lakh in Dwarka, Rohini III, IV & V and Narela.

TABLE 3.6

Zone-wise Estimated Holding Capacity of Existing Urban Area

(in '000)

Zone	Holding Capacity MPD 2001	Existing Population 2001	Holding Capacity 2021
A	420	570	570
B	630	624	630
C	751	679	788
D	755	587	813
E	1,789	2,798	2,800
F	1,278	1,717	1,975
G	1,490	1,629	1,955
H	1,865	1,226	1,865
Sub Total	**8,978**	**9,830**	**11,396**
Dwarka		579	1,700
Rohini III		96	160
Rohni IV & V		198	820
Narela		179	1,220
Sub total	**3,222**	**1,052**	**3,900**
Grand Total	**12,200**	**10,882**	**15,296**

Source: Master Plan for Delhi 2021.

The remaining population of the year 2021 will have to be accommodated in the planned new urban extensions.

Urban Extension

Out of the remaining 77 lakh (230-153 lakh) population, 29 lakh already exists in villages, census towns, unauthorised colonies and JJ clusters in the present rural areas. Therefore about 48 lakh (77-29 lakh) additional population is to be accommodated in the future urban extensions.

Due to land constraints in NCTD the area earmarked as rural/agriculture in the previous Master Plans have always been under pressure for utilisation for various urban activities and have virtually lost their original character. In future, urbanisation has to be in the areas that have development pressure/potential like the areas along the major transport corridors and fringes of already urbanised areas. Therefore it is envisaged that the area under existing designated rural would be absorbed as urban extension from time to time with due regard to balanced city development.

3.3 Sanitation

The total water supply capacity of Delhi Jal Board (DJB) as on 31 March 2006 was 675 MGD and it is proposed to increase to 850 MLD by 31 March 2008. About 80 per cent of it is estimated to go as wastewater. The main uses of 333 MGD of treated wastewater (as on 31.03.2006) are considered to be for irrigation and horticulture. Presently DJB supplies about 138 MGD of treated wastewater to the Irrigation Department, CPWD, DDA and Pragati Power Plant. The remaining water still needs to be put to beneficial uses. The actual quantity of wastewater treated is much below the installed capacity of the 16 sewage treatment plants (STP) of about 512.40 MGD (as on 31.03.2006). The treated wastewater is being largely put back into the drains and gets polluted again before flowing into the river Yamuna. The low level of capacity utilisation at the STPs is due to missing links in sewer connectivity and choking/silting of sewer lines.

DJB has a network of 6000 km of sewer lines of which 147 km are trunk sewers. About 91 km of trunk sewers require immediate desilting and rehabilitation. All the approved colonies have sewer facilities. Out of 567 unauthorised and regularised colonies, 482 colonies have this facility. Sewer lines have also been laid in all re-settlement colonies and 98 urban villages. Another 14 unauthorised/regularised colonies and 5 urban villages are likely to be covered by December 2007. There are about 504 unauthorised colonies, which are yet to be regularised and provided with the basic civic amenities.

The main contributing sources for the continued flow of untreated sewage into river Yamuna are the numerous slum clusters that have come up unauthorisedly on both the banks and in the bed of the river. The local bodies have removed some of the slum clusters from the Western Bank.

3.3.1 Garbage Management

As per the 2001 data, Delhi generates garbage at the rate of 0.68 kg. per capita per day, thus on an average about 9384 tonnes of garbage every day of which only 59 per cent was cleared and the remaining, mostly around slums and unauthorised colonies, caused unhygienic conditions. In contrast, Mumbai with total daily garbage generation of 5,800 tonnes had 86.2 per cent clearance efficiency. Kolkata generates about the same amount of garbage as Delhi but had the highest clearance efficiency of 90 per cent.

It is estimated, that at present Delhi generates garbage at the rate of 0.68 kg per capita per day. Thus the present (2001) generation of garbage is of the order of 9384 tonnes per day against the total handling capacity of MCD, NDMC and cantonment Board of about 5543 tonnes. Thus the garbage clearance efficiency in Delhi has reduced from 62.37 per cent in 1991 to 59 per cent in 2001.

3.3.2 Solid Waste Management

The quantity of municipal solid wastes generated in Delhi has been consistently rising over the years. This can be attributed to the rapid population growth, mass migration of population from rural to urban areas, increase in economic activities in general in the city and the change in lifestyle of the people. According to the Population Census 2001, the highest percentage of urban population in India is in Delhi (93.01 per cent). There has been a decadal population growth of 47.02 per cent between 1991 and 2001 as against the corresponding All-India level, which is 22.66 per cent. Along with intrinsic population growth the rural to urban mass migration account for additional population pressure on the city. Change in lifestyle of the people has resulted in increased wasteful consumption, leading to a change in the composition and increase in the quantum of solid waste generated. Urban solid waste is normally a complex mixture of household, construction, commercial, toxic industrial elements and hospital wastes. On an average, Delhi generates 4000 tonnes of municipal solid waste per day. A physical analysis reveals that it consists of about 32 per cent compostable matter. The recyclable components include paper 6.6 per cent, plastics 1.5 per cent and metals 2.5 per cent. Primarily the responsibility of solid waste management is vested upon several public sector agencies. However, various other stakeholder groups, such as waste pickers, waste dealers, recyclers and recycling unit workers play significant roles in the overall scheme of things.

The garbage from unauthorised developments, slums, JJ settlements etc., is not collected which further adds to the environmental degradation. The projected average garbage generation up to the year 2021 is at the rate of 0.68 kg per capita per day and total quantum of solid waste is 15750 tonnes/day as given in Table 3.7.

TABLE 3.7

Quantum of Municipal Solid Waste (Tonnes/Day)

Local Body Area	*Existing Capacity 2001*	*Projected Generation for 2021*
MCD	5,250	15,100
NDMC	245	550
Cantonment	48	100
Total	**5,543**	**15,750**

Source: Master Plan for Delhi 2021.

Management of solid waste involves waste generation, segregation and storage, waste collection, waste transfer/ transportation, treatment, recycle, re-use, recovery, and disposal. For effective waste management, its segregation at the community and neighbourhood level is imperative. The waste shall be segregated and collected, in separate chambers at *dalaos*. For this, involvement of rag pickers with RWAs, CBOs and NGOs is to be encouraged. The projected composition of municipal waste for the plan period is formatted as given in Table 3.8.

TABLE 3.8

Projected Composition of Total Municipal Solid Waste for 2021

Constituents	*Quantum (in tones)*	*Percentage to total waste*
Biodegradable	6,000	38
Silt	6,000	38
Recyclable	3,750	24
Total	**15,750**	**100**

Source: (i) Report on Solid Waste Management in Delhi conducted by NEERI, Nagpur through DDA;
(ii) Feasibility study in Master Pan for Optimal Waste Treatment & Disposal for the entire State of Delhi, June, 2004 by COWI Consultants appointed by MCD.

3.3.2.1 Disposal Solid Waste Management in Delhi

Three municipal bodies—the Municipal Corporation of Delhi (MCD), the New Delhi Municipal Council (NDMC) and the Delhi Cantonment Board (DCB), are responsible for solid waste management in Delhi. MCD alone manage almost 95 per cent of the total area of the city. The above authorities are supported by a number of other agencies. The Delhi Development Authority (DDA) is responsible for siting and allotment of land to MCD for sanitary land filling. Delhi Energy Development Agency (DEDA) under Delhi Administration (DA) is responsible for solid waste utilisation projects aiming at biogas or energy generation in consultation with the Department of Non-Conventional Energy Sources (DNES), and Ministry of Environment and Forests (MoEF), Govt. of India. The Department of Flood Control of Delhi Administration looks after the supply of soil to be used as cover for sanitary landfills by the MCD.

Apart from the above public agencies there are other important agents who play their part in the overall scheme of solid waste management in the city. They are private sweepers and garbage collectors employed by the people for cleaning privately owned premises, waste pickers, waste dealers and recycling industries, which consume recyclable waste to produce recycled products.

The other type of specialised waste includes biomedical waste, hazardous waste from industries, construction debris and fly ash, meat processing centre etc. Disposal of biomedical waste is to be as per biomedical waste rules and hazardous waste requires special handling according to hazardous waste handling rules. Proper dumping, recycling and re-use of construction debris and fly ash have to be linked. Meat processing centre waste is to be recycled for chicken feed etc.

Considering the nature of solid waste and the economic aspects of its disposal, major part of solid waste especially silt has to be disposed off in sanitary landfills. But wherever recycling is possible, it should be preferred than disposing of the waste in sanitary landfill sites. More viable alternative to landfill are vermiculture, fossilisation, composting etc. Waste Minimisation Circles (WMCs) should be constituted and made effective implementation and monitoring, and Biomedical Wastes (Handling & Management) Rules, 1998, for hospitals, nursing homes, and clinics should be taken up. The sites, which are filled up or are in operation, are given in Table 3.9. The filled up sites may be re-used for plantation or as recreational area. The proposed sites for sanitary landfill are given in table 3.10 and existing and proposed compost plants are as under given in Table 3.11.

TABLE 3.9

Existing Land Fill Sites for Waste Management

Sl. No.	*Location*	*Area (in Ha.)*	*Remarks*
1.	Kailash Nagar, East Delhi	1.8	Filled up
2.	Tilak Nagar, West Delhi	16.0	Filled up
3.	Subroto Park	-	Filled up
4.	Purana Quila/Bharion Road	2.7	Filled up
5.	Timarpur	16.0	Filled up
6.	Sarai Kale Khan	24.0	Filled up
7.	Gopal Pur	4.0	Filled up
8.	Chhaterpur	1.7	Filled up
9.	SGT Nagar	14.4	Filled up
10.	IP Deoit	1.8	Filled up
11.	Sunder Nagar	2.8	Filled up
12.	Tughlaqabad Extension	2.4	Filled up
13.	Haider Pur	1.6	Filled up
14.	Mandawali Fazilpur	2.8	Filled up
15.	Rohini Phase III	4.8	Filled up
16.	Near Hastal Village in West Delhi	9.6	Filled up
17.	Site near Ghazipur Dairy Farm	28.0	In operation
18.	Site near Jhangipur/Bhalswa	16.0	In operation
19.	Okhla Phase I	12.8	In operation
20.	Crossing on GT Karnal Road	3.2	In operation
21.	Jaitpur/Tajpur	-	New
22.	Near Puthkhurd	-	New
23.	Bawana to Narela Road	-	New
24.	Sultanpur Dabas (Bawana)	-	New

TABLE 3.10

Proposed Sanitary Land Sites

Sl. No.	*Location*	*Area (in Ha.)*	*Remarks*
1.	Near Jaitpur/Tajpur	50	Proposed
2.	Near Gummanhera	30	Proposed
3.	Near Bawana – Puthkhurd Road	58	Proposed
4.	Near Bawana – Narela Road	60	Proposed
5.	Near Sultanpur Dabas alnong Khanjawala Road	40	Bawana- Proposed
6.	As part of Ghazipur SLLF	5	Proposed
7.	Bakarwala		Proposed
8.	Expansion of NDMMC Okhla	-	Proposed
9.	As part of Gummanhera SLF	-	Proposed
10.	As part of SLF Bawana Puthkhurd	4	Proposed
11.	As part of SLF Bawana – Narela Road	4	Proposed
12.	As part of SLLF Bawana – Khanjawala Road	4	Proposed

TABLE 3.11

Existing and Prop Compost/Incineration Plants

Sl. No.	*Location*	*Area (in Ha.)*	*Remarks*
1.	Okhla (MCD)*	-	Existing (NIO)
2.	Okhla (NDMC)	3.6	In operation
3.	Kair Village site (Najafgarh Zone)	4.0	In operation
4.	Deorala Village site (Najafgarh Zone)	4.8	New
5.	Compost plant of SLF Bhalaswa	4.8	New
6.	Vermiculture at SLF Gazipur	0.1	New
7.	Incinerator near Timarpur	-	Existing (NIO)
8.	Gazipur meat processing centre Disposal	2.0	Waste Proposed

Note: * Not in Operation

Keeping in view the fact that finding new sanitary landfill sites in Delhi is becoming extremely difficult, there is no option, but to resort to alternative methods of waste treatment, reduction, recycle and use, which include vermiculture, fossilisation and composting.

3.3.2.2 Stakeholders Involved in Recycling of Solid Waste in Delhi

In the overall sequence of activities, starting from collection of recyclable materials to the final disposal and recycling of waste, significant contributions are made by a range of private stakeholder groups outside the municipal authorities. These stakeholder groups wheel the informal sector recycling trade activities namely segregation, collection, sale and purchase of recyclable materials, and the actual process of recycling at recycling units. Residents and shopkeepers sell recyclable items, such as newspaper, glass containers, tin cans etc. to *kabariwallas* or itinerant waste collectors. The waste pickers retrieve recyclable materials from what is discarded by households, commercial establishments and industries from municipal wastes. Larger commercial establishments and industries sell the recyclable waste (in segregated form or otherwise) to waste dealers in bulk, who then sell it to recyclers.

Waste pickers pass on the retrieved materials to waste dealers. Then there are agents who facilitate transactions between medium/large waste dealers and recycling unit owners. A typical structure of waste trade is presented in Figure 3.2.

Waste trade activities performed by these informal sector stakeholders result into very significant waste material recovery and recycling. The waste trade activities in the informal sector are crucial in the broader framework of urban waste management. It calls for only small capital investment, responds directly to local needs and demands, requires low capital investment, ensures livelihood of a significant number of urban poor and reduces the environmental burden otherwise caused due to the same quantum of solid wastes had it remained uncollected. Unfortunately, not all the stakeholders benefit proportionately from these activities. Amongst all the stakeholders the waste pickers who come from highly vulnerable background, often become victims of exploitation, despite their significant service to the environment and society at large.

FIGURE 3.2

Recycling and Movement of Waste Through the Various People Involved in the Waste Trade

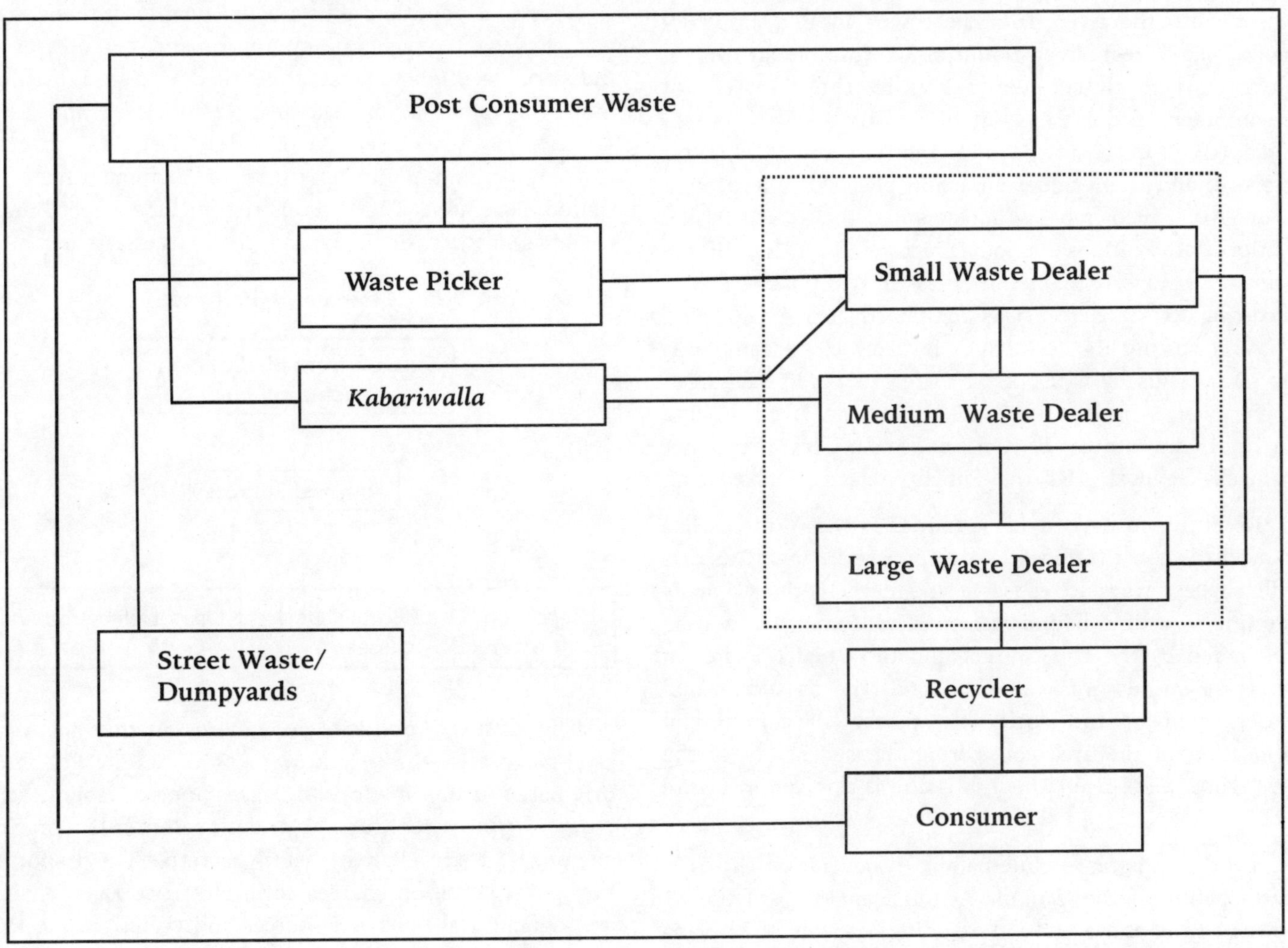

Under The "Ganga Action Plan" the clearing of the holy river Yamuna called "Yamuna Action Plan" has played a vital role in the sanitation of Delhi.

3.3.3 Yamuna Action Plan

The Yamuna, a major tributary to the holy river Ganga, is itself one of the holiest rivers of India and is used by millions as a source for drinking water besides for bathing and irrigation. In recent years, however, it has become grossly polluted due to various causes affecting human health and biodiversity of the eco-system. Emphasis is being laid on speedy execution of the Sewerage & Drainage Plan proposed by Delhi Jal Board to ensure water quality. The pollution potential in the catchment area depends on various human activities and is categorised into two groups: *Point sources of pollution & Non Point sources of pollution.* 80 per cent of the pollution load in the river comes from only 2 per cent of its catchment that lies in Delhi between Wazirabad and Okhla Barrages.

One of the main causes of pollution of the river is discharge of untreated domestic wastewater and other wastes into the river from the towns located along its banks. To arrest river pollution, certain measures of cleaning river have been taken by the Ministry of Environment and Forests (MoEF) of the Government of India (GOI) in 12 towns of Haryana, 8 towns of Uttar Pradesh, and Delhi under an action plan (Yamuna Action Plan-YAP) which is being implemented since 1993 by the National River Conservation Directorate (NRCD) of the Ministry of Environment and Forest in two phases. Phase-I costing Rs. 686 crore was completed during 2003 and Phase-II costing Rs. 624 crores is likely to be completed by 2009. Thus by 2009, Rs. 1310 crore would have been spent over a stretch of 1376 km of the river flowing through six states of Uttarakhand, Uttar Pradesh, Himachal Pradesh, Haryana, Punjab, Rajasthan, and Delhi.

Recently, to save dying Yanuna, Prime Minister has okayed the constitution of a high powered committee that will suggest ways to conserve and develop the Capital's life line in a time bound fashion. The Committee will be co-chaired by the Lt Governor and the Chief Minister of Delhi. It will also redevelop the landscape on and around the river front and decide the policy for commercial utilisation of the area considering the sensitivety of the river zone. Sewerage system of Delhi, is as given in Figure 3.3.

The Japan Bank for International Cooperation (JBIC) is participating in the Yamuna Action Plan in 15 of the 21 towns in the above status (excluding 6 towns of Haryana which included later on the direction of the Honourable Supreme Court of India) with soft loan assistance of 17.773 billion Japanese Yen (equivalent to about Rs. 700 crore) while GoI is providing the funds for the remaining 6 towns added later.

3.3.3.1 Point Sources of Pollution

The point sources of pollution are contributed at a single point in significant amount such as wastewater drain joining a water body. The point source pollution covers two major categories: domestic pollution and industrial pollution

3.3.3.2 Domestic Pollution

Sewage is discharged into the river without any treatment from the cities located along the banks of river and its tributaries. The river water does not remain suitable due to pollution, for uses like drinking, outdoor bathing, propagation of aquatic life, irrigation, and industrial purposes.

3.3.3.3 Industrial Pollution

Industrial pollution affects water quality in many ways i.e., dissolved oxygen, temperature and pH etc. Some industrial effluents cause toxicity. Large and medium industrial units—22 in Haryana, 42 in Delhi, and 17 in Uttar Pradesh—have been identified as directly discharging and polluting the river Yamuna under the Action Plan area. These industries include paper, sugar, chemical, leather, distillery and pharmaceuticals etc.

3.3.3.4 Non-Point Sources of Pollution

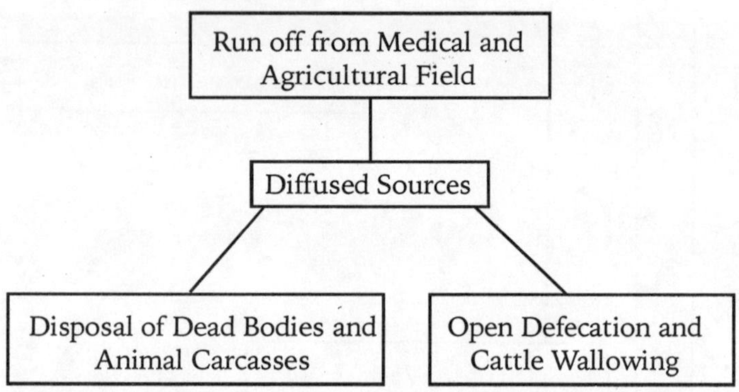

The diffused pollution originates mainly from the catchment area through movement of water. Pollutants originated from the topsoil losses include soil organic matter, plant residues, nutrient elements, organic chemicals, toxic elements, and bacteria. The important non point pollution sources contributing to river Yamuna are: agricultural pollution sources and pollution due to in stream uses of water.

FIGURE 3.3
Sewerage System of Delhi

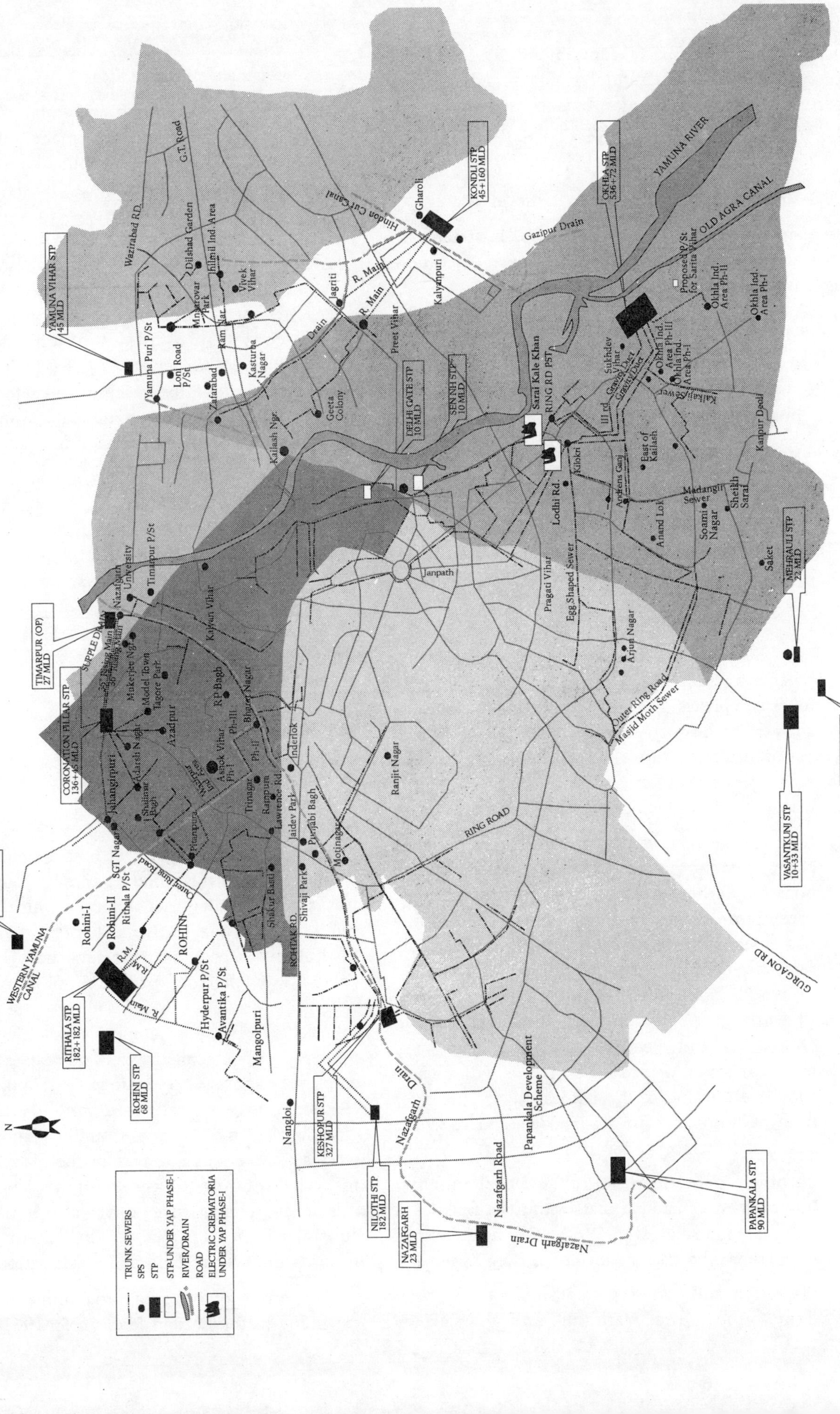

3.3.3.5 Agricultural Pollution

Agricultural pollution is contributed by following major sources: cattle, agricultural residues and fertiliser and pesticide use. The pollution load generated through above sources may be contributed to the river either as point source or as non point sources.

3.3.3.6 Pollution Due to In-stream Uses of Water

The main sources of pollution caused by in-stream use of river water are: cattle wading, bathing, open defecation, clothes washing.

3.3.4 Measures for Handling Sources of Pollution

In order to control the water pollution and improve the water quality of river Yamuna, some alternative measures are being taken up. The major components are:

(A) Sewerage Component

- Interception and diversion works including intermediate pumping stations
- Main pumping station and Raising Mains
- Sewage Treatment Plant (STP)

(B) Non-Sewerage Component

- Low Cost Sanitation: The Low Cost Sanitation scheme under YAP mainly consists of community toilet complexes provided at strategic locations in a town like bus depots, market places etc., as well as in slums and other areas inhabited by economically weaker sections (EWS) of people who do not have good sanitation facilities.
- Electric and Improved Crematoria: From religious point of view, people prefer to cremate human bodies on the banks of river, and sometimes partly burnt bodies are thrown into it. This is due to the fact that the poor are not able to afford the required quantity of wood for cremation. The firewood requirement is high per dead body. Therefore, provision of improved wood crematoria and electric crematoria have been made under YAP schemes. These will ensure complete burning of the bodies, saving the river from pollution due to dead bodies and consume less wood thereby saving trees.
- Bathing *Ghats*/River Front Developments: Improvement of bathing ghats with toilet facilities is being done in some of the YAP towns as thousands of pilgrims who take a bath in the river Yamuna.
- Plantation and Landscaping: Plantation has been done along the Yamuna and it carries considerable amount of flow around the facilities created under YAP, wherever land was available for such purposes.
- Public Participation and Public Awareness: There has been little effort made hitherto to create public awareness about the need to prevent pollution of the Yamuna. In this context, YAP has taken lead with respect to a public awareness campaign to save the river. Campaign items would include rallies, dramas, posters and pamphlets, sit and draw context for children, women's programme etc., on various aspects of conservation of water; toilet facilities; use of kitchen wastewater for gardening; composing of waste food for fertiliser; separation of combustible waste from non-combustibles and other possible topics to prevent river water pollution.

All these works are being implemented by the Uttar Pradesh Jal Nigam (UPJN) in U.P, Haryana Public Health Engineering Department (HPHED) in Haryana, Delhi Jal Board (DJB) and Municipal Corporation of Delhi (MCD) in Delhi under the coordination of National River Conservation Directorate (NRCD). The TEC-DCL Consortium (Indo-Japanese consultants) have been appointed as project consultants to monitor the progress of the schemes on a day-to-day basis.

3.4 Housing and Urban Policy

3.4.1 Evolution

The policies on urban development and housing in India have come a long way since 1950s. The pressure of urban population and lack of basic amenities were further compounded by migration of people from Pakistan. Delhi was among the few major cities, which had to bear the burden of huge influx of refugees. The existing institutional capacity at that time was grossly inadequate to deal with the problem of resettlement and rehabilitation of refugees. In the first Five Year Plan (1951-1956) therefore emphasis was given on institution building and on construction of houses for government employees and weaker sections. The Ministry of Works & Housing was constituted and National Building Organisation and Town & Country Planning Organisation were set up. A sizeable part of the plan outlay was spent for rehabilitation of the refugees from Pakistan. An Industrial Housing Scheme was also initiated. The Centre subsidised the schemes to the extent of 50 per cent towards the cost of land and construction.

The scope of housing programme for the poor was expanded in the Second Plan (1956-1961). The Industrial

Housing Scheme was widened to cover all workers. Three new schemes were introduced, namely, Rural Housing, Slum Clearance and Sweepers Housing. Town & Country Planning Legislations were enacted in many states and necessary organisations were also set up for preparation of Master Plans for important towns. The general directions for housing programmes in the Third Plan (1961-1966) were coordination of efforts of all agencies and orienting the programmes to the needs of the Low Income Groups. A scheme was introduced in 1959 to give loans to State governments for a period of 10 years for acquisition and development of land in order to make available building sites in sufficient numbers. Master Plans for major cities were prepared and the state capitals of Gandhi Nagar and Bhubaneshwar were developed.

The balanced urban growth was accorded high priority in the Fourth Plan (1969-1974). The Plan stressed the need to prevent further growth of population in large cities and need for decongestion or dispersal of population. This was envisaged to be achieved by creation of smaller towns and by planning the spatial location of economic activity. Housing & Urban Development Corporation (HUDCO) was established to fund the remunerative housing and urban development programmes, promising a quick turnover. A scheme for Environmental Improvement of Urban Slums was undertaken in the Central Sector from 1972-73 with a view to provide a minimum level of services, like, water supply, sewerage, drainage, street pavements in 11 cities with a population of 8 lakh and above. The scheme was later extended to 9 more cities.

The Fifth Plan (1974-1979) reiterated the policies of the preceding Plans to promote smaller towns in new urban centres, in order to ease the increasing pressure on urbanisation. This was to be supplemented by efforts to augment civic amenities in urban areas with particular emphasis on a comprehensive and regional approach to problems in metropolitan cities. A Task Force was set up for development of small and medium towns. The Urban Land (Ceiling & Regulation) Act was enacted to prevent concentration of land holding in urban areas and to make available urban land for construction of houses for the middle and low income groups.

The thrust of the planning in the Sixth Plan (1980-1985) was on integrated provision of services along with shelter, particularly for the poor. The Integrated Development of Small and Medium Towns (IDSMT) was launched in towns with population below one lakh for provision of roads, pavements, minor civic works, bus stands, markets, shopping complex etc. Positive inducements were proposed for setting up new industries and commercial and professional establishments in small, medium and intermediate towns.

The Seventh Plan (1985-1990) stressed on the need to entrust major responsibility of housing construction in the private sector. A three-fold role was assigned to the public sector, namely, mobilisation of resources for housing, provision for subsidised housing for the poor and acquisition and development of land. The National Housing Bank was set up to expand the base of housing finance. NBO was reconstituted and a new organisation called Building Material Technology Promotion Council (BMTPC) was set up for promoting commercial production of innovative building materials. A network of Building Centres was also set up during this Plan period. The Seventh Plan explicitly recognised the problems of the Urban poor and for the first time an Urban Poverty Alleviation Scheme known as Urban Basic Services for the Poor (UBSP) was launched.

As a follow-up of the Global Shelter Strategy (GSS), National Housing Policy (NHP) was announced in 1988. The long term goal of the NHP was to eradicate houselessness, improve the housing conditions of the inadequately housed and provide a minimum level of basic services and amenities to all. The role of the government was conceived as a provider for the poorest and vulnerable sections and as a facilitator for other income groups and private sector by the removal of constraints and the increased supply of land and services.

The National Commission on Urbanisation eloquently pointed out the reality of continuing rapid growth of the urban population as well as the scale and intensity of urbanisation, the critical deficiencies in the various items of infrastructure, the concentration of vast number of poor and deprived people, the acute disparities in the access of shelter and basic services, deteriorating environmental quality and the impact of poor governance on the income and the productivity of enterprises.

In the backdrop of this report the Eighth Plan (1992-1997) for the first time explicitly recognised the role and importance of urban sector for the national economy. While growth rate of employment in the urban areas averaged around 3.8 per cent per annum, it dropped to about 1.6 per cent in the rural areas. Therefore, the urban areas had to be enabled to absorb larger increments to the labour force. The plan identified the following key issues in the emerging urban scenario:

- The widening gap between demand and supply of infrastructural services badly hitting the poor, whose access to the basic services like drinking water, sanitation, education and basic health services is shrinking.

- Unabated growth of urban population aggravating the accumulated backlog of housing shortages, resulting in proliferation of slums and squatter settlement and decay of city environment.
- High incidence of marginal employment and urban poverty.

3.4.2 *National Housing and Habitat Policy 1998*

The National Housing and Habitat Policy of 1998 envisages that public agencies should perform the role of facilitators by providing developed land and legal and infrastructure support to enable the private sector to make heavy investments in housing. The main objectives of the policy are:

- Creation of surpluses in housing stock either on rental or ownership basis.
- Providing quality and cost effective shelter options, especially to vulnerable groups and the poor.
- Removing legal, financial and administrative barriers for facilitating access to land, finance and technology.
- Forging strong partnership among private, public and cooperative sectors to enhance the capacity of the construction industry to participate in every sphere of housing and habitat.
- Using technology for modernising the housing sector to increase efficiency, productivity and quality
- Empowering Panchayati Raj Institutions and village Cooperatives to mobilise credit for adding to the housing stock.

3.4.3 *Delhi's Shelter Policy*

Delhi's policy on "Shelter" is based on the above National Housing and Habitat Policy which has the ultimate goal of ensuring "Shelter for all". It recognises that Housing has a spatial relationship with Employment, Social Services and other urban activities. The Planning Board of the National Capital Region (NCR) has envisaged a Regional Plan Policy of "Induced Growth" of some selected settlements in the NCR through large scale housing activity to reduce population pressure on Delhi and achieve balanced development of the entire region.

3.4.4 *National Slum Policy*

In view of the enormity of the problem of slums in cities/towns at the National level, the Ministry of UD&PA has framed draft 'National Slum Policy'.

NATIONAL SLUM POLICY

Objectives

- To integrate slum settlements and the communities residing them into the urban area as a whole by creating awareness amongst the public and in government of the underlying principles that guide the process of slum development and improvement and the options that are available for bringing about the integration.
- To strengthen the legal and policy framework to facilitate the process of slum development and improvement on a sustainable basis.
- To establish a framework for involving all stakeholders for the efficient and smooth implementation of policy objectives.

Salient features

The policy preliminary endorses and promotes an upgrading and improvement approach to deal with slums and informal settlements as opposed to resettlement. It proposes that all existing planning instruments such as master plans, land use plans etc. should be modified to ensure that slums and informal settlements can properly integrated into the wider urban area.

The policy states that all physical upgrading and improvement in informal settlements should adopt a community-based approach with the active involvement of members of the community at every stage of design, implementation, and maintenance of services and assets. It sets forth specific norms and guiding principles for physical infrastructure developments and the desirability of collection of user charges.

The policy also emphasises improving access to social services, health, education, child labour and child rights and public distribution system as their effective delivery would also reduce social inequities and promote integration of people residing in slums into the social and economic networks of the city as a whole.

The policy recognises the importance of economic empowerment of the slum dweller and lays guidelines for provision of financial services for the poor and economic support/enterprise development designed to address the livelihood needs of the urban poor.

Contd...

...contd...

The policy proposes a sustainable financing mechanism for slum improvement through a Slum Development Fund at the state level, while recognising the role of private sector funding and institutional finance.

The policy proposes a consolidated Service Tax on properties located in slums. It gives measures for strengthening municipal governance and management in the context of slum areas. It also proposes establishment of a system of monitoring and evaluation at different levels of government in order to find out the extent to which the programmes under the policy are being implemented and whether the policy objectives are being achieved.

The policy is committed to a shelter upgradation approach that will enable, support and extend individual and community initiatives for housing provision.

Incorporating some of the important features outlined in the policy, the Central government has announced the Valmiki Ambedkar Malin Basti Awas Yojana (VAMBAY) for construction of dwelling units, upgrdation of slum tenements and provision of basic amenities like water supply and sanitation in slums.

Source: National Slum Policy (Draft), Ministry of Urban Development and Poverty Alleviation, October 2001

3.4.5 Delhi's Slum Policy

The broad policy adopted in Delhi is that no fresh encroachments shall be permitted on Public land and past encroachments, which had been in existence prior to 31 January 1990, will not be removed without providing alternatives. A three-pronged strategy has been adopted for dealing with the problems of *Jhuggi-Jhopris* as under:

i) Relocation of those *jhuggi* households where the land owning agencies are in a position to implement projects on the encroached land pockets as per requirements in larger public interest, and they submit requests to Slum & JJ Department for clearance of the *jhuggi* cluster for project implementation and also contribute due share towards the resettlement cost.

ii) *Insitu* upgradation of JJ Clusters and informal shelters in case of those encroached land pockets where the land owning agencies issue NOC to S&JJ Department for utilisation of land. However, the utilisation of land under this strategy is linked with the clearance of the project by the Technical Committee of the DDA.

iii) Extension of minimum basic civic amenities for community use under the scheme of Environmental Improvement in JJ Clusters and its component scheme of construction of Pay and Use '*Jansuvidha* Complexes' containing toilets and baths and also introduction of mobile toilet vans in the clusters irrespective of the status of the encroached land till their coverage under one of the aforesaid two strategies.

It can be categorically stated that the first part of this policy has remained a pipe dream and no agency i.e., the Land Owning Agencies or the Law Enforcement Agencies has made any efforts to curb fresh encroachments. Even the Government accepted this fact and therefore the earlier cut off date of 31st January 1990 for determining the eligibility for rehabilitation of squatters had to be extended to 31st December 1998.

The NCR Planning Board has suggested a joint approach with active cooperation between DDA, GNCT-Delhi and the Development Authorities of towns in the NCR (i.e. HUDA, GDA, MDA, NOIDA, etc.) wherein NCT Delhi could consider entering into necessary agreements/joint venture with them for:

i) Purchasing the existing vacant EWS plots and flats available for immediate occupancy in these towns; and/or

ii) Investing in fresh development of such facilities in these towns for resettlement and taking full advantage of the Government of India's (MOUD&PA) innovative schemes like VAMBAY etc. in establishing housing colonies for the poor and the needy.

The Board has suggested that these settlers would have to be relocated preferably close to their work places, on the rail, road transport corridors with the fast commuting transportation system.

Some isolated efforts were made for rehabilitation of slum dwellers in the NCR towns but the slum dwellers were not inclined to move to these NCR towns because of disruption of their economic means. Even within Delhi, the squatter families do not want to move out to far away locations, where they do not have any assured source of earnings. They are reluctant to shift from their more convenient central locations within the city to outlying areas, away from their places of employement, due to the distance involved and the extra transportation expenses etc. Since these migrants have their roots somewhere else, either at the place of last residence or place of work, they are very often reluctant to move and resort to squatting.

Relocation/re-settlement efforts in the past had either failed or had only limited success mainly because many newly located sites deprived the residents of the much needed job opportunities. In this context, it has also been suggested time and again that the possibility of solving the problem of slums in Delhi should be explored in the regional context.

3.5 Data Base Development and Management

While a large amount of data on housing in Delhi is generated by DDA, PWD, NDMC, MCD, Cantonment Board etc., it remains uncoordinated and often redundant to support decision making. Thus housing policy making so far has been without proper linkages between various sectors like physical Infrastructure, Business & Industry, Education, Health, Environment etc.

The process of data collection is also not within any regulatory framework. While the Indian conditions in general and Delhi's conditions in particular should govern development of such a framework, it would be desirable to consider the broad guidelines provided by the United Nations Human Settlements Programme. The indicator system for "shelter" developed by the U.N. Commission on Human Settlements (UNCHS) lists the following aspects/issues to be addressed:

i) Provision of security of tenure:
   - Indicator 1- Tenure type
   - Indicator 2- Evictions.

ii) Right to adequate housing:
   - Qualitative data- Housing rights
   - Indicator 3 – Housing price-to-income ratio

iii) Equal access to land:
   - Indicator 4 – Land price-to-income ratio

iv) Equal access to credit:
   - Indicator 5 – Mortgage and non-Mortgage

v) Access to basic services:
   - Indicator 6 – Access to Water
   - Indicator 7 – Household connections.

In case of Delhi, which attracts people from all parts of the country many more aspects need to be considered for urban planning in general and housing in particular *viz.*, employment opportunities for skilled, semi-skilled and unskilled people, public transport and over all carrying capacity of the land and other resources of the city. Carrying capacity of the city has to be assessed taking into consideration a wide range of aspects such as:

- Availability of land and optimal land use pattern.
- Existing physical infrastructure and the optional limits to which it can be expanded in future.
- Exhaustible and scarce natural resources especially surface and ground water.
- Sustainability of healthy environment and ecology.
- Internal support systems for healthy economic interdependence and social harmony.

Collecting and compiling data according to an appropriate Indicator System should be a collaborative effort since no single agency can be expected to be simultaneously conversant with all the issues involved.

Chapter 4

Infrastructure Development

ENERGY

4.1 General Features of Delhi Power Situation

4.1.1 Consumption and Load Growth

Delhi has the highest per capita power consumption among the States and Union territories of India, with a consumption of 1254 kWh per capita per annum in 2001-2002 as compared to the national average of 408 kWh. Over time, its consumption has also grown much faster than that of the country as a whole (Figure 4.1).

FIGURE 4.1

Per Capita Consumption (kWh per annum)

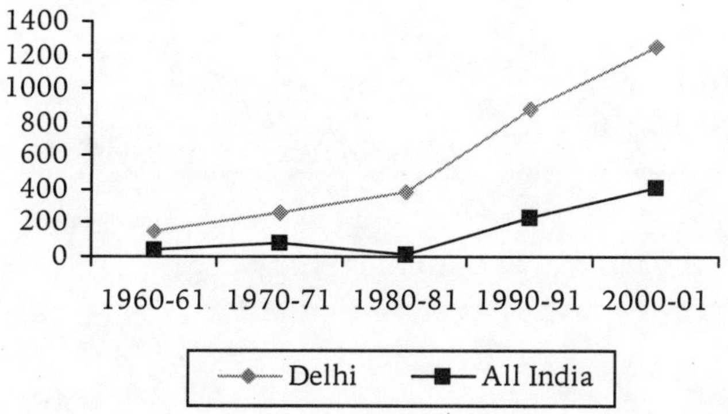

However, this is not surprising given Delhi's metropolitan character: its per capita consumption remains low compared to Bombay's.[1] Load and consumption have grown rapidly with Delhi's population. Table 4.1 shows the increase in load (megawatts).

TABLE 4.1

Maximum Load Demand Met

	1955-56	*1960-61*	*1970-71*	*1980-81*	*1990-91*	*2000-01*	*2004-05*
Max Demand Met (MW)	50	87	260	563	1437	2670	3490

Note: These are figures of demand actually met, and do not include load demand not met.

Source: Delhi Vidyut Board/Delhi Transco Limited.

Table 4.2 shows the actual consumption, the unmet requirement in terms of million units of shedding and the total requirement (being the total of the two)[2]

TABLE 4.2

Consumption, Requirement and Shedding

	1986-87	*1990-91*	*1994-95*	*1998-99*	*2001-02*	*2002-03*	*2003-04*	*2004-05*
MU Supplied	5433	8262	11862	16426	18334	19686	20385	20810
MU Shed	3	49	110	302	558	450	229	177
Total Requirement	5436	8311	11973	16728	18892	20136	20614	20987
Shed (%)	*0.06*	*0.59*	*0.92*	*1.81*	*2.95*	*2.23*	*1.11*	*0.84*

Source: Delhi Vidyut Board/Delhi Transco Limited.

Clearly, DESU/DVB had not been able to keep up with the increasing requirement, while there has been a significant improvement since unbundling. Figure 4.2 contrasts the rate of increase in transmission and distribution system capacity with the rate of increase in

1. 2620 kWh in 2002.

2. The shedding figures are compiled with reference to loss of supply reported at the level of 66/33 kW substations (including loss on a whole 11kW feeder emanating from such a substation). The loss of consumption at lower levels would be relatively insignificant in overall quantitative terms.

consumption. The 400 KV Ring around Delhi, a major project to enable Delhi to import power to meet its needs, was commenced in 1991 and not completed until 2002. Distribution transformer failure, which is another rough indicator of the adequacy of the distribution system, is shown in Table 4.3.

But it is also noteworthy that, while the peak lead has continued to increase after the unbundling of DVB, the rate of growth of consumption has decreased, and per capita consumption appears to have actually declined (Table 4.4).

FIGURE 4.2

Load, Consumption and System Capacity

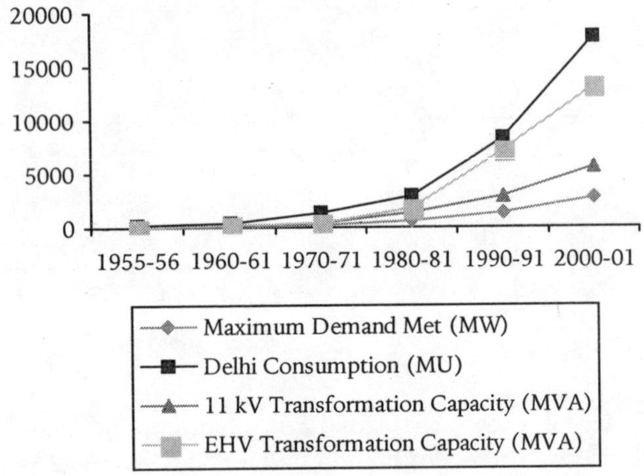

4.1.2 Peak/Off-Peak Variation

There are sharp diurnal and seasonal variations between peak and off-peak load, attributable to the climate plus the absence of agricultural and other possible sources of off-peak consumption. Figure 4.3 shows the difference between monthly maximum and minimum loads met during 2004-05. Figure 4.4 shows the peak/off-peak variation on a day in winter, when it is the highest.

FIGURE 4.3

Maximum and Minimum Load, 2004-05

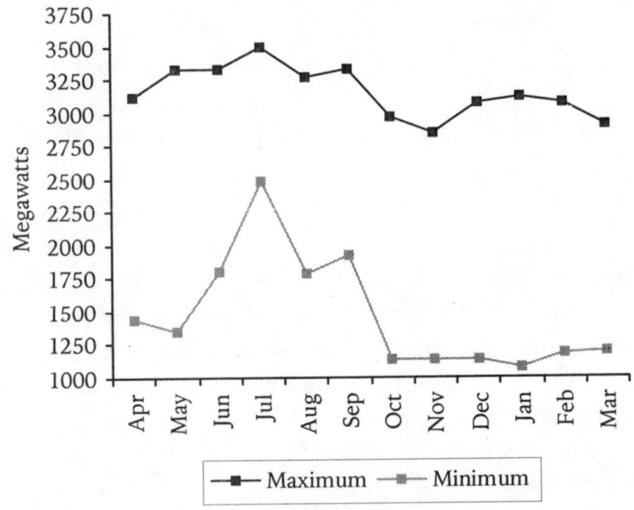

TABLE 4.3

Distribution Transformer Failures

	1990-91	*1991-92*	*1992-93*	*1993-94*	*1994-95*	*1995-96*	*1996-97*	*1997-98*	*1998-99*	*1999-00*	*2000-01*	*2001-02*
Total No. of DTs	5329	5783	5911	NA*	NA	NA	6931	7382	9152	9602	10060	10525
Number Failed	600	891	866	1346	1545	1627	1631	1706	1780	1628	1840	1533
Failed (%)	**11.26**	**15.41**	**14.65**	NA	NA	NA	**23.53**	**23.11**	**19.45**	**16.95**	**18.29**	**14.57**

Note: * NA = Data not available.
Source: Delhi Vidyut Board/Delhi Transco Limited.

TABLE 4.4

Recent Consumption Trends

	2000-01	*2001-02*	*Change (%)*	*2002-03*	*Change (%)*	*2003-04*	*Change (%)*	*2004-05*	*Change (%)*
Population (millions)	13.85	14.50	4.70	15.15	4.49	15.80	4.30	16.45	4.12
Consumption (MU)	17364	18445	6.23	19686	6.73	20385	3.55	20810	2.09
Per Capita (KWH)	1254	1272	1.46	1299	2.14	1290	-0.71	1265	-1.95

Note: Annual Population figures are estimated.
Source: Delhi Vidyut Board/Delhi Transco Limited.

FIGURE 4.4

Delhi Demand on 7-1-05

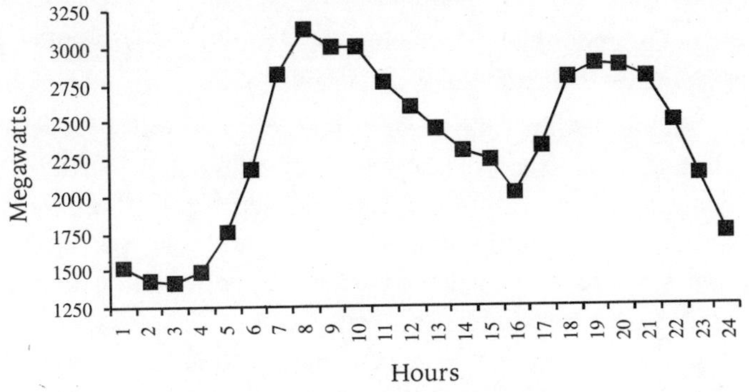

Delhi's own generation being limited, there is, therefore, an endemic peak supply problem, but less ability than in most other states to utilise capacity for off-peak consumption.

So far as the actual future requirement of Delhi is concerned, the Energy Department of the Delhi Government states (July 2007) that the requirement has been "realistically assessed on the basis of the projections made by the Central Electricity Authority/ own assessment of the Government and Power Purchase Agreements have been signed for 1200 MW of power with various Power Generating Companies over the next five years."

4.1.3 *Consumer Profile*

Table 4.5 shows the break-up of connections, sales and revenue by consumer categories in 1991-92 and in 2002-2003. The pattern remained remarkably consistent.

TABLE 4.5

Delhi Consumer Profile

	Connections (%)		*Sale of Energy (%)*		*Revenue (%)*	
	1991-92	*2002-03*	*1991-92*	*2002-03*	*1991-92*	*2002-03*
Domestic	76.86	78.09	41.07	40.80	22.32	26.14
Non-Domestic LT	17.49	15.37	9.04	6.63	11.26	10.17
Non-Domestic HT	0.02	0.03	6.51	5.90	12.35	8.19
Small Industry (LT)	4.51	5.41	17.77	22.17	18.43	29.12
Large Industry (HT)	0.03	0.04	8.64	7.87	18.58	11.84
Agriculture	0.97	0.96	0.64	1.21	0.13	0.37
Public Utilities	0.11	0.10	5.41	5.70	7.23	5.80
Licensees (NDMC+MES)			10.92	9.72	9.69	8.37

Source: Delhi Vidyut Board/Delhi Transco Limited.

However we see a decline in the proportion of energy sold to both commercial and industrial High Tension consumers, and a substantial decline in the proportion of revenue from them, which is matched by a sharp increase in the role of small industry. There has also been a noticeable increase in the proportionate contribution to total revenue by domestic consumers. Two factors appear to be at play here: firstly, planning norms discouraged the expansion of large industry and, secondly, the possibilities of cross-subsidisation to keep domestic tariffs down were saturated.

The post-privatisation position is not as clear. The break-up in respect of sale of energy in 2004-05 according to DERC's tariff orders for 2005-06 is shown in Table 4.6.

It is difficult to draw any conclusion in view of the huge difference between the picture presented by NDPL and the huge swing towards domestic consumption shown by the other two Discoms. This does have revenue implications and suggests the need for an independent audit of the billing software and data systems in use by the Discoms. However, it may be added that DERC is now understood to be seized of the matter.

4.1.4 *Urban Pattern*

Delhi's power supply network has been continuously impacted by the city's growth, much of which has been unplanned. Delhi's population grew from 1.74 million in 1951 to 4.07 million in 1971 to 13.78 million in 2001. There are about 1400 unauthorised colonies over and above 600 that have been 'regularised', and a population of about 3 million living as squatters in *jhuggi-jhopri basties*. There is also a significant mismatch between planned and actual land use.

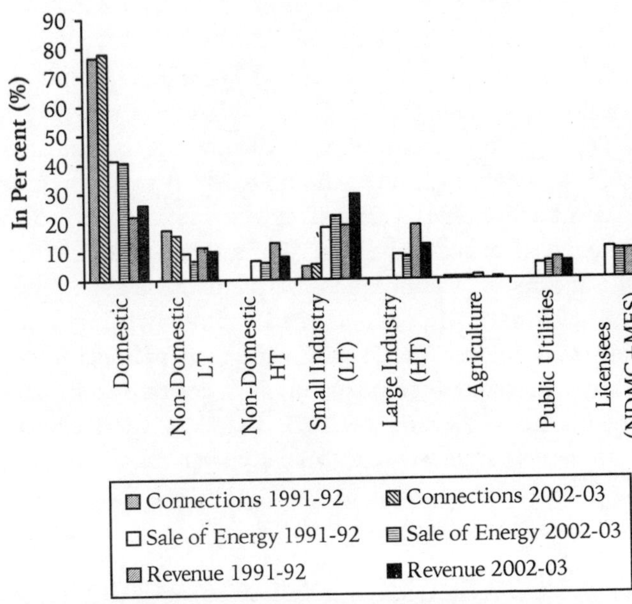

TABLE 4.6

Consumer Category-Wise Sale of Energy in 2004-05 As Per DERC

(In Per cent)

	NDPL	BRPL	BYPL	Total
Domestic	42.08	54.77	53.53	50.55
Non-Domestic	18.73	30.07	31.35	26.87
Industrial	32.40	11.17	13.23	18.22
Public Lighting	2.02	1.89	1.75	1.90
Agriculture	0.65	1.15	0.00	0.73
Railway Traction	1.50	0.67	0.00	0.77
DMRC	1.06	0.00	0.00	0.33
Others	1.55	0.28	0.14	0.64
	100.00	100.00	100.00	100.00

Source: Delhi Vidyut Board/Delhi Transco Limited.

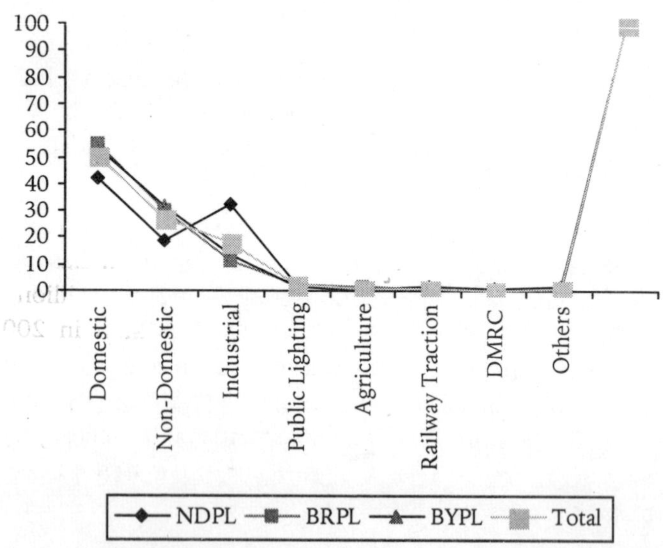

The effects of this situation were compounded by certain provisions of the Delhi Electricity Control Order (DECO) in force from 1959, until their partial withdrawal in 1999, which restrained the utility from supplying power to unauthorised structures or for unauthorised commercial or industrial use. While this proved ineffective as a means of planning control, it compelled the growing population of those excluded from lawful access to electricity to steal it, usually with tacit political support, which increased corruption and contributed to the organisational decline of DVB. In 2001, DVB estimated that about 14 per cent of Delhi's power consumption was going to the unelectrified colonies and *jhuggi basties*. A large backlog of unelectrified areas continues to exist. This situation may be contrasted with that in Bombay where BSES, the private utility supplying to most of the city, had been able to meter and provide regular supply to every squatter settlement as it came up.

Again, Delhi has been undergoing more continuous change and transformation than the other metros. A changing and unstable cityscape, with continuous road widening, changing densities and land use patterns in different areas, with new centres of load and consumption continually springing up, complicates the tasks both of maintenance and of the continual system augmentation that is required. There are continuous demands to shift lines because subsequent unauthorised development has made them dangerous; lines may have to be re-laid because of other infrastructure projects (like flyovers); cables suffer repeated interference from digging related to other services; and urgent repairs may be held up pending approval for digging from the road owning agency; transformation capacity augmentation is severely constrained by the inability to find sites for sub-stations; new transmission and distribution lines are held up on account of right-of-way issues, etc. Problems of inter-agency cooperation aggravate these difficulties.

The above factors tend to offset what is one of Delhi's undoubted advantages, so far as the operations of its power sector utilities are concerned, of having a negligible level of agricultural consumption. Its impact during the DVB period is illustrated by the findings of energy audit[3] shown in Table 4.7, in which the distribution loss at 11 KV level varied considerably between circles, correlating significantly with the level of unauthorised development:

TABLE 4.7

Distribution Loss at 11 KV Level in DVB Period

Circle	Energy Released (Dec. 1999-Nov. 2K (MU)	Energy Billed (Dec. 1999-Nov. 2K (MU)	Distribution Loss (%)
Central	1383.75	784.28	43.32
East	2848.07	1049.59	63.15
North	2459.69	1501.81	38.94
North-West	1761.85	971.63	44.85
South	3772.86	2290.50	38.29
West	2725.38	1121.53	58.37

Source: Delhi Vidyut Board/Delhi Transco Limited.

3. DESU/DVB was in fact the first SEB/State utility to meter 11KV feeders and begin introducing an energy audit, though admittedly not a wholly satisfactory one, from the late 1990s.

FIGURE 4.5

Distribution Loss at 11 KV Level in DVB Period

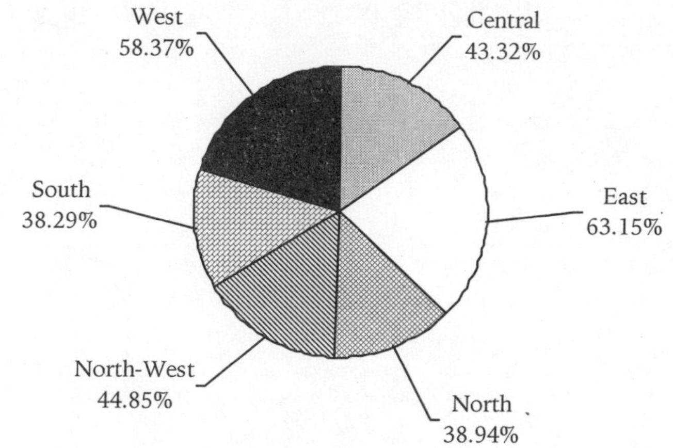

The point is illustrated even more graphically if we compare the best and the worst performing of DVB's thirty 'districts' as shown in Table 4.8.

TABLE 4.8

Distribution Loss at 11 KV level in Best and Worst Districts

Circle	*Energy Released (Dec. 1999-Nov. 2K (MU)*	*Energy Billed (Dec. 99-Nov. 2K (MU)*	*Distribution Loss (%)*
Yamuna Vihar (East Circle)	901.00	239.61	73.41
Nehru Place (South Circle)	446.10	349.31	21.70

Source: Delhi Vidyut Board/Delhi Transco Limited.

While the overall loss reduction achieved since privatisation will have reduced these disparities, the underlying fact remains that the pattern of consumption, area-wise and consumer-category-wise must always be influenced by the changing, always emerging pattern of urban development—for example, the sealing and demolition of numerous commercial establishments under Supreme Court orders in many (actual, though not planned) commercial areas in 2006, and the consequent acceleration in the development of shopping malls in other areas, would obviously have affected the local economics of power supply and also the local load conditions—and consequently local system requirements—in different parts of the city. It would be unrealistic to expect that Delhi's growth, whether overall or in its pattern of distribution, will ever be reliably predictable in the foreseeable future: certainly, no predictions made in the past have ever proved entirely accurate. Given the political—and also socioeconomic—sensitivity of power supply in different parts of Delhi, this means that some over-planning is necessary, unavoidable and actually desirable, and the tariff will have to take it into account.

4.1.5 Sourcing of Delhi's Power Supply

As Table 4.9 shows, Delhi has become increasingly dependent on external sources of power supply over the years. This issue is discussed further in Section 4.3 below.

TABLE 4.9

Share of Local Generation in Total Supply

	1952-53	*1962-63*	*1972-73*	*1982-83*	*1992-93*	*2001-02*
Units generated (MU)	158.21	248.68	1115.83	963.65	2227.28	2293.76
Units Supplied (MU)	148.57	516.16	1629.66	3483.3	11167.67	18334.07
Generated (%)	**106.49**	**48.18**	**68.47**	**27.66**	**19.94**	**12.51**

Source: Delhi Vidyut Board/Delhi Transco Limited.

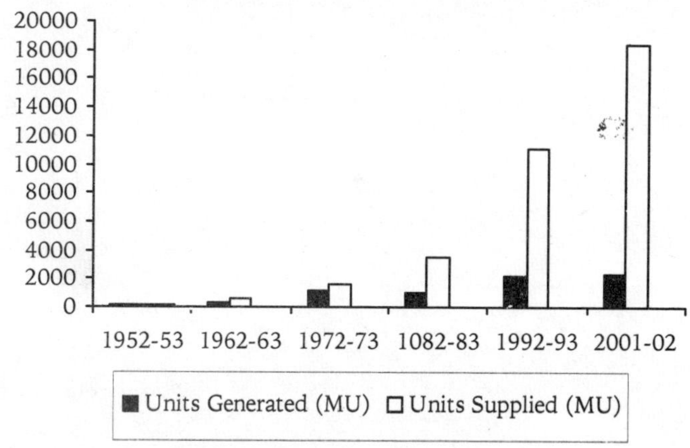

4.2 Review of Policies, Programmes and Projects

4.2.1 Organisation of the Power Sector before 2002

The Delhi Vidyut Board (DVB) came into existence in February 1997 as a State Electricity Board (SEB) under the Electricity (Supply) Act, 1948. However, its organisational history goes back to the establishment in 1951 of an earlier Delhi State Electricity Board (DSEB), which was replaced in 1958 by the Delhi Electric Supply Undertaking (DESU) created as a wing of the newly established Municipal Corporation of Delhi (MCD). The jurisdiction of MCD, and consequently of DESU and its successor DVB, did not extend to the New Delhi Municipal Council area or the Cantonment area, and the NDMC and the MES functioned separately as statutory distribution licensees, obtaining bulk supplies from DESU/DVB.

The establishment of DSEB in 1951, replacing a private utility that had been generating and supplying electricity in Delhi since 1905, was in pursuance of the 1948 Act, entrusting the power sector to State Electricity Boards. However, the subsequent (1957 and 1997) changes in the name and formal legal character of this utility were purely constitutional and political: in practice DSEB, DESU and DVB were a single, continuous organisation.

4.2.2 Analysis of DESU/DVB's Failure

Figure 4.6 shows the Transmission and Distribution (T&D) losses[4] over a period of time. At 12 per cent, DVB's T&D losses in 1976 were comparable to those of BSES, India's best-performing private distribution licensee.[5]

During the 1990s when the T&D losses reached wholly unacceptable levels, it would have been difficult to expect consumers to pay DESU/DVB's costs through the tariff, but that DESU had been losing money even in earlier decades when it was fairly efficient and when its consumers could quite reasonably have been expected to pay the cost of its services. Table 4.10 shows the operating loss and net commercial loss from 1983-84 onwards. Tariff revisions took place with effect from 1-4-87, 1-3-91, 1-10-93, 1-4-97 and 1-6-01, and the effects can be seen on Table 4.10; but while the operating losses might decrease in a particular year as a result of tariff revision or because of other efforts made, the overall losses continued to increase as a result of accumulating

FIGURE 4.6

DESU/DVB T&D Losses

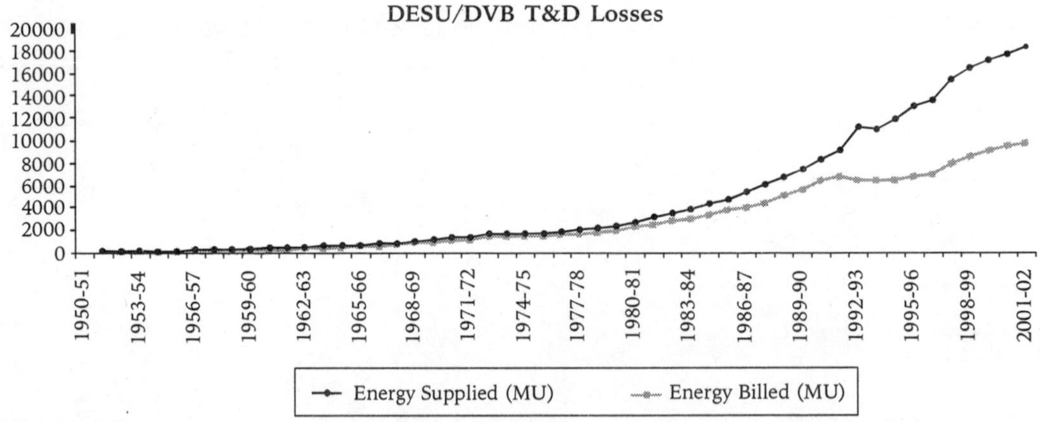

TABLE 4.10

Commercial Performance of DESU/DVB

(Rs Crores)

	FY 84	*FY 85*	*FY 86*	*FY 87*	*FY 88*	*FY 89*	*FY 90*	*FY 91*	*FY 92*	*FY 93*
	1	2	3	4	5	6	7	8	9	10
Revenues	150.36	182.96	288.17	328.23	360.63	456.08	529.09	701.16	865.00	1072.00
Operating Deficit*	63.59	73.92	4.92	52.43	165.81	165.65	199.94	150.98	15.50	216.38
Net loss	86.92	100.59	40.74	104.25	226.16	242.20	241.63	208.82	90.96	328.79

	FY 94	*FY 95*	*FY 96*	*FY 97*	*FY 98*	*FY 99*	*FY 2K*	*FY 01*	*FY 02*
	11	12	13	14	15	16	17	18	19
Revenues	1322.78	1555.09	1911.95	1970.19	2699.14	3031.99	3266.75	3554.32	4004.73
Operating Deficit*	114.14	172.95	354.35	491.81	281.98	502.23	292.72	462.63	248.04
Net loss	245.46	326.55	500.76	709.74	536.31	833.47	833.93	1104.41	1196.04

Note: * i.e. excluding interest and depreciation

Source: Annual Accounts; audited up to 1990-2001; thereafter unaudited.

4. The difference between units of energy supplied and energy billed, or unaccounted energy.
5. BSES's (now renamed Reliance Energy) T&D losses in Bombay were 11.58 per cent in FY 2002 and 13.60 per cent in FY 2003; those of CESC, Calcutta are considerably higher: 21.09 per cent in FY 2002.

liabilities. Further, when tariff increases took place they tended to be quite steep as Table 4.11 shows in respect of the domestic tariff (which is politically the most sensitive tariff category in Delhi, and the principal beneficiary of cross-subsidisation).

TABLE 4.11

Pre-Reforms Tariff Increases for Domestic Consumers

Units	*1-4-87 (Rs./ unit)*	*1-3-91 (Rs./ unit)*	*% increase*	*1-10-93 (Rs./ unit)*	*% increase*	*1-4-97 (Rs./ unit)*	*% increase*
1-100	0.27	0.40	*48.15*	0.60	*50*	1.00	*66.67*
101-200	0.32	0.50	*56.25*	1.00	*100*	1.75	*75.00*
201-300	0.75	1.50	*100.00*	1.80	*20*	2.50	*38.89*
301-400	0.75	2.00	*166.67*	2.40	*20*	3.00	*25.00*
>400	0.75	2.00	*166.67*	2.40	*20*	3.00	*25.00*

Source: Delhi Vidyut Board/Delhi Transco Limited.

Coming to the reasons, it may be suggested that DESU and its counterparts, the SEBs, were not inherently worse than other governmental organisations but proved more conspicuously unsuited to their purpose. Some of the factors affecting their management were:

• *The absence of a commercial orientation, reflecting the prevailing mindset in governance*: The reward system did not recognise good commercial performance, nor were there systems in place to provide the information that would have made it possible to fix accountability within the organisation; this implied weak and ineffective managements and made it possible for political leaders to interfere in SEBs with impunity, which made matters worse; the weakness of management, with nobody effectively in charge, made improvement difficult; widely dispersed corruption reflected all these organisational failings as, equally, it contributed to them and created vested interests in the *status quo*: to understand the deterioration of SEBs, we need to appreciate the malign synergy that works between all these interrelated factors. This state of affairs was exemplified in the fact that DESU/DVB's annual accounts were always several years behind schedule, and were finally brought up-to-date only in the last couple of years of DVB's existence (because of which they remain unaudited after 1991-2): clearly, the financial performance of this utility had not been a priority concern either of the Government's or of its own management's, whilst the absence of finalised accounts for years together compounded the consequences of non-financial management and further diluted accountability.

• *Increasing scale of operations:* Table 4.12 shows the increasing scale of operations in Delhi, and the number of employees:

TABLE 4.12

Increasing Scale of Operations

	1950-51	*1960-61*	*1970-71*	*1980-81*	*1990-91*	*2001-02*
Consumers (millions)	0.03	0.17	0.52	1.01	1.70	2.65
Peak Demand Met (MW)	27	87	260	564	1437	2879
Consumption (MU)	149	435	1306	2797	8262	18334
Number of Employees				26159	26358	22869

Source: Delhi Vidyut Board/Delhi Transco Limited.

The number of employees, which had crossed 26,000 by 1980-81, stabilised and declined slightly during DVB's last years. The utility's operations grew from a scale at which supervision and accountability were still possible through personal surveillance and inspection, to a large, anonymous one where they were not, yet there was no significant change in work methods and systems throughout this half-century; the failure to respond to the changing requirements of expanding operations with changes in organisational structure, procedures, technology, training, and information systems reflect the lack of a commercial orientation.

• *DESU/DVB's precipitate decline in the 1990s:* The accelerating deterioration in the 1990s may be seen as the cumulative effect of the factors referred to above, aggravated in the final stages by the change in Delhi's constitutional arrangements that took place in 1993: subject to the control[6] and interference of the newly elected Government of the NCT of Delhi and of its legislators, the utility saw no fewer than seven changes of chief executive during the period 1993 to 1998 and it is fair to say that by the end of that five-year period nobody was really in charge.

The widespread dissatisfaction with DVB seems to have reached a head in the difficult summer of 1998, when there were riots and disturbances in the streets. The power situation in that summer was not atypical, but the public response to it appeared to reflect accumulated discontent.

6. MCD (of which DESU was a wing) was under suspension when the new Government of NCT of Delhi came into being, and DESU became DVB before the elected MCD was restored in 1997.

4.2.3 Power Sector Restructuring, 1999-2002

The unbundling of DVB with simultaneous privatisation of its distribution business was the single most important policy transaction affecting the power sector in the city, and its lessons are of possibly seminal importance for other states. It will, therefore, need to be considered in a little detail.

4.2.3.1 Background Factors

There were three general factors that influenced the scheme of the Delhi reforms as it developed:

• *Political motivation:* The leadership of the new Government elected in December 1998 was very conscious that DVB had become a serious liability not merely for its financial losses but because of its poor image, and lost no time in bringing out a Strategy Paper in February 1999. As we shall see, the reform package evolved and developed according to the empirical requirements of the situation, throwing up several innovations. This happened because what drove the process was the force of a political mandate with a clear objective in view.

• *Necessity of a fast-track process and its implications:* To sustain political will, reforms must be likely to bear some visible fruit within the Government's term of office. In Delhi, this ruled out involvement of the World Bank or other external agencies, which would have meant a longer time frame. Secondly, a conventional asset valuation exercise as adopted in Orissa and elsewhere would, in the absence of the requisite data, have involved delays. This was a reason for adopting the Business Valuation methodology and for engaging the consultants who had innovated it (for distribution privatisation) in Kanpur.[7] The consultants derived the revenue earning potential of each of the proposed distribution companies (Discoms) by modelling based on certain assumptions about reasonable tariff increases; targeted efficiency improvements (for the business to be self-sustaining within five years); and government assistance for the transitional period. It should, however, be added that such a methodology is in any case more appropriate for the transfer of a running business. It also obviates the impact of overvaluation on retail tariff.[8]

• *Orissa Experience:* The distribution business was privatised in Orissa in 1999, thus the post-privatisation experience there unfolded contemporaneously with the unbundling process in Delhi. The issues emerging in Orissa, therefore, had to be dealt with in order to retain investor interest in Delhi.

Firstly, confidence had to be created in the data, after it had turned out in Orissa that the T&D losses were about 15 per cent higher than had been stated by the consultants.

Secondly, while the Orissa Government had sought to address the problem of political risk by creating the country's first State Electricity Regulatory Commission, the subsequent experience in that state now compelled the Delhi Government to address investor apprehensions about regulatory risk. The most important single issue in Orissa, from the investors' point of view, was the inability of the Orissa Electricity Regulatory Commission (OERC) to set tariffs on the basis of the actual T&D losses and uncertainty about future regulatory decisions, particularly about the expected trajectory of efficiency improvements.[9] Again, efforts to privatise the Kanpur Electric Supply Company proved abortive mainly because of unrealistic initial efficiency improvement targets (5 per cent T&D loss reduction fixed by the Government for the first year, which was compounded by the UP Electricity Regulatory Commission's failure to allow for any collection inefficiency). Successful privatisations in the power sector, notably in the UK and in Latin America, had normally involved an initial five or seven year period for which tariffs (or tariff-setting formulae) were fixed in advance, usually by the Government, and not left subject to regulatory uncertainty. In India, after the Orissa experience, it was clearly necessary both that efficiency improvement targets should be fixed in advance and that investors should perceive them to be achievable.

4.2.3.2 Evolution of the Reform Package

The reform package evolved through four broad stages:

First, there was the process adumbrated in the Strategy Paper issued in February 1999, which provided for the establishment of a Regulatory Commission; unbundling, which as then conceived was to start with the

7. SBI Capital Markets (SBI Caps), a subsidiary of the State Bank of India. At that time the UP Government had engaged SBI Caps to try to privatise power distribution in Kanpur. There has been subsequent audit criticism of the decision to engage SBI Caps without a full-blown tender process, though more expensive offers received from two other consultants did provide some standard of comparison. This audit criticism, which is actually quite muted in tone, does not reflect the fact that SBI Caps have been directly engaged by a number of Central and state departments and agencies in other cases, apparently without attracting audit criticism.

8. While some controversy was raised about the adoption of a business valuation methodology at the time, the Electricity Act, 2003 now mandates valuation of the assets of a State Electricity Board that is being wound up on the basis of their revenue potential.

9. In fairness to OERC it must be stated that, in the absence of transitional assistance as in Delhi, and also because of the asset valuation done, tariffs rose very steeply in Orissa. Further, it could well be argued that the investors had accepted the data provided by the consultants and were themselves responsible for their own failure in 'due diligence'.

establishment of a generating company; disinvestment of distribution; a commitment to protect the interests of staff; and some interim measures to improve DVB's performance pending its restructuring.

Second, when the Consultants gave their initial report in April 2000, it incorporated the following essential features that were to remain in the final package:

(i) Unbundling into a generation, a transmission and three distribution companies.

(ii) DVB's unserviceable liabilities (which were almost entirely payable to the Central Public Sector Undertakings, Central government and NCT government) would not be passed on to the successor entities. Correspondingly, the Discoms would not take over DVB's receivables; instead they would retain a 20 per cent collection charge for the receivables (other than those due from government-owned consumers) that they collected. (However the idea of a holding company had not yet been conceived; at this stage the idea was that these dues would be taken over by GNCTD and subsequently got written off by the Central government and GNCTD for, respectively, the DESU and DVB periods.[10])

(iii) Business Valuation. The reasons for this have already been discussed above.

(iv) Retirement benefits to be provided for: The successor entities to DVB would not be saddled with the liability for retirement benefits incurred up to the date of unbundling. A separate fund would be created for the purpose, the Government topping up the (inadequate) funds already available with DVB for the purpose.

(v) Clubbing of T&D losses and collection inefficiency. The intention was that the figure of units of electricity supplied for which payment was recovered would be accepted as a reliable figure, since the calculation of T&D losses in Orissa had been discredited.

(vi) Return on equity for Discoms: A return on equity of 16 per cent was stipulated.

(vii) The Transfer Scheme was to be given the form of delegated legislation, as statutory rules under the Delhi Electricity Reform Act, 2000 (DERA) which was enacted later in the year.

Third, there was the package that GNCTD adopted in January 2001, which incorporated the following additional features:

(i) Holding Company: It was now decided that a Holding Company would be set up to retain the unserviceable liabilities of DESU and DVB, partly because write-off by the Central government of dues to Central public sector utilities was now seen to be improbable. The Holding Company would retain the proceeds from the sale of a controlling interest in the Discoms (thus retaining this as a resource available to discharge unavoidable liabilities created by DVB, or for alternative use within the sector).

(ii) Serviceable Liabilities: The business valuation of DVB provided the basis for quantifying the serviceable liabilities of DVB; 40 per cent of this amount was issued to the Holding Company as equity by the other successor entities and the balance remained as debt to be repaid after an initial moratorium period of three (later increased to four years).

(iii) Simultaneous Unbundling and Privatisation: The new companies would be incorporated in advance, as shell companies, so that unbundling and privatisation could take place simultaneously. Besides saving time (a) there was no risk of the new companies incurring additional liabilities after unbundling but before an attempt to privatise them and (b) the Government could abort the process at any time, if satisfactory bids were not forthcoming.

(iv) Tripartite Agreement: Government would top up the available fund for terminal benefit liabilities of employees in pursuance of the Tripartite Agreement entered into between Government, DVB and the main employee unions and associations.

(v) Transitional Assistance (of Rs.2600 crores) was envisaged which the Government would release directly to the Discoms.

(vi) Five-Year Tariff Package: An important additional feature of the package at this stage was the intention to get five-year tariff setting formulae established in advance by DERC. DVB applied for five-year tariff-setting formulae (or 'principles') along with its Annual Revenue Requirement (ARR) for 2001-02. The proposal was to target T&D loss reduction at 12 per cent over the five-year period while simultaneously laying down graded annual targets for improvement in collection efficiency.[11] In addition, the Commission was requested to fix in advance the principles on which it would allow the

10. DESU, as a wing of the Municipal Corporation of Delhi, had been under the statutory control of the Central government: hence GNCTD did not own its liabilities.

11. This was only a superficial departure from the intended clubbing of T&D loss and collection inefficiency, dictated by the necessity to adhere to DERC formats for filing before DERC.

Annual Revenue Requirement (ARR) on other key parameters, taking 2001-02 as the base year and laying down in advance the basis of annual variation from it.

The final package involved several further changes:

(i) Loss reduction targets made the bidding parameter: DERC created a difficult situation that threatened the whole privatisation project when, in June 2001, it declined to issue a five-year tariff package. It was clear by now that privatisation would not be possible without the advance fixation, at the very least, of loss reduction targets. It would therefore become necessary to issue statutory Policy Directions.[12] However, it would equally have been difficult to obtain Government concurrence or popular acceptance for any achievable loss reduction targets that might be fixed in advance by the Government without regulatory concurrence. Therefore, the reform process seemed to be stuck. The way out that was devised was that reduction in the level of AT&C losses should itself be made the basis for bidding. The loss reduction targets would thus be legitimised as being the outcome of a transparent bidding process and enforced by means of Policy Directions binding the Regulatory Commission to the outcome of the bidding process.

(ii) Overachievement Incentive: It was further provided that the investor taking over any Discom would retain 50 per cent of the gain from exceeding the minimum efficiency improvement targets for any one year. The remaining half would be returned to the consumers as a rebate on the tariff.

(iii) Transitional Assistance routed through Transco: Another change was that now assistance would be routed through Transco rather than given directly to the Discoms. This was administratively and politically more convenient and also facilitated the intention to keep a common retail tariff throughout Delhi with differential bulk supply tariff for sale to each of the three Discoms (which was advisable since, as long as losses remained high differential retail tariffs would mean higher tariffs in the poorer areas, especially East Delhi, which had higher losses.)

(iv) Quantum of Transitional Assistance: The quantum of transitional assistance eventually increased from about Rs.2600 crore to Rs.3450 crore. The circumstances in which this happened are described below.

Figure 4.7 below depicts the restructuring of DVB.

FIGURE 4.7

Financial Restructuring of DVB

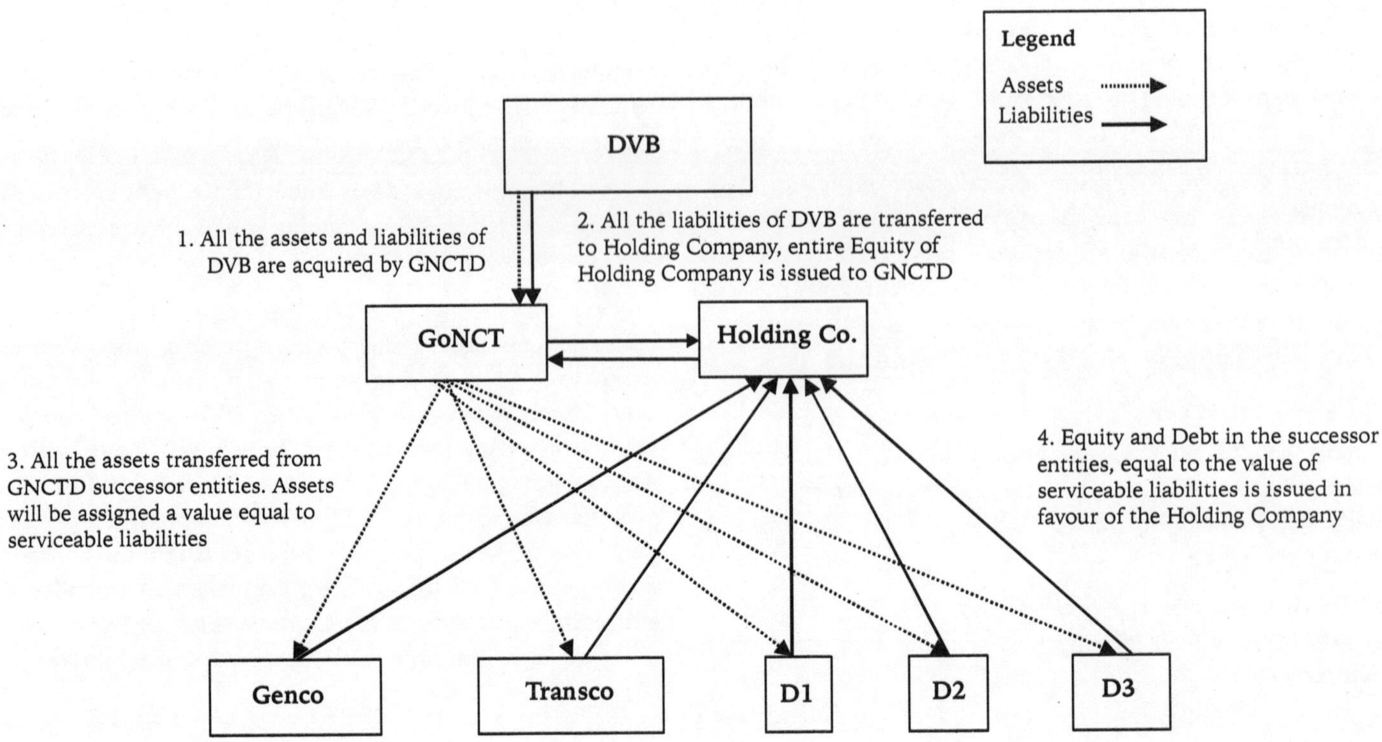

12. which GNCTD had the power to do under DERA.

4.2.4. *The Bidding Process and Completion of Restructuring*

The statutory Policy Directions and the Delhi Electricity Reform (Transfer Scheme) Rules were issued in November 2001. By this time only four eligible bidders, of the six who had been short listed, were still interested. These now began their due diligence. Meanwhile DVB applied to DERC for the bulk supply tariff for sale of power by Transco to the Discoms, and the opening loss levels. The bulk supply tariff had to be fixed retaining the existing retail tariff, but involved examining distribution level expenses in order to differentiate the tariff for sale to each Discom.[13] The Bulk Supply Tariff order with opening loss levels was issued by DERC on 22nd February 2002[14] after which minimum AT&C loss level reduction targets were fixed for the bidding. The minimum bidding targets fixed by GNCTD for each were as shown in Table 4.13.

TABLE 4.13

AT&C Loss Reduction Targets for Bidding

(In Per cent)

	2002-03	*2003-04*	*2004-05*	*2005-06*	*2006-07*
Central East*	1.50	5.00	5.00	5.00	4.25
South West**	1.25	5.00	4.50	4.50	4.00
North Northwest**	1.50	5.00	4.50	4.25	4.00

Notes: * Later renamed BSES Yamuna Power Ltd. (BYPL).
** Later renamed BSES Rajdhani Power Ltd. (BRPL).
*** Later renamed North Delhi Power Ltd. (NDPL)

Source: Delhi Vidyut Board/Delhi Transco Limited.

However only two investors, BSES and the Tata Power Company, submitted bids, and their bids were well below these targets, giving a five-year loss reduction of only 13-14 per cent. One concern was that DERC had fixed the opening loss levels at about 3 per cent below those submitted by DVB; DERC's estimates assumed that certain efficiency improvements would take place by 31 March while DVB's, being based on the actual trends, were considered more credible. Secondly, with BSES losing heavily in Orissa the bidders appeared to have lost faith in their ability to reduce losses. Thirdly, the absence of much competition would presumably have influenced the bidding.

Prolonged and difficult negotiations followed.[15] From the Government side the efficiency improvements had to be sufficient to turn the sector round within five years, otherwise privatisation would not be worthwhile. Eventually the targets shown in Table 4.14 were accepted.

TABLE 4.14

AT&C Loss Reduction Targets Accepted

(In Per cent)

	2002-03	*2003-04*	*2004-05*	*2005-06*	*2006-07*
Central East	0.75	1.75	4.00	5.65	5.10
South West	0.55	1.55	3.30	6.00	5.60
North Northwest	0.50	2.25	4.50	5.50	4.25

Source: Delhi Vidyut Board/Delhi Transco Limited.

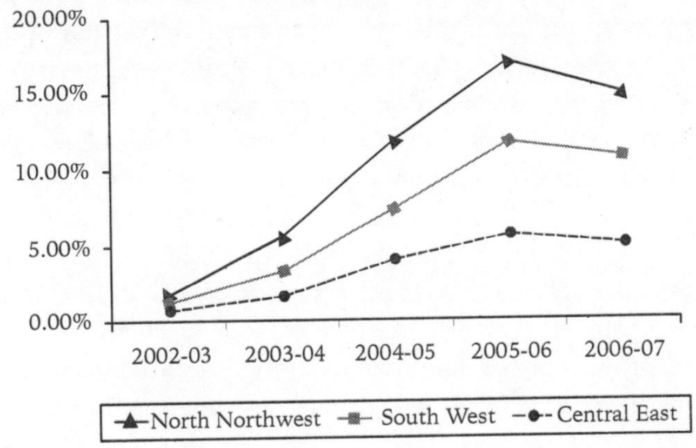

The amount of Government assistance necessary was therefore recalculated at about Rs.3450 crore, as in Table 4.15.

TABLE 4.15

Transitional Assistance Committed

(Rs. Crore)

2002-03	*2003-04*	*2004-05*	*2005-06*	*2006-07*
1364	1260	690	138	0

Source: Delhi Vidyut Board/Delhi Transco Limited.

Some other changes were also incorporated at this time, the most notable being that the period of moratorium of loans was increased from three years to four years.

4.2.5 *Discussion of the Delhi Reforms*

We may briefly take stock of the Delhi reform package and its lessons:

---

13. Since the retail tariff was to be kept uniform for the transitional period of five years.
14. The opening loss levels fixed by DERC were 57.2 per cent for one of the Discoms and 48.1 per cent for the other two; 50.7 per cent overall.
15. The negotiations were with the best bidder, in accordance with the Central Vigilance Commission guidelines, i.e. with BSES for Central-East and South-West and with TPC for North-Northwest.

Political motivation not necessarily replicable: Unlike those in many states, the reforms were not driven by any compelling necessity for the Government to obtain external assistance to extricate itself from financial difficulties, or under any external pressures from lending agencies or the Central government. While DVB was losing heavily with no prospect of a turnaround, the operational problem in terms of actual cash outflow was not unmanageable for the Delhi Government. What drove the reforms was the political decision that privatisation was the best route for improving the service on a sustainable basis and would prove popular. This combination of circumstances is not necessarily replicable.

Accurate measurement of commercial efficiency: The AT&C loss concept as the measure of commercial efficiency was a Delhi innovation. The Ministry of Power has now adopted it for distribution reform generally. However, even this calculation remains uncertain where there is continuing uncertainty about the number of units actually billed, since the figure must be derived either by dividing the number of units input by the actual billing rate or by correcting the T&D loss figure by the collection inefficiency; therefore it is not foolproof in states with a large proportion of unmetered billing. A tidier solution might be simply to go by revenue per unit input, setting utility-specific targets. The theoretical criticism of such a criterion is that it would motivate the utility to discriminate against less remunerative consumers, but it is suggested that this is a manageable risk: firstly it already happens—even SEBs discriminate by focused shedding on loss-making areas when they can—and, secondly, the political system (now supported, on this point, by the regulatory system) will not let it happen beyond a point. The real gain from the Delhi experience has perhaps been not merely the AT&C loss concept but the concern, lacking in the past, that commercial efficiency should be depicted accurately.

Success in addressing personnel issues: Delhi, alone among the states that had unbundled until then, saw no disruption of supply on account of the reforms. This shows the importance of political support: employee leaders understood that the reforms were popular with the public and, therefore, wisely focused on protecting the interests of staff within the reform process.

But this was achieved at the cost of guaranteeing existing staff against retrenchment, which is feasible in this (electricity distribution) business but may not be elsewhere. Personnel accounted for a little over 10 per cent of DVB's expenses; this was not an insignificant figure, being Rs. 429.6 crore during FY 2002 whilst BSES, serving about two million consumers in Bombay as an integrated utility, had only about 3500 employees in March 2002, who accounted for less than 5 per cent of its expenses. However, reducing staff costs would not be a crucial factor to turn the distribution business around. Firstly the importance of reducing commercial losses puts all other possible savings into the shade. Secondly, DVB had an ageing work force and a high rate of superannuation; to that extent, the problem would solve itself with time. Finally, expenses on the existing employees would normally be treated as a pass-through.

Financial savings: The Government is already a beneficiary of the reforms, since with the phasing out of transitional assistance its commitment of Plan funds to the power sector has dropped significantly, freeing resources for other purposes. The annual savings to Government have been estimated by the Delhi Government to be of the order of Rs. 1400 crores, which is conservative if anything. The elements of saving to the Government are as follows, based on the approximate level of Government expenditure on each item below during the last year of DVB (which would have continued to increase annually in each case):

- Saving of Plan expenditure on the Distribution sector (which was loan, but never actually repaid and not expected to be repaid in practice): Rs. 500 crores.
- Saving of non-Plan loan to DVB (which was actually just a loan to repay the interest annually on DVB's mounting debt to the Delhi Government, which was growing exponentially): Rs. 400 crores.
- Saving of deduction by the Central government (for payment to Central Utilities) of Delhi's Central Plan share—this was about Rs. 300 crores.
- Saving of non-plan temporary cash loans that had to be given to DVB from time to time to keep it afloat when it faced a serious payment crisis. This varied considerably, but based on the experience of DVB's last couple of years, may safely be estimated at Rs. 100 crores on the average.

The above gains do not take into account the savings to consumers (through the AT&C loss reductions achieved) of costs which would otherwise have been a burden on the tariff. These were estimated for 2004-05, by the Prayas Energy Group, Pune, a highly respected independent NGO, at Rs. 880 crore; their estimate is cited because none was made by DERC during the first three years of the five-year transition period. For 2005-06, DERC estimated the incremental savings to consumers at Rs. 252 crore, which would give a total of about 1130 crores; we have no estimate for the subsequent period, but from the further loss reductions to date it may be expected that the savings would have increased significantly (though at a lower incremental rate).

The expenditure on transitional assistance and also on the limited other subsidies given by the Delhi Government during a couple of the post-privatisation years pales into insignificance against the permanent gains of privatisation, which will continue to grow with each passing year for at least another five years. Since the unbundling of DVB and privatisation of its distribution business were conceived primarily as a financial restructuring package, it seems unfortunate that the whole process has tended to be judged on other considerations.

Need for multi-year tariff package—inadequacy of Delhi package: A basic issue that the reforms package in Delhi sought to address was that of regulatory uncertainty. Tariffs, expected improvement of commercial efficiency, and transitional finance are the three crucial inter-related issues in any distribution privatisation from a situation of high opening losses. The solution adopted in Delhi (fixing only the loss reduction targets in advance) arose from the circumstance that multi-year tariffs were not feasible at the time. The unorthodox bid procedure adopted (which has been described above) was the answer found to the problem of target setting at the time. Further, this package was made possible because of GNCTD's willingness and ability to provide transitional finance, without which the tariff would initially have had to be increased very sharply.

The concept of a multi-year tariff package has now been adopted as one of the guiding principles to be followed by regulatory commissions under section 61(f) of the Electricity Act, 2003—but it was not accepted in Delhi when it was needed. The solution found appeared to solve the problem at the time but now, in the light of subsequent experience, appears to have been insufficient: regulatory issues have since arisen (which will be referred to Section 4.4) that should preferably have been resolved upfront through a more comprehensive multi-year package such as the one DVB had suggested in early 2001. This, certainly, is a lesson for any future distribution privatisations.

Fortunately, DERC is now engaged in a process of finalising a multi-year tariff for Delhi; but unfortunately the whole exercise is, at the time of writing, a good six months behind what ought to have been the schedule (i.e., it should have been operative from April 2007) and there is no prospect of the new multi-year tariff having any genuine impact on the performance of the sector during the first post-transitional year (2007-08).

Changed context after enactment of Electricity Act, 2003: The Delhi reforms took place before enactment of the Electricity Act, 2003. Taking over the distribution business of an SEB is hardly an exciting prospect for investors, but at the time the leading Indian companies had every reason to suppose that this was the best—probably the only way to turn the power sector round and create future investment opportunities in generation and transmission for the private sector. Now, the new Act envisages a market-driven industry structure that (whatever else it may so far have achieved) has apparently changed investor perceptions. The fact that bypass has become (at least in principle) an option available both through the open access route and through the possibility of multiple distribution licenses (and, to some extent, through the liberalised definition of captive power) there has been even less investor interest in taking over State-owned distribution utilities with their legacy managerial problems; but it remains to be seen whether the new possibilities of bypass that have been created (at least in theory) do actually lead to any market-driven turnaround of the sector—as might have been expected, all the evidence so far is to the contrary.

Delhi's value as a model: The extent to which the Delhi reforms succeed in their commercial and quality-of-service objectives, and the extent to which they are perceived to have done so in comparison with the performance of other states in the region, will also determine their value as a model. In terms of commercial performance, the reforms are broadly on track, though two of the three Discoms have belied expectations by failing to overachieve the loss reduction targets, despite a strong financial incentive to do so. There have also been gains in the quality of service, but not to the point where consumers express wide satisfaction. The absence of a five-year tariff and the controversies over tariff cast a shadow over the reforms during the first five years; DERC's performance has also been criticised by independent agencies. What still casts a shadow over the whole matter, however, is the controversy generated by a recent order of the Delhi

High Court, which at the time of writing has been stayed by the Supreme Court.[16]

4.3 Current State of the Sector

4.3.1 Successor Entities to DVB

The entities operating in the power sector in Delhi, following the restructuring of the sector that came into effect from July 1, 2002, are as follows:

• *Delhi Power Supply Company Limited (DPCL).* This company, the 'Holding Company' of the Transfer Scheme,[17] is 100 per cent owned by the Government of the NCT of Delhi and, in turn, holds 100 per cent of the equity of the Indraprastha Power Generation Company Ltd (IPGCL) and Delhi Transco Ltd. (DTL); it holds 49 per cent of the equity of the three distribution companies and is represented on their Boards. It should be noted that DPCL is not a licensee under the Delhi Electricity Reforms Act 2000 or the Electricity Act, 2003, and is not subject to any direct regulation by the Delhi Electricity Regulatory Commission.

• *Generating Companies:* These are not licensed and regulated entities under the Electricity Act, 2003, which has freed the thermal generating sector entirely from licensing. However Transco's power purchases are subject to regulatory approval and, therefore, DERC does examine their performance and their revenue requirements in the course of its annual exercise of approving the price at which Transco purchases power from these companies.

• *Indraprastha Power Generation Company Ltd. (IPGCL).* This is the 'Genco' of the Transfer Scheme,[18] i.e., the company formed out of the generating wing of DVB. It operates three power stations, viz., the old and outdated Indraprastha Power Station and the Rajghat Power House (both coal-based thermal stations), and the Gas Turbine Power Station (GTPS). IPGCL's generating plants have not performed very well, though showing some improvement in the last few years, as table 4.16 shows:

TABLE 4.16

Plant Load Factor

(Per cent)

	2000-01	*2001-02*	*2002-03*	*2003-04*	*2004-05*
I.P.STN.	39.88	37.49	28.65	35.38	45.45
RPH	66.85	59.52	71.68	65.25	58.96
GTPS	49.07	49.55	49.14	49.03	62.32

Source: Delhi Vidyut Board/Delhi Transco Limited.

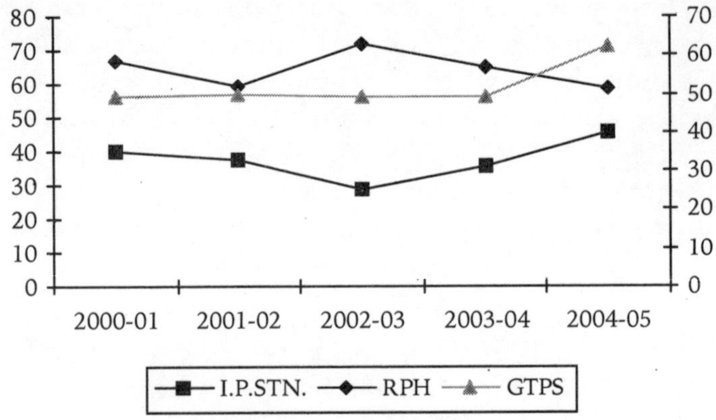

The main issues affecting the performance of IPGCL's plants may be mentioned:

- The Indraprastha Power Station is old and outdated. One of its units has been shut down. The future use of this site, *viz.*, whether for continuing the present unit after R&M or replacing it with a new plant, is under consideration.
- The performance of GTPS has been affected by two important factors. Firstly, the performance of the retrofitted Waste Heat Recovery Units has never been satisfactory; this has been an ongoing issue between the utility and the supplier (BHEL); secondly, gas allocation sufficient to run all its units has not been continuously available.

The Delhi Government has recently decided to close down the existing units of the I.P. Power Station, in the context of its poor performance, environmental concerns, and the new projects that are discussed below.

16. Order dated 7.2.07 in CWP No. 2705/2002. The Court held that the Policy Directions were unlawful and directed the Government to take steps to expedite the tabling by the Secretariat of the Delhi Assembly of the Action Taken Report submitted in reply to a highly controversial PAC report; in fact the report had been submitted long ago, but not tabled by the Secretariat for reasons which can only be speculated upon. The PAC report had, inconsistently with the report of the CAG, and after introducing numerous factual inaccuracies, questioned the motivation of the whole process and called for a CBI enquiry against the officers involved in it. The author of this chapter, who admittedly was one of those who were personally involved in the reform process, believes that the order of the Hon'ble High Court (currently stayed by the Supreme Court) is erroneous on numerous counts, and also that the Court may have taken a different view of the matter if the whole factual position had been more effectively represented to it by those who had actually been involved in the process. Unfortunately the officers concerned, who were also likely to suffer reputational damage by the publicity generated around these proceedings before the Court, were not involved in the matter and were not asked to make any submissions regarding what were, in effect, charges against them. The same applies to the proceedings before the PAC which, in any case, were necessarily political in character. The real damage has been to the cause of power sector reform and to objective assessment of the outcome of the reforms in Delhi.

17. See Figure 4.8.

18. See Figure 4.8.

• **Pragati Power Corporation Ltd. (PPCL):** The Pragati Power Project was kept formally distinct from the DVB, and registered as a separate company, primarily in order make its financing viable. The equity is wholly owned by the Delhi Government. PPCL achieved a load factor of 88.28 in 2004-05.

The combined generation and performance of these stations, shown in Figure 4.8, has been improving but clearly needs to improve further:

FIGURE 4.8

Delhi Generation Performance

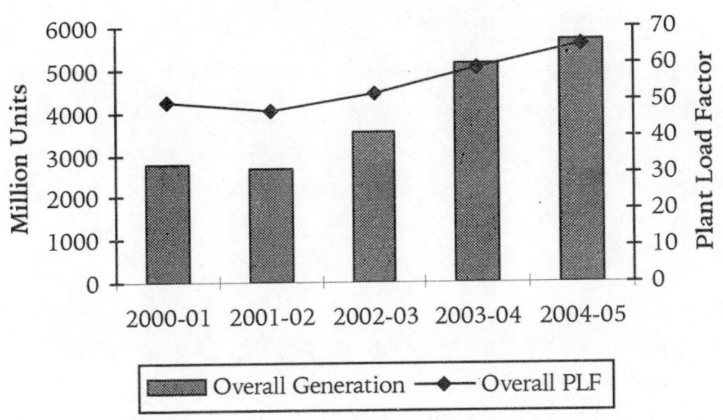

• **Delhi Transco Ltd. (Transco):** This is the company created to take over the transmission business of the erstwhile DVB. As such it is also responsible for grid management, being the State Transmission Utility (STU) under the Electricity Act, 2003; the State Load Dispatch Centre (SLDC) functions within Transco.

Further, Transco took over DVB's power procurement functions and sold power to the Discoms during the five-year transitional period ending in March 2007. This is no longer the case, and the Discoms are directly responsible for power procurement, but a Power Procurement Group has been established by the Government for purposes of coordination. The Government's transitional support was funnelled to the consumer by means of reducing the Bulk Supply Tariff at which Transco sells to the Discoms. Even during the transitional period, there was no bar in principle on the Discoms' directly purchasing power from sources they might identify and pay wheeling charges to Transco for the use of its system, but this did not happen, nor was it likely to happen, as long as Transco's Bulk Supply Tariff remains cheaper than the possible alternatives.

In fact, the third proviso to section 41 of the new Act debars transmission licensees from the business of trading in electricity; the first proviso to section 14 envisages a one-year transition period[19] but the Delhi Government was able to take the shelter of section 185(2)(e) which saved the Policy Directions issued under DERA, thus securing an extension of the transitional arrangement until the end of March 2007.

After considerable delay, and consequent past uncertainty, the Delhi Government has now finalised and implemented an appropriate trading structure. Transco no longer trades power, trading and procurement responsibilities now devolving upon the distribution companies, in terms of the provisions of the Electricity Act 2003, with effect from 1st April 2007. Now the responsibility for arranging supply of power in NCT of Delhi has been vested with the distribution companies in accordance with the provisions of the Electricity Act, 2003 and the National Electricity Policy. The Delhi Electricity Regulatory Commission has accordingly approved the assignment of the existing Power Purchase Agreements (PPAs) to the three private distribution companies in the proportion of energy drawn in 2006-07.

• **Distribution Licensees:** Most of Delhi is served by the three discoms carved out of DVB's distribution business. In addition, the New Delhi Municipal Council and the Cantonment Board are statutory licensees under their own laws; with the enactment of the Electricity Act, 2003 they have been brought under the regulatory jurisdiction of DERC.[20] The three discoms are as follows:

• **BSES Rajdhani Power Ltd. (BRPL).** This comprises what were earlier the South and West circles of DVB. It has about 8.69 lakh registered consumers. While the BSES label has been retained for the time being, the controlling interest in this discom is held by Reliance Energy Limited.

• **BSES Yamuna Power Ltd. (BYPL).** This is the second discom controlled by Reliance Energy Limited; comprises what were earlier the East and Central circles of DVB. These are among the most challenging areas to serve, and this was the discom with the highest opening AT&C loss level (57 per cent according to DERC). East Delhi includes a disproportionately large (even for Delhi) proportion of unauthorised development. Central Circle includes the most congested areas in Delhi, where capacity augmentation has to be made within the context of severe space constraints and right-of-way difficulties. This discom has about 8.49 lakh registered consumers.

19. The Act came into force on June 10, 2003.

20. The provisions of DERA did not apply to the NDMC and Cantonment areas and, as the Commission (originally constituted under the Electricity Regulatory Commissions Act, 1998) was brought under DERA, it did not exercise jurisdiction in these areas until the Electricity Act, 2003 came into force.

• **North Delhi Power Limited (NDPL).** This discom, comprising the former North and North-West circles of DVB, is controlled by the Tata Power Company and, thus, provides benchmarking competition. It serves about 8.54 lakh registered consumers.

• **Statutory licensees:** NDMC within its area and the Military Engineering Services (MES) within the Cantonment are statutory licensees under their own constitutive laws and are subject to DERC regulation as deemed licensees. Under DERA, DERC's jurisdiction did not extend to the areas of operation of these two utilities, but (as it had to consider DVB's ARR) it did fix the bulk supply tariff for DVB's supplies to them by an order dated May 31, 2002, which has yet to be revised. After the coming into force of the Electricity Act, 2003, DERC's jurisdiction extends to the whole of Delhi, and NDMC has begun to submit annual ARRs to DERC; there has been no change in its tariff. NDMC's peak load is about 270 MW and its annual consumption is about 1100 MU with over a lakh of consumers; MES's peak load is about 25-30 MW and its annual consumption about 160 MU. These are both small, efficient utilities which have not hitherto been regarded as problematic in any way, but which will now have to modernise some of their operations to comply with DERC-imposed norms, including the Billing and Metering Regulations.

4.3.2 Sourcing of Power

We may briefly consider the main factors impacting Delhi's power procurement strategy, in the context of the situation described in Section 4.1 above. Firstly, there is a continuing need to source significantly more power from year to year, merely to keep up with the steady growth in load demand. Secondly, the proportion of local generation is low; it would be very desirable to have a larger proportion of local generation in the interests of reliability and quality of supply. Thirdly, the pattern of consumption, with its steep variation between peak and off-peak requirements, impacts both investment and procurement decisions. Any decision to invest in dedicated generation has to take into account its implications for capacity utilisation; the same applies to power procurement when it is round-the-clock supply that is on offer. Finally, it is difficult to be completely self-sufficient in the context of grid and transmission constraints: even with sufficient power contracted for, it may become necessary to shed in order to maintain grid frequency, and the ability to contract for surplus power from other regions depends on the availability of transmission capacity for the purpose.

Delhi's average power purchase costs at the rates approved by DERC were Rs. 2.10 per unit in 2004-05 and Rs. 2.13 per unit in 2005-06. This was costlier than other states in the region which source more of their power from their own old thermal plants and/or hydro-electric plants. Delhi's cheapest source was the Central Generating Stations, (Rs. 1.87) and its costliest was power sourced through PTC and other trading companies (Rs. 3.61).

4.3.2.1 Core Generation

The generation capacity dedicated to Delhi and available within the National Capital Region (NCR) includes (i) the plants belonging to IPGCL and PPCL, which have been discussed in section 1.3.1 above; (ii) the Badarpur Thermal Power Station (BTPS) which belongs to the Government of India (Ministry of Power) but which is operated by NTPC under a management contract; and (iii) NTPC's own Dadri Thermal Station, 90 per cent of the capacity of which is dedicated to Delhi. It is obviously desirable to enhance Delhi's core generation capacity, for better reliability and quality of supply. About 60 per cent of Delhi's power sources fall within this category; ideally, it should be closer to 80 per cent. Certain decisions have been reported by the Delhi Government.

The Government of Delhi has approved a 1500 MW gas-based plant at Bawana and a 750 MW gas-based plant at Bamnauli. It also plans to enter into a joint venture with the Haryana Government for a 1500 MW Super Thermal project at Jhajjar, in Haryana, in which Delhi's share would be 750 MW. These plants are intended to be ready by the end of the 11th Plan, thus incidentally in time for the forthcoming Commonwealth Games in Delhi.

In the new, increasingly market-oriented character of the power sector in India, and given Delhi's peculiar demand pattern (described above) there may be some degree of long-term market risk in establishing capacity dedicated to Delhi. There is also a case for not making heavy public investments in the power sector in Delhi, at the cost of other sectors, since a fundamental objective of the reforms was to make the sector self-sustaining and IPGCL's principal customers in future will be the privately managed Discoms. The optimal solution for new projects, therefore, appears to be to identify a private investor through a transparent tariff-based bidding process in accordance with the guidelines recently issued by the Central government, with some equity issued to the Government in exchange for its contribution of the site. This will be possible if the Delhi Electricity Regulatory Commission is able to agree to the bidding process in advance, in order to give potential investors the necessary comfort regarding market risk.

It is understood that the Delhi Government is likely to adopt such an approach, of partnership with a private investor, for the Bawana and Bamnauli projects.

One further issue on which no current information appears to be available, is that of the future utilisation of the IP Station site; to consider further gas-based generation here would certainly be very cost-effective.

4.3.2.2 Non-Conventional Sources of Energy

There is limited scope for the use of non-conventional energy sources in a metropolitan city like Delhi. Firstly, the scale of the requirement is too large, and it becomes improbable that non-conventional sources can meet even a noticeable, much less a significant portion of it. Secondly, most non-conventional sources are still costly, and become economically viable where the cost of extending the grid is still costlier, as in remote areas, whereas in large cities the network costs per capita are much lower because of the high density. One possible urban source, *viz.*, generation from municipal waste, is justifiable because of the synergy it creates between these two areas of urban management, but it is unlikely to be a significant source of power generation in Delhi and, despite many proposals and the erection with foreign aid of a plant for the purpose,[21] there has been no headway in this kind of generation so far.

However, Regulatory Commissions are now bound, under section 61(h) of the Electricity Act, 2003 to promote the generation of electricity from renewable sources. In many countries the viable means of doing this has been to require utilities to purchase a certain proportion of their electricity supplies from renewable sources, and it is likely that in future the Ministry of Power will lay down policies under Section 3 of the same Act which will require this. Such an explicit policy alone will enable utilities to source some of their electricity supply from renewable sources without apprehensions about regulatory approval of the cost. Unless this happens, procurement by utilities from renewable sources (other than large and medium hydro plants) seems improbable.

4.3.2.3 Energy Conservation and Demand Side Management

At the present stage, it is difficult to set targets for conservation and supply-side management in quantitative terms; visions of the reduction that might be achieved if (say) all the incandescent bulbs in Delhi were converted to CSFL, and the like, may be facile, yet the potential is enormous. Energy conservation requires a combination of consumer education and incentivisation. The following are among the issues and measures envisaged:

- Energy Audit of Government buildings, to be followed up by appropriate conservation measures, possibly with the assistance of ESCOs. A beginning in energy audit of Government buildings was made in 2003, but needs to be followed through.
- By-laws should promote energy efficient building design, particularly in multi-storey buildings (e.g. by requiring double-glazed windows in all centrally air-conditioned buildings, etc.)
- Delhi was the first State/UT to introduce kVAh billing for bulk consumers, to motivate them to maintain the power factor, and it is DERC's policy to gradually expand the coverage of consumers under kVAh billing. The current (FY 2006) tariff specifies the tariff for non-domestic and industrial consumers at LT level above 10kw in both kwh and kVAh terms, the former continuing to be applicable wherever meters supporting the latter are yet to be installed.
- A further possible regulatory step to flatten the load curve would be the application of TOD (time of day) tariff. DERC has expressed its intention to collect data to assess the implications and then publish a discussion paper on the subject.

The Government has taken steps under the Energy Conservation Act, 2001, issuing notifications as follows:

- Making use of solar water heating in hotels and in certain public buildings compulsory.
- Incentivising domestic use of solar water heating by subsidies.
- Making the use of ISI marked equipment for pumps, capacitors and certain other equipment.
- Mandatory use of CFL bulbs and electronic chokes in public buildings.
- Modernisation of the street lighting system.
- Promoting Time of Day Metering in collaboration with TERI.

---

21. A plant set up at Timarpur in the 1980s never functioned because it was designed to European standards of solid waste, which has higher calorific value; in developing countries the solid waste has less calorific value because people discard fewer combustible items and rag pickers retrieve much of what does get discarded. Proposals to revive the plant have been mooted from time to time, but have not borne fruit.

4.3.3 Transmission System

The planning norms standardised by CEA stipulate that the transformation capacity at a 400 KV S/stn. should not normally exceed 1000MVA and 320 MVA at 220KV substations. Further, the size and number of inter-connecting transformers (ICTs) should be planned in such a way that the outage of any single unit would not overload the remaining ICT(s) or the underlying system.

Delhi Transco Limited has been able to sufficiently enhance and improve the transmission system to meet foreseeable capacity requirements.

4.3.4 Distribution System

Delhi has an extensive distribution system which has to be continually augmented to meet the annual increase in load, to cover hitherto unelectrified unauthorised colonies and *jhuggie basties*, and to improve the service by providing appropriate redundancies. This is partly reflected in the increasing number of distribution transformers as shown in Table 4.3 and Table 4.19. The quality of supply and the commercial performance of the new distribution utilities are discussed separately. The capital expenditure (capex) programmes of the Discoms are discussed below.

Discom capital expenditure for the earlier post-reform period, as approved by DERC for inclusion in the ARR subject to some further compliances and consequent adjustments, is shown in Table 4.17. NDPL has a five-year capital investment plan (2002-03 to 2007-08) of Rs. 14461 crore[22] of which capital expenditure of Rs. 336 crores had been incurred by the end of 2003-04. DERC has expressed little difficulty in approving this Discom's capex programmes, which is not the case with the two BSES Discoms. BRPL had proposed Rs. 800 crores for 2004-05 and as much as Rs. 1400 crores for 2005-06, and now claimed to have spent Rs. 911.07 crores during the former year. BYPL had proposed Rs. 700 crores for 2004-2005 (but spent only Rs. 417.81 crores) and proposed Rs. 1165 crores for 2005-06. DERC was not satisfied with the details of expenditure submitted to it, which apparently included schemes DERC had not approved, while the proportion of capitalisation was low and inventories had grown enormously (both of which suggest non-implementation). Exaggerated claims for capital expenditure, which would potentially have tariff implications and yet are not justified by improvements in service quality or efficiency that seem commensurate (taking NDPL as a benchmark) would tend to affect credibility.

TABLE 4.17

Capital Investment in Distribution System

(Rs. Crore)

	2004-05		*2005-06*	
	Petition	*DERC*	*Petition*	*DERC*
NDPL	303.26	328.42	361.11	361.11
BRPL	800.00	525.82	1400.01	477.00
BYPL	681.61	405.25	1165.00	426.00

Source: Delhi Vidyut Board/Delhi Transco Limited.

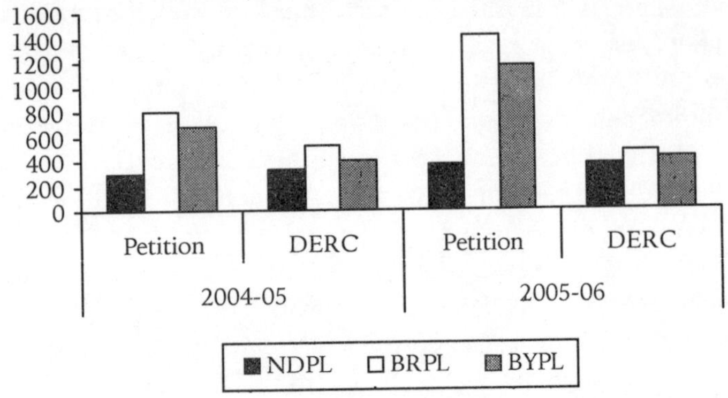

However, these issues are no longer so live, and (whatever the cost issues) it is not seriously now disputed that the distribution system has seen very significant improvement, and that the real problem for Delhi is now power procurement rather than distribution bottlenecks.

4.3.5 Quality of Service

A holistic picture of the progress being made is provided by the State-wise ratings of power sector performance made for the Ministry of Power by CRISIL and ICRA. These assign scores to States/Union Territories on the basis of six groups of parameters, the State Government related; State Electricity Regulatory Commission (SERC) related; Business Risk Analysis; Financial Risk Analysis; progress in attaining commercial viability; and an 'others' category that includes the quality of information systems, availability of audited accounts and extent of computerisation of commercial operations. Delhi was ranked third, after Andhra Pradesh and Gujarat—something that certainly could never have been expected in the days of DESU and DVB. However some questions can be raised about the adequacy of information relied on and the validity of the methodology adopted.[23] The most important outcome should be better levels of consumer satisfaction, as a result of palpable

22. Revised figure; earlier Rs. 1248 crore.

23. To cite just one simple example, the only measure adopted to judge technical performance at the distribution level is the rate of transformer burnout.

improvement in the quality of service both in terms of quality of supply and of user-friendly commercial operations. We may consider the evidence available regarding these parameters so far.

Quality of Supply: The quality of supply that consumers get is a function of the performance of the sector as a whole, *viz.*, the generation and sourcing of power, its transmission and its delivery to the end user through the distribution system. So far as the sourcing of power is concerned, a major gain is the fact that since the unbundling Delhi's suppliers have received full and timely payment for the first time in decades.

One broad indicator of continuity of supply is simply the number of units shed in relation to the total requirement. The information contained in Table 4.2 above shows a steady improvement in this parameter after the restructuring. These figures include shedding at the 33 KV level and above; they do not reflect shedding at the distribution levels; though they are a useful rough guide since, in terms of actual consumer-hours lost, the latter would amount proportionately to very little.

TABLE 4.18

Shedding: All Causes, in Million Units (MU)

		April	*May*	*June*
1999	Supplied	1554.6	1534.0	1505.9
	Shed	21.8	31.2	46.5
	Total	1576.4	1565.2	1552.4
	Shed (%)	*1.4*	*2.0*	*3.0*
2007	Supplied	1915.0	2149.9	2246.7
	Shed	6.8	3.8	5.0
	Total	1921.8	2153.7	2251.7
	Shed (%)	*0.4*	*0.2*	*0.2*

Source: Delhi Vidyut Board/Delhi Transco Limited.

Frequency is a grid-level parameter and shedding on account of under frequency is not within the control of Transco, nor are general grid restrictions. The impact of these factors is, in any case, of relatively less significance. The main improvement that has taken place is clearly because of better performance of the transmission and distribution utilities, reflecting the capacity augmentation and system upgradation that has been taking place.

We have referred in Table 4.3 to the rate of distribution transformer failure as a rough indicator of the adequacy of the distribution system's capacity. Here, there has been a really notable improvement after privatisation (Table 4.19):

TABLE 4.19

Failure of Distribution Transformers after Privatisation (All Discoms)

	No. of Transformers (11 KV)	*Number of Failures*	*Failure (%)*
2003-04	13814	533	3.86
2004-05 (1st half)	15934	100	0.63
2004-05 (annualised)	15934	200	1.26

Source: ARR submissions by Discoms to DERC.

Another source of information is consumer surveys conducted by IMRB; these were done with representative samples of about 4500 respondents drawn from different occupation and gender groups and from different parts of the city. The first was commissioned by DVB and conducted shortly before unbundling, in May 2002; the next two were committed by DPCL in May 2003 and October 2003. The dissatisfaction rate reported in these three surveys fell successively from 81 per cent to 61 per cent to 39 per cent. Subsequent information is not available. DERC has commissioned a survey in 2007 and, according to media reports, it shows a significant improvement in consumer satisfaction. However, the results have not been officially publicised.

The standard consumer-based parameters of SAIDI (System Average Interruption Duration Index) and SAIFI (System Average Interruption Frequency Index) would provide a sound basis for comparing the performance of distribution utilities and for measuring improvement or deterioration in the service, but are not yet systematically monitored in our country. According to information obtained, pertaining to NDPL, the present SAIDI is 24.7 hours against the targeted level of 2 hours while the SAIFI is 13 as against the target of 1.3.[24] These figures are not, however, confirmed by DERC or any independent third party.

The Central Electricity Authority has started to issue reports rating utilities on the basis of reports obtained from them regarding the average number and duration of incidents of tripping per feeder per month. For example in November 2004 the average number of trippings per feeder varied from 0.08 in Calcutta to 8.88 in Tamil Nadu. NDPL (0.86), BSES Rajdhani (3.32) and BSES Yamuna (4.21) ranked respectively 6th, 13th and 16th among twenty

24. The targeted levels stated are the current U.S. levels.

utilities reported on in that month. In outage duration per feeder NDPL and BSES Rajdhani were at the bottom of the list with an average outage duration per feeder of 269.35 and 381.75 minutes respectively, comparing poorly with 4.26 minutes in the part of Bombay served by Reliance Energy (formerly BSES). However, this information is available so far only for a few months and the ranking of utilities seems to get reshuffled a great deal every month. The data is apparently sourced from the utilities themselves. Hence it may be difficult to draw too many firm conclusions from it.

It is clear from the above that Delhi still has a long way to go to achieve the best Indian, much less international, standards in the quality of supply, but this should not obscure the fact that there has been some very significant improvement.

Consumer-friendly commercial operations: When considering the extent to which commercial operations have become more efficient and consumer-friendly, it is difficult to quantify the level of real consumer satisfaction and much of the evidence is anecdotal or based on media reporting. However, both companies have been replacing the old electromechanical meters with electronic ones and have introduced new billing systems.[25] Remote metering of HT consumers has been introduced. There were complaints, which at one point received a great deal of media publicity, that the new meters ran fast; this is partly because the old ones ran slow: old electromechanical meters do slow down and over half of DVB's meter population was more than ten years old. The complaints were not confirmed by either DERC's monitoring nor by the High Court in its findings; rather, they were disproved.

The impression existed that NDPL had been more successful initially; it was ahead in going on-line and enabling its consumers to access their billing history, pay their bills and get grievances resolved over the internet, it was ahead in introducing pre-paid metering experimentally in some areas, and generally it had a much better press than the other two Discoms. This general impression would also be consistent with NDPL's greatly superior performance in reducing AT&C losses. However with the introduction of new systems by all the Discoms, and with the regulatory interventions that have been taking place, it would appear that over time the commercial operations have stabilised, and are certainly more modern and consumer-friendly than in the days of DESU/DVB. A heartening report, that may be cited in conclusion is the finding of Transparency International that consumers in Delhi, unlike those in other States, no longer face corruption as a problem in dealing with their distribution utility.[26]

4.4 Implementation of the Reform Package and Prospects of Achieving Financial Viability

4.4.1 Implications of the Reform Package

The relevant elements of the reform package and the concomitant apportionment of risks and rewards may (at the cost of a little repetition) be summarised as follows:

1. The loss reduction targets for five years were fixed through the bidding process. The Discoms bore the entire risk if they underachieved these targets and get half the benefit of overachievement beyond the original minimum levels fixed by the Government before inviting bids.

2. The Discoms investors were entitled to a return of 16 per cent on the equity and free reserves each year, which the Regulatory Commission was bound to provide in the tariff. However the investors accepted full 'regulatory risk' except in respect of loss reduction targets and the related specific points stated in the Policy Directions. That is to say, it was entirely the investors' risk if the Regulatory Commission did not accept any expenses they may have incurred or were likely to incur, or did not provide for such expenses to their satisfaction, and it was entirely for them to bear the consequences; they might seek appellate remedies as provided in the relevant law, but had no claim against the Government in respect of any regulatory decisions. (It will be recalled that, as mentioned in Section 4.2 above, a comprehensive five-year tariff package was initially proposed but did not materialise; the investors knew this.)

3. In order to reduce the tariff impact of the reforms[27] by reducing the bulk supply tariff (at which Transco would sell power to the Discoms) the Government agreed to provide Transco with transitional assistance of about Rs. 3450 crores as

25. NDPL has successfully built upon a new online billing system that DVB had been developing and which was being tried out in a couple of districts at the time of unbundling; the BSES Discoms chose to develop their own system.

26. Reported in the *Hindustan Times*. The report as available at the Transparency International India website does not give utility-wise information but reports less corruption in privately managed distribution utilities generally.

27. Before the unbundling, the consumer did not bear the full cost of power supply (which itself was greatly inflated by DVB's inefficiency); this situation was reflected in DVB's annual losses and accumulating liabilities.

described above[28]. This was in the form of a loan, but the terms and conditions of repayment by Transco were to be settled later, after negotiations between Transco and the Govt.

4. The successor utilities to DVB (being the three Discoms, Transco and Genco) were to repay the Holding Company the debt they were created with,[29] amounting to Rs. 1896 crores[30] with interest at the rate of 12 per cent *per annum,* after an initial four-year moratorium.

5. The successor entities did not inherit DVB's unserviceable liabilities, nor its receivables. These remained with the Holding Company.[31]

6. As already brought out in Section 4.2 above, the modelling on which the business valuation had been done involved projections of future revenue based on the three elements of efficiency improvement, transitional support and tariff increases. The efficiency improvements committed by the Discom investors and the transitional assistance committed by the Government have been shown in Tables 4.14 and 4.15 respectively. The upward tariff revisions projected by the consultants are shown in Table 4.20.[32]

TABLE 4.20

Projected and Actual Tariff Increases

(Per cent)

	2002-03	*2003-04*	*2004-05*	*2005-06*	*2006-07*
Projected Tariff Increase	10	10	10	5	3
Actual Tariff Increase	0	5	10	6.6	0

Source: Delhi Vidyut Board/Delhi Transco Limited.

It was expected that by the end of this transitional period, the AT&C losses having come down very significantly, the tariff would stabilise and, probably, decline. It should be clearly understood that, while the figures of transitional assistance reflect a positive commitment by the Government, and the efficiency improvement targets a commitment made at their own risk by the investors, there was no commitment of any kind regarding the projected tariff increases. The latter were only projections made depending on many cost variables and were not binding on DERC, nor could the successor entities make any absolute claim based on them; though indeed DERC was expected to provide through the tariff for the utilities' reasonable costs, otherwise the 16 per cent return would be meaningless.

4.4.2 AT&C Loss Reduction

The reduction of losses and improvement of commercial efficiency was the main commercial objective of the reform package, making the sector viable and permanently benefiting consumers by reducing the actual cost of supply and eliminating a major source of upward pressure on tariffs. So far as this fundamental parameter is concerned, the reform process is a success at the end of the transitional period, as shown by Table 4.21.

TABLE 4.21

AT&C Loss Reduction

(Per cent)

	Original Level (As per DERC)	*Target Level (FY 02)*	*Actual Achievement As per Discoms (DERC finding awaited)*
NDPL	48.1	31.10	23.70
BRPL	48.1	31.10	29.92
BYPL	57.2	39.03	39.03

Source: Delhi Vidyut Board/Delhi Transco Limited.

4.4.3 Tariff Orders and Issues Arising

Of the three projected sources of additional cash flows to the distribution sector during the transitional period, *viz.*, efficiency improvements, transitional assistance and tariff revision, the first two occurred as planned—in fact the efficiency improvement targets have been exceeded. But this was not the case with tariff revision. During the period DERC adopted the questionable means of maintaining a "Regulatory Asset" rather than meeting the full cost of supply through the tariff, but was able to

28. This was a benefit to the consumers, not to the Discom investors, since the latter remained entitled only to their 16 per cent return and overachievement bonuses, and nothing else. This is obvious, but is stated again as there has been some ill-informed criticism alleging favouritism towards the Discoms through this arrangement.

29. See Figure 1.2.3.1.

30. The break us is Genco Rs 210 cr, Transco Rs 270 cr, BYPL Rs 174 cr, BRPL Rs 690 cr, NDPL Rs 552 cr.

31. Figure 1.2.3.1.

32. These were overall projections. No projections were made regarding the implications of cross-subsidy removal, which became mandatory only much later with the enactment of the Electricity Act 2003. The subsequent statutory requirement that cross-subsidy should be phased out does imply a greater relative burden of tariff increase on domestic consumers who have been the beneficiaries of cross-subsidy.

amortise the same because of the overachievement of loss reductions.

Bulk Supply Tariff: The Bulk Supply Tariff (i.e. Transco's price for supply to the distribution utilities) had necessarily to rise much more rapidly than the retail tariff, as the level of Government assistance decreased.

Regulatory Asset: DERC's justification for leaving massive and unprecedented 'regulatory assets' of nearly Rs. 700 crores in 2004-05 was that otherwise the tariff would have to go up sharply—a circumstance created by the inadequacy of the tariff increases in the previous years. The Commission's order did not hold out any specific timetable for amortisation of the regulatory asset, and the Discoms have filed a writ petition against it, alleging that it arbitrarily deprives them of the return of 16 per cent to which they are entitled under the Policy Directions. In its order for 2005-06, the Commission revised the regulatory assets on the basis of a 'truing up' exercise and partially amortised them on the basis of the additional revenue from overachievement of the loss reduction targets by each Discom—a salutary principle as it holds out the prospect of future tariff advantage for the consumers of a better-performing Discom.[33]

The Discoms have been able to obtain favourable appellate decisions, which however are of little practical import. The loss reduction has made it possible to amortise the regulatory asset fully.

Departures from Reform Package: Some of the decisions and observations contained in DERC's tariff orders are in conflict with the Transfer Scheme and Policy Directions, and potentially impose significant additional financial burdens on the Government. These are as follows:

- As already mentioned in section 4a.2 above, the Transfer Scheme placed DVB's receivables with the Holding Company[34] and allowing the Discoms to retain a 20 per cent commission on their collection.[35] While conceding that its action was contrary to the Transfer Scheme, the Commission in its tariff order for 2003-04 and onward, consistently down to the present, decided to count the arrears collected for the Holding Company towards Transco's ARR, and expressed the hope that the Government would 'revisit' the Transfer Scheme on the grounds that such arrears when collected would have counted towards DVB's ARR if there had been no unbundling, and should therefore remain available to the sector. This reasoning is questionable since, had there been no unbundling, DVB's massive liabilities would also have remained as a burden on the sector.[36] The Holding Company requires this source of revenue as one of the means of discharging DVB's liabilities, and has already utilised some of the amounts collected for this purpose. The Government has declined to revise the Transfer Scheme, but DERC has continued in both its subsequent tariff orders to underprovide Transco to the extent of its estimation of the DVB arrears likely to be collected. This means that either the Government must bear an additional, unbudgeted liability or Transco must suffer a shortfall in its revenues.
- Secondly, it will be recollected from Section 4.2 above that all the five successor utilities to DVB will have to repay their loan to the Holding Company after the moratorium of four years, with 12 per cent interest.[37] In its orders for 2005-06 DERC stated that the servicing of these loans (which does not arise in 2005-06) cannot be provided for in the ARRs of these companies and that they should "take up the matter of servicing...with the appropriate authority and make arrangements for servicing this loan without affecting the ARR...for the future years." Since regulated utilities can have no source of revenue not accounted for in their ARRs, it was difficult to see how this will be achieved without imposing an unanticipated extra burden on the shareholders, including the Government, which would be inconsistent with the reforms package.[38]

33. That is, in case there remains any unamortised regulatory asset at the end of the five-year transitional period (i.e. after 2006-07) during which the Policy Directions mandate a common retail tariff.

34. Apart from some specific exceptions including current arrears collected during the first four months.

35. This commission is not available in respect of the arrears of Government consumers. Further, it goes into the Discoms' ARR and, therefore, is not a benefit to the investors.

36. It is true that, in order to maintain consistency with the basis of calculation of opening AT&C loss levels, the collection of such arrears will have to be taken into account in counting collections towards the AT&C loss reduction targets; this fact is, however, irrelevant to the present issue and wrongly cited by DERC.

37. The loan, reflected in the opening balance sheets contained in the Transfer Scheme Rules, amounts to Rs. 270 crores in the case of Transco, Rs. 552 crores of NDPL, Rs. 690 crores of BRPL, and Rs. 174 crores of BYPL.

38. On the other hand, to write off these loans would not only affect the discharge of DVB's liabilities, but would also be perceived as conferring an undue benefit on the investors.

However, fortunately, with the decline in interest rates, the Discoms have been able to repay the entire loan in advance on the basis of refinancing—a win-win situation for all concerned.

- The same issue arises regarding the Government's transitional loan to Transco of Rs. 3450 crores. Here the Government too failed to determine the terms and conditions for repayment for far too long. Fortunately, however, the Government was eventually able to reach a very fair decision, to convert the loan into equity, thus restoring a gaping hole in Transco's balance sheet.

Other issues: The Discom investors have at times professed to be aggrieved by DERC's disregard for their stated requirements of compliance with the accounting standards obligatory under Company law. Their contention has been that if their obligations, as companies, to provide for depreciation and deferred tax liability are not considered in fixing their ARR, then they are unable to actually realise their prescribed rate of return. So far as depreciation is concerned, they have eventually succeeded in obtaining favourable appellate orders which have been upheld by the Supreme Court.

There remains an obvious force in the contention that the prescribed return is meaningless for a company unless reflected in the bottom line of its statutory profit and loss account. This is a policy issue on a quite different footing from the non-acceptance of any particular expenditure projected by a utility, and it needs to be addressed. It is certainly arguable that the Discoms have not obtained their promised return (apart from the overachievement bonuses earned by NDPL) despite overachieving their efficiency improvement targets, in terms of their statutory financial statements.

Conclusion: It should be sufficiently clear from the foregoing discussion that the whole reform package has been impacted by the tariff issue, which led DERC to leave a large uncovered 'regulatory asset'. The regulatory asset has since been amortised, but such 'back loading' tends to increase, rather than reducing the burden on the consumer in the long term. The implications are:

- Where the pain of reform should have been behind us by now, and consumers should have been able to look forward to the prospect of steadily improving service without further tariff increases, it now appears possible that the tariff may have to rise again during the current year. And as the pre-reform situation recedes in public memory, and consumers feel the new entities have had sufficient time to deliver, there is likely to be more consumer resistance to such increases in the future. This situation could have been avoided, or at least minimised, by making fairer increases in the early years, ending with the third year of the five-year transitory lustrum, and standing by them.
- DERC's disregard of certain features of the transfer scheme, referred to above, potentially imposes a continuing burden on the Government that was not envisaged.
- Investors, though they may wary of complaining too much in public, have not benefited sufficiently to motivate them, or other private players in the power sector, to be interested in taking over distribution in other States in India. To that extent, the unique achievement in loss reduction in Delhi has failed to create investor interest in the distribution sector, which is a tragedy for the power sector as a whole.

4.5 Areas of Strengths, Weaknesses and Where Intervention is Needed

4.5.1 Strengths

The greatest strength of the power sector in Delhi is the background of successful restructuring. This has freed the successor companies of DVB from the burden of the past. They are not burdened with DVB's accumulated financial losses and liabilities; the fact of restructuring and change of management has provided an opportunity to modernise and change the organisational culture, especially in the distribution part of the business where it was most needed. VRS schemes have been implemented successfully by the Discoms and also, on a more modest scale, by IPGCL. We already see a healthy competition among utilities, and the superior performance of one of the Discoms has posed a challenge for the others to meet.

Secondly, the restructuring with privatisation of distribution has created scope for private sector investment not only in the distribution sector itself but also in generation. There is every prospect of the sector becoming substantially self-sustaining and the need for public expenditure on investment and current requirements of the power sector has already come down a great deal.

As a result of these changes, as well as the enhanced power procurement ability that has come with full payments to power suppliers, the availability of power and the quality of service to the public has improved substantially and (if appropriate steps are taken regarding the sourcing of more power) is likely to continue to improve.

4.5.2 Weaknesses

The two main weaknesses of the power sector in Delhi are the failure to create a really strong feeling of consumer satisfaction, especially during the transitional period, and the continuing tariff issue described above. These two issues are interrelated. There were very high public expectations from the transfer of DVB's distribution business to the new Discoms controlled by such reputed national companies. Despite the real improvements that have taken place, the regularity and quality of supply and the quality of service available to consumers are still not up to the standards desired and there was a lot of media criticism of two of the three Discoms during the transitional period, though they too have later been able to address the major public grievances regarding their billing systems with some degree of success. It is reasonable to suggest that if all three of the Discoms had been able to perform to the level that NDPL was able to achieve especially during the second, third and fourth years after unbundling, then there may have been more willingness to accept tariff revisions as the cost of better service and, even more important, the extent of tariff revision required would have been smaller with better commercial efficiency.

Nevertheless, despite what has been said above, the Discoms cannot be faulted for their commercial performance so far since all three appear (subject to DERC's confirmation) met their committed loss reduction targets.

A consequent third weakness of the sector is the fact that the public-private partnership on which the reforms were premised has come under strain. The regulatory concerns that have been referred to have, in some cases, put Transco and the Discoms in opposite camps. Discom managements have been slow or remiss at times in making payments to Transco and DPCL in terms of the reform package (though payments for power purchase have been timely). While Discom managements may have felt at times that they were not getting sufficient cooperation in various matters, they too may need to appreciate that public and political support for them is bound to weaken unless all three Discoms are able to create a strong feeling of satisfaction among their consumers.

The Government's ability to deal with such issues as those that have been referred to is also constrained by the apprehension of audit or similar criticism. This is not the place to comment on the C&AG's report covering the privatisation process, but media reporting on it has not been consistently objective. The first draft of the C&AG's special review of the privatisation process was leaked to the press and received wide publicity; when the final report came out, dropping some of the original criticisms (notably the observation that bids should have been reinvited) the differences were not highlighted as they should have been, and the coverage has presented the report as being more critical than, on closer analysis, it actually is. In fact, the C&AG dropped its initial observation that bids should have been re-invited, and in its final report merely said that, given the financial implications of the decision taken (to accept negotiated bids) the approval of the Lieutenant Governor should have been obtained, and should now be obtained *post facto*. This criticism did not at all go to the merits of the decision, a distinction which the media failed to appreciate and explain to the public. The possibility of a negative atmosphere of opinion getting created by incomplete reporting, sometimes to the point of misinformation, has since materialised—greatly aided by the conflation in the media, presumably in the public mind, of the C&AG report with the PAC report, which went far beyond and actually contradicted the C&AG's report.

Further, Delhi's energy security in regard to the power sector remains a question mark since, three years after the reforms, neither has any project to enhance local generation been launched, nor has the opportunity of benefiting from private sector participation in generation in Delhi yet been availed of.

4.5.3. Interventions Required

Five-year tariff package: The ongoing multi-year tariff exercise, and the tariff decision for the current year, need to be expedited by DERC. They are already overdue.

Focus on consumer satisfaction: DERC needs to be proactive in dealing not only with individual consumer grievances but with overall utility performance. The existing Metering & Billing Regulations establish norms for processing individual matters and penalties for individual failure. DERC has now taken steps to monitor the performance of Discoms in the field. It should also take steps to implement the well-known objective, overall norms and standards for the quality of service provided by Discoms (especially SAIDI[39] and SAIFI[40]) with effective penalties for failure to achieve them.

39. System Average Interruption Duration Index.
40. System Average Interruption Frequency Index.

Sourcing of power: Immediate steps should be taken to expedite the allotment of the Bawana site for a generation project and for expanding the capacity of Genco; the issues have been discussed above.

4.5.4 Conclusion

Given the complexity of the whole restructuring exercise, and its dependence for success on the decisions and performance of different, independent participants—the regulator, the investors, the managements of the successor utilities and the Government itself—as well as on various external factors, it is not surprising that things have not gone exactly to plan in all respects and that the overall picture is one of partial—though very substantial—success. It is, further, to be hoped the difficulties described above will be greatly mitigated if all the Discoms are able, during the post-transitional period, to step up the level of overachievement in loss reduction, reducing pressure on the tariff (and also benefiting their own shareholders). What is most necessary during the current transitional period is to appreciate that the reforms are still an ongoing process which needs to be monitored and kept continuously on track rather than a completed transaction to be merely commented upon.

RAILWAYS AND ROADS

4.6 Introduction

4.6.1 This Section covers the development of roads and railways in the State of Delhi. Beginning with the present status of Railway and Road network, the development works planned, the works in progress, their present status, resource requirement for completion with time frame for the same have been covered. The deficiencies in the existing network and proposals for removing them and the resource requirement for the same have further been analysed.

4.6.2 The effect of multiplicity of authority in the road sector with different sectors and activities controlled by Government of NCTD, MCD, NDMC, DDA, and NHAI and the resulting mismatch in coordinated synergic approach in this sector so far and the remedial measures being taken have been detailed below.

4.6.3 The Maintenance of roads, lighting, sanitation facilities on these roads, together with the aspects of road furniture and signage has been examined.

4.6.4 The integration of rail and road transport is essential for providing optimal services to the traveling public. With the Metro Rail coming up rapidly, suitable interfaces require to be developed with the Indian Railways to meet the transportation needs of the people of NCT Delhi and those travelling to and from Delhi to neighbouring towns and to other parts of the country.

4.6.5 Delhi is the third largest city in India, surpassed in population only by Calcutta and Bombay. Delhi's history dates back to the first millennium B.C., when it was known as Indraprastha.

The long period, during which Delhi has served as the capital of India, resulted in development of a network of roads from all parts of the country to Delhi. After the advent of Railways, similarly a network of Railways developed leading to Delhi

Delhi was made a Union Territory on November 1, 1956. With the 69th Constitutional amendment, Delhi got a Legislative Assembly when the National Capital Territory Act was enacted in 1991.

Delhi is one of the fastest growing cities in the World. Here, remnants of the past survive cheek-by-jowl with skyscrapers, residential colonies and bustling commercial complexes.

4.6.6 The population of Delhi, which was around 2 million in 1971, rose to13.78 million in 2001 and is expected to reach 22 million by 2021. A large percentage of this population is made up of immigrants from other Indian states and their travel requirements are also required to be serviced by the transport system.

4.6.7 This Section outlines the growth of the road and rail network in and around Delhi, and the measures being constantly planned and taken for providing a better and more efficient road network to the people of Delhi. A large number of flyovers have been recently commissioned and several more are under construction, widening of roads has been taken up, new bypasses and slip roads are being added and other measures are being taken to improve the system. This report goes on to identify the further measures required and the action required to be taken to make both the rail and road systems adequate for the traffic they would be called upon to carry.

It also examines the main causes of environmental degradation that has taken place due to traffic and transport and reviews the earlier studies carried out by various different authorities to provide relief to the ever increasing traffic and transport problems of the city and action taken on them, as well as by the Railways and the NCR Planning Board in this connection.

4.6.8 The measures being taken to meet the objective of having a world class road and rail network as per the Master Plan Delhi 2021 have been detailed and steps to achieve the same together with the resources required for doing so, ways to raise these resources and the changes required in the existing procedures and policies for effective fulfillment of this vision have been examined and suggested.

The required Institutional Frame Work and an Action Plan for achieving systematic and scientific development, management and operation of an Integrated Multimodal Transport System in Delhi composed of railways, roads, MRT and other modes of transport capable of meeting the needs of Delhi has been identified and proposals in this regard have been made in the report.

4.7 Traffic Characteristics and Overall Transportation Scenario

4.7.1 The adequacy of any transportation network lies in its ability to allow the movement of all the traffic offered by different modes of travel smoothly and without inordinate or avoidable delays.

In a big megapolis like Delhi, people use several modes of transport like buses, cars, taxies and TSRs, rickshaws and bicycles, besides walking. Goods are ferried by trucks, tempos, trolleys and *thelas*, besides handcarts. This mix of traffic uses the same road network.

Then we have the Railways main line, suburban, and local services, and the rail based metro system.

According to the studies conducted in the recent past, the modal split (excluding walk trips) in favour of public transport was to the tune of 60 per cent followed by about 30 per cent by personalised modes. Work and education trips constituted 40 per cent and 42 per cent respectively.

Though the average trip length of all trips was 6.8 km, the average length of work trips was as high as 9.74 km, which shows an unhealthy relationship in spatial distribution of residence and work place. The increase in trip length by personalised vehicles means more exposure to pollution for the occupants and adding of more pollutants by the vehicles themselves.

4.7.2 Traffic Characteristics

In spite of roads occupying 21 per cent of the total area of the city, the continuous increase in vehicular traffic on major arterial roads is resulting in lowering of the journey speed, congestion, intersection delays and intolerable pollution levels especially during peak hours. Ring Road and Vikas Marg carry about 110000 to 120000 vehicles per day with peak hour traffic of 8 per cent and 11 per cent respectively.

Major intersections are acting as bottlenecks due to their handling of traffic volume much beyond their capacity. Though some of the major intersections have been or are in the process of being provided with grade separated facility still in the absence of any long-term policy perspective, the problem is being shifted elsewhere without much relief in the total traffic environment. The lowering of speed, congestion and traffic hold-ups on roads obviously add to the air and noise pollution levels.

4.7.3 Road Safety

Safety is a major component of the traffic environment. The phenomenal increase in the number of motor vehicles in the city coupled with limited road space, inadequate facilities for pedestrians and cyclists, irresponsible driving and violation of traffic rules has resulted in significant number of road accidents. Though the number of accidents has shown a decreasing trend in the last three years due to continuing efforts of Traffic Police, this aspect should get adequate attention in order to improve the traffic environment.

4.7.4 Transport Scenario—Growth of Motor Vehicles

The phenomenal population growth in Delhi has been accompanied by an equally rapid increase in vehicle population. Delhi had 48.30 lakh motor vehicles in March 2006, compared to 32.10 lakh motor vehicles in March 1999, eight years ago.

Delhi now has more vehicles than Mumbai, Chennai and Calcutta combined. The distribution of motor vehicles in Delhi is shown in the Table below:

TABLE 4.22

Distribution of Motor Vehicles in Delhi

Type of Vehicles	31-3-1999	31-03-2006
Cars, Jeeps	818962	1471858
Scooter, Motor cycle	2101876	3078660
Auto Rickshaw	86985	74188
Taxies	17136	20646
Buses	35254	25511
Other passenger vehicles	964	18378
Goods vehicles	150243	128193
Total	*3211420*	*4817434*

Source: The source for first column showing position on 31-03-1999 is Table 12.2 of *Economic Survey of Delhi 2003-04*, and of position as on 31-03-2006 is Table 12.2 of the *Economic Survey of Delhi 2005-06*.

This table indicates that the proportion of personalised transport *viz.*, cars, jeeps, scooters, and motor cycles has increased from 90.9 per cent in 1998-99 to 94.25 per cent in 2005-06, while the proportion of buses, taxies, auto *rickshaws* and goods vehicles has declined.

4.7.5 Availability of Roads

The availability of roads in Delhi as per last available statistics is 31183 kms in March 2006 of which 27139 kms belong to MCD, 1550 kms to NDMC, 144 kms to DCB, 182 kms of National Highway and 2168 kms of other roads. The average length of road per 100 sqm areas is 2103 and the road length per 1000 population is about 1.94 kms.

4.7.6 National Highways

Five National Highways i.e., NH-1, NH-2, NH-10, NH-8 and NH-24 pass through the National Capital Territory of Delhi, contributing significantly to the character of Delhi as a major trading and distribution centre, and as the melting pot of India. Delhi continues to stand at the cross roads of modern India, with the Grand Trunk Road built by Sher Shah Suri from Peshawar to Calcutta having been the precursor of NH-1 and NH-24.

4.7.7 Rail Network

Delhi is a major junction on the rail map of India linked with almost all Metropolitan cities directly. There are four major railway stations at New Delhi, Old Delhi, Hazrat Nizamuddin and Sarai Rohila besides a Container Depot at Tuglakabad. There are eight rail corridors in the National Capital Territory, which bring in more than 400 passenger trains and 40 goods trains each day.

4.7.8 Modes of Transport

As far as local traffic is concerned, Delhi is predominantly dependent on road transport, with the railways catering to only about 1 per cent of the commuter traffic. The ring rail network in Delhi is grossly underutilised. Buses cater to 62 per cent of the total traffic while personal vehicles account for the balance 37 per cent. Although, buses are a small percentage of the total number of vehicles, they cater to 62 per cent of the total traffic load. Among personalised vehicles, motor cycles and scooters comprise about two-third of the total number of vehicles in Delhi, while cars and jeeps account for one-fourth of the total vehicles.

Complete data about man and animal-driven vehicles in Delhi is not available. However, there were 66195 *rickshaws* registered, 422 *tongas*, 62 *rehras*, 5239 handcarts and 379 bullock carts as well as 135872 trollies/cycle carts and *rickshaws* making a total of 208169 as on 31 March 2005. The unauthorised number of such vehicles is estimated to be more than those registered with the local bodies. Registered man and animal-driven vehicles constitute about 3.5 per cent of the total vehicle population in Delhi out of which about 51 per cent are cycle rickshaws.

4.7.9 Ring Road

The Ring road, Outer Ring road and the radial roads constitute a distinct feature of the road network in Delhi. Ring road has a length of 48 km, out of which 16 km is common with Outer Ring road and NH-1. The 6-lane carriageway of the existing Ring Road had reached the saturation capacity of 75,000 PCUs per day in 1994. Traffic is projected to reach between 1.5-4 lakh PCUs by 2011, which will require creation of considerable additional capacity on the both the Ring Roads.

4.7.10 Mass Rapid Transit System (MRTS)

MRTS is an ambitious project that aims at providing an efficient rail based transport system properly integrated with road transport. The first phase of the project is currently under implementation. Considering the escalation during the period of construction, the completion cost of first phase is now estimated at Rs.10571 crore. Of this 56 per cent of the cost is to be funded by OECF of Japan, 30 per cent through equity support by Government of Delhi and Central government, 8 per cent through interest free subordinate debt and 6 per cent through property development.

In the first phase three corridors were taken up totaling 65 kms. These corridors have been completed and already operational. Work on the next phase of Metro lines development is progressing rapidly.

4.7.11 Integrated Freight Complexes

MPD-2001 envisaged the construction of four integrated freight complexes in Delhi at Madanpur Khadar (NH-2), Patparganj (NH-24), G.T. Road (NH-1), and Bhartal (NH-8). These four integrated freight complexes will consist of wholesale markets, warehousing, road (truck), and rail transport terminals so as to curtail the movement of heavy vehicles within the urban area. The freight complexes are conceived to shift wholesale trade, decongest the walled city and also cater to regional goods traffic flowing through Delhi. The project design and financing pattern is under consideration of DDA.

4.7.12 Interstate Bus Terminals (ISBTs)

MPD-2001 has suggested five ISBTs in Delhi by 2001.

With the development of two new ISBTs at Sarai Kale Khan and Anand Vihar and the existing ISBT at Kashmere Gate, three ISBTs are functioning at present. These three ISBTs cater to average 1.54 lakh passengers and 3300 buses/trips per day. Two more ISBTs are proposed to be constructed during the 9th Five Year Plan at Dwarka and in North Delhi.

4.7.13 Flyovers and Bridges

Work on the 14 flyovers has been recently completed bringing the total number of existing flyovers to 72, while 27 more flyovers are to be built.

4.7.14 Delhi Transport Corporation

DTC was taken over by Government of N.C.T. of Delhi from Government of India in August 1996. The DTC fleet comprised 3131 buses in 1998-99. As on 1 January 2006, DTC had 3110 CNG driven buses. It also has 364 diesel buses for plying on interstate routes. Replacement of over aged buses, introduction of high capacity twin buses and augmentation of the existing carrying capacity is being planned. The DTC has initiated action to procure 100 new modern low floor buses.

4.7.15 Ring Railway

The ring rail was constructed in the 1930's as the goods avoiding line but its role in intra-urban service is being emphasised for about last 40 years. The existing system, which was built at a cost of 340 million rupees and was expected to cater about 12 per cent of the total commuter load, has proved a non-starter, carrying less than 1 per cent of the load. The reasons for this are:

- Dependence on availability of goods avoiding lines
- Absence of integration with feeder bus operation
- Absence of commuter facilities at stations
- Convenient access of platforms to commuters
- Lack of development along the railway corridor
- Unattractive fare structure
- Competitive and attractive parallel bus service

A committee has examined the deficiencies in the system and subsequently it has been decided that incurring an expenditure of about Rs.900 crore and integrating it with radial lines and MRTS system could significantly improve the ring railway services.

4.8 Status of Roads and Their Development So Far

4.8.1 While the NCT of Delhi is served by both rail and road, Delhi is predominantly dependent on road transport. The road network in Delhi is being developed and maintained by many agencies, the main being the State PWD, MCD, NDMC, Delhi Cantonment Board and DDA. The road network in Delhi is 31183 kms as on 31 March 2006 (including 182 kms of National Highways). The road network has increased from 8380 km in 1971-72 to 31183 km in 2005-06.

The phenomenal population growth in Delhi has been accompanied by an equally rapid increase in vehicle population. The number of vehicles has increased from 2.14 lakh in 1971-72 to 48.30 lakh motor vehicles in March 2006.

4.8.2 In view of the steep increase in growth of traffic, and other factors, this road network is unable to meet the requirements of Delhi and due to the very heavy traffic and congestion; it is grossly inadequate and requires huge inputs to make it effective. Congestion on Delhi roads is worsening despite several local road improvement programmes. Average speeds during peak periods range from 10kmph-15kmph in central areas and 20km-40 kmph on arterial roads. Delhi does not lack road infrastructure. However, problems arise as a result of the wide variety of vehicle types including bicycles, mechanical, man-powered and animal-drawn vehicles sharing the same road space.

A much better picture can be expected only if all vehicles present can use the road space available efficiently. Reduced average speeds should result in fewer fatalities. The number of total fatalities does show a marginal decline; however, the share of pedestrian fatalities continues to rise.The decline in the average speed of motor vehicles and the increase in pollution levels in the city seem to be the two most important parameters. The transport system of NCR as of today consists of a well-knit road network and radial rail corridors catering to inter-city and intra-city commuter and long-distance traffic.

The freight traffic is also substantial in the region and this is mostly carried by road. Delhi acts as collection and distribution center for the northern region.

4.8.3 Road Network

4.8.3.1 National Highways

Delhi is served by a network of National Highways. Existing road network in the region shows convergence of five National Highways i.e., NH-1,2,8,10 & 24 on Delhi and two National Highways namely NH-58 and NH-91 meet NH-24 at Ghaziabad (Map 5.1). These National Highways have four lane divided carriageways in most of the area of NCR except Delhi-Rohtak (NH-10), Ghaziabad-Meerut (NH-58), and Ghaziabad-Bulandshahar (NH-91), which are of two lanes. Ten States Highways also serve in strengthening the regional road network.

4.8.3.2 The road network in Delhi is being developed and maintained by PWD, MCD, NDMC, Delhi Cantonment Board and DDA. The road network in Delhi was 31183 kms (including 182 kms of NHs) in March 2006. The growth of the road network in Delhi is shown in Table 4.23.

TABLE 4.23

Growth of Roads in Delhi

Agency	*1980-81*	*2002-03*	*2003-04*	*2004-05*	*2005-06*
MCD	12129	27139	27139	27139	27139
NDMC	1191	1299	1550	1550	1550
DCB	124	143	144	144	144
i) National Highway	302	182	182	182	182
ii) Other Road	570	1934	1934	2168	2168
Total	**14316**	**30697**	**30949**	**31183**	**31183**

Source: The source is Table 12.6 of *Economic Survey of Delhi 2005-06.*

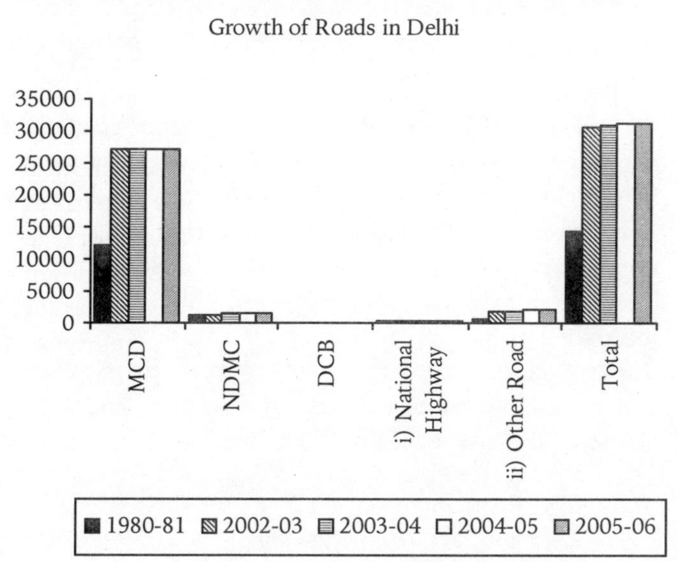

The road network has increased from 8380 km in 1971-72 to 31183 km in 2005-06, (almost four times), while the number of vehicles has increased from 2.14 lakh in 1971-72 to 48.30 lakh in 2003-04. (Almost twenty-four times).

4.8.3.3 Outer Ring Road and the radial roads constitute a distinct feature of the road network in Delhi. Ring road has a length of 48 km, out of which 16 km is common with Outer Ring Road and NH-1. The six-lane carriageway of the existing Ring Road had reached the saturation capacity of 75,000 PCUs per day in 1994. Traffic is projected to reach between 1.5-4 lakh PCUs by 2011, which will require expansion of the Ring Road to 18-24 lanes (Source: NCRPB).

TABLE 4.24

Growth of Vehicles on Delhi Roads

Vehicle	*1990-91*	*1993-94*	*1998-99*	*2003-04*	*2005-06*
Cars & Jeeps	398479	522264	818962	1267852	1471858
Motor Cycles & Scooters	1220640	1492201	2101876	2650241	3078660
Auto Rickshaws	63005	72102	86985	74906	74188
Taxies	10157	11846	17136	14941	20646
Buses	18858	24211	35254	24774	25511
Goods Vehicles	101828	116379	150243	135671	128193
Total	1812967	2239003	3210456	4168385	4799056

Source: The source is Table 12.2 of *Economic Survey of Delhi 2005-06.*

TABLE 4.25

Overall Increase in the Number of Vehicles on Delhi Roads

Items	*1990-91*	*1993-94*	*1998-99*	*2003-04*	*2005-06*
Number of Vehicles	1812967	2239003	3210456	4168385	4830136
Increase in number of Vehicles	175365	141848	177411	957929	362982
Annual (%)	10.71	6.76	5.85	5.96	5.84

Source: The source is Table 12.6 of *Economic Survey of Delhi 2005-06.*

Traffic is projected to reach between 1.5-4 lakh PCUs by 2011, which will require expansion of the Main arterial roads and the two Ring Roads considerably.

4.9 Limitations of the Existing Road System

4.9.1 The Basic Infrastructure

4.9.1.1 The road network in Delhi can be categorised on the basis of a hierarchy of roads, ranging from "Arterial Roads" designed to carry fast through traffic, to "Feeder Roads" and "Residential roads".

However, the lack of transport choices results in a pedestrian presence on all roads, regardless of the hierarchy and designated functions. The existing road design does not appear to have considered the needs of pedestrians, cyclists, or other slow moving traffic.

Service roads, if present, are not well maintained. Footpaths are either not present or are poorly maintained. Furthermore, there are no specific facilities, other than passenger waiting shelters, provided for buses. Approaches to bus shelters, dedicated bus priority lanes, continuous pedestrian paths, and separate lanes for slow vehicles like bicycles and rickshaws have not been included in the road network designs.

As a result, consequently, all road users have to share the carriageway. This often leads to unsafe conditions for pedestrians and slow moving vehicles and congested conditions for motor vehicles.

Not surprisingly, government surveys find 50 per cent of the road space in Delhi 'encroached on' by non-traffic activities. This disrupts traffic in all lanes and makes walking and cycling even more hazardous. Motor traffic does not use the kerb-side lane even when pedestrian and bicycle densities are low.

Providing a pedestrian friendly path and separate bicycle track would make more space available for motorised modes and would make walking and cycling less hazardous. All modes of transport move in sub-optimal conditions in the absence of facilities for pedestrians and non-motorised vehicles.

Even though a large number of road widening works have been done and provision of grade separators and subways have been constructed all over Delhi, as per details given elsewhere in this report, it is unfortunate that despite this, average speeds have fallen over the years. This is also due to the approaches of the flyovers continuing to be narrow as a result of which 4 lanes of traffic—two from the flyover and two from the slip road merge into 2-3 lanes. Peak hour traffic on arterial roads (most of which are two or three-lane dual carriageways) crawls through bottlenecks at major intersections, and all road users have to share the carriageway. This often leads to unsafe conditions for pedestrians and slow moving vehicles and congested conditions for motor vehicles.

The main reason for this is that the extensive road network has not been developed to serve the mixed traffic presently using the roads. State authorities and 'experts' continue to plan infrastructure, which is supposed to ensure fast movement of bus and car traffic, this in effect is at the cost of pedestrians and non-motorised vehicles. The basic needs of pedestrians have not been considered as a key part of the urban transport infrastructure.

Since pedestrians, bicycles and other non-motorised vehicles use the left side of the road; buses are unable to use the designated bus lanes and are forced to stop in the middle lane, often 4-6m away from bus stops. The carriageway between the bus and the bus stop is occupied by waiting commuters, parked rickshaws and hawkers.

The absence of safe crossing points for pedestrians leads to their trying to run across busy roads between traffic flows, slowing down the motorised traffic besides causing accidents and casualties. Even where zebra crossings have been provided, drivers of motor vehicles do not stop clear of them as a result of which pedestrians have to jay walk through a maze of parked mixed vehicles waiting at the red light in a jumbled disorganised manner.

This jumble at red light crossings also results in delay in clearance of vehicles across busy junctions. It has also been observed that vehicles in a particular traffic stream continue to cross much after the light has turned red with consequent delays in movement of other traffic streams receiving the green light.

In a recent study, pedestrians were observed at selected junctions on a major arterial road in Delhi (IIT, 2000). The study shows that nearly 70 per cent of pedestrians cross the road when it is safe for them to cross, i.e., either it is green for pedestrians or green for right turning vehicles, which makes half the crossing safe. The number of pedestrians waiting at the median is more than those waiting on the side of the road, even though there is no pedestrian island in the median. The road median does not provide any convenient space for waiting and indeed restrictive measures for pedestrians are instituted such as high medians (30-50 cm) and guard rails.

Though pedestrian subways are meant to facilitate safe crossing by pedestrians, it has been observed that more often the construction of pedestrian subways and footbridges is so located as to ensure that pedestrians do not obstruct motor traffic. These pedestrian subways continue to have low usage rates not only because of poor location, but also because they are often locked at night due to safety concerns. This leaves no option for pedestrians but to either break the median fences or run across at the risk of losing their lives.

4.9.2 The Road Improvement Plan for the City includes the Following

- Construction of a large number of grade-separated junctions/flyovers, listed elsewhere;
- Construction of subways to facilitate pedestrians; and
- Widening of arterial roads.

This has the effect of discouraging public transport use, as all commuters using buses have to cross the road at least twice for every round trip at the origin or the destination.

The area occupied by grade-separated intersections is much greater than ordinary intersections and the location of bus stops at these intersections is often changed from the previous location (close to the intersection) to the foot of the flyover. Consequently, commuters have to walk a greater distance—at least 200 metres extra when changing bus routes. In addition, because of the increase in walking distance and road widths; pedestrians and commuters are exposed to higher accident risks. This further discourages use of public transport by children, disabled people and other vulnerable road users.

Pedestrians have to contend with narrow pavements, often made narrower to increase the width of the road to reduce congestion for cars and other motor traffic. Pedestrians are expected to walk among parked cars, street fixtures such as electricity poles, telephone poles, traffic signs, litter bins, redundant phone boxes, and commercial waste.

The situation is made worse as a result of poor public management of streets and public spaces, including litter and uneven pavements. It is not wrong to say that the streets of Delhi are characterised by an absence of design.

The presence of diverse socioeconomic groups in the city is reflected in the wide variety of transport modes present on all roads. This also results in the emergence of a range of activities by different road users.

4.9.3 Roadside Vendors and Services for Road Users

4.9.3.1 Bicycles, pedestrians and bus traffic attract street vendors. Often, people selling food, drink and other goods occupy the side roads and pedestrian paths. If the wares on offer were not required at those locations, then the vendors would have no incentive to remain there.

However, road authorities and city authorities view their existence as illegal. Often the argument is made that road capacity is reduced by the presence of street vendors and hawkers. If we apply the same principle that is applied for the design of the road environment for motorised traffic, especially private cars, then vendors have a valid and legal place in the road environment.

4.9.3.2 Highway design manuals make recommendations on the frequency and design of service areas for motor vehicles. Street vendors and hawkers serve the same function for pedestrians, cyclists, and bus users. As long as our urban roads are used by these modes, street vendors, inevitably, will remain.

4.9.3.3 Main Causes of Environmental Degradation due to Traffic and Transport can be summarised as:

- Lack of appreciation of the impact of land use planning on transportation. Needs like parking space, road widening, intersection improvement etc. Absence of service roads and the road system design not catering adequately for the needs of pedestrian's cyclists and slow moving traffic.
- Haphazard growth in absence of non-conformity to actual developments with Master Plan, commercialisation of residential areas where the residential roads cannot take the traffic load and parking requirement resulting from such commercialisation.
- Tremendous increase of motor vehicles especially personalised vehicles on roads resulting in congestion, delays, accidents and pollution. The motley mix of vehicles from *thelas*, *rickshaws*, cycles, trucks, TSRs, cars, Buses, and two wheeler motorised vehicles, moving in the same lanes adds to the confusion on the roads.
- Ineffective utilisation of road space due to on-street parking, encroachments, intermixing of slow and fast modes, hawkers on the roads and lack of pedestrian facilities etc.
- The satellite towns, instead of easing the pressure on Delhi roads, add to the same, as instead of integrated development, they have mainly become residential suburbs with work places continuing to be in Delhi.
- Inadequate and inefficient public transportation system
- The absence of byepasses leading to a large number of transit vehicles entering the city and adding to the chaos on the city roads, and
- Long gestation time in the implementation of improvement schemes like bridges, flyovers and ROBs and other improvements at intersections etc., during which inadequate temporary arrangements for smooth flow of traffic lead to heavy delays and traffic jams.

4.10 Sanctioned Road Development Projects and Their Present Status, Planning for Completion and Projects in the Pipeline

4.10.1 Delhi is endowed with one of the most complex road networks in the country, which is used, by more than 10 per cent of the country's vehicular population.

Delhi Government is responsible for construction and maintenance of most of the roads of Delhi.

4.10.2 Besides road widening and improvement, the present focus is on construction of grade separations to smoothen traffic flows. PWD, Government of Delhi is using State-of-the-Art technologies for its flyover projects to minimise construction activity at busy intersections and to have better control on the quality of the works. For the first time in the country, PWD, Government of Delhi has introduced ISO-9002 standards.

It is being argued that, the flyovers at the most may provide a little relief mainly to personalised fast vehicles as the low occupancy buses, will continue to use the old at-grade routes for commuter convenience. But in the long term, they may not make much impact on the overall traffic situation and on the environmental pollution level, as the grade of the flyovers along with intersection on either side of them, will definitely have an adverse effect. However, these would definitely result in smoother traffic flows.

4.10.3 The road network linking the suburban towns to Delhi which is extensively used by commuters coming for work to Delhi is proposed to be developed in three categories:

- Primary road network—These will be the radial roads connecting important towns with Delhi. In addition to the National Highways listed above, it is proposed to upgrade Luni-Shamli State Highway to a four-lane divided carriageway. It is also proposed to strengthen the grid roads connecting various towns in the NCR.
- The secondary road network—this will consist of major districts roads.
- The tertiary road network—this will connect all the villages' work places and residential areas in the region.
- Expressways—It is proposed to develop the existing Ring Road, the outer Ring Road and the five radial roads (National Highways) upto Kundli NH-1, Ballabhgarh NH-2, Gurgaon NH-8, Bahadurgarh NH-10, and Ghaziabad NH-24 into expressway standards, if required by providing elevated roads. Access to above expressways is proposed through major arterial roads in Delhi. Feeder roads will link all business employment centers and residential areas to the arterial roads.

4.10.4 Government of Delhi has undertaken various projects for providing planned infrastructure for equitable distribution and decongestion in the city i.e., construction of flyovers, construction of Kalindi bypass to decongest Mathura Road from Ashram to Sarita Vihar and widening of major arterial roads.

4.10.5 Delhi has a massive programme involving road and intersection improvements at a number of critical designated locations. Construction of grade-separated facilities is oriented to meet predominantly the needs of cars rather than buses. Also, there is practically no dedicated infrastructure for 'development for non-motorised vehicles. Though some cycle tracks are now available in disjointed lengths, Proposals related to cycle tracks as stipulated in the Master Plan Delhi 2001 are yet to be fully implemented.

4.10.5.1 There are a number of missing links in the arterial road system of the city. Predominant missing links are the Sarita Vihar-Jamia Millia-Maharani Bagh (SJM) bypass along the western edge of the Yamuna River, and the peripheral expressway.

4.10.5.2 Comprehensive road network proposals for congested central areas (by MCD, NDMC and the Transport Department of Delhi Administration) to improve traffic operations have been pending for implementation for over two decades. Options to provide road links as alternatives to planned schemes should be explored further with emphasis on environmental issues.

4.11 Development of Roads Leading to and Bypassing Delhi

In compliance of the orders of Honourable Supreme Court of India dated 6.12.2001, the heavy traffic passing through National Capital has been banned except the vehicles destined for Delhi. As a result, sizeable commercial traffic has been diverted on other roads passing through Haryana. As a result the traffic on the following roads in Haryana has already increased manifold:

- Palwal–Sohna–Gurgaon–Jhajjar–Sampla–Kharkhauda–Murthal
- Faridabad–Gurgaon–Chandu–Badli–Bahadurgarh–Narela–NH-1.
- Kotputli–Narnaul–Mahendragarh–Dadri–Bhiwani–Jind–Kaithal.

These roads of Haryana are not capable of taking heavy traffic diverted on these routes and need immediate strengthening and widening. Otherwise the road network is bound to collapse anytime. Therefore, it is necessary to take up upgradation of these roads. In addition to above, the Haryana Government has decided to construct the 130 kms long Kundli–Manesar–Palwal Expressway which will join the National Highway-1, National Highway-10, National Highway-8, and National Highway-2, bypassing all the major towns and industrial estates of Haryana sub-region.

In addition to the above, Ministry of Road Transport & Highway, has approved the construction of elevated Highway at Badarpur on National Highway-2, to remove the frequent traffic bottlenecks. Work on this project is being taken up.

In addition to the Express Highway under construction from Dhaula-Kuan to Gurgaon, Delhi Government is also taking up widening and strengthening of Delhi-Mehrauli road upto Gurgaon border in order to ease traffic on this route. An additional road link to Gurgaon from Delhi passing through village Dera Mandi to Vasant Kunj area is also under consideration. Similarly the existing bypass along Agra Canal in Faridabad is proposed to be connected with the new road linking Sarita Vihar and Kalindi Kunj in New Delhi.

4.12 New Expressways

Work on two new expressways is being taken up to facilitate movement of traffic bypassing Delhi which now has to pass through the city.

a) Eastern Peripheral Expressway, consisting of two corridors:
    1. Faridabad-NOIDA-Ghaziabad (FNG): 56 kms
    2. Ghaziabad-Kundli (GK) Corridors: 49 km
b) Western Peripheral Expressway

The Western Peripheral Expressway having a length of 135 kms., will pass entirely through Haryana thereby linking NH-1 at Kundli to NH-2 at Faridabad via NH-10 and NH-8.

4.13 Institutional Measures

The financial investments planned under the Tenth and Eleventh Plans are proposed to be buttressed by institutional measures to ensure effective and efficient functioning of the transport system in an integrated manner. For this, it is proposed to set up an Integrated Metropolitan Transport Authority (IMTA) which will look after regulatory issues like fares and tariffs as well as provisioning and common functions/services for metro, rail and bus systems. Until IMTA is formed, a Delhi Transport Planning Group (DTPG) to be chaired by the Chief Minister may be set up. To provide technical and logistic support to the DTPG and then IMTA, a Traffic Engineering and Transport Planning cell will be set up which will function under the aegis of the Transport Department but will draw expertise from PWD, MCD, NDMC and the Traffic Police to ensure coordination and the Traffic Police to ensure coordination and implementation.

4.14 Phasing of Projects

The projects planned in the Master plan Delhi 2021 are divided into two phases—first phase 2001-2011 and second phase 2011-2021. In the first phase the following projects on roads leading to Delhi and on construction of the bypass which will result in easing the flows on Delhi roads, are planned:

a) Western Peripheral Expressway
b) Eastern Peripheral Expressway
c) Four Laning of the following road sections:
    - Bahadurgarh-Rohtak-NCR Border (NH-10)
    - Rohtak–NCR Border (NH-71)
    - Ghaziabad-Meerut-NCR Boundary (NH58)
    - Ghaziabad-Bulandshahar-Kurja-NCR Boundary (NH-91)
    - Gurgaon-Alwar (Old NH-8)

In the second phase of the plan, following projects would be taken up in the neighbouring states for easing traffic flows to and from Delhi, for implementation:

a) Ghaziabad-Meerut Expressway
b) Bhiwadi-Rewari Road
c) Rewari-Jhajjar Road
d) Jhajjar-Rohtak Road
e) Rohtak-Sonipat Road
f) Sonipat-Baghpat Road
g) Baghpat-Meerut Road
h) Meerut-Hapur Road
i) Hapur-Bulandshahar Road
j) Bulandshahar-Khurja Road
k) Khurja-Palwal Road
l) Palwal-Bhiwadi Road
m) Rohtak-Panipat Road

Phasing of the transport projects will be modified on the basis of suggestions received from the State Governments.

4.15 Multiplicity of Authority in the Road Sector and its effect on Development

4.15.1 Overview

At present the following agencies are responsible for construction and maintenance of roads, bridges and flyovers in Delhi:

- Public Works Department of Government of Delhi
- Municipal Corporation of Delhi
- New Delhi Municipal Council
- The Delhi Cantonment Board
- Delhi Development Authority
- Delhi Tourism and Travel Corporation
- Central Public Works Department
- National Highways Authority of India

Other authorities are also involved in different aspects of road administration in Delhi.

All these agencies do their own planning and execution with the result that there is little coordination. Moreover, availability of resources with different agencies being different, the completion of works by different agencies proceeds at different speeds.

Further, there is no coordination between utility providers digging up the roads for laying sewage, water supply, cables both for power and communications etc and the agencies controlling the road maintenance as a result of which the roads are frequently dug up and left in a state of disrepair, with excavated material heaped up on the carriage way obstructing the smooth flow of traffic.

Garbage heaps, stray dogs and cattle moving on the roads freely add to the problems of smooth flow of traffic. Efforts are being made by the Government of Delhi to overcome these problems but due to the multiplicity of agencies, the problems persist.

During the last four decades a number of in-depth traffic and transportation planning studies have been undertaken for metropolitan Delhi and the National Capital Region. The findings of these studies *inter alia* led to the Delhi Metro Rail Project.

All the studies have stressed the need to strengthen the institutional set up and to plan, implement, co-ordinate, fund and monitor an integrated urban transport system.

Fundamentally, the factors causing deterioration in the transport system of metropolitan Delhi are, multi-agency planning and implementation, inter-agency interests and conflicts, lack of a strong will to improve the public transport system, lack of land use-transport integration, and, above all, a non-existent public transport culture.

In the context of MP, Delhi 21, the main objective and long-term goal is to provide, promote and ensure safe, economic and efficient movement of all categories of passengers and goods, in an environment friendly manner, through an integrated multi-modal transportation system.

4.16 Institutional Framework

In order to ensure systematic and scientific development, management and operation of an integrated multi-modal transport system in the NCT an institutional framework is a basic prerequisite. The focus will be on:

- Institutional strengthening and capacity building from within the available mechanism.
- Horizontal and vertical linkages at all levels of government (Central, State and Local).
- Setting up an Urban Transport. Information System.

Pending establishment of Delhi Unified Metropolitan Transport Authority (DUMTA), an arrangement to strengthen the institutional mechanism by drawing expertise/resources from existing agencies is being set up. This unifying metropolitan transport mechanism is proposed to consist of five groups with clearly defined roles.

4.17 Policy and Planning Group

A Policy and Planning Group (PPG) should be established to function specifically at the level of NCT to plan and coordinate with agencies at the level of DMA. This group should also take into consideration, the guidelines set out by overall spatial planning for the city by the proposed Metropolitan Planning Committee (MPC). This group should also ensure community participation. To be effective the CM of Delhi should chair this group. The main functions of this group will be:

- To set out goals and formulate policy guidelines to facilitate preparation of a Strategic Transport Plan (STP) for the NCT and a multi-modal plan for linkages with the DMA/NCR.
- To coordinate activities of various groups/ agencies at the plan formulation stage.
- To regulate allocation of funds to different agencies for coordinated development.

- To ensure provision of land with focus on identification, reservation and protection for development of transport related projects.

Information based innovative pricing strategies for transport with adequate legal backing should be formulated, and based on real costs.

As part of the policy planning function an independent mechanism, on the pattern of Delhi Electricity Regulatory Commission, should be installed to appropriately price all the items of transport, parking and accessibility.

In this context there is a need to determine pricing of all public and IPT modes on sound economic, system operation and performance basis. The fares and tariffs, determined by the proposed independent mechanism, should be implemented in the entire DMA sub region. Any subsidies, should be contained and minimised and provided only to economically deserving,

4.17.1 Public Transport Group

Following the requirements of the STP, the Public Transport Group (PTG) will be responsible to prepare an action programme to achieve a sustainable and balanced public transport system and optimum multi-modal transport mix. The main agencies in this group will be Indian Railways, DMRC, DTC and private operators and Transport Department of GNCTD. Each agency will ensure provision of services, operation and management and maintenance of the system. The overall and contextual responsibility of each agency in the PTG is clearly defined ensuring functional independence.

4.17.2 Management Group

The Traffic Management Group (TMG) will prepare traffic management strategic action plans with emphasis on movement of people and goods. Area level traffic management schemes with active participation from peoples' group should be prepared for implementation according to time bound programmes.

4.17.3 Infrastructure Development Group

The Infrastructure Development Group (IDG) will comprise of professional advisors and engineering experts from agencies namely the PWD, MCD, NDMC, DDA, and Cantonment Board etc. This group will streamline construction and maintenance practices and formulate project based schemes with latest technological and management interventions. The activities of this group will be based, among other localised schemes, on the strategic transport plan.

4.17.4 Enforcement Group

The proposed Enforcement Group (EG) will have professional advisors, concerned officers from local bodies in addition to the traffic police and local residents and will evolve strategic action plans to ensure smooth and safe flow of all modes of traffic.

Once the unified authority is set up, things should look up and the people of Delhi should get roads on which traffic can move smoothly and without hinderance.

4.18 Maintenance of Roads, Signages, Street Lighting and Sanitation

4.18.1 Signages

One of the essential requirements for smooth flow of traffic in a busy megapolis like Delhi is the provision of proper signages to guide and direct the flow of traffic. Though such signages have been provided in recent years on the National Highways, Ring Road and Outer Ring Road they are often misleading which lead to more confusion. For instance on the Ring Road in Lajpat Nagar you find a signage of the "Garden of Five Senses". Though rightfully an advertisement board, as it is made in the same pattern and colours as a road signage, it misleads people. Further on the Ring Road the main entrance to Naraina Vihar is indicated as road leading to Patel Nagar. On Mathura Road the indications are similarly misleading.

Not only is it important to have signages, but they must direct the road users properly and not lead to confusion in their minds.

The Delhi Government is doing a lot in this connection and is providing luminous signages on all main roads. With the Common Wealth games coming, the thrust would be on making Delhi a beautiful and pleasant to the eye. For this, it is proposed to change the entire road fixtures including streetlights. Modern road signages and markings, meant to educate road users about road safety and rules, would be put up across the Capital.

4.18.2 Road Lighting

Though a lot of improvement has been carried out by the local bodies *viz.*, MCD and NDMC and by the Government of Delhi to provide state of the art lighting on the roads of Delhi and most flyovers have been provided with cluster lights on high masts, there is still vast scope for improvement.

In this connection, the Government of Delhi has decided to bring about a sea change in the scenario before the Commonwealth Games in 2010.

Keeping the Commonwealth Games in mind, the Central government is expected to spend nearly Rs.200 million (over $4 million) on lighting equipment alone. A state of the art illumination technology can change the way Delhi looks during the 2010 Commonwealth Games.

The idea seems to be to make Delhi can look so much better in the night by using effective lighting techniques. This would showcase the array of heritage monuments dotting the city. The city's stadiums, the flyovers and almost all other upcoming infrastructure can be made to look much more attractive with effective lighting.

An electronic lighting control system for regulating the street lights would help save energy and make maintenance easy.

4.19 Pollution

Remote sensors are now identifying gross polluters on the roads of Delhi by the Delhi Department of Transport tests devices that detect vehicle emissions in real time and driving situations.

The pilot study follows a test run of the equipment in Pune and is being demonstrated under a partnership between the city's transportation department, the Automotive Research Association of India and Environmental Systems Products (a U.S. company). The U.S. Agency for International Development's U.S.-Asia Environmental Partnership supports the public-private effort to improve existing vehicle inspection and certification methods that aim to curb air pollution from city traffic.

The remote sensing device technology detects a vehicle's emissions when it drives through an invisible light beam projected across a roadway, and can be placed at different locations around the city. The devices identify polluters and help evaluate control programmes such as the Pollution under Control (PuC) Centers.

The technology is recognised by the U.S. Environmental Protection Agency and is used by many countries around the world together with fixed station inspection and maintenance programmes to enhance mobile source pollution control efforts.

4.20 Maintenance of Roads

There are of course state-of-the-art means of transport and flyovers, but they exist along with uneven roads, overflowing with dirty sewage water and pock-marked by potholes and up to feet deep ditches.

For Delhi motorists, negotiating their way through these hazardous stretches is a torture that takes all pleasure out of the thought of the city that plans to be among the best ones in the world. Despite the issue of the wear and tear of roads taken up at the highest level during the past monsoon season and claims made by the government that quality and speed has been ensured in the construction and repair of roads, their condition, even in the VIP areas, is far from satisfactory.

There are multiple explanations for the poor state of roads in the capital. In a report, the Central Public Works Department, stated that Delhi roads were under great strain because of the density of vehicular traffic, which was the highest in the country.

Delhi Municipal Corporation has been citing lack of funds among other things as coming in the way of ensuring quality of construction and proper maintenance of roads in as much as 90 per cent of the capital's roads are with the MCD and only four per cent with the PWD and NDMC but when it comes to receiving grants, the ratio is reversed. The PWD receives Rs. 400 cr. for maintaining 4,000 km roads while the MCD receives almost the same amount for maintaining 28,000 km roads. Remedial action is required to rectify this situation.

The roads of Delhi cannot be said to be well maintained. After each monsoon there are pot holes and ruts all over the place. Of late, the Delhi Government has faced a huge problem with regard to repair and construction of bitumen roads as the Supreme Court has banned hot mix plants in the capital. Now the raw material is being brought from the hot mix plants that have come up on the periphery of the capital but these are also slowly closing down in view of the tightening of pollution norms in the National Capital Region (NCR).

In order to deal with this problem, the Delhi Government has prepared a proposal for setting up a non-polluting hot mix plants conforming to pollution standards set by the Apex Court. This kind of hot mix plants are already in operation in Gujarat and the PWD has sought information on their functioning so that they could be replicated in the capital.

The Government of Delhi proposes to establish such plants in Delhi with one of the finest technologies in the world. Approval of the Cabinet has already been given for getting such non-polluting plant installed in Delhi. In any case, the Government would first seek the permission of the Supreme Court before setting up such non-polluting hot mix plants.

Improvement of road surface by providing plastic/rubberised wearing coats on Delhi Roads is also being planned.

The Delhi Government is planning a separate Road Maintenance Corporation, which will be entrusted with the task of building and maintenance of roads in the city of Delhi. Currently, the construction and maintenance of roads, subways, bridges and flyovers in the city is looked after by various agencies and departments like the State Urban Development Department, Municipal Corporation of Delhi, State PWD, New Delhi Municipal Council, Delhi Tourism Development Corporation and DDA.

The proposed Corporation will have powers to generate its own resources for its own projects like Metro Rail and NHAI through advertising, constructing roads and flyovers, and maintaining them.

Even though Delhi's area under roads is comparable to other major cities in the World, the condition of roads leaves much to be desired. Poor drainage and heavy traffic soon create pot holes and ruts, which compounded by unplanned digging by various agencies, leads to many bottlenecks to the smooth flow of traffic. Garbage heaps, construction material, haphazard parking by buses and stray cattle on the roads obstruct traffic.

4.21 Status of Railways and Their Development So Far

4.21.1 Delhi is also well connected to all important cities and towns of India by rail. Delhi NCT currently has 156 route kms of BG lines. There are four major railway stations at New Delhi, Delhi, Hazrat Nizamuddin, and Sarai Rohilla besides container terminals at Tughlakabad. There are in all 8 rail corridors in the NCT, which bring in about 400 passenger trains and 40 goods trains every day. Delhi has a double line ring railway but the same is grossly under-utilised due to absence of proper road linkages.

4.21.2 The Railways have a number of measures planned for augmenting the services to and from Delhi. Measures for improving the utilisation of the existing rail infrastructure have also been examined together with development of an integrated road-rail-metro based transport system.

4.21.3 Delhi is now well connected to all important cities and towns of India by rail. Delhi NCT currently has 156 route kms of BG railway lines. There are 4 major railway stations at New Delhi, Delhi, Hazrat Nizamuddin, and Sarai Rohilla besides container terminals at Tughlakabad. There are in all 8 rail corridors in the NCT, which bring in about 400 passenger trains and 40 goods trains every day.

4.21.4 Delhi also has a double line ring railway but the same is grossly under utilised due to absence of proper road linkages.

4.21.5 Railways are planning to take several measures for improving the utilisation of the existing rail infrastructure together with development of an integrated road-rail-metro based transport system.

4.21.6 To upgrade the services to the people of Delhi, the Railways electrified Delhi-Howrah route in 1976 and Delhi-Mumbai Route in 1987. The first Shatabadi Express between New Delhi and Jhansi, which was the fastest train in the country, was launched in 1988.

However, despite introduction of several fast Shatabdi and Rajdhani services, which could compete with the best in the World, the people of Delhi and other cities in the country had to face lot of hardships to get reservations due to touts and employees with vested interests. The computerised passenger reservation system was introduced in 1990 at New Delhi and other Metro Cities.

Simultaneously, the steam engines were phased out which lead to considerable reduction in pollution and improvement of ambient air quality in the NCT of Delhi. The freight services were also upgraded and containerisation of Cargo Traffic brought us close to the state of the art systems in the field.

The rail network has two special features i.e., goods avoiding line (GAL) and Delhi avoiding line (DAL).

The GAL provides a direct entry from Ghaziabad to New Delhi bypassing the congested Delhi Railway Station Complex.

The DAL provides a direct passage from the major yards of Tughalakabad and Ghaziabad directly into the Delhi-Ambala-Kalka section and through Lajpat Nagar-Patel Nagar-Dayabasti and Azadpur link.

4.22 Railway Services in Delhi can be categorised as under

4.22.1 National Network Services

As far as the National network services are concerned, Railways are constantly upgrading the same and adding new trains, increasing capacity of existing trains and speeding up trains to provide better services to the people traveling to and from Delhi.

With a view to develop Indian Railways as a World Class Railway an Integrated Railway Modernisation Plan spaning 5 years upto 2010 has been formulated. Under this plan, running of 150 kms of per hour train on New Delhi-Howrah and New Delhi-Chennai routes is envisaged. On the freight side speeds on Delhi-Mumbai-Delhi-Kolkata and Delhi-Chennai routes are being raised to 100 kmph.

These services are by and large adequate for the traffic offered during most parts of the year except during the summer rush period when the Railways have to run a number of holidays specials to meet the demand. With capacity augmentation works on all saturated sections being taken up on priority and funded out of the Railway Budget/through public private partnership via the RVNL route, the Railways would be able to cope with the projected increase in traffic on the National network link to Delhi.

In order to reduce passenger concentration and resultant discomfort at the existing 3 terminals of Delhi, New Delhi and Nizamuddin, new directional terminals are planned at Holambikalan, Bijwasan, Anand Vihar, and Tughlakabad. A number of capacity enhancement works in the region are under implementation.

The upgradation of New Delhi station to a World Class terminal is in the planning and consultancy stage. At this station arrivals and departures would be segregated, proper parking and terminal facilities similar to those provided in the state of the art modern stations in other world capital cities and metros. The upgradation of Delhi main station and Nizamuddin station is also under implementation.

4.22.2 Commuter Services to Surrounding Towns like Ghaziabad, Faridabad, Rohtak, Panipat and other NCR Towns:

Though suburban trains are already in operation between Delhi and its neighbouring towns, EMU/DMU services are operating between Delhi-New Delhi and these surrounding suburban towns but these carry only a small percentage of the commuters, most of who continue to travel by bus as the service is inadequate, unreliable and inconvenient due to the lack of feeder services from trip end points.

This is on account of limited path availability on the railway lines since the Railways have to fit in these services on available paths between Mail, Express and passenger trains on the same busy routes. Moreover, since these trains travel only upto Delhi, New Delhi and Nizamuddin stations, commuters have to again travel by bus to their destinations.

This service needs major augmentation by construction of additional dedicated local lines with electrification from Delhi to Ghaziabad, Faridabad, Gurgaon, Rohtak, Sonepat and new electrified suburban lines to NOIDA/Greater NOIDA. Thereafter EMU services can be introduced as in Greater Mumbai and Kolkata.

However, to attract the commuters away from road, which consume 6 times more energy for carrying the same amount of traffic as a railway and occupy 4 times more land, it would be essential to introduce an Integrated Rail-cum-Bus Transportation System (IRBT).

The proposal for integrated Rail-cum-Bus Transportation System has already been approved by the NCR Planning Board in its meeting held on January 16, 2004. This proposal is under the consideration of the Government of India. Integrated Rail-cum-Bus Transportation System project is a part of Regional Rapid Transit System (RRTS), which is proposed to be implemented. The following two corridors have been proposed in the first phase of the IRBT project:

- Pulbangash-Sabzimandi-Narela
- Badarpur–Tilak bridge

These corridors are proposed to be implemented by forming two joint venture companies (Special Purpose Vehicles) between Ministry of Urban Development/ National Capital Region Planning Board, Ministry of Railways (MOR), GNCT-Delhi, Government of Haryana and Government of Uttar Pradesh. RITES have completed the technical and economic feasibility for this project. The financing pattern will be on debt equity ratio of 1:1. The equity will be shared such that a third each is borne by the Ministry of Urban Development, Ministry of Railways and by the respective State Governments.

4.22.3 Local Train Services for the Citizens of Delhi

These services are primarily on the ring railway. The ring railway, which was expected to carry 12 per cent of the commuter load, at present, carries less than 1 per cent, with only 12 services.

The main hurdles are limited capacity especially in the northern portion of the ring, inadequate feeder services, commuter inconvenience and lack of integration with radial lines.

A preliminary survey indicated that there was virtually no scope for improving the capacity of northern portion of the ring (between Tilak Bridge and New Delhi station) but it would be possible to augment the capacity in, the southern ring.

The strengthening project (98 kms out of 144 kms of ring railway and radials within NCT) will facilitate operation of Electric Multiple Units (EMU) with frequent services in peak hours.

4.23 Sanctioned Railway Projects and Their Present Status

4.23.1 Development of road network alone will not be able to meet the transport demand of Delhi and the neighbouring towns; hence a supportive rail system will be necessary.

The corridors, which have to be strengthened/ provided by the railways, are listed in the Table 4.26. The regional rail network will also require to be extended by constructing new links in the region. In this connection rail links have been suggested between Rewari and Bhiwadi and between Rohtak and Hansi.

TABLE 4.26

Proposed Rail Network Development Plan in Delhi (As per RITES Report of March 1999)

	Section	*Work*
1.	Shahdara-Sahibabad	Dedicated BG double line & electrified (on MRTS standards)
2.	Sahibabad-New Delhi Railway station	Dedicated BG double line & electrified
3.	Holambi Kalan-Narela	Dedicated BG double line & electrified (on MRTS standards)
4.	Dayabasti-Bijwasan	Dedicated BG double line & electrified
5.	Tilak Bridge-Tughlakabad	Dedicated BG double line & electrified
6.	Patel Nagar to Shakurbasti	Dedicated BG double line & electrified
7.	Brar square to Delhi Cantt station	Dedicated BG double line & electrified
8.	Terminal at Tilak Bridge	EMU terminal
9.	New Tilak Bridge to Mayur Vihar (Delhi Border) part of New Tilak Bridge Noida Greater Noida new rail link	Dedicated BG double line & electrified

The above works were originally targeted for completion in 2005-06 but have got delayed on account of scarcity of resources. They will be completed in the coming years.

In addition there are 15 projects for developing the rail network in the NCR region, which will facilitate travel from neighbouring towns to and from Delhi.

4.23.2 Studies done for the Augmentation of the Railway System in Delhi

Northern Railway conducted a study on Commuter Travel in NCR and Delhi in 1998. The major findings and recommendations of the study were:

- Out of an estimated 2 million inter-city trips per day in 1998 only 20 per cent was by rail while 50 per cent was by bus
- Total inter-city trips were projected to grow to 85 lakhs per day in 2025 respectively
- 15 sections at regional level and 12 sections including (3 sections for MRTS) at city level were proposed. Most of the lines in Delhi area were proposed as "Dedicated Electrified BG Double Line".

Due to involvement of multiple agencies including various 'state governments, not much headway has been made so far, except the ongoing construction work of the MRTS.

4.23.3 Regional Rail Projects Connecting Delhi and NCR Towns

A number of regional rail projects, which aim at strengthenmg the existing rail infrastructure and include provision of dedicated electrified corridors, Additional terminals, and automatic signaling facilities. additional stations, rolling stock, power supply, etc., are being implemented in a phased manner.

4.23.4 Revitalisation of Ring Railway

The ring rail originally constructed in the 1930s as a city bypass line for goods traffic was suggested by DDA in 1962 to be developed as an important public transport mode. However, the system, which was initially expected to carry 12 per cent of commuter load, carries less than 1 per cent at present.

Subsequent evaluation of the system identified the main hurdles as limited capacity in the northern portion of the ring, inadequate feeder service, integration with radial lines and above all non-conforming land use along the corridor to attract passenger use. Considering the near —saturated road traffic condition revitalisation of the system is an immediate necessity.

Data collected through Household Travel Surveys for MRTS (1994) and Commuter Travel in NCR and Delhi by Northern Railways (1998) will serve as a base for travel pattern assessment. The scope of the work will include land-use corrections along the corridor, demand estimation and projection, working out rolling stock requirements and service frequency, provision of feeder service, capacity augmentation and integration.

4.23.5 *Strengthening Rail Service to DMA and NCR Towns*

The study on Commuter Travel in NCR and Delhi by Northern Railways (1998) estimated about 2 million inter-city trips per day of which only 20 per cent was carried by rail. Considering the developments in DMA and other NCR towns there is need to strengthen the available service capacity along the tracks. Moreover land use correction along the corridors and integration arrangements with Ring Rail/MATS needs adequate attention.

Prioritisation of the corridors to be developed is to be made in such a way so that the road traffic impact of this rail based traffic within the city remains minimal.

4.24 Traffic Management

4.24.1 *Traffic Engineering and Improvement Schemes*

There is a need to strengthen the technical capability of agencies to facilitate the preparation of traffic engineering improvement schemes. The inherent deficiencies in traffic management in metropolitan Delhi are the absence of a clearly defined road hierarchy, lack of access control, inadequate traffic design and road equipment, and above all, the lack of road user discipline.

Some area-wide traffic management schemes have been commissioned in places such as Connaught Circus and India Gate. Based on the experience of SCOOT (Split Cycle Off-Set Optimisation Technique), implemented by Delhi Traffic Police for 50 intersections in New Delhi area with Central Computer Center at Teen Murti. Similar other areas with critical problems should also be covered with such systems. At a number of locations pedestrian subways are not being used optimally due to poor siting and poor maintenance. Actions are necessary to improve their utilisation.

4.24.2 *Road Safety*

Safety is a major component of the traffic environment. The phenomenal increase in the number of motor vehicles in the city coupled with limited road space, inadequate facilities for pedestrians and cyclists, irresponsible driving and violation of traffic rules has resulted in significant number of road accidents. Though the number of accidents has shown a decreasing trend in the last three years due to continuing efforts of Traffic Police, this aspect should get adequate attention in order to improve the traffic environments. Public safety forms an integral part of the sections that follow.

In addition, there is need for a GNCTD policy regarding road safety education in schools so that children can be made aware of the dangers of road traffic and learn the proper rules of the road and Highway Code.

4.24.3 *Parking*

Increasing parking demand together with limited parking supply and absence of a parking policy is an impediment to the smooth flow of traffic, especially in and around major commercial areas/activity centres. With the basic objective of reducing the parking demand (especially for personalised vehicles), parking pricing is a major tool for environmental improvement Moreover, provision of 'Park and Ride' facilities, additional parking supply in critical areas with optimal private sector participation, employers participation in transport demand management, and stringent controls in zoned areas are key policy issues.

The Government of Delhi is, at present, engaged in finalising the parking policy. Through this policy, efforts will be made to wean away the users of personalised vehicles to "public transport" so that the demand for parking is contained to an extent. It is also being envisaged to raise the "parking fees" to enable such fees reflects the economic cost of land.

Under the "Parking policy", it is proposed to provide "Park & Ride" services with access to important commercial centers etc. so that the customers could park their vehicles at convenient locations and commute to their destination by using the "Park and ride" vehicles.

4.24.4 *Enforcement*

The traffic police have to bear the difficult responsibility of managing and controlling traffic flow. Difficulties are made worse due to lack of coordination from local and road maintenance agencies. Local expertise is required to facilitate formulation of low cost and viable area-wide traffic management schemes. Vehicle pollution control can be assisted through technological advances and strict enforcement of regulations.

4.24.5 *Transport System for Special Areas*

Preparation of a strategic action plan is needed for special areas and specialised markets to determine a framework for functional optimisation and relocation. Car-free zones with support from non-motorised vehicles and environment friendly medium capacity transport modes, like battery operated buses, should be established with the provision of parking at the periphery. To conserve the historic character of the walled city, pedestrian zones should be reinstated. Entry of vehicles for the servicing of shops and establishments would only be permitted outside certain entry timings, at night, for example, between 8 pm and 8 am.

4.24.6 Urban Transport Information System

Update and revision of available data, filling data gaps and preparation of urban transport information system.

Traffic, travel, network and land use data are generally collected by various agencies like PWD, DDA, DTC, NDMC, MCD, GNCTD etc., with reference to some specific project. For travel characteristics, the Household Travel Surveys for MRTS (1994) and Commuter Travel in NCR and Delhi by Northern Railways (1998) form base line data. DCA is also in the process of preparing the MPC-2021 from where existing and proposed land-use maps will be available. Enough traffic and network related data is available from PWD, NDMC and MCD, though much of it needs updating. With all this availability of data, no effort has been made so far to consolidate the entire data base and make it available to decision makers, researchers and transport specialists so that planning and policy interventions are coordinated for an effective and efficient transport system. The Urban Transport Information System will be a giant step towards this direction. The scope of the work *inter-alia* will cover consolidation of recent available data, collection and updating of information, bridging data gaps, computerisation and making them available through the electronic media.

It is recommended that the agencies that collect data/ information about transport systems in Delhi and NCR should make it available to all the other agencies so that coordination in their activities could be established.

4.24.7 Recommendations in this regard are:

This report has attempted to present future directions and actions that need to be initiated in the traffic and transport sector in the context of the objective to provide, promote and ensure, safe, economic and efficient movement of all categories of passengers and goods, in an integrated multi-modal transportation system.

The exclusive bus ways and Traffic Management schemes can offer almost immediate relief at much lesser cost and should therefore be given immediate attention.

A unifying mechanism has been proposed which needs to be established as soon as possible. This mechanism can be replaced by DUMTA in due course. The various groups under this mechanism need to initiate actions in their own spheres, which will get continuously reviewed, and improvements will get introduced on the basis of the experience gained.

The information base, the policy formulation and review and monitoring will automatically keep this sector active in its own sphere and also activate others concerned, such as the land-use planners and those in charge of development control, those responsible for implementation of construction for traffic improvement etc. The mechanism can review traffic flows on various arteries and through various junctions. It can suggest local and linked improvements in the interest of best flows and initiate many such other actions especially in the operation of the public sector transport systems of different types of modes and their operation in a linked manner.

Special attention also needs to be provided to the green modes—for the cyclists and pedestrians. Such proposals and progress on their implementation needs to be reviewed periodically at the highest level. We are of the view that the Master Plan should have provision for these. Since the process is dynamic many more plans and actions might get generated and implemented in the future. Unlike the past, it is to be hoped that Delhi will be a much more livable city in terms of traffic and transportation achievements in a very short period - much before the expectations as expressed in Delhi–21 i.e. much before 2021.

The Ministry of Urban Development is preparing a draft Bill for constituting the Delhi Metropolitan Transport Authority (DMTA) and till that is finalised, a Coordination Committee, known as Delhi Metropolitan Transport Coordination Committee, will function to secure compliance for inter agency requests and coordinate the inter-agency activities.

4.25 Salient Features of the Report of the Committee on Sustainable Transport

The main recommendations are to provide *interse* priority in descending order to:

- Mass transport
- Non-Motorised Transport (NMT) namely bicycles, cycle-rickshaws, pedestrians etc.
- Intermediate Public Transport (IPT) namely auto-rickshaws, taxi etc., and
- Personalised motor transport

An integrated Metropolitan Transport Authority (IMTA) should be set up not only for setting fares and tariffs but also to provide provisioning and common services for bus, metro and commuter rail as well as IPT modes. There should be one authority for all modes of transport.

Pending the setting up of IMTA, a Delhi Transport Planning Group (DTPG) should be constituted. A technical cell of qualified and trained professionals from all concerned departments may support the DTPG.

4.26 Further Recommendations

Work on the Phase I of the commuter rail system called the Integrated Rail and Bus transit (IRBT) along three existing railway lines needs to be speeded up.While the Metro is coming up fast, even after a fully developed rail based Mass Rapid Transit System has come into existence, the bus system will continue to play the role of the main mass transport system provider.

Development of bus terminals is very important for efficient operation of any bus system. Three directional Inter State Bus Terminals (ISBTs) have already been provided and two more are to be taken up at Dwarka and Narela. The services at the existing ISBTs at Kashmere Gate, Anand Vihar, and Sarai Kale Khan need to be further improved.

IPT modes will continue to play an important role even in the future as feeder services to the main mass transport system and providing accessible movement in pre-designated areas. Therefore, steps have to be taken to strengthen this system by proper regulation and discipline.

Several low cost and quickly implementable transport system management (TSM) measures are being given a lot of importance in order to improve traffic flow. TSM plans are being prepared for various corridors and will be taken up for implementation.

4.27 Integration Issues

Integration of all modes of transport is necessary to achieve the potential of each mode. Feeder systems to metro and commuter rail will be provided. Facilities for parking of personalised modes, autos and taxis are proposed at all stations. Timetable and fare integration for metro rail and buses are also contemplated.

4.28 Vision for the State and Policy Action Required for Achieving the Same

4.28.1 As per the Master Plan of Delhi, the vision of the Government is that Delhi should be a well-managed, clean and dynamic city serving its citizens as a model capital city.

The mission is to provide safe, eco-friendly, cost-effective and efficient modes of transportation through a well-integrated multi-modal transport system.

4.28.1.1 In order to strike the appropriate modal balance, an extensive mass transport system including a metro, commuter rail and buses will be required. Considering this, the Delhi Metro is being rapidly progressed within the NCT as per details above and also connecting to Gurgaon, Noida, and Faridabad and later to Greater Noida which will help commuter traffic. In addition, Phase I of the commuter rail system called the Integrated Rail and Bus transit (IRBT) along three existing railway lines is also being taken up in partnership with neighbouring State Governments of Haryana and Uttar Pradesh and the Government of India.

4.24.1.2 Even after a fully developed rail based Mass Rapid Transit System has come into existence; the bus system will continue to play the role of the main mass transport system provider. The bus system is proposed to be augmented to 10000 CNG buses within a year on Stage Carriage to be supplemented with about 4000 CNG buses on chartered and premium services. Premium bus services will be introduced on selected routes. High Capacity Bus Systems on selected corridors for 100 km is planned. In addition, on 32 km of selected corridors, Electric Trolley Buses will also be introduced in order to reduce congestion and pollution. A Light Rail Transit for the walled city is being considered. In order to improve the bus system dedicated busways/lanes are being planned on designated road corridors.

4.28.1.3 Development of bus terminals is very important for efficient operation of any bus system. Three directional Inter State Bus Terminals (ISBTs) have already been provided and two more are to. IPT modes will continue to play an important role even in the future as feeder services to the main mass transport system and providing accessible movement in pre-designated areas. Therefore, steps are being taken to strengthen this system by proper regulation and discipline.

4.28.2 *Perspective for Future Needs: Travel Demand by 2021*

Based on the existing situation and trends the transport scenario for 2021 appears to be quite alarming. The various indicators for assessment of travel demand are shown in Table 4.27.

4.28.3 *Traffic and Transport Management and Environment*

The Goals laid down in the Master Plan for Delhi 2021 are

Delhi should be free of environmental problems from this sector. From this angle the following goals can be set for traffic and transportation sector:

TABLE 4.27

Perspective for Future Needs: Travel Demand by 2021

Population	13.78 million in 2001 22 million in 2021
Vehicles	3.3 million in 1999 Over 8 million in 2021
Per capita trip rate (mechanical modes)	0.79 in 1993 1.2 in 2021
Avg. Trip Length (km)	Car 11.28 in 1993 17.74 in 2021 Bus 10.66 in 1993 14.58 in 2021

- Traffic levels on roads within environmental capacity (with respect to physical, noise and air pollution).
- Efficient handling of traffic through traffic engineering and management, schemes about 80 per cent patronage for public transport (both road based and rail based).
- Adequate facilities for pedestrians and cyclists.
- Effective use of parking spaces.
- Use of cleaner fuels.
- Segregation of local and regional traffic.
- Transport sector management—unified transport authority (DUMTA).
- Improvement of connectivity to DMA & NCR towns.
- Private investments in transport infrastructure. Decongestion of metropolitan city centre.

4.28.4 Policy Framework—Regional Transport Linkages

The solution to Delhi's transport problems does not only lie just in the NCT. It also depends on the linkages to DMA towns, in particular, and to the NCR towns in general. Though suburban trains are already in operation between Delhi and its neighbouring towns, the service is inadequate, unreliable and inconvenient.These sections need to be strengthened and services augmented.

Further, in absence of any suitable bypass for the city the intermixing of local and regional traffic acts as a major deterrence factor for smooth flow of traffic in the city. The peripheral expressways as conceptualised will decongest the roads significantly.

4.28.5 Future Directions

A well-functioning road infrastructure must fulfill the requirements of all road users. In the context of the present socioeconomic realities in most developing countries, pedestrians, cyclists and other slow moving vehicles cannot be eliminated from the urban landscape. The needs of pedestrians have been ignored in conventional planning strategies and have been assigned lower importance compared with other vehicles on the road. However, the experience from environments where 'captive pedestrians' are present makes a very strong case for.re-thinking the conventional hierarchy of road users. It is clear that present investment patterns focused on improving conditions for cars are not giving the desired results.

Congestion continues to worsen along with a shift away from walking, bicycles and public transport– the desirable modes for sustainability. A reversal of this trend is possible. It is possible to create pedestrian, bicycle and public transport friendly urban roads without increasing the right of way of existing arterial roads in Delhi. The guiding principle of such a design is meeting the needs of pedestrians, cyclists and public transport commuters in that order.

Given that there is not much space available to expand existing roads, future mobility needs are best met by increasing the capacity of the existing road network. This can only be achieved by encouraging modes, which are more efficient in terms of space utilisation. If pedestrian friendly paths are constructed, together with a separate segregated lane for bicycles, the kerbside lane (which is currently used by cyclists) becomes available to motorised traffic.

4.29 What Ails Delhi Roads

4.29.1 In order to achieve the above aims, the foremost requirement would be to study the factors that ail Delhi Roads at present. There are of course state-of-the-art means of transport and flyovers, but they exist along with uneven roads, overflowing with dirty sewage water and pock-marked by potholes and up to feet deep ditches.

4.29.2 For Delhi motorists, negotiating their way through these hazardous stretches is a torture that takes all pleasure out of the thought of the city that plans to be among the best ones in the world. Despite the issue of the wear and tear of roads taken up at the highest level during the past monsoon season and claims made by the government that quality and speed has been ensured in the construction and repair of roads, their condition, even in the VIP areas, is far from satisfactory.

4.29.3 There are multiple explanations for the poor state of roads in the capital. The Central Public Works

Department says that Delhi roads were under great strain because of the density of vehicular traffic, which was the highest in the country.

4.29.4 Various service providers like MTNL, private Telecom operators and others for laying their cables was one of the main reasons for the deteriorating condition of roads as after doing their work, they do not do the repairs properly. However, the system is going to end shortly. The service providers will now leave the scene after digging and it is MCD, which will do the repairs, and the cost will be charged from the service providers.

4.29.5 Leakage and poor drainage was also an important cause of early wear and tear of roads as per Delhi PWD and the NDMC has expressed agreement on this count.

4.29.6 It is felt that in order to improve maintenance as well as to optimise construction costs, quality and accountability, all roads in Delhi except National Highways and those in Cantonment area, should be given to one agency, the most suited is the PWD. This agency should be responsible for construction, improvement and maintainance. Legal issues will be there but these could be sorted out.

4.29.7 Development of Directional Terminals and Freight Complexes

The MPD 2001 proposals for terminals and freight complexes are yet to be implemented fully. The proposed locations need to be reviewed in the light of present movement patterns and road/rail development projects. The scope of the proposed project will include assessment of movement patterns for passengers and goods, identification/validation of locations, layout clans and designs, private sector participation options. Integration with the total system. Implementation and operation.

DRINKING WATER SUPPLY

4.30 Current Status and Resource Assessment

4.30.1 Water Supply and Demand

4.30.1.1 Water—A Precious Resource

Water is a precious natural resource, next to air only, vital for sustaining all forms of life on the earth. Three-fourth of the earth's surface area is under water and yet only 3 per cent of it is usable, the balance 97 per cent being in the oceans. Therefore, being an exhaustible resource and with the associated problems of maintenance of its quality due to environmental degradation, management of this resource has been a matter of concern for the civic authorities. Although, India receives an average rainfall equivalent to about 4,000 billion cubic meters (BCM) annually, it is unevenly distributed both spatially and temporally. Nearly three-fourth of the annual rainfall is concentrated in the four months of monsoon, most of which flows down the sea as river runoff due to non-availability of adequate storage in upstream river basins.

Surface water resources such as rivers and lakes are the major sources of drinking water for majority of the urban population. Due to problems of uneven distribution of precipitation, abstraction of large quantities of water for irrigation and growing anthropogenic pressures leading to environmental degradation of the surface water resources, availability of drinking water is becoming difficult day-by-day. Every third person in the country does not have access to safe drinking water. Despite the growing problem of its scarcity and deteriorating quality, water in India is still managed as a 'cheap resource' rather than a 'productive asset' with an economic value attached to it. This goes against the very concept of conservation amongst various consumptive and non-consumptive uses of this precious resource.

4.30.1.2 Population of Delhi

According to the Census of India 2001, population of Delhi is 13.85 million comprising 7.57 million (55 per cent) males and 6.28 million (45 per cent) females. The density of population is 9,294, which is the highest amongst all States and Union Territories. The growth of population during the decade 1991-2001 was 46.31 per cent which portrays an annual rate of 4.63 per cent as against the national average growth rate of 3.12 per cent in the urban areas. According to the sources of the Ministry of Urban Development, nearly 50 per cent of the growth in population is on account of people migrating into the city every year from other states for employment opportunities. The current literacy level is 81.82 per cent as compared to 75.29 per cent in 1991.

Nearly 31 per cent of the current population of Delhi lives in *Jhuggi-Jhopri* (JJ) clusters, unauthorised colonies and villages of various categories and does not have access to the piped water supply and sewerage system. Of these, about 3 million people live in about 600,000 shanties comprising JJ clusters spread all over the city.

4.30.1.3 The Delhi Jal Board

The Delhi Jal Board (DJB) is entrusted with the responsibility of production and supply of potable water in Delhi. The DJB was constituted in April 1998 through an Act of the Delhi Legislative Assembly incorporating the then Delhi Water Supply and Sewage Disposal Undertaking. Besides managing drinking water, DJB is also responsible for collection, disposal and treatment of municipal sewage in the capital. The Board provides water in bulk quantity to the areas covered under the New Delhi Municipal Corporation (NDMC) and the Delhi Cantonment Board. Water supply in the remaining parts of Delhi is handled by DJB directly.

DJB functions under the Chief Minister of Delhi as its Chairperson. The Vice-Chairperson of the Board is nominated by the Speaker of the Legislative Assembly from amongst the Members. The executive functions of the Board are vested in the Chief Executive Officer. The Board meetings are held once in a month. The full constitution of the DJB is at Annexure A-4.1. The organisational setup of DJB is at Annexure A-4.2.

Currently, DJB has a staff strength of about 26000 for both water and sewerage sectors. The distribution of manpower is reported to be in the ratio of about 40:60 between these two sectors. Accordingly, the current manpower for handling water supply is about 10500, which makes DJB a considerably oversized organisation in comparison with those handling similar services in Mumbai, Chennai and Kolkata.

4.30.1.4 Rate of Water Supply

DJB has adopted a per capita water supply rate for domestic consumption as per the Central Public Health Engineering and Environment Organisation (CPHEEO) Manual 1999 on water supply. The Manual prescribes a rate of 150 lpcd (litres/capita/day). For metropolitan and mega cities, the manual also provides an allowance of 15 per cent over this rate towards losses. For assessing the water demand for other uses, the rates prescribed in the Master Plan Document-2001 have been followed. Accordingly, the per capita water requirement works out to 275 lpcd as calculated below under Table 4.28.

TABLE 4.28

Rate of Water Supply

	Type of Use	*Rate (in lpcd)*
(a)	Domestic (150 lpcd + 15% towards losses)	172
(b)	Industrial, commercial and community requirement @ 45,00 per ha. per day	47
(c)	Special uses, embassies, hotels, airport, railway stations, floating population etc.	52
(d)	Fire protection @ 1% of total demand	3
	Total	274

Note: Say 275 lpcd or 60 gallons/capita/day (gpcd)

The supply rate is reckoned at the source of production. In the calculation, there is no provision for use of potable water for parks, lawns, horticulture and agriculture due to shortage of water.

This rate compares well with that of Mumbai and important cities like London of the developed countries. However, the Delhi Development Authority (DDA), which is the nodal agency for preparation of the Master Plan of Delhi, has adopted a rate of 80 gpcd for the Master Plan Document-2021, which appears to be non-achievable, given the constraint of raw water availability for Delhi during the Master Plan period.

4.30.1.5 Potable Water Demand

Based on the projections of the Master Plan Document-2021, the current population (2005) of Delhi is estimated at 16 million. Thus, the total demand of drinking water at the rate of 60 gpcd is estimated at 960 mgd.

4.30.1.6 Sources of Raw Water

The water treatment capacity is governed by the availability of raw water. Another factor that has bearing on it is the losses that occur during the transit of raw water from the source to the treatment plant.

Delhi depends on several sources of raw water to meet its drinking water needs. The main sources are Yamuna, Ganga and Bhakra Byas Management Board (BBMB). Besides these, Delhi also draws ground water equivalent to about 15 per cent of its present treatment capacity through a battery of ranney wells and tube wells.

The share of Delhi in Yamuna water as per MoU dated 12 May 1994 signed by the riparian states is 0.724 BCM, which is subject to construction of storage dams in the upper reaches. Meanwhile, seasonal allocations are made by the Upper Yamuna River Board (UYRB) and the lean period allocation of Delhi during March to June is 0.076 BCM or 750 cusec of which 495 cusec is returned as wastewater to Yamuna river. This quantity is allocated at two points, namely: 381 cusec at Tajewala for Haiderpur WTP and 369 cusec at Wazirabad for Wazirabad and Chandrawal WTPs. The allocation of 381 cusec at Tajewala is carried through the Western Yamuna Canal (WYC) and Delhi sub-branch. In this passage, there are 13 per cent losses from Tajewala to Munak and 30 per cent losses from Munak to Haiderpur. The total transit losses are estimated at 148 cusec or 80 mgd. Thus, the net raw water availability from the Yamuna is about 600 cusec or 325 mgd. To save the losses from Munak to Haiderpur, the work of construction of parallel channel has been entrusted to the Irrigation Department of

Haryana. This will help Delhi to save about 80 mgd of water for which DJB has planned for construction of a WTP of equivalent capacity.

The Ganga water for Delhi measuring 200 cusec or 108 mgd is released through the Upper Ganga Canal (UGC) system at Muradnagar in District Ghaziabad about 40 km from Delhi. Water from Muradnagar is conveyed through a closed conduit to the Bhagirathi WTP and hence there are no en route transit losses.

A total quantity of 431 cusec (233 mgd) is released by BBMB at Nangal in Punjab and is supplied through the Narwana branch and WYC system. The transit losses are 13 per cent from Nangal to Munak and 30 per cent from Munak to Haiderpur. In the Haryana portion, it is supplied through the same WYC as in the case of Yamuna water. The transit losses on the route are estimated at about 150 cusec or 80 mgd leaving the net quantity available at the treatment plants as only about 280 cusec or 153 mgd.

In addition to the above, about 185 cusec or 100 mgd is extracted from groundwater through a number of Ranney wells and tube wells.

Thus, the current raw water availability for Delhi from different sources is 686 mgd. Of this, 586 mgd is river/canal water and the remaining 100 mgd is from groundwater. The details of the source-wise availability of raw water and the transit losses are as given in the Table 4.29.

TABLE 4.29

Installed Capacity and the Sources of Raw Water

Sl. No.	*Raw Water Source*	*Quantity*		*Transit Losses (mgd)*	*Net Quantity (mgd)*
		In cusec	*In mgd*		
1.	Yamuna	750	405	80	325
2.	Ganga	200	108	Nil	108
3.	BBMB	431	233	80	153
4.	Ground Water	185	100	Nil	100
	Total	**1566**	**846**	**160**	**686**

4.30.1.7 Current Water Treatment Capacity

Raw water from river/canal is first treated in a WTP to the desired quality level before it is supplied to consumers as potable water. On the other hand, groundwater is extracted from only those aquifers, which conform to the potable grade quality. Therefore, it is supplied direct to the consumers.

As against the raw water availability of 686 mgd, the present installed capacity is 650 mgd comprising 550 mgd from WTPs and 100 mgd from groundwater. Plant-wise details of the installed capacity and the sources of raw water are given in the Table 4.30.

TABLE 4.30

Current Water Treatment Capacity

Sl. No.	*Source of Raw Water*	*Water Treatment Plant*	*Installed Capacity (mgd)*
1.	Yamuna	Chandrawal I & II	90
2.	Yamuna	Wazirabad I, II & III	120
3.	BBMB	Haiderpur I	100
4.	Yamuna	Haiderpur II	100
5.	BBMB	Nangloi	40
6.	Ganga	Bhagirathi	100
7.	Groundwater	Ranney Wells/Tube Wells	100
		Total	**650**

A map showing the revenue zones of DJB and locations of the various WTPs is at Annexure A-4.3.

Although the installed capacity of the Nangloi WTP is 40 mgd, it is presently operating at half the capacity at 20 mgd only due to the constraint of raw water availability. The Government of Haryana is presently taking up some improvement works on WYC. These works were scheduled to be completed by the end of March 2004 but have not completed so far. Full supply of 40 mgd would be restored only after completion of these works.

With the optimisation of capacity of WTPs, DJB presently produces about 670 mgd of potable water to meet the drinking water needs of the current population of 16 million.

Of the total water produced, bulk supply of potable water is given to NDMC and the Delhi Cantonment Board under an existing agreement. Presently, about 26 to 27 mgd is supplied to NDMC and 7.5 mgd to the Cantonment area. The population of these two segments is about 0.6 million. The balance quantity of about 636 mgd is supplied as drinking water to the remaining population of about 15.4 million. Of this, nearly 3 million people live in JJ clusters, which do not have service connections for piped water supply. The rate of water supply to these JJ clusters is not more than 10 gpcd. In addition, it is estimated that at least another 2 million people living in unauthorised colonies and rural villages also get water at the rate of not more than 10 gpcd. The total water supplied to this segment of the population is thus about 60 mgd only. Therefore, the balance quantity of 576 mgd (636 mgd–60 mgd) is supplied to a population of 9.4 million, which accounts for a supply rate of about 65 gpcd.

4.30.1.8 Shortfall in Supply

As mentioned in Para 4.1.1.5, the current water demand is 960 mgd against which the production of potable water is 670 mgd. Therefore, there is a shortfall of 290 mgd at present.

The delay in commissioning of the 140 mgd Sonia Vihar WTP is responsible largely for the shortfall in treatment capacity. This treatment plant is to get 300 cusec or 162 mgd of raw water from Tehri Dam. After en route losses of 30 cusec, the net availability through the UGC system at Muradnagar will be 270 cusec. From Muradnagar, raw water will be carried through a 3200 mm conduit, which has already been completed. This plant was to be put in operation by December 2004 but has been delayed due to delay in the supply of raw water from the Tehri Dam. DJB has made arrangements with the Government of UP for providing 80 cusec of Ganga water for flushing the treatment system. DJB now expects this WTP to be commissioned by July 2006 when the supply of raw water from Tehri would start on a regular basis.

With the availability of raw water and commissioning of the Sonia Vihar WTP, the present total operating capacity would become 790 mgd and the shortfall in the water supply would accordingly come down.

4.30.1.9 Other Problems of Water Supply

All the WTPs are located West and Northeast Zones of Delhi. The locations were selected in consideration of the nearness to the source of raw water. The WTPs and distribution network were designed to cater to the population of the command area on an equitable basis. However, in the course of time, several new colonies have come up in the respective command areas increasing the load on the distribution network. As a result, the consumers located at the tail end of the distribution network suffer on account of water shortage. This phenomenon is more prominently reflected in the South and Southwest zones. The delay in the commissioning of the Sonia Vihar WTP has compounded the problem of water shortage further in these revenue zones.

Another related problem of water supply in the residential areas, particularly the group housing colonies, is the supply pressure. Although, the distribution system in such colonies were designed to ensure supply at the desired pressure, the overall shortage of water supply has led the consumers to put online boosters. As a result, supply pressures in such colonies have remained low. Putting online booster is illegal under the DJB Act.

4.30.1.10 Water Supply-24 X 7

Currently, DJB supplies water on an intermittent basis. However, in line with the practice followed in the developed countries, DJB plans to switch over to the 24 hours supply system.

This system would be introduced in a phased manner after a careful study in select pilot areas. The programme would seek to have a mix of supply side interventions and demand side measure to achieve this goal. The supply side interventions would basically include effective leakage management and NRW (non-revenue water) reduction. The demand side measures would comprise 100 per cent metering and volumetric pricing.

On the basis of the experience gained during the first phase, the coverage of the scheme would be extended to other zones of the city.

4.30.2 Water Treatment Process

The DJB has adopted universally proven technologies at its WTPs. Raw water lifted from canal or river is pre-chlorinated to destroy the organic impurities and algae and then taken to a clarifloculator to remove the inorganic impurities by alum dosing. Clear water then passes over rapid sand filters to remove the remaining inorganic impurities. A pre-calculated dose of chlorine is added to the filtered water to destroy the traces of organic matters up to the consumer end.

DJB has also introduced a modern technique, namely the Biological Nitrification and Ozone Treatment at Okhla WTP to treat contaminated potable water before supplying to the network to improve its colour, taste and bacteriological characteristics.

The recently constructed 140 mgd Sonia Vihar WTP uses some of the state-of-the-art technologies like Pulsator Clarifiers and Aquazur V Filters for treatment of raw water. The pulsator clarifier operates under the principles of an up-flow current through a suspended sludge blanket for the removal of colloids, plankton and algae. This method is extremely efficient (95-99 per cent) for removal of impurities as compared to the other conventional clarifiers. Aquazur V filter uses a single layer of homogenous sand and is suitable for high rate filtration and extended filtration cycle due to its in-depth clogging capacity.

DJB is one of the few public utilities to undertake extensive work on Geographical Information System (GIS), mapping of its various utilities like the numerous water and sewage treatment plants, water transmissions, mains, underground reservoirs, overhead tanks, ranney wells, tubewells and several other appurtenant works. The attributes pertaining to the various objects are both spatial as well as non-spatial to their maximum useful aspects. The modeling and analysing tools are also purposed to be put in place subsequently.

4.30.3 Quality Control

The drinking water supplied by DJB is potable, wholesome and conforms to the BIS 10500 of the Bureau of Indian Standards and the standards prescribed by the CPHEEO of the Ministry of Urban Development. The quality of water is checked at every stage of treatment right from the raw water stage up to storage in service reservoirs and also in the distribution system at the consumers' end.

Water supplied from ranney wells and tubewells is also tested on regular basis to ensure that it conforms to the BIS 10500 and no contamination takes place during transmission of water through water mains.

Besides nine laboratories at the WTPs, there are six zonal laboratories manned by a staff of 200 persons comprising, among others, qualified chemists. Approximately 300 to 400 water samples are lifted daily from the distribution system, individual taps, public hydrants, etc. for ensuring the desired water quality in the distribution system. Of these, only about 2-3 per cent failures are reported, where remedial measures are immediately taken to rectify the cause of failure. In order to avoid contamination of water, all ground reservoirs, overhead tanks and dead ends in the distribution system are flushed and cleaned periodically.

Despite these quality checks, complaints of contaminated water are often reported from users. Sewer and water mains have been closely laid in the residential areas. Leakage occurs in both these mains. Because of intermittent water supply system, the water mains suck sewage through leaking joints resulting in the contamination of water. In order to curb this problem, a more stringent inspection of the vulnerable areas and sealing of leaking joints is necessary.

4.30.4 Water Conservation Measures and Public Participation

4.30.4.1 Leakage Control

Leakage is one of the components of water losses and comprises physical losses from old and damaged pipes, joints and fittings and also overflows from service reservoirs. These losses could be severe and may go undetected for months or even years. The larger losses are usually from burst pipes or from sudden rupture of a joint. Leakage losses are sometimes referred to as 'Unaccounted for Water' or 'Non-Revenue Water'.

Delhi has a network of about 9,000 Kms. of water supply mains of which, a significant portion is as old as 40 to 50 years and prone to higher leakage losses. Normally water losses are calculated by water billed or consumed subtracted from the water produced. In the case of Delhi, water billed or consumed and leakage losses therefrom can not be calculated exactly as a majority of houses do not have working meters. According to the estimates of DJB, the total distribution losses are of the order of 40 per cent of the total water supplied. These are quite high as compared to 10-20 per cent in the developing countries. The distribution losses include losses due (a) leaking pipes and (b) theft of water through unauthorised connections. The CPHEEO Manual on water supply prescribes 15 per cent distribution losses.

DJB has taken several steps to minimise leakage losses. To address this problem, a leak detection and investigation (LDI) cell was set up in 1978 to provide assistance in leak detection and to monitor leakage repairs in transmission and distribution network. Initially, the leak detection cell started functioning with the help of a very few conventional equipments *viz.*, sounding rods, micro-correlates and pipe/cable locators. More sophisticated sonic and electronic equipments were subsequently acquired and are now being used regularly. During 2002-03, a total of 12000 leaking points were repaired which resulted in the saving of potable water at the rate of 2.5 million gallons/hr. In addition, the Board has replaced about 1200 km length of the old, damaged and leaking water mains during the last five years. DJB has also started monitoring water thefts through unauthorised connections. As a result of these initiatives, the Board expects to bring down the distribution losses to 20 per cent level in the near future.

4.30.4.2 Metering of Supply

Metering of water supply, be it domestic or for other uses, is an important step towards conserving water besides increasing the revenue of DJB.

The total number of water connections provided by DJB at present is about 1.5 million in all categories. Of these, nearly 1.32 million connections are in the domestic category. Of these, there are about 322,000 connections mostly in the rural areas where meters are not to be provided. Tariffs in these areas are on a flat rate. Thus, there are about 1 million connections where the water supply is to be metered. Of these, nearly 0.53 million connections have either defective meters or no meters at all. These connections will require installation of new meters.

To enable the consumers to purchase and install the meters directly, DJB has circulated the specifications of water meters and the details of test houses where such meters are to be tested for ensuring accuracy. Institutions like the National Physical Laboratory Delhi have been entrusted with the responsibility of testing the meters. This will ensure the quality of meters and metering of domestic water consumption in a reliable manner. Despite these measures and quality checks, there are frequent complaints from users about non-functioning of newly installed meters. DJB needs to address this problem expeditiously.

4.30.4.3 Water Tariffs

Water is a precious but exhaustible resource for sustaining life. Its price, therefore, should be so fixed that it facilitates motivating the consumers to conserve this commodity and the production agency is not unduly burdened financially. At the same time, under the prevalent socioeconomic scenario, where nearly 31 per cent population lives in JJ clusters and unauthorised colonies and a sizeable population falling under 'below poverty line', the price of water should be affordable to consumers from these sections of society also.

The water tariffs applicable hitherto were introduced in July 1998 and were considerably subsidised. According to that tariff plan, a family of say four persons consuming about 30 Kl. per month was charged at the rate of Rs.1.50 per kilo-litre under the domestic category with the total pay out amounting to Rs.45 per month only including 50 per cent additional charge. Thus, on an average, the cost of water was being charged at the rate of Re.1/Kl. only as against the estimated cost of production of Rs.7/Kl. Thus, the tariffs were highly subsidised and provided no incentives for conservation of this commodity. This also put a severe financial burden on an already much oversized DJB. Under such situations, quality of water also gets adversely affected. The impact of the establishment cost of DJB on the cost of production of water can be very well appreciated from the fact that as against the production cost of Rs.7/Kl. in DJB, it is Rs.2.40/Kl. in Mumbai, which has a lot of similarity with Delhi in terms of water supply operations and treatment capacity. The present manpower strength of DJB makes it a highly oversized organisation as compared to the similar organisations in the other mega-cities of Mumbai, Chennai, Bangalore, Kolkata, and Hyderabad. The annual establishment cost of the water supply set up of DJB is estimated at Rs.260 crore as against the revenue of Rs.75.47 crore only generated from the sale of water on 1998 tariffs.

In this background, the DJB has revised the water tariffs vide its notification dated 29 January 2005. The revised water tariffs are in two parts as against the single rate under the 1998 plan. The revised plan consists of a fixed service charge in one-part and water use charges on the basis of actual consumption in the other part. Fixed service charges are payable by all registered consumers towards the cost of accessing the network and for its operation and maintenance.

For purposes of fixing tariffs, consumers have been divided in three categories, namely CI, CII and CIII. The category CI includes all types of domestic consumers, whereas category CII and CIII cover non-domestic premises like shops, schools, and government institutions (CII) and hotels, cinema halls, factories etc. (CIII). The fixed service charges in the domestic category (CI) vary from Rs.40 (for premises with built up area less than 200 m^2) to Rs.120 per month (for premises with built up area more than 200 m^2). In categories CII and CIII, these charges have been fixed at Rs.250 and Rs.650 per month respectively. The fixed service charges as per the revised tariffs are applicable from 1 December 2004. The water charges are applicable from 1 April 2005.

The water usage charges have been fixed in different categories for different slabs of consumption on a sliding scale. Under CI, there are four slabs, namely up to 6 Kl/month, above 6 to 20 Kl, above 20 to 40 Kl and above 40 Kl/month. The new tariffs per Kl. for these slabs are nil, Rs.2, Rs.5 and Rs.10 respectively. For a family size of say 4 persons consuming 30 Kl/month, the revised tariff calculations are given in Table 4.31.

TABLE 4.31

Revised Tariff Calculations

Consumption Slab (in Kl/month)	*Rate (Rs./Kl)*	*Total usage charges (Rs./month)*
Upto 6	Nil	Nil
Above 6 and up to 20	2.00	28
Above 20 and up to 30	7.00	70
Total	9.00	98

The water bill will be calculated as under:
Fixed Service Charges + 1.5 X Usage Charges or
Rs.40 + 1.5 X Rs.98 or Rs.187 per month.

The factor 1.5 to the usage charge is towards maintenance of sewerage system, which means that 50 per cent of the total usage charge of Rs.98 in this case goes for sewerage. Therefore, out of the total monthly bill of Rs.187, the amounts for water and sewerage are Rs.138 and Rs.49 respectively.

It would, thus, be seen that a consumer in the middle level category under the revised plan would be required to pay an amount of Rs.138 per month as compared to Rs.30 per month (for water alone) in the previous plan. Even after the implementation of the new tariff structure, DJB would be able to meet about 80 per cent of the operating cost only from user charges.

The revised tariff on the volumetric usage charges will be effective from 1.4.2005. DJB has also introduced a one-time charge for new connections, which are Rs.2500, Rs.4000 and Rs.6000 for categories I, II and III respectively. It is felt that the revised tariffs will significantly help DJB in tiding over the revenue deficit and would, therefore, go a long way in sustaining the water supply operations in terms of both quality and quantity. These measures will also facilitate motivating the consumers for conserving water.

4.30.4.4 Rainwater Harvesting

Rapid urbanisation has put tremendous pressure on the existing civic services, more so, on the supply of drinking water in Delhi. Shortage of canal/river water has led to the large-scale withdrawal of ground water. As a result, the water table in Delhi has been going down at a fast rate particularly in the South and South-West revenue zones. The Central Ground Water Authority (CGWA) is the nodal agency under the Ministry of Water Resources for regulation and control of ground water management in the country. Despite the legislation being in place and banning of drilling of tube wells in the notified areas of Delhi, there is hardly any let up in the depletion of groundwater aquifers. There are reportedly a numerous farmhouses and industrial establishments in Delhi, which continue to draw large quantities of groundwater in the notified areas.

With a view to addressing this issue, DJB has initiated a scheme of rainwater harvesting in Delhi. A special cell has been created for this purpose, which is managed by qualified personnel. This cell creates public awareness on rainwater harvesting in the NCT of Delhi and provides technical assistance to schools, institutions, resident welfare associations (RWAs), cooperative group housing societies (CGHS) and individuals. As a first step in this direction, DJB has installed rainwater-harvesting structures at its own Head Quarters, Varunalaya besides nearly 180 of its other installations in different parts of Delhi.

With a view to promoting the rainwater harvesting, DJB provides financial assistance to the extent of 50 per cent of the total cost of structures or Rs.50,000 whichever is less. According to DJB, out of total 193 proposals of rainwater harvesting received till December 2005, 129 proposals had been approved and the remaining 64 proposals were under active consideration. The Government of NCT of Delhi has already passed legislation where all new buildings with covered area more than 100 m^2 are required to provide rainwater-harvesting structure.

4.30.4.5 Rationalisation of Water Distribution

With a view to rationalising distribution of water in the NCT of Delhi, DJB plans to construct a number of underground reservoirs (UGRs) and bulk pumping stations. This would help increase the storage capacity of the UGRs from the present 177 million gallons to 348 million gallons and the transmission mains network from the present 568 kms to 818 kms.

4.30.4.6 Bhagidari

The Government of NCT of Delhi had earlier started an innovative scheme of 'Bhagidari' for public participation in various utility and civic services in January 2002. At the time of its launch, there were only 20 RWAs covered under the scheme. Today, it has a number of over 1600 RWAs, traders' bodies and industry associations and many more are joining. These institutions now have a much louder voice in the decision making process in respect of various civic services including water supply. On the whole, the 'Bhagidari' scheme has generated a movement in Delhi that has expanded numerically, spatially and thematically.

Under the water sector, RWAs and various associations are actively participating with DJB in the following areas:

(a) Rainwater harvesting

(b) Replacement of old/leaking service pipes

(c) Curbing wastage of water

(d) Distribution of water through tankers

(e) Payment and collection of water bills

4.31 Vision 2021

4.31.1 Demand Projections

Keeping in view the present shortfall of 150 mgd in the water treatment capacity (after commissioning of the

Sonia Vihar WTP), DJB has taken up a number of initiatives to meet the growing demand of drinking water in Delhi. For this purpose, demand projections and water resource assessment have been made for 2006, 2007, 2011, and 2021 on the basis of water supply rate of 60 gpcd.

The DDA, as the nodal agency for preparation of the Master Plan-2021, has projected the population of Delhi as 23 million in 2021. On this basis, the population and water demand for the above four scenarios have been projected as given in Table 4.32.

TABLE 4.32

Population and Water Demand

Year	*Anticipated Population (in million)*	*Total Water Demand (in mgd)*
2006	165	990
2007	175	1050
1011	190	1140
2021	230	1380

4.31.2 Sources of Water

As mentioned earlier, Delhi gets its raw water from Yamuna, Ganga and BBMB. At present, out of the total installed capacity of 650 mgd on canal/river water (Table-4.30), 56.4 per cent of it is on Yamuna water, 18.2 per cent on Ganga water and the remaining 25.4 per cent is on the BBMB water. After the commissioning of the already completed Sonia Vihar WTP, the share of Yamuna, Ganga and BBMB water in the installed capacity would become as 44.9 per cent, 34.8 per cent, and 20.3 per cent respectively. Thus, Yamuna remains the largest source of water for Delhi and the additional water supply of Delhi to meet its future demand is also largely dependent on this source only.

No possibility of augmentation is seen in the near future, as far as Ganga and BBMB sources of raw water are concerned.

Yamuna water is shared amongst Haryana, Uttar Pradesh, Rajasthan, Himachal Pradesh, and Delhi in terms of a Memorandum of Understanding (MoU) signed by these states in May 1994. According to that MoU, 75 per cent dependable notional virgin flow in the Yamuna upto Okhla has been assessed as 11.70 BCM and the mean year availability has been assessed as 13 BCM. The annual shares of the five basin states in the utilisable flow of Yamuna have been agreed to as given below in Table 4.33.

TABLE 4.33

Yamuna Water is Shared Amongst

Sl. No.	*State*	*Share (in BCM)*	*Share (%)*
(i)	Haryana	5.730	47.82
(ii)	Uttar Pradesh	4.032	33.65
(iii)	Rajasthan	1.119	09.34
(iv)	Himachal Pradesh	0.378	03.15
(v)	Delhi	0.724	06.04
	Total	11.983	100.00

To maximise the utilisation of surface flow of Yamuna, a number of storage projects in the upper reaches of the river have been identified. Pending construction of these projects, the interim seasonal allocation of the annual utilisable flow have been envisaged in the MoU as in the Table 4.34.

TABLE 4.34

Annual Utilisable Flow envisaged in the MoU

Sl. No.	*States*	*Allocation (BCM)*			*Total (BCM)*
		July to Oct.	*Nov. to Feb.*	*Mar. to June*	
1.	Haryana	4.107	0.686	0.937	5.730
2.	Uttar Pradesh	3.216	0.343	0.473	4.032
3.	Rajasthan	0.963	0.070	0.086	1.119
4.	Himachal Pradesh	0.190	0.108	0.080	0.378
5.	Delhi	0.580 (Consumptive) (1926+495 return flow) or =2421 cusec	0.068 (Consumptive) (231+495 return flow) or =726 cusec	0.076 (Consumptive) (255+495 return flow) =750 cusec	0.724 (Consumptive) (806+495 return flow) =2350 cusec

The Upper Yamuna River Board (UYRB) within the overall framework of the aforesaid MoU regulates the allocations amongst the beneficiary states.

As would be observed from the above table, the share of Delhi in Yamuna water is 0.724 BCM per annum (consumptive), which is equivalent to 2350 cusec. It is, however, subject to the construction of storage dams in the upper reaches of Yamuuna. This allocation is reckoned at Tajewala in Haryana where the Yamuna water is distributed amongst the major riparian states. It is important to note that the entire allocation of Delhi is for drinking purposes, of which only about 20 per cent of it is for consumptive use and the balance 80 per cent is returned to the river as treated wastewater. According to the MoU, out of the present supply of 750 cusec of raw water from Yamuna, Delhi is required to return 495 cusec (267 mgd) of treated wastewater into the river after fulfilling the lean season consumptive requirement of 255 cusec (138 mgd). However, Delhi is returning much larger quantity of treated wastewater than envisaged under the MoU as the entire treated wastewater generated from the city is discharged into the river. The return flow, in any case, is used by the downstream states for irrigation. Thus, in real terms, the share of Delhi in the overall allocation of Yamuna water is only 1.2 per cent on consumptive use basis. On the other hand, in case of the other four states, the allocations are mostly for irrigation purpose, which is non-consumptive in nature. DJB has been taking up this matter with the UYRB to reckon the entire allocation of 0.724 BCM for consumptive use as far as sharing of Yamuna water is concerned.

During the lean period from November to June, the total allocation on an average is only 735 cusec. After considering the transmission losses of 130 cusec, the availability of raw water during the lean period is just sufficient for the present installed capacity of 310 mgd of water treatment dependent upon the Yamuna water. However, Haryana, at times, curtail water supplies whenever availability is less, although the MoU gives priority to Delhi's drinking water. Para 7 of the MoU mentions that when the availability of water is less than the assessed quantity, first the drinking water requirement of Delhi is to be met and the balance will be distributed amongst the other states in proportion to their respective allocation.

4.31.3 Measures for Managing Shortfall

With the limitation of availability of raw water and in order to meet the growing demand of water supply for Delhi in the years to come, DJB has shortlisted a number of measures for conservation and more efficient management of the water resources. DJB is making preparations to deal with the growing water demand for the following three scenarios.

4.31.3.1 Scenario 2007

The projected water demand for 2007 is 1050 mgd. As against this, the present installed capacity inclusive of the 140 mgd Sonia Vihar WTP and water obtained through ranney wells and tube wells is 790 mgd, the break up of which is as given in the Table 4.35.

The Sonia Vihar WTP is to get raw water from the Tehri Dam in Uttranchal through UGC system at Muradnagar. This plant is ready for commissioning. About 80 cusec (43 mgd) of raw water for this purpose is being supplied by U.P. The regular supply of 300 cusec (162 mgd) of raw water from Tehri Dam is expected to start from July 2006 after which the WTP would be commissioned for regular operation.

Although, the installed capacity of the Nangloi WTP is 40 mgd, it is presently operating at 20 mgd only due to shortage of raw water. Raw water for this plant is supplied by the BBMB and conveyed through the canal carrier system in Punjab and Haryana. For this purpose, two aqua-ducts are under construction by the Government of Haryana on the WYC as deposit work of Delhi at a cost of Rs.9 crore. These structures were scheduled to be completed by December 2004. However, only one aqua-duct has been completed so far. DJB has been pursuing with the Government of Haryana to complete the work expeditiously. After commissioning of the second aqua duct, the Nangloi WTP would start operating at the design capacity of 40 mgd.

TABLE 4.35

Sonia Vihar WTP and Water Obtained

Sl. No.	*Source of Raw Water*	*Water Treatment Plant*	*Installed Capacity (mgd)*
1.	Yamuna	Chandrawal I & II	90
2.	Yamuna	Wazirabad I, II & III	120
3.	BBMB	Haiderpur I	100
4.	Yamuna	Haiderpur II	100
5.	BBMB	Nangloi	40
6.	Ganga	Bhagirathi	100
7.	Ganga (Tehri Water)	Sonia Vihar	140
8.	Groundwater	Ranney Wells/Tube Wells	100
		Total	790

During the treatment process, sand filters are to be frequently back-washed. Nearly 6 to 8 per cent water is lost in this activity. The backwash water contains impurities like alum, sand, silt and clay and is presently drained out as wastewater. The total quantity of backwash water at present is about 46 mgd, which is larger than the installed capacity of the Nangloi WTP. DJB is now planning to treat and recycle the backwash water. The first project of recycling of 16 mgd of backwash water for the Haiderpur WTP is expected to be ready by March 2007. With this additional quantity and with capacity optimisation, it would be possible to produce 216 mgd of potable water from the 200 mgd Haiderpur WTP. The other two recycling projects at Wazirabad (11 mgd) and at

Bhagirathi (10 mgd) are also expected to be ready by March 2007. This measure will help providing an additional capacity of 37 mgd within one year.

DJB has a proposal to further augment the quantity of sub-surface water from the present 100 mgd. For this purpose, it is proposed to dig a battery of tube wells in the flood plains of Yamuna in the Palla (Wazirabad upstream) region. At present, there are 100 operating tube wells in this region.

These measures would help increase the total availability of potable water to 842 mgd only by March 2007 as given in the Table 4.36.

TABLE 4.36

Total Availability of Potable Water to 842 mgd only by March 2007

Sl. No.	*Source of Raw Water*	*Water Treatment Plant*	*Installed Capacity (mgd)*
1.	Yamuna	Chandrawal I & II	90
2.	Yamuna	Wazirabad I, II & III	120
3.	BBMB	Haiderpur I	100
4.	Yamuna	Haiderpur II	100
5.	BBMB	Nangloi	40
6.	Ganga	Bhagirathi	100
7.	Ganga (Tehri Water)	Sonia Vihar	140
8.	Groundwater	Ranney Wells/Tube Wells	115
9.	Recycling backwash water	Haiderpur, Wazirabad and Bhagirathi	37
		Total	842

This would still leave a gap of about 200 mgd between demand and supply in March 2007, which can only be met, if an additional quantity of 350 cusec (190 mgd) of raw water is allocated to Delhi during the lean period. For this purpose, it is necessary for the Government of NCT of Delhi to approach the Ministry of Water Resources as soon as possible. If the additional quantity of water is made available, DJB has to start preparing for installation of the additional treatment capacity, which will take at least three years for completion.

4.31.3.2 Scenario 2011

The projected demand of potable water for 2011 is 1140 mgd for a population of 19 million. It will be possible to augment the treatment capacity from 790 mgd (optimised to 842 mgd on account of recycling of backwash water) to 921 mgd through the following measures currently in hand.

Raw water from Yamuna and BBMB for the Haiderpur WTP is presently received through an unlined channel from Munak in Haryana. This results in seepage losses to the tune of 30 per cent of the total quantity. With a view to saving water on this account, a parallel lined channel is presently under construction by the Government of Haryana as a deposit work on behalf of Government of NCT of Delhi. The entire cost of the project amounting to Rs.315 crore is borne by Delhi. This project was to be completed by May 2004 but as of now only about 65 per cent work of the channel has been completed. The project is now expected to be ready by December 2006. This measure would help save 160 cusec (86 mgd) of raw water.

In anticipation of these savings, DJB has undertaken construction of an additional 20 mgd WTP at Bawana. About 98 per cent of work of this plant has been completed. However, it can be commissioned only in December 2006 when the work of the aforementioned parallel lined channel will be completed and raw water out of the savings from en route losses would be available.

In order to utilise the remaining quantity of water likely to be saved out of en route losses, DJB proposes to construct a 40 mgd plant at Dwarka and a 20 mgd plant at Okhla. It may be mentioned that a huge township has already come up in Dwarka, which has no assured supply of potable water at present. The Dwarka WTP is proposed in two phases. The first phase of 20 mgd is expected by 2011 and the second one of another 20 mgd by 2021. The 20 mgd Okhla WTP is expected by 2011.

The savings of additional 9 mgd from recycling of backwash process water (out of a total 46 mgd, 37 mgd to be commissioned by March 2007) would be utilised to augment the capacity of Chandrawal, WTP by 2011.

The steps taken by the Government of NCT of Delhi for rainwater harvesting through DJB would not only help in sustaining the current withdrawals from groundwater aquifers but also in providing additional 10 mgd of water by 2011. It is proposed to extract 5 mgd of water from the flood plains of Yamuna along Okhla barrage-Kalindi Kunj reach through a battery of 25 tube wells.

Delhi is hosting the mega event of the Commonwealth Games in 2010. For this purpose a Commonwealth Village is likely to come up near the Swamy Narain Mandir close to the Nizamuddin Yamuna Bridge. Continued efforts towards rainwater harvesting would help in extracting another 5 mgd of water along the Swamy Narayan Mandir-Nizamuddin Bridge reach through a battery of 25 tube wells to meet the requirement of the

Commonwealth Games. DJB is planning to put up a 5 mgd treatment plant for this purpose and has requested DDA to allot 3 ha. land for the WTP in the vicinity of the area.

By undertaking these initiatives, it will be possible for DJB to produce 921 mgd of potable water by 2011 as given in detail in the Table 4.37.

TABLE 4.37

DJB to Produce 921 mgd of Potable Water by 2011

Sl. No.	*Source of Raw Water*	*Water Treatment Plant*	*Installed Capacity (mgd)*
1.	Yamuna	Chandrawal I & II	90
2.	Yamuna	Wazirabad I, II & III	120
3.	BBMB	Haiderpur I	100
4.	Yamuna	Haiderpur II	100
5.	BBMB	Nangloi	40
6.	Ganga	Bhagirathi	100
7.	Ganga (Tehri Water)	Sonia Vihar	140
8.	Savings from Seepage losses	Bawana	20
9.	-do-	Dwarka	20
10.	-do-	Okhla	20
11.	Groundwater	Ranney Wells/Tube Wells	125
12.	Recycling of Backwash water	Haiderpur, Chandrawal, Bhagirathi & Wazirabad	46
		Total	921

Although an additional quantity of 20 mgd of raw water would be available out of the savings from en route losses, this will be utilised to augment the capacity of the Dwarka WTP to 40 mgd by 2021.

DJB has moved DDA to explore the possibility of introducing the duel plumbing system to separate the two types of wastewater in all new colonies and group housing societies. The population of Delhi in 2011 is projected as 19 million, which means that the increase over the 2006 population would be of the order of 2.5 million. With the policy of relocating the slums and make Delhi a clean city before the 2010 Commonwealth Games, it is presumed that the additional population will come up in new planned colonies only. Out of the water supply rate of 60 gpcd, it is presumed that sullage would account for about 25 per cent per capita water supply. On a conservative basis, this would aggregate to a saving of 30 mgd of water. This is a water conservation measure and would help in offsetting the demand of potable water from 1140 mgd to 1110 in 2011. However, a project of this kind is being considered for the first time not only in Delhi but also perhaps in the whole country. This would require a meticulous planning by DDA and public cooperation, which has to bear the extra cost of plumbing. But in the given scenario of the acute scarcity of water, which would only aggravate further with the passage of time, such measures are absolutely essential. On this positive note, it is presumed that DDA would be able to implement this project and effect a saving of 30 mgd by segregating the use of potable water for non-potable applications.

With the demand of potable water being 1110 mgd and the installed capacity as 921 mgd, there would be a shortfall of 189 mgd in 2011. The following additional measures if allowed to be exploited may help in bridging the shortfall. These will, however, require the consent of Haryana and U.P.

There appears to be no scope of further augmenting the availability of sub-surface water in the NCT of Delhi beyond the present level of 125 mgd due to the constraint of both quantity and quality of water. However, the prospects of groundwater exploitation in the NCR region appear to be promising. It may, therefore, be possible to meet the entire projected shortfall of 189 mgd by developing a system of tube wells in the following areas of NCR:

(a) Yamuna Flood Plains

This area falls in the Panipat and Sonepat districts of Haryana and Baghpat districts of Uttar Pradesh and extends from Kairana in the North to Palla in the South.

(b) Area along Upper Ganga Canal

This area extends from Jani on Baghpat-Meerut road in the North to Muradnagar in South. The demarcated area that can be exploited for extraction of sub-surface water is in a length and width of about 20 Kms. and 50 Kms. respectively on either side of the Upper Ganga Canal.

(c) Ganga Flood Plains

The CGWB has earmarked the Ganga river flood plains as one of the potential areas for development of groundwater to meet the drinking water requirements of Delhi. The demarcated area is on the western side of the Ganga river and extends up to 15 Kms. from Parikshatgarh in the North to Syana in the South. The area is bound by the Madhya Ganga Canal in the West and Ganga River in the East and falls in the Parikshatgarh Block of Ghaziabad district in Uttar Pradesh.

The raw water supply from Ganga to the Bhagirathi WTP and Tehri dam to the Sonia Vihar WTP is through the unlined UGC system. The en route transit losses from these sources are of the order of 200 cusec (108 mgd). The Governments of Uttar Pradesh and NCT of Delhi are considering a proposal for lining of the canal to avoid these losses. According to a detailed study carried out by the IIT Roorkee, the cost of this project is estimated at Rs.1200 crore. However, the matter of sharing the project cost between U.P. and Delhi has not been finalised yet.

Alternatively, the Government of NCT of Delhi needs to approach the Ministry of Water Resources and the UYRB to increase the allocation of Delhi from Yamuna water by 350 cusec (190 mgd) over the present supply of 750 cusec to meet the drinking water requirements during the lean period.

DJB is also exploring the possibility of reclamation of sewage on the lines of NE Water, Singapore by using ultra-filtration, reverse osmosis and UV treatment through a pilot project of 6 mgd at Okhla STP. If the pilot project trials are found techno-economically viable then large-scale reclamation of sewage at other STPs can be taken up in phases. According to DJB, the first tertiary treatment plant of this kind would be set up at Rithala STP which can produce 40 mgd of treated water which can be taken to the Haiderpur WTP for mixing with raw water.

It would, therefore, observed that DJB is exploring several alternatives to tide over the problem of shortage of raw water in 2011. To meet the growing demand of drinking water, these alternatives are to be explored singly or severally. The existing corridor for transportation of raw water after the lining of the WYC and completion of the parallel lined channel would be sufficient to carry additional water for 2011. However, the planning for construction of the matching water treatment capacity, which has a gestation period of five years, needs to start before long. About 345 acres of land would be required for new WTPs, which is to be allocated by DDA keeping in view the locations of the new developing colonies and the sources of raw water.

4.31.3.3 Scenario 2021

The projected population of Delhi in 2021 is 23 million and the total water demand at the rate of 60 gpcd is 1380 mgd. Considering that the water demand of 2011 estimated at 1140 mgd, only 920 could be met through the existing installed capacity and various other alternatives discussed above. Therefore, new sources of raw water would have to be explored to fulfil the shortfall of 219 MGD in 2011 and 460 MGD by 2021. Of this, the capacity augmentation of the Dwarka WTP from 20 mgd in 2011 to 40 mgd in 2021 has been proposed. Raw water for this plant would be available from the savings from en route losses from Munak to Haiderpur as explained above. This would increase the installed capacity 921 mgd to 941 mgd as given in Table 4.38 for which the raw water availability is almost assured through various water conservation measures already in hand.

TABLE 4.38

Increase in the Installed Capacity 921 mgd to 941 mgd

Sl. No.	*Source of Raw Water*	*Water Treatment Plant*	*Installed Capacity (mgd)*
1.	Yamuna	Chandrawal I & II	90
2.	Yamuna	Wazirabad I, II & III	120
3.	BBMB	Haiderpur I	100
4.	Yamuna	Haiderpur II	100
5.	BBMB	Nangloi	40
6.	Ganga	Bhagirathi	100
7.	Ganga (Tehri Water)	Sonia Vihar	140
8.	Savings from Seepage losses	Bawana	20
9.	-do-	Dwarka	40
10.	-do-	Okhla	20
11.	Groundwater	Ranney Wells/Tube Wells	125
12.	Recycling of Backwash water	Haiderpur I and II	46
		Total	**941**

This would still leave a gap of about 440 mgd between the projected demand and supply in 2021. There seems to be no other alternative to meet this shortfall but to get additional equivalent allocation out of the utilisable surface flow of river Yamuna. While the raw water availability from Yamuna during the period from July to October is sufficient, it is the lean period from November to June when the shortfall becomes acute.

The proposals for construction of three reservoirs, namely Ranuka, Kishau and Lakhwar Vyasi in the upstream of Yamuna river are under consideration for nearly the past two decades. Even today these projects are in the preliminary stages only. Their current status is as given below:

(a) Renuka

The Renuka dam is proposed to be constructed on

Yamuna in Himachal Pradesh. A provision of 275 mgd of water has been made for Delhi in this project.

The revised cost of this project is Rs.1225 crore. The revised proposal was discussed in January 2000 in the 72nd meeting of Advisory Committee on Irrigation, Floods and Multipurpose Projects in the Central Water Commission (CWC). The Committee decided to approve the project on the conditions that clearance of the Ministry of Environment and Forests is obtained expeditiously and project cost is shared between the Governments of NCT of Delhi and Himachal Pradesh. In a subsequent meeting held in December 2000 between the Chief Secretary, Government of NCT of Delhi and senior officials of Government of Himachal Pradesh, both sides agreed, in principle that the cost of the power component of the project is to be borne by Himachal Pradesh and the remaining cost by Delhi.

According to CWC, a 50 ha. wildlife corridor is falling within the command area of the project as a result of which, the clearance by the Ministry of Environment and Forests (MoEF) has been held up. In view of this, the project authorities are exploring an alternative site to meet the requirement of MoEF.

(b) Kishau

Kishau dam is proposed to be constructed on river Tons, a tributary of Yamuna in Uttaranchal. Dellhi's share of water in this project is 372 mgd.

The CWC, at its first stage scrutiny, found the project techno-economically viable. The project cost at December 1998 price level was estimated at Rs.3566 crore. The project was taken up for consideration by the Advisory Committee on Irrigation, Floods and Multipurpose Projects at its 72nd meeting held in January 2000. The Committee, after discussion, decided to defer the project until a more elaborate economic viability has been established and project cost apportioned among the irrigation, water supply and power components. According to the latest information from the Government of Uttaranchal, a MoU has already been signed with the Tehri Hydroelectric Development Corporation (THDC) for construction of the Dam. THDC has now to prepare a fresh bankable DPR for the project and submit it to the Central Electricity Authority after obtaining the Forest and Environment clearance from MoEF.

(c) Lakhwar Vyasi

The Lakhwar Vyasi dam is to be constructed on Yamuna in Uttaranchal. A quantity of 135 mgd of water has been earmarked for Delhi in this reservoir. The revised cost of the project at November 2004 price level is Rs.3700 crore, with the share of Delhi being Rs.1080 crore. As per CWC, a fresh bankable DPR is necessary in this case also, which is to be submitted to them by the project authorities after obtaining the clearance of MOEF.

According to the information obtained from the Government of Uttaranchal, negotiations are in progress with the National Hydroelectric Power Corporation for taking up the work.

4.32 Policy Interventions and Recommendations

4.32.1 Need For Policy Action

It would be observed from the foregoing Para that despite a number of water conservation and augmentation measures undertaken by DJB, there is going to be a huge shortfall between the demand and supply in the above three scenarios as given below in Table 4.39.

TABLE 4.39

Need for Policy Action

Year	*Shortfall (mgd)*
2006	169
2011	189
2021	220

In order to meet the demand of potable water in future, a multi-pronged approach is essential to explore all possible avenues of conservation and augmentation of water resources on one hand and recycling of wastewater on the other. This would require long-term and short term interventions at the Central government level, basin states level and last but not the least at the cutting edge, where public has to play a major supportive role.

Both surface and groundwater are scarce and finite natural resource. Therefore, planning, development and management of this life support substance need to be governed by the national perspectives.

4.32.2 Long Term Measures

4.32.2.1 Management of Surface Water

Groundwater cannot serve as a perennial source for a city of the size of Delhi due to its own problems of quantity and quality. Therefore, all hopes of Delhi are concentrated on surface water to meet its future demand.

Amongst the three sources presently supplying raw water, Delhi has riparian rites only on Yamuna water. Therefore, it is this source only that needs to be developed and managed effectively to meet the growing demand of water in Delhi. It also needs to be appreciated that besides being the capital of India, a sizeable population migrates to Delhi from other states every year in search of employment opportunities. Therefore, it is all the more necessary to address the water supply issue of the city from a national perspective.

In the absence of adequate storage in the upper reaches, large quantities of water during monsoon months flow down the river without serving any useful purpose as far as Delhi is concerned. The first charge, therefore, should be on expediting the construction of the three reservoirs, which has been pending for some reason or the other since the past two decades. For this purpose, interventions at the levels of the Planning Commission and the Ministry of Water Resources are necessary. The project authorities are also required not only to prepare the DPRs and addresses the inter-state issues expeditiously, but also move the Ministry of Environment and Forests to obtain the necessary clearances. These are multipurpose projects involving power and irrigation components besides water for Delhi. The delay in construction is, therefore, adversely impacting on all the beneficiary states including Delhi in one way or the other. Considering a long gestation period in construction, it is necessary that approval of these mega-projects is processed on top priority.

Requirement of capital funds for these projects is the next important issue that needs to be addressed at appropriate level. Although, the cost estimates are not yet firmed-up, if the available data are any indication, the share of Delhi in the capital cost would be anywhere around Rs.5000 crore. It is too large an outlay to be managed by a small state like Delhi out of its own resources. Therefore, once the projects are cleared, support of the Planning Commission is necessary for earmarking adequate funds for Delhi in their Annual/Five Year Plans. Funding from multilateral/bilateral donors like the World Bank, Japan Bank for International Cooperation or Asian Development Bank also needs to be explored.

The National Water Policy 2002 has allocated first priority to the drinking water amongst various consumptive and non-consumptive uses of fresh water. The MoU on sharing of Yamuna water amongst the basin states also gives priority to drinking water for Delhi. It needs to be appreciated that unlike the other four basin States, the entire present allocation of 0.724 BCM or 806 cusec of water of Delhi is for consumptive use. Delhi has no other option but to return about 80 per cent of it back to the river as return wastewater, which is picked up at Okhla by other basin states for irrigation purposes. As a matter of fact, Delhi is returning the wastewater to the river even from those water revenue zones also, where WTPs are operating on Ganga and BBMB water. Delhi is, therefore, at a great disadvantage *vis-à-vis* other four basin States in so far as utilisation of Yamuna water is concerned. Therefore, a more pragmatic approach needs to be adopted on sharing the available surface flow of the river amongst the basin States to ensure that Delhi gets enough water to meet the growing demand.

4.32.3 Short Term Measure

4.32.3.1 Commissioning of Sonia Vihar WTP

There are several uncertainties associated with the availability of raw water for the Sonia Vihar WTP. Being an interstate matter, intervention of the Central government at appropriate level is necessary so that this plant gets full quantity of water from Tehri dam at least by mid-July 2006.

4.32.3.2 Management of Groundwater

Keeping in view the fact that DJB draws over 100 mgd of groundwater, it is necessary that its withdrawal is regulated under a strict regime. Presently, there is no control over extraction of groundwater except banning of new bore wells in some selected pockets of South and Southwest Delhi. In several parts of the city, unauthorised extraction of large quantities of groundwater takes place round the year. Due to meager rains and fewer rainwater harvesting activities, groundwater recharge is minimal. As a result, the water table is falling at an alarming rate. This will eventually have adverse impact on the water supply of Delhi. The nodal agency for regulation, development and management of groundwater is CGWA under the Ministry of Water Resource. DJB with its widespread network can assist CGWA in checking unauthorised exploitation of groundwater in Delhi. CGWA may, therefore, consider delegating necessary powers to DJB in this regard on the lines of Chandigarh.

4.32.3.3 Conservation Measures

(i) Leakage Control

Distribution losses in Delhi are very high at about 40 per cent as compared to other mega-cities. With a fairly large gap between demand and supply of water, this area assumes greater significance, as quick results can be possible with smaller interventions. DJB has already taken several steps to minimise leakage losses. The target should be to bring the losses within 15 per cent as set out by CPHEEO as quickly as possible. It is, therefore, necessary to prepare a comprehensive action plan to complete the whole work in a given time frame.

(ii) Metering of Supply

With the recent increase in the water tariffs, concurrent action on metering of supply can act as a good deterrent against misuse or wastage of water. The work of replacing the defective meters is already in hand. DJB should ensure that it is completed expeditiously and meters function on a sustainable basis.

(iii) Water for Horticulture

Water for parks, lawns and horticulture is extracted from underground aquifers in significant quantities in several parts of Delhi. Due to fast depletion of the water table, most of the bore wells, particularly in South and Southwest Delhi, have gone dry. As a result, parks in Delhi are starving for water and loosing the greenery. Most of these parks are in the neighbourhood of group housing societies. These parks can be maintained comfortably, if treated sewage from the neighbourhood is used for watering them. Presently, the Sewerage wing of DJB collects sewage from such areas and conveys it through a long network of sewers to STPs at a significant cost. The problem can be addressed in a more simplistic and economic manner by providing small decentralised STPs in such neighbourhoods from where sewage, treated to the desired standards, can be used for horticulture and other similar purposes in the same area. This approach will render multiple benefits. Firstly, it will reduce the load on the sewerage system and STPs and save in the conveying cost. Secondly, it will provide a zero pollution system in a local area. Thirdly, it will help in conserving the fast depleting groundwater table. Lastly, it will help save potable water where it is used for watering the parks and lawns. To begin with, DJB should plan to put up such decentralised systems on demonstration basis in some parts of Delhi.

In many areas of New Delhi falling under NDMC, potable water is used for watering the lawns and parks. In several of these areas, pipe network for supply of treated sewage for such purposes already exists. However, according to the available reports, this system is seldom used due to various reasons like foul smell, undependable supply, leakage etc. All these bottlenecks can be easily removed. DJB may consider reviewing this option on priority, which can save a considerable quantity of potable water.

(iv) Plugging of Transit Losses

Nearly 30-35 per cent water is lost in transit in the WYC and UGC. The work of lining of the WYC from Munak to Haiderpur is already in progress. This work needs to be expedited so that it is completed by the revised schedule of May 2006. This will result in the saving of about 160 cusec (86 mgd) of raw water. Similarly, seepage losses in UGC, which carries raw water for Bhagirathi and the Sonia Vihar WTP, are of the order of 200 cusec. This quantity can be made available to Delhi, if, like the WYC, this canal is also lined. This proposal is techno-economically viable and, therefore, needs to be considered on priority. Interventions at the Planning Commission/Central government level are necessary to finalise the matter of sharing of the project cost between U.P. and Delhi early.

To utilise the savings from en route transit losses in the WYC, DJB is planning to construct a 40 mgd WTP at Dwarka and a 20 mgd WTP at Okhla. Considering the gestation period involved, these projects need to be taken up on priority.

The Government of Haryana is constructing two aquaducts on the WYC, which carries water for the 40 mgd Nangloi WTP. The progress of this work is very slow. The matter needs to be taken up with the Government of Haryana so that this project is completed without further delay and the Nangloi WTP is operated at its full capacity.

DJB should also ensure that the project of recycling of backwash water is completed as per schedule. This measure would help conserve 46 mgd of water, which is presently discharged as wastewater.

(v) Recycling of Sullage

Recycling the treated sullage in the new colonies planned by DDA by providing duel-plumbing system is an innovative project towards conserving water and needs to be encouraged by all the concerned agencies. Similarly, the proposal for reclamation and recycling of sewage through tertiary treatment is also a novel idea and needs to be taken up on priority.

DDA is the land use planning and development agency for Delhi. There are instances like Dwarka, where a huge colony has been developed without the matching provision of water and sewerage utilities. Keeping in view the constraint of raw water availability, all new colonies need to be planned only when matching availability of water is ensured.

About 17.5 per cent of the total water supplied is used for industrial, commercial and community purposes. Although firm data are not available, a sizeable quantity in this category is used in the high-rise buildings and complexes housing offices of government and public/ private sector companies. These offices generate a significant quantity of wastewater in the form of mixed sewage and sullage, which is discharged into the nearby sewerage system. On the other hand many of these offices have centralised cooling system, for which fresh water either from DJB or from underground aquifers is used adding to the problems of DJB during the lean months of summer. Such requirements can also be met by recycling the treated sewage from the complex. For instance, the entire sewage of CGO complex can be collected and treated to tertiary level and used for such purposes as cooling or flushing of toilets or horticulture. These types of plants are in operation in a number of high-rise buildings in Mumbai. In order to motivate the agencies to adopt this approach, the water tariffs may be fixed in such a way that the recycling option is more economic than using DJB water.

4.32.3.4 Public Participation

Although, the programmes of public participation covering rainwater harvesting, curbing wastage of water, identification and replacement of old/leaking service pipes, payment and collection of water bills etc. have already been started by DJB, it is necessary to step up public awareness about these programmes. There is a tremendous scope of public involvement in these areas, which can not only help in water conservation activities but also help DJB to improve its service and increase revenue generation. RWAs and various other bodies under the Bhagidari scheme can be more actively involved in these programmes. Some of the areas where a focussed public awareness programme can bring good results are as under:

(i) Nearly 20 litres of water is used in flushing of toilets. About 10 per cent water can be saved in this activity simply by putting a two-litre plastic bottle in the flushing cistern. There are about 13 lakh domestic connections in Delhi. Considering that a toilet is used at least five times a day, every household can save an average 10 litres/day that makes the total saving as 3 mgd from a single measure without any investment. Secondly, in the new construction, public needs to be educated and motivated to use smaller cisterns in the toilets. Water can be saved by not running the tap continuously, as many people do, while brushing the teeth or washing hands. A car can be washed with a bucket of water, whereas many use a hosepipe wasting a significant quantity of water. People need to be sensitised about such facts. These ideas are no new and are known to a common man. But in practice, these norms are not followed. Sensitising public in a focused manner is the only way to achieve results in this regard. RWAs can be of immense help in such initiatives.

(ii) A significant quantity of water is wasted through overflows in the desert coolers during summer, when water demand is at its peak. Although, the increase in tariffs now proposed by DJB is likely to act as a deterrent in this regard, it is necessary to sensitise the consumer to minimise wastage in the national interest. Similarly, in several areas, the service reservoirs provided in the residential colonies overflow resulting in the wastage of a significant quantity of potable water. Such type of wastage can be controlled through the involvement of RWAs. DJB may devise a system wherein the pump operators posted at such reservoirs are made accountable to the RWAs operation of the water supply system.

(iii) RWAs are a valuable resource in helping the civic authorities in maintaining a better standard of services. This resource must be utilised intelligently and fruitfully. DJB, on its part, should take steps to provide incentives for good work done by the RWAs. This would inculcate a spirit of competition amongst such bodies to show better performance.

4.33 Conclusion

Controlling operation and maintenance costs, while providing appropriate levels of service to customers, is an important part of achieving an efficient water utility. To that end, DJB is developing innovative measures to address the complex problems associated with the water supply of Delhi. However, the main problem of Delhi, as far as water supply is concerned, is the uncontrolled influx of migrating population from other states and non-availability of matching quantity of raw water to meet the growing demand. Although, to decongest Delhi, the National Capital Region is being developed, its progress so far has been slow. Therefore, this issue needs to be addressed at appropriate level early. Meanwhile, implementation of the above measures in a planned and time-bound manner can greatly help in managing the water supply of Delhi in a more efficient manner and bridging the gap between the supply and demand of potable water.

Measures including water conservation, loss reduction, dual plumbing, water recycling need to be strengthened and implemented rigorously.

There is significant reduction in river-flows during the lean periods. The proposals for construction of the reservoirs on Yamuna river need to be considered urgently and implemented.

The Ministry of Water Resources should intervene and resolve the matter of availability of raw water for Sonia Vihar Water Treatment Plant.

The withdrawal of ground water should be regulated. Central Ground Water Authority may consider delegating necessary powers to bring the management and development of groundwater under DJB.

A decentralised approach for treating sewage may be more economic. The treated water from such STPs may be used for horticulture, parks and greening of Delhi.

All the works and other measures in hand to augment and conserve water should be completed on priority.

On the lines of Mumbai, wastewater from the high rise building should be treated *insitu* to the prescribed standards and re-used for air conditioning and other industrial applications.

Public awareness and education through the Bhagidari Scheme should be encouraged for conserving and managing potable water optimally.

Delhi may have to depend on Yamuna only to meet the demand projected in the Master Plan Document-2021. An additional quantity of 350 cusec needs to be made available by the UYRB during the lean period.

There is need to construct dams to minimise the shortfall during the lean periods. UYRB should be persuaded to treat the allocation of Yamuna water for consumptive use only.

The web site of DJB is available at *www.delhijalboard.com*. However, the information on the web is old. DJB needs to update the site regularly so that people of Delhi know more about what is happening on the waterfront.

TELECOMMUNICATIONS

4.34 Introduction

Telecommunication is an essential infrastructure of modern day society. It acts as a catalyst to economic development and leads to faster growth. It also leads to improvement in education, health, environment, governance, entertainment, social benefits etc. The legal framework for the provision of telecommunication services is provided by the following Acts.

a) The Indian Telegraph Act, 1885

b) The Indian Wireless Telegraphy Act, 1933

c) The Telegraph Wires (Unlawful Possession) Act, 1950

d) The Cable Television Networks (Regulation) Act, 1995

e) The Telecom Regulatory Authority of India Act, 1997

f) The Information Technology Act, 2000

4.35 Telecommunication Policy

Under the Indian Telegraph Act, 1885 the telecommunication services can be provided by Central government or an entity licensed by the government. Telecommunication services in India were earlier provided by Central government or Government PSUs. In early 90s, a beginning was made and private service providers started offering value-added services. About ten years back licences were given to private service operators for Mobile Telephone service. In 1994 the government announced Telecommunication Policy, which further liberalised the telecom sector and opened Basic (Fixed) Telephone service for private service operators. This was further followed by New Telecom Policy 1999 which fully opened the telecom sector for competition by allowing private service operators in all telecom service. In the process private service providers started offering Mobile telephone, Fixed telephone and Internet services in late 1990s followed by National Long Distance (STD) in year 2000 and International Long Distance (ISD) in year 2002. There are limitations on foreign direct investment (FDI) which varies from 49 per cent (recently announced by government to be increased to 74 per cent) in basic, mobile and long distance services to 100 per cent in Internet and value-added services.

4.36 Major Telecom Services

The major telecom services include

a) Basic (Fixed) Telephone Service

b) Mobile Telephone Service

b) National Long Distance Service

c) International Long Distance Service

d) Internet Service

e) Other Data Service

f) Value-Added Service

g) VSAT Service

h) Private Mobile Radio Trunking Service (PMRTS)

i) Paging Service

j) Provision of bandwidth to different users

k) Broadband Service etc.

A Unified Access licence category defined about two years ago combines Basic and Mobile services. A further unified licensing regime to consolidate further is being considered by the government.

4.37 Teledensity Status

At present (end-March 2007), there are about 206 million telephones in India which consist of 46 million Fixed telephones and 160 million Mobile telephones. This means a teledensity of about 18.3 (i.e., 18.3 telephones per 100 population). The number of telephones has increased from about 9 million telephones in year 1995 and 27 million telephones in year 2000. The telephones are working both in urban and rural areas but majority of telephones are provided in urban area. In rural area only about 13 million fixed telephones and 33 million Mobile Telephones are working which is equivalent to a teledensity of 6, whereas the urban teledensity is about 50. It can be seen that telecommunication sector is growing very fast with growth touching almost 40 per cent in year 2003-04, 29 per cent in year 2004-05, 42 per cent in year 2005-06 and 47 per cent in year 2006-07. In Delhi also the growth of telecommunication has been significant. At present (end-March 2007), there are about 14.36 million telephones in Delhi consisting of 2.87 million Fixed telephones and 11.49 million Mobile telephones. This is equivalent to teledensity of about 85 Telephones per 100 population. The growth of telephones in Delhi during last 5 years (since beginning of 10th Five Year Plan) can be seen from Table 4.40.

TABLE 4.40

Teledensity Status

(In millions)

	March 2002	*March 2003*	*March 2004*	*March 2005*	*March 2006*	*March 2007*
Fixed	2.10	2.21	2.23	2.41	2.87	2.79
Mobile	1.07	1.85	4.23	5.57	8.07	11.57
Total	3.17	4.06	6.46	7.98	10.94	14.36

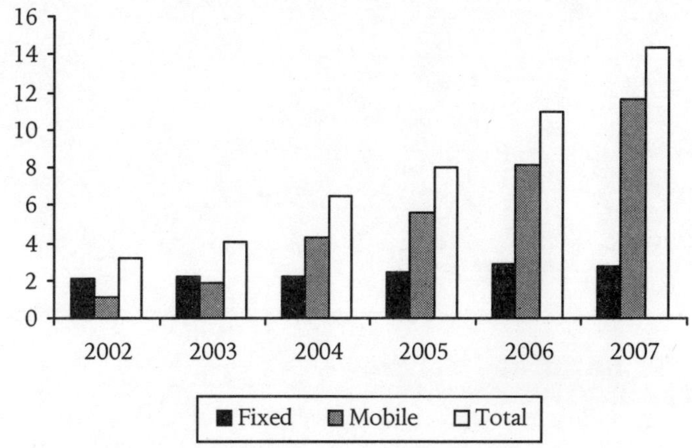

This can be compared with growth of telephones on all India basis during same period of 5 years:

(In millions)

	March 2002	*March 2003*	*March 2004*	*March 2005*	*March 2006*	*March 2007*
Fixed	38.43	41.48	42.48	46.19	48.23	46.48
Mobile	6.54	13.00	33.69	52.22	92.23	160.35
Total	44.97	54.48	76.53	98.41	140.46	206.83

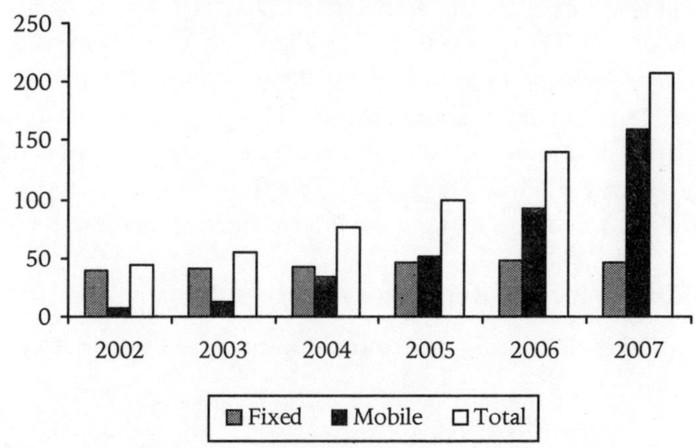

It can be seen that about 7 per cent of all India telephone is in Delhi. Also growth of telephone facilities is taking place at a very fast pace. The major contribution in this fast growth is the very rapid increase in Mobile telephones. It can also be mentioned that almost 3/4th of Mobile subscribers are 'Prepaid' type and only 1/4th subscribers are 'Postpaid' type. This has also contributed to rapid growth of Mobile telephone services.

The Service providers who are providing Fixed and Mobile telephone services along with their contribution of telephone lines as on 31 March 2007 is given below:

(In millions)

Service Provider	*No. of Subscribers*		
	Fixed	*Mobile*	*Total*
MTNL	1.58	1.42	3.00
Bharti	0.61	3.04	3.65
Hutch	0.00	2.37	2.37
Reliance	0.06	1.65	1.71
Idea	0.00	1.45	1.45
TATA	0.54	1.64	2.18
Total	2.79	11.57	14.36

4.38 Broadband Service

In addition to individual telephones, there has been a tremendous growth of Public Call Offices (Also called Public telephones or Payphones or PCOs) where people who do not own a telephone or persons in transit can go and make telephone calls to their family, friend, office, or anywhere. On all India basis the number of PCOs have increased from 0.23 millions in 1995 to 0.66 millions in 2000 to more than 5.55 millions in 2007. In early 90s the government had decided to franchise operation of PCOs to unemployed and educated youth on commission basis which will also result in generating employment. This was very successful in generating convenience to public in addition to generating employment. The fast growth led to about 5.55 million PCOs in urban India as mentioned above besides 0.55 million Village Public Telephones (VPTs). In Delhi about 240,000 PCOs are working in different areas, 92000 of these are provided by the government PSU Mahanagar Telephone Nigam Limited (MTNL) and the balance by Private Sector operators.

4.39 Telecom Regulatory Authority

Other significant telecommunication facilities in Delhi are:

a. Internet service

b. Public Mobile Radio Trunking service (PMRTS)

c. Value Added service

d. Broadband service.

Telecommunication infrastructures are also being used to provide facilities for call centres, BPOs, video distribution, tele-education, tele-health, e-governance etc.

4.40 Private Sector Participation

Broadband service is in its infancy. Based on the report of CII (India's Broadband Economy: Vision 2010) and views of different stakeholders the telecom regulator TRAI gave its recommendations to government on Broadband Policy. A Broadband Policy was announced by the government in October 2004. Broadband service will provide facility for "Triple Play" which means simultaneous transmission of voice, video and data (high speed Internet). The broadband Policy puts a target of 9 million connections by year 2007 and 20 million connections by year 2010. If we estimate the target for Delhi on same proportion as telephones (with all India figures), the target for Delhi will be 0.7 million and 1.5 million in year 2007 and year 2010 respectively.

In Delhi Broadband service is being provided mainly by Bharti and MTNL using wired technology and Reliance is using wireless technology for high speed Internet. Optical Fibre Cable will also be used to provide Broadband service in big offices, residential complexes etc.

The growth of Internet service during last couple of years on all India basis can be seen below:

(In millions)

	March 2003	*March 2004*	*March 2005*	*March 2006*	*March 2007*
Internet	3.64	4.55	5.55	6.94	9.27
Broadband	-	-	0.18	1.35	2.34

It can be seen that at present Broadband service in limited form to provide only high speed Internet service is basically being provided in Delhi and all over India. The number of such connections is also very low but is likely to grow significantly in coming years. Availability of different contents and applications will also increase in future for Broadband service to make it more useful for subscribers and the society in general.

4.41 Long Term Goal

The two major thrust area in telecommunication for future growth are:

a) Mobile service and

b) Broadband service

In addition, value-added service, diverse applications, IT enabled services eg. tele-education, tele-health, e-governance etc., and entertainment using telecommunication infrastructure and facilities will also grow significantly and provide help to society and lead to economic development. Broadband service can give facility to work from home or nearby office in many cases such as banking, insurance, software development, IT enabled services etc. This can result in lesser strain on transport sector and will thus be also eco-friendly. Growth of Broadband services is also likely to lead to greater employment, both direct and indirect.

4.42 E-governance Schemes

Growth of telecommunication services in Delhi have been fuelled by provisioning of resources by many telecommunication operators. The major telecommunication operators in Delhi are

a) MTNL

b) Bharti

c) Hutch

d) Idea

e) Reliance

f) Tata Teleservices

They have been investing resources in the telecom sector by utilising partly from their revenue generation and partly from market in the form of equity or borrowings. Fast changing technology affects the cost of equipment and also leads to newer applications and services. This makes it difficult to estimate the requirement of resources for growth in telecommunication sector accurately. However, as a rough estimate, about a few thousand crores Rupees investments are required every year for the next five years in Delhi for good growth of telecommunication infrastructure and facilities. There should not be any problem for telecommunication operators to invest the required resources as the telecommunication sector, if managed properly, provides good return and profit even in a competitive environment.

4.43 Policy Formulation

With the coming of competition in telecommunication sector in the last 10 years, the government set up an independent regulator called TRAI (Telecom Regulatory Authority of India) in 1997 under the TRAI Act, 1997 (which was significantly amended in 2000). The major activities of TRAI include:

a) setting up tariff of different telecom services

b) ensuring compliance of terms and conditions of licence

c) dealing with interconnection issues between service providers

d) regulating sharing of revenue between service providers

e) ensuring quality of service provided to consumers

f) giving recommendations to government on different issues including spectrum etc.

Telecom Dispute Settlement and Appellate Tribunal (TDSAT) was also set up as per TRAI Act 1997 to hear and decide

a) dispute between government as licensor and licensee (service provider)

b) dispute between two or more service providers

c) dispute between a service provider and a group of consumers

d) appeal against any decision or order of TRAI

The appeal against judgment of TDSAT can be challenged in Supreme Court only.

4.44 Private Sector Participation

Opening of the telecommunication sector to private operators has helped the sector in many ways These can be summarised

a) faster growth of telecom sector

b) new services and applications

c) reduced tariff

d) improved quality of service etc.

As mentioned above, is one of the major advantages to consumers due to competition. For example, the Mobile telephone tariff which was Rs. 8.40 per minute (Rs. 16.80 per minute at peak hours) in Delhi in 1997 has come down to almost Re. 1 per minute. Similarly domestic call long distance call say from Delhi to Mumbai has come down from Rs. 42 per minute to less than Rs. 2 per minute and an international call say from India to USA has come down from Rs. 84 per minute to about Rs. 6 per minute. These sharp reductions of rates has led to more demand of telecom facilities and also increased traffic. The large spurt in demand for Mobile Telephones in Delhi and whole of India is mainly due to reduced tariffs. This has helped the consumers both for domestic as well as business purposes. One can see plumbers, electricians, carpenters, taxi drivers, etc. all carrying mobile telephones in Delhi.

4.45 Long Term Goal

The long term goal should be to provide Broadband service connection (with triple play of voice data and video) to all households in Delhi by year 2015. In addition, Mobile telephone connection should be available to everyone needing it. And tariff should be such that these services are affordable to the general masses. The services should include value-added services and applications, IT enabled services and entertainment. Growth of tele-education, tele-health, and e-governance can be very useful to the society. Also growth of Broadband services can lead to tele-working (i.e., working from home or even other towns and villages) which can lessen the load on transport sector and hopefully on other infrastructures.

Another important goal is to make the whole of Delhi a completely Wi-Fi enabled area using Wi-Max or other relevant technologies which will allow the use of Laptop and other devices in any part of the city and also while on move.

The quality of service especially for Mobile Telephone service needs lot of improvement. All the service providers have to work on this area. The Central government has to release additional spectrum for telecommunication growth and improvement of quality of service.

4.46 e-Governance

Delhi State Government is actively working for the last few years to promote e-Governance schemes to make efficiency in government functioning and also to make citizen's interaction easy and fruitful.

NIC has been actively supporting Delhi government in e-Governance project including software development for many applications. Some of the important software developed by NIC includes:

a) Automation of District Administration for Land Record Computerisation, Registration of Documents, Certificate Issue Management System

b) Automation of District Courts

c) Land and Building

d) Industries

e) Pay and Accounts

f) Food Adulteration

g) Planning

h) Registrar of Cooperative Societies

i) Social Welfare

j) Transport

k) Common Applications for Citizens use etc.

A citizen centric web portal of Delhi government was started in April 2003 to provide different services to citizens. The aim of the portal was to make people interact with the government electronically and to gradually make most of the services available online. The following online services are available.

a) Online filing of applications for 11 types of certificates

b) Online birth, death, marriage certificate

c) Tender Notice Information System

d) Online registration of new vehicles etc.

Many other applications have been developed. These include Computerisation of Driving Licences, Computerisation of RC of Vehicles, Online Sales Tax, Details of Old Age Pension, etc. Some more applications are being developed.

The Delhi government should take further initiatives in this area to make e-Governance project more useful and friendly to citizens. Some of important areas are:

a) Give proper publicity of services to citizens by newspaper and TV media.

b) Ensure opening of Cyber Facility Centre, where citizens can avail these online services. Such cyber centres can be opened by participation of private sector on Revenue sharing model.

c) Assessment of existing services and requirement of new needs of citizens by methods of survey etc.

d) Development of new applications and services e.g. payment of bills of water, electricity, telephone, house tax payment.

4.47 Suggestions

Delhi State government is not directly involved in Policy formulation of Tele communication sector as it is within the ambit of Central government. However, State government can play a number of major roles to see that growth in telecommunication sector takes place properly and is instrumental in leading to benefit the people and the society. Some of the important aspects are:

a) Mobile service requires large number of antennas and towers. Possibility of sharing of towers at some critical areas by different service providers; provision of antennas and towers in high rise buildings; aesthetic provisioning of these are some of the issues.

b) Road digging by different service providers is minimised by provisioning of ducts for cable laying especially on major roads. Of course, road digging for maintenance cannot be ruled out completely.

c) Moral issues concerning undesirable use of some telecommunication facilities in schools, hotels and other places require attention.

d) State government along with Central government can deal with some Policy issues especially dealing with privacy aspects.

   One example is unauthorised passing of individual's data by other agencies eg., telemarketing, insurance companies, banks etc.

e) State government can actively promote IT enabled services like e-governance, tele-education etc. The objective should be to make citizen's interaction with government as little as possible but the interaction required is easy and friendly. In addition to availability of applications and services, this will require re-engineering of many government processes.

f) State government along with Central government can promote to make the whole of Delhi city a Wi-Fi enabled city.

ANNEXURE A-4.1

Composition of Delhi Jal Board

(i) A chairperson who shall be the minister in-charge of the subject matter of the government and a vice chairperson to be nominated by speaker from amongst members as per clause 2 of the Act.

(ii) A Chief Executive Officer to be nominated by the Government who shall be an officer drawing pay in the scale not less than that of a Joint Secretary to the Government of India.

(iii) Three Members of the legislative assembly of the National Capital Territory of Delhi to be nominated by the speaker.

(iv) Two members of the Municipal Corporation of Delhi, Ex-officio.

(v) The Commissioner of the Municipal Corporation of Delhi, Ex-Officio.

(vi) The Chairperson of the New Delhi Municipal Council, Ex-officio.

(vii) A Member (Water Supply) to be nominated by government who shall be an engineer, drawing pay not less than that of a Joint Secretary to the Government of India, having specialised knowledge and experience in the matters relating to water supply.

(viii) A Member (Drainage) to be nominated by government who shall be an engineer, drawing pay in scale not less than that of a Joint Secretary to the Government of India, having specialised knowledge and experience in the matters relating to drainage.

(ix) A Member (Finance) to be nominated by the government drawing pay in the scale not less than that of a Joint Secretary to the Government of India, having specialised knowledge and practical experience of accounting and financial matters.

(x) A Member (administration) to be nominated by the Government drawing pay in the scale not less than that of a Joint Secretary to the Government of India, having specialised knowledge ad practical experience of personnel and administrative matters.

(xi) Secretary-In-Charge of the Department of the Government dealing with the Board, Ex-officio.

(xii) A representative of the Ministry of Urban Affairs & Employment, Government of India who shall not be below the rank of Joint Secretary to the Government of India, to be nominated by the Central Government.

(xiii) One representative of the Delhi Cantonment Board, preferably an elected representative of the Delhi Cantonment Board, to be nominated by its President.

(xiv) A representative of the Central Ground Water Authority who shall not be below the rank of a Chief Engineer, to be nominated by the Central government.

ANNEXURE A-4.2

Organisational Setup of DJB

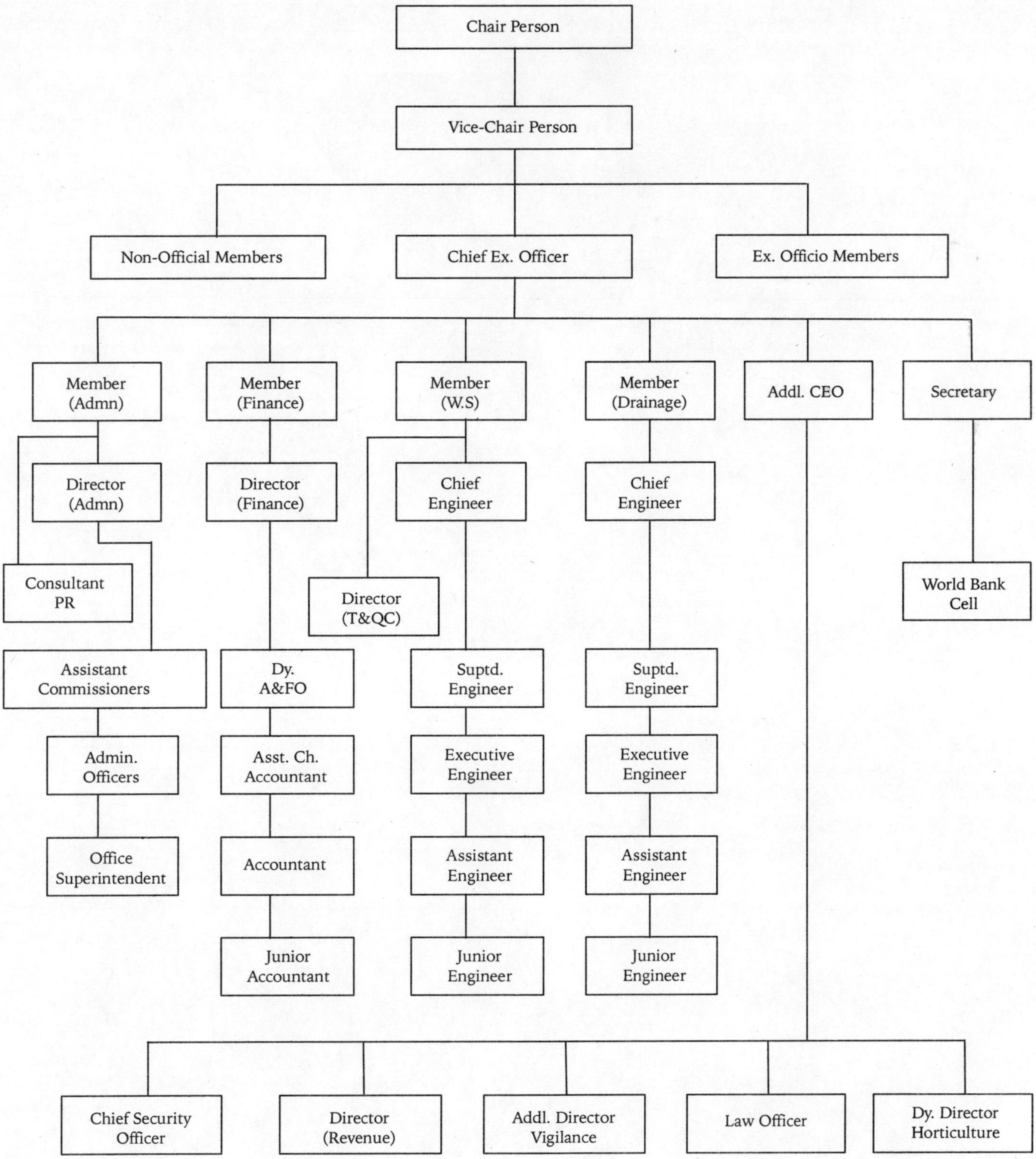

ANNEXURE A-4.3

Zonal Boundaries of DJB and Location of WTPs

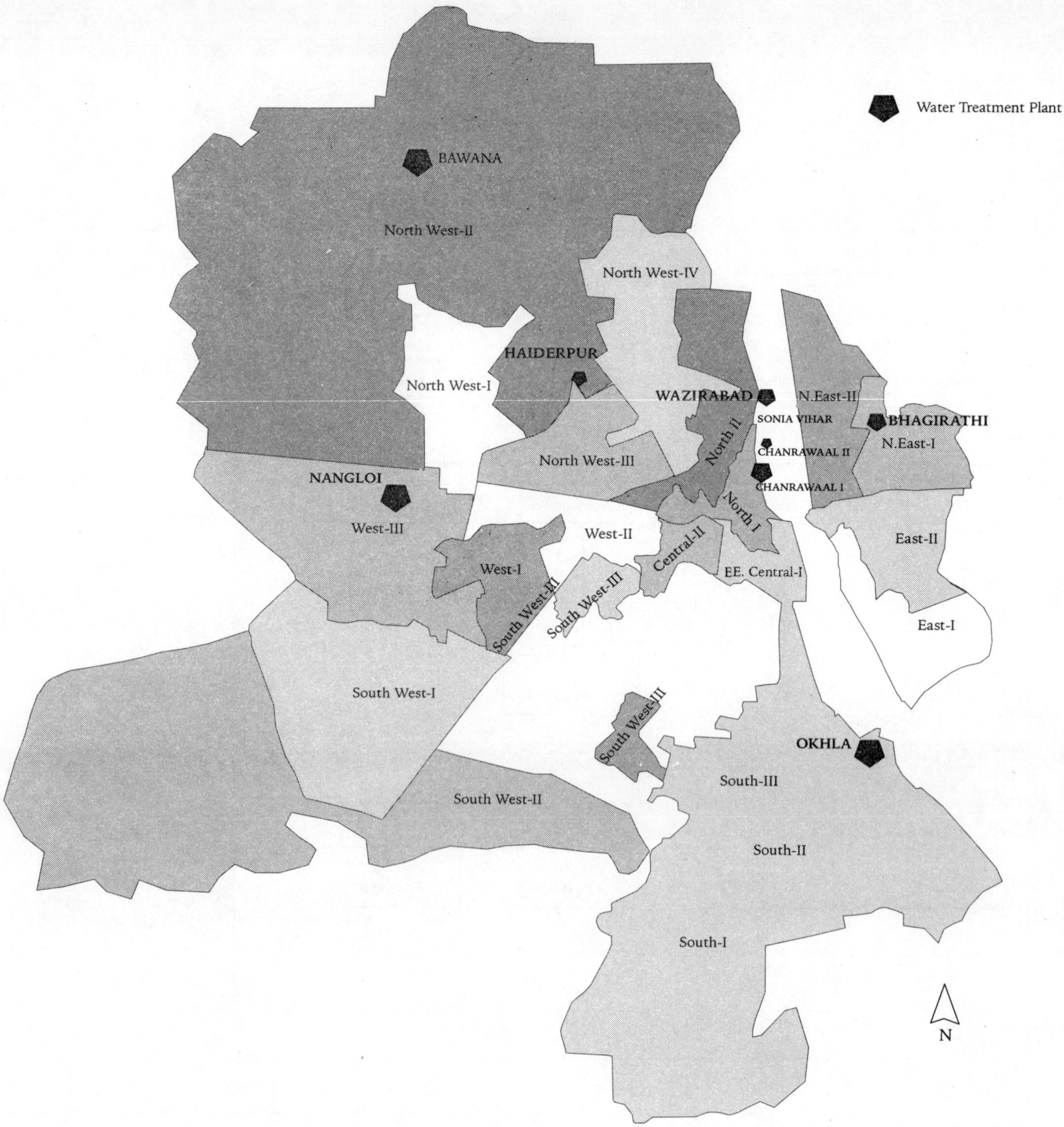

Chapter 5

Environment Management

5.1 Land Use

5.1.1 Urbanisation and Changing Land Use

The total area of NCT of Delhi was 1,483 sq km with an urban segment of 685.34 sq km in the year 1991. Urban population grew at 51.53 per cent from 1991-2001, as compared to the same period. The population density has increased to 9,294 person per sq km (the highest in the country) in the year 2001 against 6,352 persons per sq km in 1991 (GNCTD, 2002).

Urbanisation and industrialisation affected agriculture in the urban areas, as population pressure resulted in changes in land use from agriculture to urban land use, be it for housing, commercial, industrial or other purposes. To accommodate the growing population, successive master plans of NCT of Delhi suggested an increase in the population holding capacity of the area within urbanisable limits and the further extension of present urbanisable limits to rural-use zones. The master plan envisaged that each planning area should have only one use. However, the process of urbanisation followed a mixed pattern of commercial and residential use leading to unplanned growth of city.

Non-agricultural uses such as built up area, housing and roads have grown from 742 (50 per cent of the geographical area of NCT of Delhi) sq km in 1990-91 to 897 (60.5 per cent of the geographical area of NCT of Delhi) sq km in 2000-2001–amounting to around 21 per cent growth in urban area. Per capita floor area availability has also reduced to 52 square metres. This indicates the rapidity of urban expansion in NCT of Delhi. Urban expansion is mainly occurring at the expense of agriculture land in the rural-use zones and areas such as parks, open spaces and green area been earmarked for recreational purposes.

The changing land use pattern in NCT Delhi (Table 5.1) indicates that till 1990-91, agricultural lands (fallow land, cropped area and other uncultivable land) represented 49 per cent of the total area while non-

TABLE 5.1

Changing Land Use in NCT of Delhi

Land Use	*Area (sq. km.)* *1990-91*	*Area (sq. km.)* *2000-2001*	*Percentage change*
Total area	1483	1483	Nil
Rural area	797.66	591.91	-25.8
Urban area	685.34	891.09	30
Forest area	16	111	594
Built up area (as per IRS IC LISS III Satellite)	488	702	43.85
Non-agricultural land (including build up area)	742	897	20.90
Other uncultivated land	128	112	-12.5
Fallow land	128	115	-10.16
Cropped area	469	248	-47.12

Source: Government of National Capital Territory of Delhi.

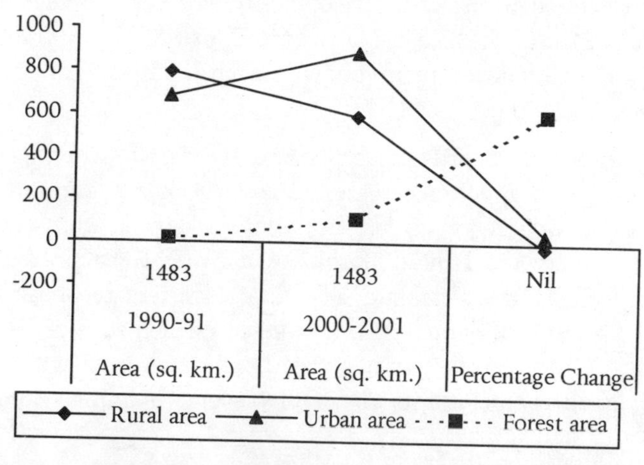

agricultural land 50 per cent of the total. The data also indicate that agriculture was a major land use in and around Delhi. However, by 2000-01, agricultural lands had fallen to 32 per cent of total area while non-agricultural land had risen to 68 per cent of the total.

5.1.2 *Forest Cover and Biodiversity*

In the recent years, the forest cover in NCT of Delhi has shown an increasing trend. As against 16 sq km in 1990-91 (GNCTD, 2001) it had increased to 88 sq km in 1993. Out of the 88 sq km, dense forest accounted for 35 sq km and open forest 53 sq km. According to the State of Forests report (2003), Delhi has 170 sq km of forest cover and 98 sq km of tree cover. Total tree and forest cover constitutes 18.07 per cent of geographical area under green cover (table 5.2) The green cover in NCT of Delhi has increased due to various initiatives taken by the government.

TABLE 5.2

Forest Cover–Percentage of Total Geographical Area

Area	*Area (sq. km.)*	*Per cent of Total Geographical Area*
Geographical Area	1,483	100
Forest Cover	170	11.46
Tree Cover	98	6.61
Forest & Tree Cover	268	18.07

Source : *http://www.forest.delhigovt.nic.in/delhi_state.html*, 2004

The Delhi Ridge, an extension of Aravalli range, serves as the green lungs for NCT of Delhi. The main native tree species of the Ridge forests include *Anogeissus penult, Ziziphus mauritana, Ehretia laevis,* and *Balanites aegyptiaca*. The faunal species found in Delhi ridge are *nilgai* (blue bull), mongoose, porcupine, monkeys, monitor lizard, and jackal. About 250 species of birds can still be spotted. However, the ridge areas have been under pressure due to increasing urbanisation/development activities. To tackle this pressure, the Ridge Management Board has been set up by Delhi government under the chairmanship of the Chief Secretary.

Historical records from 1883 onwards of wild pigs, foxes, hares and mugger are available from the Yamuna; *chinkara*, wolves, *nilgai*, leopard, and black buck, from the Ridge areas and around Tughlaqabad have been reported. More than 580 vertebrate and 1200 invertebrate species have been documented. While large carnivores such as the leopard and wolves may have been extirpated from within the geographical limits of Delhi, several mammals and significant species of birds are yet found here. The southern areas of the Ridge (within Asola-Bhatti Wildlife Sanctuary) retain small numbers of *nilgai*, ruddy mongoose, porcupine, rufous tailed hare, and the jungle cat. Several lists prepared by birdwatchers indicate between 403 to 449 species within the geographical limits of Delhi. The wetlands of Delhi region also harbour significant populations of resident and migratory waterfowl.

The Delhi Ridge (7,777 ha in four remnant patches) is a continuation of the Aravalli Range which extends into Delhi from Haryana at the Tughlaqabad–Dera-Mandi axis moving northwards covering areas of the Asola-Bhatti Wildlife Sanctuary, parts of Delhi Cantonment and the Lutyens Zone terminating at Delhi University covering the Kamala Nehru Ridge. The original area of the ridge was believed to be 15,046 ha. Concerns over the rapidly decreasing cover on account of infrastructure and settlement expansion and mining led to declaration of the remaining four patches that constitute the Delhi Ridge as Reserved Forest in 1994 under the Indian Forest Act (1927): (i) Northern (87 ha, under Delhi Development Authority, DDA) (ii) Central (864 ha, under Forest Department (iii) South Central (626 ha, under Municipal Corporation of Delhi, DDA and Forest Department, FD) (iv) Southern (6200 ha, under the FD).

The Asola-Bhatti Wildlife Sanctuary (ABWLS) was created with the notification of community land of villages (Asola, Sahurpur and Maidangarhi, covering 4704 acres) during 1986 and Bhatti (2167 acres) as Wildlife Sanctuary. The areas are dominated by exposed irregularly distributed boulders of Precambrian, quartzite base that yield quartzite rocks of high quality silica locally known as 'Badarpur' or 'Bajri'. Due to the presence of such mineral resources within the area, it has been subjected to extensive mining and till date faces problems of illegal mining.

5.1.3 *Action Points*

From a settlement of 7 Lakh in 1947, Delhi's population increased to 138 lakh in 2001. As a result, there is a tremendous pressure on land, housing, transportation network and infrastructural services. Of the total geographical area, about 50 per cent has already been urbanised and the rest is under heavy pressure of urbanisation. According to estimates, to cater to a projected population of 224 lakh by year 2021, the urban areas of NCT of Delhi (70,162 ha) will need to be increased by around 25,000-30,000 ha (Table 5.3). From a settlement of 7 lakh in 1947, Delhi's population increased to 138 lakh in 2001.

TABLE 5.3

Population Growth and Land Requirement in NCT of Delhi

S.No.	*Land*	*Area (ha.)*	*Per cent to total area (ha.)*
1.	Total Geographical Area-NCT, Delhi	1,48,300	100
2.	Build up area (As per IRS IC III Satellite Data-1999)	70,162	47.31
3.	Natural features to be conserved (Forest, Other water bodies/drains)	19,509	13.16
4.	Sub-total (Build-up + Natural Features)	89,671	60.47
5.	Balance land available in NCT-Delhi	58,629	39.53
6.	Proposed land for urbanisation	27.629	18.63
7.	Total urbanisable area 2021 (including built-up area 1999)	97.791	65.94

Source: National Capital Region Planning Board, 2002.

To ensure planned development and to avoid delays and litigation in land acquisition, it is necessary to seek a suitable alternative to the existing policy of large-scale acquisition and disposal of land. The policy approach should also be geared to mobilise the public private partnership arrangements in urban development. The example set up by Haryana, which has a land development act that has invited large-scale private involvement in land development and has increased the availability of land, can be thought for Delhi too. Alongside, due cognisance should be taken for providing basic amenities to vulnerable section of the community. Regulatory and enforcement arrangements have to be strengthened to arrest the growth of unauthorised colonies and *jhuggi-jhopri* (JJ) clusters. The concept of land pooling in agricultural lands/areas and Transferable Development Rights (TDR) for urban areas can be integrated along with compulsory acquisition of land.

5.2 Water Supply and Sanitation

5.2.1 Urban Growth and Water Consumption

A considerable part of fresh water supply (86 per cent) in NCT of Delhi is drawn from surface water. The river Yamuna provides the major share of this supply. Delhi's share of this river's resources, as per interstate agreement, is 4.6 per cent. Other sources of water supply to Delhi through different interstate agreements include the Himalayan Rivers and sub-surface sources like ranney wells and tube-wells. Delhi receives a normal rainfall of 611.8 mm in 27 rainy days. In the absence of adequate storage structures in the catchment areas, the unutilised rainwater runoff is 193 MCM (Central Ground Water Authority 2001). Dynamic groundwater resources in Delhi have been assessed as 292 MCM, while the present withdrawal is 312 MCM; thus resulting in depletion of fresh water lenses. The total renewable fresh water availability in NCT of Delhi is estimated at 1442 MCM per year (1150 MCM/year surface water and 292 MCM/year ground water). As of today, per capita freshwater availability for NCT of Delhi is 105 cubic metres per year, indicating a water stress scenario.

Based on a norm of 70 gallon per capita per day prescribed by MPD-2001, the water requirement for population in 2000-01 was 966 Million gallon per day (MGD). Even if the water requirement for the population in rural areas and slums (including JJ clusters/walled city), estimated at about 4.5 million (estimated slum population 3.5 million and rural 1 million), is calculated at the lower norm of 30 gallons per day, the demand for water in Delhi in 2000-2001 was estimated as 786 MGD as compared to 538 MGD in 1990-91.

The primary source of municipal/domestic water is surface water (86 per cent) and other sources include the sub-surface and ground water. Due to rapid urbanisation, the domestic consumption of supply water increased from 401.3 million kilolitres in 1990-91 to 929.6 million kilolitres in 2001-02, a growth of 131 per cent (Delhi Jal Board). Per capita consumption of water per day increased from 145 litres (32.07 gallons) during 1980-81 to 223 litres (49.03 gallons) in 1990-91 but dropped to 183 litres (40 gallons) per day in 2001-2002 (after deducting the water losses) (Delhi Statistical Handbook, 2002).

Delhi had 3.131 million household (13.8 million populations) in 2001. In the urban area, 78.37 per cent of the households had piped water supply, 17.88 per cent depended on handpumps or tubewell and the remaining 3.75 per cent households used wells, rivers and canals for their drinking water. In the rural areas, 48.38 per cent of the households had piped water supply, 42.62 per cent depended on handpumps or tubewells and the remaining 9 per cent used wells, rivers canals for drinking water. Thus, in aggregate, 75.72 per cent of the households in Delhi had piped water supply, 20.06 per cent depended on handpumps/tubewells and the remaining 4.22 per cent used wells, rivers and canals for drinking water in 1991 (Directorate of Economics and Statistics, 2002).

5.2.2 *Commercial/Industrial Growth and the Demand for Water*

Groundwater/supply water is the main source for meeting the water needs of commercial activities/industries in Delhi, where industrial growth has been high, from 81,000 in 1990 to 126,000 in 1996 (Directorate of Industries, Government of National Capital Territory of Delhi). The water demand of commercial and industrial activities went up from 52.7 million kilolitres in 1990-91 to 164 million kilolitres in 2001-02, a growth of 211 per cent (Delhi Jal Board). The environmental cost of such rapid commercial and industrial growth has been the contamination of water resources, including pollution of groundwater and surface water.

The rapid growth in the State's population has resulted in a decline in the annual per capita availability of freshwater, from 153 cubic metres per year in 1990-91 to 105 cubic metres per year in 2001-02. Chronic shortages of freshwater of adequate quality are already being experienced. Water quality has been degrading due to combination of factors such as draining of sewage and industrial and urban effluents into water sources, and saline intrusion.

In several areas of the State, the misuse of water resources has resulted in depletion of aquifers, resulted in shrinking inland lakes and streams to unsafe levels. Per capita consumption figures are generally based on quantity supplied to the water distribution network in urban areas. But the distribution systems are obsolete and operational wastages are high. For NCT of Delhi, the average loss is estimated at 15 per cent.

The treatment capacities have increased from 42 MGD (million gallon per day) in 1951 to 337 MBD in 1991 and 600 MGD in 2002 (Delhi Jal Board). Despite this, the average current short fall is about 276 MGD (as calculated using the Delhi Jal Board's supply norms and average losses estimated at 15 per cent). However, the percentage of unaccounted-for-water calculated from the difference between water produced and pumped is a high 35-40 per cent (GHK International Ltd., 2000). This situation can be rectified through better maintenance systems, which can enhance the per capita availability.

5.2.3 Over-extraction on Groundwater

The State has been experiencing a fall in ground water levels and deteriorating water quality on account of over-exploitation. Groundwater withdrawals have exceeded the rate of recharge and as a result there is a increase in salinity, lowering groundwater table and chemical concentration. A comparison of existing groundwater levels in the different administrative blocks with level in 1960 shows a decline of 2-30 m. Levels in Alipur and Kanjhawala blocks have declined by 2-6m, in Najafgarh block by 10m and in Mehrauli by 20 m. In the flood plain of river Yamuna, freshwater generally exists at a depth of 35-45m. However, there is scope of further ground water development in the Yamuna flood plain area and in some other areas of the Delhi NCT (Central Ground Water Authority, 2001). Chemical quality of ground water in Delhi varies with depth and space. Brackish water at shallow depth exists in Kanjhawala and Najafgarh blocks and in some minor patches of Alipur and city blocks.

5.2.4 Wastewater Generation and Sewerage System

5.2.4.1 Wastewater Generation

With the high population growth and rapid urbanisation, the amount of domestic wastewater generated has increased from 260 million litres per day in 1961 to 930 million litres per day in 1991 and 2650 million litres per day in 2001. This is despite the fact that more than 45 per cent of the population currently has no access to sewerage services and traditional on site sanitation and open defecation if practised. The growing lag between increased wastewater discharges and treatment capacities will worsen the quality of existing raw water sources and increase the costs of treatment. Further, due to inadequate infrastructure for wastewater collection and other operational problems, even the current STP capacity is underutilised.

Unabated discharge of partially treated and untreated wastewater from different sources is responsible for deterioration of water quality. Domestic sources contribute maximum to wastewater discharges. Industrial discharges are, however, maximum in the Rithala and Keshopur zones (Central Pollution Control Board). Deterioration of surface (Yamuna River) and ground water quality is one of the most serious environmental problems for NCT of Delhi. High population densities, rapid urbanisation, increasing commercialisation/industrialisation and a general lack of pollution control facilities are exerting growing pressure on water resources.

Delhi, the capital of India, has a population of over 13.9 million (Approx. 14 m). It has grown by more than 300 per cent since 1971. The population density in the city is also widely divergent, ranging from 1300 persons per sq km to 70,000 persons per sq km. The population growth pattern of Delhi is the single most important factor that affects the level quantity of water supply and sewerage services available to its habitants Delhi Jal Board (DJB) is the authority responsible for planning, designing and execution of water supply and waste water management facilities within its jurisdiction in the National Capital Territory of Delhi. About 40 per cent of the population of Delhi (JJ Clusters, MCD area, unauthorised colonies and rural villages) lives in unsewered areas. Presently, about 650 mgd (2955 mld) water is distributed by the DJB in Delhi. Additional 90 mgd water supply is estimated from ground water. In future the demand is projected by DJB as 845 mgd (3841 mld) by the year 2006 and 950 mgd (4319 mld) in 2011. In absence of any additional source of water, no further significant increase is expected up to 2021. The population that has been projected by Delhi Development Authority (DDA) by 2021 is 23 million.

5.2.4.2 Sewerage System

The development of sewerage system in Delhi started soon after New Delhi was built in 1938. A Sewage Treatment Plant (STP) of 82 nld capacity was constructed at Okhla. By 1956, the capacity of this plant was augmented to 164 mld. Additional STPs were later constructed at coronation pillar (55 mld) in 1957 and 1960 respectilvely. The treatment capacity in creased from 273 mld in 1961 to 1273 mld in 1993. The present sewage treatment capacity in Delhi stands at around 2330. Presently, the urban area of Delhi is served by a gravity collection sewers, sewerage system involving a large network of branch sewers, intercepting sewers, peripheral and trunk sewers, of about 6000 km length. As per DJB there are 28 main trunk sewers with size ranging from 700 mm to over 2400 mm diameter with a total length of round 140 km. The balance length comprises peripheral sewers with smaller diameter with the smallest internal sewers having diameter of 150 mm.

There are 36 major waste water pumping stations of capacities ranging from 6 MLD to 455 mld. Even today, only about 60 per cent of the population of Delhi is served by the sewerage system. For the purposes of sewerage and drainage, Delhi is served by the sewerage system. For the purposes of sewerage and drainage, Delhi can be divided into six zones: 1) Rithala; 2) Coronation Pillar; 3) Keshopur; 4) Okhla; 5) Trans Yamuna; and 6) Outer Delhi. Besides this, there are newly developed areas or urban extensions mostly contiguous with urban limits such as Narela, Pappan Kalan, Nazafgarh, Ghitorni, Vasant Kunj, Mehrauli, and Sarita Vihar. At present STPs are located at 17 different places in Delhi with a cumulative treatment capacity of 2330 mld (512.5 mgd).

5.2.5 Surface Water Contamination

The River Yamuna passing through Delhi receives nearly 200 million litres of untreated sewage every day. As per the data generated by Central Pollution Control Board from monitoring stations in Delhi segment of Yamuna from 1971-2001, the minimum and maximum coliform values have demonstrated 150-fold and 10,00,000-fold increases, thus indicating the severity of the pollution.

The longitudinal profile of the main water bodies flowing through Delhi highlights a drastic deterioration in water quality as observed at stations upstream, within and downstream of Delhi (Central Pollution Control Board 2000). Depletion in Dissolved Oxygen (DO), increased Biochemical Oxygen Demand (BOD) and increased faecal coliform levels are characteristics of the stretch of Yamuna passing through Delhi. During the non-monsoon period, when the demand is high and adequate dilution water is not available, the river stretch catering to Delhi's needs gets worse and becomes unfit for beneficial use.

5.2.6 Impact on Groundwater Quality

Groundwater, which has long been the primary alternative to polluted surface water, is being increasingly contaminated by human waste and leaching of chemicals, as a result of over-extraction. According to a latest study, conducted by Delhi Pollution Control Committee (DPCC) in January 2004, presence of high TDS and hardness has been reported near the industrial areas municipal solid waste dump site, which indicates that the ground water is receiving some contaminants from the industrial areas either through leachate or the drains in the area. Iron content in the groundwater has been found to be higher in some samples through there is near absence of heavy metal contamination.

5.2.7 Water Quality and Changes in Land Use

Changes in land use patterns brought about by urbanisation affect the recharge of groundwater. Urban run-off that collects toxic compounds from sewage, vehicular exhaust and industrial pollution severely degrades the water quality. Groundwater in most urban areas of NCT of Delhi is contaminated due to polluted run-off that percolates down.

5.2.8 Action Points

Rationalising water pricing: Demand management initiatives in the water sector are important, considering demand from various sectors. Demand management policies are normally constrained due to the existing pricing system from piped water supply in domestic and commercial/industrial sector. The tariffs are very old and do not even meet the operational costs. Moreover, the unaccounted for water wastage needs to be reduced by rehabilitating the existing infrastructure (leak detection, replacement of meters, reduction in un-metered connections, involvement of stakeholders in operation, production and consumption, etc).

There have been no incentives for water conservation or for improving water use efficiency. Technology development and transfer programmes can help in reducing water usage and wastage. The augmentation of water supply through rainwater harvesting and recycling of wastewater also helps in meeting the water requirement to some extent. Appropriate tariffs structure for water services will have to be evolved to encourage wise usage of the resource and generate additional support for the fund starved service providers. Additionally, there is a need to develop and implement cost-effective water appliances such as low-flow cisterns and faucets and formulate citizen groups to encourage and raise awareness on water conservation.

Rainwater harvesting: The amount of runoff generated from 910 MCM of precipitation in NCT of Delhi is 193 MCM. This can be tapped and stored in both surface and sub-surface reservoirs. When clubbed with the 282 MCM runoff in the Yamuna, the non-committed flow is 475 MCM. This can be stored in the regenerated quarries and lakes for creating additional water storage for small communities (GHK International Ltd., 2000).The harvested rainwater can also be used to recharge the groundwater through injection wells, recharge-pits, shafts and trenches. The Yamuna Flood Plain also offers excellent opportunities for future groundwater development besides the ongoing process in different hydro-geological locations (CGWA, 2001). PWD and DJB have started rainwater-harvesting measures in government office buildings. Cooperative Group Societies are also being persuaded to adopt rainwater harvesting in their complexes. Building byelaws have been amended to ensure rainwater-harvesting measures in all new buildings with 1000 sq metres and above size plot.

Participatory approach: A participatory approach is an important prerequisite for sustainable water resources management. There is an urgent need for an awareness campaign to share experiences on the critical aspects of availability of water resource in terms of quality and quantity, conservation, etc. To achieve this, the services of Civil Society Organisations (CSOs) can provide a very important link between communities and government institutions. The CSOs can offer their services in capacity building of the relevant stakeholders, R&D for low-cost and effective water supply and sanitation facilities, and enforcement of policies.

Integrated water resource management: Integrated all aspects of water management—namely, water allocation, pollution control, protection of water resources and mobilisation of financial resources—is important. An analysis of the availability of utilisable water resources, demand levels and consumption patterns is also needed. Such an analysis would help in developing a Water Zoning Atlas to guide decisions related to sitting of commercial/industrial and other economic activities. The treated wastewater can also be provided as a dual source of supply for supply for bulk users such as institutions, industries and for areas with greater water demands. However, this requires identifying users for pilot implementation and conducting studies to find the potential cost of such provisions, cost/benefit ratio and user acceptability.

The other methods of water management include introducing water-saving technologies (such as sprinkler and drip irrigation technologies) for commercial/ industrial and domestic use, reviving the traditional wisdom of water harvesting system for storage and utilisation, micro-catchments planning through involvement of stakeholders at all levels.

Wastewater Management

There are two sources of pollution; domestic and industrial. The domestic sources are mainly domestic sewage and toilet wastewater; whereas industrial pollution source is mainly from Industrial estates. Normally 80 per cent of water supply is generated as sewage. However, the flow of wastewater in various drains was observed as 3900 mld, which confirms the use of ground water for drinking and other purposes. Presently, a large part of the sewage flows through open sewer drains. Due to ineffective conveyance system coupled with inadequate sewage treatment capacity, untreated sewage from sewered areas flows into 18 drains/*nallahs* which were meant to carry only storm water and outfall directly into the Yamuna.

There are 31 planned industrial estates in Delhi. The industrial effluents from most of the industrial estates flow through open surface drains ultimately finding access into the River Yamuna. Some of the examples are Wazirpur Industrial Area, G.T. Karnal Road Industrial Area, Rajasthan Udyog, Jhilmil Industrial Area. The gross population caused by effluents from these Industrial Estates was taken note by Hon'ble Supreme Court of India and the court ordered construction of 15 Common Effluent Treatment Plans (CETP) in Delhi out of which 10 CETPs have been completed.

The DJB has 30 STPs at 17 locations in the NCT of Delhi along with sewage pumping stations. The sewerage network comprises 5600 kms of sewer lines including trunk sewers and branch sewers (peripheral/internal sewers). This includes 28 main trunk sewers of a total length of 130 kms. For sewage management, Delhi is divided into five drainage zones of Okhla, Keshopur, Rithala-Rohinil, Coronation and Shahdara. In addition, there are newly sewered areas of Pappan Kalan (Dwarka), Vasant Kunj, Sarita Vihar, and Narela.

Serious efforts are needed to ensure effective operation and maintenance of the CETPs and STPs. Future action plans should also take into account the rise in wastewater generation in proportion to the projected rise. Even if piped water is supplied for the entire population of Delhi as per the aim of the government, the amount of domestic sewage generated will also rise proportionately. Various forms of public-private partnerships for different levels of services such as water supply metering should be introduced. The feasibility of having cost effective package treatment system for all communities located in outer Delhi zone needs to be assessed.

5.3 Solid Wastes Management

5.3.1 Sources and Quantum of Solid Wastes

Municipal solid waste: With the exponential growth of population in Delhi where half a million people are added every year, the quantum of municipal solid waste generation has considerably increased. It is estimated that the present per capita waste generation, which is 450-500 grams, will go up to 900-1000 grams by 2021 (a projection based on an additional 8.6 million people added to Delhi's population). The present municipal solid waste generation in Delhi is 7,000 to 7,500 metric tonne per day, which is likely to increase in the range of 17,000 to 25,000 metric tonne by 2021 (NEERI). The waste generation in MCD (Municipal Corporation of Delhi), NDMC (New Delhi Municipal Corporation) and the Cantonment Board are about 7,000 metric tonnes, 300-350 metric tonnes, and 60 metric tonnes per day, respectively.

Industrial waste: Industrial activities and treatment of industrial effluents (sludge generation) are the major sources of hazardous waste generation. As per the survey conducted by NPC-NCAER in 2002-2003, about 23000 industrial units have been identified in the 31 approved industrial areas. As per the above report, 1777 industrial units are hazardous waste generating units. The hazardous waste generation is around 50,000 kg/day (i.e., approximate 15,000 tonnes per year).

In addition, the generation of fly ash from three coal based thermal power plants in Delhi is 2,893,179 tonnes in the year 2005. There was a decrease in fly ash generation during 1998-2000 due to the use of coal with lower ash content (34 per cent as against 40 per cent used earlier) and partly fuel substitution from coal to natural gas. Further, siginificant reduction in the fly ash accumulation has been observed at Rajghat Thermal Power Plant and IP Thermal Power plant fly ash is being used for various construction and landfill purposes.

Hospital waste: As per DHS report 2005, Delhi Government has 31 hospitals; MCD has 59 hospitals; NDMC has 4 hospitals; 23 hospitals belong to Government of India/public sector unit or associated institutions besides AIIMS. In addition, 562 private nursing homes are also registered with DHS.

As per the report, the total bed strength is about 32,760. Out of this, 12,381 beds are with private sector and the rest is with the government/autonomous bodies.

As per the annual report of DPCC 2005, about 8.5 tonnes per day of biomedical waste is collected and treated per day.

5.3.2 Management Systems and Status

Municipal solid waste management: According to the records available and as per the annual report submitted by MCD, NDMC and the Cantonment Board, on average, 15-20 per cent of the municipal solid waste generated remains uncollected. Out of the collected municipal solid waste, only 10-15 per cent is used for composting and the remaining is disposed at various landfills.

MCD generates around 7,000 metric tonnes of municipal solid waste per day. Out of the generated waste, 6,000 to 6,500 metric tonnes per day gets collected. Around 650 metric tonnes of waste per day is composted in existing three composting plants and the remaining goes for land filling. The estimated amount of waste that remains uncollected is 500 to 1,000 metric tonnes per day.

NDMC generates around 300-350 metric tonnes of municipal solid waste per day and the whole amount gets collected. NDMC has its compost plant of 200 metric tonnes of garbage handling capacity per day in Okhla, which runs for 3 shifts. This plant was commissioned in 1985 and is functioning presently with garbage handling capacity of 80-90 metric tonnes per day in two shifts. The remaining waste goes for land filling at Okhla landfill site.

The Cantonment Board generates around 60 metric tonnes of municipal solid waste per day and whole amount is getting collected also. The Cantonment Board does not have composting plants and the whole amount goes for land filling at Okhla landfill site.

The disposal of solid waste is presently carried out at four disposal sites—Okhla Phase–1, X-ing GT Karnal

Road, Bhalswa, and Gazipur. The balance life of these sites has reached a critical stage, and there is an urgent need to identify and acquire more sites that would last for the next 20-25 years. The total capacity of the proposed disposal sites to manage MSW in Delhi is 22,55,000 sq/ mtr (228500 m^2). The projected quantities of solid waste to be disposed by 2021 are 100 MT, requiring a land area of 600-800 ha.

The phenomenal increase in use of plastics in Delhi started in the 80s. Although plastic waste contributes to only 6 per cent of the total municipal solid waste generated in NCT of Delhi, its management, especially of discarded polythene bags, leaves much to be desired. These bags are disposed in a haphazard manner, thus choking sewage drains and destroying the landscape in cities. Waste polythene bags are picked by rag pickers and sent for recycling. Repeated recycling deteriorates the quality of the bags produced, and pigments used to impart colour to these bags poses health hazard to people engaged in recycling because of the outdated technologies used. Unsafe storage of waste plastics also poses a fire hazard as was evident in the 1995 fire accident at Jwalapuri in which resources worth crores were lost in addition to emission of large amounts of toxic fumes. The government has taken initiatives to introduce guidelines on the use of food-grade plastics and use of recycled plastic, and also minimising littering of waste.

Industrial waste management: Most of the industrial units in Delhi are in the unorganised sector and much of the hazardous waste is in the form of sludge from CETPs and individual ETPs. The biggest problem is small scale pickling units, electroplating and anodising, dyeing units and vehicle service stations. As per the study conducted by NPC/NCAER, the hazardous waste generation is around 50,000 kg/day (i.e., a 15,000 tonnes/year). These wastes are required to be disposed off in a safe manner as specified in the Hazardous Waste (Management and Handling) Rules, 1989.

In NCT of Delhi, the main industrial non-hazardous waste is fly ash from coal based power plants that emitted about 2.89 million tonnes in the year 2005. Out of the total fly ash generated from the coal based thermal power plants, huge quantity of fly ash is utilised mainly for landfill, road embankments and brick making. Land is now being allotted to three brick-manufacturing units near Rajghat and Indraprastha thermal power stations so that additional fly ash from these plants can be utilised. At the same time, the use of beneficiated/washed coal may reduce the amount of fly ash generated by thermal power plants.

Hospital waste management: Most of the large hospitals in Delhi have incineration facilities and in some cases autoclaving facilities but these are close to residential areas and are potential health and environmental hazards. Private nursing homes and small hospitals do not have arrangements to treat hospital waste. At present 54 incinerators, 18 autoclaves, and 2 microwaves are in operation.

5.3.3 Action Points

Waste inventorisation: Detailed waste inventorisation is one of the first steps in designing a proper and scientific waste management plan for any site. Considering the limited financial capability of the local bodies, it is indispensable for them to utilise the resources fully to have savings in overall cost. In order to distribute the resources optimally to various sanitary wards of NCT of Delhi and to regularise the operations to provide better service consistently, a detailed survey would be required which will have following objectives.

- Assessment of quantity and quality of solid waste generated in each sanitary ward by different sources;
- Assessment of community needs, perception and willingness to pay for improved collection service;
- Selection of suitable waste disposal sites; and,
- Route optimisation for minimisation of collection and transportation cost

Waste minimisation: Waste, which is costly to manage must be reduced as much as is economical through waste recycling and minimisation. Some of the waste minimisation options are as follow:

- Incentives for use of cloth and paper bags;
- Segregating wastes in the house with the municipality to prove separate containers for recyclable waste;
- Large plot holders to have small compost pits in their own landscaped areas; and
- Separate collection from large generators of organic wastes, like *mandis*, sent for composting. Combustible wastes from timber markets or industries sent to 'waste to energy' generating centres.

Private sector participation: Private Sector Participation (PSP) may be used as an agent for change. The privatisation process should initially be targeted towards profit making centres, such as the following:

- Door-to-door collection and transportation of wastes from restaurants and commercial centres, hospitals and nursing homes;
- House to house collection of wastes in high income areas;
- Operation of waste processing/utilisation systems in selected areas.

The above-mentioned activities can be introduced on full cost recovery basis with positives cash flow. The procedure for handling and disposal of restaurants/hotel was waste is entirely different from that of hospital wastes. So also is the case with industrial wastes. Therefore, municipal corporations should ensure appropriate systems for collection, transportation, processing and disposal of these wastes.

Public participation: Cooperation and participation of the community is essential in implementing any waste management strategy. Reduction, reuse and recycling of waste cannot be performed without active public participation. Community involvement in the decision-making process in developing solid waste management strategies should be encouraged at the inception and during the implementation of waste management programme. The State policies should be aimed at reduction of waste by encouraging procedures and consumers through education and awareness. Sorting of waste at source plays an important role for getting private sector partnership in solid waste management, especially in the recycling industry. The growing volume of waste spawned by the consumption inherent in city life is a formidable challenge for low-income areas; the main solid waste problem is how to extend the collection services to the poor.

Technological interventions: For disposal of solid wastes, the following technological options can be considered:

- Composting;
- Sanitary landfill;
- Anaerobic digestion; and,
- Incineration.

To meet the recurring expenditure towards salary of the staff, operation and maintenance of vehicles and workshop facilities, overheads and for purchase of tools and equipment for improvement in collection and transportation services and for development of new sanitary landfill sites, the possibility of introducing a separate solid waste management tax may be considered. This tax initially be so levied that the recurring cost of salary and operation and maintenance to be completely recovered. The rates of tax could be based on property value and frequency of service provided.

5.4 Air Quality

5.4.1 Causes of Air Pollution

The principal sources of air pollution in the city of Delhi are the transport, power plants, industry and domestic sectors. Besides the anthropogenic sources, climate and natural sources too has played an important role in the increasing pollution levels. Delhi has a semi-arid climate, with an extremely hot summer, average rainfall and very cold winters. Mean monthly temperatures range from 14.3°C in January (Minimum 3°C) to 34.5°C in June (Maximum 47°C).

The monsoon season witnesses the least pollution due to washout of pollutants along with rains. Mixing height is one of the important parameters that influence the dilution of pollutants. It follows diurnal and seasonal variations. During winter, ground-based temperature inversions are a regular feature that restricts mixing height to low levels. Lower temperatures, calm conditions, lower mixing height, and temperature inversions during winter restrict and confine pollutant dispersion and dispersal. Winter evenings have higher pollution build-up because of frequent calm conditions with temperature inversions resulting in poor natural ventilation and high emission loads due to evening traffic peaks. The situation in Delhi during winter is therefore more critical as compared to Mumbai, Chennai, and Kolkata as the effect of natural sea breeze is absent resulting in virtually no dilution of pollutant. In the summer season, there are frequent pre-monsoon dust storms, when strong westerly winds from Rajasthan desert deposit large concentration of dust particles in Delhi's atmosphere.

Vehicular pollution: Although Delhi has the longest road length amongst the Indian cities (1284 km per 100 sq km of area) the total number of registered vehicles in Delhi is about 40 lakhs, which is more than the sum total of vehicles registered in 3 other metropolitan cities *viz.*, Calcutta, Mumbai, and Chennai. As many as 500 vehicles exist for every kilometre of the road stretch in Delhi whereas the figure for Mumbai and Kolkata is 350, and for Chennai, this figure is less than 100 vehicles. About two-thirds of the registered vehicles in Delhi are two-wheelers. Cars and jeeps account for about 27 per cent o the total vehicular population auto-rickshaws constitute about 2.5 per cent. Buses constitute 1 per cent of the total registered vehicles and goods carrying vehicles account for 4.5 per cent (Table 5.4).

TABLE 5.4

Growth of Registered Vehicles in Delhi

Name of Vehicle	*1971*	*1981*	*1991*	*1994*	*2001-02*
Cars/Jeeps	56450	119495	398479	522264	968894
Motor cycles and Scooters	93263	345109	1220640	1492201	2265955
Auto rickshaws	10221	20379	63005	72102	86985
Taxis	3842	6385	10157	11846	20628
Buses	3038	8044	18858	24211	47578
Goods vehicles	13620	36599	101828	116379	161650

Source: Delhi Statistical Handbook 2002.

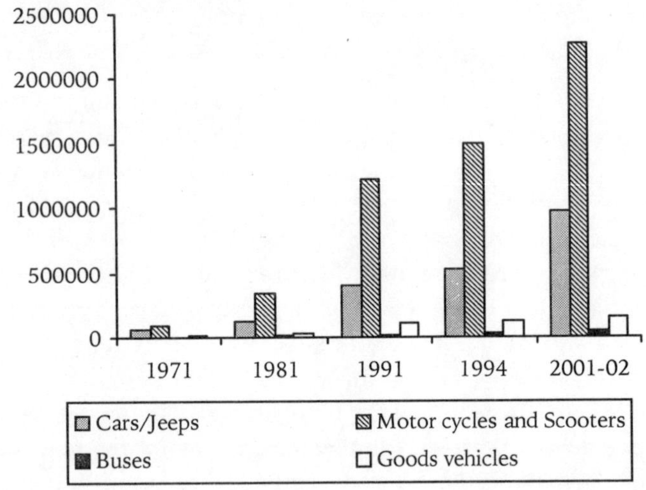

Although the vehicular population in Delhi is still relatively low compared to several European cities and the U.S., the travel demand and the per capita trip rate in Delhi is one of the highest among the developing countries. Hence, the vehicular pollution has become a serious problem. The factors which contribute to vehicular pollution include increase in travel demand, increase in the number of vehicles, constrained road space, over loading, types of engines used, over aged vehicles, quality of fuel, poor road conditions etc.

Industrial pollution: Amongst the various types of industries that mushroomed in the city, the most polluting ones were stone crushers, hot mix plants, potteries, induction furnaces, etc., besides the above important industrial air pollution sources, coal-fired boilers, foundries, forging units, etc. also contributed significantly to air pollution. In addition, significant pollution was also caused by a large number of Diesel Generating (DG) sets, which were installed in various commercial and industrial establishments. The erratic power supply caused phenomenal increase in the number and use of DG sets. In addition to these industries, emission from thermal power plants located in the heart of the city also adds to air pollution.

Pollution from the domestic sector: The various types of energy sources used in urban households include liquefied petroleum gas (LPG), kerosene, soft coke, electricity, firewood and other biomass fuels. LPG and electricity are generally used by the higher income groups, while the lower income brackets choose kerosene, coal and biomass fuels. The main concern in the domestic sector is the use of inefficient and highly polluting fuels in the poorer households/urban slums, leading to deterioration in the indoor air quality and health.

The burning of biomass fuels in inefficient cook-stoves and in the absence of chimneys and windows lead to high levels of indoor air pollution causing a variety of eye and lung diseases; especially among the women and children. The CO, CO_2, SPM emissions from fuel use are fairly significant and are inadequately dispersed. This brings about high exposure and risk to the slum dwellers. Pollutants from slow combustion of miscellaneous combustible materials by domestic and commercial sources account for 8 per cent of the total pollution. Sulphur dioxide is the major pollutant emitted. Moreover, since these emissions take place at low heights, the problems due to domestic burning need proper attention in order to avoid any undesirable health effects.

5.4.2 Health Impacts

A study on The Health Effects of Air Pollution in Delhi, India (Cropper *et al., 1997*) reported the results relating levels of particulate matter to daily death in Delhi between 1991 and 1994. During the study period, the average total suspended particulate (TSP) level in Delhi was 378 micrograms per cubic metre—approximately five times the World Health Organisation's (WHO) annual average standard. Furthermore, TSP levels in Delhi during this time period exceeded the WHO 24-hour standard on 97 per cent of all days on which reading were taken. The major findings of the study reveal the following:

- In general, these impacts are smaller than those estimated for other countries, where on average a 100 microgram per cubic meter increase in total suspended particulates (TSP) leads to a 6 per cent increase in no traumatic mortality. In Delhi, such an increase in TSP is associated with a 2.3 per cent increase in death.
- The differences in magnitudes of the effects are most likely explained by difference in distribution

of age at death and cause of death, as most deaths in Delhi occur before the age of 65 and are not attributed to causes with a strong association with air pollution.

- Although air pollution seems to have less impact on mortality counts in Delhi, the number of life-years saved per death avoided is greater in Delhi that in the U.S. cities—because the age distribution of impacts in these two places varies. In the United States the particulates have the greatest influence on daily deaths among persons in the age of 65 and older. In Delhi, they have the greatest impact in the 15 to 44 age group.

The traffic policemen posted at road intersections of Delhi have also been victims of the increasing number of vehicles in the city as evident from three studies conducted in the 1990s. The first, in collaboration with the Central Road Research Institute (CRRI) and the All India Institute of Medical Sciences (AIIMS), studied the effects of pollution on traffic policemen performing duties at traffic intersections. The second study followed up in association with the Patel Chest Institute of Delhi University with a continual programme till 1997 for diagnosis and treatment of traffic policemen's lungs and other respiratory diseases. In the third study, the local Majidia Hospital in 1999 volunteered to provide free treatment to traffic policemen affected with such ailments. All the three studies revealed that traffic policemen working in adverse environmental conditions are affected both in the short and long-run, and their health and efficiency are impacted. Eye irritation, throat infections, respiratory discomfort, skin ailments, impaired hearing, chest diseases, excessive carboxyl-haemoglobin, and annoyance with noise are some of the ailments they suffer from. A local survey has indicated that the incidence of respiratory diseases in Delhi is 12 times the national average, and 30 per cent of Delhi's population suffers from respiratory disorders due to air pollution.

5.4.3 Steps Taken to Improve Air Quality

Improvement in transport system: To provide a better public transport service, a large number of private buses (Blue line, White line, etc.) have been initiated since 1993 in a phased manner in addition to the DTC buses. Till the late 90s, the DTC and other buses contributed heavily towards the air pollution load of the city as most of buses were old and poorly maintained. However, conversion of the diesel driven public transport and the commercial vehicles (buses, autos, taxis etc.) to CNG have resulted in reduction of air pollution substantially. Also, to meet the complex and ever growing transportation requirements of the city, an integrated Mass Rapid Transit System (MRTS) is being executed.

Thermal power plants: All the three thermal power plants have installed electrostatic precipitators in all their units to control particulate matter emissions. Consistent efforts for environmental improvement have resulted in installation of new high efficiency Electrostatic Precipitator in unit no. 5 of I.P. Power Station. Besides this, the Power Plants are using beneficiated coal (ash content less than 34 per cent) since 1999 as against the coal used earlier (ash content above 40 per cent) to reduce pollution. DPCC has further directed these power plants to achieve stricter norms of 50 mg/Nm^3 as against the standards of 150 mg/Nm^3 notified by the Ministry of Environment and Forests, Government of India.

Two gas based power plants namely I.P. Gas Turbine Power Plant and Pragati Power Station have been commissioned to augment the power generation capacity from 1087 MW to 1700 MW. Since, these plants are based on natural gas, there is no significant addition to the existing air pollution levels as particulate emissions are virtually absent in gas based plants. In addition, low NO_X burners have been installed at Pragati (gas-based) power plant.

Small-scale industries: In 1996, Honourble Supreme Court while hearing a Public Interest Litigation passed various orders to close down the 1328 'H' category units, i.e., Hot mix plants, lead smelting units, stone crushers, pesticides, heavy foundries, steel rolling mills etc. Subsequently, DPCC also issued closer orders in respect of 118 industrial units, which were engaged in 'H' category. In 2000, Hon'ble Supreme Court ordered the closure of polluting industrial units in non-conforming/ industrial areas under the supervision of Ministry of Urban Development, Government of India as a Nodal Agency. Based on the criteria of polluting industries, evolved by the Nodal Agency and Expert Committee constituted by the Government of Delhi, 5046 units have been closed down by Government of Delhi. Acting on similar lines, Delhi Pollution Control Committee has also identified 557 such industries and ordered their closure. In addition, Delhi Pollution Control Committee directed several industrial units to install pollution control devices, which were found polluting during the course of action of implementation of Air (Prevention and Control of Pollution) Act, 1981.

In order to check the pollution from DG sets, Government of Delhi, on December 10, 2001 authorised all

Deputy Commissioners, SDMs and other Police officers to implement the norms pertaining to DG sets. These officers were asked to ensure that the DG Sets above 5 KVS capacity do not operate in residential areas, between 10.00 p.m. to 6.00 a.m. (except Group Housing Societies and Multi Storied Complexes) and ensure that these DG sets meet the prescribed emission norms.

5.4.3.1 Steps Taken to Control Vehicular Pollution

To control vehicular pollution, the important steps which have been taken in recent years include the following:

- Stringent Emission Norms.
- Phasing out/Conversion of vehicles.
- Fuel Quality Improvement.
- Introduction of Clean Fuel.
- Delhi is the only city in the world with over 0.1 million fleet of CNG driven vehicles.The various vehicular pollution control measures which have been taken from time to time are given in the following Table 5.5.

Other Measures

- Pollution under control (PuC) certificate mandatory for all vehicles every 3 months.
- Improvement in traffic management through flyover construction at major traffic intersections and synchronisation of traffic signals.
- Introduction of Mass Rapid Transport System i.e., Metro Rail.

5.4.4 Air Quality Trends

The analysis of ambient air quality data of last five years i.e., 2000 to 2005 (up to December 2005) of Delhi has witnessed a significant reduction in pollution levels. Sulphur Dioxide levels have fallen by 51 per cent in 2005 (up to December, 2005) as compared to 2000. The concentration of other pollutants like Lead and Benzene have also registered marked decline. The levels of Suspended Particulate Matter (SPM) have fallen by 23 per cent (2000-2005) and levels of Respirable Suspended Particulate Matter (RSPM) have fallen by 6.7 per cent during the same period. Despite the phenomenal growth in vehicular population, Nitrogen Dioxide levels have remained more or less constant.

TABLE 5.5

Vehicular Pollution Control Measures Taken in Delhi

Measures Taken	*1996*	*1998*	*2000*	*2001*	*2002 & 2003*	*2004 & 2005*
Emission Norms of Vehicles	Emission norms made stringent as compared to 1991.	· Emission norms for catalytic converter fitted vehicle made stringent.	· Euro-1 equivalent norms for all type of vehicles except passenger vehicles which are Euro-II equivalent. · Hot start replaced by Cold start test which gives less emission.	· CNG/LPG norms finalised.	· Euro-II in Goods Vehicles from 1st Oct. 2002.	· Euro-III norms mandatory for all four wheelers w.e.f. 1st April 2005. · Euro-II norms mandatory for all Two and Three wheelers w.e.f. 1st April 2005.
Fuel Quality Improvement	· Fuel quality specification notified under EPA for the first time. Lead content (g/l)=0.15 Diesel Sulphur =0.5 per cent Gasoline Benzene= 5.0 per cent	· Diesel sulphur reduced to 0.25 per cent. · Gasoline Benzene reduced to 3.0 per cent Gasoline Lead phased out.	· Diesel sulphur reduced to 0.05 per cent in selected outlets. · Gasoline benzene reduced to 1.0 per cent. · Gasoline sulphur with 0.05 per cent maximum sulphur in all outlet. · Low smoke 2-T oil introduce.	· Diesel with 0.05 per cent sulphur throughout retail outlets in NCT.		· 0.035 per cent Sulphur in Diesel w.e.f. 1st April 2005. · 0.015 per cent Sulphur in Petrol w.e.f. 1st April 2005.
Other Measures	Govt. vehicle to run CNG/ Catalytic Converter.	· 15 years old commercial vehicle banned. · Pre-mix 2-T oil in retail outlets.	· Buses more than 8 years phased out. · Replacement of pre-1990 auto/taxis with vehicle on clean fuels. · Conversion of post 1990 autos to CNG initiated. · Fuel testing laboratory established.	· All taxis/ Auto and buses to run on CNG.		· Stringent Emission Norms for in use vehicles w.e.f. June 5, 2005.

Source: Transport Department (n.d.). *Auto Fuel Policy, 2002*. New Delhi: GNTCD.

5.4.5 Action Points

Transport Sector

- For facilitating the shift from personal to mass transport, policy measures/programmes should focus on providing a flexible and affordable mass transport service system with decreased levels of pollution, overcrowding and fuel consumption.
- Grade separation or additional lanes by road widening for heavily polluting intersections and high-density corridors needs to be provided.
- Alternative environment friendly modes of transport such as, battery powered electric vehicles need to be promoted to the maximum extent.
- The road layout and traffic management need modernisation because the inadequate road network is unable to meet the increasing transportation load in Delhi. Lack of adequate control on proper land use and development has added to the traffic congestion and increased pollution. While planning the future extension pockets of Delhi, adequate area would have to be kept reserved under transportation use.
- The ring railway should be strengthened. The land-use along the ring railway and existing/ proposed MRTS alignment may be studied in details so that the location of traffic-generating activities such as offices, business centres and educational (higher) institutions are along their routes. Delhi's Master Plan may be modified to locate District Centres along/near rail-lines.

Industrial Sector

- Identification of unregistered small-scale industries located in various parts of the city.
- Steps to enforce compliance with pollution standards for the polluting units. Dust control measures such as cyclones, etc., especially in small-scale industries to be enforced.
- Green belts to be promoted around industrial estates.
- Environmental audit to be enforced with immediate effect.
- Delineate adequate sites and shift nonconforming industries (small as well as large) along with enforcement of adequate pollution control devices.
- Industries to adopt recycling and waste recovery technologies. Incentives to be looked into in order to promote recycle and re-use.
- Energy conservation techniques such as co-generation and waste heat utilisation techniques to be actively promoted.

Domestic Sector

- Demand side management through optimum electricity consumption by replacement of conventional bulbs (incandescent and fluorescent) with compact fluorescent lamps (CFL). Even though the use of CFLs involves much lower electricity usage than conventional systems, the higher upfront costs act as a deterrent to their ready acceptability with consumers. It is therefore required to formulate strategic plans, including financing, for affecting such change.

5.5 Cleaning the River Yamuna

5.5.1 The Hon'ble Supreme Court, in its order dated 4 August 2004, expressed concern regarding deteriorating water quality in the river Yamuna and inadequacy of various measures so far taken to improve the situation. Pursuant to the Court order, a High Powered Committee was constituted to determine the quantum of water/waste water generation, sources of pollution and to suggest the mode and manner of improving the quality in the river. The Committee has drawn up an Action Plan; the components of which include the following:

- Maintenance of flows in the river;
- Water and waste water handling capacities;
- Refurbishment of trunk sewer age system;
- Treatment of the flows in Najafgarh and Shahdara drains;
- Laying of sewer lines in the unsewered areas of Delhi;
- Slum cluster on the river bed;
- Treatment of industrial effluents;
- Utilisation of treated effluents; and,
- Removal of coliform in the sewage treatment plants.

5.5.2 *Flows in River Yamuna*: For improvement in water quality, the water flow should be adequate and continuous. To this end, the riparian States need to contribute their share for maintaining a minimum flow in the river stretch. Based on the recommendation of a minimum flow of 10 cumecs earlier made, the Committee has determined the shares of different States in the raw water to be released in the river which are as follow:

- 4.54 cumecs should continue to be released by the Government of Haryana at Tajewala;
- More than 10 cumecs should continue to be released by the Government of Haryana through Munak escape; and,
- 4 cumecs being released by the Government of Haryana at Najafgarh drain outfall should be continued.

5.5.3 *Water and Waste Water Handling Capacities*: The present installed capacity for water treatment is 640 mgd which is proposed to be augmented by another 140 mgd by 2005 and another 80 mgd by 2008, thereby raising the installed capacity to 860 mgd. The existing capacity of sewage treatment is 512 mgd which is proposed to be increased to 640 mgd by 2008 and to 835 mgd by 2015.

5.5.4 *Refurbishment of Trunk Sewerage System*: The Delhi Jal Board (DJB) has a network of 130 km sewerage system to convey the collected sewage to treatment plants. It is reported that nearly 91 km of the sewer lines are in dilapidated condition and are silted to the extent of 50-70 per cent in different stretches. The rehabilitation work in 30 km of sewer lines has been completed and the work on 19.5 km is in progress. The work on the remaining 41 km is proposed to be completed by 2008.

5.5.5 *Treatment of Flows in Najafgarh and Shahdara Drains*: The Najafgarh drain contributes around 60 per cent flow by volume and 39 per cent in terms of pollution load. The Shahdara drain contributes around 20 per cent flow by volume and 37 per cent by pollution load .Thus, these two drains contribute as much as 80 per cent to the flow and 76 per cent to the pollution load in the river stretch The Najafgarh drain carries a total flow of 1778.20 MLD including the flow from the Haryana sewage treatment plants, treated effluents from 8 Sewage Treatment Plants(STPs) operated by the Delhi Jal Board, raw water from the Western Yamuna Canal, Hyderpur waste water outfall, waste water from industries and 342.20 MLD of untreated sewage. Nearly 76 MLD of untreated sewage is contributed by the unauthorised colonies which are unsewered The Shahdara drain carries a total flow of 467 MLD consisting of 190 MLD treated effluent from two STPs and 277 MLD of untreated sewage.

5.5.6 *Yamuna Action Plan Phase–II*

A number of projects have been finalised under the Yamuna Action Plan Phase-II (YAP-II) to reduce pollution load in Yamuna. The total project cost of the sanctioned projects is Rs 387.17 Crores under scheme of "Yamuna Action Plan Phase-II" in Delhi. The cost of the scheme is to be shared on 85:15 basis between the Government of India and Government of Delhi. A few study projects are also covered in YAP-II, which will be implemented under scheme YAP-III. Implementation of this scheme is now started by concerned Implementing Agencies.

Detail of Projects under Yamuna Action Plan Phase–II (YAP–II)

Proposals Finalised by MOEF	*Cost (Rs.) in Crores*
324 MLD (72 MGD) Keshopur, STP rehabilitation, Pumping station and rising main in Keshopur STP Pilot plant for electricity generation from biogas	66.36
Okhla STP augmentation with electricity generation plant for 170 MGD STP	85.27
Ring Road trunk sewer rehabilitation	90.07
Wazirabad road trunk sewer settlement	64.20
Bela Road trunk sewer rehabilitation	17.47
DPR Preparation including Pilot Plant implementation for YAP-III	35.00
Misc. e.g. Slum Rehabilitation, Public Participation and Awareness and Capacity Building/PR	28.80
Total	387.17

5.5.7 *Laying of Sewer Lines in Unsewered Areas*: The Delhi Jal Board has laid internal sewerage system in 482 unauthorised/regularised colonies and in 98 urban villages of Delhi. The sewerage systems in 496 unauthorised/ regularised colonies and in 103 urban villages are likely to be laid by the end of 2005. In 516 unauthorised/ regularised colonies and 105 urban villages, sewer systems are expected to be completed by May 2006.

5.5.8 *Removal of Slum Clusters on the River Bed*: The slum clusters on the eastern and western banks of the river contribute to the untreated waste water flow. The Municipal Corporation of Delhi (MCD) and the Delhi Development Authority have removed the slums from time to time. However, as per reports, 4330 *jhuggies* are still there on the western bank and nearly 12200 *jhuggies* are still there on the eastern bank of the river. It proposed to remove all such settlements by December 2006.

5.5.9 *Treatment of Industrial Effluents*: The Delhi Small Industries Development Corporation (DSIDC) has constructed 10 Common Effluent Treatment Plants (CETPs) with an installed capacity of 133 MLD for treatment of industrial waste water before discharge into the river. DSIDC is also constructing two treatment plants—one at Naraina with a capacity of 21.6 MLD and the other at Najafgarh having capacity of 9.6 MLD. As of now, the CETPs are treating only 53 MLD of industrial effluents. The low utilisation of the installed capacity is on account of the provision made for handling the volume of industrial effluents till 2021 besides the absence of conveyance system at some places. It is proposed to lay the conveyance system at Wazirpur, Friends Colony, and Okhla Industrial Area, in addition to de-silting of Mangalpuri sewerage system which expected to increase the waste water flow in the CETPs.

5.5.10 *Utilisation of Treated Effluent*: Presently, 109.5 MGD of treated effluent is supplied to various agencies and an additional amount of 241 MGD is available for other user agencies. Occasional break down of conveyance systems, irregular supply and offensive odour of the treated effluent are among the reasons for limited use of treated waste water.

5.5.11 *Removal of Coliform at STPs*: An Expert Group headed by the Chairman, Central Pollution Control Board (CPCB) has examined the issues relating permissible level of coliform in the treated waste water and the process required to achieve the desired levels. The Expert Group has held that dilution available in the river is very little and the fresh water available is less than the quantity of sewage discharge. Hence, it is necessary to collect the total effluent and treat it to achieve Biochemical Oxygen Demand (BOD) of 20mg/l and Suspended Solids (SS) not exceeding 30mg/l. Thereafter, in the second phase, sewage treatment plants should be upgraded to reduce BOD and SS to 10mg/l and 15mg/l respectively. The process for achieving the limits may also remove coliform to the extent of MPN 2500 per 100ml, which is the maximum permissible limit for bathing as notified under the Environment (Protection) Act, 1986.

5.5.12 *Action Points*

Besides the aforesaid targets and activities as proposed in the Action Plan, it will be useful to address the following issues:

- Assured availability of water in the river is vital for improvement of water quality. Along with the proposed measures for contribution of water from Haryana, which are of interim nature, it will be useful to explore the possibilities for sustainable sources of water in the river. In this context, the three water storage projects which were planned in the upper reaches of Yamuna at Kishau, Renuka and Lakhwar Vyasi should be revisited. Such projects, if implemented, will help in maintenance of a regular flow particularly during the lean seasons:
- For ensuring adequate flow, the ground water development potential in and around Delhi and possibilities for ground water recharge need to seriously looked into;
- Rain water harvesting activities, which are now sporadically undertaken, need to be geared up; and,
- Concerted efforts are needed for promoting the use of water saving devices in house holds, commercial establishments, industries and in agriculture.

5.6 Storm Water and Flood Control

5.6.1 The territory of Delhi has been experiencing floods mainly from Sahibi Nadi and Yamuna River. The Sahibi River originates in Jaipur District of Rajasthan. After passing through Alwar District in Rajasthan and Gurgaon District in Haryana, it enters Delhi near Dhansa. Sahibi River belongs to a special category of rivers in arid and semi arid areas in Rajasthan. The Sahibi River occasionally rises when its flood water travels down, up to Yamuna through Rajasthan, Haryana, and Delhi. In Delhi, flooding and consequent damage is caused mainly in the rural area of Delhi in and around Najafgarh Jheel. It also causes damage to the urban areas situated along the banks of the Najafgarh Drain.

5.6.2 In order to cope up with the monsoons, Irrigation and Flood Control Department of the Government of NCT of Delhi undertakes pre-monsoon anti water-logging and flood control measures. These include desilting of all the trunk drains, restoration of anti erosion works like spurs, installation of control rooms and check post at various stations etc.

5.6.3 An Apex Committee has been constituted under the Chairmanship of Chief Minister, Delhi to recommend, supervise and co-ordinate the flood control measures. NCT of Delhi has been divided into nine districts with a sector committee for each district, which has come into existence from 15 June 2005. A Central Flood Control Room is established to assist the Apex Committee. Following are the functions of the Central Flood Control Room:

a) To receive flood warnings and other related information.

b) To submit flood situation reports to the Chief Minister, Chief Secretary, Divisional Commissioner and Secretary (I&F)

c) To convey flood situation reports and orders relating to flood control measures to the sector officers/sector control rooms and the concerned organisations/departments of the administration (through their liaison officers)

d) To issue necessary flood warnings and directions for evacuation

e) To arrange necessary food articles and relief supplies

f) To maintain liaison with Upper Yamuna Division of the Central Water Commission (CWC), and Army/Air Force, when required.

g) To maintain a fleet of vehicles needed for mobility of staff and the relief measures

5.6.4 Dahisara bund upstream of R.M.E. near Palla is under the control of Haryana Irrigation Department. A proper watch needs to be kept on this embankment during high floods for ensuring the safety of rural areas of Delhi located on the North of Bawana Escape up to Diversion drain No. 8 and East of G.T: Road up to R.M.E. Right marginal embankment near Jhangola and Burari needs a close watch, as the active course of the river is quite close to the main marginal embankment at these locations.

5.6.5 The three ramps on Jagatpur bund acting as spurs need constant watch during floods, requires a close watch due to the eroding tendency of the river in this reach. Left forward bund near R.D. 1350 mts. where active course of the river is only 92 mts. away from the main embankment. A constant watch has to be kept on the right side connecting bund between Okhla Barrage and Right Marginal Embankment downstream of Okhla Barrage near villages Madanpur Khadar and Jaitpur, since this portion of bund is lower than the left side bund and is under control of UP. Irrigation Department Yamuna Bazar wall near Nigam Bodh Ghat will have to be kept under constant vigil during high floods.

5.6.6 Left marginal bund between Old Railway Bridge and ITO Barrage shall also need to be kept under watch during high floods, since active course of river is running very close to this embankment. Special watch will have to be kept on H.T: Pylon structure between Spur Nos. 17 and 18. The bund protecting Gas Turbine Power Station shall have to be kept under watch during floods as river course is flowing quite close to this bund.

5.6.7 *Operation of Barrages*: At present, the operation of barrages across river Yamuna in Delhi Territory is under the control of following authorities:

(i)	Wazirabad Barrage	Delhi Jal Board
(ii)	I.T.O. Barrage	Haryana Irrigation Department
(iii)	Okhla Barrage	U.P. Irrigation Department

5.6.8 Rural Drainage: Rural drains in Delhi territory have been planned to drain out low lying rural areas (agricultural). These areas are being served by important drains like Mungeshpur drain, Nangloi Drain, Drain No.6, Burari Creek, Karari Suleman Nagar Drain, portion of supplementary drain below GT Road, Bankner Drain, Sanoth Link Drain, Shahdara drainage system and other small drains. Improvements in these drains by clearance of silt where ever required, cleaning of opening in pipe culvert/bridges etc. shall be ensured before the flood season by I&F Department. However, link drains from village ponds to these trunk drains are under the control of MCD and the responsibility of ensuring proper functioning of storm water drainage of entire rural area of Delhi has been vested with the M.C.D.

5.6.9 *Drainage of Unauthorised Colonies*: Proper drainage system within the unauthorised colonies has not been developed so far, resulting in stagnation of storm water in pools and low lying plots. For drainage of these ponds, a battery of pumps has to be installed to link the colony water to nearby drains. These pumps shall be deployed by MCD in all the unauthorised colonies outside the development area of DDA. In the unauthorised colonies falling within its jurisdiction, DDA has to make necessary arrangements.

5.6.10 *Urban Drainage*: For monitoring the activities of desilting of storm water drains, connecting drainage/ sewerage and for other related problems, an Operation Mission has been constituted by Urban Development Department, Government of Delhi. The Operation Mission will have to monitor the following activities:

(i) Desilting of storm water drains.

(ii) Desilting of sewers.

iii) Tackling the problems of drainage congestion wherever required.

iv) Delinking the sewer system from storm water drains.

5.6.11 *Responsibilities of Concerned Agencies*

(a) *Provision of Wireless Sets*: Although adequate Wireless sets are available in Irrigation and Flood Control Department the Civil Defence Volunteers/Home Guards will need to be provided with supplemental support by setting up wireless stations at the strategic places such as Flood Control Room, L.M. Bund office of Deputy Commissioner (East) and various sectors as per requirements of the Divisional Commissioner Delhi. All these wireless stations will be manned by the Civil Defence Volunteers.

(b) *Home Guards and Civil Defence Volunteers*: Home Guards will have to be deployed for patrolling duties on bunds and regulators when required/called for, to guard against sabotage and for initiating rescue operations of marooned villages. Civil Defence volunteers will be deployed for camp management, distribution of rations, etc.

(c) *Medical Arrangements*: On receipt of requisition from the Divisional Commissioner, Delhi, Secretary (Medical), Government of Delhi would make arrangements for setting up first-aid posts/mobile dispensaries at relief camps and arrange visits of medical team to the flood affected areas. For such purposes, the Medical Department would plan and make provisions for sufficient stores of essential medicines in advance. In case of need, Secretary (Medical) may seek the assistance from the Chief Medical Officer, NDMC/MCD.

(d) *Sanitation etc.*: M.C.D. would provide temporary latrines, urinals and street lighting at camp site. Supply of drinking water would be arranged by D.J.B. in flood affected areas/relief camps.

(e) *Support of Animal Husbandry Wing*: On receipt of the requisition from the Divisional Commissioner Delhi, the animal husbandry wing of the Development Department would send a medical team of veterinary staff in the flood affected areas and cattle camps.

(f) *Transport*: Commissioner (Transport), Government of Delhi would arrange adequate number of trucks or other category of vehicles as may be needed by Divisional Commissioner, Delhi.

5.6.12 *Action Points*

An elaborate institutional mechanism has been put in place for storm water and flood control. However, some of the basic preventive measures which need to be given priority attention include the following:

- Control on encroachment of the river banks for unauthorised human settlements and commercial activities;
- Restrictions on construction activities in the flood plains;
- Collaboration with the neighbouring states for creation of upstream water storage structures and for flood water management systems; and,
- Preparation of a long term plan for storm water and flood control.

References

Chhabra, Sunil K., Pragati Chhabra, Sanjay Rajpal, Rajiv K. Gupta (2001). "Ambient Air Pollution and Chronic Respiratory Morbidity in Delhi", *Achieves of Environmental Health*, January.

Cropper, Maureen L., Nathalie B. Simon, Anna Alberini, and P.K. Sharma (1997). "The Health Effects of Air Pollution in Delhi, India", *Policy Research Working Paper*. World Bank, December.

Delhi Pollution Control Committee (n.d.). *Towards Cleaner Air, A Case Study of* Delhi. New Delhi: Dept. of Environment, GNCTD. *http://www.dpcc.delhigovt.nic.in*

Directorate of Economics and Statistics, 2002. *Delhi Statistical Hand Book, 2002*. Delhi: Government of National Capital Territory of Delhi.

GNCTD (2001). *Status Report for Delhi 21*. New Delhi: Government of National Capital Territory of Delhi.

———. (2002). *Economic Survey of Delhi, 2001-02*. New Delhi: Planning Department.

http://www.forest.delhigovt.nic.in/delhi_state.html

Ministry of Environment and Forests (MoEF) (n.d.). *State of Forest Report, 1999*. Chapter 3

Protecting traffic policemen from the hazards of pollution *www.delhitrafficpolice.nic.in/art8.htm*

Chapter 6

Public Distribution System

6.1 Evolution of PDS

Public Distribution System has its origin in the 'rationing' system introduced by the British during the World War II. The system began in 1939 in Bombay and was subsequently extended to other cities and towns. It was really the generation of the World War's own compulsions that forced the then British Government to introduce the first structured public distribution of cereals in India. There was a rationing system—sale of a fixed quantity of ration (rice or wheat) to entitled families (ration card holders) in specified cities/towns.

6.1.1 Creation of Department of Food

In the year 1942, a department was created to take care of the matters related to food and distribution of food called—The Department of Food. But in the year 1945, when the World War II had ended, India, like many other countries, abolished the rationing system. However, on attaining Independence, concern for increasing malnourished population and due to already prevailing high global prices of food grains, India was forced to reintroduce it in 1950. Public distribution of foodgrains was retained as a deliberate social policy by Indian Government.

6.1.2 Growth of the System

During the First Five-Year Plan (1951-1956), the system, which was essentially urban based till then, was extended to all rural areas suffering from chronic food shortages. It was also decided to have two variations of the system, Statutory Rationing Areas, where foodgrains availability was supposed to be only through the ration shops and Non-Statutory Rationing Areas, where such shops would only supplement the open market availability. 1958 marked the addition of other essential commodities like sugar, cooking coal, kerosene oil and a rapid increase in the ration shops (now being increasingly called the Fair Price Shops-FPSs). Thus, by the end of the Second Five Year Plan, PDS had changed from the typical rationing system to a social safety system making food grains available at a 'fair price' and to keep a check on the speculative tendencies in the market.

6.1.3 Food Corporation of India

In the year 1965, the position of PDS was strengthened by creation of Food Corporation of India and Agricultural Prices Commission. It was in this year that government planned to announce a minimum support price (MSP) for wheat and paddy and procurement of quantities that could not fetch even such minimum prices in the market. The policy of MSP was designed primarily with the objective of providing food security to the poor and simultaneously fixing remunerative prices to the producers. This was

TABLE 6.1

Year-wise MSP, CIP and Range of Open Market Prices for Wheat and Rice

(Rs. per quintal)

Year	*Common Rice*			*Wheat*		
	MSP	*CIP*	*Market Price*	*MSP*	*CIP*	*Market Price*
1992	270	377	450-650	275	280	260-575
1993	310	437	420-780	330	330	260-580
1994	340	537	290-850	350	402	350-600
1995	360	537	550-950	360	402	375-750
1996	380	537	650-1250	380	402	460-825
1997	415	550 (APL) 350 (BPL)	650-1150	475	450 (APL) 250 (BPL)	500-850
1998	440	550 (APL) 350 (BPL)	650-1020	510	450 (APL) 250 (BPL)	525-1100
1999	490	700 (APL) 350 (BPL)	700-1280	550	650	550-1100

Source: Report of the Comptroller and Auditor General of India for the year ended March 1999; p.9.

done in order to prevent farmers to resort to distress sale due to the weak bargaining power and monopoly market functionaries and also to their demands. It also targeted to build buffer stocks to face the scarcity situation. For this the government even had to resort to imports to honour its charge to PDS consumers.

In June 1992, the Government of India launched the Revamped Public Distribution System in 1775 blocks and Targeted Public Distribution System from June 1997 with a view to target the disadvantaged and the poor across the country.

The salient features of RPDS and TPDS are given in Table 6.2.

Currently the focus of PDS is on the poor population in all areas. The Ninth Plan (1997-2002) targeted primarily people below the poverty line and enunciated a broader view of food security, which also includes nutritional security by ensuring availability, accessibility, acceptability and affordability of balanced food and nutrition for all.

6.1.4 Present Magnitude of PDS

According to the Department of Food and Public Distribution, the quantities of food grains allocated to all states and Union Territories, under various schemes of PDS, from September 2004 to March 2005 is 28,77,073 tonnes of rice and 31,23,824 tonnes of wheat i.e., a total of 60,00,897 tonnes of foodgrains.

6.1.5 Problems of PDS

Overcoming the 1987 drought, considered the worst in the century, with dignity and effectiveness has been seen as the PDS's biggest success. PDS is one of the most widely implemented schemes, involves major distribution of resources and coordination of departments. Therefore, PDS is always subjected to continuous monitoring and evaluation. And the results of both formal and non-formal feedback systems are used to make PDS an increasingly people friendly policy.

However, the evaluation studies have pointed out several shortcomings in the functioning of PDS. According to *Business Week* (2001)(*www.greenaction.org.il/lib/greenrev.html*), "even though Indian granaries are overflowing now, thanks to the success of Green Revolution, raising wheat and rice yields, 5000 children die each day out of malnutrition, one third of India's 900 million people are poverty stricken." Since the poor cannot afford to buy what is produced, the government is left trying to store millions of tonnes of food. Some are rotting and there is concern that rotten grains would find its way to public markets. Some other problems include:

- Urban and pro-rich bias of the system and its ineffectiveness in reaching the poor and the poorest of the poor population.

FIGURE 6.1

Overall Allocation of Foodgrains (in '000 tonnes) September 2004 to March 2005

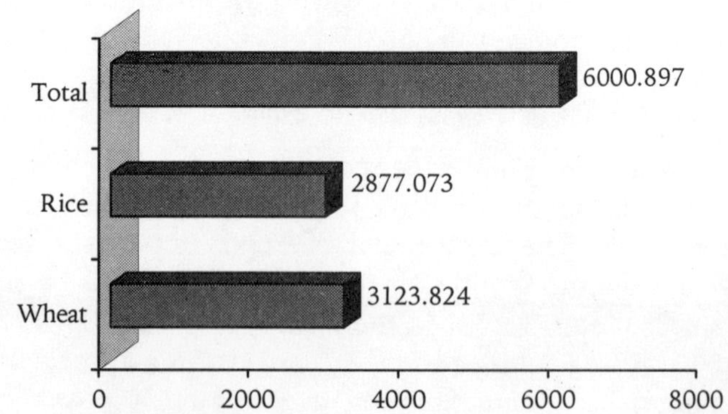

Source: Data & Information was provided by "Food & Supplies Department, Govt. of NCT of Delh

TABLE 6.2

Salient Features of RPDS and TPDS

S.No.		*RPDS*	*TPDS*
1.	Target Group	All persons in poor areas approach. Covered 1775 blocks in tribal and hilly, drought prone and remotely located areas.	Poor persons in all areas approach. Focused on people below poverty line throughout the country. Initially TPDS adopted the number of poor household as estimated by the Expert Group of Planning Commission.
2.	Scale of Ration	5 kg. per head subject to maximum of 20 kg. per family per month.	The foodgrains supplied to cardholders is 35 kg. (25 Kg. wheat + 10 Kg. rice) per BPL household per month.
3.	Issue Price	Food grains were issued at 50 paise below the CIP and the states were asked to issue the same at the margin of not more than 50 paise per kg.	The rate of wheat under BPL is Rs.465 per quintal and Rs.615 per quintal for rice. Under AAY, Rs.2/ Rs.3 for wheat and rice respectively.

Source: Report of the Comptroller and Auditor General of India, March 1999; p.5.

- Issues in identification of targeted families specially the BPL and the poorest of poor.
- The lack of effective contribution towards complete household food security.
- Expensive system due to 'wasteful' movements of grain and high storage losses.
- Issues related to distribution and quality of essential commodities.
- Marginal impact or very low impact, as far as income transfer to poor households is concerned.
- Problems related to issuance of ration card.
- Regulating the licensing of Fair Price Shops.

Despite such flaws in the PDS, official circles adopted the typical insensitive approach and declared that, the system has, however, come to stay, notwithstanding its shortcomings, because millions of India's poor derive direct or indirect benefits from the very existence of this system. All they suggested was some tinkering.

6.2 Public Distribution System in Delhi

The government of National Capital Territory is selling essential commodities through PDS. To maintain transparency the names and prices of these commodities are specified by gazette notification from time to time. In the past, a number of items like iodised salt, R.B.D. Palm oil, candles, Panghat *Ghee* and control cloth etc., have been distributed through PDS. However, at present, PDS in Delhi is confined to two cereals, wheat and rice, and two other essential commodities *viz.*, sugar and kerosene oil.

6.2.1 Food, Supplies and Consumer Affairs Department

The Department of Food Supplies and Consumer Affairs, Delhi takes care of the Public Distribution System for the NCT of Delhi. The department also enforces provisions of Control Orders made u/s 3 of the Essential Commodities Act, 1955 regulating trade in specified essential commodities by keeping a close watch on stocks, prices, quality and availability of these commodities. Enforcement consists of collection of information and evidence of contravention of provisions of the relevant Control Orders and action taken against them under the provisions of Essential Commodities Act.

The department has three important functions related to effective functioning of PDS:

1. PDS of Essential Commodities under Essential Commodities Act, 1955 and various control orders thereunder.
2. Consumer Affairs—for better protection of the consumer's interests through State Commission and District Forums under the Consumer Protection Act, 1986.
3. Enforcement of the standard of Weights & Measures Act, 1976 and Weights and Measures (Enforcement) Act, 1985 and rules made thereunder.

6.2.2 Territorial Division of NCT of Delhi

The NCT of Delhi is divided in 9 Zones that are further divided in 70 circles. Each circle is headed by Food & Supplies Officer and each Zone is headed by Assistant Commissioner.

FIGURE 6.2

Territorial Division of NCT of Delhi

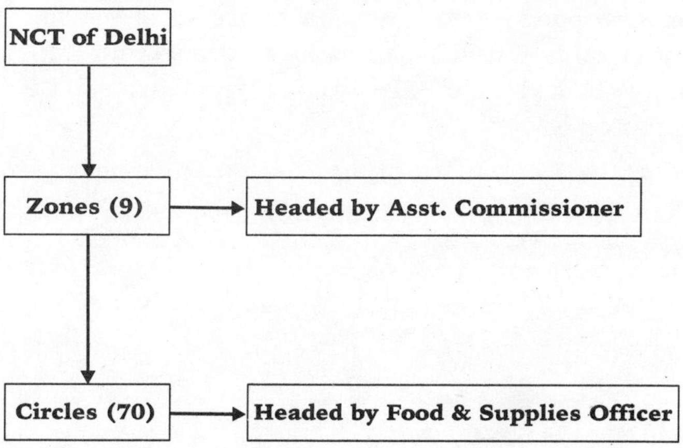

The complete organisational structure is attached as Annexure A-6.1

6.2.3 Objectives of the Department

The main aim of the Department is to make PDS more transparent, accountable and ensure food security to the vulnerable segments of the population.

6.2.4 Public Distribution System in Delhi

In Delhi, PDS comprises of a network of Fair Price Shops (popularly known as ration shops) and Kerosene Oil Depots for making available specified articles at controlled prices through Household Consumer Cards, commonly called ration cards. The distribution of kerosene oil is through a separate consumer card called Blue Card issued to persons who are not using LPG.

According to the data available there are 2745 fair price shops operating in Delhi and 2443 licensed kerosene oil shops.

TABLE 6.3

Fair Price Shops and Licensed Kerosene Oil Shops Operating in Delhi

(in number)

S. No.	Item	1992-93	2000-01	2001-02	2002-03	2003-04	2004-05	2005-06
1(i.)	FPS in Urban Areas	3394	2818	2583	2562	-		
1(ii)	FPS in Rural Areas	153	347	392	391	-		
	Total FPS	3547	3165	2975	2953	3129	3114	2745
2	Licensed Kerosene Oil Shops	1931	2501	2508	2521	2476	2443	2443

Source: Data & Information was provided by "Food & Supplies Department, Govt. of NCT of Delh

6.2.5 *Ration Cards*

A ration card is a document that certifies the bearer's right to purchase rationed goods. The total number of ration cards issued under various schemes in Delhi is about 26 lakh. Each FPS handles approximately 1,000 ration cards.

According to data available as on 19 March 2006 more than 22 lakh ration cards have been issued to the consumers 'Above Poverty Line'.

TABLE 6.4

Issue of Ration Cards

S.No.	Category	Figures
1.	No of APL Ration Cards*	22,85,513 (as on 31.12.2006)
2.	No. of BPL Ration cards**	3,78,947 (as on 31.12.2006)
3.	Antyodaya Anna Yojana***	57,336 (as on 31.12.2006)
4.	Annapurna Yojana****	128 (as on 31.12.2006)
5.	Total No. of Food Cards	27,21,924
6.	K.Oil cards	13,47,785

Source: http://delhigovt.nic.in/dept/food/fpds4.asp

The cardholders are supplied ration through a network of 2745 Fair Price Shops and kerosene oil through 2443 Kerosene Oil Depots.

* **Above Poverty Line:** The consumers in the category of 'Above Poverty Line'/APL are those with an annual income above Rs.24200.

** **Below Poverty Line:** The consumers in the category of 'Below Poverty Line'/ BPL are defined as those with an annual income below Rs.24200. This needs to be redefined as a family of 4 can't survive in this limit of Rs.24200 pa.
Source: Minutes of DDR Workshop

*** **Antyodaya Anna Yojna:** The Consumers in the category of 'Antyodaya Anna Yojna'/AAY are the poorest of the poor among BPL. This constitutes about 30 per cent of BPL families. 57,336 persons/families have been identified under this scheme.
Source: http://delhigovt.nic.in/dept/food/fpds6.asp

**** **Annapurna Scheme:** This scheme caters to destitute person of more than 65 years of age having no regular source of income. 128 persons have been identified under this scheme.
Source: http://delhigovt.nic.in/dept/food/fpds7.asp

Foodgrain at BPL Rates to Welfare Institutions

As per Government of India Scheme, Delhi Government has decided to provide foodgrain at BPL rates to indigent/destitute people living in Welfare Institutions such as beggar home, hostels for SC/ST and OBC students, home for street children, neglected and delinquent and abandoned children, juvenile, older persons, *nari niketan* etc. The foodgrain would be made available to these welfare institutions, depending on the rates at which the allocation is received from Government of India. Applications can be obtained from Circle Offices. Till now 42 such institutions are registered with the Department. Priests, Maulvis, and Imams with income less than Rs.24,200 are also being covered under BPL for which they shall contact their zonal ACs.

Issue of Kerosene Oil to Para-Military Forces, Social/Religious Organisations etc.

Special kerosene oil permits are issued to para-military forces, social/religious organisations etc. as per their requirement at PDS rates. These permits are issued/ renewed on quarterly basis.

Source: http://delhigovt.nic.in/dept/food/fpds8.asp

6.2.5.2 Issuance of Ration Cards

As on 1 June 2004, there were approximately 36 lakh APL cards. The renewal of APL cards started in August 2004. The process of renewal of APL cards closed on 31 December 2006 and the number of APL ration cards have come down by 14 lakh to about 22 lakh (cards distributed).

The Department estimated about 14 lakh cards and has now changed the mode of preparation of new APL Cards, wherein strict scrutiny is done and the approval of Commissioner Food & Supply (CFS) is obtained for issue of a new APL card.

6.2.5.3 Tatkal Ration Cards

This scheme has been withdrawn/cancelled.

6.2.6 *Scale of Entitlement*

The Government of NCT of Delhi has a marked categorisation of the household consumers on the following basis:

- Wheat or rice eater.
- LPG or kerosene user.
- *Jhuggi* ration card holder (JRC) and permanent ration card holder (PRC).

TABLE 6.5

Scale of Entitlement

S.No.	Category	Entitlement (for APL, BPL, Antyodaya)
1.	Wheat eating	wheat-25 kg per card per month, and rice-10 kg per card per month.
2	Rice eating	rice-25 kg per card per month and wheat-10 kg per card per month.
3.	Sugar	Above poverty line (APL): Nil. Below poverty line (BPL): 6000 grams per unit per month.
4.	Kerosene Oil	The entitlement of kerosene oil is 22 ltrs per K.Oil card per month @ Rs. 9.09/lt in r/o BPL/AAY cards & 9 ltrs per K.Oil card per month @ Rs. 9.09/lt in r/o APL cards.

Source: http://delhigovt.nic.in/dept/food/fpds2.asp

6.2.7 Scale of Distribution

It is decided to sell the essential commodities and duties of Fair Price Shops as per the following prices and quantity category wise:

TABLE 6.6

Scale of Distribution of Cereals

Families Categories	*Quantity of Wheat/ Issue price/kg.*	*Quantity of Rice/Issue price/kg.*	*Quantity of Sugar/Issue price/kg.*	*Quantity of Kerosene (Per litre)*
APL	25 Kg. @Rs.6.80	10 Kg. @Rs.9.00	Nil	9.09
BPL	25 Kg. @Rs.4.65	10 Kg. @Rs.6.15 per Kg.	1200 gm per person on a BPL/ AAY card	9.09
AAY	25 Kg. @Rs.2.00	10 Kg. @Rs.3.00 per Kg.	@Rs.13.50 per Kg.	9.09
Annapurna	10 Kg. free of cost	-	Nil	

Source: http://delhigovt.nic.in/dept/food/fpds3.asp

FIGURE 6.3

A) Category Wise Distribution of Foodgrains (per cent) 2003-2004

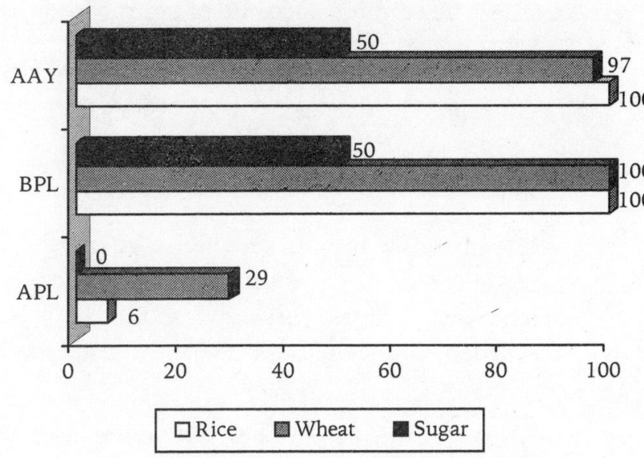

B) Category Wise Distribution of Foodgrains (per cent) 2004-2005

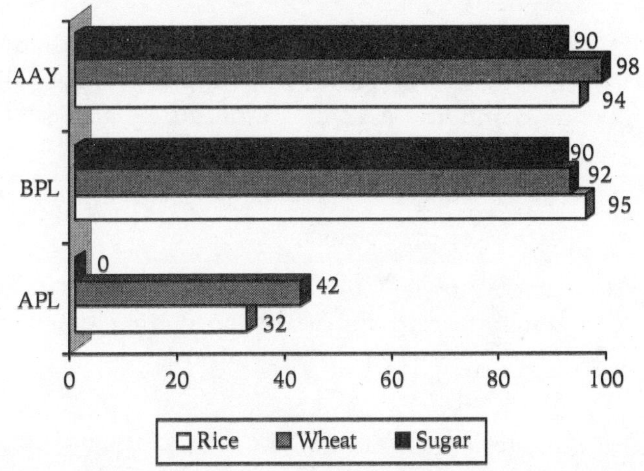

Source: Data & Information was provided by "Food & Supplies Department, Govt. of NCT of Delh

TABLE 6.7

Scale of Distribution of Cereals in Delhi 2003-04 and 2004-05

S No.	Description	2003-04 Rice	2003-04 Wheat	2003-04 Sugar	2004-05 Rice	2004-05 Wheat	2004-05 Sugar
		Items (Qtls)					
A	**Quantity Allotted**						
	1. Above Poverty Line	2823930	10709700	-	2824200	7140960	-
	2. Below Poverty Line	452400	1131000	258017	448659	1121610	356080
	3. Antyodaya Anna Yojana	37061	91407		42150	105390	
B	**Quantity Lifted For Distribution**						
	1. Above Poverty Line	183012	3095926	-	910041	2972788	
	2. Below Poverty Line	452400	1131000	129089	413694	1064016	320647
	3. Antyodaya Anna Yojana	37061	89106		41074	98701	
C	**Percentage Distributed**			-			
	1. Above Poverty Line	6	29	-	32	42	
	2. Below Poverty Line	100	100	50	95	92	90
	3. Antyodaya Anna Yojana	100	97		94	98	

Source: Economic Survey of Delhi 2003-04 (www.delhiplanning.nic.in/economic%20survey/ecosur2003-04/ch19.pdf)

6.2.7.2 Scale of Distribution of Kerosene Oil

The entitlement of kerosene oil is 22 litre per Kerosene Oil Card per month at the rate of Rs. 9.08/litre in respect of BPL/AAY cards and 6 litres per month at the rate of Rs.9.08/litre in respect of APL cards.

6.2.8 Guidelines for Cardholders

- Ration Card should be kept safely and should not be given to others.
- While drawing ration, the FPS owners should make an entry in the ration card and the receipt of the commodities purchased should be taken. The ration card should not be handed over to FPS owner.
- Recheck the quality of the commodity with the samples available in the shop.
- Proper attention should be given at the time of weighing of the commodities.
- Any BPL cardholder, whose annual income exceeds Rs. 24,200 has to surrender his/her BPL card and any AAY card immediately and get the card prepared under APL.
- No unauthorised alteration should be made in the entries of the consumer card.
- In case of loss or damages of the ration card, duplicate card can be obtained from the Circle office on payment of prescribed fees.
- In the event of death of any member of the family or staying out of Delhi for more than one month, the names of such persons should be got struck off from the ration card and the prescribed commodities should not be drawn from FPS.
- Any change in the parameters on the basis of which consumer card was issued like change in the units owing to increase or decrease in the number of members of the family and change in the age of family members or issue of gas connections in the name of any member of the family shall be immediately reported to the concerned Food & Supplies Officer.

6.3 Targeted Public Distribution (TPDS)

It was always realised that there were operational inadequacies in the existing Public Distribution System till late 80s. There were problems of irregular supply of Essential Commodities to FPS and inturn to consumers, poor quality leading to non-drawal, non-lifting of sanctioned quotas by FPS in rural areas and general pessimism expressed by FPS dealers about profitability of running FPS, etc. Therefore in year 1992, the Essential Supplies Programme gave way to Revamped PDS (RPDS) with focus on corrective measures to ensure better functioning of overall PDS. RPDS had sought to improve targeting with its emphasis 'on all persons in poor areas'.

It was observed that there still existed gap between the fair quantity and fair price or the very socio-economically backward section of the society. The TPDS was implemented in the year 2001 in Delhi to benefit the poor and to raise the unit subsidy and ration subsidy considerably for the targeted consumers defined as 'Below Poverty Line' or BPL. This system aimed to modify the scope and coverage by adopting the principle of 'poor in all areas'. Therefore for an effective implementation of TPDS, identification of population Below Poverty Line was critical.

Based on the report of 'Expert Group on estimation of Proportion and number of Poor' for the year 1993-94, State government was asked to adopt the provisional estimates of BPL households.

TABLE 6.8

Poverty Line in Delhi

(no. in Lakh)

Year	*Rural*	*Urban*	*Combined*
1983	0.44 (7.66 %)	17.95 (27.89%)	18.39 (26.22%)
1987-1988	0.10 (1.29%)	10.15 (13.56%)	10.25 (12.41%)
1993-1994	0.19 (1.90%)	15.32 (16.03%)	15.51 (14.69%)
1999-2000	0.07 (0.40%)	11.42 (9.42%)	11.49 (8.23%)

Source: Report of the Expert Group on Estimation of Proportion and Number of Poor. Planning Commission, Government of India.

Later it was found in audits that significant time overrun has occurred in identification of BPL families in most of the states and Union Territories. The then government of NCT of Delhi blames the delay in implementation of PDS on the following two reasons. Firstly, there was a non-availability of authentic data on identification of BPL families. Secondly, the state government of NCT of Delhi wanted to make the scheme broader by inclusion of all *Jhuggi* ration cardholder as beneficiary of the scheme. However, as these issues were taking time, the government of NCT of Delhi realised that genuine BPL Population was suffering the loss of subsidised rations in the state. So, it went ahead and implemented the scheme to all whose income was up to Rs.24,200 per annum.

TABLE 6.9

Features of TPDS in Delhi

S.No.	Particulars	Figures	
1	Estimated Number of persons (in lakhs)	11.49	BPL families
2	Number of targeted persons (in lakh)	4.09	Only BPL
3	Number of BPL cards (in lakh)	3.84	
4	Number of AAY cards (in lakh)	0.56	
5	Number of BPL families covered	4.40	
6	Quantity of cereals supplied per household (Kg/per month)	35 Kg	

Source: Data & Information was provided by "Food & Supplies Department, Govt. of NCT of Delh

6.4 Other Schemes

6.4.1 Antyodaya Anna Yojna

National Sample Survey Exercise points out that about 5 per cent of the total Indian population can not afford two square meals a day. Their purchasing power is so low that they are not in a position to buy food grains round the year even at BPL rates. It is this 5 per cent of out population (5 crores of people or 1 crore families) that constitutes the target group of Antyodaya Anna Yojana.

The Antyodaya Anna Yojana is an important milestone in providing foodgrains to poor. This scheme started in six States—Himachal Pradesh, Rajasthan, Madhya Pradesh, Chhattisgarh, Andhra Pradesh, Uttar Pradesh and the UT of Dadra and Nagar Haveli. About 36 lakh families in these states were identified and given distinctive Antyodaya ration cards. Later this scheme was extended to most of the states. As far as Government of National Capital Territory of Delhi is concerned, the scheme was started in the year 2001-02. At present there are 56249 beneficiaries. The Government has also started the 3rd phase for identification of additional 1 lakh beneficiaries. But as on 27 March 2006, 64982 applications were received out of which about 10771 were found to be complete. Instructions have been issued to the concerned field officers to issue cards to these eligible applicants immediately.

The states/UTs are required to bear the distribution cost, including margin to dealers and retailers as well as the transportation cost. Thus the entire food subsidy is being passed on to the consumers under the scheme.

TABLE 6.10

Latest Lifting Figures for the Year 2005-06 up to January 2006

Category	Month	Allocation by Govt.	Allocation to Zone	Lifted by FPS	Balance to Lift
Wheat	**January 2005**	**11130**	**11130**	**13524**	**+ 2394 (Excess)**
	February 2005	11130	11130	8678	- 2454
	March 2005	11130	11130	12643	+ 1513 (Excess)
	up to January 2006	138,800	138,800	133,434	- 5366
Rice	**January 2005**	**4450**	**4450**	**5381**	**+ 931 (Excess)**
	February 2005	4450	4450	3098	- 1352
	March 2005	4450	4450	5609	+ 1159 (Excess)
	up to January 2006	55500	55500	51420	- 4080

Lifting of Wheat & Rice

(Figures in Lakh M.T.)

	APL		BPL		AAY		ANNAPURNA	TOTAL	
	W	R	W	R	W	R	W	W	R
2001-2002	0.071	0.163	0.516	0.094	0.009	0.01	0.0000064	0.596	0.027
2002-2003	1.19	0.1095	0.924	0.342	0.083	0.031	0.000039	2.197	0.483
2003-2004	3.096	0.183	1.169	0.460	0.091	0.036	0.000102	4.357	0.679
2004-2005	2.932	0.880	1.069	0.398	0.099	0.039	0.000045	4.100	1.317
2005-2006	2.407	0.541	1.036	0.413	0.160	0.062	0.000121	3.603	1.015
2006-2007	2.812	0.954	1.022	0.433	0.166	0.066	0.0000172	4.000	1.453
2007-2008 (up to May'07)	0.39	0.20	0.17	0.01	0.03	0.01	0.0	0.59	0.22

W: Wheat

R: Rice

Source: http://dscsc.delhigovt.nic.in/

6.4.1.2 Expansions of Antyodaya Anna Yojna

Ever since the scheme was announced there have been continuous expansions. In line with the National Common Minimum Programme (NCMP) of the UPA Government and the announcement made by the Hon'ble Finance Minister in the Union Budget 2004-05, the Antyodaya Anna Yojana (AAY) was expanded with effect from 1 August 2004 by adding 50 lakh BPL families by including *interalia* all households at the risk of hunger.

In Delhi the expansion was started in September 2005, but due to stringent scrutiny only 64982 applications were received till 27 March 2006. Out of these only 10771 were found to be complete. To ensure that only genuine and needy poorest of the poor is selected, the department had insisted on income certificate issued by the area SDM. Now only eligible persons are submitting these applications.

The following are the other criteria adopted for identification of additional Antyodaya families:

(a) Landless agriculture labourers, marginal farmers, rural artisans/craftsmen such as potters, tanners, weavers, blacksmiths, carpenters, slum dwellers, and persons earning their livelihood on daily basis in the informal sector like porters, coolies, rickshaw pullers, hand cart pullers, fruit and flower sellers, snake charmers, rag pickers, cobblers, destitutes and other similar categories in both rural and urban areas.

(b) Households headed by widows or terminally ill persons/disabled persons/persons aged 60 years or more with no assured means of subsistence or societal support.

(c) Widows or terminally ill persons or disabled persons or persons aged 60 years or more or single women or single men with no family or societal support or assured means of subsistence.

6.4.1.3 Objectives of the Scheme

Antyodaya Anna Yojana reflects the commitment of the Government of India to ensure food security for all and create a hunger free India. The objective of the scheme is to reform and improve the Public Distribution System so as to serve the poorest of the poor in rural and urban areas. It is for the poorest of poor that the Antyodya Anna Yojana has been conserved.

6.4.1.4 Scale and Issue Price

Antyodaya Anna Yojana contemplates identification of one crore families out of the number of BPL families who would be provided foodgrains at the rate of 35 kg. per family per month. The approximate annual requirement of food grains for Antyodaya families would be 30 lakh tonnes. The food grains will be issued by the Government of India at the rate of Rs.2 per kg. for wheat and Rs. 3 per kg. for rice. The Government of India suggests that in view of the abject poverty of this group of beneficiaries, the state government may ensure that the end retail price is retained at Rs.2 per kg. for wheat and Rs.3 per kg. for rice.

As far as Delhi is concerned, about 1,00,000 additional beneficiaries are to be identified in addition to present 56249 beneficiaries. Therefore the total requirement of food grains would be 5.46 lakh qtls. per month.

6.4.1.5 Issue of Ration Cards

After the identification of Antyodaya families, distinctive ration cards known as "Antyodaya Ration Card" are issued to the Antyodaya families by the designated authority. The ration card has the necessary details about the Antyodaya family, scale of ration etc. There is no application form and no fees for applying for Antyodaya Cards.

6.4.2 Annapurna Scheme

The Annapurna scheme aims at providing food security to meet the requirement of those senior citizens who though eligible have remained uncovered under the National Old Age Pension Scheme (NOAPS). This scheme addresses senior citizens of the country who are above 65 years of age and are not receiving any pension. The objective of the scheme is to ensure food security for the aged destitutes of the state. A "destitute person" is defined, as the person who has no regular source of income or financial support and therefore it is difficult for him to support himself.

6.4.2.2 Eligibility Criteria

Central assistance under Annapurna Scheme are provided to the beneficiaries fulfilling the following criteria:

a) The age of the applicant (male or female) should be 65 years or above.

b) The applicant must be "destitute" in the sense of having little or no regular means of subsistence from his/her own source of income or through financial support from family members or other sources. In order to determine destitution, the criteria (if any) currently in force in the state/UTs could also be followed.

c) The applicant should not be in receipt of pension under the NOAPS or State Pension Scheme.

The number of beneficiaries at present is 142. The main reason for this low number is:

- Most of senior citizens are availing benefits under NAOPS.
- People prefer AAY cards to Annapurna cards as there is no restriction of pensionnary benefits in AAY. Moreover they get 35 kg. of foodgrains at very low rate.

6.4.2.3 Benefits under the Scheme

The benefits under this scheme are

a) Supply of foodgrains–10 kg. per head per month

b) Issuing of free of cost ration cards.

6.4.2.4 Review of the Annapurna Scheme

After review of the National Old Age Pension Scheme about 8,915 persons were identified as eligible for getting this benefit. Despite a wide publicity and promotion, the total number of applications received was a mere 406 applications. Out of which only 170 Persons have been found eligible beneficiaries and were issued a card under the scheme. The main reason, which has been observed as the cause of such low number of beneficiaries, is that a lot of persons are already availing benefits of National Old Age Pension Scheme.

6.4.3 GPS System for PDS Management

In order to eliminate the pilferage and diversion of Specified Food Articles in the PDS system, the Corporation planned to introduce a web based GPS system for monitoring the movement of trucks carrying the SFAs. It was hoped a barcode base system along with GPS will ensure timely delivery of allocated quantity of food items at Fair Price Shops. The objectives of this planned system were to:

- Stop diversion
- Monitor vehicle movement online
- Track and analyse route deviation by vehicles
- Tighter control on goods movement

However, the proposal of GPS system has been kept suspended temporarily as it was not very cost effective.

6.4.4 Procurement of SFAS from Mandis

The Corporation also gave active consideration to procure wheat and rice directly from *mandis* at government approved rates to ensure better quality and uninterrupted supply to the citizens in order to increase the profitability of the corporation by saving on account of storage and manpower. However, this proposal at present has been kept in abeyance due to administrative reasons.

6.4.5 Weighing System at FCI

To stop pilferage at godowns an automatic weighing system has been introduced. This ensures correct weighing and one can monitor the weighing process completely online. Also with the online MIS, weighing database will be integrated. There will be surveillance cameras to deter malpractices.

6.4.6 Renewal of APL Cards

The Department has started the process of renewal of APL cards so that the problem of bogus cards, unused cards can be sorted and a better estimate of food security subsidies and issues can be made.

TABLE 6.11

Report of APL Renewal and Distribution as on 27.3.2006

Zones	*APL Cards before APL Renewal*	*Total Application Received for Renewal of APL (i+ii phase)*	*Total Percentage of Renewal of APL Ration Cards*	*Card Received by AC from CMC*	*No. of forms Rejected*	*Card Distributed*	*Percentage of Distribution*
South	466,760	283,057	61	276,095	6,214	180,720	65
South West	262,232	138,258	53	131,719	6,247	129,600	98
West	742,206	540,984	73	519,649	21,579	510,035	98
North West	645,230	491,197	76	449,131	33,548	441,669	98
East	393,911	280,944	71	271,966	7,902	264,233	97
North East	413,816	318,169	77	287,724	20,316	275,652	96
New Delhi	178,137	71,949	40	69,581	670	65,669	94
Central	275,126	164,039	60	153,332	4,397	149,131	97
North	249,406	147,093	59	144,301	1,837	142,077	98
Total	36,26,824	2,435,690	67	2,303,498	102,710	2,158,786	94

Source: Food Supplies and Consumer Affairs Department.

FIGURE 6.4

District-wise APL Card Renewal (Per cent)

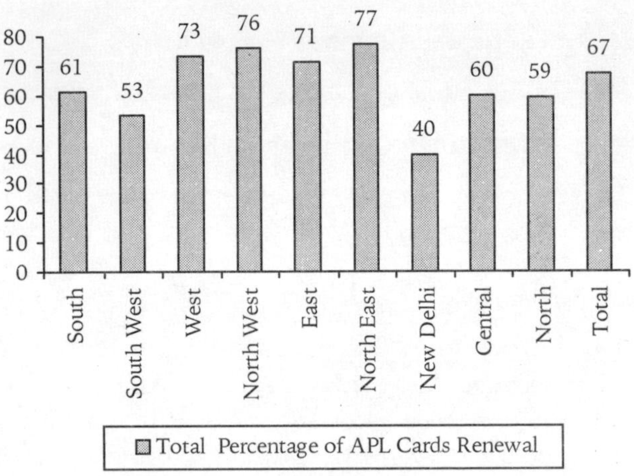

Source: Data & Information was provided by "Food & Supplies Department, Govt. of NCT of Delhi.

6.4.6.2 Process of Renewal of APL Cards

The APL renewal cards are available with the concerned authorities and are also available online. The form, duly filled in are required to be submitted/sent to the concerned Circle office within 15 days along with two black and white photographs (One unattested photograph, to be pasted on the form and one attested photograph, to be attached with the form) of the applicant and other supporting documents duly signed along with a fee of Rs. 20 + Re.1.

The forms are received in Circle offices/counter between 10.00 a.m. and 4.00 p.m. from Monday to Saturday (except 2nd Saturday of the month) and the acknowledgement receipt against each application form be taken from the office which will also authorise the ration card holder to obtain SFAs and kerosene oil for a period of 30 days on the said receipt. The cardholder will have to produce the receipt at the time of delivery of the ration card.

Following documents are required to be attached along with the application form:

1. Original old Ration Card and Blue Card for kerosene oil.
2. Photocopy of Election I-card.
3. One passport size photograph affixed on the form and one spare duly attested by Gazette officer.

Applicants providing any wrong information in this form will be liable to punishment or penalty. The renewal of Ration Cards and Blue Cards is being done in phases.

6.5 Circle Advisory Committee

The beneficiaries under BPL, Antyodaya Yojana and Annapurna are finalised by Circle Advisory Committee consisting of :

- Area MLA
- Members of Municipal Committee
- Seven Eminent Persons of Locality
- Food & Supplies Officers of the Circle.

6.6 Grievances Related to PDS

Food Security stands for the availability of food at all the times, in adequate quantity and quality to all the people. It is indicated by physical and economic accessibility of food. The Public Distribution System or PDS is the strategic way to ensure 'Food Security' to the people. Unfortunately though, in a welfare state like India, PDS has crossed more than 6 decades of working as a public policy but the problem of hunger, starvation, malnutrition, poverty and food security of the poor and vulnerable sections of the society still haunts. Over the years various important steps have been taken and various policies have been put in place for effective functioning of the system. The major concern for the country today is not inadequate quantity of foodgrains but the distribution of the good quality food grains in the right quantity to the more vulnerable and poor section of the society.

6.6.1 Micro-level Food Security

One of the significant objectives of PDS was to ensure Micro Level Food Security. The CAG report revealed that inefficient targeting has affected targeted PDS, under which 10 kg. (now 20 kg.) foodgrains per month per family was to be provided to the households below the poverty line at about half the normal PDS price. Many state governments failed to translate this objective into action.

In a large number of cases, the CAG report stated, the BPL families did not get the prescribed quantity of 10 kg. ration at the special subsidised rates and were charged higher rates. The state governments did not absorb the cost over and above that was provided by the Union Government towards handling, transportation, etc. The higher cost was passed on to the consumers, "thereby defeating the main objective" of the targeted PDS.

The quantity of mere 10-20 kg. per family at the special BPL price, according to the report, was also not significant to provide food security at affordable price, since it did not fulfill the monthly requirement of about

53 kg. of foodgrains for an average size family of five members.

The average per household per month was as low as mere 6.5 kg. "Thus, while the cost to the exchequer was enormous, the gains to the consumer were marginal."

During a good harvest time general public and also BPL depends on PDS for a very small quantity of total requirement, as the PDS prices are generally higher than the market prices. And therefore a very meagre income transfer.

6.6.2 Food and Nutritional Security

Low availability of food grains through PDS assumed importance in the face of acute nutritional inadequacy in diet and very low per capita calorie intake of BPL population in the country. Several studies have indicated that the per capita cereal consumption of the poor had remained the same despite a significant improvement in their real per capita expenditure and decline in the cereal prices compared to non-cereal food, which is attributed to the change in the preference of the people to non-cereal food.

6.6.3 Identification of Target Group

One of the major problems with the functioning of PDS is the problem of identification of the right target group. There is no availability of authentic data for classification of population in APL, BPL and other relevant categories. There still exists a gap between the targeted number of beneficiaries *vis-à-vis* actual beneficiaries. Approximately only about 57 per cent of the BPL households are covered by TPDS.

6.6.4 Distribution Network

The PDS chain starts with the Departments of Food and Civil Supplies that monitor and look after various policy matters, followed by Food Corporation of India (FCI) taking care of the procurement of foodgrains from producers, their storage and also the import of other means food items. But the arm that directly reaches the target group is the Fair Price Shop Owners (FPS). Their number is directly proportional to the number of targeted population living in that particular area. Due to callous attitude or low profit associated with PDS, these FPS owners resort to illegal and mis-appropriate means and ways:

- Excess issuances of ration cards to increase margins. Many FPSs have large number of ghost cards in order to get more quantity of foodgrains and earn huge profit by selling them in the open market.
- As a result of low annual turnover some of FPS owners indulge in leakage of commodities and diversion of subsidised grains available with them.
- Irregularities in opening and closing of FPS.
- Harassment to the card holders.
- Entries of the commodity sold to the beneficiary is not made.
- Commodities sold are not weighed properly.
- Over charging from consumers.
- Good quality commodities replaced by poor quality foodgrains/kerosene.
- Lacunae in the licensing and selection of FPS. Marked irregularities have been found in allotment of licence to FPS.
- Inaccessible location of FPS from the BPL or Antyodaya beneficiaries.

6.6.5 Leakages

A significant portion of subsidised food grains and other essential commodities do not reach the beneficiaries due to their diversion. The review of the scheme by Comptroller and Auditor General of India has also disclosed significant number of cases of diversion of PDS commodities, undue benefit to millers losses in transit and storage, existence of large number of bogus ration cards, excess charging from the consumers compared to the maximum price prescribed by the Central government and poor quality of foodgrains supplied which reduced the efficacy of the PDS.

6.6.5.1 Ration Cards as Identity Proof

There are a number of ration cards issued by government not been used for years together but exist for the sake of personal identity. This leads to mis-planned targets for food distribution and lot of subsidy and resources get wasted due to such cards. The Supreme Court has strictly issued the order that no ration card will be treated as 'Identity Proof'. The department has already issued circular to this effect that ration cards shall not be issued as proof of identification.

6.6.5.2 Bogus Ration Cards

To deal with the problem of bogus ration cards, which cause large scale diversion to open market of foodgrains, sugar, etc., the Department has recently concluded the renewal of APL cards wherein the number of cards has been brought down by 14 lakh from 36 lakh to 22 lakh. It is also proposed to start revive/renewal of BPL cards soon. The current number of BPL cards issued is 28 lakh. This exercise will eliminate ghost cards or ineligible beneficiaries.

6.6.6 *Lack of Awareness*

The department issues press advertisements to inform beneficiaries about the prescribed rates/quantity entitlement on a card. It has also been made mandatory to paste/paint or put up notice boards displaying rates etc. at all fixed price shops and in and around *Jhuggi*-clusters to make them aware of their rights. All these corrective actions have started showing positive result and they needs to be repeated at regular intervals, as still there is significant lack of awareness among the beneficiaries about the process to avail it and also regarding grievance redressal mechanism.

6.6.7 *Quality Issues*

The Government of NCT of Delhi tries to ensure that good quality foodgrains should reach people but it is found unscrupulous dealers exchange good quality products received from the F.C.I. with inferior stock.

The department in order to deal with this problem conducts quality checking at Fixed Price Shops and the sample received from FCI godowns is tallied with foodgrains available at FPS. What is needed is more frequent checking by the department and handing out strict punishment and fine to those indulging in such malpractice.

6.6.8 *Inadequate Number of Fair Price Shops*

As per the policy there should be one Fair Price Shop per 1000 persons. Unfortunately there is inadequate number of Fair Price Shops *vis-à-vis* population in a given area resulting in the problem of right quantity for each ration card, which in turn breeds dissatisfaction with FPSs among people.

The government is initiating action to rationalise FPS in each circle. Also due to decrease in number of APL cards, the requirement of FPS has also come down.

6.6.9 *Storage Facility*

Under RPDS, construction of godowns for facilitating storage and availability of good quality foodgrains was contemplated. Currently there are 6 FCI godowns, which cater to the storage requirement of foodgrains.

6.6.10 *Financial Viability of FPS*

Even the financial viability of FPS is under question. By viability, we mean an annual return of 12 per cent or more on the working capital. Since financial viability of FPSs is critical to the success of TPDS, a simulation exercise was carried out with respect to alternate values of the relevant parameters that affect the operations of FPS. Only about 22.7 per cent of the FPSs were found to be earning a return of 12 per cent on capital. To make the FPS financially more viable the department is considering various options such as rationalisation of cards, increasing the FPS margin, etc.

6.7 Initiatives for Improving Efficiency

The Department continuously takes initiative for streamlining and improving the efficiency of Public Distribution System. The Finance Minister Mr. P.

TABLE 6.12

Prices of Commodities Issued to the Cardholders & FPS under PDS

Category	*Central Issue Price (Rs./Qtl.)*			*Transportation Charges (Rs./Qtl.)*			*FPS Holder Margin (Rs./Qtl.)*			*Retail Issue Price (Rs./Qtl.)*		
	W	*R*	*S*	*W*	*R*	*S*	*W*	*R*	*S*	*W*	*R*	*S*
APL	610	830		35	35		35	35		680	900	
BPL	415	565		15	15		35	35		465	615	
Antyodaya	200	300	1329/60	15*	15*	10/32	35*	35*	10/08	200	300	1350
Annapurna	Free of Cost (10kg Per Head)									Free of Cost		

* to be paid by Delhi Government

Note: In regards of Annapurna Yojna, the DSCSC Ltd. deposits the draft @ Rs.415 per Qtl. to FCI and then FCI issues the stock of wheat to the concerned FPSs.

Thereafter DSCSC claim the amount of stock transportation charges and FPS Margin (Rs.415 + Rs.15+Rs.35 = Rs.465 per Qtl.) to F&S Department.

Source: http://dscsc.delhigovt.nic.in/

Chidambaram had announced in his budgetary speech that a policy will be developed for "comprehensive medium-term strategy for food and nutrition security for all". Government of Delhi has been working continuously towards meeting the set objective and strengthening of the PDS. The Chief Minister of Delhi has ensured the following:

- There is a periodical checking of FPSs and mechanism of issuance of ration cards to identify and eliminate bogus rations cards.
- To take stern action against persons found guilty of misusing the TPDS benefit.
- The cardholders should get their entitled allotment on any day any time/on the dates indicated in the card.

6.7.1 Fair Price Shops

According to an order by Hon'ble Supreme Court of India of India ration card shops shall remain open throughout the month during fixed hours and the details of which shall be displayed on their notice board. Also, they should display the following information on a notice board at a prominent place in the shop:

- Display of information on the wall outside the Fair Price Shops/Kerosene Oil Depots.
- Licence name and number of authority letter.
- Entitlement of essential commodities.
- Stock as on date.
  - Stock of essential commodities received during the month.
  - Opening and closing stock of essential commodities, and
- Rates of commodities.
- Sample of sugar, wheat, rice.
- Timings of opening and closing office of Fair Price Shop/Kerosene Oil Depots.
- Weekly off.
- He should have a complete list of BPL and Antyodaya beneficiaries.
- Procedure for making complaints indicating the authorities for redressal of grievance of the consumer.
- Maintaining a complaint register for recording complaints with regard to quality/quantity of stocks.

6.7.2 Area Vigilance Committee

To suggest objective methods for deletion of inflated and ineligible units and to suggest ways and means for preventing diversion of SFAs and kerosene oil, Area Vigilance Committee has been constituted consisting of the following members

- Area MLA – Chairman.
- Members of Municipal Committee of both the wards of the area.
- Seven Eminent Persons of Locality (including ladies, social workers, RWA and members of SC/ST) nominated by area MLA.
- Food & Supplies Officers of the Circle—Secretary.

6.7.3 Monthly Inspection

Besides other measures taken to ensure proper functioning of FPS, there is a team of Inspection staff who keeps a close eye on FPS. The Food Commissioner of Delhi is a vigilant officer himself and to keep everyone agile, he leaves nothing to chance. He himself goes for sudden visits to take an overall assessment of the area. He personally visits all the FPS and in case of any irregularity or problem, he gives warning to the FPS owner and still if the problem persists he files an FIR and calls the police. It has been ordered that the officers of the Department will conduct monthly random inspection of FPSs/KODs as follows:

Area Inspector	:	15
FSO	:	10
Assistant Commissioner	:	7
Addl. Commissioner	:	5

6.7.4 Public Audit

The present Food Commissioner of Delhi Mr. K.S. Mehra has introduced a system of 'Public Audit'. This is a very interesting mechanism to keep a check on the issues of distribution. This programme began with North and Northeast of Delhi as pilot districts. The reason for selection of these areas was that there is a greater number of slums and BPL population compared to other districts in Delhi. This project was conceived by Mr. Mehra himself in the month of February 2005 and it started immediately in March 2005.

Initially it was made that Fair Price Shop (FPS) owners will show the records to public as and when asked. But later it was observed that FPS owners used to intimidate the people and the purpose of the programme was getting defeated. After much deliberation, the programme was given a little twist with a day fixed as 'Public Audit Day'. This is the day when people can come and check the records in the office of Food Commissioner. For this the FPS owners will have to submit the records a day in advance of the public audit. Also, to be emphasised is the fact the FPS owners will have no entry on that day.

These audits are held on every Saturday of the month and FSOs are to submit their reports on Friday of every month. Public Audits are available for public scrutiny between 12:00 a.m. and 1:00 a.m. every working day and are called as the 'Public Hours'.

Public hearing by all the Food & Supplies Officers in their circles and Assistant Commissioners in their Districts on 1st and 3rd Saturday of the month between 2:00 p.m. and 5:00 p.m.

6.7.4.1 Inspection of the Following Records

Beneficiaries of the TPDS under the categories of BPL, AAY and Annapurna Scheme can inspect following records free of cost.

1. Stock Register
2. Sale Register
3. Master Register (Ration Card Register)
4. Cash Memos

6.7.4.2 Sale Register

The format of the sale register maintained in the fair Price Shops/Kerosene Oil Depots has been revised to indicate ration card number, registration number, quantity of specified food articles (SFAs) issued, amount received and signature/thumb impression of the person who received the SFAs and relationship with the ration card holder.

6.7.5 Prevention of Diversification of Food Articles

To prevent diversification of food articles -

- Procedure for opening the sale before commencement of sale prescribed.
- FPS owner to report the arrival of SFAs in writing within 3 hours of the receipt of the stock indicating the quantity and time.
- Circle FSO to note the same in the Intimation Register.
- Area Inspector to inspect FPS within 3 hours of receipt of information.
- Area Inspector to record his visit in the receipt column of the Stock Register.

6.7.6 Penalties

- In case of minor variation of stock upto 50 kg. of SFAs, a penalty of Rs. 5000 to be imposed.
- In case variation is more than 50 kg. of all the articles combined together, licence to be suspended for 3 months, initiation of quasi-judicial proceedings at the level of Zonal Assistant Commissioner.
- In case variation is more than 100 kg. of all the articles put together, licence to be suspended and FIR to be lodged under Section 7/10 of Essential Commodities Act, 1955.
- In case of over charging and other violations, immediate suspension of licence.

6.7.7 Complaints

All complaints to be disposed of in a time bound manner. All Assistant Commissioners/FSOs to fix a complaint box in their office complex which is to be opened by the concerned officer daily in the morning and the complaints are to be registered in the Complaint Register.

TABLE 6.13

Institution and Disposal of Cases since Inception up to March 2005

Institution	*Filed*	*Disposed*	*Pending*	*Percentage*
		State Commission		
Complaints	5548	4488	1060	80.89
Appeals	17435	14798	2637	84.87
		District Fora		
Cases	151612	141610	10002	93.40

Source: Food Supplies and Consumer Affairs Department.

FIGURE 6.5

Disposal of Cases since Inception up to March 2005 of State Commission

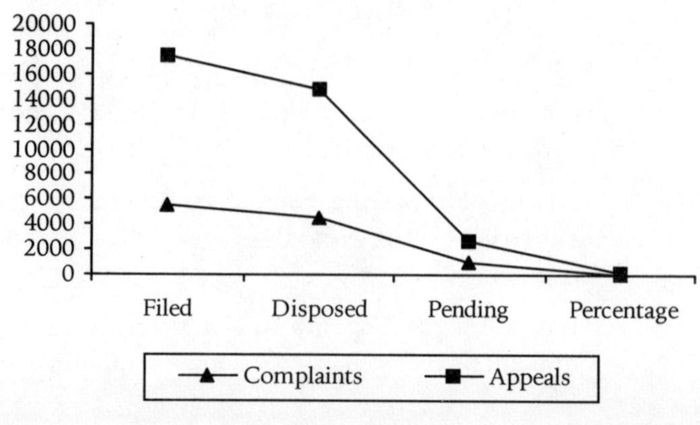

6.7.8 Citizen Charter

Citizen Charter of the Department provides following:

Getting a new ration card	:	30 days
Surrender of ration Card	:	Same day
Addition/Deletion of name	:	10 days
Tatkal Ration Card	:	This scheme has been withdrawn

6.7.9 Feedback Forms

Each Cardholder is asked to fill in a feed back form provided by the Food and Civil Supplies Department, Delhi. This form is kept very simple and all questions are asked in a direct manner. This form deals with the behaviour of FPS owner, quality and quantity of the food items purchased and other related issues

6.7.10 Other Instructions

- All the FSOs to give certificate that FPSs/KODs in their jurisdiction are being run by the authorised person.
- All the PDS outlets to give undertaking relating to the authorised salesman/representative.
- Only authorised representative to unload the SFAs.
- Photo Identity Card of the Salesman/Authorised representative to be displayed.
- Instructions have been issued to allow senior citizens to get their work done on priority by forming separate queues.
- It has been decided to keep the records of the FPS/KOD such as stock register, sale register, master register, cash memos, etc. open to allow the bonafide card holders to see the records and satisfy themselves whether they have received the same quantity, etc.

6.8 Futuristic Approach

The Consumer Affairs Department, Delhi has set priorities for today and action points for tomorrow. They believe in an interactive and participatory mechanism that leads to lesser grievances. Some of the futuristic steps by them are:

- Setting up consumer clubs.
- Setting up of district consumer information centres.
- Financial assistance for consumer welfare activities.
- Meeting the expenses of district consumer protection councils.
- Sponsoring NGOs for grants-in-aid.
- Setting up consumer clubs.
- Educating students in schools on consumer related matters.
- Setting up consumer information centres for spreading consumer awareness.
- Create awareness about consumer related matter, rights, grievance-handling mechanism, etc. through mass media like newspapers, posters, brochures, etc. Also to be involved in this is the civil society. They are expected to organise seminars, street plays, ***nukkad nataks***, puppet shows, essay competitions, etc.
- One more district forum by bifurcation of District South will start functioning shortly. And there is a proposal to open three more district forums.
- There is a proposal to open one more bench of the State Commission

6.9 Right to Information

To make sure that each cardholder knows his rights and has his faith restored in the system, the working of the department is made absolutely transparent. Each FPS will display information such as beneficiaries' entitlement of various essential commodities, the issue prices, periodicity at which ration can be drawn, name of Fair Price Shopkeeper, timings of opening and closing of FPS and weekly closing days, stock position, etc. at a conspicuous place.

The process is designed keeping in mind that the cardholder should not get scared to ask for any information and the entire necessary information is always on display. This is leading to number of grievance cases coming down, as the information is readily available.

Since the inception of Delhi Right to Information Act, 2001, a total of 569 applications were received upto February 2005 of which 565 applications have been disposed of.

There used to be only one competent authority under the Delhi Right to Information Act as the Headquarter, Office of Commissioner (Food & Supplies). However, w.e.f 1 June 2004, all the Zonal Assistant Commissioners have been notified as the competent authority under the Delhi Right to Information Act.

To ensure that there is proper awareness regarding the grievance redressal system it is compulsory for the FPS to also display procedure for lodging the complaints with reference to quality and quantity of ration, other problems being faced by the beneficiaries during the course of getting their ration. And to ensure success of this, the departments has made all the officers equipped enough to answer all queries. Even the officers of other departments who are not aware of the rules and guidelines related to PDS and its functioning are made aware.

The department has specially prepared a ready reckoner, which is made available to all the officers for ready reference. Even the directions by Supreme Court and other important papers are included.

Besides the above, the consumer who is listed in the list of the FPS is entitled to inspect the stock register, sales register and ration card register at the shop.

6.10 Role of Civil Society

The role of civil society is indispensable in making any public welfare policy work. It has been observed that when civil society takes up the challenges to make a programme success, it can ensure complete people participation and put the desired pressure on the government for the rights of the people.

It is well understood that the government has a limited reach to people. It is physically impossible for the government to be present at each and every place whereas civil societies are grass root people and they interact with common public day in and out. They can understand the grievance of the people better and explain it to the government as desired by the cardholders. Therefore, they can play the role of a mediator and inform government of the issues pending with people.

In a landscape where exists an inadequate implementation of government regulations, long-standing, un-addressed grievances, it is natural that people will go on losing faith in the overall system of Public Distribution. In Delhi various Non-Profit organisations like 'Parivartan' are working towards restoring the lost faith in the system. But civil society has to play a balanced role. They can serve as a vehicle for informing the most uninformed public and mobilising them to make the much criticised 'system' accountable.

Government wants civil society to play a participatory role in planning, executing, monitoring and evaluating public policies relevant to Public Distribution System. Only a participatory approach will give the government's policies on food and food security a more humane shape and a much-needed impetus.

6.11 Some Suggestions

- **Reward/Recognition**
  - Reward for the meritorious and honest officers who are vigilant and care for people's needs.
  - Recognition or annual award for the FSPs so that more and more shop owners would try to follow the system.
- **Legalised Ways to make Profit**
  - As there are low margins in the running of FPS, there should be legalised and genuine ways to earn profit for an honest business.
  - There can be a provision for the supply of other essential items like tea, soap, matchbox etc. be made available through FPS.
  - There can be various Tax exemption provisions in procurement and distribution of other essential commodities to encourage the concept of providing complete service to people.
- **Quantity/Quality/Timeliness of Foodgrains**
  - A timely arrival of foodgrains at FPS can ensure timely distribution of essential commodities. It is interesting to note that most of the people get their wages/salaries in the first seven days of the month so the system should be such that it ensures the supply of food grains during that period. Failing which people will buy from the commercial outfits leading to non-lifting of the quota and diversion of supply to black marketeers.
  - The supply should be in adequate quantity keeping in mind the number of consumers registered with the FPS owners. Inadequate quantity of food grains leads to shaking of the trust of the consumer in the FPS owner and hence the whole Public Distribution System.
- **Licence to FPS**
  - The mechanism of allotment of FPS licence should be made more stringent. People from economically weaker section should be given opportunity.

Last but not the least, people's participation should be sought for successful functioning of PDS. Voluntary organisations should also actively be involved for better functioning of the system. A vigilant and cooperative public will go a long way in making this system more viable and effective.

The department is considering these proposals for reward/recognition to the honest officials, and the FPS licensees who adopt fair practices and legalised way to make profit.

Strict instruction/monitoring is done on quantity/quality/timeliness of foodgrains.

Mechanism of allotment of FPS licence has also been made more stringent. The Chairman of Selection Committee is D.C. (Revenue) who is from the other department and hence selection is more transparent and based on merit.

ANNEXURE A.6.1

Organisational Structure

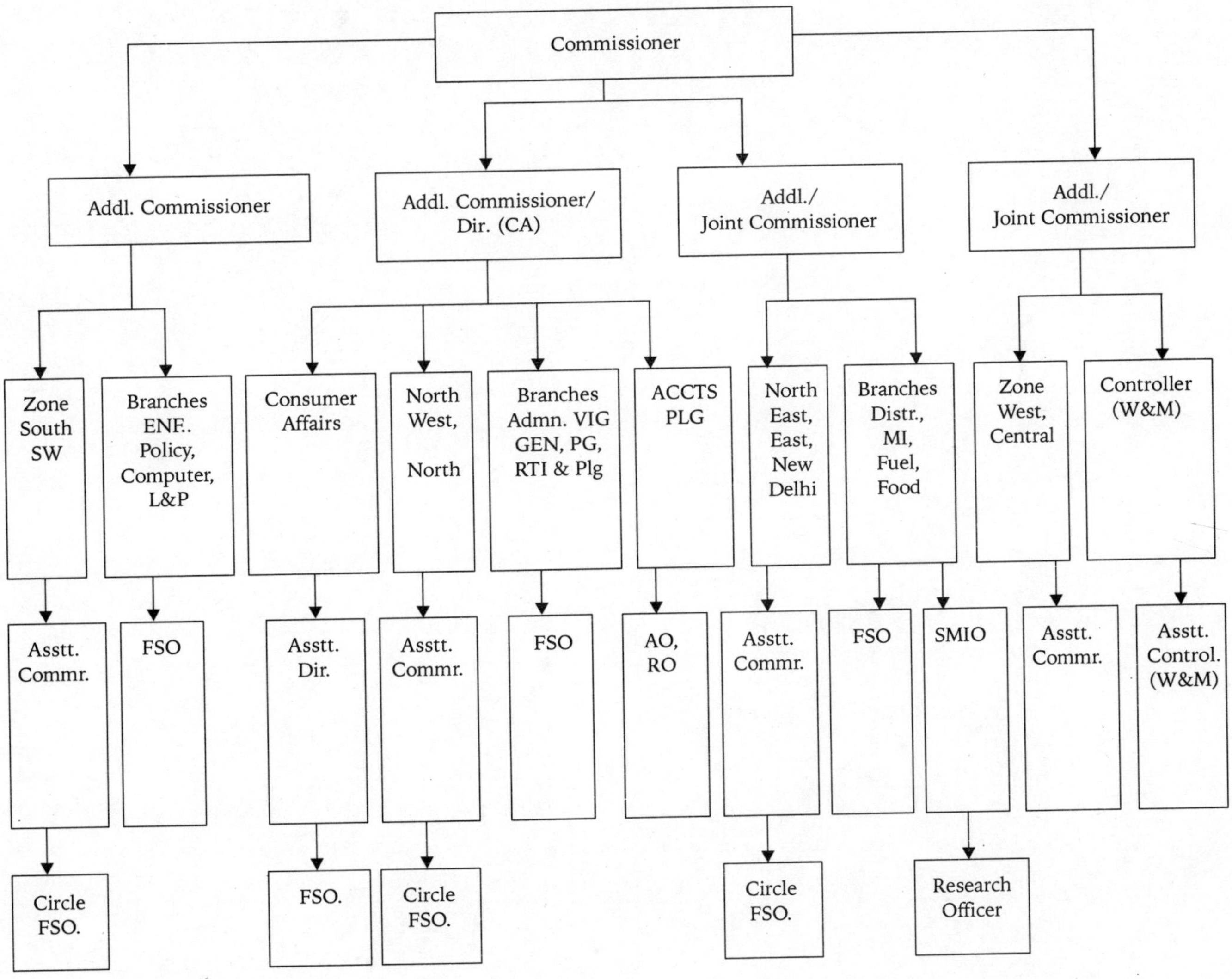

Source: http://delhigovt.nic.in/dept/food/forg.asp

Chapter 7

Forest, Tree Crop Management, Greening of Delhi

7.1 Introduction

7.1.1 Background

The National Capital of Delhi continues to occupy an unenviable position in the world's most polluted cities list despite the efforts of "Greening Delhi". Although the introduction of CNG and *Van Mahotsav* has made an impact, still more solutions are sought for improving the environment of the city. This chapter reviews the forestry status, plantation trends, and potentiality of new species and suggests policy measures to increase the green cover of Delhi. The study is based on published literature on the subject and secondary data collected from the reports of Forest Survey of India, Green Action Plan of Delhi, websites of different organisations and meeting stake-holders like the forest department and concerned officers of Delhi administration.

Delhi finds prominent reference in pre-historic times right from the epic Mahabharat. Later, Delhi went on passing from one kingdom to another beginning with the Maurayas, Guptas and Palas of Central India and finally to the Chauhans in the 12th century, followed by Afghan Muslim invasions and Mughal rule. The British took control of Delhi in 1803 and in 1911 it was made the capital of British India and it got the position of its present prestige. Delhi, which was having a status of a single large district/Union Territory, has been assigned the status of National Capital Territory in 1991.

7.1.2 Geographical Location

The National Capital Territory of Delhi, situated between the Himalayas and the Aravallis, lies between $28^0 24'$ to $28^0 53'$ N latitudes and $76^0 50'$ and $77^0 20'$ E longitudes. The altitude varies between 243 and 305m above sea level.

FIGURE 7.1

District Map of Delhi

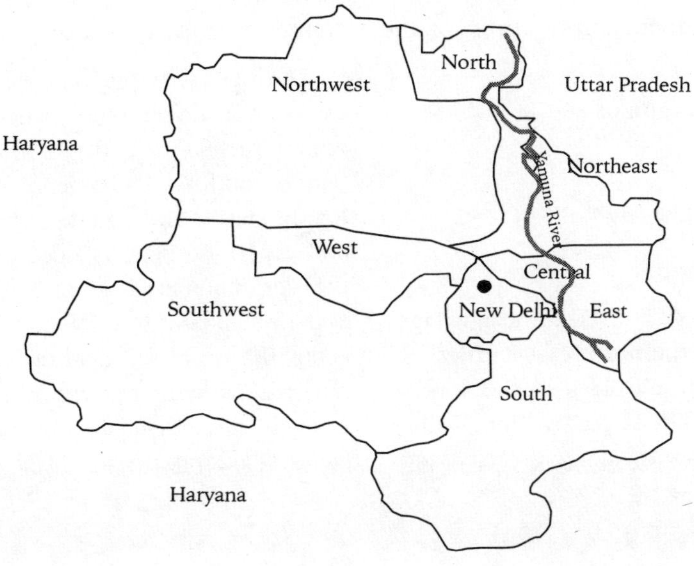

Haryana surrounds Delhi in all sides except east where Uttar Pradesh touches it. The major part of the territory is on the western side of the Yamuna. It covers a geographical area of 1,483 sq. km. The human population of the state is 13.78 million (1.3 per cent of the country's population) that comprises of 7 per cent of rural and 93 per cent of urban population. Its population density of 9,294 persons per sq. km. is the highest in the country. The livestock population is only 0.3 million. The state ranks 15th among all the states in respect of percentage of geographical area under tree cover.

7.1.3 Climate

The climate of the region is semi-arid, characterised by hot summers and cold winters and marked by diurnal temperature differences and moderately low rainfall. It is markedly periodic and is characterised by a dry and increasingly hot season from March to June, warm monsoon period from July to September and a dry and cold winter from October to February.

The important factors influencing the climate of the region are rainfall, temperature and wind. The normal annual rainfall is 66.6 cm, of which nearly 80 per cent is received during the period of three months from mid-June to mid-September. Temperature is one of the most characteristic features of the climate of Delhi, which is marked by extremities. Normally the temperature ranges between 18.7° C (mean minimum) and 40.3° C (mean maximum). Wind is another important climatic factor for Delhi. Winds are strongest in the month of June and lightest in November. In summer months hot and dust raising winds, popularly known as "loo" are commonly experienced and may result in thunderstorms or dust storms. To sum up, it is unfavourable for the growth of luxuriant vegetation.

7.1.4 Topography

The NCT of Delhi can be divided into three main physiographic segments:

i. The Flood plains of the Yamuna;

ii. The Ridge; and

iii. The plains including the irrigated area.

7.1.4.1 Flood Plains of the Yamuna

The river Yamuna enters the NCT of Delhi near village Bakhtawarpur of Alipur Block in the north-east and leaves Delhi near village Jaifpur of Mehrauli block in the south-east after meandering about 45 km stretch within Delhi. The river flows from north to south along the city and divides it into smaller eastern part (Trans-Yamuna) and bigger western part (Cis-Yamuna). The river occupies flood plain area of about 97 sq. km. (Anon., 2000). The flood plains are somewhat low-lying, sandy and subject to recurrent floods. The river water has been blocked by Wazirabad barrage constructed to maintain water level and to store water for municipal supply. The quantity of water extracted in Wazirabad is approximately 350 million cubic metres per day. Due to scarce water situation, hardly any water is allowed to flow in the Yamuna through the barrage during the lean season, thus the river is left with almost no clean water to flow. However, during monsoon season, Wazirabad barrage is opened to avoid floods in upstream reaches of the Yamuna.

Agriculture is practised extensively along the stretch of river. The entire region falls within the suburban pocket of Delhi. Most of the native vegetation has been cleared for the purpose of agriculture and farming. However, the areas, which are not fit for agriculture, are used as grazing grounds when the flood water recedes. The anthropogenic pressures, in the form of encroachments and conversion of land for various purposes, on the riparian habitat particularly the flood plain areas have led to threatened status of the riverine ecosystem.

The soil along the river is silt to sandy loam in texture, with pH from 8-8.5, more alkaline with the depth and is generally fertile and suitable for cultivation. The 'new alluvium' thrown up by the river and submerged by annual floods for several feet each year, until raised above the surface of the water by successive deposits of silt, becomes covered in the first place by seedlings of *Tamarix indica* and *T. dioica*, the former being more common than the latter. These soon establish themselves in a dense crop either in pure formation or mixed with *Alhagi pseudalhagi* and others. Such alluvial *Tamarix* forests are generally disappearing from these tracts, as more and more area adjoining the riverbed is being brought under plantation and cultivation.

During the monsoon i.e., from July-October, the river assumes a violent appearance, bringing down lot of silt, which raises its bed. As the water recedes during the winter months, a characteristic flora comprising of water loving herbs and sedges and species of higher altitudes and colder regions, is observed. On these muddy islands, the common species are *Riccia discolor, Equisetum arvense, Marsilea minuta* (all lower plants). *Ranunculus sceleratus, Anagallis arvensis, Centaurium ramosissimum, Verbascum chinense, Lathyrus aphaca, Mililotus indica, Potentilla supina, Grangea maderaspatana, Conyza aegyptiaca, Vicoa vestita, V. indica, Pulicaria crispa, Gnaphalium indicum, G. luteo-album,*

Veronica anagallis-aquatica, Mazus japonicus, Salvia plebeia, Polygonum plebeium, Juncus bufonius, sedges like *Scirpus tuberosus, S. affanis, Cyperus pygmaeus, Fimbristylis dichotoma* and grass *Polypogon monspeliensis*.

Due to its poor water-holding capacity, the silt loses its moisture content and these muddy flats soon organise into temporary dunes. According to Maheshwari (1963), many plants that were recorded from Yamuna ravines near Delhi in Royle's time (1839) but have since then remained unnoticed. They include *Ranunculus aquatilis, Anisochilus carnosus, Polygala telephioides, Dicoma tomentosa* and *Pulicaria angustifolia*. However, Naithani *et. al.* (2004) has rediscovered *Dicomma tomentosa* and *Pulicaria augustifolia* from the Ridge.

Aquatic plant species found in the Yamuna have reduced dramatically due to excessive pollution and heavy infestation by water hyacinth (*Eichhornia crassipes*).

7.1.4.2 The Ridge

Aravallis are the oldest of all the mountains in India and probably originated about 1500 million years ago. The range was apparently as high as the Himalayas but erosions have worn out the hills over the ages and reduced the once lofty ranges to near sea levels. The range is very significant from the conservation point of view due to its merger with the Indo-gangetic plains in the east (Sawarkar and Uniyal, 1995).

The Aravallis enter Delhi from Haryana in the south in the form of the Ridge. The ridge emerges as the most dominating physiographic feature. Historically, it has played a vital role in the affairs of Delhi. All the seven cities that were built and destroyed in what today forms the National Capital Territory came up in the triangle of land formed by the Ridge and the Yamuna River.

The difference between the highest point (near Bhati at 320 m) and the bed of the Yamuna at the old railway bridge is about 110 m. "The Ridge" a green patch of land approximately 7,782 hectares, which is about 6 per cent of Delhi's geographical area, has been considered as the "Breathing lung" for Delhi. The District Gazetteer of Delhi (1883-84) records that "in the later part of the last century, the best drinking water was obtained from springs on the Ridge" (Ganguli, 1975). However, at present there are no permanent natural water bodies, though few artificial ones are available. Aravalli Hills, entering from Gurgaon in south sprawl towards Delhi in the form of a tableland, some five kilometers across and break into four distinctive spurs now known as Northern, Central, South Central, and Southern Ridge.

7.1.4.2.1 The North Ridge or Old Delhi Ridge

About 87 ha. at present, is the smallest section bound by Delhi University in the north, Kamla Nagar in the south, Rajpur Road in the east, and Malka Ganj in the west. The area is dominated by cultivated and exotic species.

7.1.4.2.2 The Central or New Delhi Ridge

More popularly known as Dhaulakuan Ridge is 869 ha. in area and is bordered in the north, south, east and west by Link Road, Dhaulakuan, Mandir Marg, and Naraina Industrial Area, respectively.

7.1.4.2.3 The South Central Ridge (Vasant Kunj)

It is about 626 ha. in area and flanked by Mehrauli Industrial area, Mahipalpur, Sri Aurobindo Marg, and Jawahar Lal Nehru University Road, in north, south, east and west, respectively.

7.1.4.2.4 The Southern Ridge

About 6,200 ha. in area, where a substantial tree cover is found in Sanjay Van or Kishangarh forest and the Jahanpanah City Forest. The remainder of the southern Ridge is under the Indira Priyadarshini (Asola-Bhati) Wildlife Sanctuary, but has been largely degraded owing to mining and grazing activities. It is estimated that about 72 per cent of the Ridge area has been encroached leaving only 28 per cent green area. Other areas falling under Southern Ridge as a reserve forest area include Devli, Dera Mandi, Jonapur, Rajokri, and Gittorni.

TABLE 7.1

The Ridges in Delhi

S.No.	*Name of Ridge*	*Area in(Ha)*	*Jurisdiction*
1.	North Ridge or old Delhi Ridge	87	DDA
2.	Central Ridge or New Delhi Ridge (Dhaula Kuan)	868*	CPWD
3.	South Central Ridge (Vasant Kunj)	626	MCD, DDA and Forest Deptt.
4.	Southern Ridge	6,200	Forest Deptt.
	Total	**7,781**	

Note: * In some places the Central Ridge has been stated to be 864 ha. in that case total area would be 7,777 ha.

Delhi has always the privilege of being a city of considerable importance for many centuries. It is therefore not surprising that the tree growth on the hills in the neighbourhood has been completely destroyed except where especially protected near temples or mosques, or other such places. The Gazetteer of the District (1912) described the hills as "Their surface is generally bare supporting little or no vegetation, save a stunted *Kikar* (*Acacia nilotica ssp. indica*), *Karil* (*Capparis decidua*) or the small bush of the *Ber* (*Ziziphus nummularia*), which with its prickly thorn is inhospitable to the pedestrian. The surface of the ground is sprinkled with thin laminae of mica, which shine in the sunlight like gold. The stone, which juts up from the ground here and there, is hard and often sharp-edged. Water, of course, lies very deep, and irrigation by well almost everywhere impracticable. A moderate pasture is obtained by flocks of sheep and goats herded by Gujar boys." Parker (1920) gave a complete list of plants growing in the Ridge, which included 69 species *viz.*, 23 trees, 9 climbers, 36 shrubs and one palm. Out of these, 5 species were planted *viz.*, *Ailanthus excelsa*, *Albizia lebbeck*, *Dalbergia sissoo*, *Dodonoea viscosa*, and *Tamarindus indica*. He also recommended some species for plantation *viz.*, *Acacia modesta*, *A. catechu*, *Boswellia serrata*, *Dichrostachys cinerarea*, *Sterculia urens* as well as *Agave*, *Euphorbia* and *Cacti*, which would probably grow very well in Ridge.

7.1.4.2.5 *The Vegetation and Floristic Composition of the Ridge*

The Ridge basically is a 6B/C Tropical Dry Thorn Forest as classified by Champion and Seth (1968) and comprises of groups of scattered trees with thorny shrubs. Main species are given in Table 7.2.

TABLE 7.2

Species in the Ridge

Trees	*Acacia leucophloea*, *Acacia Senegal*, *Azadirachta indica*, *Balanites roxburghii*, *Butea monosperma*, *Holoptelia integrifolia*, *Flacourtia indica*, *Maytenus senegalensis*, *Prosopis cineraria*
Shrubs	*Capparis deciduas*, *Calotropis procera*, *Grewia tenax*, *Ziziphus nummularia*
Herbs/ Grasses	*Aristida spp.*, *Crotolaria burhia*, *Eragrostis spp.*, *Heteropogon contortus*

The Ridge and its neighbouring hilly tracts represent the characteristic, natural flora of the state. The vegetation presents an open appearance as the trees and shrubs are widely spaced. The bulk of the vegetation consists of co-dominant, spinous shrubs and trees, capable of great drought resistance, and may be classified under two broad categories:

(i) Permanent vegetation occurring throughout the year.

(ii) Temporary vegetation consisting of the annuals growing mainly during the short, rainy season.

Correspondingly the Ridge, vegetation presents two distinct, seasonal aspects:

(a) The summer and winter aspect when most of the trees and some of the shrubs flower and soil is devoid of any ground cover.

(b) The rainy season when the vegetation is at its best and the soil, which is otherwise bare, is covered by a vivid green carpet of temporary vegetation. The latter flower and fruit in a short time and disappear as soon as the surface layer of the soil dries up and winter sets in.

The permanent vegetation is xerophytic in character and shows various xeromorphic features such as thick tomentum, succulence, stunted growth, coating of wax, thick cuticle, protected stomata, etc. The plants occur in open, clump formations with plenty of vacant spaces between trees and shrubs. Most of the woody species of the Ridge and those growing in similar arid regions regenerate vegetatively by throwing out root suckers and coppicing shoots and some propagate even by natural layering. These features appear to be common in dry situations. The noteworthy examples are: *Prosopis cineraria*, *Acacia spp.*, *Butea monosperma*, *Balanites roxburghii*, *Grewia tenax*, *Capparis decidua*, *Ziziphus nummularia* and *Anogeissus pendula*. The trees comprising the perennial vegetation of Ridge are both indigenous and introduced. The former are represented primarily by *Prosopis cineraria*, *Acacia leucophloea*, *A. modesta*, *A. senegal*, *A. nilotica ssp. indica*, *A. catechu*, *Butea monosperma*, *Anogeissus pendula*, *Salvadora oleoides*, *Wrightia tinctoria*, *Cordia dichotoma*, *Ehretia laevis*, *Tecomella undulata*, and *Balanites roxburghii*. Among the latter, the most noteworthy example is *Prosopis juliflora*, an evergreen, spiny, tree, which has the capacity to survive in harsh environments. This tree is so useful, that Reddy (1978) stated that if Teak has been the Royal Timber, *Prosopis juliflora* has been the Loyal Timber of the poor. It is very common on the Ridge and has become a part and parcel of the native flora. Other successfully introduced trees are: *Azadirachta indica*, whose self-sown seedlings are common, *Feronia limonia* occurring in a semi-wild state, *Dalbergia sissoo*, *Parkinsonia aculeata*, *Cassia fistula*, *Albizia lebbeck*, *A. amara*, *Mitragyna parvifolia*, *Holoptelea integrifolia*, and *Prosopis glandulosa*. Among the shrubs, *Jatropha gossypifolia*, native of Brazil, and *Opuntia dillenii*, native of South America, have become naturalised on the Ridge.

The thorny shrubs occur in widely spaced clumps supporting a number of twiners and climbers. Of these, *Capparis sepiaria* is very common and abundant, growing alone or associated with *Grewia tenax*, *Securinega leucopyrus*, *Carissa opaca*, *Flacourtia indica*, *Maytenus senegalensis*, *Clerodendrum phlomidis*, and *Capparis decidua*. Other shrubs in localised, isolated patches include *Dichrostachys cinerea*, *Mimosa hamata* and *Diospyros cordifolia*. There are no epiphytes because of adverse climate but few lianas like *Maerua oblongiafolia*, and *Cryptostegia grandiflora* are known to occur on the common trees. A very common and gregarious undershrub *Adhatoda zeylanica*, grows as a co-dominant with *Capparis sepiaria*. It flowers from December to March and adds to the winter aspect of the Ridge. Other undershrubs which come into vigour and growth after the rains are: *Indigofera tinctoria*, *I. astragalina*, *Tephrosia purpurea*, *T. villosa*, *Hibiscus ovalifolius*, and *Ocimum americanum* (Naithani *et. al.*, 2004).

The Asola area is dominated by *Anogeissus pendula* and *Butea monosperma*, although other trees and shrubs like *Acacia leucophloea*, *Grewia tenax*, *Balanites aegyptiaca*, *Wrightia tinctoria*, and *Dalbergia sissoo* are also common. In some places like Jonapur, Gittorni, and Aayanagar, Acacia tortilis has invaded.

A marked change is induced by the monsoon when the Ridge wears a new cloak of green and the whole ground is carpeted with a variety of herbs, with a vivid green colour. These plants complete their life history in three to four months after the rains. They help in increasing the humus content of the soil and help in extending the vegetation to barren areas. The commonest and most successful annuals are: *Triumfetta rhomboidea*, *Corchorus aestuans*, *Tribulus terrestris*, *Cleome viscosa*, *Trianthema portulacastrum*, *Vernonia cinerea*, *Bidens biternata*, *Blainvillea latifolia*, *Trichodesma amplexicaule*, *Sesamum orientale*, *Martynia annua*, *Elytraria acaulis*, *Peristrophe paniculata*, *Justicia simplex*, *Boerhavia diffusa*, *Digera alternifolia*, *Achyranthes aspera*, *Pupalia lappcea*, *Euphorbia hirta*, *Phyllanthus fraternus*, *Asphodelus tenuifolius*, *Commelina forskalii*, *C. benghalensis*, *Cyperus rotundus*, *C. triceps*, *C. compressus*, *C. bulbosus*, *Evolvulus alsonoides*, *Heteropogon contortus*, *Melanocenchris jacquemontii*, *Cenchrus setigerus*, *C. ciliaris*, *Setaria verticillata*, *Tragus biflorus*, *Oropetium thomaeum*, *Eragrostis poaeoides*, *E. cilianensis*, *Digitaria ciliaris*, *Eleusine verticillata*, *E. compressa*, *Dichanthium annulatum*, *Brachiaria ramosa*, *Tetrapogon tenellus*, *Dactyloctenium aegyptium*, *Aristida adscensionis*, *A. hystrix*, *Chrysopogon serrulatus*, *Sporobolus diander*. Besides, a number of annual and perennial twiners and climbers add to the rainy season aspect of the Ridge, such as *Ipomoea pilosa* and other *Ipomoea spp.*, *Rivea hypocrateriformis*, *Trichosanthes cucumerina*, *Coccinia cordifolia*, *Mukia maderaspatana*, *Cayratia trifolia*, *Rhynchosia minima*, *Cryptostegia grandiflora*, *Pergularia daemia*, and *Telosma pallida* (Naithani *et. al.*, 2004).

In areas, where soil consists of gravel or a thin, superficial mantle of soil over the rock, *Oropetium thomaeum* forms a dense, tufted growth, in association with *Riccia discolor* and moss like *Fussaria spp.* All these form a pioneer plant community on the parent rock, later associated with *Cyperus triceps*, *Melanocenchris jacquemontii*, and others. *Sesamum orientale*, cultivated in the plains for its oil, has become naturalised on the Ridge along roadsides and amongst the thorny bushes and shrubs, but the seeds produced are much harder than those of the cultivated types. Amongst introduced weeds, Mart*ynia annua* thrives commonly in depressed areas or more often along roadsides and paths and *Elytraria acaulis a scapigerous*, rosette-leaved herb, grows on hilly tracts in open places and shades of bushes on gravelly or stony soil. Among monocotyledonous annuals *Commelina forskalii*, apparently a new record from the north Indian plains occurs commonly in sandy depressions and grows alone or associated with *C. benghalensis*. Both these are elegant herbs with sky-blue or bluish-violet flowers and produce aerial and underground flowers, where the top soil is moist for a slightly longer period. There are also some perennial weeds, which occur almost all round the year, such as *Calotropis procera*, *Withania somnifera*, and *Abutilon indicum*.

Among recent introductions on the sandy and silty soils of the Ridge, the following deserve mention: *Phyla nudiflora*, *Alternanthera sessilis*, *A. pungens*, *Fagonia cretica*, *Erigeron bonariensis*, *Carthamus oxyacantha*, and *Nicotiana plumbaginifolia*.

7.1.4.3 The Plains

Leaving aside the Yamuna flood plain (*Khadar*) and the ridge, the entire area of the NCT of Delhi is categorised as *Bangar* or the plain. A major proportion of the area of Delhi is plain and on this area are located Delhi, New Delhi and Delhi cantonment along with a vast stretch of numerous villages. The land of the plain is mostly fertile.

7.1.5 Fauna

Delhi had diverse fauna in the past, which has now become the victim of exploding metropolis. There have been records of the presence of lions in and around Delhi region in 1875 (Gogate, 2001). The Gazetteer of Delhi District of 1912 described principal wild animals found in Delhi, *viz.*, blackbuck, chinkara, wild boar, hyena, wolf, fox, jackal, hare, monkey, porcupine, and occasional sittings of leopards. Black bucks were then seen in large herds, sometimes with over one hundred heads, in the Najafgarh tract and the south of Ballabgarh. Foxes and jackals abounded everywhere. Porcupines were common and they infested vegetable and horticulture gardens. Hog deer and Chinkaras were seen in small numbers. In 1877, measures were taken to discourage shooting on the Ridge during the close season from 15th March to 15th September with tax proposals for killing wild game e.g., 8 annas on Grey and Black Partridge and Re. 1 on Hare. Rewards were paid for destruction of dangerous animals; for leopards Rs. 5, for male wolves Rs. 3, and Rs. 5 for female wolves were given. Of the poisonous snakes, cobra and krait were the most common. Wild animals then caused considerable number of human deaths.

Birds listed in the Gazetteer of 1912 included:— partidges, pigeons, teals, ducks, geese, barbets, sunbirds, Indian roller, kingfisher, hornbill, hoopoe, nightjar, hawk, cuckoo, crow, parakeets, owls, owlets, eagles, vultures, falcons, kites, black drongo, mynas, shrikes, aurioles, tailorbirds, doves, weaver birds, fly-catchers, blue throats, robins, swallows, swifts, babblers, bulbul, chats, larks, wagtails, herons, coots, moorhens, Indian dartyer birds, cormorants, sand pipers, terns, spoonbills, adjutants, storks, egrets, etc.

Many kinds of fish were found in river Yamuna *viz.*, *mahseer, rohu, bachwa, mulley, tengra, silund, mohi, mirga, kalbans, chilwa* and *gunch*. The best-known fishing ground then was Okhla. The entire river was infested with corcodiles, both *gharial* and the *magar*. Turtle abounded in both river and lakes.

Many faunal species have now become the victims of exploding metropolis. One can no longer see black bucks, hyenas, and chinkaras in the forests of Delhi, nor can be seen the fish and crocodiles in the Yamuna. Yet, there still are large numbers of wildlives in the forests of Delhi. Delhi now has 32 species of mammals, 25 species of reptiles, and 434 species of resident and other birds. In all 585 species of vertebra and 1202 species of invertebra have been listed in Delhi by the Zoological Survey of India in 1997 (Kumar, 1997).

7.2 Green Cover and its Current Status

Forests are life support system of nature that sustain various life forms on earth. Tree cover is essential for soil and water conservation, climate amelioration and a host of other watershed and ecological functions. It serves to meet both economic and ecological needs of the society.

In urban areas, trees and green spaces play an important role in improving the living conditions by providing a host of climate buffering services, besides contributing to the aesthetic appeal of cities. Without trees cities are hotter and drier, the air pollution is worse, the wind stronger, dust more damaging, energy consumption increases and people less comfortable and less healthy (Tewari, 1994).

With the ever-increasing trend of urbanisation, the burden on Delhi's environment and green cover has steadily increased. It needs to increase its green cover at a faster rate. According to the State of Forests Report (2003), Delhi has 170 sq. km. of forest cover and 98 sq. km. of tree cover (Table 7.4 and Table 7.5), which constitutes 18.07 per cent of geographical area under green cover (Figure 7.2) much less than 33 per cent as envisaged by National Forest Policy, 1988.

FIGURE 7.2

Forest Map of Delhi

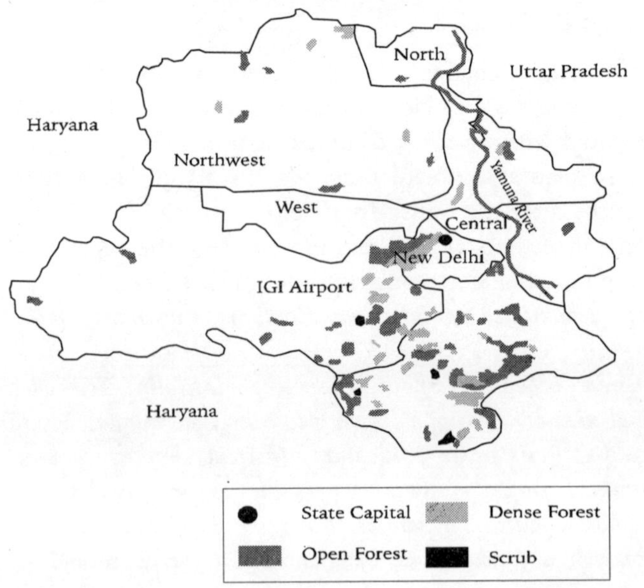

Source: SFR, 2003.

TABLE 7.3

Recorded Forest Area of Delhi

Reserve Forest (R.F.)	78 km^2
Protected Forest (P.F.)	7 km^2
Total	85 km^2
Per cent of total geographical area of the state	5.73%
Per cent of total forest area of the country	0.01%

Source: SFR, 2003.

TABLE 7.4

Forest Cover of Delhi

Dense Forest	52 km^2
Open Forest	118 km^2
Total	170 km^2

Source: SFR, 2003.

TABLE 7.5

Tree Cover of Delhi

Culturable Non-Forest Area (CNFA)	1278 km^2
No. of trees per ha (CNFA)	24.9
Tree Cover	98 km^2

Source: SFR, 2003.

FIGURE 7.3

Details of the Forest Area

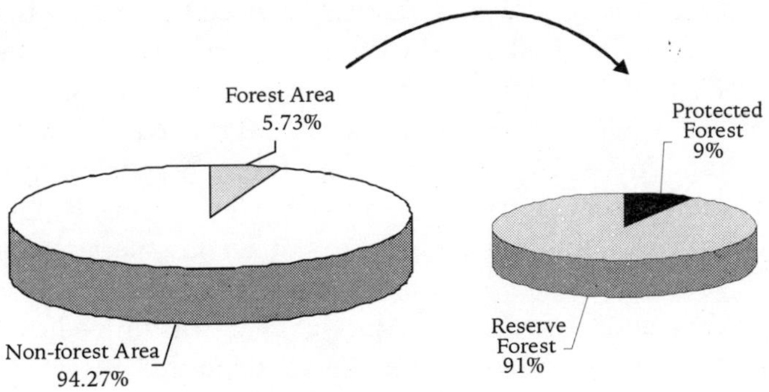

The district-wise forest cover of Delhi is also presented in table 7.6. It reveals that 78.80 per cent of the forest cover is in south and south-west Delhi and New Delhi alone having a total area of 134.10 sq. km under forest cover. On the other hand east Delhi, which supports one-third of the city's population, has a forest cover of mere 2.94 sq. km. Similarly north as well as northeast Delhi also have very less green cover. It shows that the tree cover is unevenly distributed, although the capital has 24.9 trees per ha., as against the national average of 11. Thus, there is a need to expand the green cover to west and north Delhi as well besides the eastern region.

FIGURE 7.4

Distribution of Forest Cover

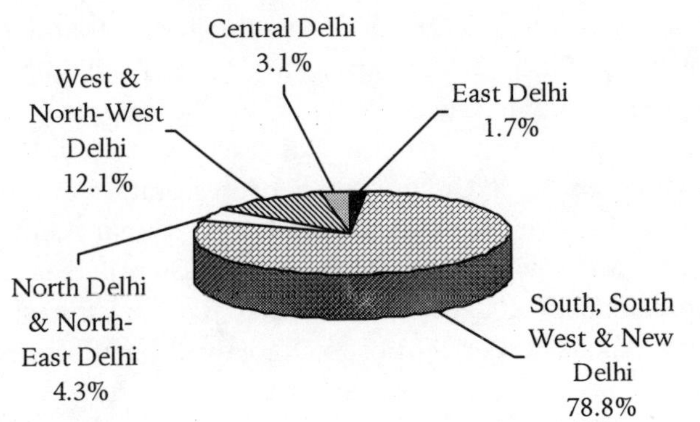

7.2.1 Management Initiatives

Although Delhi seems to be overwhelmingly green at some places but most of its area is devoid of green cover.

TABLE 7.6

District-wise Forest Cover of Delhi

District	*Geographic Area (Km^2)*	*Forest Cover*				*Per cent*	*Change*
		Very Dense	*Moderately Dense*	*Open Forest*	*Total Forest*		
Central Delhi	24.68	0	2.8	2.4	5.2	21.07	2.93
East Delhi	63.76	0	0.98	1.96	2.94	4.61	1.37
New Delhi	34.90	0	6.97	7.57	14.54	41.66	4.81
North Delhi	59.16	0	3.02	1.68	4.7	7.94	1.52
North East Delhi	60.29	0	1.1	1.6	2.7	4.48	0.85
North West Delhi	440.31	0	6.63	8.84	15.47	3.51	7.1
South Delhi	249.85	0	13.88	26.73	40.61	9.66	10.52
South West Delhi	420.54	0	15.02	63.93	78.95	31.60	26.44
West Delhi	129.52	0	1.62	3.44	5.06	3.91	3.3
Total	**1,483.01**	**0**	**52.02**	**118.15**	**170.17**	**11.46**	**58.84**

Source: SFR, 2003.

The spatial air pollution pattern confirms the number of existing hotspots impacting Delhi's dwindling flora. Various initiatives have been taken to manage this in the past. As a result, a large portion of the ridge was declared as protected zone to enhance the protection and conservation of the city's floral and faunal diversity. Some part of the Southern Ridge has been converted into the sanctuary, created artificially through innovative measures. Legal status of sanctuary was uncertain till 1986 when 1,883 ha community land of Asola, Sahurpur, and Maidangarhi villages was notified in 1986 and 867 ha. land in Bhati was notified in 1991 as sanctuary. Subsequently, large chunks of land on the ridge have also been notified as reserve forest under section 4 of the Indian Forest Act, 1927 in 1994 on the recommendations of Lovraj Committee.

The area was adversely affected by the mining activities undergoing on Haryana side all along the boundary of sanctuary. Since 2002, mining in Haryana adjoining the state of Delhi has been stopped by the Supreme Court order. Recently, a scheme has been initiated by the Government of NCT of Delhi for restoration of Bhatti mines through Eco-task force, Forest Department and Centre for Environment (University of Delhi). Every year approximately 200 ha. area is taken up for afforestation work. About 60 per cent of total area will be afforested by indigenous trees as well as medicinal plants by using appropriate soil and moisture conservation techniques, 30 per cent area will be developed as grass lands in consultation with Centre for Environment to increase biomass and organic matter in the soil and the remaining 10 per cent area consisting of abandoned mine pits to be developed as natural water bodies.

The enactment of Delhi Tree Preservation Act, 1994 was another step taken for the preservation of existing trees. It laid down heavy penalties on individuals, posh clubs, educational and religious institutions, etc., if found culprit of tree felling.

Besides all this, the Greening Delhi Action Plan is regularly launched every year to undertake additional plantation in Delhi. It has brought different controlling agencies together for afforestation in a coordinated manner. A task force has been constituted under the chairmanship of the Conservator of Forests, Government of NCT, Delhi to delineate zone wise plantation plans and implementation mechanism. Since then, large areas of the city have been brought under plantation schemes and thereby the total area under green cover in Delhi has increased significantly (Anon, 2001b).

The plantation scales in the recent past have increased from around one lakh seedlings per year in mid-nineties to about 11 lakhs presently (Anon, 2004b). But the survival rate of plantation is low due to biotic pressure and developmental activities. However, there is still tremendous scope to enhance the green areas in the city and improve the quality of the existing green spaces designated and being developed under the Master Plan of Delhi. The target for tree plantation in Delhi for 2007-08 by all greening agencies has been fixed at 18.9 lakhs which includes 5.0 lakh seedlings to be distributed free of cost.

7.2.2 *Past Afforestation*

Plantation forestry has been known in India since the middle of the 19th century and the oldest plantation date back to 1842 when teak was artificially raised in Nilambur (Kerala). The other species is *Eucalyptus globolus*. As per the municipal records of Delhi about 3000 neem (*Azadirachta indica*) and Babul (*Acacia nilotica ssp. indica*) were planted between 1878 and 1879. However, the real impetus came in 1912 when Delhi became the capital and Lutyens arrived to design the new city. The Delhi Town Planning Committee and the newly formed Delhi Administration took up afforestation of the Delhi Ridge. Afforestation of the North Ridge began in 1913, and a year later, experimental afforestation commenced on the New Delhi Ridge. Initially planting was confined to indigenous species such as *Prosopis cineraria, Acacia nilotica ssp. indica, Salvadora oleoides* and *S.persica*. *Prosopis juliflora* was introduced later, which has shown good drought resistant properties. Gradually the Ridge was covered with this, and by 1938 had more trees as a part of forest community. In recent past seeds of *Prosopis juliflora* were broadcast in Bhati mine area in 1991-92 and in 1996-1997, Forest Department planted 1,77,658 tree saplings in the Ridge (Naithani *et. al.*, 2004).

The major portion of the Delhi Ridge falls in the arid and semi-arid tracts. Many sites, *viz.*, Asola, Deoli, Bhati are quite inhospitable for the growth of forest crop and special efforts are therefore, needed for afforestation on an extensive scale.

Trees like *Acacia catechu, A. farnesiana, A. leucophloea, A. modesta, A. nilotica ssp. indica, A. senegal, A. tortalis, Ailanthus excessa, Albizia amara, A. lebbeck, Anogeissus pendula, Azadirachta indica, Balanites roxburghii, Bombax ceiba, Butea monosperma, Cassia fistula, Cordia dichotoma, C. rothii, Crataeva adansonii ssp. odora, Dalbergia sissoo, Dichrostachys cinerea, Diospyros cordifolia, Ehretia laevis, Eucalyptus microtheca, Feronia limonia, Ficus benghalensis, F. palmata, F. racemosa, F. religiosa, F. virens, Flacourtia indica, Holoptelea integrifolia, Leucaena leucocephala, Manilkara hexandra, Mitragyna parvifolia, Moringa oleifera, Pithecellobium dulce, Parkinsonia aculeate, Prosopis glanduiosa, P. juliflora. P. cineraria, Salvadora oleoides, Sesbania sesban, Syzygium cumini, Tecomella undulata* and *Wrightia tinctoria* are already known to occur in the Ridge area.

7.2.3 Impediments

The presence of adequate number of trees on the avenues and in parks enhances the city's physical environment and aesthetic beauty. However, the forests and tree cover always remain vulnerable to development activities, new townships, upcoming new residential colonies, over bridges, illegal constructional activities and various other forms of developmental interventions. For instance, Delhi Metro Rail Corporation project that comprises of a network of underground, elevated and surface corridors is also adding to the concretisation of the area. Although it is an eco-friendly project and the necessity of the time, yet it has spoiled the aesthetic view of the city. Besides this, it has even done harm to the ground water level because thousands of heavy stones have been filled up along the river that prevents the water movement beneath the land leading to depletion of ground water level (Kumar, 2004).

Another fact is that the provisions and plans made by the first Master Plan (MPD) for a network of green areas have been grossly violated. Large chunks of land earmarked for recreational use have been lost to other uses, considerable sections have been encroached upon by squatters, DDA has increasingly gone in for exotic, fast growing species of low ecological value and worse of all, natural forest areas have been systematically converted into parks (Anon., 1995).

The MPD-62 had allotted 23.7 per cent of the urbanisable land for recreational use. This was to encompass district, regional and neighbourhood parks, refuse grounds and city forests. The greening of city was conceived as a system of linked open spaces and district parks penetrating through residential and work areas with the development of natural features such as the Ridge and the river front. But during the implementation of the plan (1961-1981), 34 per cent of all the allocated green space was taken over for all kinds of development. The green zones have been desecrated by road widening, construction, illegal encroachment, garbage dumping and grazing (Anon., 1995). According to the State of Environment Report (Anon., 2001a), both plans could not be achieved due to lack of clear policies and strategies and also because of poor implementation and monitoring.

In addition to this, the involvement of multiple agencies like forest department, CPWD, DDA and MCD in enhancing and maintaining the green space further aggravates the existing threats due to lack of coordination in making uniform planning and implementation. They even have competing and conflicting responsibilities.

Other constraints include the lack of lands, environmental stress and lack of trained manpower, extension and communication. The lack of adequate infrastructure facilities including tractors, tankers, trucks etc., is an added impediment for proper development and upkeep of forests, tree cover and wildlife. The limited availability of land is a key constraint to the efforts of increasing the forest cover. Environmental stress refers to the site conditions that reduce the vigour of many tree species and increase their susceptibility to disease and pest infestation. Urban trees are subject to poor soils, air and water pollution. Another important constraint is the lack of training, extension and communication, which require practical approaches to involve citizens.

7.2.4 Working Agencies and their Role

The Master plan of Delhi (2001) has earmarked an area of 8,422 hectares for green purposes out of a total area of 44,777 hectares. This area is being managed by various government and non-government agencies, *viz.*, Forest Department, Delhi Development Authority (DDA), Municipal Corporation of Delhi (MCD), Public Works Department, Horticulture, Development Department, Central Public Works Department (CPWD), New Delhi Municipal Committee (NDMC), Delhi Cantonment Board (DCB), Irrigation and Flood Control Department (IFCD), Delhi Transport Corporation (DTC), Delhi Jal Board (DJB), Delhi State Industrial Development Corporation (DSIDC), Resident Welfare Associations and Eco task force. The achievements and targets of these agencies are presented in Table 7.7.

The Forest Department has taken up the work of development of forest areas across the city. It has been actively involved in the protection and preservation of trees in Delhi by taking up multifarious activities to improve and increase the forest cover through massive plantation along railway tracks, drains, roadsides, Gaon Sabha lands, city forests, ridge, Asola Bhati wildlife sanctuary and along the banks of the Yamuna. The department is also carrying out enrichment planting in ridge area to augment the natural regeneration. It has identified about 1,400 acres in different zones to develop into mini forests in addition to the ridge. The department

TABLE 7.7

Achievements and Targets of Greening Agencies

(Saplings in lacs)

S. No.	Agency	Targets 2006-07	Achievements 2006-07	Targets 2007-08
1.	Forest Department	3.60	3.50	4.00
2.	DDA	1.80	1.76	1.85
3.	MCD	1.75	1.99	2.00
4.	Eco Task force	1.40	1.40	2.00
5.	P.W.D (Hort.)	0.45	0.36	0.45
6.	DSIDC	1.00	0.55	1.00
7.	Development Department (Hort.)	0.50	0.53	0.60
8.	N.D.M.C.	0.20	0.11	0.20
9.	C.P.W.D.	0.20	0.23	0.25
10.	Delhi Jal Board	0.21	0.42	0.25
11.	Airport Authority of India	0.20	0.00	0.05
12.	I&FCD	0.60	0.54	0.60
13.	Delhi Cantonment Board	0.10	0.12	0.15
14.	DTC	0.03	0.006	0.01
15.	Health Department	0.02	0.02	0.04
16.	Indraprastha Generation Company Ltd.	0.15	0.04	0.15
17.	Education Department	0.10	0.12	0.15
18.	Delhi Metro Rail	0.10	0.10	0.15
	Total	**12.41**	**11.796**	**13.9**
Free distribution of saplings		4.70	6.79	5.00
Grand total		**17.11**	**18.586**	**18.90**

Source: Greening Delhi Action Plan 2007-08.

TABLE 7.8

Nine New City Forests

Village	Area in Ha	District
Issapur	66.25	SW
Rewla Khanpur	22.85	SW
Kharkhari Jatmal	50.00	SW
Sultanpur Dabbas	24.76	NW
Auchindi	0.5	NW
Mungesh Pur	13.5	NW
Qutab Garh	27.77	NW
Hindon Cut Ghazipur	5.0	East
Harewali	24.80	NW

has set up a target of planting 3.50 lakh saplings and distributing 4.50 lakh saplings to various institutions in the current year.

Besides, the Department of Forests and Wildlife is also developing nine new city forests over and above the existing fourteen city forests (2.88 lakh seedlings) which will be complteted within the current financial year.

DDA is another agency that plays a major role in making Delhi green, as about 5,050 ha area is under its jurisdiction. Its greening project involves development of regional parks, district parks, neighbourhood parks, city forests, historical landscapes, sport complexes and green belts. If a residential colony is developed, the maintenance of green-park in that area is shifted to the local civic bodies while the bigger green areas are retained by DDA for up-keep and maintenance. In addition to this, DDA has taken up the work of development of Yamuna River front into a green area. It is also working in collaboration with the Department of Botany, Delhi University to develop a Biodiversity park along the Yamuna river-bed in North Delhi. It has fixed a target of planting 1.80 lakh trees during 2006-07 (Anon., 2007).

The Municipal Corporation of Delhi (MCD) undertakes plantation in various areas such as schools, parks, bus stands and along road sides. It has also set a target of planting 1.75 lakh saplings in the ongoing year (Anon., 2007).

The New Delhi Municipal Committee (NDMC) has nearly 42 sq. km. area under its jurisdiction. It encompasses Lutyen's Delhi with tree plantation along the wide roads, apart from residential areas, parks, etc. It proposes to plant 20,000 trees during 2006-07 (Anon., 2007).

Other agencies involved in plantation work include the Central Public Works Department, Department of Horticulture, Public Works Department, Irrigation and Flood Control Department, Health Department, Delhi Transport Corporation, Delhi Jal Board, and Delhi Cantonment Board, which are responsible for undertaking plantations in their respective areas.

Thus, under plantation programme the government agencies with the help of Residents Welfare Associations (RWAs), Market Traders Associations (MTAs), Non-governmental organisations and schools have planted 90 lakh seedlings in the last four years (*http:// delhigovt.nic.in/ environment.asp*).

Apart from this, 1500 Eco-clubs have been established in various schools/colleges of Delhi. These clubs conduct various environmental activities every year. These activities include motivating students to undertake plantations and for this Forest Department provide free seedlings.

7.3 Greening of Delhi—Vision 2015

In the next ten years Delhi should become one of the most green and clean city of the world providing its people a safe and healthy environment thus setting an example of a modern metropolis. The twin objectives of greening Delhi and combating pollution can be achieved in a meaningful way only through combined efforts of various Government and non-government agencies and the active participation of the people. Following strategic actions have been suggested in this regard.

7.3.1 Expanding Green Area

The geographical area of Delhi is 1,483 sq. km., out of this 268 sq. km. or 18.07 of percent area is under the forest and tree cover (SFR, 2003). In the existing scenario there is no scope of expanding the green cover because of non-availability of land for this purpose. Around eleven lakh seedlings are being planted every year by the various agencies in their respective areas to expand the green cover (Anon., 2004b). Although these small blocks of plantations, road side trees, gardens and parks are providing good services to the people even than they cannot be compared with the natural forests which have altogether different composition and purpose to serve. Another problem with such trees or plantations is that sooner or later they become prey to some development activity, *viz.*, road widening, pavement repair, social gathering, etc. The needs and the perception of the society keep on changing with the passage of time and trees are not a priority for most of the people. Thus there is no possibility of expanding green area through such activities. However, if there is a will there is a way to achieve this. The two possible options are mentioned below:

i. Developing 1 km. wide green belt on both sides of the Yamuna River; and

ii. Acquisition of atleast 2 km. wide strip of land along Haryana border and developing it into forest.

In the present scenario both of these options may look wild or absurd. Although land acquisition is an expensive propostion but both the dreams can be made true if government is really keen to make Delhi green.

The flood plain area of Yamuna River constitutes 97 sq. km. (Anon., 2000). Agriculture is practiced extensively along the stretch of river and most of the native vegetation has been cleared for agriculture and farming. The areas not fit for agriculture are used as grazing grounds when flood water recedes.

The advantage with Yamuna bank is that most of the area is still under the possession of government. However, the area is getting decreased day by day due to encroachments and developmental activities and if the same trend continues, the whole area might get converted into the jungle of concrete after few years. The government should take a bold decision of handing all available area to the forest department to plant suitable species on both sides of the river. It would be a great service to the people of the whole country and shall be remembered in the years to come.

The plantation of native trees, shrubs, reeds and grasses along the natural levee would check erosion and bank cutting and help in restoration of the floodplains. An increase in habitat diversity and the vegetation is expected to revive the natural fisheries as well as other biodiversity (birds, amphibia, reptiles, molluscs and macro-invertebrates) that once occurred in the area (Gopal, 2003). The loss of agricultural production will be more than compensated by the potential for fisheries and the production of forage and fuel. Additional benefits will accrue in terms of improvement in water quality due to the reduction in the application of agrochemicals and through nutrient transformation in the restored floodplain wetlands. A programme of rehabilitation by providing alternate opportunities for livelihood to people who own or cultivate the land in floodplain should be formulated. Efforts can be made to involve these people in the restoration and follow-up management activities, and motivate them to take up fisheries and prawn culture that are economically profitable.

Since river Yamuna is an ecological feature with high conservation value for NCT of Delhi and its surrounding area, its safeguard from encroachments and urbanisation is of paramount importance. The rehabilitation of people who cultivate there is but a small price the government has to shell out for the survival of the Yamuna till posterity.

As suggested above, after taking over the complete flood plain area of river Yamuna by Forest Department and rehabilitating the oustees, the actual area available needs to be worked out and annual targets for future plantations should be fixed including the 1 km. wide green belt on both sides of the river Yamuna.

The Delhi Ridge, an extension of Aravalli range, serves as green lungs for NCT Delhi and is ecologically very important with immense conservation value. The original area of the ridge is believed to be 15,046 ha which is at present 7,782 ha. (some refer it as 7777 ha. for the sake of convenience). There are more than 580 species of vertebrates and 1200 species of invertebrates that inhabit the ridge area besides supporting a significant population of resident and migratory waterfowl and more than 400 species of birds in the wetland areas. Due to rapid urbanisation and encroachment the ridge area has not only been severely ravaged but also reduced to 4 remnant patches which have ultimately been declared reserved forests in 1994.

Although the Ridge area has been regularly planted and restoration initiatives of the department including curbing of fresh encroachments and bestowing reserved status have led to a gradual increase in green cover but still fresh plantation of suitable species at regular intervals is needed for restoration of these 4 remnant ridges and included in the annual plan of operations of respective departments who exercise control over these ridges.

Apart from increasing the green cover, another challenge is to protect Delhi from desertification from southwest direction, which can be checked only by massive afforestation on private and public lands through some workable mechanism. The state government should acquire atleast 2 km. wide strip of land all along the border of Haryana and develop it into a green belt. The cost of acquiring land for green belt may seem high at present but it would go a long way in ameliorating the environment in and around Delhi in the years to come. It would serve the dual purpose of checking expansion of desertification from Haryana side as well as protecting the flood plains from further encroachment and degradation otherwise the days are not far when Delhites will have to drive 200-300 km. to get a feel of forest.

7.3.2 Raising Plantation in New Areas

The total area of NCT of Delhi is 1483 sq. km. An analysis of changing land use show that although forest area has increased to 7.5 per cent, the agricultural land has fallen to 32 per cent of the total area while non-agricultural land has risen to 68 per cent of the total in the last decade. Table 7.9 shows the changing land use pattern over the last decade.

TABLE 7.9

Changing Land Use Pattern

Land Use	*1990-91*		*2000-01*	
	Area (Sq. km.)	*Per cent of total area*	*Area (Sq. km.)*	*Per cent of total area*
Total Area	1483		1483	
Forest Area	16	1	111	7.5
Non-agricultural land (including build up area)	742	50	897	60.5
Other uncultivated land	128		112	
Fallow land	128	49	115	32
Cropped Area	469		248	

Source: State of the Environment and Action Points, Delhi Development Report, March 4, 2005, NCT Delhi.

From a settlement of 7 lakh in 1947, Delhi's population has increased to 138 lakh in 2001 and is expected to increase to 224 lakh by 2021 thereby increasing the need for urbanisation manifold. Therefore there will be tremendous pressure on land for the burgeoning populace and is expected to be in the range of 25,000-30,000 ha. Already 50 per cent of the land is under urbanised category while 10 per cent is under natural features like water bodies, drains etc., which need to be conserved. The supportive infrastructure for the ever increasing population will obviously need to be developed from the balance 40 per cent land. Hence at least 50 per cent of the uncultivable land including fallow land and cropped up area has to be earmarked for greening Delhi and saved from encroachments by enacting suitable legislations.

The Table 7.10 below shows the alarming situation lurking round the corner of the next decade to enable us to come out of the slumber.

TABLE 7.10

Alarming Situation

S.No.	*Land Use*	*Area (Sq. km.)*	*Per cent of Total Area*
1.	Total Geographical Area	1,483	—
2.	Build up Area (as per IRS IC LISS III Satellite)	702	47
3.	Natural features to be conserved (Forest, water bodies, drains)	195	13
4.	Sub total (Build up + Natural Features)	897	60
5	Balance land available to NCT	586	40
6	At least 50 per cent to be earmarked for afforestation/greening Delhi through requisite regulations	293	20

Afforestation of all available areas such as waste lands, parks and gardens, educational institutions, road sides, along railway lines, ponds, water bodies, industrial areas, cremation grounds and other vacant lands must be done on a priority basis. Stress should be laid on development of multi-strata forests. For avenue plantations there could be single to three lines, shorter trees close to road and shade giving tall trees away from the road. Post plantation care and regular monitoring should be there for ensuring higher survival.

7.3.2.1 Pollution Hardy Species

The tremendous influx of population, heavy pressure on city resources, environmental degradation in terms of air, noise and water pollution has earned Delhi the dubious distinction of being the fourth most polluted city in the world. This has led to a deterioration of ambient air quality, inversion phenomena and higher incidence of respiratory diseases.

There has also been a significant increase of suspended particulate matter (SPM) due to air pollution. The city which boasts of a registered vehicle population more than the combined registered vehicle population of other three mega polis *viz*. Mumbai, Chennai, and Kolkata, noise pollution of the city is an obvious corollary. The changing land use pattern due to urbanisation has affected the recharge of groundwater too. Urban run-offs collect toxic compounds from sewage, vehicular exhaust, industrial pollution, etc and severely degrade the water quality. The increase of domestic consumption of water from 401.3 million kilolitres in 90-91 to 929.6 million kilolitres in 2001-02 at a growth of 131 per cent has compounded the problem. The amount of wastewater generated has increased from 260 million litres per day in 1961 to 930 million litres in 1991 to 2650 million litres per day in 2001 despite the fact that more than 45 per cent of population currently has no access to sewerage service. The growing lag between increased wastewater discharges and treatment capacities are bound to further worsen the quality of existing water sources.

Therefore there is an urgent need to address these issues as well. The detailed mitigation measures shall be available in the relevant chapter on environment. But forests are traditionally known to act as a sink for many pollutants, air purifier and supplier of oxygen. The vegetation cleans the air, conserves soil and moisture and also acts as a moderator of climate. One hectare of woodland (about 1000 trees) absorbs 3.7 tonnes of carbon dioxide from atmosphere and releases 2.5 tonnes of life sustaining oxygen. A full grown Peepal tree is, for instance, estimated to give out 600 kg. of oxygen in 24 hours. Thus it can be safely concluded that forest cover help in amelioration of environment in following ways.

- Effective Carbon sink.
- Green lungs of the city.
- Acts as dust filter/collector.
- Act as a shelter belt and dissipates sound/ noise.
- Pollution scavenger.
- Absorbs gases and gather particulate matter.

Planting of such species will be useful for the air pollution control. Thus tolerant plants, which can withstand ill effects of pollution, could be used to landscape polluted area. Similarly plants, identified for dust trapping ability, without having negative effects on its growth and development, could be used as dust traps. Table 7.11 presents the list of pollution resistant species, which can easily be adapted to Delhi's environment.

TABLE 7.11

List of Pollution Hardy Species

S. No.	*Trees*	*Shrubs*	*Herbs and Grasses*
1.	*Acacia leucophloea*	*Adhatoda zeylanica*	*Argemone mixicana*
2.	*A. modesta*	*Calotropis procera*	*Dichanthium annulatum*
3.	*A. nilotica ssp. indica*	*Capparis decidua*	*Euphorbia hirta*
4.	*A. senegal*	*Carissa opaca*	*Leucus aspera*
5.	*A. tortilis*	*Grewia tenax*	*Ocimum basilicum*
6.	*Albizia lebbeck*	*Ipomoea carnea*	-
7.	*Ailanthus excelsa*	*Maytenus senegalensis*	-
8.	*Anogeissus pendula*	*Ricinus communis*	-
9.	*Azadirachta indica*	*Salvadora oleoides*	-
10.	*Balanites aegyptiaca*	*Solanum surattense*	-
11.	*Bombax ceiba*	*Ziziphus nummularia*	-
12.	*Butea monosperma*	-	-
13.	*Cassia fistula*	-	-
14.	*Cordia dichotoma*	-	-
15.	*Dalbergia sissoo*	-	-
16.	*Ehretia laevis*	-	-
17.	*Ficus benghalensis*	-	-
18.	*F. racemosa*	-	-
19.	*F. religiosa*	-	-
20.	*F. virens*	-	-
21.	*Holoptelea integrifolia*	-	-
22.	*Leucaena leucocephala*	-	-
23.	*Mimusops elengi*	-	-
24.	*Moringa oleifera*	-	-
25.	*Morus alba*	-	-
26.	*Pithecellobium dulce*	-	-
27.	*Prosopis juliflora*	-	-
28.	*Tecomella undulata*	-	-

Source: Naithani *et. al.*, 2004.

7.3.2.2 Plantation Models of Jatropha, Bamboo and Medicinal Plant

7.3.2.2.1 Jatropha

Jatropha curcas is a drought resistant, perennial, growing well on marginal and poor soil. It is easy to establish, grows relatively quickly and produce seeds for long periods. It is adapted to less fertile sites and alkaline soils and can be grown with little effort. Its water requirement is extremely low and it can stand long periods of drought by shedding most of its leaves. It prevents soil erosion and shifting of sand dunes. Thus it can play an important role in meeting the challenge of afforestation in Delhi.

Jatropha is a small, deciduous tree or shrub with smooth, grey bark, which exudes whitish coloured, watery latex when cut. Normally, it grows between 3-5 m in height but can attain a height of upto 8-10 m under favourable conditions. Flowering occurs during the wet season. The seeds mature about 3 months after flowering.

Nurseries can be set up by forest department to supply seedlings for afforestation to ensure success of plantation. Seedlings are generally planted at 2m X 2m spacing. Early growth is fast and with good rainfall conditions nursery plants may bear fruits after the first rainy season, direct sown plants after the 2nd rainy season.

The seeds are rich in oil having properties of an excellent fuel and are thus a good source of bio-diesel. Besides this, various parts of the plant are of medicinal value. In addition, the plantation removes carbon from the atmosphere, stores it in the woody tissues and assists in the build up of soil carbon. It is thus environment friendly also.

7.3.2.2.2 Bamboo

Bamboo is a cultural feature of south-east Asia. No country in the region is without an indigenous bamboo flora. Its plethora of essential uses has led to the use of term such as "bamboo culture", "green gold", "poor man's timber", "bamboo friend of the people" and "the cradle to coffin timber". It is the fastest growing plant amongst the woody species, attaining harvestable maturity in less than five years. In India 120 species belonging to 23 genera are distributed (Naithani, 1993). *Dendrocalamus strictus* and *Bambusa bambos* (*B. arundinaecea*) are the most commonly planted species in the country. Figure 7.5 presents different plantation techniques of Bamboo.

An experiment conducted at the Forestry Research Centre (FRC) of The Energy and Resource Institute (TERI), Gaul Pahari, Gurgaon, Haryana, showed that *Dendrocalamus strictus* and *Acacia nilotica ssp. indica* as mixed plantation (6mX5m) bring about significant improvements in degraded lands and demonstrated the scope of production of wood as well as bamboos in high degraded lands. The site was an agriculture land with severly eroded slopes, active soil erosion and devoid of vegetation cover. The sandy loam soil was very poor in nitrogen, phosphorous and organic carbon. Rehabilitation of mined areas through bamboo afforestation has been tried in two villages located in the upper stream of the confluence of the Ganga and the Yamuna rivers at Allahabad. In this area rampant mining of topsoil by the brick industries over long period had ravaged the land. Bamboo helped in reclaiming the degraded land and micro-watershed. It prevented the loss of topsoil, rejuvenated the degraded soil, conserved moisture, and increased the vegetal cover (Tewari and Kumar, 2002).

Recently aerial seeding was done in the Palani Reserve forest in Dindigul Forest Division, Tamilnadu. This area is classified as a degraded, dry deciduous and thorny forest. Out of the species selected for seeding, *Acacia ferruginea, A. leucophloea, A. palnifrons,* and *D. strictus* emerged as the successful species capable of withstanding the limiting factors. The high success of *D. strictus* is attributed to its ability of better withstand adverse conditions and to the presence of rhizome that facilitates recovery and reestablishment (Rao, 2002). As the conditions of Delhi are similar to Palni, the introduction of *D. strictus* may be quite useful in restoring the green cover in the degraded area.

7.3.2.2.3 Medicinal Plants

NCT of Delhi has a good potential of Medicinal plants. Out of 31 plant species, which are in high demand both in domestic and international markets eleven species are found in Delhi. These are: *Emblica officinalis, Saraca asoka, Withania sominifera, Aegle marmelos, Phyllanthus amarus, Tinospora cordifolia, Andrographis paniculata, Solanum nigrum, Rauvolfia serpentina, Asparagus racemosus* and *Ocimum sanctum*. The National Medicinal Plant Board, Government of India has recommended these species to bring into cultivation status, as these constitute a bulk of the ingredients used in the preparation of ISM & H and herbal products. The demand of raw material is increasing day by day at national as well as in global markets. Therefore, cultivation of selected species can be promoted in a big way.

The National Medicinal Plant Board has developed a medicinal Herbal Garden in the Rashtrapati Bhawan where about 200 species have been planted. The garden is elliplitical in shape, divided into eight sectors; each sector dedicated to a specific therapeutic category. These sectors represent eight organ systems, *viz.*, Digestive system, Blood and Circulatory system, Skeleto Muscular system, Skin Care system, Urinogenital system, Respiratory system, Inflammations and fevers and Nervous system. In addition, four thematic corners are developed at the periphery of the garden. These corners have plants specifically used under *Bal Ayurvedam* (medicinal plants useful in the treatment of diseases of the children, *Nari Ayurvedam* (medicinal plants used for curing gynaecological disorders and specific cosmetic purposes), *Pashu Ayurvedam* (medicinal plants used in treating animals and cattle) and *Vruksha Ayurvedam* (medicinal plants used to prevent trees and plants from diseases and pests). The State government should develop few such gardens at appropriate places to create awareness among the society. 21 species of medicinal plants have been recommended for cultivation in Delhi (Anon, 2004a).

7.3.3 Replacement of Old Trees

Trees do not grow forever. They too die after attaining a certain age. Pollution and other developmental pressure are making their life shorter. Therefore, the old, dried, dead and over matured trees need replacement as a cyclic process to sustain environment. Following measures have been suggested by the State Forest Department under the replacement policy for trees (Anon., 2004b).

i. Identification of trees, which are likely to be replaced in the next 10 years.

ii. Replacement of these trees should be planned in such a manner that at the time of removal of old tree the new tree should atleast be 5-10 yrs old or the crown of tree is developed enough to provide shade and mature enough to withstand various climatic and biotic pressures. Make sure that there are sufficiently large trees of different species available in the nurseries, which can be transplanted at the time of need.

FIGURE 7.5

Cultivation Techniques of Bamboo

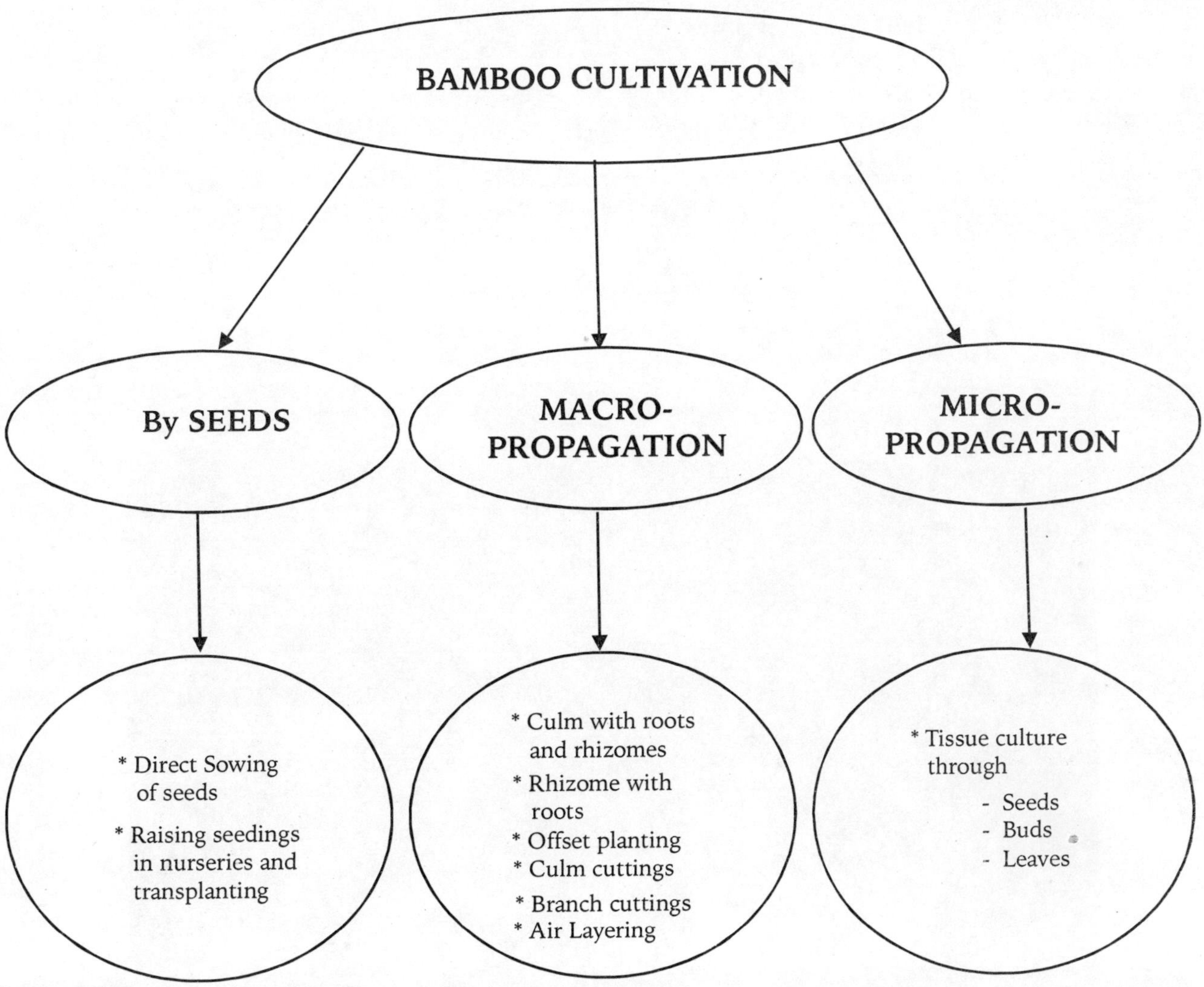

iii. Tall saplings of 6 ft. and above should be used so as to reduce establishment period and maintenance cost. Seedlings can be raised in modern nurseries using root trainers in place of polythene bags or by using gunny bags along with wire mesh placing the seedlings over a suitable platform so that roots do not strike the soil and get self pruned.

At the time of replacement planting it should be ensured that sapling of same species are planted to maintain symmetry. Sufficient protection measures should be taken to avoid casualties, which normally results into gaps and gives uneven look to the avenue. All the greening agencies should prepare an action plan for replacement of old trees, in consultation with forest department of Delhi, for their respective areas.

7.3.4 Protection and Maintenance of the Existing Trees/Green Cover

Protection and maintenance of existing tree cover requires strict enforcement of the provisions of " The Delhi Preservation of Tree Act, 1994", which regulates the felling of trees in Delhi. Delhi Ridge should be made to accommodate various combinations, in which trees, shrubs and Rerbs co-exist as multi-layered vegetation. Assisted natural regeneration cum enrichment planting can be useful in conserving and protecting the biodiversity of this region.

7.3.5 Rejuvenation of Degraded Areas

The ecologically and environmentally sensitive sites need to be specially examined and suitable provisions be made for them in the perspective plans. The reclamation of degraded Bhati areas through afforestation and grassland development being undertaken by Eco-Task Force for last couple of years has been a success and needs to be replicated. Figures 7.6 and 7.7 present the picture of Bhati mines area before and after afforestation.

7.3.6 Compensatory Plantations

Compensatory plantations should be ensured in case trees are felled on account of various developmental activities. Concept of the land bank as adopted in other states may be followed to ensure the availability of area for raising compensatory plantations. Appropriate measures already exist in Delhi Tree Preservation Act, 1994 which should be enforced strictly.

7.3.7 Public Awareness

Mass awareness programmes among the citizens about the importance of trees should be organised to motivate communities, resident welfare associations, school

FIGURE 7.6

Mine Area before Afforestation

FIGURE 7.7

Mine Area after Afforestation

children, non-government organisations, corporate sector to plant trees and engage themselves in post plantation care. The expertise of the non-governmental organisations, who are engaged in the environment related activities, can be utilised for developing various programmes and activities for afforestation and protection of existing tree cover.

7.3.8 *Coordinated Planning for City, Metropolitan Area and NCR*

Agencies whose remit is to increase and maintain green cover in Delhi needs to be capable of planning site specific projects through participation of private sector and land owners. Strategic planning for new development should include a clear definition of the boundaries of rural areas and green belts together with the type of development that can be permitted in these regions.

The agencies maintaining the trees in and around the city and planners should work together to effectively plan the greening of the capital. Construction sites in the past were often cleared of all existing trees, shrubs, and the organic matter. Now there has been efforts to keep some of the existing trees which usually die due to soil compaction, root disturbance, change in soil texture and composition, and surface becoming impervious which reduces or prohibits infiltration and water uptake by tree roots. City planners and contractors need to work with the green squads to determine which trees should be preserved on a given site and the best ways to minimise damaging these trees.

Green areas need to be enlarged following modern urban development codes. Every new residential colony to be developed should have atleast 30 per cent of the total area for green cover. The areas between sidewalks and roads need to be wide enough to sustain the root system of a tree or plants in a parking lot should be large enough to ensure that the trees have enough nutrients and water to maintain its vigour and health.

Another significant fact is that the greening programme is mainly focused on planting of trees, while post plantation care is not given adequate attention. This results into very low survival percentage and is thus a sheer wastage of infrastructure. About 18.5 lakh seedlings are planted every year. This is a good enough number but how many of them survive is a point to be noted. Thus, instead of laying emphasis on increasing the number of seedlings to be planted, impetus should be given to ensure maximum survival. The savings can be diverted to research and development of new techniques. Following factors should be kept in mind during the planning phase:

- Availability of sufficient space for planting and growth of the trees.
- Emphasis should be laid on planting tall seedlings of atleast 4-5 years old especially on the avenues to ensure its establishment and survival. The cost of seedlings may be higher in this case but it would ensure cent per cent survival.
- Plantation as well as nursery raising is a specialised job. There are so many agencies

involved in planting trees. Many of them do not even have specialised manpower to carry out the plantations and maintain them. Such agencies should be removed and only specialised agencies should be handed over the task.

A considerable degree of forward planning is required for effective use of available funds. Funds should be allocated for long-term maintenance of trees.

Thus a strategic overview is required so that the planning and management of the green areas is closely coordinated across the different agencies that have a role to play.

7.3.9 Establishment of GIS Cell

The geographic information system (GIS) is a computer based information system that is designed to work with data referenced by spatial or geographic coordinates. The use of GIS is rapidly increasing, as city, regional and environmental planners, resource managers and the scientific community become aware of the capabilities these systems have to offer (Wood, 1990).

A GIS allows the user the ability to quickly manipulate, analyse, display geographic or spatial data and take advantage of existing spatial information (Miller, 1997). GIS has long been recognised as a useful tool in the management of natural resource development, land use planning, wildlife management, environmental planning, and forestry planning. The use of tree inventories is essential for the management of trees in an urban community. The street tree inventories can be greatly enhanced by using a geographic information system. This would help the urban foresters and planners to make more thorough and cost effective management decisions to better manage and maintain healthy urban forests.

A GIS cell should be established immediately to create a database of all the area under forest and tree cover for regular monitoring. The benefits of GIS would exceed the initial costs of the software and digital data that is needed. Updating data in a GIS is much more cost efficient and less time consuming than having to manually redraw maps. This would give up-to-date information, which can be used by urban and environmental planners during planning and policy formulation. Based on the database, remedial measure, if any, can be suggested without any loss of time.

7.4 Policy Framework

There are lots of issues regarding the causes and consequences of degradation of green cover in Delhi. However, a strategic, integrated and coordinated institutional approach is not in place to address these issues. There is clear lack of focus both in terms of policy, priorities and intervention. The government and non-government agencies and communities must integrate, develop and achieve a shared vision for increasing the green cover. Some of the issues, which may be useful in deciding policy framework, are mentioned below:

- There are various agencies involved in the task of afforestation and maintenance of green space, which leads to administrative confusion in planning and implementation. Handing over the task to one body with the sole objective of protecting and increasing the green cover would reduce the complexity.
- Conversion of recreational areas to other uses should not be permitted at all.
- In all the developmental processes, visual characteristics should be given consideration. In the planning of " New Delhi" in 1961, the central vista was conceived as a landscaped stretch to form continuity between the ridge and the river Yamuna. But the new developments are more on the basis of division of land for different uses and lack spatial qualities (Anon., 1990). Thus policies should be framed to support urban design, giving importance to the aesthetic view besides the developmental activities.
- Recently the MoEF has issued guidelines making it mandatory for development projects, government or private (hotels, hospitals, industrial estates, office and commercial complexes, new townships etc.) to obtain environmental clearance if it caters to the needs of 1,000 persons or more, discharging sewage of 50,000 litres a day or more, with an investment of Rs. 50 crores or more. These guidelines should be followed strictly.
- Regular survey of user's attitude and expectations and of potential for increased community involvement in creating and managing green spaces should be conducted.
- Management of each area of green belt and recreational land should be made fully transparent and accountable, with appropriate rewards for

effective management and penalties for mismanagement.

- Ring road and rail corridors have the potential to acquire an additional dimension of visual quality and integration.
- The banners, hoarding, signboards, bill boards etc., should not be allowed to be placed on trees. These not only harm the trees but spoil the visual quality also.
- On the basis of the study conducted by Central Water Pollution Control and Prevention Board, six areas, *viz.*, Najafgarh road, Lawrence Road, Wazirpur, Kirti Nagar, DLF Industries area, and Moti Nagar have been declared as Pollution Control Areas under the Air (Prevention and Control of Pollution) act, 1981 (Anon., 1990). Thus emphasis on pollution hardy species should be laid especially in these areas for pollution abatement.
- A green buffer should be developed along the major roads, commercial areas like shopping complexes and cultural centres for controlling noise pollution.
- Trees in the periphery of airport should be short statured to avoid birds, which are a menace to air safety.
- Avenue trees should be strong enough to withstand heavy wind, pleasing crown shape and have attractive flowers. Trees bearing edible fruits or fodder leaves are prone to be damaged heavily.
- In "Make Bangalore Green" campaign, to avoid the cost of tree guards, industries were approached to adopt avenues and use the space for the advertisement of their logos (Sunder, 1986). Another step taken by the forest Department was to involve individuals for extension work and for protecting the seedlings and tree guards. They in turn were appointed as 'Honorary Tree Wardens', which later became a status symbol. This approach can be adopted in Delhi as well.
- Local authorities should encourage formation of neighbourhood watch organisations for green areas in their purview.
- The achievements of local groups and people who care for their local green spaces should be acknowledged. For this community award can be instituted to encourage and reward the efforts of local communities.
- 'Delhi Green Spaces Taskforce' should be set up for developing and maintaining green areas in the city.
- Non-governmental organisations can work in conjunction with the forest department to come ahead and motivate people to plant trees in their surroundings on special occasions such as birthdays, anniversaries, wedding, and valentine's day etc. This would make their days memorable besides adding to the aesthetic appeal of the place.
- Students should also be involved in planting trees and to look after them in and around school and college campuses. In short the concept of "Tree Police" as proposed by the Green Delhi Action Plan should be realised.
- Local initiatives and partnerships should be encouraged to promote greater involvement of local people, optimise the capacity of communities, foster a greater sense of individual responsibility and citizenship and give communities a sense of ownership of their green spaces, all leading to more cohesive and sustainable communities.

Policies in accordance with the National Forest Policy, 1988 need to be formulated with the aim to have a minimum of one-third of total land area of the city under forest or tree cover. Thus, protection, afforestation and maintenance of existing tree cover should be strongly supported by enabling policy decisions whether on strengthening the existing rules and regulations, staff strength, training, research, funding, etc.

7.5 Conclusion

The responsibility of making Delhi green is not a duty of one department alone. It is an obligation on all. Government departments, public authorities, non-government organisations and communities each have a fundamental role to play. Hence concerted efforts are required by all to make Delhi one of the most attractive and appealing cities of the world. The suggestions contained in this report will provide a better focus and building blocks for all those involved in planning, managing and maintaining green spaces in Delhi to identify the important issues and develop consensus and priorities for further action.

References

Anonymous (2001a). *State of Environment Report for Delhi*, Tata Energy and Research Institute. Delhi.

———. (2001b). *State of Forest Report, 2001*. Forest Survey of India. Kaulagarh Road, Dehra Dun.

———. (2004a). *Agrotechniques and Economics of Some Important Medicinal Plants of India*. National Medicinal Plants Board, Department of Ayush. Ministry of Health and Family Welfare, Government of India.

———. (2004b). *Greening Delhi Action Plan, 2004-05*. Department of Forest and Wildlife, Government of NCT of Delhi.

———. (2007). *Greening Delhi Action Plan, 2007-08*. Department of Forest and Wildlife, Government of NCT of Delhi.

———. (1912). *Delhi Gazetteer*.

———. (1990). *What will be Delhi in 2001*. Delhi Master Plan August 1990, Delhi: Akalank Publications. pp. 37-40.

———. (1995). *Delhi Environment Status Report*. World wide fund for Nature-India. Department of Environment, Government of NCT, Delhi.

———. (2000). *Environmental Management Plan for rejuvenation of river Yamuna in NCT*. National Environmental Engineering Research Institute.

Champion, H.G. & S.K. Seth (1968). *A Revised Survey of the Forest Types of India*. Government of India Publ. Delhi. p.404.

Ganguli, U. (1975). *A Guide to the Birds of the Delhi Area*, I.C.A.R., New Delhi.

Gogate, V.G. (2001). *Impact of Urbanisation on Delhi Fauna with special reference to Avifauna*. 13-15. CENDE & Dept of Environment, Delhi.

Gopal, B. (2003). *State of Degradation and Approaches to Restoration of Floodplain Rivers in India*. Proceedings of the second international symposium on the management of large rivers for fisheries: Sustaining livelihoods and biodiversity in new millennium. Vol II. 11th–14th Feb. 2003, Phnom Phen, Cambodia.

Kumar, A. (1997). *Fauna of Delhi: An overview* 1-15. Zoological Survey of India. Calcutta.

Kumar, P. (2004). *Ecosystem Services of Floodplains: An Exploration of Water Recharge Potential of the Yamuna Floodplain for Delhi*. Draft Version. Paper Presented at the conference on Market Development of Water & Waste Technologies through Environmental Economics, 28th-29th May 2004, Paris. p.6.

Maheshwari, J.K. (1963). *The Flora of Delhi 1-947*, C.S.I.R., New Delhi.

Miller, R.W. (1997). *Urban Forestry: Planning and Managing Urban Greenspaces*. 2nd ed. Englewood cliffs, New Jersey: Prentice Hall. p. 105-130.

Naithani, H.B. (1993). *Contributions to the Taxonomic studies of Indian Bamboos*. Vol. I and II. Ph.D. Thesis submitted to the HNB Garhwal University, Srinagar, Garhwal.

Naithani, H.B., M. Pal, Sumer Chandra and V.P. Khanduri (2004). *Vegetational Survey and Inventorisation of Species in the Ridge Forest of Delhi*. Report. Submitted to Department of Forest and Wildlife, Government of NCT of Delhi.

Parker, R.N. (1920). *Afforestation of the Ridge at Delhi*. Indian Forester. 46 (1): 21-28.

Rao, M.J. (2002). *Technology for Large Scale Propagation of Bamboo through Aerial Seeding*. pp 323-331. In Kumar A., Ramanuja Rao, I.V. and Sastry, Ch. (Eds.) Bamboo for Sustainable Development. INBAR Proc. No. 7, Netherlands.

Reddy, C.V.K. (1978). *Prosopis Juliflora*. The Precious Child of the Plant World. Indian Forester. 104: 14-18.

Sawarkar, V.B. and V.K. Uniyal (1995). *Management Planning of Asola Bhati Wildlife Sanctuary*. Wildlife Institute of India, Dehra Dun.

Sunder, S.S. (1986). *Urban Tree Planting-Foresters Efforts in Bangalore*. Indian Forester. 112: 296-304.

Tewari, D.N. (1994). *Urban Forestry. Indian Forester*. 120: 647- 657.

Tewari, D.N and K. Kumar (2002). *Rehabilitation of Mined Areas through Bamboo Afforestation: A Case Study*. pp. 777-782. ibid.

Wood, J.P. (1990). *Tree Inventories and GIS in Urban Forestry*. Project report submitted to the Faculty of the Virginia Polytechnic Institute and State University in partial fulfillment of the requirements for the degree of Master in Forestry in Forest Biology, Blacksburg, Virginia.

Chapter 8

Wildlife Management and Biodiversity Conservation

8.1 Introduction

A metropolis like Delhi may not be typically associated with significant wildlife values, however pressures associated with rapid urbanisation have brought such issues into sharp focus. While areas such as the Delhi Ridge on the one hand, are regarded as the green lungs of the city and have been the focus of conservation efforts over the last few decades, rhesus macaques have been involved in serious incidents of harassment and injury to humans, on the other. The primary responsibility of managing wildlife rests with the Department of Forest and Wildlife of the Government of National Capital Territory (NCT) of Delhi. There are also significant initiatives from NGOs and educational bodies especially with regard to Wildlife Conservation, Education and Awareness. This chapter examines the current status of areas and programmes significant for wildlife conservation and management and puts forth recommendations and policy actions for achieving desirable outcomes, primarily for the Department of Forest and Wildlife of Government of NCT of Delhi.

8.2 Status of Wildlife

The areas encompassed within the NCT of Delhi (hereinafter referred to as Delhi) have undergone successive changes since its origin dating back to the 1st century B.C. and the subsequent period of growth 11 century A.D. onwards under the Rajput Dynasty kings. The ruins of atleast eight capitals are scattered over an area of about 181 km^2 around the Yamuna. Yet another phase of settlement since 1911 has resulted in the rapid expansion of areas around the ancient capital sites and the consequent degradation of the two main topographical features, the Delhi Ridge and the Yamuna River (Figure 8.1).

Delhi's population has grown about 33 per cent per annum since 1901 during the 20th century and according to the 2001 census is 137.83 lakh with a density of 9294 persons per km^2. The expanding settlements have direct consequences on the forest and tree cover. Of the total area of 1483 km^2 the forest and tree cover constitutes only about 18.07 per cent (268 km^2) and about 6.5 per cent constituted by the Yamuna (between Wazirabad and Okhla) that is significant from the wildlife management and biodiversity conservation point of view.

8.2.1 Fauna of Delhi

Historical records from 1883 onwards of wild pigs, foxes, hares and mugger are available from the Yamuna; *chinkara*, wolves, *nilgai*, leopard, black buck from the Ridge areas and around Tughlaqabad have been reported. Kumar (1997) gives an overview of the fauna of Delhi wherein about 585 vertebrate and 1200 invertebrate species have been documented. While large carnivores such as the leopard and wolves may have been extirpated from within the geographical limits of Delhi, several mammals and significant species of birds are yet found here. The southern areas of the Ridge (within Asola-Bhatti Wildlife Sanctuary) retain small numbers of Nilgai, Ruddy mongoose (*Herspestes smithi*), Small Indian Civet, Jungle Cat, Small Indian Mongoose, Porcupine, Rufous tailed hare and the jungle cat. Several lists prepared by birdwatchers indicate between 403 to 449 species within the geographical limits of Delhi. The wetlands of Delhi region also harbour significant populations of resident and migratory waterfowl. The following are areas of consequence to wildlife management and biodiversity conservation in Delhi.

FIGURE 8.1

Salient Forest/Wildlife Conservation Sites in NCT in Delhi

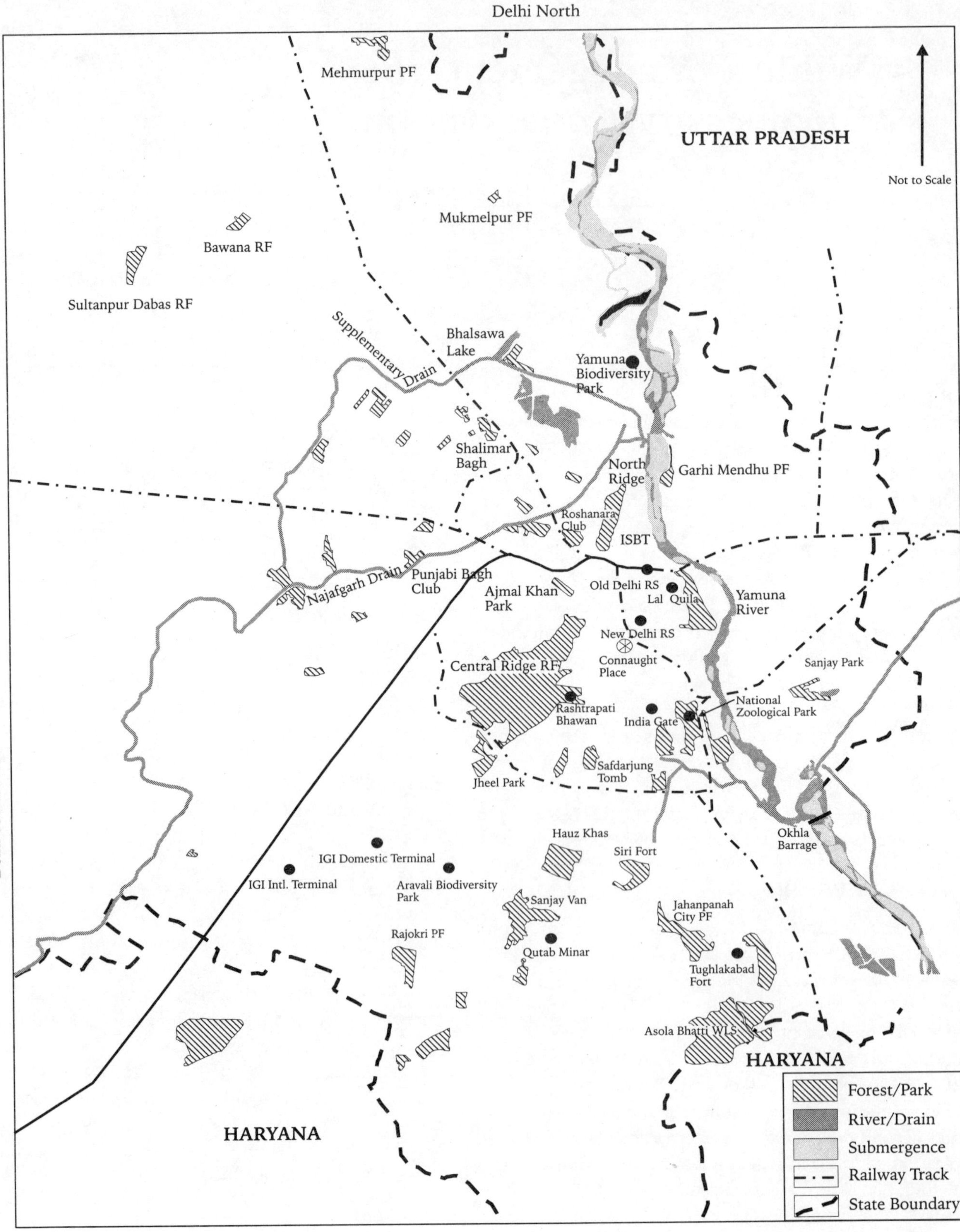

8.2.2 Delhi Ridge

The Delhi Ridge (7,777 ha. in four remnant patches) is a continuation of the Aravalli Range which extends into Delhi from Haryana at the Tughlaqabad — Dera-Mandi axis moving northwards covering areas of the Asola-Bhatti Wildlife Sanctuary, parts of Delhi Cantonment and the Lutyens Zone terminating at Delhi University covering the Kamla Nehru Ridge (Thapliyal, 1987). The original area of the ridge was believed to be 15,046 ha (Madan, 2002). Concerns over the rapidly decreasing cover on account of infrastructure and settlement expansion and mining led to declaration of the remaining four patches that constitute the Delhi Ridge as Reserved Forest in 1994 under the Indian Forest Act (1927): (i) Northern (87 ha, under Delhi Development Authority, DDA); (ii) Central (864 ha, under Central Public Works Department, CPWD); (iii) South Central (626 ha, under Municipal Corporation of Delhi, DDA and Forest Department, FD); and (iv) Southern (6200 ha, under the FD).

The vegetation is typical Northern Tropical Thorn Forest Type (Champion and Seth, 1968). Among trees Acacias such as *A. nilotica, A. leucophloea, A. catechu, A. modesta, Butea monosperma* (Dhak), *Cassia fistula* (Amaltas), *Salvadora persica* are prominent. There are patches of *Anogeissus latifolia* while *Prosopis juliflora* is abundant. Shrubs include *Capparis sepiaria, C.decidua, Zizyphus aenoplia, Croton sparaiflorus*. Herbaceous flora includes *Calotropis procera, Withania somnifera, Achyranthes aspera, Alysicarpus vaginalis, and Peistrophe bicalyculata*. The main grasses are *Cenchrus ciliaris, Aristida, Eragrostis poaeioides, Saccharum spontaneum* (Kumar and Khanna, 1997).

Among the notable avian species of the ridge areas are Grey-breasted Prinias, Small Minivets, Common Wood-shrike, Paradise Flycatcher, several barbets and woodpeckers. In winter Olive-backed Pipits are regular in several places and several buntings (notably White-capped) have been recorded. Peafowl and Grey Francolin are numerous and Eurasian Thick-knees are also noted to breed in good numbers (*www.Delhibird.org*, retrieved on 27/12/2004). The only Protected Area (PA) Asola – Bhatti Wildlife Sanctuary constituting the Southern Patch of Delhi Ridge harbours significant wildlife species.

8.2.2 Asola-Bhatti Wildlife Sanctuary

The Asola–Bhatti Wildlife Sanctuary (ABWLS) was created with the notification of community land of villages (Asola, Sahurpur and Maidangarhi, 4704 acres) during 1986 and Bhatti (2167 acres) during 1991 as Wildlife Sanctuary. The area is dominated by exposed irregularly distributed boulders of Precambrian, quartzite base that yield quartzite rocks of high quality silica locally known as 'Badarpur' or 'Bajri' (Sawarkar and Hussain, 1997). Due to the presence of such mineral resources within the area it had been subjected to extensive mining and till date faces problems of illegal mining. As part of the extensive habitat recovery activities of the Department of Forests and Wildlife along with the Eco-Task Force of the Territorial Army since 2001-2002 over 7 lakh indigenous trees have been planted in the Bhatti area (2500 acres) including over 1.4 lakh trees in the Dera Mandi area for recovery of the tree cover.

Historical records indicate that before 1900 A.D. there were abundant populations of Black Buck, Nilgai, and Chinkara along with reported sightings of Wolf, Hyena and Leopard as late as 1940. However, due to the extreme anthropogenic pressures that the areas have been subjected to, the species now found are Nilgai, Common Mongoose, Small Indian Civet, Jungle Cat, Small Indian Mongoose, Porcupine, Palm Squirrel, Spiny Tailed Lizard, and the Rufous tailed Hare. Records indicate between 110 and 200 species of resident and migratory birds including Little Grebe, Little Cormorant, Cattle Egret, Peregrine Falcon, Grey Francolin, Brown-headed Barbet, Coppersmith Barbet, Indian Grey Hornbill, Common Hoopoe, Indian Roller, Sirkeer Malkoha, Alexandrine Parakeet, Spotted Owlet, Spotted Dove, Common Kestrel, Common Myna, and Jungle Prinia among others.

8.2.3 Yamuna Flood Plains

Floodplains are the most widespread of the wetland ecosystems present in the Yamuna river corridor in the Delhi stretch from Wazirabad to Okhla, comprising approximately 95 per cent of the total area (Babu *et. al.*, 2001). The remainder area comprises marshy areas and seasonal pools that are of critical importance in providing nurseries for fish fries and nesting sites for the migrating waterfowl respectively. Floodplains are the stretch of flat land between the manmade embankments and the levee of the river channel that is regularly inundated with floodwater during the monsoons. Ecosystem goods and services provided by wetlands include fish, water supply for domestic, industrial and agricultural purposes, fodder and other utilisable plant species, fuel wood, recreation and tourism. Existence of the wetland ecosystems in the Yamuna river corridor however is threatened due to the immense anthropogenic pressures including civic infrastructure development and construction, pollution and discharge of raw sewage into the river, change in nature of vegetation, over-exploitation of species and agriculture. According to an estimate (Kumar, 2001), the capitalised value of 3250 ha land of floodplain varies from

Rs. 72620 lakh to Rs. 12103 lakh. In terms of per ha the range of value comes to be Rs. 22.34 lakh to Rs. 3.72 lakh. The range depends upon the rate of discount applied.

S. munja—a characteristic plant species of floodplains is found in small pockets near Wazirabad barrage. Marshy areas are predominantly present from Chilla regulator to Okhla barrage and *Typha angustata* is the dominant plant species here. Field surveys indicate that 115 plant species belonging to 27 families were identified and categorised (Babu *et. al.*, 2001).

Marshy areas present in the Yamuna river corridor provide nesting and feeding grounds for many migrating waterfowl species. Thus these sites are of prime importance with respect to their potential to act as waterfowl habitat. Most of the birds remain in the Yamuna corridors for about 4 winter months on an average which makes the wetlands of the river to function as wildlife habitats. Of the 97 species visiting the wetlands, 47 species (about 46 per cent) of birds are resident and breed in and around the areas of the wetlands (Babu *et. al.*, 2001). With the development of the Yamuna Biodiversity Park, the biodiversity of the region is expected to receive a considerable boost.

8.2.4 Okhla Barrage

The construction of a barrage on the Yamuna near Okhla in 1986 created a large water body that is shared between Delhi and the adjoining state of Uttar Pradesh. The area is rich in avian diversity wherein 302 bird species have been recorded (Urfi, 2003). During winter, between 14,000 to 20,000 water birds are recorded including two critically 'Endangered Species', nine 'Vulnerable Species' and one 'Conservation Dependent' species. Bird species that have shown a decline across the country and in the Okhla area include the Sarus Crane (*Grus antigone*), Indian Skimmer (*Rynchops albicollis*) and the Black Neck Stork (*Ephippiorhynchus asiaticus*). Among the winter migratory species are the Northern Shoveller (*Anas clypeata*), Northern Pintail (*Anas acuta*) and Ruddy Shelduck (*Tadorna ferruginea*) and Graylag Goose (*Anser anser*). The Okhla barrage is an important feeding ground for the hundreds of Painted Storks that breed in the vicinity of the National Zoological Park (Islam and Rahamani, 2004.).

8.2.5 National Zoological Park

The National Zoological Park or Delhi Zoo as it is popularly known is yet another resource of consequence to wildlife and biodiversity with obvious *ex-situ* implications. The administrative control of the zoo is with the Government of India, Ministry of Environment and Forests. However, as the resource is located within the NCT of Delhi it is taken up for consideration in this chapter. A vital function served by the zoo is that of promoting education and awareness among people regarding wildlife and biodiversity conservation. Also the zoo provides veterinary care and rehabilitation facilities to rescued animals in and around Delhi. The zoo was visited by 13.35 lakh persons in the year 2003-2004, thus exposing them to several facets of wildlife conservation. Several programmes for education and awareness were carried out for students and teachers during the same period such as painting competition, primate and bat conservation programmes among the notable. The zoo is also home to a number of free living birds such as Peafowl, Cormorants, Comb Duck, Shoveller, Spotbill Duck, Cattle and Little Egrets, White Ibis, Indian Moorhen, and Painted Stork.

8.2.6 Other Urban Forest Patches

There exist several smaller forest patches around Delhi that provide shelter to several bird species. Some of the notable forest patches are Mitraon Protected Forest (PF, 105 acres), Sultanpur PF (120 acres), Mukhmelpur PF (133 acres), Rajokri PF (600 acres) that are under the administrative control of the Forest and Wildlife Department. There are 21 other PF patches under the control of Delhi Development Authority and Defence lands that comprise a total area of 3186.9 acres. Another notable patch of city forest is that near Nasirpur (28 ha) along with 10 other patches occupying a total of 741 acres. Several gardens along with these urban forest patches have the potential to harbour significant bird populations that add to the biodiversity of the region.

An appraisal of the policies and programmes pertaining to wildlife and biodiversity conservation is considered next.

8.3 Multi-Agency Programmes and Areas

In this section we consider areas and programmes that are not under the direct administrative and executive control of the Forest and Wildlife Department of Government of NCT of Delhi but are managed by other agencies or involve joint efforts. These areas and programmes as listed earlier are significant from the wildlife and biodiversity point of view for the NCT of Delhi.

8.3.1 Okhla Barrage

The stretch of Yamuna River between Wazirabad (the

entry point into Delhi) and Okhla Barrage (the exit point) has enormous volumes of raw sewage and other industrial pollutants being emptied into it. This is the most critical factor affecting the floral and faunal communities of the wetland created by the barrage. It is pertinent to note here that dabbling ducks such as the Shovlers and Pintails, the diving ducks and grazing ducks (Graylag and Barheaded Geese) have different feeding ecology within the same area. Besides providing irrigation to the adjacent crop fields the wetland provides flood and storm damage protection, groundwater recharge, fish and shellfish habitat, water source for fish and wildlife and recreation in the form of boating and fishing.

The Forest Department could take the lead in improving the water quality in this stretch of Yamuna along with the ongoing efforts of the Yamuna River Authority, the Central Pollution Control Board and agencies like the Delhi Jal Board and Municipal Corporation of Delhi. Apart from the pollution the barrage is choking with *Eichhorina crassipes* covering more than 35-45 per cent of the water during February and March which affects the migrating ducks and geese population (Wildlife Institute of India, 2002). Regular discharge of the water from the main gate of the barrage so as to get rid of the *Eichhorina* mats along with manual removal of the weeds needs to be undertaken during the months of May and June.

Fishing and grass cutting are two important benefits being derived by the people along with use by the washer men. These important sources of livelihood need to be taken care of in the absence of any alternative areas while according a Wildlife Sanctuary status to the parts of the area within Delhi. It is desirable from the wildlife and biodiversity conservation viewpoint that the Okhla islands along with the stretch upto Yamuna Bridge/Noida Toll Bridge is accorded the status of Wildlife Sanctuary on par with the existing status on the Uttar Pradesh (Ghaziabad district) side. Declaration of requisite areas upstream and down stream of the barrage as buffer zones will not only augment the pollution control efforts but also allow the pollution load to be removed by the natural wetland ecosystem process. While it will be extremely difficult to completely stop the discharge of effluents and raw sewage into the river stretch between Wazirabad and Okhla, minimising such discharge will enable the wetland ecosystem to remove this load provided adequate flow of volume is available. Also enhancing the recreational use of the area needs to be carefully planned in order to manage the tourist potential of the area.

8.3.2 Yamuna and Aravalli Biodiversity Parks

The River Yamuna and the Aravalli Mountains or the Delhi Ridge are the two life support systems. However, they are severely degraded and face high biotic pressure due to over exploitation, fragmentation and conversion of habitat, pollution, biological invasions and rapid population growth. These environmental resources have almost lost their life supporting potential and ecosystems have lost their resilience and natural self-sustaining ameliorative capabilities. Recognising this, the Centre for Environmental Management of Degraded Ecosystems, University of Delhi and the Delhi Development Authority initiated the project on establishing a network of biodiversity parks in the form of Yamuna and Aravalli Biodiversity Parks at a total project cost of about Rs. 19 crores over ten years. Natural ecosystems characteristic of the Yamuna River Basin and Aravalli Mountain System are being developed in these parks respectively with the help of extensive landscaping and planting of native and indigenous species. Some of the key functions of the biodiversity parks are (Anon, 2005):

- Augmentation of freshwater availability by acting as a catchment area, enhancing groundwater recharge and increasing the groundwater table
- Positively impacting local weather patterns by buffering ambient temperatures by reducing albedo
- An ideal alternative habitat for migratory and resident bird species
- An important venue for ecotourism for the people of Delhi
- Provide a place for coexistence of nature and culture
- An ideal medium for environmental education at every level
- Research opportunities for closely understanding and documenting birth of lost ecosystems
- Linkages with other parks and botanical gardens for promoting conservation efforts at national and international level
- Reducing pollution load of the city
- Sequestering atmospheric carbon dioxide
- Trapping dust coming with westerly desert winds
- Checking advancing of deserts

Yamuna Biodiversity Park is adjacent to the river stretch upstream of the Wazirabad Bridge across the river (Figure 8.1). The project initiated in 2002 over an area of 157 acres is now slated to be extended to an adjacent area of 300 acres which will be developed in the second phase of the plan. An Information Centre has already been opened on the site, displaying the plan of the park, the aim and other related information. One of the major challenges faced at the park site was to deal with excess alkalinity of the soil coupled with saline water. To overcome this problem, first year works focused on improvement of the soil environment for paving the way for introduction of indigenous species of the Yamuna river basin that are characteristic of biotic communities of the river basin. The Yamuna Biodiversity Park will eventually be home to 10 ecosystems (Anon, 2005).

A total of about 30 biotic communities, that are most prominent ones in the entire Yamuna River basin, are planned for introduction and development in the park. Some of these communities under development are: Mixed deciduous with bamboo, Mixed deciduous without bamboo, Sal dominated mixed evergreen, Teak dominated mixed deciduous, Sal Dominated mixed deciduous, Acacia Woodlands, Grasslands, Thorn-scrub forests, Shallow Wetland communities, Deep Wetland Communities, Semi-Evergreen low-lying forest, Broad-leaved mixed communities, Marshy communities, Riparian communities, Peripheral Plantations, and Island communities (*Acacia nilotica*-grasses). Plants that were collected and brought to the park from the wild have added to the increase in the number of species. A total of about 450 plant species are now existing in the park. Further areas such as Sacred Grove, Herbal Garden, Fruit Orchard are being developed along with a site for camping. The major purpose of conservation awareness will be served through visits of groups and individuals to these areas within the park.

A narrow wetland designed like a river with a total length of 1.8 km was created through artificial digging of soil in 2002 with plantation being completed in 2003. Another deeper wetland of about 2.5 hectares has been created in July 2004 for providing habitat particularly for the migratory birds. About 500 individuals of *Rana* sp. (3 sp.), 1000 fish fingerlings collected from local wetlands and 1,50,000 fish fingerlings of various carp species have been introduced in the wetlands resulting in a resident population of Cormorants.

With improvement in the habitat quality, and the development of the wetlands, a number of faunal species have started appearing. The diversity is relatively higher in the case with birds. During early 2002, when plantation work was started, there were about 30 species of common birds found in the area. After the development of the wetlands, the number of bird species has gone to over 160 with over 40 species of birds nesting in the park. The Red Crested Pochard, a migratory bird from Siberia is being seen in Delhi in the Yamuna Biodiversity Park after a gap of almost five years. This bird is an indicator of good water quality. Besides increase in the avifauna, the number of species recorded for mammals has also gone up. The following animals have been sighted/indirect evidence observed in the park site: Fruit Bats, Wild Pig, Nilgai, Black Napped Hare, Porcupine, Gerbil, Cobra—Brown and Black, Checkered Keel Back, Wolf Snake, Rat Snake and Common Krait (Anon, 2005)

Aravalli Biodiversity Park located between Vasant Kunj and Vasant Vihar is spread over 692 acres with plans for water bodies, a rock garden, a butterfly park and a safari park. This park is intended to highlight flora and fauna that are characteristic of a desert. Communities under development in the Aravalli Biodiversity Park are: Anogeissus-Boswelia, Mixed deciduous forest, Sacred Grove, Butea dominated deciduous, Mixed semi-evergreen community, and Wetlands. A total number of 230 plant species belonging to 53 families and 152 genera and 90 species of birds have been sighted in the park. Mammals such as Nilgai, Jackal, Brown hare, Jackals and Hyena and five snake species (Cobra, Banded krait, Russell's viper, Rat snake and Water snake) are the notable fauna of the area. Water harvesting has already started in the Aravalli Biodiversity Park and waste-water from the Mahipalpur Dairy is being diverted to the park.

While the progress made in the case of Yamuna Biodiversity Park has been considerable, the Aravalli Biodiversity Park is embroiled in a controversy. Residents and NGOs filed complaints with the Supreme Court Central Empowered Committee (CEC) claiming that the development of the park was in violation of the designated green area. Although the Supreme Court Central Empowered Committee consequently has cleared the project, doubts have been raised on the environmental feasibility of both the parks. In the interim, it would suffice to view the development of the biodiversity parks as a vital opportunity to demonstrate the regenerative potential of sites which have otherwise been subject to immense anthropogenic pressures. In this regard, the case of Yamuna Biodiversity Park is of special interest as there could be vital lessons to be learnt for the development of the Yamuna Floodplains as a whole. This should be seen in light of the earlier recommendation for Okhla Barrage pertaining to the need to provide opportunities for the wetland system to thrive along the entire stretch of the Yamuna. The ability of wetlands to remove the pollution load from the water and other associated benefits provide tangible benefits to society at large. While it may be too early to comment on the intensity and extent of replication of the Yamuna Biodiversity Park experience along the stretch of the Yamuna within Delhi and elsewhere, the project is expected to yield vital insights for the evolving of an integrated water management plan. Also, the contribution of such parks towards increasing awareness regarding wildlife and biodiversity conservation cannot be overstated.

8.3.3 Wildlife Conservation Awareness

The initiatives by the Forest and Wildlife Department, NGOs and members of civil society towards improvement of their environs have been aided by the enormous growth in media. The cable revolution within the last decade has brought wildlife and environment related entertainment right into the homes of the ordinary urban citizen. Cable TV channels like the National Geographic and Discovery have provided the opportunity to millions of viewers to appreciate matters related to the environment in general and wildlife specifically. Those households that have access to the Internet have an additional source of information and entertainment that is being made available on the World Wide Web.

An environment and ecology related programme of awareness was initiated during 1998-1999 by the Environment Department of the Government of NCT of Delhi and at present is operational in 1560 schools and colleges of Delhi. An eco-club was established in each institution with the objective of promoting an ethos of conservation, creating awareness regarding waste generation and recycling, sensitising students to minimise use of polythene bags, organise tree plantation with the Forest Department and awareness generation through organising quizzes, painting competition, rally, street plays on environmental issues. An evaluation conducted by the Planning Department has put forth some encouraging results for the continuation and augmentation of this scheme (Anon, 2002). Some of the major highlights of the findings of the evaluation include: 28 per cent of the sampled eco-clubs were formed of the initiatives of the students themselves; 63 per cent of the eco-clubs gave 1-3 hours/week and 3 per cent more than 6 hours/week for various activities; 99 per cent of the eco-clubs have conducted plantation activities, 89 per cent drawing and poster competitions, 63 per cent debates and 66 per cent have organised rallies. It is encouraging to note that 92 per cent of the student members shared views regarding eco-clubs with their friends and family and 65 per cent members continued activities since the formation in 1999-2000. With a total of Rs. 94.87 lakh having been spent on the scheme the evaluation indicated some recommendations for the continuation and improved working of the scheme.

Several NGOs are active in the area of wildlife conservation awareness and have on occasion joined forces to highlight issues like the ban on Shatoosh, illegal trade in wildlife, plight of captive animals etc. Some of the NGOs taking leadership roles in awareness generation within Delhi and outside are Wildlife Trust of India, Wildlife Protection Society of India, World Wide Fund for Nature-India, ATREE and CEE. While it is not possible to comment on the investment of these organisations in terms of resources both monetary and human, it is desirable that partnerships for such awareness towards wildlife conservation between the government agencies, NGOs and industrial houses are strengthened.

The education section of the National Zoological Park has been actively pursuing the task of awareness building among its visitors. Among the major activities and budget heads listed are: (a) printing of guide maps, brochures, posters, stickers and pamphlets; (b) preparation and installation of signage's for interpretation; (c) celebration of wildlife week, van mahotsav and other events; (d) educational seminars; and (e) purchase of books, periodicals and other equipment. A sum of Rs. 11.6 lakh (4.64 per cent of total outlay) is proposed to be spent on educational and awareness related activities (for 2004-2005) by the zoo authorities. A permanent kiosk for selling educational material is proposed to be put up in the premises in the near future. The effectiveness of the various educational and awareness activities in the past however are not ascertainable and hence any comments on the matter are not attempted at this juncture.

The Forest Department itself is also involved in wildlife conservation awareness raising activities. The Forest Department funds for publicity are primarily utilised for forestry activities wherein publicity activities are being targeted at specific groups such as school and colleges, parents of school children, market associations and resident welfare associations. The publicity efforts are carried via radio, newspapers, posters, kiosks and panels on buses and bus shelters and animated display systems. Also the active participation of NGOs, Voluntary bodies, Resident Welfare Associations and the corporate sector is sought for the distribution and planting of saplings throughout Delhi. However, a beginning is being made for wildlife conservation awareness in the ABWLS with the involvement of Bombay Natural History Society for establishing a 2 km trail and a Conservation Education Centre within the sanctuary which is discussed in the subsequent section of appraisal of the scheme pertaining to ABWLS.

8.3.3 Illegal Trade in Wildlife Products

The trade of wild fauna and flora has severe implications for the survival of endangered species such as tigers, elephants, and rhinoceros. While these are large charismatic species there is a very real threat posed for numerous other wild floral and faunal species. Delhi has emerged as a major hub for the illegal trade in such species and their products. Provisions of the Wildlife (Protection) Act 1972, the Import and Export Policy of the Government of India and the Customs Act 1962 along with the provisions of the Convention on International Trade in Endangered Species of Wild Fauna and Flora (CITES) are available to the enforcement agencies for regulation of trade in wild fauna and flora.

Hunting of wild animals has been prohibited under Sec. 9 of WPA 1972 as also is the collection or trade in specified plants (whether alive or dead or part or derivative) under Sec. 17A. The Import-Export Policy announced periodically by the Ministry of Commerce enlists wild species and products derived from such wild species that are prohibited or permitted along with the conditions of compliance with CITES. This policy is brought out under the provisions of the Foreign Trade (Development and Regulation) Act 1992 and is enforced through the provisions of the Customs Act 1962. The number of wildlife offence cases detected by the Office of the Dy. Director, Wildlife, Northern Region in Delhi under the Customs Act since 1995 is shown in Figure 8.2.

The number of cases detected in Delhi might show a decline over the last five years but this in no way can be construed as indicative of a decline in the overall trade for wild fauna and flora. The Wildlife Wing of the Forest and Wildlife Department has till date been able to register 93 seizures till date. While the arrest of 71 persons and a conviction rate of almost 85 per cent is most encouraging, 52 cases are still pending in the courts.

Major bottlenecks exist in the effective enforcement of the provisions of the law. Raids and seizures need to be planned and coordinated among the Wildlife Wing of the state government, the police, Directorate of Revenue Intelligence the Central Bureau of Investigation and the Customs. While the occasional seizure at entry and exit

FIGURE 8.2

Number of Wildlife Offence Cases Detected in Delhi

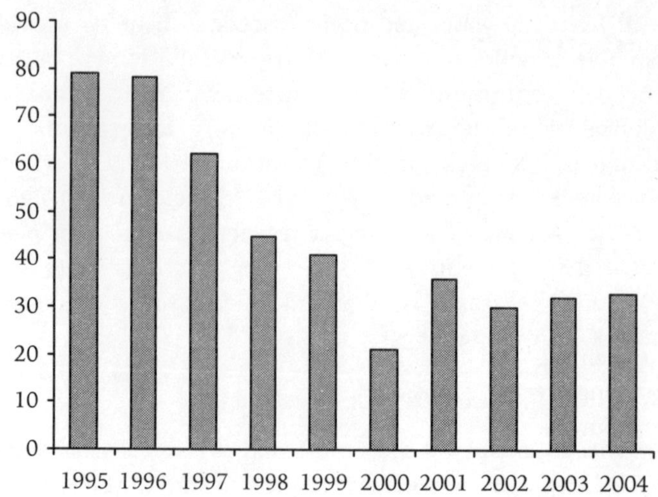

Source: Office of the Dy. Director, Wildlife, Northern Region, 2004

ports may be purely opportunistic there is always scope for well planned operations landing the major operators. However, due to the legal procedures and the associated delays only few cases culminate in a conviction. Lack of sufficient manpower and resources is also another major hurdle in providing an effective deterrent to would be traders.

There is a lack of access to identification material and relevant skills with the enforcement agencies like the police and the customs. Training in Wildlife forensics related to the trade and the legal aspects is urgently required for the personnel of the Wildlife Wing along with the requisite grounding on all aspects of recording evidence and preparation of the charge sheets.

A host of NGOs have taken active part in intelligence gathering and trapping poachers and traders. Such efforts need to be strengthened and better coordination with the enforcement agencies is highly desirable. NGOs like the WWF, in particular TRAFFIC India and the Wildlife Protection Society of India (WPSI) have played a key role in highlighting the issue of illegal wildlife trade in the capital and provided enforcement assistance from time to time in form of enforceable intelligence on wildlife criminals, as well as identification tools, kits, handbooks, posters, TV spots etc.

Government of India has established an inter agency consultative body for periodic review of wildlife crime situation especially as it pertains to control of illegal trade in wildlife in the country. This high level body is headed by the Secretary of the Ministry of Environment and

Forests, MOEF and includes representatives of all relevant agencies and Ministries at the union level. It is desirable that such mechanisms are replicated at the state level also, where at present information gathering and coordination exist mostly at an informal level based on the perceived urgency of specific cases. A coordination committee with representatives of Police, Customs and Central Excise, Railways, Forests and NGOs and nominees of the Hon'ble Chief Justice of Delhi High Court has been constituted during 2006-07 for effective implementation of the Wildlife (Protection) Act. The revival of the Central Sector Scheme relating to Control of Poaching and Illegal Trade that had been transferred during the 8th Plan to the State sector will augment the resources at the disposal of the enforcement agencies.

8.3.4 Managing Monkey and Captive Elephant Populations in Delhi

A major issue of concern relates to the management of macaque populations within Delhi. At present the Animal Welfare department is responsible for managing this issue and the Department of Forest and Wildlife maintains captive monkeys at a holding facility at Rajokri PF.

8.3.4.1 Background

According to an estimate, there are more than 4500 rhesus macaques (*Macaca mulatta*) (hereinafter called 'monkeys') in Delhi who share urban habitat with human populations in residential colonies, markets and office premises. This interface invariably results into conflicts, and sometime quite fatal too.

The primary reason prompting monkeys to use urban environ as their inseparable habitat is related basically with their commensal behaviour (capacity to share human inhabited habitations) being put into practice by them to compensate for shortage of food (or as substitute of) and cover following large scale destruction of their natural habitat (the sylvan environ). This rather forced entry of monkeys into the urban environ, over a period of time, has got further fortified due to the presence of freely available provisioned food (both as solid waste material across the urban environ and as offerings by devotees of Hanuman God). Apart from being easily available (the monkeys do not need to range for longer distances to procure stomach full of food as they have to do while in forest habitat), the provisioned food is also very rich in its nutritional values. The ensured supply of rich provisioned food, absence of natural predators and availability of extra time with the adult males to practice promiscuity, saw their population booming (compared to the population growth within the groups of their counterparts in forest habitat) and occupying all available nook and corners of the urban habitat before long. True to their innate behaviour, any resistance faced subsequently by monkeys in easy procurement of provisioned food and cover was countered by them with depredation activities—be it destruction of properties or inflicting injuries on the person. For them, the only aim left is to meet their basic requirements for food and cover.

8.3.4.2 Management Strategies

The management strategies for mitigation of monkey menace involve adopting an integrated approach of both short- and long-term measures. One major step in the entire mitigation strategy is to first categorise monkey populations based on their behavioural traits. Broadly the monkeys fall into three categories; obligatory urban monkeys, facultative urban monkeys and semi-wild monkeys. It is believed that major populations of monkeys in Delhi belong to obligatory urban category.

The monkeys in each of these categories would have to be treated with separate set of strategies. The most hostile groups of monkeys that are causing severe depredation in and around the human habitations can be captured and translocated at alternate sites (forested habitat) as a short-term relief measure. However, this would have to be preceded with a thorough assessment of possible impacts of the released monkeys on native flora and fauna at the release site. This would also require proper facilities for appropriate health care and other quarantine measures before release of monkeys in the wild. The long-term measures would include facilitating resurrection of their lost natural habitat, complete check on the availability of provisioned food to the monkeys in the urban environ (this will slowly allow them to switch over to natural food), population control/management with the aim of reduction in the population growth (through application of anti-fertility measures and physical capture of males using non-lethal methods), and education and awareness among the public to attempt at shunning all such activities that would help minimising the chances of confrontation with monkeys.

Behaviourally, the obligatory urban monkeys are virtually at a point of no return (to the wilderness areas) and would have to be removed physically from the urban environ. Realising the fact that their health (it is suspected that they might have contracted many zoonotic diseases) and behaviour would not allow their release in the wild habitat straightaway, it may be worthwhile to have specially created monkey sanctuaries in suburban areas for those groups of monkeys for health check-up, various quarantine regulations and for habituating them to live in a forest habitat. These sanctuaries would also have facilities for religious feeding by the devotees after clamping a total ban on religious feeding in and around temples premises. The free availability of provisioned food in these sanctuaries would also help lure the obligatory and facultative groups of monkeys reducing their populations from the urban areas. The monkeys in these sanctuaries, after proper health treatments, can also be supplied to various laboratories across the country as experimental animals after observing relevant rules and regulations to this effect. Simultaneously, the population growth of these monkey groups inside the sanctuary will have to be checked with the application of appropriate sterilisation techniques.

The facultative group of monkeys mostly occupy peripheral areas of the urban environ (mostly the temple sites and the road-sides). These monkeys mostly act as a transitory stage between the obligatory and semi-wild groups of monkeys. If appropriate measures are not taken, the void created following translocation of above mentioned obligatory urban monkey populations will be filled in no time by the facultative group of monkeys. The strategy to deal with these monkey groups primarily rests with the effective management of solid waste across their habitation range to ensure non-availability of provisioned food and resurrection of their lost wild habitat to allow them to switch over to natural diet: being facultative these monkeys are still left with wild instincts and can be forced to home-coming in absence of provisioned food. Also, the strategy of physical capture and translocation as in the case of obligatory monkeys can also be adopted for those stubborn individuals (mainly the alpha males) who would resist return to the wild with all their might from these facultative groups of monkeys.

The semi-wild monkey groups are mostly confronted as road-side beggars with the difference that they are choosers too. Though occupying the forested habitat (whatever little is available in Delhi on ridge areas and other greens) for cover, they would prefer provisioned food either through begging (road-side) or snatching (in temple locations) to supplement the natural food available close to their roosting places. These groups are the easiest to control compared to above two categories. Main strategy would be to strengthen the forest habitat and convert them into a kind of conservation reserves with major food species of their choice. This has to be done in conjunction with putting a complete ban on the availability of provisioned food on the road/temple/residential colonies sites by invoking relevant Acts/Rules and Regulations of Traffic Department, Municipality/City Development Authority, Forests and Wildlife Department, etc.

A common strategy to deal with all the three different categories of monkey groups relate with creation of awareness about the health hazards associated with feeding and messing up with monkeys and learning among the local residents, motorists, devotees, staff and officers working in different office premises on how to co-exist with these forced non-human city dwellers till they are helped to vacate unnatural urban environ in favour of their natural forested habitat.

In pursuance of the orders of the Hon'ble Delhi High Court, monkeys are being trapped by MCD and NDMC from Delhi and are being released in the ABWLS. As the forest area is deficient in fruit bearing trees, arrangements have been made for feeding as also tall saplings of fruit bearing trees are being planted. About 800 monkeys have been relocated to ABWLS. Public awareness about the ban on feeding by members of the public is also being attempted through advertisements.

8.3.4.3 Captive Elephants

There has been increasing concern with respect to the captive elephants in Delhi. The captive elephants are viewed as a traffic hazard, and movement of these animals on the arterial roads is cause for concern to all. There are a total of 37 captive elephants in Delhi on last count. The elephants were primarily kept on the banks of the Yamuna adjacent to the ITO bridge area but since their eviction from here have scattered across the city. These elephants are engaged in weddings and other special occasions such as the Republic Day Parade.

Due to unavailability of the specific costs of maintenance and the earnings from such employment by the owners it is extremely difficult to comment on the status of welfare of these captive elephants. Only 20 elephants have been implanted with an identifying microchip and 19 ownership certificates have been issued. The rest of the cases are under review with the Wildlife Wing. In view of the scant information available it is only recommended that the Chief Wildlife Wardens of the adjacent states do not issue any transit permits without verifying the ownership certificates. On the issue of a requisite welfare and housing policy for the elephants, the Kerala Captive Elephant (Management and Maintenance) Rules 2003 could be referred to for necessary guidelines.

8.4 Appraisal of Policy and Programmes

The Wildlife (Protection) Act of 1972 and the Delhi Wildlife Protection Rules 1973 are the overarching statutes under which the wildlife management activities are primarily defined. Additionally, provisions within the

Indian Forest Act (1927), Forest Conservation Act (1980), Environment (Protection) Act 1986 and the Delhi Preservation of Tree Act (1994) are applicable. This section will not critically peruse the Act(s) and rules per se, as that is beyond the scope of the present report. Instead, the focus is on the specific programmes within the purview of the wildlife domain.

8.4.1 Schemes Under the Department of Forest and Wildlife Government of NCT of Delhi

The Department of Forest and Wildlife, Government of NCT of Delhi was set up in 1987 vide Delhi Administrations Order No F.57/4/87_S.I. The work relating to Environment, Forests and Wildlife was till then being looked after by the Development Department. The Wildlife Section and the Forest Department however continued to be under the charge of the Deputy Commissioners' Revenue and Development respectively and the duties of the Chief Wildlife Warden (CWLW) were being discharged by the Deputy Commissioner. The Wildlife section and Forest Department were merged only in 1996 and placed under the charge of a Conservator of Forests (CF and CWLW). At present the department has the following personnel: one CF, four DCFs, one ACF, one Soil Conservation Officer, three Rangers, 14 Deputy Forest Rangers, 59 Forest Guards, and 744 labourers. The personnel manning the Wildlife Wing include: 1 Senior Wildlife Inspector, 5 Wildlife Inspectors, 1 Game Inspector and 10 Wildlife Guards/Watchers. Hence only the 9th Five Year Plan Period onwards the Department mirrors the usual setup of a Department of Forest and Wildlife elsewhere in the country. Nevertheless, certain aberrations that continue to exist as a result of the erstwhile administrative setup are discussed later.

The 10th Five Year Plan has brought with it some changes to the schemes being implemented by the Department of Forest and Wildlife. The Grant in Aid to Delhi Wastelands Development Board and the Road side plantation schemes have been discontinued since the beginning of the 9th Five Year Plan. Three schemes namely Plantation and Distribution of Seedlings, Preservation and Maintenance of Ridges and Development of City forest have been merged as also the wildlife related schemes of Strengthening of Wildlife Section and Birds cum Wildlife Sanctuary. A perusal of the performance of the FD in general and the three prevalent schemes follows. The annual approved and revised outlays as well as expenditure for the period 1997-2006 are given in Figure 8.3.

FIGURE 8.3

Forest Department Approved Outlay (AO), Revised Outlay (RO) and Expenditure (EXP)

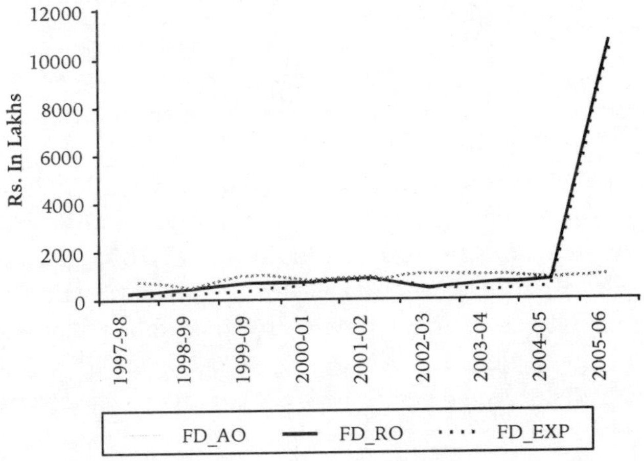

Source: Planning Department, Govt. of NCT of Delhi, 2006.

The decline in revised Plan Outlays and Plan Expenditure after 2001-2002 is on account of the fact that Forest and Wildlife are not accorded a priority status. The ratios of Approved Outlays and Expenditure of the Department to Total Approved Outlay and Expenditure of the Government of NCT of Delhi respectively are given in Figure 8.4.

FIGURE 8.4

Ratio of FD Approved Outlay and Expenditure to Total Approved Outlay and Expenditure

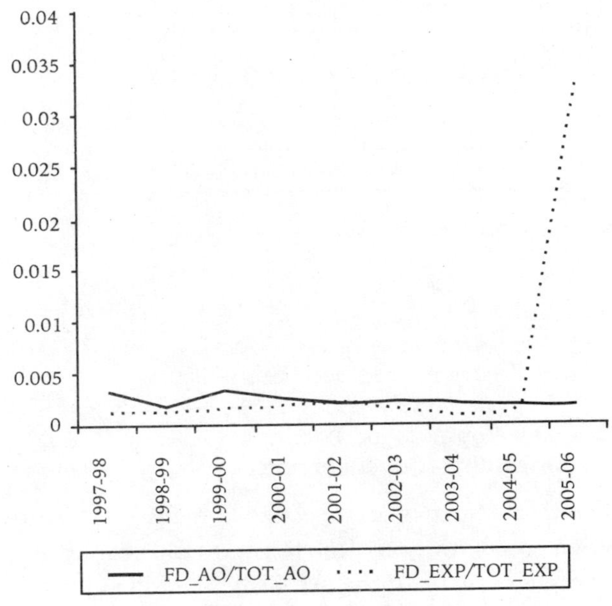

Source: Planning Department, Govt. of NCT of Delhi, 2006.

The miniscule share of Forest and Wildlife Department outlays and expenditures is further declining and is again indicative of the lowly priority accorded to this sector. The figures if adjusted for inflation may reveal a decline in allocation in real terms.

A major criteria indicative of the performance of the Forest Department in terms of utilisation of funds and is rated poor according to the evaluation criteria (80 per cent to 50 per cent). The subsequent years 2002-2004 have shown a marked decline in the utilisation ratio with an average of 0.782 for the period 1997–2006 (Figure 8.5). It is also evident from Figure 8.5 that utilisation of revenue allocations have been better than funds allocated under the capital heads with the exception of FY 2005-2006. While utilisation of revenue allocations have been above 80 per cent considerable attention is required to be devoted to the capital funds utilisation.

FIGURE 8.5

Ratio of Revised Outlay and Expenditure of Forest Department

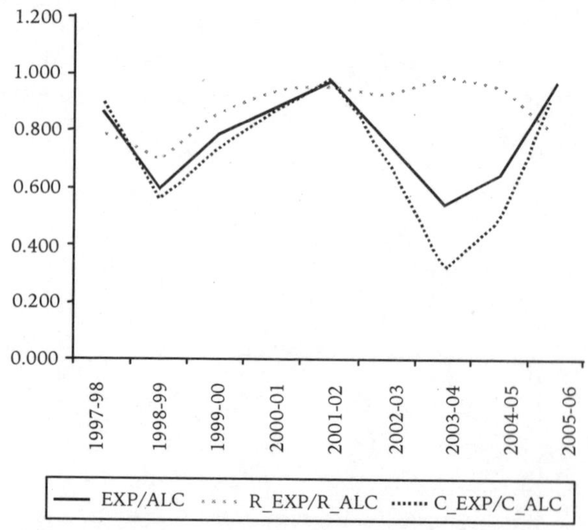

Source: Deptt. of Forest & Wildlife, Govt. of NCT of Delhi, 2006.

There may be several reasons for the poor utilisation and we shall examine the specific schemes under which the plan allocations have been utilised.

8.4.1.1 Development of Forests Including Consolidation

The performance of the department in terms of achievement of the physical targets has been extremely encouraging. Against the 9th Five Year Plan target of plantation of 5 lakh seedlings a total of 13.28 lakh seedlings were planted. Againts the 9th Five Year plan target of free distribution of 40 lakh seedlings only 14 lakh could be distributed. The recent performance in this regard is better with an achievement of 3 lakh seedlings as against a target of 2.5 lakh seedling distribution. Considerable progress was also achieved with respect to the Preservation and Maintenance of Ridge in the 9th Five Year Plan Period. Demarcation of 600 acres along with plantation in 500 *bighas* of 2.02 lakh seedlings was carried out. Erection of barbed wire fencing in Dera Mandi and Ghitorni was completed and newer areas in Neb Sarai were taken up for fencing. Alipur and Hauzrani city forests were developed by planting 22000 tall plants of height more than 6 inches. Several green houses and allied facilities like gensets were set up during the 9th Five Year Plan Period.

FIGURE 8.6

Utilisation Ratios of Expenditure and allocation for Development of Forests including consolidation

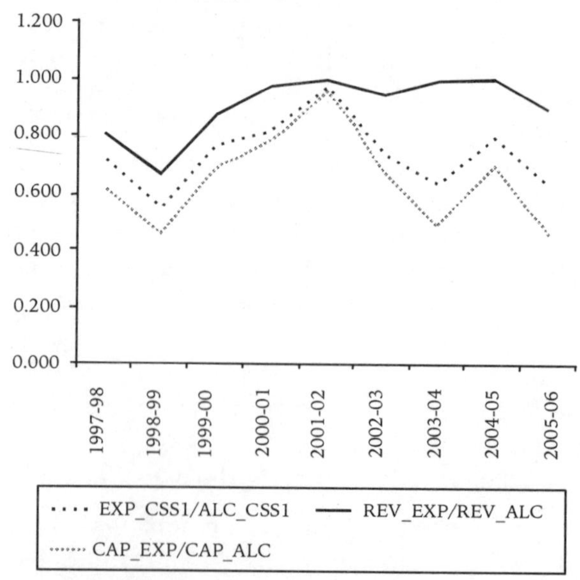

Source: Deptt. of Forest & Wildlife, Govt. of NCT of Delhi, 2006

Objectives of this scheme for the 10th Plan Period are:

1. To raise and maintain plantations on wastelands, *gaon sabha* lands, along road sides, railway tracks, drains, *bunds* etc., in order to increase forest cover of Delhi to 10 per cent of total area (addition of 60 sq. km in 5 years).

2. To raise the seedlings of suitable forestry and ornamental species in the nurseries which can be planted on private lands, school compounds, institutional areas, avenues etc.,

3. To distribute the raised seedlings free of cost to

general public, institutions/organisations, government and semi-government departments and public especially in rural areas to augment income.

4. Demarcation, protection and enrichment of existing forest areas by providing fencing/ construction of boundary wall and then planting of valuable species to enrich the floral composition of the existing forests to make it more effective as a carbon sink and green lung of the city besides increasing their value, environmentally and aesthetically by forestry and allied activities.
5. To develop more city forests.
6. To preserve and manage the Delhi Ridge, demarcate and survey the existing land use on various ridges.
7. Preparation of maps, to contain the further encroachment and vacate old encroachment.
8. To undertake water conservation and water harvesting measures in the forest areas.
9. Preparation of Management/working plans for the Ridge.
10. To improve the quality of forests by planting indigenous species.

Programme Contents:

a) Planting of tall plants particularly on the road junction, banks of river Yamuna, drains, *Gaon Sabha* land etc., which are heavily polluted besides other areas.

b) Demarcation, protection, fencing, and enrichment of existing forest areas by providing fencing/ boundary walls and enrichment plantation to improve the floral composition of the existing forests. Development of more forest areas through protection of area by fencing and construction of water ponds, enrichment of forest composition by planting, developing water sources through tube wells and beautification of these forest areas.

c) For better survival of the tree saplings, watering the plant is an important requisite. Three mini trucks will be purchased for transportation of seedlings and watering the plants in the field.

d) Digging of tube wells, maintenance of diesel sets and hand pumps in the nurseries and forest areas and laying of hydrants besides providing electric connection in all nurseries and city forest.

e) Maintenance of the fencing and boundary walls of nurseries and forest areas.

f) Development of adequate number of additional nurseries and introduction of improved nursery technology, i.e., use of root trainer etc.

g) Labour sheds and basic facilities will be created for smooth and efficient functioning of the nursery works.

h) Development of Water Harvesting structures in the forest area to conserve moisture and to check the water loss due to runoff.

i) Scheme plan for development of city forests, Block planting of various species, establishment of arboretum, developing a core zone of forests, providing jogging and cycles track for the visitors, planting of flowering and ornamental trees, developing a Cacti house and green house, establishment of a orchid house and nature interpretation centre, Planning informal recreational facilities as per action plan.

TABLE 8.1

Approved Plan Outlay 10th Five Year Plan (2002-2007)

(Rs. in lakh)

	2002-03	*2003-04*	*2004-05*	*2005-06*	*2006-07*
REV.	150.00	140.00	150.00	160.00	170.00
CAP.	400.00	310.00	320.00	300.00	300.00
TOTAL	550.00	450.00	470.00	460.00	470.00

Source: Deptt. of Forest & Wildlife, Govt. of NCT of Delhi.

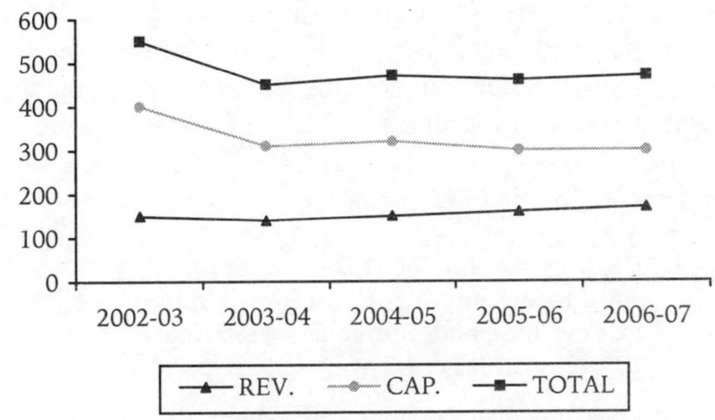

The development of 14 city forests is taken up during the 10th Five Year Plan Period. An outlay of Rs.2400 lakh has been earmarked for this scheme under the 10th Five Year Plan. However the revised outlays for 2002-2003 and

2003-04 were reduced to Rs. 530 lakh and Rs. 378 lakh respectively.

The activities planned for the year 2004-05 include:

(i) Afforestation on lands made available for the purpose including raising of medicinal plants.

(ii) Free distribution of saplings to public.

(iii) Survey, demarcation, consolidation of plantation/forest area. Protection from encroachment, construction of boundary wall and fencing of the plantation area.

(iv) Preservation of Southern Ridge.

(v) Preparation of management/working plans of forest area, improvement of existing forests through planting of indigenous trees.

(vi) To undertake soil and water conservation measures in forest/plantation area.

(vii) Development and maintenance of city forests for improvement of environment and recreation of local population.

Physical targets of planting 3.30 lakh saplings and distribution of 3.6 lakh saplings, development of nurseries, and protection of forest area through fencing are set for the period 2004-05. The total plan outlay for the financial year 2004-05 is approved to be Rs. 450 lakh out of which Rs.150 lakh is approved under Revenue Head and Rs.300 lakh under the Capital Head.

Presently continuation of 688 posts have been sanctioned for Plantation and Distribution of seedlings and these will continue during 2004-05 as well. However, additional posts of labourers may be required to be created to absorb the ex-laborers on the direction of various courts. While there is great demand for ornamental and decorative plants, mostly forestry species are promoted under this scheme, thereby decreasing the seedling offtake by people. The lack of trained technical persons proves to be a major impediment in the implementation of this scheme.

8.4.1.2 Strengthening of Administration Management, Infrastructure, Training of Personnel and Publicity Measures for Forest and Forestry

The measure of success of this scheme is the increase in total forest cover within the NCT region from 88 km^2 in 1999 to 111 km^2 in 2001 (FSI, 2002). This has been possible due to the concerted efforts of the Forest Department on several fronts through initiatives like the Greening Delhi Action Plans.

Utilisation of funds under this scheme is the best among the three schemes. The entire sum of allocation under this scheme is under the revenue head and is consistently over 80 per cent. Also the trend in utilisation for the period 1999-2000 onwards has shown an upward trend that has seen a decline after 2004.

FIGURE 8.7

Utilisation Ratio of Revenue Funds for Strengthening of Administration Management, Infrastructure, Training of Personnel and Publicity Measures for Forest and Forestry

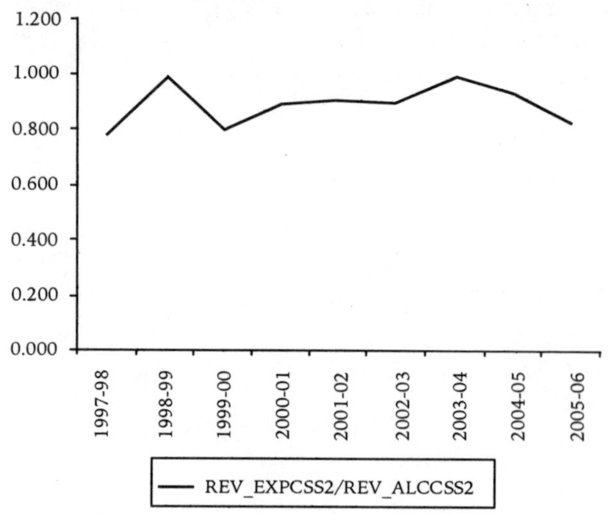

Source: Deptt. of Forest & Wildlife, Govt. of NCT of Delhi, 2006.

Objectives envisaged for the 10th Five Year Plan are:

1. To strengthen the Administration of forest department in NCT of Delhi.
2. To ensure better forest management of Ridge areas and City Forests.
3. To create awareness among people about importance of ridge and forests in general through various means of publicity.
4. To increase the mobility of the field staff by providing vehicles/motorcycles.
5. Training of staff to enhance skill and efficiency.

Programme contents:

1. To create the supporting posts in the Office and field for the effective functioning of Conservator of Forests/Head of the Department and Deputy Conservator of Forests heading three territorial divisions so as to achieve better Forest management.

2. Salary of the 41 posts created for effective functioning of the Department.
3. Providing office equipment such as computer, fax, photocopiers, etc., for effective documentation and communication thereby achieving higher efficiency.
4. Printing and publishing of material.
5. Preparation of documentary films.
6. Organising debates, symposium, exhibitions, workshops drawing and photo competition and other publicity measure for arousing public consciousness in protecting trees and forests.
7. Replacement of 1 jeep, 1 gypsy, 1 truck and purchase of 6 motorcycles.
8. Training of staff.

The responsibilities of the Forest Department having increased manifold, there is need to increase to strengthen the administration by providing office of the Conservator of Forests supporting staff in office as well as in the field. Also constant upgradation of skills through training related to wildlife management is imperative for effective discharge of functions. Increased participation of the citizens is obtained through awareness campaigns. For the plantation activities effective media coverage is highly desirable.

TABLE 8.2

Additional Posts Required

S.No.	Post	Numbers
1.	A.AO/J.A.O	03
2.	Admn.Officer	01
3.	Superintendent	01
4.	Head Clerk	03
5.	U.D.C/Cashier/Store Keeper	08
6.	Peon	07
7.	*Chowkidar*	16
8.	Sweeper	04
9.	Draft Man/Tracer	01
10.	*Dakman*	04

Source: Deptt. of Forest & Wildlife, Govt. of NCT of Delhi.

A total of 41 posts have been created during 1996-1997 under this scheme, however an additional requirement of 50 posts is put forth.

8.4.1.3 Development of Wildlife Sanctuary and Strengthening of Wildlife Section

Crucial work related to the protection of ABWLS was undertaken during the 9th Five Year Plan Period. This included construction of boundary wall, peripheral road, a tubewell, 50 ponds, plantation of 0.40 lakh seedlings, development of a lake, development of two nurseries, development of two mother tree groves and completion of 13 check dams. Bhatti area was handed over to Eco Task Force for reclamation of 300 acres along with plantation of 71434 saplings. The Forest and Wildlife Department has entered into an agreement with the Bombay Natural History Society (BNHS) for setting up a Conservation Education Centre at ABWLS. The centre will initially be run by the BNHS for three years. It will impart natural education and provide facilities for research and conservation to the young generation, students, teachers, non-government organisations, policy planners and the eco-clubs in various school and colleges. The aim of this centre is to create awareness of conservation of nature, natural resources, biodiversity, and rare and endangered flora and fauna in the city. The technical expertise of the Centre for Environmental Management of Degraded Ecosystems, University of Delhi is also being actively sought for restoration of the previously mined and degraded areas within the sanctuary.

FIGURE 8.8

Utilisation Ratio of Capital and Revenue Allocations for Development of Wildlife Sanctuary & Strengthening of Wildlife Section

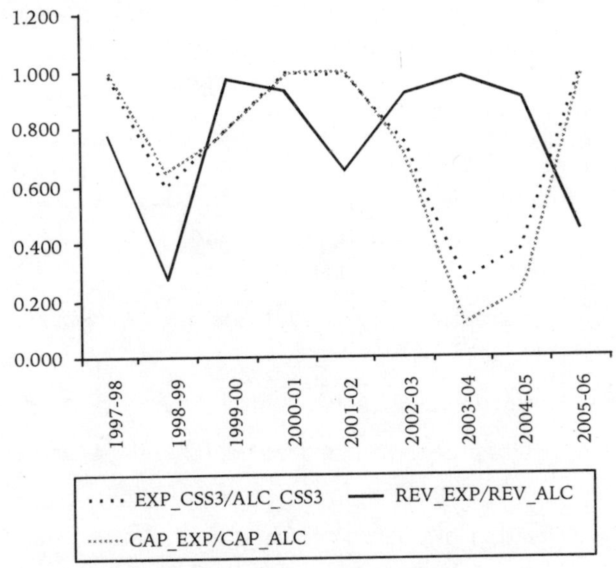

Source: Deptt. of Forest & Wildlife, Govt. of NCT of Delhi, 2006.

The utilisation of allocation under the capital head has been particularly weak in this scheme as is evident from Figure 8.8 and has only improved in the last FY i.e., 2005-2006. The bulk of funds under this scheme are earmarked under the capital head which results in the overall utilisation ratio being weighted by the poor performance of the capital allocation utilisation. Some of the major impediments and bottlenecks are identified and discussed in the next section.

The targets for 10th Five Year Plan Period include afforestation of 2100 acres through planting 8 lakh saplings as also the construction of 15 check dams.

Objectives of the scheme for the 10th Plan period include:

i) To strengthen wildlife section with more manpower and other infrastructure for more effective enforcement of Wildlife (Protection) Act, 1972.

ii) To provide sufficient mobility and communication facilities.

iii) To evolve a formidable strategy to counter the latest modus operandi of the smugglers/poachers.

iv) To establish fruitful coordination with other government agencies and NGOs engaged in enforcement activities and conservation.

v) To educate the masses about the utility of wildlife.

vi) To improve an effective intelligence network to get information regarding poaching and smuggling of wild animals/articles and finally the stringent enforcement of Wildlife (Protection) Act, 1972 and its allied amendments and notifications.

vii) Protection and maintenance of ABWLS, and improvement and development of habitat to make the sanctuary conducive and hospitable for indigenous faunal species.

vii) Reclamation and development of sanctuary through Eco Task force.

ix) Development of Eco Tourism.

The activities proposed under the 10th Five Year Plan are:

i) Creation of additional posts

ii) Purchase of vehicles and other modern communication facilities.

iii) Construction of a building to house Wildlife office, stores/godown for seized property, a lock-up and central room.

iv) Purchase of computers, quick-productive cameras and publicity requisites.

v) Strengthening of intelligence network and coordination with other Govt. and NGOs engaged in Wildlife enforcement and conservation.

vi) Construction of roads, boundary walls, water reservoirs, watch towers.

vii) Setting up of nature interpretation centre.

viii) Habitat improvement through natural regeneration supplemented by enrichment planting combined with *in-situ* soil and water conservation works like trenching cum-pits, check dams, percolation tanks, small pounds etc.

ix) Reclamation and development of Sanctuary through ECO Task Force.

TABLE 8.3

Approved Plan Outlay for 10th Plan Period

(Rs. in lakh)

	2002-03	*2003-04*	*2004-05*	*2005-06*	*2006-07*
REV.	50.00	150.00	150.00	150.00	150.00
CAP.	300.00	360.00	370.00	350.00	370.00
TOTAL	350.00	510.00	520.00	500.00	520.00

Source: Deptt. of Forest & Wildlife, Govt. of NCT of Delhi.

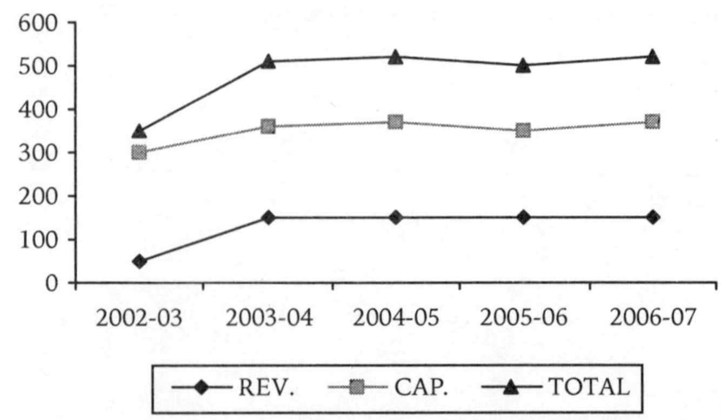

An outlay of Rs. 2500 lakh is earmarked for the 10th Five Year plan out of which Rs. 750 lakhs is earmarked under Revenue Head and Rs. 1750 lakh under the Capital Head. However, the revised outlays for the annual periods 2002-2003 and 2003-2004 were reduced to Rs. 300 lakh and Rs. 245 lakh respectively. The total plan outlay for the financial year 2004-05 is proposed to be Rs. 310 lakh out of which Rs. 60 lakh is proposed under Revenue Head and Rs. 250 lakh under the Capital Head.

Only two posts of Wildlife Inspector are sanctioned under Strengthening of Wildlife Section scheme. Keeping in view the extent and intensity of threat to the ABWLS and the urgent need for tackling the illegal trade in wildlife products the additional posts are to be created after due appraisal.

The threat of illegal mining and encroachment is ever present on the fringes of ABWLS. However there are severe limitations being faced by the staff of ABWLS. The lack of sufficient logistical capability severely hampers patrolling work and there is urgent need for purchase of vehicles. There is need for full time scientists to carry on the long term work of restoration of degraded habitats. Also, the Wildlife Wing plans to bring under its purview the National Zoological Park, New Delhi, which is presently under Ministry of Environment and Forest, Government of India. This however should be deferred in view of the already stretched manpower resources and the lack of sufficient technical expertise.

8.5 Recommendations for Department of Forest and Wildlife

While it is eminently desirable that the Department of Forest and Wildlife, Government of NCT of Delhi take a lead role in the multi-agency programmes for wildlife management as also biodiversity conservation, there are certain structural impediments that need to be recognised and acted upon. The personnel of the department are stretched to the capacity with a large quantum of their work time being taken up in legal matters.

There are about 100 cases relating to land encroachments, 20 cases relating to the Delhi Tree Preservation Act (1994) and 60 grievance cases that are being handled by the department. This is in addition to over 6000 Declaration cases and about 175 Wildlife (Protection) Act cases that are at several stages of the legal process. Proper handling of these cases requires a dedicated pool of personnel that is not holding primary charge of an area at the same time. To this effect it is recommended that all legal matters are handled by a duly appointed Law Officer along with adequate ministerial staff.

The staffing pattern of the department reveals a narrow hierarchy of mostly single officers down to the Ranger level. The vertical linkage is one to one from the DCFs of the four divisions through the ACF upto the Ranger. The lower rungs also have a peculiar structure wherein the vital link of Forester is missing between the Forest Guard and the Forest Ranger. Also, there are several instances of personnel stagnating at the Senior Wildlife Inspector level. A coherent policy of promotions and parity in pay scales with other Union Territories is therefore desirable. These structural impediments to a smooth chain of command and incentives for a motivated work force require streamlining.

Regular upgradation of skills and expertise available to the personnel of the department is a must. To this effect the earlier sections have noted the need for adequate training in Wildlife Forensics and preparation of legal cases. Specific inputs for the restoration work in ABWLS require training of the personnel for such technical work. Further, personnel of the wildlife wing would benefit from training on legal matters and wildlife management. It is also noted that some of the criteria for availing training with external agencies and institutes may have to be relaxed in the case of personnel of the department as they may have exceeded the prescribed age limit.

Demarcation of physical boundaries for the acquired lands in a developed urban environment such as Delhi is proving to be a major task. Problems related to part of the Khasra plot not being physically acquired and remaining encroached and absence of markers in the form of boundary pillars or other such clearly identifiable landmarks are being encountered. The personnel of the department do not have a grounding in such matters. Therefore, it is recommended that that cases be either handled by deputation of adequate personnel from the Revenue Department or a Land Cell be created within the department. This could be staffed by an officer of the rank of ACF, a Range Officer, one Field *Kanungo* and two *Patwaris*.

Policy with respect to the Ridge areas has been articulated by the H'ble Supreme Court in the M.C. Mehta *versus* Union of India order on securing protection of the Ridge. The restoration of the Ridge areas that are under the control of the Department and other agencies is accorded the highest priority. However, due to the multiplicity of handling agencies adequate and timely action may not be possible. In this regard it is recommended that the Forest and Wildlife Department take an active lead role and coordinate the actions of other agencies. Also for the Yamuna floodplains management, it is only logical that the department is entrusted with the overall responsibility of management of this vital wetland ecosystem. To this end synergies with the functions related to environmental matters is vital. Coordination with other agencies such as the DDA, Delhi Jal Board, NDMC and other stake holders such as Corporate and Voluntary bodies and NGOs should be primarily handled by the department. Coordination in intelligence gathering and operations related to illegal trade in Wildlife Products is urgently needed and should be moved from the informal case to case basis to a regular exercise.

Last but not the least there is enormous scope for improvement in the funds utilisation especially the capital funds allocated to the Department. The tremendous pressures in terms of work load in the face of a lack of a coherent activity plan have led to the poor utilisation of funds. A target of minimum 85 per cent to 90 per cent utilisation is highly desirable for the remainder of the 10th Five Year Plan Period.

References

Anon (2002). *Evaluation Study Report on Eco-clubs in Schools*, Evaluation Unit, Planning Department, Government of NCT of Delhi. Delhi.

———. (2004). *Greening Delhi Action Plan*, Department of Forests and Wildlife, Government of NCT of Delhi. New Delhi.

———. (2005). *Status Report, Yamuna and Aravalli Biodiversity Parks*, Centre for Management of Degraded Ecosystems. Delhi: Delhi University.

Babu, C.R., Pushpam Kumar, Lallan Prasad and Rashmi Agrawal (2001). "Valuation of Ecological Functions and Benefits: A Case Study of Wetland Ecosystems along the Yamuna River Corridors of Delhi Region", *EERC Working Paper* Series:WB-6, Indira Gandhi Institute of Development Research, Mumbai.

Champion, H.G. and S.K. Seth (1968). Revised *Forest Types of India*, Government of India Publication, New Delhi< *http://www.delhibird.org/checklists/Delhi/checklists_delhi.htm*>

Forest Survey of India (2002). *State of Forest Report, 2001*, Forest Survey of India, Ministry of Environment and Forests, Dehradun.

Islam, M.Z. and A.R. Rahamani (2004). *Important Bird Areas in India: Priority sites for Conservation*. Indian Bird Conservation Network: Bombay Natural History Society and Birdlife International (U.K.) pp.357-359.

Kumar, Arun (1997). "Fauna of Delhi: An Overview", in *Fauna of Delhi*, State Fauna Series 6, Calcutta: Zoological Survey of India, pp.1-15.

Kumar, A. and V. Khanna (1997). "Biogeography of Delhi", in *Fauna of Delhi*, State Fauna Series 6. Calcutta: Zoological Survey of India, pp. 17-44.

Kumar Pushpam (2001). Cost of Wetland Conversion: A case study of Floodplain Wetland Ecosystems along the Yamuna River Corridors of Delhi Region, Presented at the Open Meeting of the Global Environmental Change Research Community, October 6-8, 2001, Rio de Janeiro.

Madan, Mohan (2002). GIS-Based Spatial Information Integration, Modeling and Digital Mapping: A New Blend of Tool for Geospatial Environmental Health Analysis for Delhi Ridge, FIG XXII International Congress, April 19-26 2002, Washington D.C. USA.

Sawarkar, V.B. and S.A. Hussain (1997). "Problems and Prospects in conserving Asola-Bhatti Wildlife Sanctuary: Some Management Strategies", in *Fauna of Delhi*, State Fauna Series 6. Calcutta: Zoological Survey of India, pp.1-15.

Thapliyal, U.P. (1987). *Gazetteer of Rural Delhi*, Gazetteer Unit, Delhi Administration. Delhi.

Urfi, A.J. (2003). "The Birds of Okhla Barrage Bird Sanctuary". Delhi, India. *Forktail* 19:39-50.

Wildlife Institute of India (2002). Report on the Ecological social and hydrological factors affecting the management of wetland systems in Uttar Pradesh with special reference to Vijay Sagar and Associated water bodies in Ghaziabad district, Bakhira Bird Sanctuary and Nawabganj Bird Sanctuary, Dehradun.

Chapter 9

Education Status Report of Delhi

9.0 Introduction

Education plays a crucial role in empowering the disadvantaged sections of our society. Apart from knowledge being important in itself, there is a more pragmatic need for education in today's world since it helps to make people more articulate, better able to make choices and better equipped to participate in the development process through improved employment opportunities. The importance of education for women, in particular, can hardly be overemphasised since a large gamut of social issues and reforms are linked with it. Here, too, education can be interpreted as an empowering tool for improving women's lot and for broadening their horizon of opportunities.

Recognising the overriding importance of education in our country, the Indian government has stated two major goals of the Tenth Five Year Plan as:

i) Universalisation of elementary education (UEE), and

ii) Eradication of illiteracy.

UEE has three main aspects:

i) Universal access and enrolment.

ii) Universal education for children up to age 14.

iii) Substantial improvement in quality of education to allow all children to achieve essential levels of learning.

It is against this backdrop that we take a look at the present state of education in Delhi. In addition we look at higher levels of education. To the extent possible, we have used data from government sources like Economic Survey, NSSO surveys, Sixth All India Educational Survey, Delhi Statistical Handbook, Government statistics published by the Directorate of Education, Delhi, etc. But the Education Department does not provide information regarding government and private school facilities separately. Again, data on enrolment is available from government sources, but pertains to recognised schools only. Moreover enrolment data over various years occasionally show unexplained trend and major fluctuations in certain years (Table 9.6).[1] Delhi Government had undertaken a recent household survey focusing on school participation among 6 to 14 year old children which has provided a major source of input for elementary education, as has the background paper on education for Delhi Human Development Report. The paper has also drawn from different field surveys in Delhi, from reports published in the media as well as from interviews with service providers and government officials regarding problems in education and recent initiatives of the government.

9.1 Trends in Literacy Rates in Delhi since Independence

At present the literacy rate in Delhi is high at around 82 per cent but is still lower than Mumbai (87 per cent). Literacy rates have been increasing sharply over time as seen from different Censuses. Between 1961 and 1981, the growth in literacy was relatively slow, followed by a sharp increase in the next decade. It has grown slowly in the last decade again, perhaps indicating a tendency of leveling off. Female literacy rates have always been lower than that for males, but have largely followed the pattern for males. The literacy rates for males and females in Delhi in 2001 were 87.4 per cent and 75 per cent respectively (*Economic Survey 2001-02*). Within Delhi the

1. Any meaningful exercise in planning requires systematically collected data. There appeared to be a major gap in this respect.

literacy rates vary from 78 per cent to 85 per cent, north-east Delhi has the lowest literacy rate and east Delhi the highest.

Figure 9.1

Literacy Rates in Delhi

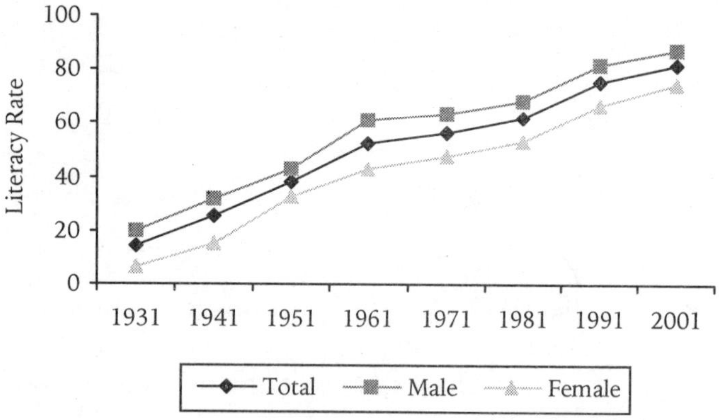

Source: Government of Delhi (2002). *Delhi Statistical Hand Book*. Directorate of Economics and Statistics, NCT of Delhi.

Population has increased very fast in Delhi (partly due to immigration), as a result of which illiteracy has grown in absolute numbers in spite of growth in literacy. By 2001, the illiterate population in Delhi was above 4 million (Figure 9.2).

Figure 9.2

Illiterate Population in Delhi

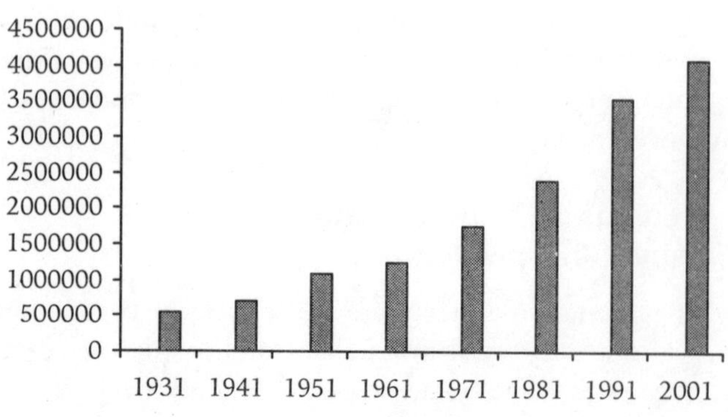

Source: Government of Delhi (2002). *Delhi Statistical Hand Book*. Directorate of Economics and Statistics, NCT of Delhi.

In percentage terms, the share of illiterate people in urban Delhi is around 13.7 per cent of the total (Table 9.1) although the Delhi figure is much better compared to the urban India average of 20.2 per cent. The table also shows the educational performance of urban Delhi *vis-à-vis* urban India. Delhi performs better than all-India (urban) as seen from the lower proportion of illiteracy and the higher proportion of people who have completed secondary and higher levels.

TABLE 9.1

Education Levels of Population in 7+ Age Group in Urban Delhi and India, 1999

(Per cent)

	Urban Delhi			*Urban India*		
	Male	*Female*	*Total*	*Male*	*Female*	*Total*
Not literate	8.3	19.8	13.7	13.5	27.7	20.2
Literate, below primary	14.0	13.1	13.6	16.4	15.7	16.1
Primary	13.6	13.0	13.3	14.9	14.3	14.7
Middle	13.8	10.6	12.3	17.7	15.3	16.5
Secondary	15.1	13.2	14.2	15.1	11.7	13.5
Higher secondary	11.5	10.8	11.2	9.7	7.1	8.5
Graduate and above	23.6	19.5	21.7	12.7	8.2	10.5
Total	100	100	100	100	100	100

Source: NSSO 55th round, 1999

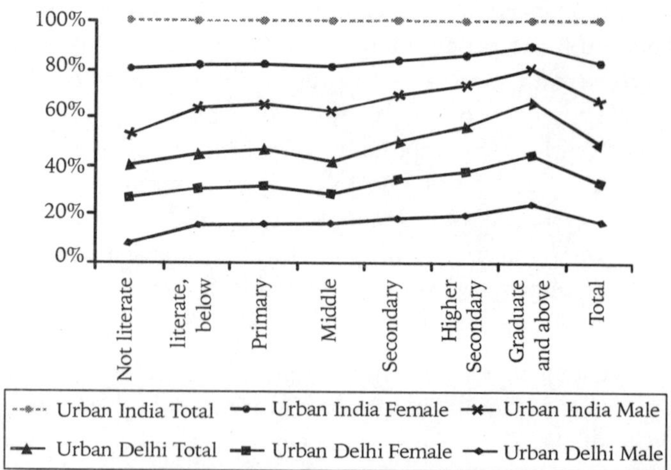

9.1.1 Migration Issues

The performance indicated above does not reflect an even performance by all sections of the society. This distinction is particularly important for Delhi because this city has a large migrant population and the education scenario here is impacted by not only population growth but also by migration. Delhi acts as a magnet to people from different socioeconomic strata. It offers the maximum opportunities for higher education among all Indian metros and education at the higher levels reflects a large student body which comes into Delhi for higher education. But Delhi also attracts a very large size of illiterate and semi-literate people who come here in search of jobs. The relatively poor performance of this section affects Delhi's educational performance. The issue of migration and its impact on Delhi's education scenario is discussed in this section.

By 2000, an estimated 25 per cent of Delhi's population was living in slums.[2] The decadal growth rates in population in Delhi have been as high as 53.2 per cent (1971-1981), 51.4 per cent (1981-1991) and 46.5 per cent (1991-2001).[3] The large contribution due to migration exceeded that due to natural increases (from neighbouring and faraway states, as well from other countries e.g. Bangladesh and Nepal) as can be gauged from the Table 9.2.

TABLE 9.2

Population Statistics for Delhi

(in millions)

	Population as on 1st July	*Increase in Population over previous year*	*Natural increase in Population*	*Increase in Population due to Migration*
1991	9.55	0.389	0.211	0.178
1995	11.17	0.424	0.206	0.218
1999	12.98	0.468	0.209	0.259
2000	13.46	0.478	0.237	0.241

Source: Delhi Government, Planning Department.

As may be expected, the educational attainment is very poor (relative to urban India average or urban Delhi average) for disadvantaged groups such as the scheduled castes, minority groups and families of casual labourers. There are some differences in educational attainments in

Figure 9.3

Educational Attainments of Disadvantaged Groups in Delhi, 1999

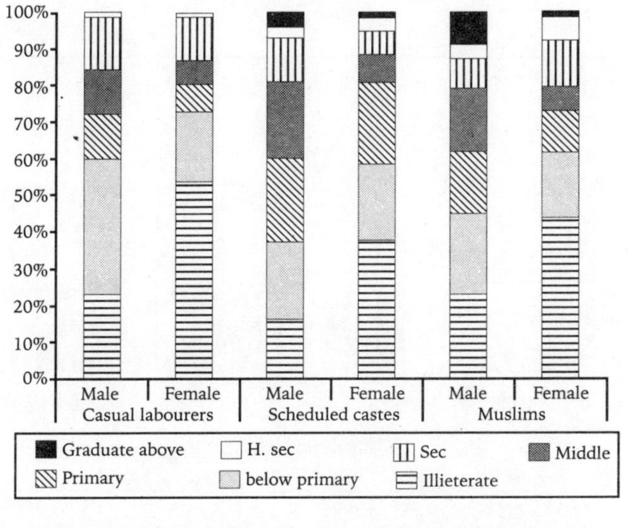

Source: National Sample Survey (1999). *Employment and Unemployment among Social Groups in India*. 55th round, Directorate of Economics and Statistics, Delhi.

different socio-economically disadvantaged groups. But overall, they are far below the average standards for urban Delhi and urban India. The background paper on school education for Delhi HDR sums up the problem facing the education planners in Delhi very well: "Given the rapidly changing population of Delhi, its uneven spread in districts surrounding the central part of Delhi, fast increasing slum populations of new migrants to the city, it is a challenge for a city to meet and keep up with the growing demands of provision and coverage of basic educational facilities."

9.2 Delhi Education Scenario

9.2.1 Structure

Government schools in Delhi are usually primary (classes I to V) or secondary/higher secondary (classes V to X/XII). Primary schools are managed by Municipal

TABLE 9.3

Schools in Delhi

		2000	*2004-05*
	Number of Schools	4618	4862
A.	Government + Aided Schools	3216	3173
1.	Directorate of Education	1227	1149
	(i) Middle	180	107
	(ii) Secondary	221	246
	(iii) Senior Secondary	826	796
2.	M.C.D.		
	(i) Primary	1850	1896
3.	N.D.M.C.	114	80
	(i) Primary + Nursery	82	55
	(ii) Middle	14	10
	(iii) Secondary	10	9
	(iv) Senior Secondary	8	6
4.	Delhi Cantonment	6	8
	(i) Primary	3	2
	(ii) Middle	3	3
	(iii) Secondary		3
B.	Unaided Schools	1402	1689
1.	Directorate of Education	950	1127
	(i) Middle	469	515
	(ii) Secondary	174	246
	(iii) Senior Secondary	307	366
2.	M.C.D.		
	(i) Primary	452	562
C	Kendriya Vidyalaya Sangathan	40	40
	(i) Primary	0	0
	(ii) Middle	0	0
	(iii) Secondary	0	0
	(iv) Sr. Secondary	40	40

Source: Planning Cell, Directorate of Education, Government of Delhi.

2. DDA slum wing, Chugh, 2004.
3. From final population total of Census 1991 and 2001, as given in draft of background paper on school education for Delhi HDR.

Corporation of Delhi (MCD) and other local bodies in their areas of jurisdiction.[4] Education beyond primary level (and up to secondary level) is provided by Directorate of Education. Majority of the government schools are up to secondary or senior secondary level. Earlier there were middle schools too with classes VI to VIII, but now they are mostly upgraded to class X or XII. In the late nineties some secondary and senior secondary schools have expanded to include primary classes.[5] There are some aided schools too, largely secondary or higher secondary, with classes beginning from I or VI. There is also a very large and growing unaided sector—there are about 1500 recognised private unaided schools educating about a third of Delhi's school going children. In all, these schools are divided into 11 districts and 28 educational zones. The number of schools under different management is given in Table 9.3.

How is Delhi coping with the demand for education, a demand that stems from a vast and heterogeneous population? In the year 2000[6] there were 2422 primary schools, 669 middle schools and 1550 secondary and higher secondary schools. The growth in the number of schools has also been the highest for Secondary and Senior Secondary level, though it has increased for other levels too. One possible reason for the unusually high growth at this level is that many primary and middle schools have been upgraded to secondary and senior Secondary schools.

9.2.2 *Enrolment*

9.2.2.1 Enrolment in Different Stages

The enrolment of students and the number of schools in Delhi are shown in Table 9.5 for 1980-81, 1996-97, 2000-01 and 2004-05. The available data for different years shows sudden irregularities making it difficult to analyse the growth in enrolment. The enrolment data for the year 1996-97 shows that the enrolment in different classes in secondary and higher secondary stages (11.36 lakhs in classes IX to XII) is larger than that in the middle stage (5.39 lakhs in classes 6 to 8). This is contrary to the expected pyramid structure in class-wise enrolment—especially since the dropout rates are also fairly high. The 2004-05 figures are very different, showing a drastic reduction in enrolment in higher secondary stages and the

TABLE 9.4

Changes in Number of Schools

Types of School	*Number of Schools*		
	1980-81	*2000-01*	*2004-05*
Primary	1726	2422	2515
Middle	326	669	635
Sec. & Senior Sec.	704	1550	1712
Total	2756	4641	4862

Source: Directorate of Education.

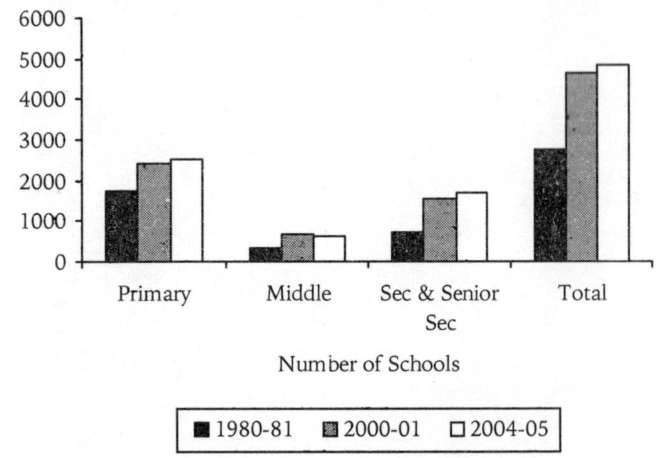

TABLE 9.5

Enrolment in Different Stages in Delhi

Stages of Schooling	*Enrolment (in lakhs)*			
	1980-81	1996-7	2000-1	2004-5
Primary	6.68	12.70	14.32	15.29
Middle	3.23	5.39	7.55	8.22
Secondary & Senior Secondary	2.54	11.36	5.43	6.69
Total	12.45	29.45	27.30	30.20

Source: Delhi Government data.

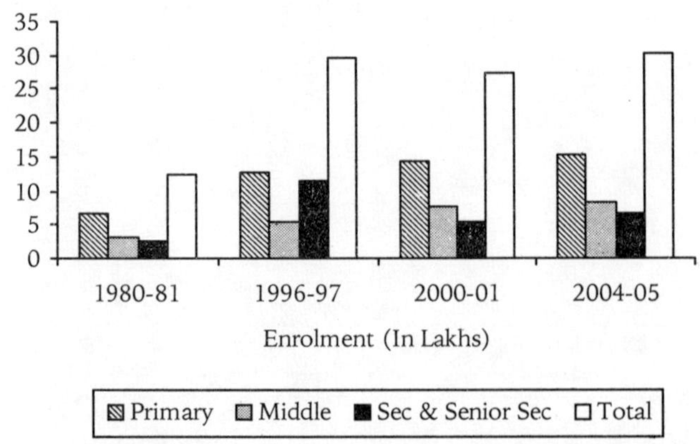

4. New Delhi Municipal Council (NDMC) and Delhi Cantonment Board (DCB).
5. These schools are thought of as model schools and often have an English medium section. These are the Sarvodaya Schools and mostly include classes I to XII—primary classes have been introduced in 364 Sarvodaya Vidyalayas in Delhi.
6. According to the 2001-02 Economic Survey, Delhi has 2416 primary schools, 715 middle schools and 1576 secondary/senior secondary schools. We have used data for previous year, because management-wise breakup was available for that year.

usual pyramid structure. This is a very serious problem, particularly for planners.[7] Reliable data about enrolment and school participation are essential for undertaking concrete plans to improve the schooling situation, and fortunately the Directorate has taken steps to address this (see section on recent initiatives).

9.2.2.2 Enrolment in Private Schools

Non-government institutions play a significant role in managing school education. Most of the non-government schools are at least upper primary, and a large number are even up to senior secondary level. Table 9.6 shows enrolment data for 1997, which indicate that the share of private sector in schooling in Delhi increases sharply at the secondary and higher secondary stages. This corroborates the hypothesis that for many government school students, schooling cannot be sustained. These data do not take into account enrolment in unrecognised private schools in Delhi.

TABLE 9.6

Share of Enrolment in Private Schools in Delhi, 1997

Share of Private Sector	*Enrolment (lakh)*	*% of Total Enrolment*
Primary schools	3.4	26.7
Upper primary schools	1.1	17.8
Secondary schools	4.0	53.7
Higher Secondary schools	3.1	60.2

Source: Chugh (2004) and Directorate of Education NCT Delhi, 1997.

The dominance of government schools in the primary and middle stages as opposed to private schools is supported by the results of another survey. As a part of Sarva Shiksha Abhiyan, Delhi Government had conducted a survey[8] in 2003. The survey also showed that although nearly one-third of students enrolled go to private schools at the primary level, this share drops to around 25 per cent at the middle level. So, government schools dominate at the early stages of education.

TABLE 9.7

Share of Enrolment in Private Schools in Delhi, 1997

(*in Lakhs*)

Classes	*Government*	*Private*	*Total*
Primary	8.62 (68.7%)	3.92 (31.3%)	12.54
Middle	4.40 (75.1%)	1.46 (24.9 %)	5.87

Note: Percentage shares are given in brackets.
Source: Delhi Government Household Survey (2003).

9.2.2.3 Gender Distribution of Enrolment:

Data from different sources contradict each other, regarding proportion of girls' education. The Delhi Government Household Survey (2003) indicates that the proportion of male students is higher than females at primary and middle levels (Table 9.8). So, some gender bias is observed against the education of the girl child.

TABLE 9.8

Enrolment in Government and Private Delhi Schools in 2003

(*in Lakhs*)

Classes	*Boys*	*Girls*	*Total*
Primary	6.78 (54.1%)	5.76 (45.9%)	12.54
Middle	3.13 (53.4%)	2.74 (46.6 %)	5.87

Note: Percentage shares are given in brackets.
Source: Delhi Government Household Survey (2003).

Data from the Directorate of Education for the year 1999 however indicates a different gender-wise distribution of enrolment. Annexure Table A-9.1 annexures presents enrolment data for boys and girls for different stages of schooling. Except at the primary level, there is a relatively higher enrolment for girls (*vis-à-vis* boys) at all other levels. The difference between girls and boys is the highest (in percentage terms) at the senior secondary stage. Table 9.9, based on Selected Educational statistics, bears similar evidence.

According to the Directorate of Education, Government of NCT of Delhi enrolment data for 2004-05 shows that girls constitute 49 per cent of total students at primary level and by and large this ratio is maintained up to senior secondary level.

7. It is possible that in certain years enrolment by types of schools (a secondary school may have classes I to X or classes VI to X) are given rather than by stages (classes I – V, VI – VIII, IX – XII). So the data for different years are not strictly comparable.

8. As a part of the Sarva Shiksha Abhiyan, Delhi Government has conducted a household survey according to geographical units called "*kshetras*" and compiled a disaggregated database for education-related statistics. The *kshetra* approximately corresponds to the catchment area of a municipal primary school.

TABLE 9.9

Enrolment of Children (All Communities and Scheduled Castes), 1998-99

Number of Children Enrolled in	All Communities			Scheduled Castes		
	Boys	Girls	All	Boys	Girls	All
Primary stage	693870	630556	1324426	146647	123808	269455 (20.3%)
Upper primary stage	292712	330423	623135	49466	57475	108941 (17.5%)
Secondary stage	370372	410651	781023	47729	61446	109175 (14.0%)

Source: Selected Educational Statistics, 1998.

9.2.2.4 Enrolment of Disadvantaged Communities

As expected, the disadvantaged communities have a long way to go to catch up with the rest of Delhi. While more than 20 per cent of those enrolled at primary stage belong to the disadvantaged communities, at the secondary stage this proportion is reduced to 14 per cent. Sustained efforts are required to improve the participation of the backward communities.

9.2.3 Participation and Achievement

9.2.3.1 School Participation

In this section, we discuss the extent of school participation of children in Delhi and the achievement of those who are already part of the education process. The Delhi Government household survey (2003) indicated that 1.04 lakh children in 6-10 age group (6.39 per cent of total 6-10 children) and 0.84 lakh children in 11-14 age group (7.12 per cent of total 11-14 children) were out of school in 2003. In the lower age group, 50.6 per cent and in the higher age group, 51.6 per cent of the out of school children were male. No marked gender difference was observed. It was also found that the out of school children are concentrated in certain districts of Delhi (South and North-East) and within these, in certain pockets. The survey has not distinguished between dropouts and never enrolled children. Evidence from other field data suggests that a higher proportion of boys are ever enrolled, but high dropout rates lead to similar proportion as girls being out of school.

The achievement in the area of education can be assessed in two ways: (i) retention of children in school and (ii) educational performance. The assessment is done in this present section for elementary level (primary and upper primary) and for the secondary and higher secondary level.

9.2.3.2 Achievement at the Elementary Level

The retention of children in government schools in Delhi is fairly good in proportionate terms, although the absolute number of out of school children is quite high. It has been observed from Government statistics that at an all-India level, 40 per cent of children enrolled in primary schools do not complete standard V. In a 2000 study by Planning Department of Delhi Government, comparing enrolment in Std I in 1996 with that in standard V in 2000, there were 25 per cent less children in 2000 (29 per cent for girls *vis-à-vis* 24 per cent for boys). So the situation in Delhi can be said to be relatively better than the national average. Pratham[9] have found comparable figures in a study which tracks "survival" of cohorts through the primary stage for MCD schools for 1989, 1993, and 1999. For 1993 and 1999, the percentage of cohorts surviving till standard V were 75 per cent and 82 per cent respectively for boys and 68 per cent and 68 per cent respectively for girls. Contrary to expectations, there were "drop-outs" even at lower standards like I and II. In particular, for girls, the surviving percentage for the 1993 cohort in standard II was 90 per cent, which declined to 84 per cent for the 1999 cohort. For the boys, however, the same percentage rose from 91 per cent to 92 per cent. Clearly, there is pressing need to address the issue of retention right from the primary stage of education.

It is difficult to assess the educational performance at the primary level since there is no system of examination till class III. But results of different achievement tests (Aggarwal, 2000 and Chugh, 2003) based on a selected sample suggest that the schooling achievement is lower for government school students than private school students. Within government schools slum children have poorer achievements. So home factors seem to crucially impact learning achievements of children. For the poorer children, the problems begin from class I itself.

In 2004, Pratham conducted a simple test (a "dipstick survey") on a sample of 3000 children in the 7 to 14 age group, distributed over all districts in Delhi. Their aim was to judge the literacy and numeracy skills of children. The sample included out-of-school children as well as children in government and private schools. Some of the broad patterns that have emerged is that vast majority of out-of school children were not able to read words, this is also true for dropout children in the older age groups. In addition, in the younger age groups (7 to 10) barely

9. Source: Pratham (Delhi HDR, 2004).

half have acquired the necessary verbal and number skills. In the older age group (11 to 14) though most were fluent readers about 30 per cent of government school children in class 6 could not read fluently. About 15 per cent in government school and 5 per cent in private schools could not even recognise numbers and do simple operations.

9.2.3.3 Achievement at the Secondary and Senior Secondary Level

The achievement in educational performance is quite low for the higher stages in schooling as well. Over the last few years, roughly half of those who appeared for Class X exams and nearly 70 per cent of those who appeared for higher secondary examinations passed (Table 9.10).

TABLE 9.10

Pass Percentage in Class X and XII CBSE Boards

Year	*Class X*	*Class XII*
1997	48.99	69.29
1998	46.07	66.83
1999	48.78	68.86
2000	50.03	71.48

Source: Delhi Statistical Handbook, 2000.

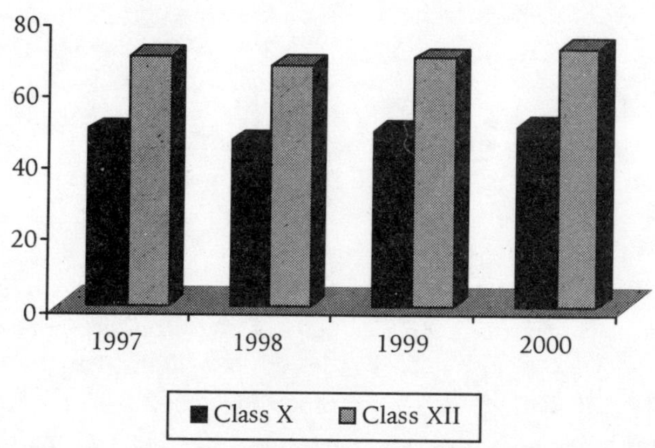

Class X pass percentage has always been lower than Class XII pass percentage as has been the number of students appearing for the board examinations.

The two main reasons for this trend are:

1. Many children do not continue further studies after passing Class X, because for many parents as well as children, especially from disadvantaged communities, Class X is seen as the highest desired level of education. Many jobs both in the private and government sector require only matriculates. An additional factor for girls is that marriage is considered as the next step after passing the secondary level.
2. The lower number of children is also on account of higher failure rate in Class X, which effectively debars many children from pursuing further studies. The latter reason holds true especially for government school children accessed by poor households since the pass percentage in these schools is very low, in the lower 30s (Table 9.11).

TABLE 9.11

Pass Percentage in Class X and XII CBSE Boards for Government School Students

Year	*Class X*	*Class XII*
1997-98	32.10	63.45
1998-99	34.67	68.11
1999-2000	38.97	72.54
2000-01	40.13	70.21
2001-02	46.23	71.23
2002-03	48.87	77.02
2003-04	50.78	77.87
2004-05	48.00	76.44
2005-06	59.73	78.07
2006-07	77.12	82.73

Source: Delhi Directorate data.

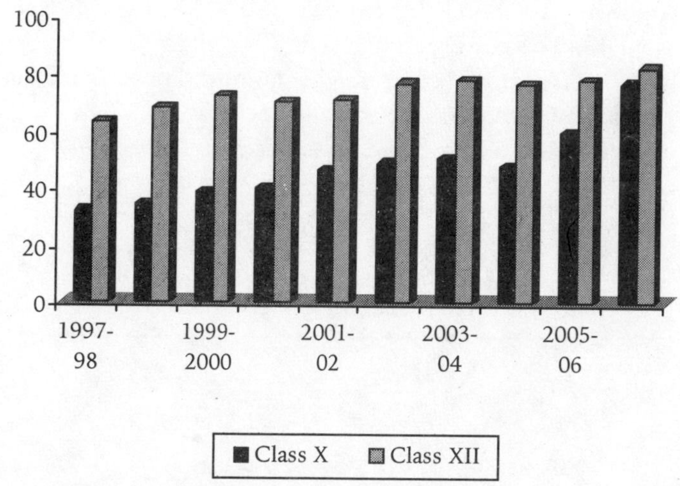

While considering the pass percentages, it is important to keep in mind that the low pass percentage at board level is actually the tip of the iceberg. In general, there is quite a high failure rate throughout the different stages of schooling in Delhi, which is why a pyramid-like enrolment structure is observed as one moves on to higher and higher classes. This is particularly true for government schools. Field surveys also support the high failures and poor achievement status of government school children. According to one estimate,[10] the total number of children in class VI came down by 30 to 50 per cent by the time the cohort reached class VIII. Again, although young adolescents in class IX had smaller class size and better teaching/learning experiences, fifty per cent of class IX adolescents also failed. A very low pass percentage in class X boards speaks very poorly of teaching standards in these schools till the year 2005.

The table indicates there have been a steady increase in pass percentage in class X in the recent years in government schools, However, in past two years a sudden jump has taken place in pass percentage especially of class X which as per Directorate of education is result of better management techniques and increased accountability of teachers. Directorate of education has initiated several steps (discussed in greater details in section 9.4 in present paper). Analysis of results revealed that the students mainly fail in English and Mathematics. Special workshops for the maths teachers were held and new incentives are being introduced for those who have better attainment levels.[11] Question banks are being prepared and circulated among the students. Instead of having school specific examination in lower classes, common question papers are being used. This is particularly useful for pre-boards classes as the students get to practice on question papers set by CBSE.

There has been a growth of 14 per cent of students appearing for class X boards over 1997-2000 as seen from table 13. The corresponding figure for class XII is higher at 19 per cent. In contrast the number appearing from government schools have actually declined at class X level, and grown at a lower rate at senior secondary level.

TABLE 9.12

Number of Students Appearing for Class X and XII CBSE Boards

Year	Class X		Class XII	
	Government school	All school	Government school	All schools
1997	88846	177270	38033	91269
1998	89746	182725	44918	95609
1999	81392	195719	41828	111359
2000	72287	202252	44044	108744

Source: Delhi Statistical Handbook, 2000, Delhi Directorate.

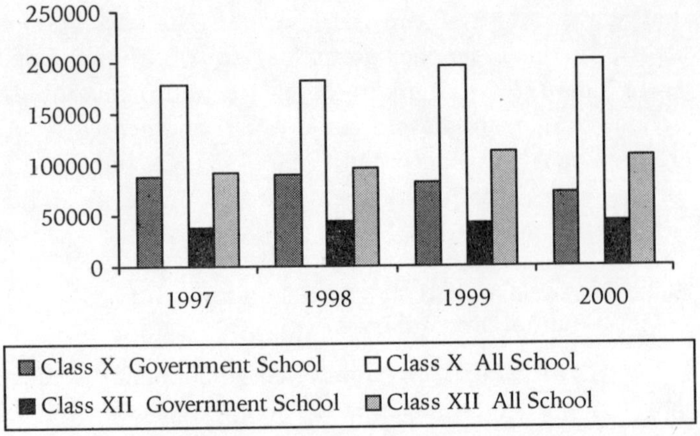

The lower pass percentage for government school students (compared to overall pass percentage) indicate that private schools perform much better. It was difficult to get comparative data for schools of different management. Annexure Table A-9.2 presents some comparative data, as given by a dated report from Delhi Directorate. It indicates a sharp difference in pass percentages at secondary level between government and aided schools. However the overall figures do not match those given by the statistical handbook, and hence its reliability is questionable.

It is perhaps not fair to compare results of government and private schools. Private schools can control their student quality through selection at admission stage. Government schools have no such choice. In spite of this some government schools do have very good performance. The pass percentage of Pratibha Vikas Vidyalaya is almost 100 per cent.[12]

The gender-distribution of students appearing for the board exams is indicated in the Annexure Table A-9.3. The percentage share of boys and girls appearing for board exams have remained remarkably steady over the years 1997-2000. There is a slight gender-bias with girls comprising around 46 per cent of the students appearing for class X exam. This bias is reduced slightly at the class XII level, with their share improving to 47 per cent of the total. It is also observed that there has been a growth of 14 per cent of students appearing for class X boards over 1997-2000. The corresponding figure for class XII is higher at 19 per cent.

Lack of learning achievements in the recognised school system has led to emergence of an unrecognised sector—through unrecognised schools at elementary level, and

10. See survey conducted by CORD for adolescent children in Delhi.
11. Continuous and comprehensive evaluation of students is carried out 3 to 4 times a year. The performance of students is linked with the teachers teaching different subjects. It is expected that once the system (being developed on MIS) is in place it would be easier to ensure teacher accountability.
12. There is a great rush for admission in these schools, but only those who had at least 2 years in government schools are considered.

coaching classes at higher levels. In addition taking private tuition, some from schoolteachers but largely from the educated unemployed, has become a common phenomenon among all income groups. These are the available alternatives for the parents to support their children's education. Being unrecognised, there is no way of estimating their overall impact, though there are ample evidence as seen from hoardings, leaflets, and newspaper advertisements. It is even more difficult to ensure any degree of quality control. While this may have helped some students to improve their performance in exams, it has led to large increases in household expenditure, as seen from different household surveys. This is a very disturbing development, especially when it becomes a necessary part of school education, and goes against the government's commitment towards 8 years of free and compulsory education.

9.3 Possible Causes behind Poor Achievement

9.3.1 Shortage of Facilities

A major reason for so many children still being out of school is shortage in schooling facilities. This includes shortage of schools, of infrastructural facilities in existing schools and of teachers. The problems for the elementary stage are discussed first.

9.3.1.1 Elementary Education

(i) Schools: A very large portion of children in Delhi go to government schools, and though the government has attempted to create adequate number of schools and classrooms, it has not been able to keep pace with increase in enrolment (as seen from Tables 9.3 and 9.5). As a result the schools have increased in size and are often very crowded. Not only are primary schools not enough to enrol all children, the facilities for upper primary education (which are part of secondary schools) are insufficient. In the background paper for Delhi HDR the researchers demonstrated (through a sample study) how a large drop in enrolment occurs in the transitional phase between classes V and VI. The capacity to admit students in class VI in the government schools is much lower than the enrolment in class V in all its feeder schools.

Setting up new schools is not always easy. The Master Plan for Delhi as developed by DDA specifies the norms for the provision of primary education in the urban areas. These provisions have generally been made in colonies that are developed according to master plan. However, a parallel growth of unauthorised colonies had resulted in a situation where it is difficult to allocate land according to prescribed norms for primary schools. Physical acquisition of land and development of social infrastructure is a difficult problem in a metropolitan city like Delhi. MCD has to acquire land from DDA, *Gram Sabhas* and other agencies for opening primary schools. Many schools were sanctioned long back but could not be started because of unavailability of land at suitable places. There are many complicated issues involved in land acquisition, thus creating problems regarding easy access to primary schools. These problems are aggravated in unauthorised colonies.

(ii) Infrastructure: On the positive side it should be noted that infrastructure in secondary and senior secondary schools is reasonably good as compared to primary schools. Still many of the infrastructural problems are applicable to primary as well as to secondary and senior secondary schools. Several features of the Delhi MCD and government schools have been observed in a field survey (Prahtam—HDR, 2004). First, many government schools work in two shifts: morning and afternoon. Second, schooling for children and adolescents in the sample areas was a gender-segregated experience. Third, almost all children experienced a transition from primary school (class I-V) to secondary school i.e., they had to move to a different school, upper primary or secondary. In some cases they had to move even three times: primary-upper, primary-secondary and sometimes, a fourth time – to senior secondary school. At present efforts are on to open more schools of secondary and senior secondary level (and to upgrade middle schools) and to convert them to single shift as far as possible.

The morning shift functioned from 7.30 a.m. to 12.30 p.m. It was usually for girls, and mostly had female teachers and headteachers. The second shift ran from 1 p.m. to 5 p.m. and was usually for boys with mostly male teachers and male headteachers. The shift system was found to lead to deterioration in school quality due to reduced teaching time (often girls were grouped fifteen minutes earlier for the final dismissal to avoid any problems with the boys who come in for the second shift). There was no time for extra classes or remedial classes for the girls. There is also little time to clean the school between the shifts. As a result these boys have to study in filthy, paper strewn class rooms. With the second shift finishing only at 6 p.m., again the time was not conducive for extra classes or remedial classes for the boys. The second factor relates to the lack of sense of belonging to the schools for students as well as teachers e.g., there was reduced accountability for maintenance of the premises.

The girls schools' functioning was generally good to average. Although the schools were often overcrowded, very little bunking and violence was reported. There were closed and guarded gates and official timings were followed. The children could be seen to be at work. There was organised timetable and school activities as well as signs of achievement displayed in trophy cupboards. Functioning at the boys' school was generally poor to average. Half-filled classrooms, almost empty classrooms were observed, especially after recess. There was major bunking and violence. The gates of the school were often left open. In many cases, schools closed two hours early. Rarely did they have an organised timetable and school activities.

(iii) Teachers: The availability of teachers at Delhi schools varies according to the administration. The teacher-pupil ratio at the primary stage at MCD schools is 1:52 while it is much better at 1:34 for DOE Government of Delhi schools. The *Economic Survey 2001-02* indicates that the number of teachers employed (as on 31.12.2000) with Directorate of Education, M.C.D., N.D.M.C., and Delhi Cantonment were 43342, 21572, 2012, and 87 respectively, with a total of 67013.

A major problem in improving quality of teaching was the absence of indicators of teaching quality. Teaching accountability was not there at all except for teachers at boards level. This is particularly true for earlier classes. Poor teaching and poor achievement at earlier levels is often the main reason for poor retention. Yet the system has no provision for monitoring teaching, and few accountability measures.

According to the Director of Education, Government of NCT of Delhi, to introduce teacher accountability continuous and comprehensive evaluation of students is carried out three to four times in a year and performance of students is linked to teachers who are teaching them different subjects. The system is being developed on MIS and since the system is in place, it would be easier to identify non performers and make them accountable.

9.3.1.2 Secondary and Senior Secondary Education

Table 9.13 provides an idea about the number of schools in Delhi (schools that operate under Directorate of Education) according to the premises from which they operate. As can be seen, as many as 21 schools function from tents and 94 from SPS/tents. A field survey (Pratham—HDR, 2004) has also observed that although impressive double storeyed or three-storeyed structures with wide corridors were commonly found in senior secondary schools, secondary schools sometimes ran in tin sheds or tents. The same survey indicated that other basic facilities were also often in short supply for all schools e.g., schools rarely had enough functional toilets or even an adequate supply of drinking water in a city which is hot and dry for the major part of the year. Water supply was a major problem and accounted for the non-functional toilets. Electricity supply was also fitful and erratic. Buildings were poorly maintained; piles of paper, broken desks and chairs were common occurrences.

TABLE 9.13

No. of Schools Functioning (DOE) in Various Premises

Premises	*No. as on 31.12.2000*
Pacca school buiding + SPS	511
SPS school building + SPS	325
SPS/Tents	94
Tents	21
In MCD premises	59
Rented	8

Source: Planning Cell, Directorate of Education, Government of Delhi.

The basic facilities reported by the average government school student were very poor.[13] It must be noted that the poorest facilities were found in east, north east and North West Delhi schools. Here the pressure on school facilities from a rapidly increasing slum population appears most acute. Even senior secondary schools, (elsewhere found in big three storeyed buildings) were in tents and tin sheds in this segment. Facilities were also generally poorer the lower the level of schooling i.e, upper primary was worse off than secondary and the latter was worse off than senior secondary schools.

The survey referred to earlier also indicated that lower the class, poorer were the class room condition. The class-size in class VI was found to be usually as high as 60-70 and in many cases this could be worse.[14] Classroom conditions were also inevitably the worst in the school i.e. if the secondary level—class IX and X had desks, the young sixths were often on dusty, torn durries or even on the dusty floor. If class IX and X had pukka classrooms class VI often had tin sheds. Perhaps class IX was special since it was the prelude to the great Board examination in class X—the pass percentage at class X Board level being

13. Based on a survey of 40 randomly selected government schools in Delhi by an independent research group.

14. Many teachers reported that owing to the number of teachers absent on a day added to the staff shortage, 2 sections were combined. Thus numbers could go up to 120 per teacher.

an easily visible measure of school performance. Multi-section teaching is relatively much more common for class VI than for class IX.

These impressions are on the basis of a dated survey (2001). At present according to the directorate "school is opened only when appropriate place has been identified. Portable cabins are erected when additional space is required. No schools run from tin sheds. Almost all schools have facilities like drinking water, electric connection and toilet facilities. At one or two places, in unauthorised colonies where appropriate water lines have not been laid, water is made available through tankers". However the findings from field studies suggest that close monitoring is necessary to ensure that these facilities remain usable and are used. Government has also provided a large amount of money (Rs.1.20 lakh) to each of the head of school every year to carry out repairs through Vidyalaya Kalyan Samitis (which has representatives of RWA and PTA). This should help in maintaining the school infrastructure if utilised properly.

9.3.1.3 Overcrowding and Need for Planning

The previous discussion points out to the various shortcomings in the existing education system, and the government's initiatives to address them. Ideally a planning exercise should have been done to estimate unmet requirements of schools and infrastructure. Such an exercise has not been attempted, primarily for two reasons.

Firstly, there is lack of reliable school level data in the private domain, which is of first importance for any planning exercise. Without information about the number of schools under different management, enrolment in different stages and their infrastructural facilities, no planning is possible. This is especially so since a significant section of Delhi's population is dependent on schools under private management.[15]

Secondly, the Directorate of Education had prepared a micro-level planning document identifying the schooling requirements in different area. This was based on the household survey in 2003 (which has been referred to in the earlier sections) and also a school survey. Their estimates can be used for planning purposes.

What comes through, from their findings and from other field surveys, is that at the primary level, shortages are marked in specific areas, and there is an overall inefficiency in supply conditions resulting in empty classrooms in certain areas and overcrowded classrooms in other areas. In some of these schools children are forced to study in the open, in balconies outside the classrooms or in tin sheds. The survey of directorate of education indicated how overcrowding and lack of schools is a greater problem in certain zones (Table 9.14). The pupil teacher ratios also vary a lot—many schools are forced to work with contract teachers.

TABLE 9.14

Variations in Overcrowding in MCD Zones

Zone	*Total Schools*	*Schools with Enrolment > 1000*	*Per cent of Overcrowded Schools*
Nazafgarh	255	42	16.47
Central	170	28	16.47
Shahadra North	198	30	15.15
Rohini	155	16	10.32
Civil Lines	169	17	10.06
West	164	10	6.10
Karol bagh	87	5	5.75
Shahadra South	205	8	3.90
Narela	119	4	3.36
South	154	5	3.25
City	87	0	0
Sader Paharganj	86.	0	0

Source: Government of Delhi (2003). Survey conducted by Directorate of Education, National Capital Territory of Delhi.

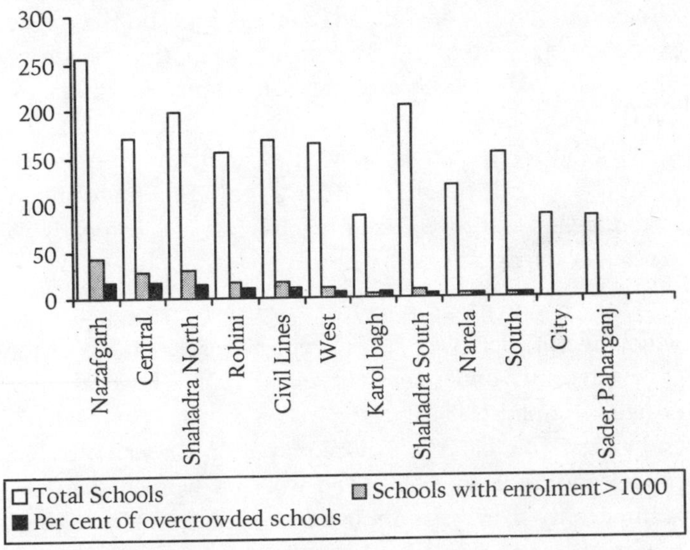

The shortage is much more severe in the higher stages of schooling. In the context of eight years of compulsory education, this has serious implications in terms of budget and manpower.

The overall pupil teacher ratios in secondary/higher secondary schools do not look very high. But in reality the

15. A very crude attempt at estimating school requirements is available in the Appendix A-9.4.

situation is much worse. In most government schools enrolment is in a pyramid shape and classes VI and VII have very large class sizes. So pupil teacher ratios in these classes are very adverse.

What is of first importance for proper planning is introduction of a reliable system of data collection from all schools. This is essential for both planning and monitoring. Fortunately this is being done. The directorate of education had a planned approach. Attempts are being made to get the out-of-school children back to school. But what appears as the major problem is the poor retention and poor learning achievements. For this, higher budgetary allocations are necessary, but are not enough. Solving these problems is much more complicated. Also one of the causes for poor retention like Dyslexia are totally overlooked in government schools which with simple methods of identification can be pinpointed. This identification can help a child in exams where he/she can get extra time as it is identified by CBSE.

The other issues like no provisions for free note books to students of all levels, and no support for uniforms at pre primary levels and fees at pre primary level are the ones that discourages students to come to school as they add extra costs.

Delhi has one of the largest per capita financial allocations. But centralised control and bureaucratic procedure (arisen partly to prevent corruption) leads to unnecessary delay—shortages remain even when funds are available. The main problem is setting up an accountability mechanism as well as a support system for principals and teachers. Many policies have been introduced to improve accountability, but it is too early to assess its impact.

There is one more issue that is of pre school education which is not discussed in the report because it does not come presently under the purview of DOE. However after Ganguly Committee's report now the scenario has changed and gives a free hand to private players in the name of pre school education in Delhi. The working women who are granted only three months maternity leave, solely rely on the crèches and pre schools for rearing of their children who are the future of this country. This is an established fact that education of a child starts with the time of their entry in this world. The DOE should step in as a regulating and monitoring authority deciding parameters regarding the safety and education of these children as the pre school environment forms the base for the development of future human resources of the country.

9.4 Initiatives in Improving the Education Scenario in Delhi

9.4.1 Government Initiative

Delhi Government has been very active in the last few years. It has taken several initiatives to achieve the EFA (Education for All) objectives. The household survey to assess the school participation status of 6 to 14 year olds formed the base of their intervention. The directorate of education had done a planning exercise indicating the number of primary and secondary schools required in different areas. However, since there are a variety of reasons why children remain out-of-school and "there is great heterogeneity among these out of school children" the directorate have decided on mainstreaming through bridge courses. These courses are taught in learning centres which are run by various NGOs already working in education sector. The objective is to bring these out-of-school children upto appropriate competency levels through condensed courses and get them admitted into appropriate grades in formal schools.

These learning centres are of at least 4 hours duration and the teacher was required to put in an extra hour of preparation time. The government has tried to coordinate NGO activities in a manner to ensure EFA. On the basis of the survey the required number of centres and their location has been identified and different NGOs have been allotted some centres in the districts where they are active. There are provisions for monitoring by the community (Kshetra Education Committee were formed for that purpose). Government supplied the teaching learning materials and paid a certain amount per student to cover Centre's cost (Rs. 845 annually per child at primary level and 1200 per child at upper primary level. The teachers were required to have formal training—1 for primary level students and 2 for upper primary level)

About 3000 learning centres are there in Delhi, run by about 200 NGOs. Nearly a lakh of out-of-school children are in these centres. In the first year of its functioning about 8000 children were mainstreamed. A major problem faced by these learning centres is that sufficient schools or classrooms have not come up. So the problem of mainstreaming remains. Without improvement in school conditions these children will not remain in the schools. The situation is visibly improving as in the year 2004, out of 187,000 out-of-school children identified, 134,000 have been brought under the ambit of the learning centres. Till the year 2005-06, 32000 children have been mainstreamed.

In an attempt to reach the hitherto unreached groups of children, particularly those at construction sites, the government is experimenting with the concept of mobile learning centres. At present two vans are put into action which are fully equipped with teaching-learning materials, teachers, mid-day meals, and CAL unit.

The Directorate is busy at present constructing additional classrooms and toilets under SSA. This enhanced space will be useful to start CRCs and ECCEs in the school complex. ECCEs will specially target the 3 to 5 year olds and focus on their play, health, nutrition and joyful learning. It will be very useful for young girls who remain out-of-school in order to take care of younger siblings.

Delhi government has sought cooperation from private sector as well in its attempt to improve school availability. The private unaided schools in Delhi are also non-profit organisations. Delhi High Court had ordered that they are to reserve 20 per cent of the seats for the economically disadvantaged children—and grant them freeship. Initially this reservation was applicable for the new admissions, but over time this will allow many children from weaker section access to quality schools. It will reduce pressure on government schools too. Not all schools have complied with this order in 2004—and so around 7000 students were admitted through this reservation in the first year. But better result is expected in the next year.

It is too early to assess the impact of these initiatives, but they appear to be in the right direction. However there is need for careful monitoring of activities of the NGOs—without proper accountability mechanisms, these NGOs may also fail to deliver. Also with high migration rates and a shifting population, the household survey may be required to be repeated.

Improving Learning Achievement and School Functioning of Government Schools

Continuous and Comprehensive Evaluation

The directorate has been concerned with providing quality education in their schools. So far the Boards results were the only accountability measure for teachers, and gave a performance appraisal for teachers who taught in class X or XII. Nothing much was known about learning level and teaching quality in other classes. For this purpose the directorate took a major step to reform the examination system. In addition to the 3 terminal tests, 4 additional tests were introduced for students of class III to class XII. Each exam was to cover a quarter of syllabus taught in the relevant quarter, and was in the form of objective type tests. The answer sheets are evaluated through optical readers so that feedback is available immediately. This scheme of Continuous and Comprehensive Evaluation helped keeping track of the children's progress. The school and the teachers were not to receive results of individual child but an analysis of the learning levels in the class. It also forms a basis of evaluation of teachers, taking into account the performance level of children as well as their improvement.

Computerising Information System

The directorate has developed web based MIS where data on schools, students and teachers are stored. Information is easily accessible not only for the planners but also the other stakeholders.

All postings and transfers are carried out electronically. Budgetary allocations and sanctions are also issued electronically. This has helped in better utilisation of manpower and physical infrastructure and exercised control on financial resources.

Admissions are done on-line. School leaving certificates are also issued electronically. All students from class V in MCD schools or other feeder schools are automatically admitted to class VI of government school. This has reduced dropout rates at transition.

It is planned that marksheets will be generated through computers with in-built logos, from next year. This is expected to eliminate the market for fake marksheets.

A tracking system has been brought in place. Through online monitoring of all children enrolled in bridge courses and Learning centres is expected to improve enrolment and attendance.

Improve Retention and Learning Achievements

Several projects are being implemented in the government schools to make schools enjoyable and meaningful. YUVA has been introduced in government schools with twin objectives—to make sure that the school is a safer and happier place for the students and that they are taught to be responsible adults. So it would give basic education on all subjects like HIV-AIDS, career counseling etc. Project RAKSHA was launched to teach self defense skills to the girl students. For this purpose the female Physical Education teachers were trained by Delhi Police, Computer aided learning (CAL) is also introduced in class VI last year. The course content of different subjects like English, Mathematics, Science, and

Social Science are presented through interactive cartoon characters. This is also expected to make learning an easier and enjoyable process. BALA (Building as Learning Aid) is introduced to improve the learning environment of the students in which school buildings will be suitably developed with architectural designs in such a way that building itself acts as a learning aid. Computer education project (CEP) started for classes VI to XII in government schools in year 2000.

In primary schools a hot cooked mid-day meal is served in all schools. Close monitoring has ensured successful implementation of the incentive. It has significantly impacted regularity of attendance. Free text books and school uniforms are also given to primary students, and goes a long way towards reducing cost of schooling.

Among the different reasons for poor retention, lack of achievement was found to be a major one. Pratham has conducted a dipstick survey to estimate the literacy and numeracy skills of the enrolled children. They have also been trying to improve achievement, and a major initiative is their learning to read programme. Activities of Pratham in the area of education are at present focused on "learning achievement".

Pratham has a small programme for *"bal shramiks"*, for around 1000 children in Delhi. In another kind of programme, Pratham carries out "catalytic programmes" for training teachers in South Shahdara zone (of the MCD zonal divisions in Delhi).

Community Participation

Initiatives have been taken to encourage the community to participate in developmental activities such as *Dakhila Abhiyan*, awareness programmes related to Polio, Dengue, participation in bhagidari melas and workshop, maintenance of schools through Vidyalaya Kalyan Samiti (VKS). VKS is authorised for minor repair works for which a developmental related fund of Rupees four lakh is proposed to be deposited in the account of the building incharge, however the effectiveness lies on the timely release of grant.

Sports and Other Activities

Government schools of Delhi stood number one in National School Games held in year 2005-06 and 2006-07. The first ever floodlit day-and-night cricket ground for a school was opened in Bharat Nagar school.

In addition to the above initiatives steps have been taken to sensitise environmental education in schools. Cultural events like cultural quest are also promoted where students of Pratibha Vikas Vidyalayas are linked with students in USA. Study tours are also initiated in schools.

Education of Disabled Children

A special cell has been created and a survey is undertaken to identify disabled children of orthopedic handicap, visual hearing and speech impairments, mental retardedness (educable) and cerebral palsy in nine districts of Delhi.

9.4.2 Vocational Education

Secondary and higher secondary education are important terminal stages in the system of general education because it is at these points that an adolescent decides on whether to pursue higher education, opt for technical training or join the workforce. Educationists and experts have consistently recommended that education at these stages should be given a vocational bias to link it with the world of employment. In accordance with the recommendations of the Kothari Commission, the Directorate of Education, Delhi, started the Vocational Education Programme in the year 1977-78 by introducing vocational stream at the +2 stage.

Under the Revised National Policy on Education, the priority has been assigned to vocational education. The target was to enrol 25 per cent of students at the senior secondary level in the vocational stream by 2000. Initially it was started in 15 Senior Secondary Schools with 9 Vocational Courses at the +2 stage in vocational stream. The programme has undergone vast expansion since then and presently 16 vocational courses are being taught in 197 Government and 7 Government Aided Senior Secondary Schools scattered over Delhi. The enrolment under vocational education programme is nearly 10657 students in Government and Government Aided Schools. However, in percentage term only 1.5 per cent students enrolled for vocational education (using the base as total enrolment in secondary and senior secondary schools provided in Annexure A-9.1).

Besides the above courses DoE is planning to introduce that skill based training for the students in earlier classes. Since the CBSE does not do this, the Directorate of Education stepped in to fill this gap. It is therefore proposed that in partnership with the CII, skill based courses should be introduced for students from standard VIII or IX, and also part of standard X, if necessary.

TABLE 9.15

Courses Offered under Vocational Education and Pre-Vocational levels

S.N	Name of Course
1.	Electrical Technology
2.	Automobile
3.	AC & Refrigeration Technology
4.	Electronics
5.	Stenography (English)
6.	Stenography (Hindi)
7.	Banking
8.	Food Service &Management
9.	Fashion Design & Clothing Construction
10.	Textile Designing
11.	Health Care & Beauty Culture
12.	Medical Lab. Technology
13.	Tourism & Travel Technique
14.	Horticulture
15.	Information Technology/Computer Application
16.	Library Information Science
Pre-Vocational Courses offered to classes VIII to IX	
1.	Cutting & Tailoring
2.	B. Office Practice
3.	Skin & Beauty Care
4.	Silk & Screen printing

Source: DoE

There is hardly any provision for vocational stream in private schools of Delhi which limits the students option of selection A course at plus two level.

Possible Causes behind Poor Performance of Vocational Education

The selection of course is the most important aspect of vocationalisation. The relevance of course in world of work and quality of training makes it marketable. The poor enrolment in these courses indicates that either the good courses are not offered to students or those which are offered are not perceived as a marketable vocation. There may be several other reasons for that, such as selection and updating of courses, lack a continuous and comprehensive market research for skills in demand, non availability of proper trainers, competency building of trainers, lack of higher academic prospects of these courses etc., which DoE has to find out in order to achieve the desired number of enrolments.

Initiatives to Improve Vocationalisation by Government

Research to evaluate vocational education Programme : The Directorate of Education, Government of Delhi had commissioned Delhi School of Social Work, Delhi University to conduct an evaluation study of the Vocational Education Programme in schools to explore new areas of the Vocational Occupation. The study report has been submitted to the department and necessary action on the report is yet to be taken.

Capacity Building of Vocational Teachers

In order to revamp vocational education in Delhi schools training of teachers that was not organised for the last 10 years is initiated. Following that key to success of vocational programmes is the involvement of organisations and agencies of excellence working in the respective fields, the help of National Institute of Fashion Technology (NIFT) for fashion designing course and Institute of Secretarial Training and Management (ISTM) for stenography and office procedures course is being sought and two training programmes for the teachers of fashion designing and clothing construction and one training programme for stenography and office procedure were organised by SCERT. The main emphasis of the training was to orient the trainees about the demands of the growing industry and changing market and develop their skills to fulfill those demands.

Introduction of pre-vocational Courses in Schools in partnership with Confederation of Indian Industry (CII)

All CBSE courses on vocational education are for students of standards XI and XII only and the subjects taught till standard X do not really teach any skill, and so it was felt that skill based training should be introduced for the students in earlier classes. And for that purpose in partnership with the CII, skill based courses for students from standard VIII or IX and also part of standard X (if necessary) will be initiated.

The final syllabus and curriculum for the skill based (job oriented) courses at pre vocational level would be jointly evolved by the CII and the Directorate of Education, based largely in consultation of existing material provided by National Open School, Department of Technical Education, Delhi and CBSE. It is proposed that trainers would be those persons who are already running trades. The training will be held outside the school and school hours preferable at the trainer's work place or at their training centers. The certification of training is proposed to be done jointly by the Government of Delhi and the CII. However, to arrest drop-out all certificates under this training would be given to the students only after they appear for the standard X exams.

9.5 Strategies, Choices and Issues in the Field of Education for Delhi of Tomorrow

9.5.1 Vocational Education

The above discussion suggests that supply led as well as demand fed restrictions slowed down the growth of vocationalisation at school level. Schools either do not have teachers to impart training or students to learn the skill. Vocationalisation lacks planning for selection of courses and training. One time study is not solution to keep pace with the changing market scenario. It needs proper, continuous and comprehensive research. For selection of the vocation in which training be imparted the approach should be at macro level means that planners should take into account the different industry reports and their skill requirements, as well as reports of different commissions addressing the skill requirement of the industry in the concerned area. This would avoid the oversupplying of popular skills as well as the shortage of relatively less popular but useful and remunerative skills in the industry.

As far as training is concerned then the best option of training is hands on experience on the job itself. However, the past experience suggests that all the employers do not take training in very good spirit as it has heavy opportunity costs. The apprenticeship Act also has lost his relevance in the modern type of industry set up where number of manpower is reduced. In other words, largely, present nature of industry has no obligation to have apprentices. Therefore the need of hour is to sensitise this issue among the users as the ultimate user of skills is industry only. This could be achieved only through regular interaction with the industry.

9.5.2 Higher Education

Amongst all cities of India, Delhi is considered to be the most favourable destination for pursuing higher education. The city is home to several renowned universities, which attract students from all parts of the globe.

Government Universities: There are five Government Universities in Delhi which include the University of Delhi (DU), Jawaharlal Nehru University (JNU), Guru Gobind Singh Indraprastha University (GGSIPU), Jamia Millia University (JMU), and Jamia Hamdard.

The latest and the Delhi Government initiative in this list is of GGSIP university. The establishment of GGSIP university which is purely a Delhi Government initiative came into existence because of the fact that demand for higher education in Delhi had increased tremendously and the Delhi University was not enthusiastic of opening new colleges or granting affiliation to private colleges. In order to fill this gap GGSIPU is established as a teaching and affiliating university. Through this the government of Delhi has also promoted the private initiative in higher education.

At present there are 68 self-financing institutions, and nine Government managed engineering institutions are affiliated with the University in the diverse areas of engineering/technology, management, computer applications, mass communications, bachelor of education physiotherapy, homeopathy, heritage and conservation management & LLD (Hons.).This includes Mahila Institute of Technology, one of the first institutions offering engineering, programme exclusively for women and five privately managed engineering colleges. Eighty-five per cent of seats in the institution located in NCR of Delhi were reserved for Delhi Students. A total intake capacity of about 9000 seats in different disciplines was created. However this is a matter of research that out of approximately 6.69 lakh of enrolment at secondary and senior secondary level how many can have a seat in higher education institutions in their state.

Private Universities: Among private universities in the capital are the Amity University and Rai University.

Open University: Delhi is also home to the largest open university of the world i.e., The Indira Gandhi National Open University, commonly known as IGNOU.

In total 7 universities and 131 degree colleges are there in Delhi. Of these, 82 colleges are affiliated with Delhi University and the remaining 49 colleges are affiliated with GGSIPU. The Delhi Government sponsors 40 Delhi University Colleges, of which 20 are fully funded by Delhi Government.

Deemed Universities: In addition to the above, there are ten deemed universities in the capital namely the Indian Agricultural Research Institute (IARI), Indian Institute of Foreign Trade (IIFT), Indian Law Institute (ILI), National Museum Institute of History of Art, Conversation and Museology, National School of Drama (NSD), Rashtriya Sanskrit Sansthana, School of Planning and Architecture (SPA), Shri Lal Bahadur Shastri Rashtriya Sanskrit Vidyapeeth, TERI School of Advanced Studies, and

National University of Educational Planning and Administration (NUEPA).

9.5.3 *Achievement at the Higher Education Level*

Promotion of Private Initiative in the field of Higher Education: The government has encouraged and promoted the private initiative in the field of higher education through affiliation to GGSIP. The private institutes or self financing institutes are funded by endowments and fees and not by profit motive.

Reservation to students of Delhi: Eighty-five per cent seats are reserved for students of Delhi in the institutes under GGSIP located in NCT of Delhi thereby giving them more opportunities to study in their own state. The University is running 8 schools of its own. It has two centres of learning and has given affiliation to 10 government institutions and 63 privately managed self-financing institutions. The total intake of the university is now more than 9000 seats.

Introduction of Professional Courses: In order to keep pace with the changing industry environment the government proposes to initiate courses like Biotechnology, Genetics Plant Molecular Biology, Environment studies etc., in the colleges fully funded by Delhi Government.

Introduction of Vocational Courses : To keep pace with the growing demands of the present day situation, the University of Delhi has included in its curriculum a good number of vocational courses. Under the Delhi University umbrella, College of Vocational Studies is the premier institution, which offers the following subjects like Tourism, Book publishing, Retailing and Trade, Secretarial Courses, Store Management, Insurance, and Office Management and Secretarial Practice.

9.5.4 *Strategies*

In order to keep pace with the knowledge economy, directorate of higher education is preparing comprehensive policy for Higher Education for next 5 years, opening new Degree Colleges in various localities of Delhi, also proposes to open Indira Gandhi Institute Of Technology under GGSIP as an emergent need is felt seeing the regional imbalance in the facilities available for undergraduate level Technical Education in the country (only 7 per cent intake facilities in north-west region comprising Chandigarh, Haryana, HP, Delhi, Rajasthan, and J&K in total technical intake of the country).

The issues related to better management of higher education such as strengthening of the Directorate of Higher Education, directing colleges for proper utilisation of funds, financial audits for their proper uses, acquisition of new sites for opening of various colleges, opening of more new hostels for girls are addressed in new policy.

In addition to these to encourage meritorious students studying in Government colleges to motivate intelligent and serious students of general stream education i.e., Science, Commerce, and Arts, in a three years Degree Course with two segments *viz.*, Honours and General Pass courses a cash award of Rs. 5000 each is proposed.

9.5.5 *Technical Education*

Delhi has 8 technical education institutions at the degree/post-graduation level. Eleven diploma level institutions (polytechnics) and 14 certificate level institutions (ITIs) impart technical education under the administrative control of the Government of Delhi. Apart from these government institutions 46 other institutes are affiliated to the Board of Technical Education

TABLE 9.16

Intake Capacity of Technical Institutions

Institutions	*Number*	*Total Student Intake*
Degree level/post-graduate level	8	1758
Diploma level	11	2966
Certificate level (ITI)	14	9108

Source: Department of Training and Technical Education GNCT Delhi.

These institutes not only run their routine courses but also run several short term courses especially of lower level vocational courses for the underprivileged under different schemes of Government.

9.5.6 *Achievements, Issues and Strategies*

The efforts in the direction of expansion of technical colleges are reflected in the shape of upcoming new colleges—Government Engineering College at Jaffarpur, Delhi Integrated Institute of Technology at Dwarka, construction of Engineering College at Geeta Colony, Delhi, ITI at Ranhola and ITI at Chatterpur.

Constitution of Takniki Shiksha Sansthan Kalyan Samiti in each Government run technical institutes i.e., diploma level institutes, CSI, BTC, and ITIs have been envisaged to address various immediate local level maintenance needs of the Institution. The TSSKS proposes to address the objectives such as up keep and maintenance of buildings, equipment, furniture, environment etc. of the institute, to suggest restructuring of the curriculum in coordination with the industry making it compatible with the requirement of the growing market of the country so as to transfer the latest technological developments enabling upgradation of skill and bring exposure to the new emerging areas. To arrange for industrial visits/industrial training for the trainees/ students, to generate revenue for the institute by obtaining job works, services, consultancy etc. from industry/market, to explore the possibilities of more gainful employment for the students/trainees, to conduct tailor made short-term courses/seminars/workshops for the employees of industry and the entrepreneurs to associate the alumni/ex-students in getting constructive feedback for the improvement of training standard. To suggest special training to faculty and other staff in industries for upgrading their knowledge and skill, to organise seminars, workshops, exhibitions, competitions and guest lectures involving society and industry.

Introduction of Technical Education Community Outreach Scheme (TECOS): The TECOS comprises of a public and private partnership based provision of training and technical education services to the poor and needy segments of society in Delhi. The basic aim behind the scheme is to enable people from the poorer sections of the society to earn their livelihood through self/wage employment. The scheme is an effort at harmonising the livelihood needs of the impoverished and the production oriented requirements of manufacturers and service provider agencies through a network of stakeholder partners, including therein the government departments, Bhagidari Cell of the CM's Secretariat, NGOs, industries, service provider organisations and low skilled impoverished citizen.

The placement of students in gainful employment shows the effectiveness of course. Hence, it is necessary that one should have authentic and reliable data regarding placement. The given data (see Annexure 9.5) shows discrepancies like students passed are some times more than appeared/intake. Placement in more than 25 per cent courses is nil. However, it does not conclude that courses are not popular. The possibility may be that the student is absorbed immediately by industry or engaged in self employment. Therefore there is an urgent need to undertake an in-depth data collection exercise. Analysis of this will elicit information as to which courses are to be initiated and which ones need improvement.

9.6 Issues in Education—Delhi

The industrial policy and the changing pattern of world of work indicate that in the coming years the economy of Delhi would be dominated by the services. The NSSO data also suggest that maximum workers are engaged in activities pertaining to trade, hotels and restaurants, transport, communication, finance and business activities which mainly fall in the service sector as shown in the table (9.17)) and this trend will continue in the coming years. The demand of skills from the industries under this sector will definitely exert pressure on the education system of Delhi. Therefore the steps should be initiated to introduce more and more courses as per the demand of job market, since education directly and through its multiplier effect is a dominant player in the economic activities and thereby growth of the state as well as country. The foregoing discussion raises certain issues (discussed below). The response to these issues will decide the future of educational policy in Delhi.

TABLE 9.17

Activity-wise Workers

S.No.	*Activities*	*48th Round*	*55th Round*
1	2	3	4
1.	Agriculture	0.92 (2.82)	0.60 (1.54)
2.	Mining	-	-
3.	Manufacturing	7.84 (24.04)	8.78 (22.55)
4.	Electricity, Gas, Water etc.	0.09 (0.28)	0.11 (0.29)
5.	Construction	1.78 (5.46)	2.26 (5.78)
6.	Trade, Hotel and Restaurants	6.85 (21.0)	11.31 (29.05)
7.	Transport, Communication etc.	2.59 (7.94)	2.91 (7.47)
8.	Finance and Business Activities	1.53 (4.69)	2.49 (6.34)
9.	Public Admn. Education, Health etc.	11.01 (33.76)	10.48 (26.92)
	Total	32.61 (100.00)	38.94 (100.00)

Source: National Sample Survey (Various Years), Directorate of Economics and Statistics, Delhi.

General Education vs. Vocational and Technical education: While general education adds to quality of civic life, vocational and technical education are value adding and productivity drivers. It is the time that government should give appropriate weightage to both as per the requirement of emerging industries. The decision then should be supported by allocation of funds and sound planning for short-term and long-term goals subject to timely revision based on the pre decided policy parameters and achievements yardsticks

Role of State vs. Market Forces: The privatisation as well as internationalisation of education is increasing at all levels starting from pre school. More and more centres of learning by private players and foreign universities are coming up in Delhi. This may affect quality of education and in turn the nature and quality of future human resources. In the absence of proper monitoring it could distort the demand and supply of different skills in the national market. Therefore, the state should remain the pioneer and prime mover and should hold the responsibility of monitoring and control of quality. magnitude and degree of commercialisation. It is suggested that DoE role should be extended and it should cover the regulation and monitoring of pre school to the higher most level of education with proper transparency methods in place.

State subsidy vs. Users Charges: It is an established fact that investment in education leads to development of economies. The government has to decide that under constraints of resources what share of education out of the total subsidy pool be there and to whom. This is very important because future returns in the borderless knowledge society solely accrue to timely investment in education. Same time relevance of users charges also be examined keeping in mind the equity concerns.

Annexures

ANNEXURE 9.1

Gender-wise Student Enrolment in Delhi during 1999-2000

Stages of Schooling	*Boys (lakh)*	*Girls (lakh)*	*Total (lakh)*
Pre-primary	0.69 (48.3%)	0.74 (51.7%)	1.43
Primary	6.94 (52.4%)	6.30 (47.6%)	13.24
Middle	2.93 (47.0%)	3.30 (53.0%)	6.23
Secondary	3.70 (47.4%)	4.11 (52.6%)	7.81
Senior secondary	2.42 (45.5%)	2.90 (54.5%)	5.32
Total	16.68 (49.0%)	17.35 (51.0%)	34.03

Note: Percentage shares are given in brackets.

Source: Directorate of Education, GNCTD.

ANNEXURE 9.2

Management-wise Secondary and Senior Secondary Level Board Results

	Secondary level			*Senior Secondary level*		
	Govt.	*Aided*	*Unaided*	*Govt.*	*Aided*	*Unaided*
			1995			
Students appeared	77479	15357	32166	42153	15357	32166
Students passed	27815	8815	29367	26820	8815	29367
Pass percentage	33.9	57.4	91.3	63.6	58.7	88.1
			1997			
Students appeared	86490	17072	38226	36379	11122	28046
Students passed	30461	9311	33623	25065	8130	24820
Pass percentage	35.2	54.5	87.9	68.9	73.1	88.5
			1999			
Students appeared	89103	16458	45067	43902	11876	33308
Students passed	30179	8949	38908	29664	8783	29647
Pass percentage	33.9	54.4	86.3	67.6	73.9	89.0

Source: Delhi Directorate.

ANNEXURE 9.3

Number of Students Appearing for Class X and XII CBSE Boards

Year	*Class X*			*Class XII*		
	Boys	*Girls*	*Total*	*Boys*	*Girls*	*Total*
1997	94961 (53.6)	82309 (46.4)	177270	48888 (53.6)	42381 (46.4)	91269
1998	97104 (53.1)	85621 (46.9)	182725	50302 (52.6)	45307 (47.4)	95609
1999	105319 (53.8)	90400 (46.2)	195719	58783 (52.8)	52576 (47.2)	111359
2000	108125 (53.5)	94127 (46.5)	202252	57048 (52.5)	51696 (47.5)	108744

Note: Figures in brackets indicate percentage in total.

Source: Delhi Statistical Handbook, 2000.

A simplistic planning exercise has been attempted. It is clear that number of government and aided schools are far short of requirements at the primary stage, but the shortage is much more acute at the middle stage. At the primary stage if we consider unaided schools as well, there do not seem to be a shortage in absolute numbers. But the fact that a significant proportion of children is still out of school indicates that there are supply problems as well. Very possibly the shortages are in specific clusters, or the unaided schools do not help the situation because of its high fees. The situation is very different in the middle stage where the shortage is very acute, and a substantial capital investment is required at this stage.

ANNEXURE 9.4

An Estimate of Schools Availability (in number)

Children in 6 to 11 age group	*Schools with primary stage required*	*Government and aided schools with primary stage*	*Total Schools with primary stage*	*Children enrolled in primary stage*
(1)	*(2)*	*(3)*	*(4)*	*(5)*
1650173	3300	1967 (2217)	3369 (3619)	14225508
Children in 11 to 14 age group	Schools with middle stage required	Government and aided schools with Middle stage	Total Schools with middle stage	Children enrolled in middle stage
1024470	3414	1262	2212	834908

Notes:

Col. 1: VIIth All India Education Survey, 2001.

Col. 2: Assuming a typical school has two sections in each class of 50 students—and so schools with primary stage have strength of 500 students in the stage and schools with middle stage have enrolment of 300 students at that stage. Norms are based on existing pupil teacher ratios in MCD schools.

Col. 3: Table 9.3 present paper: 2000. The figure in brackets derived by adding one-fifth of higher schools, as the Sarvodaya government schools (secondary and higher secondary) have primary classes as well.

Col. 4: Table 9.3 present paper: 2000. Calculated by adding government schools with all private unaided schools (as almost all such schools begin from the primary stage). Calcualtions are in the next table.

Col. 5: VIIth All India Education Survey, 2001.

Type of schools	Number of schools with classes	
	1 – 5	6 – 8
Government and aided	1967 (2217)	1262
Private unaided	1402	950
Total	3369 (3619)	2212

ANNEXURE 9.5

INTAKE/ADMITTED/PASSED/PLACED

ITI- Name	Courses	Year	Intake	Appeared	Passed	Placed	Remarks
(1)	(2)	(3)	(4)	(5)	(6)	(7)	(8)
BTC Pusa	Litho Offset Mechine Minder	2005	32	15	15	0	
BTC Pusa	Desktop Publishing	2005	16	9	9	0	
BTC Pusa	Steward	2005	16	14	14	0	
BTC Pusa	Plate Maker cum Impositor	2005	16	3	2	0	
BTC Pusa	Welder (Gas & Electric)	2005	12	9	8	0	
BTC Pusa	Cutting & Sewing	2005	80	46	42	0	
Subzi Mandi	Auto Electrician	2005	16	17	14	6	
Subzi Mandi	Cutting & Sewing	2005	144	91	90	31	
Subzi Mandi	Carpenter	2005	16	6	6	1	
Subzi Mandi	Dress Designing	2005	16	15	13	7	
Subzi Mandi	Electrician	2005	16	14	12	8	
Subzi Mandi	Embroidery & Needle Work	2005	32	17	17	8	
Subzi Mandi	Fitter	2005	32	35	31	20	
Subzi Mandi	Instrument Mechanic	2005	16	13	9	3	
Subzi Mandi	Mech. Motor Vehicle	2005	32	24	13	10	
Subzi Mandi	Painter	2005	16	11	9	3	
Subzi Mandi	Radio & T.V. Mech.	2005	16	7	7	6	
Subzi Mandi	Ref. & A.C. Mechanic	2005	16	14	12	7	
Subzi Mandi	Steno (English)	2005	64	42	6	1	
Subzi Mandi	Tool & Die Maker	2005	16	0	0	0	
Subzi Mandi	Turner	2005	12	8	3	2	
Subzi Mandi	Welder (Gas & Electric)	2005	12	21	14	8	
Subzi Mandi	Wire Man	2005	16	13	9	7	
Khichripur	D/Man (Civil)	2005	16	15	14	10	
Khichripur	Electrician	2005	16	16	11	8	
Khichripur	Plumber	2005	16	17	8	3	
Khichripur	Plastic Processing Operator	2005	32	29	25	20	
Khichripur	Fitter	2005	16	18	17	8	
Khichripur	Mech. Motor Vehicle	2005	16	15	8	8	
Khichripur	Cutting & Sewing	2005	32	27	27	22	
Khichripur	Electronics Mechanic	2005	16	17	17	16	
Khichripur	Computer Operator & Programming Asstt.	2005	40	36	25	20	
Khichripur	Turner	2005	12	12	9	7	
Khichripur	Ref. & A.C. Mechanic	2005	16	11	11	8	
Khichripur	Steno (Hindi)	2005	32	22	22	15	
Khichripur	Steno (English)	2005	32	22	11	10	
Khichripur	Information Technology & Electronics System Maintenance	2005	16	14	4	4	
Narela	D/Man (Civil)	2005	16	12	3	0	
Narela	Wire Man	2005	16	12	7	0	
Narela	Fitter	2005	16	18	9	0	
Narela	Turner	2005	12	11	8	0	
Narela	Electronics Mechanic	2005	16	13	11	0	
Narela	Ref. & A.C. Mechanic	2005	16	14	10	0	

Contd...

...contd...

(1)	(2)	(3)	(4)	(5)	(6)	(7)	(8)
Narela	Mech. Motor Vehicle	2005	16	17	5	0	
Narela	Painter	2005	16	7	6	0	
Narela	Plumber	2005	16	16	8	0	
Narela	Welder (Gas & Electric)	2005	12	8	6	0	
Narela	Mechanic Tractor	2005	16	15	7	0	
Narela	Scooter & Auto Cycle Mechanic	2005	16	17	13	0	
Narela	Steel Fabricator	2005	16	8	7	0	
Narela	Embroidery & Needle Work	2005	16	5	5	0	
Narela	Cutting & Sewing	2005	32	30	30	0	
Narela	Computer Operator & Programming Asstt.	2005	40	38	31	0	
Narela	Steno (English)	2005	32	22	1	0	
Jaffarpur	D/Man (Civil)	2005	16	16	8	6	
Jaffarpur	Electronics Mechanic	2005	16	11	11	9	
Jaffarpur	D/Man (Mech.)	2005	16	12	12	0	
Jaffarpur	Cutting & Sewing	2005	48	44	41	30	
Jaffarpur	Embroidery & Needle Work	2005	16	7	7	2	
Jaffarpur	Dress Designing	2005	16	7	7	3	
Jaffarpur	Computer Operator & Programming Asstt.	2005	40	36	35	25	
Jaffarpur	Plumber	2005	16	10	8	6	
Jaffarpur	Steel Fabricator	2005	16	9	8	5	
Jaffarpur	Scooter & Auto Cycle Mechanic	2005	16	15	15	0	
Jaffarpur	Steno (Hindi)	2005	16	9	8	4	
Jaffarpur	Steno (English)	2005	16	14	12	7	
Pusa	Machinist	2005	48	32	28	13	
Pusa	Ref. & A.C. Mechanic	2005	32	28	18	7	
Pusa	Electrician	2005	48	44	18	8	
Pusa	Radio & T.V. Mech.	2005	16	13	11	3	
Pusa	Fitter	2005	48	44	36	21	
Pusa	Computer Operator & Programming Asstt.	2005	40	39	34	18	
Pusa	Mech. Motor Vehicle	2005	32	33	17	14	
Pusa	Welder (Gas & Electric)	2005	24	24	12	6	
Pusa	Surveyor	2005	16	14	14	5	
Pusa	Mechanic Tractor	2005	32	30	6	0	
Pusa	Turner	2005	36	24	14	4	
Pusa	Instrument Mechanic	2005	16	5	5	3	
Pusa	Steno (English)	2005	96	61	27	15	
Pusa	Mechanic Diesel	2005	32	36	32	18	
Pusa	Electronics Mechanic	2005	16	15	15	8	
Pusa	Cutting & Sewing	2005	32	26	25	17	
Pusa	Carpenter	2005	16	12	5	2	
Pusa	Steno (Hindi)	2005	32	30	27	11	
Pusa	Wire Man	2005	16	16	13	4	
Pusa	D/Man (Mech.)	2005	32	28	26	12	
Pusa	Sheet Metal Worker	2005	16	12	3	1	
Pusa	Plastic Processing Operator	2005	32	21	17	8	
Pusa	D/Man (Civil)	2005	16	15	7	3	
Pusa	Commercial Art	2005	16	13	13	6	
Pusa	Dent Beating & Spray Printing	2005	16	15	15	7	

Contd...

...contd...

(1)	(2)	(3)	(4)	(5)	(6)	(7)	(8)
Pusa	Information Technology & Electronics System Maintenance	2005	16	12	4	0	
Shahdara	Tool & Die Maker	2005	0	0	0	0	Junior Section
Shahdara	D/Man (Civil)	2005	19	16	12	12	
Shahdara	D/Man (Mech.)	2005	0	0	0	0	Junior Section
Shahdara	Electronics Mechanic	2005	0	2	2	2	
Shahdara	Ref. & A.C. Mechanic	2005	19	16	15	10	
Shahdara	Machinist Grinder	2005	14	3	3	2	
Shahdara	Mech. Motor Vehicle	2005	58	52	39	30	
Shahdara	Electrician	2005	38	33	25	25	
Shahdara	Instrument Mechanic	2005	19	10	9	6	
Shahdara	Fitter	2005	58	62	45	39	
Shahdara	Machinist	2005	58	45	43	36	
Shahdara	Turner	2005	43	28	16	12	
Shahdara	Painter	2005	19	9	2	2	
Shahdara	Wire Man	2005	19	17	7	5	
Shahdara	Auto Electrician	2005	19	10	9	6	
Shahdara	Welder (Gas & Electric)	2005	29	28	13	10	
Shahdara	Mechanic Diesel	2005	19	21	17	8	
Shahdara	Mechanic Tractor	2005	58	29	23	6	
Shahdara	Foundry Man (Moulder)	2005	19	13	7	4	
Shahdara	Plumber	2005	19	20	9	2	
Shahdara	Carpenter	2005	19	10	6	2	
Shahdara	Scooter & Auto Cycle Mechanic	2005	19	12	12	6	
Shahdara	Cutting & Sewing	2005	35	31	31	10	
Shahdara	Embroidery & Needle Work	2005	18	13	13	1	
Shahdara	Steno (English)	2005	35	15	13	2	
Shahdara	Steno (Hindi)	2005	35	26	26	2	
Siri Fort	Information Technology & Electronics System Maintenance	2005	16	8	5	6	
Siri Fort	D/Man (Civil)	2005	64	29	21	9	
Siri Fort	Electronics Mechanic	2005	16	0	0	0	
Siri Fort	Steno (English)	2005	64	54	36	4	
Siri Fort	Steno (Hindi)	2005	32	26	23	0	
Siri Fort	Secretarial Practice (English)	2005	16	9	8	2	
Siri Fort	Hair & Skin Care	2005	48	41	39	0	Self employment
Siri Fort	Textile Designing	2005	32	30	30	6	
Siri Fort	Commercial Art	2005	16	13	12	2	
Siri Fort	C.C. & Home Management	2005	16	12	12	0	Self employment
Siri Fort	Dress Designing	2005	48	40	39	0	Self employment
Siri Fort	Fashion Designing	2005	16	15	9	2	
Siri Fort	Embroidery & Needle Work	2005	32	26	26	2	
Siri Fort	Cutting & Sewing	2005	160	145	144	0	Self employment
Siri Fort	Computer Operator & Programming Asstt.	2005	40	35	33	4	
Arab-ki-Sarai	Tool & Die Maker	2005	16	10	10	8	
Arab-ki-Sarai	D/Man (Civil)	2005	16	15	10	8	
Arab-ki-Sarai	D/Man (Mech.)	2005	16	21	20	15	
Arab-ki-Sarai	Electronics Mechanic	2005	16	15	15	51	
Arab-ki-Sarai	Ref. & A.C. Mechanic	2005	32	24	20	1	
Arab-ki-Sarai	Machinist Grinder	2005	12	13	7	0	

Contd...

...contd...

(1)	(2)	(3)	(4)	(5)	(6)	(7)	(8)
Arab-ki-Sarai	Mech. Motor Vehicle	2005	32	28	15	11	
Arab-ki-Sarai	Electrician	2005	32	37	9	62	
Arab-ki-Sarai	Radio & T.V. Mech.	2005	16	15	12	17	
Arab-ki-Sarai	Instrument Mechanic	2005	16	10	7	0	
Arab-ki-Sarai	Fitter	2005	48	52	35	80	
Arab-ki-Sarai	Machinist	2005	24	26	16	21	
Arab-ki-Sarai	Turner	2005	24	23	18	4	
Arab-ki-Sarai	Wire Man	2005	16	15	12	6	
Arab-ki-Sarai	Electroplator	2005	16	11	7	3	
Arab-ki-Sarai	Painter (General)	2005	16	8	5	9	
Arab-ki-Sarai	Sheet Metal Worker	2005	32	19	11	0	
Arab-ki-Sarai	Welder (Gas & Electric)	2005	36	35	28	14	
Arab-ki-Sarai	Scooter & Auto Cycle Mechanic	2005	16	15	15	0	
Arab-ki-Sarai	Steel Fabricator	2005	48	35	32	11	
Arab-ki-Sarai	Carpenter	2005	16	13	6	5	
Arab-ki-Sarai	Plumber	2005	16	18	8	13	
Arab-ki-Sarai	Computer Operator & Programming Asstt.	2005	40	34	33	9	
Arab-ki-Sarai	Steno (English)	2005	96	59	39	4	
Arab-ki-Sarai	Process Cameraman	2005	16	6	6	0	
Arab-ki-Sarai	Book Binder	2005	16	1	1	0	
Arab-ki-Sarai	Cutting & Sewing	2005	32	18	18	1	
Arab-ki-Sarai	Dress Designing	2005	16	12	12	0	
Arab-ki-Sarai	Health Sanitary Inspector	2005	20	20	18	0	
Tilak Nagar	Cutting & Sewing	2005	16	16	13	0	
Tilak Nagar	Textile Designing	2005	16	15	15	0	
Tilak Nagar	Commercial Art	2005	16	14	14	0	
Tilak Nagar	Dress Designing	2005	16	10	10	0	
Tilak Nagar	Hair & Skin Care	2005	16	10	10	0	
Tilak Nagar	Steno (English)	2005	32	22	14	0	
Tilak Nagar	Computer Operator & Programming Asstt.	2005	44	40	34	0	
Tilak Nagar	D/Man (Civil)	2005	16	0	0	0	
Jahangirpuri	Cutting & Sewing	2005	76	53	53	10	
Jahangirpuri	Steno (English)	2005	38	19	6	3	
Jahangirpuri	Photographer	2005	19	12	11	3	
Jahangirpuri	Plumber	2005	19	17	2	2	
Jahangirpuri	Welder (Gas & Electric)	2005	29	25	10	6	
Jahangirpuri	Mechanic Tractor	2005	19	17	9	4	
Jahangirpuri	Scooter & Auto Cycle Mechanic	2005	38	29	29	10	
Jahangirpuri	Turner	2005	14	9	9	6	
Jahangirpuri	Machinist	2005	29	19	17	12	
Jahangirpuri	Fitter	2005	38	33	30	20	
Jahangirpuri	Mech. Motor Vehicle	2005	19	11	6	5	
Jahangirpuri	D/Man (Mech.)	2005	19	15	13	7	
Jahangirpuri	D/Man (Civil)	2005	19	14	7	3	
Jahangirpuri	Electronics Mechanic	2005	19	14	14	8	
Jahangirpuri	Painter (General)	2005	19	8	0	8	
Jahangirpuri	Ref. & A.C. Mechanic	2005	19	14	8	7	
Jahangirpuri	Electrician	2005	19	18	14	13	

Source: Department of Technical Education, Government of Delhi.

Chapter 10

Health and Family Welfare, RCH, Ayush and Nutrition

10.1 Background

Physical, mental, social, financial and spiritual growth of human beings is a continuous process that is essential for ensuring development of full potential of human capabilities in any given society, state or the country, as a whole. Standards for these parameters denote the development level of the human race in the defined group. Human development is a continuous process and the HDI is a relative indicator of the same. Parameters that currently form the base for HDI include: i) Longevity, ii) Knowledge, and iii) Income. At the given point of time, the Index certainly helps in determining the relative levels of growth and development in a defined group of population—country wise, region wise or in any other suitable defined group to determine the apparent deprivation in a given group of population for initiating appropriate measures accordingly. Ranking for India in the latest HDR of 2004 is dismal 127th out of 175 countries and it has remained at the same rank as that of the last year.

10.2 Peculiarities of Delhi—The Capital State

Delhi is the national capital of the largest and one of the most vibrant democracies in the world, and also it is one of the most rapidly expanding economies. A city of hopes and promises for a common man—leading to a common belief that whatever was not possible at their local place could be achieved in Delhi—a trust that needs to be upheld. The city has its own share of problems too—partly inherent and partly due to a large number of in-migrations of people from other states with hope and expectations (on daily floating basis as well as on long-term/permanent basis)—leading to unusually very high population density of over 9000 persons/sq. km (93 per cent urban) compared to the national average of about 350 persons/sq. km (25 per cent urban). This extra share of population load puts additional pressure on all the infrastructure facilities that are already overstretched to their extreme. There is a lot of stress on the public facilities in Delhi—especially on the Health sector. Medical care and treatment cannot be denied to a fellow countryman on any ground. No restriction can be made on any basis.

Health care facilities in the adjoining regions, unfortunately, remain very poor leading to extra load on Delhi necessitating provision of adequate infrastructure to shoulder this additional responsibility. The geographic distribution of people in Delhi varies from those staying in posh urban localities with well-developed infrastructure to those who are homeless or live in slums with complete absence of basic facilities. A large number of urbanised villages (*Lal Dora* areas) also lack basic infrastructure and/or proper planning of the residential areas leading to over crowding with unhealthy surroundings. About 15 per cent of Delhi's population lives in slums. As per the Census of 2001, the population of Delhi is about 13.8 million with a projection of 17.7 million by 2007, if the present trend of migration of population from the adjoining states continues. Though during the last decade, the birth rate has fallen from 28.52 to 23.33 per 1,000, the growth rate of Delhi has remained unaffected due to continued in-migration.

The health of people anywhere is largely dependent upon their living conditions and lifestyles. The factors in our everyday life, which significantly influence our health status, are called "health determinants". Health determinants include water supply, sanitation, nutrition, food safety, health services, housing conditions, working conditions, education, lifestyles, population changes, income, and so on. They form the physical, social and economic environments that surround us. The Hon'ble Chief Minister has a long cherished dream to make Delhi as 'the role model' city in the country for health care infrastructure.

10.3 Health Care Delivery System in Delhi

Delhi has fairly well established health care infrastructure for its people with one of the highest bed capacity (1.98 beds/1000 persons) compared to the national average of about 0.7 beds per 1000 persons. However, the real benefits of this infrastructure, most of the times, get diluted in accommodating the additional load of patients from adjoining states. There is multiplicity of agencies operating their health care outlets in different areas or for defined subset of populations in different areas like Delhi Government, MCD, NDMC, CGHS, DGHS, ESI, and Army etc., leading to some overlaps/duplications of services with wastage of efforts and resources on one-hand and deficient services on the other.

Health has always been one of the priority sectors of Plan Development of Delhi Government as it is the major provider of health care and, thereto is responsible for ensuring its effective delivery to the citizen of Delhi. Public health expenditure of the Government of Delhi has consistently remained above 6 per cent of the total plan budget during the last 20 years reaching upto 10.35 per cent of the plan outlay for the 10th Plan (2002-2007)—the highest for any state government in the country. Health & Family Welfare Department caters to health needs of nearly 14 million population of this ever-growing metropolis and also has to share the burden of migratory as well as floating population from neighbouring states which constitute nearly 33 per cent of total intake at major hospitals in Delhi.

Delhi was a Uni-district Union Territory at the time of 1991 Census. It is only recently that the administrative set up of Delhi has changed significantly and now the NCT of Delhi comprises of nine districts and twenty-seven sub-divisions (*Tehsils*). However, very little health information is available at the district/sub-district levels, as on date. Directorate of Health Services is the nodal agency among the health care providers of Government of NCT of Delhi in the matters of establishment of hospitals and dispensaries, implementation of various National and State programmes related to Medical & Public Health and for prevention, control and eradication of major diseases.

Similarly, the Directorate of Family Welfare, GNCT of Delhi, is responsible for carrying out the Family Welfare Programmes. Health and Family Welfare Department, Government of NCT of Delhi plays a significant role and is committed to provide health care facilities to the people of Delhi by providing primary, tertiary and super specialty services in the health system and by implementation of various State level and National level Programmes under Medical and Public Health Sector for prevention and control of various diseases; by opening new hospitals and dispensaries/health centres in deficient areas to remove geographical imbalance; to ensure that health care facilities are provided to the people at a reasonable distance and incorporating Indian System of Medicine & Homeopathy (ISM&H) in the main system. The Department is providing services through a network of existing 31 hospitals including 3 hospitals under ISM&H, 174 Allopathic Dispensaries, 70 Mobile Van Dispensaries, 433 School Health Clinics, 20 Ayurvedic Dispensaries, 62 Homeopathic Dispensaries, and 8 Unani Dispensaries. The growth of medical institutions operating under all agencies in Delhi during the past 10 years is indicated in Table 10.1.

10.4 Growth of Medical Institutions in Delhi since 1992

According to the recommendations of the World Health Organisation, the bed population ratio to be achieved by

TABLE 10.1

Growth of Medical Institutions in Delhi since 1992

Year	*No. of Hospitals*	*PHCs*	*No. of Dispensaries*	*No. of Maternity Home, M&CW Centres & SCs*	*Poly clinics*	*No. of Registered Nursing Homes*	*No. of Special Clinics*	*Total No. of Institutions*
1992	82	8	656	219	10	105	45	1125
1995	84	8	675	209	11	132	37	1156
1996	86	8	740	214	11	136	43	1233
2002	70	8	808	203	04	460	43	1596
2004	87	7	993	209	05	559	44	1904
2005	86*	7	972**	204	05	558	44	1876

Note: * One health facility under Social Welfare Deptt does not have any indoor beds now hence the total number of hospitals has reduced by 1 as compared to last year.

** The number of dispensaries has decreased because, school health clinics at 70 location are being run by 16 functional teams only and existing clinics have closed due to handing over of the scheme to NGOs.

Source: Directorate of Health Services, GNCTD, *Economic Survey of Delhi*, 2005-2006 p.192.

2000 AD was 5 per thousand persons. As of March 2005, the bed-population ratio in Delhi was 2.08. The growth in the number of beds in Delhi from 1982 onwards and agency-wise distribution of beds is shown in Figure 10.1 and 10.2.

FIGURE 10.1

Growth of Beds Capacity since 1982

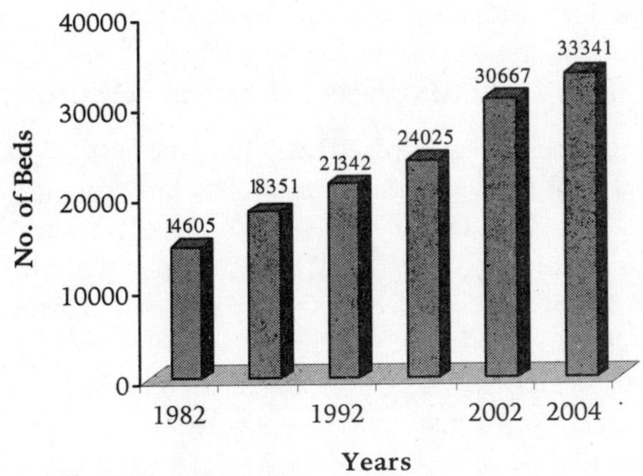

Source: Directorate of Health Services. GNCTD.

In the 22 years from 1982 till March 2004, 18,736 new beds were added in all the health care institutions in Delhi. During this period, on an average 851 beds were added each year. However, there was not much change in bed-population ratio in Delhi and it remained around 2.2/ 1000 for last 20 years but during 2004-05 only 645 beds were added thus bringing down the bed-population ratio to 2.08.

FIGURE 10.2

Agency-wise Distribution of Hospital Beds

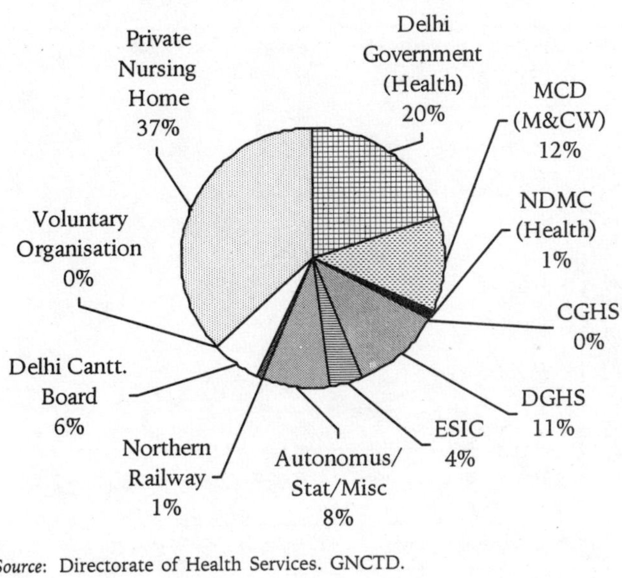

Source: Directorate of Health Services. GNCTD.

10.5 Life Expectancy at Birth

There are several determinants that indicate the health status of any given society. However, Life Expectancy at Birth, as the single parameter, provides a fairly broad indication of the same. This parameter is independent of the economic development of the country and hence it is a fair pointer of true health status of its people. For instance, Sri Lanka with a per capita GNP of $380 p.a. had a life expectancy at birth as 70 years compared to that of just 54 years for Oman with per capita GNP of $6,730 p.a. Hence, Life Expectancy at Birth has been included as the sole parameter for assessment of health status in evaluating the Human Development Index for any country/society.

The Sample Registration System (SRS) estimate (1995-1999) for Life Expectancy at Birth for Delhi's population is 68.6 years—comprising of 68.7 years for urban and 67.0 years for rural populations—compared to an all India average of 60.7 years. Further subdivisions of this indicator or the previous trends for Delhi State are not apparently available. Hence, it is necessary to undertake a planned study to evaluate the life expectancy at birth under various parameters like the gender, educational levels, region, religion, caste, community, socio-economic status occupation, etc. to be able to get more meaningful inputs for improving the human development with equal opportunities for all.

Hence, it is necessary to undertake a planned study to evaluate the life expectancy at birth under various parameters like the gender, educational levels, region, religion, caste, community, socio-economic status, occupation, etc., to be able to get more meaningful inputs for improving the human development with equal opportunities for all.

TABLE 10.2

Death Rate (per thousand)

Year	*Total*	*Rural*	*Urban*
1994	7.0	6.4	7.0
1995	6.0	4.9	6.1
1996	5.7	5.7	5.7
1997	5.4	5.4	5.4
1998	5.3	5.3	5.3
1999	4.8	4.5	4.9
2000	5.1	5.0	5.1
2001	5.0	5.4	5.0
2003	5.0	5.5	4.8
2004	4.7	5.4	4.6
2005	4.6	5.5	4.5

Source: Compiled by contributors from various SRS Reports and report of Directorate of Economics & Statistics and office of Chief Registrar (Birth & Deaths) GNCTD.

Death Rate

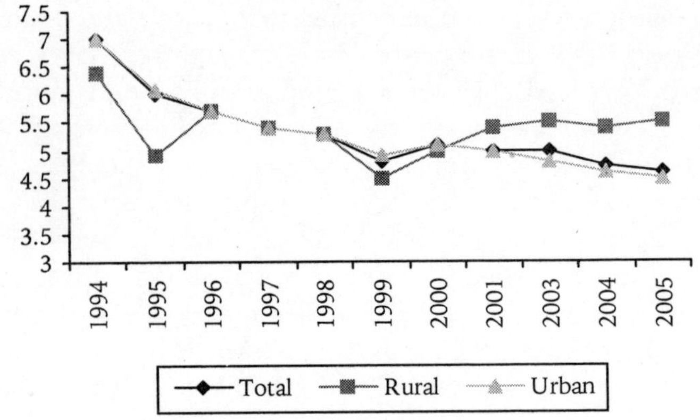

10.6 Other Indicators for Health in the Society that Ultimately Influence the Longevity

10.6.1 Crude Death Rate

Death Rate of Delhi shows a declining trend since 1991, but from 1994 onwards it shows a smooth line of graph. The death rate in Delhi is 5.59/1000 (SRS, 2004). The rural urban differential is almost non-existent. The overall death rate in Delhi is even lower than that in Kerala State (8.4), which is the most frequently quoted successful model of achieving demographic transition. As per the latest report of Directorate of Economics and Statistics and Office of Chief Registrar (Births and Deaths) Government of NCT of Delhi, the death ratio in 2004 is 5.59/1000.

10.6.2 Infant Mortality Rate (IMR)

Infant mortality rate is one of the most sensitive indicators of health. IMR is very sensitive to changes that have a bearing on the quality of life, particularly, on the health and longevity of people. It is taken as one the best indicator for assessment of basic health care, quality and reach of health services and other crucial health determinants like environment, education, nutrition etc.

As per the SRS records, Delhi has managed to bring down its IMR from 43 per thousand live births in 1990 to 29 in 2001. The decline is seen for both males and females. According to the 2001 SRS estimates, Delhi has IMR of 30 for males and 27 for females per thousand live births. Though the IMR in Delhi is much below the national, which is 66, but still it is very high while compared to developed countries where IMR is less than 10. Even Kerala, according to the 2001 SRS estimates, has managed to bring down its IMR to 11 per thousand live births. However as per SRS report 2005 the IMR in Delhi

TABLE 10.3

Infant Mortality Rate by Sex

Year	*Total*	*Male*	*Female*
1997	35	37	33
1998	36	35	37
1999	31	29	31
2000	32	29	35
2001	29	30	27
2003	28	28	29
2004	32	32	32
2005	35	33	37

Source: Compiled by contributors from various SRS Reports and report of Directorate of Economics & Statistics and office of Chief Registrar (Birth & Deaths) GNCTD.

Infant Mortality Rate by Sex

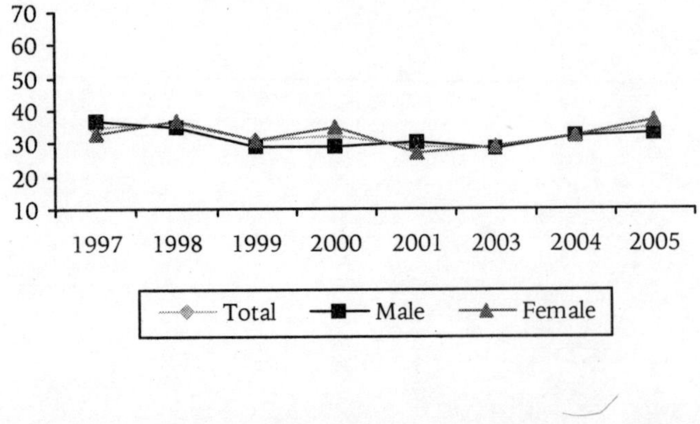

TABLE 10.4

Infant Mortality Rate by Residence

Year	*Total*	*Rural*	*Urban*
1999	31	32	31
2000	32	32	32
2001	29	34	28
2002	32	31	32*
2003	28	32	28
2004	32	48	30
2005	35	44	33

Source: Compiled by contributors from various SRS Reports and report of Directorate of Economics & Statistics and office of Chief Registrar (Birth & Deaths) GNCTD.

Infant Mortality Rate by Residence

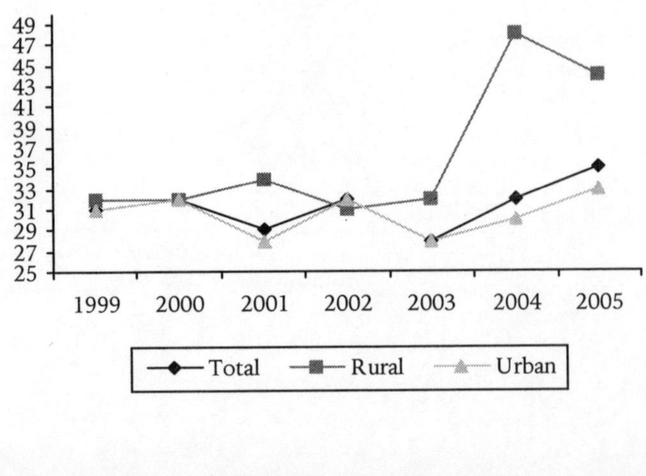

has gone up to 35 for total with 33 for male and 37 for female. As per the report of Chief Registrar (Birth & Death) Government of NCT, Delhi, the infant mortality ratio of Delhi has come down to 13.08 per 1000 in 2004.

TABLE 10.5

Trends of Various Health Indices in Delhi over the Years

Year	IMR*	CBR*	CDR*	Female Births per 1000 Male Births	Natural Growth Rate
1994	54.1	24.8	7.0	840	17.8
1995	35.5	23.3	6.0	744	17.3
1996	40.7	21.6	5.7	839	15.9
1997	29.1	21.1	5.4	852	15.7
1998	33.1	19.4	5.3	899	14.2
1999	25.4	20.3	4.8	837	15.5
2000	31.8	20.3	5.1	820	15.1
2001	29.0	18.7	5.0	821	13.6
2004	13.08	20.03	5.59	823*	13.7
2005	35.0***	18.6***	4.6***	NA	13.9
All India	**58.0*** **	**23.8*** **	**7.6*** **	**935** **	16.3***

Note: * Based on Civil registration system of birth and death.
** National Human Development Report 2001.
*** SRS Bulletin October 2006.

Source: Compiled by contributors from various SRS Reports and report of Directorate of Economics & Statistics and office of Chief Registrar (Birth & Deaths) GNCTD.

10.7 Fertility, Birth Rates and Maternal Health

10.7.1 Fertility and Family Planning

Fertility continues to decline in Delhi. At current fertility levels, women will have an average of 1.6 children each throughout their childbearing years, one of the lowest levels in India. Fertility rate in Kerala is 1.8. At the time of NFHS-1, the total fertility rate was 3.0 children per women.

NCT of Delhi has already achieved the replacement level of fertility. However, owing to large migration from neighbouring states, the decadal growth rate is higher than the national level. The sex ratio at 821 is low; sex ratio in 0-6 years is 865. Sincere efforts are required by all to reverse the present sex ratio in Delhi.

Use following sentence. "The overall use of contraceptive has gone up since NFHS-2 when it was 63.8 per cent. As per NFHS-3 the total unmet need for family planning is only 8 per cent, much less than the figures of NFHS-2 when it was 13.4 per cent. The use of contraceptive has gone up since NFHS-2 when it was 63.8 per cent. The total unmet need for family planning is only 8 per cent, much less than the figures of NFHS-2 when it was 13.4 per cent.

10.7.2 Demographic Indices

TABLE 10.6

Demographic Indices

	CBR (SRS Oct. 2006)	CDR (SRS Oct. 2006)	IMR (SRS Oct. 2006)	Sex Ratio (Census 2001)	Sex Ratio 0-6 (Census 2001)	Decadal Growth Rate	Likely year of achieving NRR
Delhi	18.6	4.6	35	821	865	46.31	Achieved
India	23.8	7.6	58	933	927	21.34	2026

Source: Compiled by contributors from various SRS Reports and report of Directorate of Economics & Statistics and office of Chief Registrar (Birth & Deaths) GNCTD.

Though replacement level of fertility has already been reached in Delhi, there is still an unmet need for both spacing and terminal methods of contraception.

10.7.3 Birth Rate

The demographic pattern in Delhi shows that from 1994 onwards Delhi has been experiencing an overall declining trend in birth rate for both rural and urban areas, with significant rural urban gap. According to the 2006 SRS data, the overall birth rate in Delhi is 18.6, which is significantly lower than the national average of 23.8.

TABLE 10.7

Birth Rate

Year	Total	Rural	Urban
1994	24.8	27.5	24.4
1995	23.3	24.9	23.2
1996	21.6	25.5	21.2
1997	21.1	22.7	20.9
1998	19.4	20.9	19.3
1999	20.3	20.7	20.3
2000	20.3	21.4	20.1
2001	18.7	23.2	18.1
2003	17.3	21.3	16.8
2004	18.4	18.4	18.4
2005	18.6	19.0	18.5

Source: Compiled by contributors from various SRS Reports and report of Directorate of Economics & Statistics and office of Chief Registrar (Birth & Deaths) GNCTD.

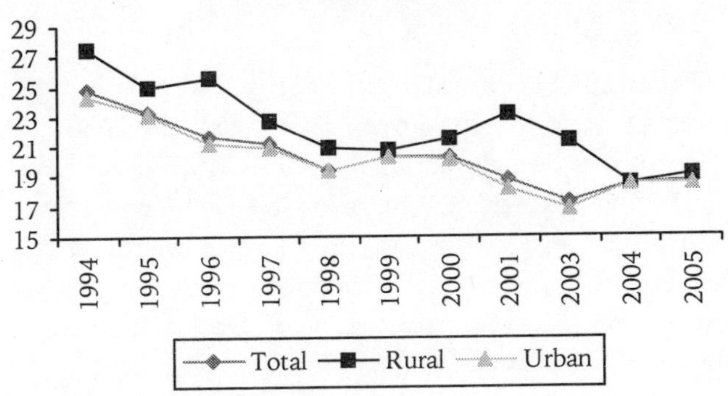

10.8 Natural Growth Rate

Delhi shows an overall-declining trend in terms of natural growth rate since 1992 till 2001 except for the year 1999 when the natural growth rate had increased marginally. Though, a marginal difference between rural and urban growth rate over the period could be observed, the year 2001 shows a significant difference between rural and urban growth rate. Rural Natural Growth Rate is showing an upward trend since 1999.

TABLE 10.8

Natural Growth Rate

Year	*Total*	*Rural*	*Urban*
1994	17.8	21.1	17.4
1995	17.3	20.0	17.1
1996	15.9	19.8	15.5
1997	15.7	17.4	15.5
1998	14.2	15.7	14.0
1999	15.5	16.2	15.4
2000	15.1	16.4	15.0
2001	13.6	17.8	13.1
2003	12.4	15.8	11.9
2004	13.7	13.0	13.8
2005	13.9	13.5	14.0

Source: Compiled by contributors from various SRS Reports and report of Directorate of Economics & Statistics and office of Chief Registrar (Birth & Deaths) GNCTD.

Natural Growth Rate

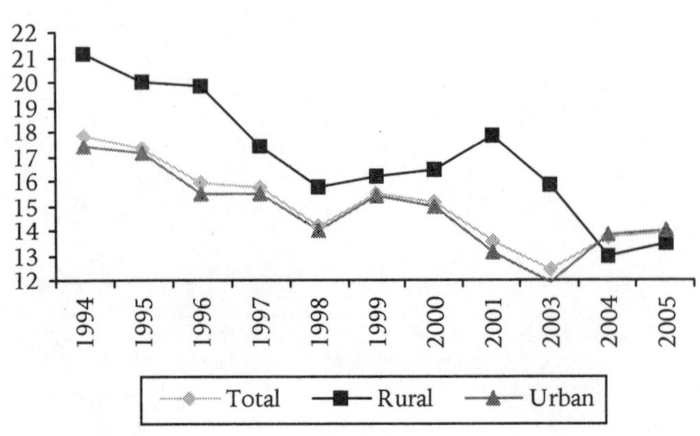

10.9 Sex Ratio

Since 1951 sex ratio in Delhi was showing an increasing trend moving from 768 in 1951 to 827 in 1991. But there has been a marginal decline in 2001, i.e., down to 821. The sex ratio is quite low in Delhi and it needs attention at various levels. As per the birth & death registration (Deptt. of Economics and Statistics) Government of NCT, sex ratio of Delhi in 2004 has improved to 823.

FIGURE 10.3

Sex Ratio (Over All), Delhi, 2001

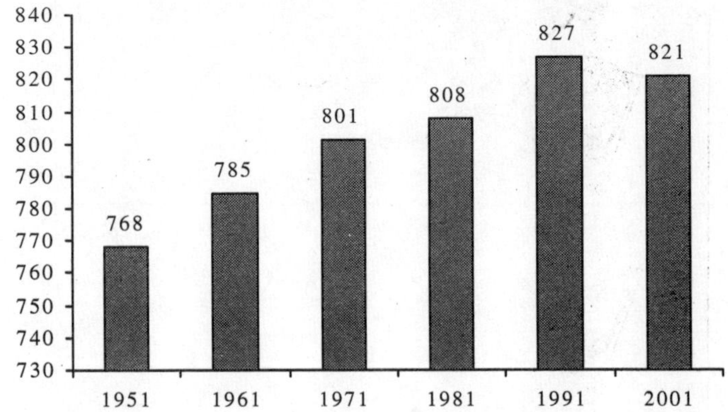

The comparison of the sex ratio of 1991 and 2001 census revealed that except for two districts i.e., North and North East, all other seven districts in Delhi show a declining trend. As per 2001 census, the highest sex ratio is recorded in North East district at 851 whereas it is lowest in South West district at 783. The 2001 census also shows a significant rural–urban differential. It is 806 females per thousand males in the rural areas as against 822 females in the urban areas. This difference could be observed in most of the districts.

FIGURE 10.4

Sex Ratio by Residence, 2001

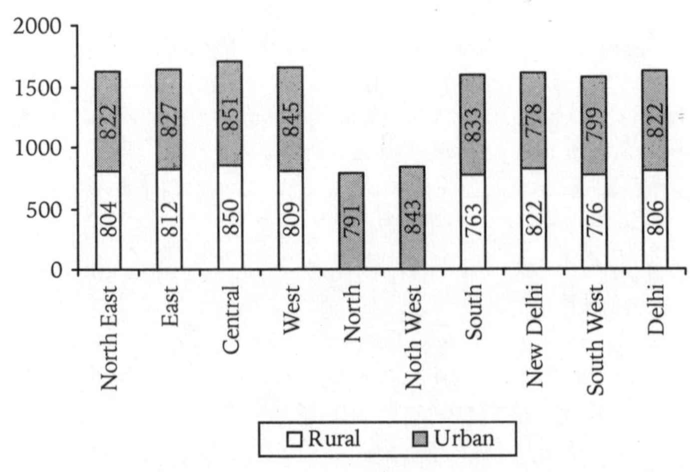

10.9.1 The Sex Ratio in the Age Group 0-6 Years

The sex ratio in the age group 0-6 years shows a sharp decline in Delhi from 915 in 1991 to 865 in 2001. This decline is seen in all the districts of Delhi. According to 2001 census, Central district has the highest sex ratio with 902 females per 1000 males in 0-6 years age group whereas South West district is lowest with a sex ratio of 845.

FIGURE 10.5

Sex Ratio (0-6 Years)

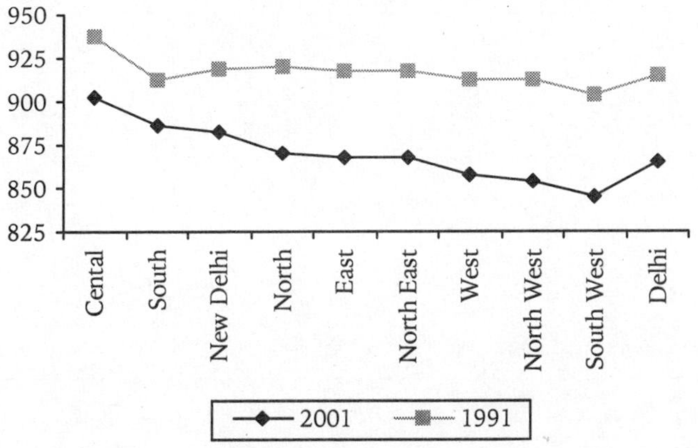

10.9.2 Sex Ratio (0-6years) in Four Metro Cities

TABLE 10.9

Sex Ratio (0-6years) in Four Metro Cities

	City/Urban Agglomeration	*Sex Ratio*	
		1991	*2001*
1.	Delhi Urban Agglomeration	830	822
2.	Mumbai Urban Agglomeration	828	823
3.	Kolkata Urban Agglomeration	830	869
4.	Chennai Urban Agglomeration	932	950

Source: Calculated by Contributors from Census 2001 report.

Comparison of sex ratio among four metros shows that Delhi has the most adverse sex ratio amongst all. Sex ratio in Delhi and Mumbai has deteriorated further between 1991 and 2001, while it has improved in Kolkata and Chennai during the same period. Among the four metros, Chennai has the highest number of females vs. male population (950:1000 in 2001).

Analysis of data of births registered, as available through civil registration system, shows that sex ratio at birth continues to be pernicious for Delhi. In the year 2000, there were 820 female births per 1000 male births—further decline of 79 from the 1998 figures of 899. Analysis of overall sex ratio, sex ratio in 0-6 year, as well as M:F ratio at birth shows inverse ratio in all the three categories. This shows that this inverse sex ratio is not because of migration alone. There is every possibility of sex-selective abortion and female foeticide being practised.

The declining female to male ratio in the state of Delhi is a cause of concern. With the advent of modern advance technology and its misuse by professionals in collusion with society and individuals due to various religious beliefs, social and economic reasons, we have reached a dangerous situation. To correct this imbalance, Pre-Natal Diagnostic Techniques (Regulation and Prevention of Misuse) Act, 1994 was enacted by Government of India. This Act has been amended in 2002 and is now called as the Pre-Conception and Pre-Natal Diagnostic Techniques (Prohibition of Sex Selection) Act.

10.9.3 Sex Ratio at Birth in Delhi

TABLE 10.10

Number of Female Births per 1000 Male Births

Year	*No. of female births per thousand male births (Delhi)*
1991	867
1992	862
1993	856
1994	840
1995	744
1996	839
1997	852
1998	899
1999	837
2000	820
2001	821
2004*	823

Note: *Birth and Death registration, Deptt. of Economics & Statistics, Govt. of NCT.

Source: Calculated by contributors from *Birth and Death registration, Deptt. of Economics & Statistics, Govt. of NCT.

10.10 Morbidity Patterns

From all available information it is clear that Delhi is in the process of epidemiological transition facing the double burden of diseases. The exact rates of morbidity or affliction of diseases are difficult to estimate, as there is no centralised system of recording and reporting. Various agencies maintain records as per their requirements. Most of the data available is based on hospital records. From analysis of the records, it emerged that communicable diseases are still a major cause of morbidity

Hospital data of 2003 shows that communicable diseases were responsible for almost 21 per cent of all outdoor patients and 26 per cent of indoor admissions. Acute Respiratory infections and diarrhoea were two major diseases among communicable diseases. However, with economic transitions in the society, one can also see a rising trend of lifestyle diseases in the society like cardiovascular diseases, cancer, diabetes, mental ailments as well as the road traffic accidents etc.

Hence, even though for the present we need to handle a larger load of communicable/infective diseases compared

TABLE 10.11

Incidence of Cholera Cases and Deaths

1996		1997		1998		1999		2000		2001		2002		2003		2004		2005	
C	D	C	D	C	D	C	D	C	D	C	D	C	D	C	D	C	D	C	D
900	0	956	0	1903	8	1396	0	959	0	1267	0	833	0	1527	1	1784	0	945	0

Note: C- Cases, D- Death

Source: Various reports of DGHS GNCTD.

TABLE 10.12

Incidence of Gastro-Enteritis Cases and Deaths

1998		1999		2000		2001		2002		2003		2004		2005	
C	D	C	D	C	D	C	D	C	D	C	D	C	D	C	D
66313	15	68250	21	69287	0	69139	0	70656	0	71844	0	77355	0	67101	0

Source: Various reports of DGHS GNCTD.

to the lifestyle or age related diseases, but this trend is rapidly changing and is expected to get reversed soon—within the next few years.

10.11 Some Programmes related with Health Problems in Delhi

10.11.1 National Tuberculosis Control Programme

Tuberculosis is still a major public health problem in Delhi. As per NFHS2, the prevalence of Tuberculosis in Delhi is 511 per 100,000 population. This is slightly less than national estimate of 544.

A special drive on control of tuberculosis under Revised National T.B. Control programme (RNTCP) has been launched in Delhi in 1993. Delhi Tapedic Unmulan Samiti has been formed under which there are fourteen district level T.B. control societies. The drugs are given free to the patient, as per DOTS (Directly Observed Treatment Supervised) strategy through the DOTS Centre near to their homes. At present there are 20 chest clinics functioning under this programme. Under the chest clinics, 325 DOTS Centres and 120 microscopy centres are functioning. Apart from this, 57 NGOs and 23 Private Practitioners are also participating in RNTCP.

10.12 Water Borne Diseases

10.12.1 Cholera and Gastro-enteritis

Information regarding Cholera and Gastro-enteritis is being collected (including 22 index hospital), and compiled, and the report is being submitted to all concerned. Health Department of MCD is collecting information from Allopathic Dispensaries through Zonal Deputy Health Officers. Medical Superintendents of major hospitals have nominated one medical officer, who is to investigate the death cases due to Gastro-enteritis/Cholera in their hospitals.

From the available data it appears that Cholera is still an endemic disease in Delhi. Though the numbers of Cholera cases declined in 2005 the Gastro-enteritis cases have continued to show increasing trend. The major reason for these cases is contaminated water.

10.13 Polio

Delhi was the first state to start pulse polio immunisation in 1994 for polio eradication. The number of polio cases has been significantly reduced ever since then. After initial good results, programme received a kind of setback in 2002 when polio cases increased to 24 from 3 in the previous two years. However, the number again came down to 3 in 2003.

TABLE 10.13

Number of Polio Cases

Year	India	Delhi
1994	34950	476
1998	1934	47
1999	1126	73
2000	265	3
2001	268	3
2002	1600	24
2003	225	3
2004	134	2
2005	66	

Source: Various reports of MNOHFW GOI.

10.14 Vector Borne Diseases in NCT of Delhi

Malaria and Dengue are two important vector borne diseases in NCT of Delhi. The NCT-Delhi is situated in a zone, which is prone to periodic fulminate epidemics of malaria. From 1940s till early 1960s Delhi was virtually free from Malaria. The situation began to turn worse again from 1971 onwards. In 1978, a record number of 3,75,077 malaria cases were recorded in Delhi.

TABLE 10.14

Incidence and Deaths due to Malaria and Dengue Cases in Delhi

Year	Malaria				Dengue	
	P. vivax	P. falciparum	Total Cases	Deaths	Total Cases	Deaths
1996	9970	682	10652	Nil	10252	423
1997	8072	122	8194	Nil	273	1
1998	4197	25	4222	Nil	333	5
1999	3800	196	3996	Nil	168	2
2000	2382	249	2631	Nil	180	2
2001	1470	14	1484	Nil	322	3
2002	688	6	694	Nil	42	0
2003	812	27	839	Nil	2882	35
2004	393	2	395	Nil	606	03
2005	588	5	593	Nil	1022	09
2006*	1072	61	1133	Nil	3366	65

Note: * Provisional

Source: Various reports of NVBDCP MOHFW GOI.

In 1996, a focal outbreak attributable to excessive rains and population movement was encountered in few areas of Delhi. Two species, *Anopheles culicifacies* and *Anopheles stephensi* transmit malaria in Delhi. The former breeds in burrows, pits, pools, along river margins, canal seepage's and quarry pits, while the latter breeds in stored water in overhead tanks, cisterns and unused wells *etc*.

Apparently, it seems that the overall situation against malaria is improving, as there is a continuous decline in cases. However, Delhi still has many sites that are suitable for breeding of mosquitoes especially in slums, around open drains and around construction sites etc. The geography and weather conditions of Delhi are highly congenial for rapid growth of mosquitoes and hence, any laxity in this direction makes the city vulnerable for epidemics in future.

10.15 Dengue

Delhi has been endemic for Dengue for past several years. The first Dengue Haemorrhagic Fever (DHF) outbreak was reported in 1988 with 33 per cent mortality among children admitted in hospitals. Another Outbreak of Dengue hemorrhagic fever swept National Capital Territory, Delhi in 1996. More than 10,000 cases and 423 deaths due to DHF were recorded in various parts of Delhi.

Again, in 2003, 2882 cases and 35 deaths from DHF were reported in Delhi. The maximum cases (37 per cent) were reported from Central, Shahadra South and Shahadra North zone. Najafgarh, Delhi Cant and Railway Hospital reported 14 per cent dengue cases. Rohini zone reported 8 per cent of dengue cases. The *Aedes aegypti* mosquito population, the vector responsible for Dengue, was found to be prevalent in all the localities in Delhi.

Effective steps, including punitive measures against defaulters, are being taken under the Vector Control Strategy Programme of the Government for control of Malaria and Dengue menace in the State.

10.16 Maternal and Child Health Programmes

Promotion of maternal and child health has been one of the most important components of the Reproductive and Child Health Programme (RCH) of the Government of India. The goal for each pregnant woman is to receive at least three antenatal check-ups, two tetanus toxoid injections and a full course of iron and folic acid supplementation. In Delhi as per NFHS-3 74.4 per cent of mothers had at least 3 anti-natal care visit for their last child birth. This is an improvement over the figures of NFHS-2, which were only 68.9 per cent. NFHS-3 shows that 60.7 per cent births in Delhi were institutional deliveries and 50 per cent women received post-natal care from doctor/nurse/LHV/ANM/other health personnel within 2>days of delivery for their last child birth.

Overall, these results show that health services in Delhi are reaching many more women during pregnancy than during delivery or after childbirth. They also point to the important role of traditional birth attendants for the substantial proportion of births that occur at home. To improve the maternal health, Delhi Government has launched special programme called Stree Shakti Programme and also conduct campaign under *Matri Suraksha Abhiyan*. The goal of these programmes is to reduce MMR through provision of comprehensive health care to all mothers during antenatal, natal and postnatal period.

As far as immunisation of children is concerned, as per NFHS-33, 63.2 per cent children received complete immunisation (3 doses each of Polio, DPT, BCG, Measles). This is slightly less than the figures of NFHS-2, which was 69.8 per cent.

10.17 HIV/AIDS

Delhi falls under low Prevalence State for HIV/AIDS. However, 42,000 HIV positive cases are estimated till January 2006, a total of 2759 cases were reported till August 2006 while 322 deaths were reported till January 2006. The sentinel data from antenatal clinic shows that the HIV infection is still within 1 per cent in Delhi. It is feared that the HIV infection would percolate down from various high-risk groups to general population in the State, if effective awareness and control programmes were not initiated.

Data from various STD Sentinel Sites shows that over the year, the HIV infection has been progressing rapidly among STD clinic attendees and is steadily spreading in low risk population. The time lag for HIV infection to spread from High Risk groups to low risk groups is between 3 to 5 years, as the infection will spread from High Risk groups to their clients, which act as bridge population and then to wives of these clients during this period. Among Intravenous Drug Users, the HIV infection has shown increasing trend. It can be concluded from above trends that there is an urgent need to start more Targeted Intervention Project among High Risk groups in Delhi.

Targeted Intervention is one of the core strategies for the prevention of HIV in India under NACP-II. Targeted Interventions in HIV/AIDS context are a set of activities and approaches aimed at reducing the risk of HIV infection amount people practising high-risk behaviour. There are various sub-population groups such as commercial sex workers, truckers, street children migrant labourers, intravenous drug users etc., who are highly vulnerable to the transmission of HIV by virtue of their high risk behaviour and socio-economic conditions. As of now 29 such programmes are being implemented. In addition, School AIDS programme is also being implemented in 450 schools.

In Delhi, 3 lakh delivery occurs per year. Considering 0.3 per cent HIV prevalence in ANC women and 30 per cent transmission rate about 240 children are born every year with HIV. Considering 0.3 per cent HIV prevalence in ANC women and 30 per cent transmission rate about 240 children are born every year with HIV. Government of Delhi has launched a special drive for prevention of HIV transmission from an infected mother to the foetus.

- Fourteen Centres have been set up under the Prevention of Parent to Child Transmission Programme along with antenatal check-up clinics in various hospitals. Four more will shortly be opened. Another ten will be started at Maternal & Child Welfare Centre (MCW centre) of MCD. This way the programme can penetrate at the grass root level.
- 28 Voluntary Counseling & Testing Centre (VCTC) have been established out of which 3 (VCTC) is established in 3 Universities of Delhi (DU, Jamia Millia Islamia, & JNU). In addition, health care dispenser are also set up in the Universities. But to reach more number of population DSACS proposes to open Integrated Counseling & Testing Centres at non-conventional sites like ISBT, railway platforms.
- Mobile Integrated Testing & Wellness Access (MITWA) is providing outreach services to slums & JJ Cluster through 13 Mobile van and the package include syndromic treatment of STD, free condom distribution and counseling and test for HIV.
- There are 52 Licensed Blood Bank out of which 8 are Regional Blood Transfusion Centre.
- 3 Community Care Centre
- 6 ART Centre.
- Tele-Counseling services.
- Workplace intervention is a new initiative of DSACS in Collaboration with ILO.

10.18 Non-Communicable Diseases (NCDs)

Worldwide, the most serious non-communicable diseases are cardiovascular diseases (CVD), cerebrovascular diseases (including stroke and hypertension), cancer, diabetes, and respiratory diseases. Mental disorders, diseases of the bones and joints such as osteoporosis and osteoarthritis and dental diseases are also emerging as major non-communicable diseases.

As life expectancy increases and fertility rates decline, the overall burden of NCDs is expected to increase in our country, too. Given the present trends, an explosion of non-communicable diseases in developing countries is projected between now and the year 2015. By then, for example, the ratio of deaths from NCDs to deaths from infectious and parasitic diseases would be 4:1 in Asia. According to these projections, three times more people will die from NCDs than from infectious and parasitic diseases in the developing countries, and in absolute terms, twice as many deaths due to NCDs will occur in developing countries than in the industrialised world.

In public-health terminology, India is going through an epidemiological transition. Changes in the demographic profile and other determinants are shifting the burden of disease, disability, and death away from infectious and nutritional disorders to chronic and non-communicable diseases. The former disorders, which contributed 56 per cent of the disability adjusted life year (DALY) loss in 1990, are projected to decline to 25 per cent by 2020. The non-communicable diseases, on the other hand, are expected to rise from 29 per cent to 57 per cent during the same period. Such projections are based on demographic trends, when the proportion of the population aged more than 35 years is expected to reach from 28 per cent in 1981 to 42 per cent by 2021. Urbanisation too is expected to accelerate during this period—the urban component of the population is expected to rise from 23 per cent to 42 per cent.

National level data shows that incidence of heart diseases in India has doubled in the past 30 years, especially in the urban population. Incidence of cancers, diabetes and fatal traffic accidents etc., are also seen more in the urban population. Delhi with 93 per cent urban population is more vulnerable to such diseases.

10.19 Accidents and Trauma

Accidents are becoming a major cause of mortality and morbidity. The phenomenal increase in the number of motor vehicles in the city coupled with limited road space, inadequate facilities for pedestrians and cyclists, irresponsible driving and violation of traffic rules has resulted in a significant number of road accidents. Though the number of accidents has shown a decreasing trend in the last three years due to continuing efforts of all concerned agencies, there is a need and room for vast improvement in traffic regulations and management.

TABLE 10.15

Deaths in Road Accidents in Delhi

	2003	*2004*	*2005 (till 31st October 2005)*
Fatal Accidents	1771	1782	1455
Person Killed	1841	1832	1536

Source: Delhi Traffic Police Web Site.

Details of accidents reveal that pedestrians, cyclists and two wheeler riders are the major victims. The fatality mostly occurred among pedestrians followed by two wheeler riders. One of the most vulnerable groups is school children. Moreover, in the absence of adequate manpower/infrastructure facilities and procedural delays, handling of accident victims is not prompt or efficient leading to unacceptably higher incidence of morbidity and mortality compared with the international standards. The Government has launched the services of well-equipped ambulances under Centralised Accident and Trauma Service (CATS) for prompt and proper transport of the accident victims. However, further steps need to be taken in this direction including enforcing strict traffic discipline upon drivers to reduce the incidence and setting up of dedicated Trauma Centres along the main highways approaching Delhi for proper management of the trauma victims.

10.20 Other Health Determinants

Health is determined by many other factors that are personal, economic and social in nature. Quantity and qualities of nutrition, water supply, electrification, sanitation, literacy standards, health awareness, environmental pollution, social norms/practices etc., are some of the other factors that influence health of an individual directly or indirectly and thus influence the average longevity of any community/state or the country.

10.21 Water Supply and Sanitation

Water is one of the most precious and vital resources for health in daily life. Contaminated water or water from uncontrolled sources is one of the major causes for a large number of water borne diseases in the state like typhoid, jaundice, cholera, gastro-enteritis, polio etc., assuming epidemics proportions at times taking a heavy toll on the morbidity and mortality of otherwise young and healthy individuals leading to totally avoidable but grave financial loss, productivity loss and social loss with undue strain on the existing public health system which is already reeling under large loads of patients.

Delhi had 2.55 million households (13.8 million populations) in 2001. On an average, 75.72 per cent of the households in Delhi had piped water supply, 20.06 per cent depended on hand pumps/tubewells and the remaining 4.22 per cent used wells, rivers and canals for drinking water *(Delhi Statistical Handbook, 2002)*.

However, despite 75 per cent of the houses having been connected to piped water supply system, the quantity and quality of the water supply is far from satisfactory. The rapid growth in the State's population has resulted in a decline in the annual per capita availability of freshwater, from 153 MGD per year in 1990-91 to 105 MGD per year in 2001-02. Chronic shortages of freshwater of adequate quality are already being experienced. Water quality has been degrading due to a combination of factors such as draining of sewage and industrial and urban effluents into water sources and saline intrusion.

Although the treatment capacities have increased from 42 MGD (million gallons per day) in 1951 to 337 MGD in 1991 and to 600 MGD in 2000 despite this, the average current shortfall is about 276 MGD. However, the percentage of unaccounted water due to losses during pumping and distribution is as high as 35-40 per cent (GHK International Ltd., 2000). This situation needs to be rectified through better maintenance systems, which can enhance the per capita availability.

Deteriorating surface (Yamuna River) and ground water quality is one of the most serious environmental problems for NCT of Delhi. High population densities, rapid urbanisation, increasing commercialisation/ industrialisation and a general lack of pollution control facilities are exerting growing pressure on the water resources. If allowed to persist, this increased pollution will further reduce the amount of water available for human use in future. Continuous supply of adequate quantities of potable water, thus, must be a primary basic aim of the social infrastructure system to minimise undue morbidity/mortality and to improve health of the people.

10.22 Environmental Pollution

Air, water, soil or noise pollutions, whether at home, outside or at work place, have serious effects on the overall health status of an individual, directly or indirectly. Several acute and chronic diseases have been linked with pollutions in various constituents of our environment. The World Health Report 2002 attributes environmental risks especially the urban air pollution, lead exposure and climate changes as some of the causes for the poor Disability Adjusted Life Years (DALY).

The Government of NCT of Delhi is already seized of the problem and has specially constituted Delhi Pollution Control Board to initiate measures for control of the same. Several initiatives have already been taken up by the Government to reduce the environmental pollution in the State with very favourable results. Conversion of public transport system to CNG based system, introduction of Metro Rail, Yamuna Action Plan, relocation of hazardous industries are some of the steps that have been initiated in this direction. High levels of fluorides in water have been a major cause for health morbidity in some parts of Delhi. The Government of Delhi has already launched Fluorosis Mitigation Programme to control this menace.

10.23 Private Sector in Health Care

Although health is a state subject and is an important constitutional responsibility upon the governments to provide the necessary infrastructure facilities for the same to its subjects, but this indeed becomes a mammoth task for a country like India. Unfortunately, despite the constitutional responsibility, health has never been given due priority by various governments ever since Independence. In a recent HDR (2004), it has been observed that the public spending on health in our country is only 0.9 per cent of the GDP, ranking 171 out of the 175 countries studied, while the private spending has been upto 4.2 per cent of the GDP.

Delhi has a fairly well established representation of the private entrepreneurs in health sector. Their range of practice varies from individual practice and small nursing homes to large charitable and corporate hospitals. As on date, there are nearly 562 registered private nursing homes/hospitals with bed strength of over 12,000. The private sector is providing range of services from simple, out patient treatments to sophisticated super-specialised surgeries like organ transplantation etc. Within the private sector, there is another group of non-profit group who extend medical services in the State. Delhi has a

TABLE 10.16

Distribution of Households by Source of Drinking Water, 2001

	Total	*Source of Drinking Water (Per cent)*							
Rural/ Urban	*Number (in Thousands)*	*Tap*	*Hand-pump*	*Tube-well*	*Well*	*Tank, Pond, Lake*	*River, Canal*	*Spring*	*Any other*
Rural	169,528	**51.56**	33.52	5.00	0.36	1.89	0.03	0.04	7.60
Urban	2,384,621	**77.02**	17.62	3.11	0.02	0.60	0.00	0.02	1.61

Source: Census Report 2001.

strong presence of non-profit institutions run by various charitable organisations and NGOs for providing free/ subsidised health services to the poor. At present, approximately 70 per cent patients are being looked after in the private sector in Delhi. Some of the problems identified with this sector are unregulated growth, lack of effective standards for quality of care leading to overuse of procedures and diagnostic services, on many occasions. This calls for a better professional management of the Government run hospitals too as this is expected that well-managed Government infrastructure shall automatically bring in the attitude of ethical and competitive practice by the private hospitals and nursing homes.

Another very serious menace identified in this sector is the large numbers of unregistered and unqualified practitioners i.e., medical quacks who generally operate in slums and in other underdeveloped colonies and prey upon poor people in the society with disastrous results at times.

10.24 Drug Policy

The Delhi State Drug Policy was initiated in 1994 with the efforts of Delhi Society for Promotion of Rational drug Use and the Delhi State Government. The State Drug Policy is based on the well-accepted principles of Rational Drug Policy and clearly articulated by WHO. The State Drug Policy is applicable for the government institutions in Delhi under the Delhi State Government.

In the process, Graded Essential Drug List was brought out for different levels of health expertise and health institutions e.g. some drugs were for primary level, some for secondary and some for tertiary level. Delhi State Drug Formulary and standard treatment guidelines with information on drugs, their dosages, side effects, special precautions, adverse drug reactions, standard treatment guidelines giving indications for usage of the drugs was released to encourage rational use of drugs.

10.24.1 Results of the Rational Use of Drugs programme

- Better availability of drugs in the hospital.
- Drug prices controlled over the years—drugs could be purchased at 35 per cent cheaper rates with pooled procurement.
- 90 per cent of prescribed drugs used were from list of essential medicines.
- Drug prescription quality improved.
- Over prescription curtailed.

WHO has hailed the Delhi State Drug Policy as an exemplary model drug policy.

10.25 Delhi Prohibition of Smoking and Non-Smoker Health Protection Act, 1996

Delhi Government implemented Anti-Smoking Act with effect from 26.1.97. No smoking day is observed on 31 May, every year. Under this programme various I.E.C. activities are being carried out to educate the general people about the various ill effects of smoking. The Directorate of Health Services deployed special Enforcement squads in 8 districts in Delhi to impose penalty for violating the said Act by smoking in public places and public service vehicles. By March 2003, raids were conducted at 14,694 public places, 73,738 public vehicles and a fine of Rs. 19,199 was imposed.

10.26 Resource Allocation for Health

The State has constantly allocated more than 7 per cent of the Plan outlay to the Health sector and has utilised more than 80 per cent of the outlay. Outlays for nutrition have been increased in the Tenth Plan. The Government has included both ICDS/PMGY and mid-day meals under the nutrition sector.

TABLE 10.17

Outlay under Health Sector (Delhi)

Plan	*Period*	*Total Plan Expenditure (Rs. in Crores)*	*Expenditure on Health Sector (Rs. in Crores)*	*% of Total Plan Expenditure*
Sixth Five – Year Plan	1980-85	1042.07	77.14	7.40
Seventh Five– Year Plan	1985-90	2631.47	207.20	7.87
Eighth Five – Year Plan	1990-95	6208.32	407.36	6.56
9th Five – Year Plan	1997-2002	15541.28 (Outlay)	1101.40 (Outlay)	7.09
10th Five Year Plan	2002-07	23,000.00 (Outlay)	2381.50	10.35
Annual Plan	2002-03	4405.89	330.43	7.50
Annual Plan	2003-04	4609.21	389.42	8.45
Annual Plan	2004-05	4260.53	469.89	11.03
Annual Plan	2005-06	4280.87	543.33	12.69

Source: Economic Survey of Delhi, 2005-06.

TABLE 10.18

Per Capita Expenditure on Health (Delhi)

Year	*Per capita Expenditure (in Rupees)- Delhi*	*All India*
2003-04	492.20	159.46
2004-05	568.87	163.79
2005-06	616.87	189.39

Source: Economic Survey of Delhi, 2005-06.

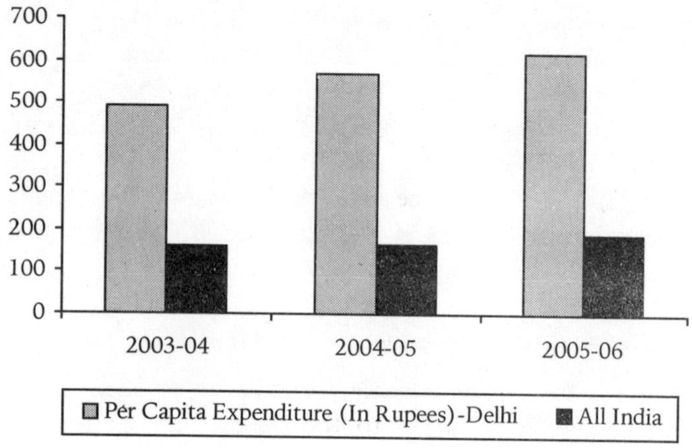

During the 8th Five year plan the total plan expenditure on Health (Medical Sector, Public Health and Nutrition) was Rs.459.4 crore (7.41 per cent) out of the total plan expenditure of Rs.6208.32 crores, while in the 10th Plan the outlay for the health sector has been planned at Rs.2318.5 crore (10.35 per cent) out of total plan outlay of Rs.23,000 crore.

10.27 Access and Utilisation of Health Services

National Council of Applied Economic Research has carried out a study on "The Burden of Ill Health among the Urban Poor" in the slums and resettlement colonies in Delhi and Chennai. As per their findings in general:

Slums and resettlement colonies in Delhi have good access to health facilities with almost all of them having some public or private facility within a distance of 2 km. However, only 38 per cent of sample slums in Delhi, reported presence of a public hospital within 2 km.

The slums appear to be better served by non-governmental organisations providing health services and by mobile health care services.

Greater proportions of sick males obtain treatment relative to sick females—92 per cent to 87 per cent.

Sick individuals belonging to the richest 20 per cent of the population are more likely to obtain treatment compared to the poorer ones.

The main self-reported reasons for not obtaining treatment were that the illness was "not considered serious", financial constraints, and a lack of time/long waits to obtain treatment. The last two reasons were especially common in cases of non-treatment among females and the elderly (60-plus years) population.

However, when treatment is sought, there is a substantial reliance on public services, accounting for about half the cases of outpatient treatment.

Private care is, however, also quite significant, and inclusive of charitable services, amounting to about 45 per cent of the total cases of outpatient care. Self-treatment by purchase of medicines at chemist shops is small, but still quite important, at about 5 per cent of all cases.

The main gender related finding is that in Delhi, a much greater proportion of treatments for males were at government facilities, compared to females.

Another key finding is that in comparison to outpatient care, slum and resettlement colony residents make much greater use of public facilities for inpatient care. Eighty per cent of the reported hospitalisations by the sample population in Delhi took place in public facilities.

The survey data confirms the standard view that public services serve as a major source of subsidised care to poor people. On the other hand, private services are used either because they are considered of high quality, or because of their proximity to the household's residence.

10.28 Health Care Expenditures

In Delhi, the average out-of-pocket spending for a non-hospitalised illness was Rs 124 pa. Analysis of the pattern of spending on out-of-pocket illness reveals several noteworthy features. First, out-of-pocket spending by those using public care was much lower than using private outpatient care. Faith healers, used by many in slums were particularly expensive and at times a cause for anti-social activities, too. Second, most of the spending on outpatient care took the form of expenses on fees and medicines, clinical tests, and transportation. Fees and medicines accounted for 62 per cent of all spending in Delhi. Third, average out-of-pocket spending increased with per capita income, with the average per episode expenditure being Rs 72 for the lowest per capita income and Rs 165 for the highest quintile.

In contrast to outpatient care, inpatient care was significantly more burdensome on the pocket, being nearly Rs 1,230 per case of hospitalisation. Inpatient care at private hospitals was more expensive than inpatient care at charitable hospitals, which, in turn, was more expensive than inpatient care at public hospitals. Thus public health facilities appear to provide some sort of insurance against the expensive inpatient care needs of the slum and resettlement colony populations.

Similarly, data available from NFHS-2 shows that most households in Delhi (53 per cent) go to a private doctor for treatment when a family member is ill. Overall, 29 per cent use the public medical sector, and 70 per cent use the private medical sector (including private doctors, private hospitals and clinics and other facilities). Even among households with a low standard of living, only 33 per cent normally use the public medical sector when members become ill. Most respondents are generally satisfied with the health care they receive. Ratings on quality of services are lower for public-sector facilities than for private-sector facilities. In the case of public-sector facilities, about half of the respondents are somewhat critical of staff attitudes and cleanliness of the facilities.

10.29 Vulnerable Areas of Delhi

The research team of VHAI working under the guidance of Prof. Ashish Bose has constructed a new Index to measure the extent of vulnerability in regard to Health Indicators, called Vulnerable Health Index (VHI). The following five sensitive indicators of health are chosen, to construct this index:

I. Per cent of pregnant women who did not receive full antenatal care (ANC),

II. Per cent of women who did not have the facility for safe delivery,

III. Per cent of children (0-6 age group) who did not receive full immunisation (all the three rounds of vaccination),

IV. Per cent of couples in the reproductive age group not using any family-planning method, and

V. Female illiteracy percentage (population 7 years and above).

The team has not used the usual statistical indicators like birth rate, death rate, infant mortality rate etc., as the focus is on the delivery of primary health care through the government health system. If women are not getting antenatal care or children are not being immunised against killer diseases or the couples are not practising family planning in spite of five decades of efforts, it is certainly a reflection on the malfunctioning of the huge infrastructure set up by the government. The centrality of health in development efforts along with restructuring of budgetary allocations for the health sector is the need of this hour. Research team has also taken female illiteracy rate as a sensitive indicator because the health of women and children is greatly influenced by the lack of literacy and education among women. Human resource development is not possible without more emphasis and funds being devoted to curbing ill health and illiteracy.

To measure the extent of deprivation, team has put values (V-1, V-2, V-3, and V-4) for each indicator in each district and state in the country. Research team has also worked out a composite Vulnerability Index based on the following:

V-1: > 75 per cent persons (women, children or couples as the case may be) in this category

V-2 = 50 - 75 per cent persons in this category

V-3 = 25 - 50 per cent persons in this category

V-4 = less that 25 per cent persons in this category

These values have been worked out for each of the 5 indicators. The composite index is the total score of these values. V-1 represents the highest vulnerability followed by V-2, V-3 and V-4 - the last representing the lowest vulnerability.

TABLE 10.19

Delhi: Health Indicators

S. No.	Districts	% of Women Without Full ANC	% of Women Without Safe Delivery	Percentage of Children Without Full Immuni-sation	% of Couples not Using any Family Planning Method
		2001	2001	2001	2001
01	South	74.0	35.5	60.0	37.8
02	New Delhi	69.2	28.8	58.2	40.0
03	North West	65.6	29.5	38.8	37.9
04	West	62.9	32.9	28.8	34.0
05	North East	57.6	22.1	31.7	35.2
06	South West*	27.9	16.4	15.3	29.2
07	East*	27.9	16.4	15.3	29.2
08	North	27.9	16.4	15.3	29.2
09	Central*	27.9	16.4	15.3	29.2

Note: * RCH 1998-99

Source: Calculated by contributors from District level Household survey & RCH Survey for Delhi 2001.

TABLE 10.20

Delhi: Weaker Sections

S. No	Districts	% SC	% ST	% of Illiterate Females
		2001	2001	2001
01	Central	23.33	0	24.1
02	East	16.33	0	20.6
03	New Delhi	22.22	0	25.4
04	North	17.23	0	25.8
05	North East	16.69	0	30.0
06	North West	19.34	0	26.7
07	South	15.63	0	25.3
08	South West	14.75	0	24.0
09	West	14.92	0	22.1

Source: Census 2001.

TABLE 10.21

Per cent of Female Illiteracy and Girls Married Below 18 Years of Age

India/Uts		% of Girls Marrying Below Age 18
All India	45.8	36.9
Delhi	25.0	6.4

Source: Census 2001.

On the basis of this index it has been found that none of the districts of Delhi fall into V-1 and V-2 category, however there are still 5 districts that fall under V-3 category:

V-3 Districts:New Delhi, North East, North West, South, West

V-4 Districts: East, Central, North, South West

10.30 Vulnerable Populations of Delhi

10.30.1 The Homeless

Delhi has the largest migrant population of all cities in India. Many of these migrants join the ranks of "Urban Poor" with the homeless people occupying the lowest stratum in the society. They sleep on the pavements, *rickshaws*, handcarts, *rehris* etc., and live a life under extreme constraints with constant fear, hatred, contempt and prejudice.

As per a head count survey (collaboratively conducted by Aashray Adhikar Abhiyan - AAA and Institute of Human Behaviour & Allied Sciences, Shahdara) in the year 2000, there were 52,765 homeless on the streets of Delhi. The government has built Night Shelters (or *Ren Baseras)* for the homeless. Due to conditions of abject poverty, these people have several complex problems, especially related to health.

High proportions of homeless people suffer from preventable diseases, which are caused by poor sanitation and hygiene, poor living conditions, lifestyle and environmental pollution.

Special programmes are required to identify these people and attend to their health needs accordingly. Help of NGOs like Sulabh International and others in the field may be taken in providing essential basic facilities and in adequate rehabilitation of these people. Some of these homeless people could even be helped to return back to their homes, wherever feasible.

10.30.2 People Living in Delhi Slums

Approximately 15 per cent people of Delhi's population live in slums under conditions of overcrowding, poor environmental sanitation, very little or totally non-existent infrastructure facilities like sewage lines, potable water, drainage systems with an alarming degree of crime and other maladies arising out of a poor socio-economic situation. Identified slum population in Delhi as per 2001 census is 20,25,890 comprising of 11,03,863 males and 8,87,827 females.

Some revealing morbidity figures reported in studies conducted in the slums showed that major prevalent diseases are ARIs, TB, Malaria and Filaria. There is a high morbidity rate of 11-15 per cent for children with numbers of annual episodes of diarrhoea range from 6-12. Diarrhoea is responsible for about 60 per cent deaths in children followed by ARI (27 per cent). Children are especially trapped in the vicious cycle of malnutrition and poor immunity. Slums have the highest proportion of people with low body weight and severe malnutrition. IMR in slums was 213 per 1000 in 2002. Child Mortality Rate was 27 per 1000 in the same year, which is 40 per cent higher than the national average.

10.30.3 Government Programmes for Slums

Government of Delhi and the Union Government have, from time to time, introduced and implemented various programmes for slums, however, they do not cover all slums and nor are they implemented effectively. A large number of NGO groups have been working in these areas to alleviate the sufferings of people in slums, but many of times they are working without any coordination with each other leading to duplication of services in some areas and deficiency and/or wastage of efforts in the others. It is essential to clearly identify the problems of these people and take appropriate actions in a coordinated manner in collaboration with various NGO groups working in these areas to improve the status of slum dwellers as outlined below:

- Coordination among various players.
- To organise themselves as a single front to address the health needs in slums in holistic manner.
- To evolve suitable plans for their own coordinated activities.
- To avoid overlapping and conserve resources.
- To connect people together to help themselves.

Mapping the areas and developing database

Children as change agents

- Potential of children as change agents should be fully tapped. Various suitable media forms should be used as per the response or effectiveness like skits, puppetry, and magic shows etc.
- Setting up and strengthening *Bal Panchayats* in slums by partners can be very effective in local campaigns on health issues. They can be used for low cost state level campaigns.
- Children are also very effective in conducting surveys. They should be fully involved in the same.

Organising State level consultations for betterment of living conditions in slums to look into:

- Health needs in slums.
- Identifying vulnerable and their special needs.
- Documenting people's aspirations.
- Making suggestions for addressing these needs and aspirations at Government, NGOs and Corporate levels.
- Identifying advocacy issues.

10.30.4 Minimising Risk Factors

- The government must set up a mechanism for early warning for impending hazards like floods.
- Legal electricity connections must be granted. This will not only reduce fire hazards but also increase revenue of the government by discouraging theft through illegal tapping.
- Provision of safe drinking water and sanitation facilities must be a priority.
- Recreation facilities should be provided for children, and coverage of *'Anganwadi'* should be complete.
- Awareness of legal rights needs to be generated and CBOs need to make efforts for establishing good working relations with the government departments (and officials). This should also cover legal housing rights.
- CBOs like Federation of Slum Dwellers and Mahila Mandal Societies must be strengthened. They may also be very effectively used for lobbying for their land titles and other rights as well as serve as watchdogs for effective implementation of various government programmes.
- Shifting of slum dwellers to new areas must not be abrupt but in a phased manner.
- Efforts towards communal harmony in slums must be encouraged. Inter-religion and inter cultural dialogue must be encouraged.

10.30.5 Sustainability

- For long-term sustainability of health programmes in slums, services should not be given free. For this reason, a training of personnel involved in social marketing and social entrepreneurship is must.
- Services based on regular house visits are very effective and need to be incorporated in the programmes.

10.31 The Way Forward

From the information given in previous sections it is clear that there is wide variation in the health status of different population segments. On an average, Delhi seems to enjoy better healthcare system as compared to other parts of the country. But still there are areas of marked imbalances. Delhi is still vulnerable to epidemics like dengue, cholera, gastro-enteritis, and hepatitis etc. There is also increasing threat from age-related and lifestyle diseases like cardiovascular disorders, diabetes, cancer, HIV/AIDS etc.

10.31.1 Health Promotion

Health promotion is an organised way of going about improving the health of a population. It is based on the assumption that, through improving the health of the population, the health of individuals within that population will benefit. Looking at Delhi health scenario it is clear that there is need for massive efforts for promoting health.

10.31.2 Health Promotion in Hospitals

A combination of services and health education is the most effective way in bringing about positive, health-related behavioural changes. Hospitals and clinics, along with medical personnel and students, play a major role in health education. Health education in a hospital/clinic can be tied up with the curative care provided by medical and nursing personnel who should be concerned about total well being of the patient. There needs to be a total change in the work culture of the hospitals, especially the public hospitals. Even an informal conversation between the patient and clinical staff can promote positive health practices. For the patient, health education should start from the time he/she enters, to the time of departure. On the patient's discharge slip, a column for health education acts as useful reminder of the necessary health precautions to be observed by the discharged patient and the drug regimen to be followed.

10.31.3 Health Promotion in Schools

Schools and colleges provide excellent platforms for educating the children towards the healthy and hygienic habits and towards proper lifestyle for them to enjoy healthy life in future. Children can also be an important force for educating their parents especially if the parents are illiterate. It would, therefore, be extremely economical and beneficial in long run to include proper health education in school/college curricula.

10.31.4 Health Education and Awareness

Aggressive health education programmes should be integrated with health and medical care programmes with emphasis on:

- Environmental health
- Personal hygiene
- Nutrition education
- Healthy habits

Although the responsibility for comprehensive health care lies with government agencies, a close partnership between voluntary organisations, private practitioners and local government infrastructure networks, is absolutely essential for successful percolation of the health programmes into the society. The Bhagidari Scheme introduced by Government of Delhi is one such example of collaborative approach.

10.31.5 Health Care Delivery System:

The state of Delhi has presently multiplicity of health implementing agencies like MCD, NDMC, ESI, Delhi Cantonment Board etc., with little coordination and sharing of resources. Because of lack of desired coordination, there is a tendency in not shouldering the responsibility in the wake of epidemic outbreak and other disaster requiring immediate concerted efforts. Further there may be duplication of services, which leads to wastage of resources. There is an immediate need for a single unit of command for coordinating these multiple health agencies and all these agencies should be reporting to this common single health authority dealing with:

a) Policy decisions on health issues

b) Creation/relocation of health facilities

c) Implementation of various health programmes/ campaigns, public health acts like Nursing Home Act, MTP Act, Prenatal Diagnostic Test Act, Antiquackery Act, Delhi Prohibition of Smoking and Non-smokers Health Protection Act etc.

d) Imbalances into reporting of health information

e) Projection of health manpower requirements

10.31.6 Primary Health Care Approach

In spite of the better availability of health facilities in the urban areas as compared to that of the rural areas, and the relative proximity of hospitals and other medical facilities, the standard of health care falls far below reasonable minimum levels for slum residents. The actual implementation of primary health care in the urban areas poses special problems.

It is extremely essential to have intersectoral coordination between relevant departments, including those dealing with water and sanitation, education, nutrition, housing, public works, transport, industry, income generation control of pollution, crime and delinquency, and mental and physical health.

Health facilities in the district need to be developed in such a way so as make district a self-sustained unit having its own referral system at district level. Patients attending secondary and tertiary health facilities will need to be referred by the primary health care unit or private practitioners of any system of medicine duly registered with the state councils except in emergency situations.

The proposed facilities should meet the preventive, promotive, curative and referral requirements of the population living in the defined area. This concept of Urban Health Centre is based upon the recommendations of Committee headed by Sh. SV Krishnan set up by Government of India for improving the quality of health care services and outreach services in urban area.

10.31.7 Hospital Care

WHO had suggested a need for 5 hospital beds per 1000 population. The establishment and maintenance of this vast infrastructure involves a huge sum including manpower, equipment etc., that may not be possible. Therefore in draft master plan Delhi 2021 it is proposed to achieve 3.5 beds per 1000 population by 2021 with measures to reduce the stay of indoor patients through promotion of day care facilities and back referral system. Based upon this norm of 3.5 beds per thousand populations the bed requirement for the year 2021 for 26 million population of Delhi shall be around 91,000. Currently Delhi is having around 33,000 beds in various governmental and non-governmental hospitals. Thus it is needed to add around 58,000 beds over the next 17 years; i.e., almost 3400 beds every year. This translates into establishment of four new 500-bedded hospitals and seven new 200-bedded hospitals every year. Thus at current costs, the total investment would be around 640 crores per year for establishment of hospitals alone.

To decongest the increasing load on facilities in Delhi, one needs to encourage development of high-class health care infrastructure in NCR towns as well as in the neighbouring states of Delhi through incentives and/or soft loans to entrepreneurs ensuring comparable quality at competitive costs. Besides, professional management of Government hospitals is essential for better efficiency of services and duly qualified hospital administrators should be placed as heads of institutions and selection should be based on performance, efficiency, skill, dynamism, vision and ideas and not merely on length of service or seniority basis. Well-managed Government infrastructure shall also automatically bring in the attitude of ethical and competitive practice by the private hospitals and nursing homes.

Proper planning of newer set ups is necessary that are more efficient, practical, economical and friendly towards the needs of the patients, as per the modern trends. Similarly, networking of various hospitals shall help in better coordination of patient care with efficiency and economy. Integration of the local area family practitioners with the Government hospitals and dispensaries in the area for two-way referrals, closer coordination amongst healthcare infrastructures of various civic bodies shall ensure seamless cover without wastage or duplication.

10.31.8 Public Health

Though there has been considerable improvement in certain areas, such as control of malaria and other vector borne diseases, water borne diseases like diarrhoea, cholera, typhoid, hepatitis etc., but the problems keep on emerging from time to time with considerable morbidity though the mortality has been contained to a significant extent.

Adequate financial and manpower resources need to be allocated to decentralise the activities for containment of the diseases. The state needs to strengthen its disease surveillance network to effectively detect any impending outbreak and control it. Diseases surveillance network needs to be strengthened at all levels with better interagency coordination. Control of water borne and vector borne diseases is possible only through intersectoral collaborations, as most of the factors that lead to increased risk of these diseases and preventive measures, are not directly in the ambit of the health department. Proper and adequate potable water supply system, sewerage/sanitation system and electric supply infrastructure is essential to permanently minimise the incidence, morbidity and mortality of infective diseases like typhoid, cholera, gastro-enteritis, jaundice, malaria, polio, etc. in the community.

Stray animals like cattle and dogs etc. are a major nuisance on the streets and roads of Delhi. Many a times, they lead to serious traffic accidents and traffic obstructions on the roads unnecessarily increasing the trauma cases resulting in loss of man-hours due to the associated morbidity and mortality besides the treatment costs. A large number of dog bite cases on the streets of Delhi also lead to a wasteful expenditure on anti-rabies vaccine in large majority of cases in addition to the associated morbidity. It is estimated that an amount of Rs. 3-5 crores is spent annually by the State Government only on the purchase of anti-rabies vaccine by its hospital. Effective measures, to control the stray animals and dogs, need to be initiated to save the vaccine cost, morbidity/ mortality arising out of the accidents, bites and other diseases caused by these animals; besides averting the international humiliation arising out of the situation.

Lifestyle diseases (hypertension, diabetes, ischaemic heart disease, cancer, nutritional diseases etc.) are emerging as, major health issues in the developing countries too, due to changing epidemiological factors.

The State needs to allocate adequate resource and manpower to develop a system for addressing the emerging problems of hypertension, diabetes, ischaemic heart disease, cancer etc., in the urban population. All secondary level government hospitals should be equipped for prevention, early detection and comprehensive management for these lifestyle diseases.

10.31.9 Health Information System

Currently the health information system in the state is unorganised with poor coordination because of poor conceptualisation and multiplicity of agencies involved in health care delivery system of the state.

There is need to strengthen its existing Health Information System to make it efficient and responsible to state health needs and all health implementing agencies should contribute to a common database system reporting to a single agency to manage this comprehensive health data base. This system may incorporate Geographical Information System as well. The Health Information System in the state needs to be developed in such a way so as to aid referral process. The system should be providing access to the health information at various levels of patient care and hospital management according to the needs.

10.31.10 Private Sector in Health Care

Partnerships with the private sector can greatly enhance the efficacy of public health programmes of the Government. However, to check unregulated growth and ensure quality of services an accreditation council can be set-up. Council may include different stakeholders like representative of private hospitals owners, professional bodies, consumer organisations, NGOs etc.

10.31.11 Participatory Approach

Meeting the basic health needs of people requires a participative approach that involves not only various levels of government and service providers, but also the active involvement of the people. Improvement in basic health is determined not only by the availability and usage of medical services, but also, and possibly more, by the practice of preventive measures, good hygiene and lifestyle choices. Some of these measures involve delivery of medical services, such as immunisation, but most involve individual initiative and are intimately related to their daily routine. As such, increasing awareness of good health practice is a key ingredient. Awareness-building programmes would therefore form an integral part of any strategy for the enhancement of basic health. Family physicians can play significant role in this direction by delivering the necessary health information directly to the public in their catchment areas. It is, hence, essential to integrate the entire health system involving the public health infrastructure with the private institutions, family physicians, NGOs, Resident Welfare Associations (RWAs), media, corporate world, local leaders and religious heads etc to form a seamless cover of service, knowledge and awareness about the health and disease in the society.

10.31.12 Bhagidari Scheme of Government of Delhi

The Government of Delhi has outlined a philosophy for governance, which is responsive and participative. This has specifically emerged from the belief that Government must work in partnership with the people and the citizens also must feel that successful and meaningful governance cannot be achieved without their involvement and without their role. In view of this the concept of 'Bhagidari': the citizen—government partnership was evolved and the 'My Delhi—I care' drive initiated. This scheme is one of the effective ways of ensuring community participation. Through this scheme RWAs can be involved in awareness generation as well as in taking certain preventive steps like cleaning of water coolers, clearing of stagnant water, sanitation, garbage segregation etc. Active RWA members can even be made part of health centre/hospital welfare committee.

10.31.13 Involvement of NGOs

NGOs in Delhi are playing a major role in supplementing government services and raising general awareness. Their work can be classified into following categories:

- Health services, health education and health awareness.
- Health research and health advocacy.
- Allied services like blood banks, ambulance, hearse, Dharamshalas for outstation patients and their families etc.

Under the above broad categories, major contribution of NGOs working in the field of health is in the following areas:

- Catering to health needs of slum population. This is especially significant in view of the fact that many slums in Delhi are unauthorised and fall beyond the service area of the government.
- Providing low cost health services through charitable hospitals.

- Implementing RCH programme of the government as Mother NGOs, service NGOs and also taking up innovative programmes.
- A whole range of activities pertaining to prevention, management and control of HIV/AIDS, especially targeted interventions in collaboration with Delhi State AIDS Control Society.
- Disability: working both for physically and mentally challenged.
- Working for the health and well being of elderly population.
- Providing health services to refugee population in Delhi.
- Water and sanitation, as these have direct relation with high morbidity seen due to contamination of water and environmental pollution.
- Activities related to Children's health, education and rights.
- Women's health and empowerment, gender relations and equity in health.
- Health research and advocacy.
- Helping the government in operation of National Health and Population Policy.

Apart from these, there are NGOs providing services like ambulance, hearse van, Dharamshalas etc. Some NGOs also take up consumer related issues in health services. There is need for providing more support to NGOs and treat them as partners in improving the health of the community.

10.32 Suggestions for Improving Health Status of People in Delhi

1. Professional management of Government hospitals for better efficiency of services—qualified hospital administrators to be placed as heads of institutions. Well-managed Government infrastructure shall also automatically bring in the attitude of ethical values and competitiveness in the practices followed by the private hospitals and nursing homes as a result of improved and quality health care in government's hospitals.
2. Need for higher proportion of public spending on health. As per the latest Human Development Report (2004), public spending on health is merely 0.9 per cent of the GDP in India, which ranks at poor 171st position out of the 175 countries studied. Only 4 countries, namely Nigeria, Indonesia, Sudan, and Myanmar rank below India in the tally. This is in contrast to the figures of 8.1 per cent of GDP for Germany, 7.3 per cent for France, 6.2 per cent for USA, 3.2 per cent for Brazil, and 2.0 per cent for China for public spending on health. On the other hand, private spending on health in India is 4.2 per cent of the GDP and ranks 18th in the world tally compared to 7.7 per cent in USA and 4.4 per cent in Brazil. In the country with a large number of poor people as ours, the public health spending is disproportionately very low that deprives the masses from availing of proper and timely medical aid in cases of need, thus affecting their health, efficiency, compliance to treatment and ultimately their chance of survival, in case of any serious ailment. This also leads to their falling prey to quacks and such other orthodox or unapproved methods of treatments risking their health and lives.
3. Proper planning of newer set-ups to make them more considerate and friendly towards the needs of the patients, as per the modern trends.
4. Networking of various hospitals for better coordination of patient care.
5. Integration of the local area family practitioners with the Government hospitals and dispensaries in the area for two-way referrals.
6. Closer coordination amongst healthcare infrastructures of all Government agencies and various civic bodies to ensure seamless cover without wastage or duplicacy.
7. Encourage development of high-class health care infrastructure in NCR towns as well as in the neighbouring states of Delhi through incentives and/or soft loans to entrepreneurs ensuring comparable quality at competitive costs.
8. Proper and adequate potable water supply system, sewerage/sanitation system and electric supply infrastructure to permanently minimise the incidence, morbidity and mortality of infective diseases like typhoid, cholera, gastro-enteritis, jaundice, malaria, polio, etc., in the community.
9. Health education of public through various means of media with emphasis on prevention aspects of infective diseases, hygiene, dietary habits, addictions etc.

10. Inclusion of health related topics in school and college curricula.
11. Improve general literacy status of the population with proper definition of a literate persons having ability to read newspaper, write letters and perform simple calculations (instead of the present criteria of just the ability to sign one's name). It is expected that a literate person would understand the health needs and family planning requirements better than the illiterates.
12. Strict control of food items and strict compliance of laws for control of food/water borne infections and adulterations.
13. Proper housing policy with adequate living space per person with healthy surroundings and with adequate infrastructure support system.
14. Policy about in-migration of people to control the population growth of Delhi may require strengthening of infrastructure facilities in NCR towns, creation of well developed satellite towns with rapid mass transport systems etc.
15. Well-equipped and dedicated trauma centers along the main highways entering Delhi.
16. Widening of Health Insurance sector base and Corporate support to their employees for medical check ups and treatments.
17. Shifting of industries to outskirts to reduce health hazards, accidents, pollution and traffic congestion in the heart of the city.
18. Control of stray dogs and stray animals to minimise traffic hazards/accidents and to reduce the cost of superfluous use of Anti Rabies vaccine, besides indirect saving on the man-hours. (Annual expenditure on ARV in GNCTD Hospital is approx. Rs. 3-5 crores).

Chapter 11

Tourism including Health Tourism

11.0 Methodology

Broad picture of the tourism scenario in general and of Delhi in particular is being given.The description will identify selected areas of the tourism sector with inputs from related organisation. Recent reports and data would also be referred to in respect of the selected sectors.

An overview of the National Tourism scene during the Ninth and Tenth Plan period will be provided and the Delhi tourism scenario will be seen in the context of this over view.

The selected Tourism sectors will be covered as follows:

1. Heritage Culture Tourism
2. Business Tourism and Conference and Conventional Tourism
3. Rural Tourism Handicraft etc.
4. Medical and Wellness related Tourism
5. Sports related Tourism
6. Shopping related Tourism
7. Adventure Tourism
8. Hub destination Tourism
9. Human Resource Development

Each of the above selected sectors of tourism would be examined and evaluated and recommendation made with a view to generate growth in the Tenth Five Year Plan period as well as the special opportunity for development linked to the Commonwealth Games 2010.

The conclusion of the Report will give the 'way forward' and provide a 'vision' for Delhi tourism in the coming years.

11.1 National Tourism Scene (Ninth Five Year Plan)

Over the years, tourism has emerged as a major segment of Indian economy contributing substantially to the foreign exchange earnings, which have increased from Rs. 66110 crore in 1993 to Rs. 164290 crore in 2003. The direct employment in the sector during 1995-96 was about 8.5 million persons, accounting for about 2.4 per cent of the total labour force. In 2003 the employment figure is 25 million. There was a gradual increase in the Central Plan outlay for tourism over the Plan periods from Rs. 1.58 crore in the Second Plan to Rs. 272.00 crore in the Eighth Plan. The details of the expenditure during the Eighth Plan period for the Department of Tourism and ITDC are given in the Table 11.1.

As against the Eighth Plan outlay of Rs. 272 crore (1991-92 prices), the expenditure during the period was Rs. 490.42 (current prices). The entire Plan expenditure of ITDC from the year 1994-95 onwards was met from internal and extra budgetary resources. Bulk of the expenditure of the Department of Tourism was incurred on tourism publicity.

The major schemes of the Department of Tourism relate to Promotion and Publicity, Central Assistance for the Development of Tourism Infrastructure, Human Resource Development and Incentives. The Central government investment for the improvement and creation of tourist facilities is channelised through State/UT Government on a cost-sharing basis. Under this pattern of funding, the Central Department of Tourism meets almost the entire expenditure, except the cost of land and interior decoration in the case of construction projects.

In order to finance major projects fro development of tourist infrastructure, a new pattern of financing was conceived during the Eighth plan. Apart from the State

TABLE 11.1

Eighth Plan Expenditure—Tourism

(Rs. Crore)

Sub-head	*8th Plan outlay (1991-92 Prices)*	*1992-93 Exp.*	*1993-94 Exp.*	*1994-95 Exp.*	*1995-96 Exp.*	*1996-97 Exp.*	*8th Plan Exp. (Current Prices)*
Deptt. of Tourism	236	73.57	86.48	89.11	97.87	89.66	436.59
ITDC	36 (32)	5.84 (0.84)	7.28 (2.28)	8.82 (8.82)	14.20 (14.20)	17.69 (17.69)	53.83 (43.83)
Total	272 (32)	79.41 (0.84)	93.76 (2.28)	97.93 (8.82)	112.07 (14.20)	107.35 (17.69)	490.42 (43.83)

Note: Figure in bracket indicates Internal and Extra Budgetary Resources (IEBR).

Eight Plan Expenditure-Tourism

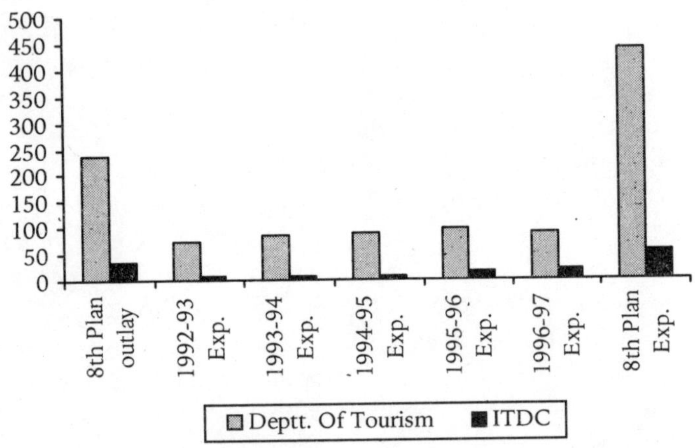

and the Central government contributing towards the funding of projects, the new scheme, known as Equity scheme, envisaged a major role for the financial institutions. As the state government could not formulate bankable projects, the scheme could not, however, make much headway in the Eighth Plan.

The Eighth Plan envisaged a growth of 9 per cent to 10 per cent per annum in international tourist arrivals and about 2.75 million tourist arrivals were anticipated by the end of the Eighth Plan. The target, however, could not be achieved due to various reasons such as armed conflict in the Gulf region, reduction in international outbound traffic during the period, law and order problems and health hazards in some parts of the country. The number of tourists who visited India during the Eighth Plan period increased from 1.78 million in 1991-92 to 2.33 million in 1996-97.

The main emphasis in the Eighth Plan for the ITDC was on consolidation rather than on expansion of accommodation. The Corporation, which earned a net profit of Rs. 3.11 crore in 1991-92 improved the financial performance during the Eighth Plan period and earned a net profit of Rs. 55.8 crore in 1996-97.

11.2 Policy Framework for the Ninth Plan

The policy objective in the Ninth Plan was to work towards creating a tourism product that provides the persons traveling to various places a pleasant experience on their trips, through an environment of peace, stability, security and an integrated system of physical infrastructure that does not fail. Tourism should become a unifying force nationally and internationally, fostering better understanding through travel. It should also help to preserve, retain and enrich our world-view and lifestyle, our cultural expression and heritage in all its manifestations.

It is important to realise that development of tourism has an important indigenous dimension. The number of middle and lower middle class tourists visiting distant places in the country is on the increase. The captive tourism around the places of pilgrimage is also increasing fast. There is a need for creating adequate, hygienic, decent, low-cost facilities for such tourists. The measures for ensuring safety, particularly in difficult places of pilgrimage at high altitudes, should be emphasised. Many of these places of captive tourism are in the regions, which are economically poor. Development of tourism in these areas, therefore, will accelerate the economic development of these regions.

The diversity of the tourism product in India makes it imperative that the development of tourism has to be a joint of all the infrastructural Departments, public sector undertakings, state governments and the private sector. The approach to tourism development in the Ninth Plan was accordingly on coordinated efforts by the public and private sector and the major thrust was on selected areas of tourism under as heritage tourism, youth adventure tourism, pilgrim tourism etc.

People's participation in tourism development including Panchyati Raj Institutions, local bodies, non-governmental organisations and enterprising local youth was to be encouraged to create public awareness and to achieve a wider spread of tourist facilities. But this was on a very limited seat.

The infrastructure projects, which are commercially viable, will be funded by the Government under the Equity Scheme except in the North Eastern States and selected hill districts in the country. The existing pattern of funding would generally be applicable only to purely promotional and product development projects and in the North East Region and selected hill districts where the equity funding pattern is not insisted upon.

The main schemes of the Department of Tourism, namely Central Assistance for Development of Tourism Infrastructure and Promotion and Marketing would continue in the Ninth Plan. Efforts would be made to make them more effective.

In order to give boost to foreign exchange earnings, employment and income generation through tourism activities, export house status was granted to tourism units.

ITDC continued its existing activities. The performance of ITDC improved through restructuring of the existing properties and improving the quality of service. No project relating to construction of new hotels was taken up during the Ninth Plan period.

The Ninth Plan period also saw initiatives being taken in manpower development by strengthening the training facilities. This was achieved by improving government run institutes as well as by encouraging private institutes to set up training facilities.

Effort was also made to improve coordination with related sectors such as Civil Aviation, Railways, ASI, etc.

The Tenth Plan approach for Tourism signified a distinct shift from that adopted in earlier Plans. The new Tourism policy 2002 to be implemented during the Tenth Plan lays emphasis on the benefit of the tourism for the host population. It will motivate State Government to use tourism for achieving socio-economic objectives. It will encourage private sector investment and will provide legislative and regulatory support for sustainable tourism and also to protect the industry and the consumer. Special encouragement will be given in promoting Rural, Heritage, Adventure and Eco tourism. Emphasis would be on creating "products" and "destinations". The policy would endeavor to remove barriers to growth and resolve contradictions so as to achieve inter-sectoral convergence of activities that will go to help the growth of the tourism sector.

11.3 Tourism Scene (Tenth Five Year Plan)

The Tenth Plan approach toward tourism signifies a distinct shift from the approach adopted in earlier Plans. Apart from acknowledging the well-accepted advantages of developing tourism for the promotion of national integration, international understanding and earning foreign exchange, the Tenth Plan recognises the vast employment generating potential of tourism and the role it can play in furthering the socio-economic objectives of the Plan. In order to create a supportive environment for the promotion of tourism, the New Tourism Policy, 2002, that is to be implemented during the Tenth Plan, will generate awareness about the benefits of tourism for the host population. It will mobilise state government to use tourism as a means for achieving their socio-economic objectives; encourage the private sector to enhance investment in tourism and provide legislative and regulatory support for sustainable tourism and to protect the interests of the industry and the consumer. The policy envisages involving the rural sector in the promotion of rural, heritage, and adventure and eco-tourism and will promote the development of competitive high quality products and destinations. Most importantly, it will remove the barriers to growth and resolve contradictions in policy to achieve inter-sectoral convergence in activities that help the growth of tourism.

The initiatives taken by the state so far have not yielded the desired result and India's tourism performance has failed to match its potential even as countries its natural and cultural endowments have taken the lead in reaping the benefits of tourism development for their people. The reasons for this poor performance need to be speedily addressed to enable tourism to make an appropriate contribution to national development.

As observed in the Planning Commission Report of the National Committee on Tourism (1988), the public sector made a significant contribution to the growth of tourism in the initial stages of planned development by providing a reasonable infrastructure base. During the Ninth Plan it was recognised that a reappraisal of the role of the State in tourism development and the extent of its participation was needed as it is neither necessary nor feasible for the State to make large investments in areas that are best left to the initiative of the private sector. The state can contribute through infrastructure development, the planning of broad development strategies, the provision of fiscal and monetary incentives to catalyse private sector investment and devise an effective regulatory and supervisory mechanism to protect the interests of the industry and the consumer. The acceptance of this view also led to the commencement of the process of disinvestments in 18 hotels of the India Tourism Development Corporation (ITDC) hotels.

The ITDC will have to redefine its role in the Tenth Plan. The state can also play an effective role in ensuring that tourism development does not harm the environment. The interaction between tourism and environmental pollution requires sensitive handling. There is complementarily, not conflict, between the high quality environmental requirements of tourism and the imperatives of maintaining the ecological balance.

11.4 Global Status and Trends

Although global recession and the 11 September 2001, events are estimates to have resulted in a temporary decline in travel and tourism demand in 2001-02, the international and domestic tourism is expected to boom over the next two decades. The World Travel and Tourism Council (WTTC) estimates as 4.5 per annum increase in the total amount of travel and tourism economic activity between 2002 and 2012. This is largely attributed to a rise in global wealth, liberalisation of international airspace, cheaper flights and the use of the Internet as a travel tool. The earnings from tourism have made it one of the world's largest industries and the fastest growing sectors of global trade accounting for 10.7 per cent of global gross domestic product (GDP), 12.8 per cent of global exports, 8.2 per cent of global employment (or one in every 12.2 jobs), and 9.4 per cent of global capital investment.

Tourism in the least developed countries is growing faster than the world average, holding the promise of prosperity for many. International tourist arrivals worldwide reached 698 million in 2000, generating $595 billion revenues. International tourism flows are expected to reach 1.5 billion. Today, only 3.5 per cent of the world population travels internationally but the number of Asian, particularly Chinese tourism is predicted to grow enormously as the region becomes more integrated with the global economy.

The scale of world domestic tourism, on the other hand, exceeds world international tourism by a ratio of 10:1. In India, for every international tourism, there are 80 domestic tourists. Domestic tourism can form the basis of a viable and sustainable tourism industry in India.

11.4.1 Global Market Trends

Consumer trends in tourism are gradually changing and require an appropriate response in terms of both policy formulation and investment. Current market trends indicate that:

- Long haul travel will grow faster than inter-regional travel. A growth of 24 per cent is expected by 2020.
- People with less time for leisure are likely to take more frequent but shorter trips nearer home, opening up opportunities for 'neighbouring country' tourism.
- The experienced traveller was authentic, off-the-beaten-track vacations in remote and less well-known places as against luxurious five-state vacations, leading to an interest in rural and ethnic tourism.
- The increase in the number of people with lots of money but little leisure time has resulted in a growing emphasis on rest and relaxation, and 'wellness' 'health' and holidays.
- The elderly population in key tourism generating markets has shown a preference for cultural tourism against sun-and-sand vacations.
- There is notable and increasing interest in spiritualism.
- The demand for eco-tourism and nature-based holidays is expected to double and even triple in the next 20 years.
- Sports and adventure holidays continue to be popular with the young.

TABLE 11.2

Contribution of Travel and Tourism to GDP and Employment

Contribution	*World Average (%)*	*India (%)*	*World Rank*
Contribution of Tourism and Travel Economy to GDP	10.7	5.3	140
Contribution of Tourism and Travel Industry to GDP	4.2	2.5	124
Contribution of Tourism and Travel Economy Employment	8	5.6	140

Source: WTTC, Department of Tourism, Government of India.

The increased interest in cultural tourism, spiritualism, 'wellness' holidays, eco-tourism and rural tourism would benefit Indian tourism, provided the country can avail of the opportunities offered to maximise its natural advantages in these areas. The development of new tourism products and destinations during the Tenth Plan must be based on market research and demand, keeping the source markets and the age groups of the tourists in mind. At the same time, the government must develop new source markets nearer home and make India a safer destination, especially for women tourists and family holidays.

11.4.2 India's Place in World Tourism

The World Tourism Organisation forecast indicates an increasing tourism preference towards East Asia, the

Pacific, West Asia and South Asia, although Europe and America still remain the world's foremost tourism destinations commanding 77 per cent of global market. East Asia/Pacific achieved highest rate of growth of 14.5 per cent in tourism and travel in 2000 followed by West Asia and South Asia (Table 11.3).

TABLE 11.3

International Tourist Arrivals

	Million		*Growth Rate (%)*		*Market Share (%)*	
	1999	*2000**	*1999/ 1998*	*2000*/ 1999*	*1999*	*2000**
World	650.0	698.3	3.8	7.4	100	100
Africa	26.5	26.9	6.1	1.5	4.1	3.8
America	122.3	130.2	2.3	6.5	18.8	18.6
East Asia/ Pacific	97.6	111.7	10.8	14.5	15.0	16.0
Europe	379.8	403.3	1.7	6.2	58.4	57.8
Middle East	18.1	20.0	18.1	10.2	2.8	2.9
South Asia	5.8	6.3	10.7	9.0	0.9	0.9

Source: World Tourism Organisation *as collected from WTO database in Jan 2001.

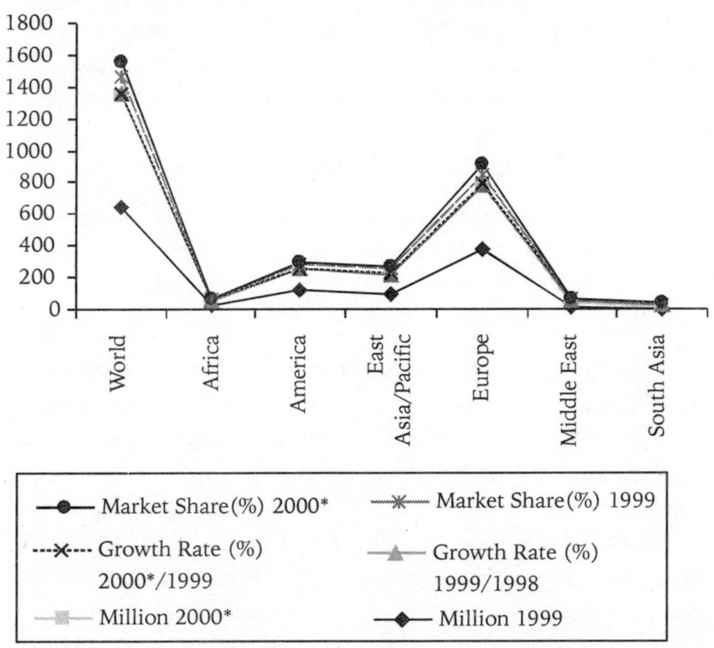

With this gradual shift in focus, the outlook for the growth of tourism in the region is promising. In Asia, China has emerged as a leading tourist destination and is poised to become the world's top tourist destination by 2020.

The WTTC has identified India as one of the world's foremost tourist growth centres in the coming decade. After Turkey, India is expected to achieve the fastest rate of growth of the total amount of economic activity likely to be generated by travel and tourism, at 9.7 per cent over the next 10 years. Also, the largest employment creation after China is expected to take place in India over the same period. The growth in 'visitor exports' or spending by international tourists, it likely to be the highest in India at 14.3 per cent per annum over the next decade. On the whole, the WTTC forecast for India is promising, subject to key policy issues that affect the growth of the sector being addressed.

TABLE 11.4

Contribution of Travel & Tourism to Exports & Receipts

(in Per cent)

	World Average	*India*	*World Rank*
Total tourism exports as percentage of total exports	12.15	9.5	3.1
Tourist Receipts	5.2	11.8	29

Source: WTTC, Department of Tourism, Government of India.

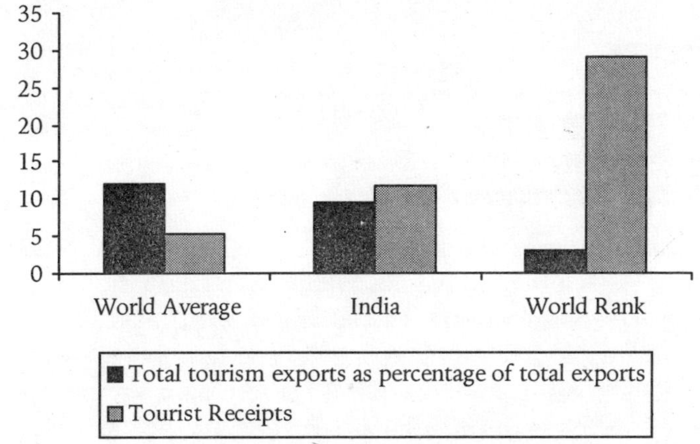

If India is to realise its full potential in tourism it must create world-class tourism products and destinations that can compete successfully for a larger share of the Asian tourism market.

Today, outbound tourism from India far exceeds visitor traffic to the country partly because there is a lack of world-class destinations within the country and partly because the domestic tourism policy has been largely directed towards those in the lower end of the spending spectrum. The high spender from India prefers to visit neighbouring countries as he gets better value for money. The scope and reach of domestic tourism will have to be broadened in the Tenth Plan through the development of competitive destinations that match international standards in terms of price and quality and also satisfy the international traveller.

India's international arrival figures have not been able to keep pace with neighbouring countries and have been exceeded by Thailand, Malaysia, Indonesia, Dubai, and the Maldives. Since 1995, India's share of the world market has remained virtually stagnant at 0.38 per cent, while domestic tourism has grown at a phenomenal rate and India now accounts for 4.6 per cent share of domestic tourism worldwide. In terms of tourism receipts, India has shown relative buoyancy because of the interest shown by visitors in traditional handicraft items—and particularly in diamond jewellery. The Tenth Plan visualises a mutually supportive role for tourism and handicrafts by encouraging *'haats'* and *'shilpgrams'* and recognising shopping as an integral part of the tourism experience to promote the 'Made in India' brand.

TABLE 11.5

International and Domestic Tourism

	World	*India*	*Percentage share of India (%)*
International Arrivals	698 million	2.64 million	0.38
Tourism Receipts	$595 billion	$3.2 billion	0.69
Domestic Tourism Worldwide	6,980 million	210 million	4.6

Source: Data as collected from WTO database in Jan 2001.

11.4.3 India's Tourist Profile

India receives the largest number of overseas tourists from the United Kingdom, which is its largest source market, followed by the United States, Sri Lanka, France, Germany, Canada, Japan, Australia, and Singapore. Of the tourists coming to India, 27.5 per cent are in the age group of 35-44 years, 23.4 per cent in the age group of 25-35 years and 20.8 per cent in the age group of 45-54 years. Women constitute only 30.5 per cent of India's total international arrivals. Repeat visitors account for 44.9 per cent of the overseas visitors. A substantial number of these may be non-resident Indians, as hotel reservations do not correspond to the number of international arrivals in the country. The average length of stay of foreign tourists in the country in 1998 was 31.2 days. Domestic tourism, on the other hand, is largely pilgrimage-oriented and requires improvement in travel facilities and pilgrim destination.

11.5 Tenth Plan Objective

Tourism in India has tended to be regarded as an elitist activity conducted primarily for the purpose of earning foreign exchange. Its vast potential as an engine of growth and employment generator has remained largely untapped. Although, with 25 million jobs, India ranks second in terms of number of persons employed in travel and tourism, yet the contribution of the sector as a percentage share of all employment is amongst the lowest in the world. The Tenth Plan objective is to integrate tourism with the socio-economic objectives of the Plan by creating 3.6 million jobs a year though the promotion of domestic and international tourism and to enhance India's share of international arrivals from 0.38 per cent to at least 0.62 per cent by 2007.

11.5.1 Role of the Department of Tourism

Being the nodal agency for the development of tourism in the country, the department of tourism needs to make greater efforts to coordinate and integrate the policies of central ministries that have an impact on the development of tourism and to mobilise state governments and the private sector to develop unique and competitive tourism products and destinations. Crucial decisions affecting tourism are taken by other ministries *viz.,* the Ministries of Finance, Home, Civil Aviation, Surface Transport, Environment and Forests, Urban Development, Rural Development, Ocean Development etc. The Department of Tourism has tended to concentrate largely on its role as the promoter of international tourism and generator of foreign exchange earnings while paying relatively less attention to all-important development of tourism infrastructure and product quality.

In the Tenth Plan, the department will redefine and expand its role and work towards inter-sector convergence and policy integration to remove the barriers to the growth of tourism.

There are several factors that are responsible for the inadequate growth of the tourism sector in India. These are barriers relate to mindset and approach, barriers that discourage private investment, factors that affect competitiveness and factors that affect the long-term sustainability of tourism. The effective and early removal of these barriers during the Tenth Plan is an essential determinant for the success of the New Tourism Policy. The need for a national consensus on the role and level of tourism development in the country has been voiced repeatedly but a concerted effort to achieve a consensus has not been made. Tourism should not be limited by state or regional boundaries if distortions in policies are to be avoided. It is evolved through the National Development Council (NDC) and the barriers to the growth of tourism removed.

Tourism has been denied the priority it deserves over successive Plan periods because its potential as an engine of economic growth has not been appreciated. This is visible in the low allocation of resources. Allocation to tourism has averaged 0.16 per cent of the total Plan outlay from the Third Plan to the Ninth Plan. In the Tenth Plan, it is likely to receive an allocation of 0.72 per cent of the plan budget allocation. According to the WTTC, India is one of the lowest spenders on tourism—153rd out of 160 countries—while its neighbouring competitors and China invest far more: Malaysia (5.1 per cent), Nepal (5 per cent), China (3.8 per cent). The growing domestic and international demand, which is set to boom, reinforces the need for higher investment. Failure to measure up to additional investment demand for domestic tourism is likely to lead to the over-exploitation of existing facilities, discouraging foreign visitors while leading to an increase in the outflow of high-spending domestic tourists from the country.

Most state governments give scant importance to tourism even though they virtually control the tourism product located within their boundaries, They are responsible for creating the local infrastructure, transport systems, sanitation and hygiene, leisure and recreation, law and order, the upkeep of local monuments and the general well-being of the tourist. Their support and participation is essential for tourism to succeed and spread its benefits among the host population. Their lack of interest has resulted in an unprofessional ad hoc approach that acts as a deterrent to growth of tourism. The approach of the state governments needs to be focused, highly professional and result-oriented if India is to avail of the opportunity that the currently favorable market trends have to offer.

Apart from the state government, the private sector plays a vital role in the growth and development of tourism. Although the Central government and certain state governments have, from to time, announced incentives to involve the private sector in tourism development, the results achieved have fallen short of expectations. To provide a conducive environment for private sector investment, it is important to realise that the travel and tourism sector is adversely affected by the lack of synergy in inter-sectoral policies. The growth of the sector requires well-integrated and cocoordinated policies and stability in approach. Contradictions and arbitrary changes in policy send confused signals to the investor. Unless infirmities in policy are expeditiously removed well before the end of the Tenth Plan period, the New Tourism Policy is unlikely to succeed.

Being a 'long haul' destination, India is more conveniently accessible by air and cannot be easily reached by rail or road. A restrictive air transport policy has a very deleterious effect on tourist traffic. There are insufficient connections to most tourism destinations. The situation could be eased if the large number of regional airports could open up as international airports. The existing international and national airports also require improvement. The price of aviation turbine fuel needs to be lowered to make air transport competitive and affordable. Today, it is cheaper to travel by air to neighboring countries from India than to travel to certain parts of India itself. A more liberal aviation bilateral regime and a new aviation policy to benefit the economy of the country as a whole rather than the national carriers alone would greatly aid the development of tourism. Central and state governments need to evolve a taxation regime, which is revenue generating without being burden some. Accommodation and transport taxes tend to be very heavy in certain states while the excise policy in others is extremely harsh. The land policy in some states makes the setting up of a hotel a formidable exercise and as many as 48 clearances are required for the construction and running of a hotel. Such policies deter private sector investment. The importance of protecting private investment in tourism must also be appreciated and activities such as mining, unauthorised construction, encroachments and haphazard development around tourist resorts must be prevented through appropriate legislation and public support.

As tourism is a highly competitive industry, the traveller has a wide range of choices and looks for good value for money. The lack of quality infrastructure, uncompetitive rates, indifferent or poor product quality, difficulty in getting access to information on travel and tourist destinations, untrained service providers, and above all, the lack of hygiene, have an enormously negative effect on the competitiveness of the tourism product. A world class destination requires professional planning to prevent haphazard, uncontrolled growth, spatial and land use planning, strict architectural controls, sewerage infrastructure and water treatment plants. It requires improvement of entry points and appropriate facilitation services. The lack of a visa-on-arrival regime on account of security consideration places India at a disadvantage *vis-à-vis* its competitors. It is necessary that India strikes a balance between security considerations and the need for tourism development and reviews its visa policy to permit tourists from its major source markets to obtain visas on arrival. Equally important is the behaviour of the host population. Training programmes are required not only for hotel managers but also for tourist guides, taxi-drivers, staff at eating places, porters etc., as the manner in which they conduct themselves affects the tourist's experience of the country. Important 'do's' and 'don'ts' in terms of a code of ethics need to be inculcated among the service providers. During the Tenth Plan, the Department of Tourism will organise capacity building programmes for service providers through mobile training units.

A major impediment to the growth of tourism in India has been the lack of awareness about the benefits that it can bestow upon the host population. Unless the host population, both in the rural and urban areas, is supportive of tourism, it cannot become a vibrant economic force. The rural sector, in particular, has been largely ignored in tourism development and had consequently been deprived of the benefits of employment and income generation accruing from tourism. The Tenth Plan would create wide interest in rural tourism. While awareness campaign that elicits local support for travel and tourism is essential for the long-term growth of the sector, it is also important to create awareness about the environmental impact of tourism by generating respect for the carrying as excessive exposure of ecologically fragile areas to human interference can lead to irreparable environmental degradation. As the demand for eco-tourism is expected to grow enormously in the next decade, it is important to have regulations in place to prevent such damage. The local population must be convinced of the need to support such regulations in the interest of long-term sustainability. India's hill resorts have already suffered seriously from a lack of concern for their carrying capacities and the unchecked influx of tourists during the summer months. If India's forest sanctuaries and pristine beaches are not to suffer the same fate, attention will have to be paid during the Tenth Plan to obtaining regulatory and public support for sustainability concerns.

11.5.2 The Tenth Plan Strategy

The Tenth Plan strategy is to work towards a national consensus on the role of tourism in national development and to focus on the removal of barriers that hamper its growth. To make public sector investment more effective, it is necessary to work towards the inter-sectoral convergence of policies and programmes that could benefit tourism. The New Tourism Policy envisages a framework, which is government-led, private sector driven and oriented towards community welfare, with the basic infrastructure for tourism development, the private sector providing the quality product and the community providing active support. The overall vision of the development of tourism in the new policy will be achieved through five key strategic objectives. These are:

i. Positioning tourism as a national priority.
ii. Enhancing India's competitiveness as a tourist destination.
iii. Improving and expanding product development.
iv. Creation of world-class infrastructure.
v. Effective marketing plans and programmes.

Positioning Tourism as a National Priority

A concerted effort will be made, through the NDC, to arrive at a consensus on the role of tourism in the development agenda of the nation. Inclusion of tourism in the Concurrent List of the Constitution will provide constitutional recognition to the tourism sector and enable the central government to legislate for tourism development. A proposal to this effect has been circulated by the Department of Tourism to the state governments for comments and has also been discussed at a Chief Ministers' conference and a majority of the states have agreed to the proposal. Other initiatives include the setting up of Tourism Advisory Council with key stakeholders functioning as a think tank and the constitution of a Group of Ministers on Tourism to improve policy integration and coordination. The adoption of a tourism satellite accounting system is underway to gauge more precisely the contribution of tourism to the national economy. A national awareness campaign in order to create a popular movement in favour of tourism is being planned through a professionally managed communication strategy. Most importantly, efficiency of public investment in tourism supporting activities will be improved through inter sector coordination and prioritisation.

Enhancing India's Competitiveness as a Tourist Destination

As air capacity available to India is woefully short during the peak travel months, ranging from October to March, especially for the main tourism originating regions such as North America, Western Europe and South Asia, it is necessary to open India's skies so as to increase capacity and help enhance tourism. Additional air seat capacity and help in enhancing tourism generating destinations would significantly benefit the national economy and provide a major impetus to tourism. Improvement in the standard of facilities and services at the international and national airports will need to be speeded up by employing professional management agencies and by privatising and leasing out airports.

To enhance India's competitiveness as a tourist destination, it is proposed to simplify the visa procedures and consider strategies for the speedy issue of visas including electronic visas and visas on arrival. An attempt will be made, through a consensus, to reduce the heavy and multiple taxes that reduce the competitiveness of the Indian tourism product. Special tourism police will be deployed at major tourist destinations during the Tenth Plan to provide security to travellers and promote India as a safe destination.

Improving and Expanding Product Development

Product development strategy during the Tenth Plan will be related to the special interests of tourist target markets.

- Cultural and heritage tourism will be expanded. India has a vast array of protected monuments with 22 world heritage sites, 16 of which are monuments. The integrated development of areas around these monuments provides an opportunity for the development of cultural tourism in India.
- For the development of beach and coastal tourism, a number of sites on the west coast of India will be identified for the development as beach resorts by the private sector. The sites will be offered on long term lease at preferential terms. These sites will primarily be on the beaches of Goa, Kerala, and North Karnataka because of easier access by air. During the Tenth Plan Kochi in Kerala and the Andaman and Nicobar Islands will be developed as international cruise destinations because of their proximity to international cruise routes and their exotic appeal.
- India's unmatched variety of cuisine is becoming increasingly popular in the world and will be developed as a special attraction. It is proposed to create a highly skilled workforce of culinary professionals through an innovative incentive scheme not only for India but also to promote Indian cuisine internationally.
- Village tourism will be promoted as the primary tourism product of India to spread tourism and its socio-economic benefits to rural areas.
- India's great wildlife variety has not been developed as a tourist attraction. Wildlife sanctuaries and national parks will become an integral part of the Indian tourism product. Priority will be given to the preparation of site and visitor management plans for key parks. The quality of tourist facilities available at the parks will be enhanced after a prioritisation of parks. Tentatively these will be: Corbett National Park, Kaziranga, Mudhumalai, Bharatput, Periyar, Ranthambore, Little Rann of Kutch, Chilka, and the Sunderbans.
- India has the greatest adventure tourism assets in the world in the Himalayas and its rivers. Mountain-based adventure activities will be developed and promoted. Regulations and certification for adventure tourism operators will be introduced so that the minimum standards of safety and conservation are met.
- India receives only a minuscule proportion of the global meetings, conventions and exhibition market. It is important that India develops a world-class international convention city not just for the sake of tourism development but also for international and domestic trade and commerce.
- India's most unique tourism product during the Tenth Plan will be holistic healing and rejuvenation packages. In focusing on this, it will capture the essence of Indian culture for international and Indian visitors alike.
- India's fairs and festivals, some of which are already well established such as the Pushkar mela, the Desert Festival at Jaisalmer, the Kumbh Mela etc., will be promoted as unique products of India. The Festivals of India programme will be re-introduced in the top 12 future markets for India initially with an annual event in the United Kingdom and the United States, to be followed by triennial events in the other markets.
- Shopping will be recognised as an integral part of tourism. The development of dedicated shopping centres for traditional crafts designed along the lines of village *haats* such as Dilli Haat and Shilpgram will be encouraged and information on where to procure specific crafts made available through shopping guides.
- Delhi will be positioned as the cultural capital of India supported by an ongoing and vibrant calendar of cultural events. The development of such a niche-based special interest product mix will position India as a unique and competitive destination.

Creation of World Class Infrastructure

The need for physical infrastructure for tourism ranges from ports of entry to modes of transport to destinations (airways, roadways, railways or waterways), to urban infrastructure such as access roads, power, water supply, sewage and telecommunication. This underscores the need for inter-sectoral convergence of infrastructural schemes and programmes that could support tourist destinations.

The road network is vital for tourism as almost 70 per cent of passengers in India travel by road. Many tourist circuits are entirely dependent on roads. The current government plan for the road system in the country covering both interstate highways and improvements to rural roads directly supports tourism development. There is urgent need to construct and improve highways linking the 22 world heritage sites and places of tourist significance. The Ministry of Road Transport and National Highways will collaborate with the Ministry of Tourism in this effort.

The Indian railway system can also become an enormous asset to the development of the tourism and hospitality industry in the country. The railways hold a special fascination for foreign tourists who wish to travel the country. For the vast majority of domestic tourists also, the railway is the most affordable means of travel linking the length and breadth of the country. Introduction of special tourist trains with pre-set itineraries and private sector participation will be encouraged.

The Indian Railways plan to establish 100 hotels at railways stations to serve specific tourist centers. The private sector will be given incentives to operate these hotels on long-terms leases. These hotels will provide clean and inexpensive accommodation for budget tourists. The Indian Railways also owns a number of heritage structures, which, if affectively maintained and marketed, could serve, both as railway stations and places of tourist interest. India has five hill railways, which compare with the best hill railway systems in the world. The enormous tourist potential of these products will be tapped during the Tenth Plan. As steam-hauled trains like the Royal Orient, Buddha Parikrama, Place-On-Wheels and Fairy Queen are extremely popular with tourists, steam traction for special tourist segments will be continued. Trains like the Shatabdi and the Rajdhani with a special tourism and hospitality focus will be planned both for foreign and domestic tourists.

India's 7,000km coastline and her mighty rivers will be tapped for the promotion of cruises. Care will be taken to develop world-class tourism products. As the Ministry of Tourism's financial assistance to the states has not been able to have the desired impact in terms of creating of world-class tourism infrastructure, the emphasis must shift to the development of specific travel circuits as internationally competitive destinations and the convergence of resources and expertise for these circuits.

The availability of trained manpower is essential to achieve excellence in the tourism sector. At present, there are 21 institutes of Hotel and 13 Food Craft Institutes in the country. In addition, a good number of accredited institutes also cater to the growing demand in the service sector. It is estimated that only 50 per cent of the requirement of the market is met by these institutes. Five new institutes of hotel management would be set up in the Tenth Plan—three in the newly created state of Uttarakhand, Jharkhand, and Chhattisgarh and two in the northeast. In addition, 15 more Food Crafts Institutes will be set up in the Tenth Plan, and efforts will be made to take culinary crafts and training to the rural areas through mobile training units. A new scheme on capacity building to train service providers in the unorganised sector such as small hotels, *dhabas*, restaurants and other eating joints is also proposed.

Strategy for Effective Marketing

As there is fierce competition for tourists from India's source markets, India needs to change its traditional marketing approach to one that is more competitive and modern. It needs to develop a unique market position, image and brand, which cannot be held by any other competitor. India's positioning statement will capture the essence of its tourism product to convey an 'image' of the product to a potential customer. This image will be related not only to its ancient Vedic civilisation with a cultural heritage that continues to thrive especially in its rural areas but also to its essentially secular nature.

In the Tenth Plan, an extensive market research programme will be launched in the target source markets and tourism products developed to cater to the interests of each source market. An effective and ongoing market representation presence will be established with the travel trade in each source market and an internet portal set up in various languages to provide information, a description of the product and the product requirements of the target market segments. The Internet has a great impact on the marketing of travel and tourism. It has already established itself as a channel through which tourism organisations can promote their destinations and products. Indian tourism will utilise both the internet and other emerging interactive technologies to avail of the benefits to be gained.

11.6 The Path Ahead

The tourism sector needs a national consensus on the role and place of tourism in national development and the early removal of impediments that have hitherto handicapped its growth. The Tenth Plan target of the creation of 18 million jobs through tourism requires a substantial investment of Rs. 38,800 crore at the rate of 47 jobs per one million rupees of investment, both from the public and the private sector. The central sector outlay for tourism during the 10th Five Year Plan is Rs. 2,900 crore.

Public sector investment, though limited, can be made more efficient through the inter-sectoral convergence of policies and programmes supportive of tourism. An integrated inter-sectoral investment plan that provides effective infrastructural support to tourism through the Ministries of Railways, Surface Transport, Shipping, Civil Aviation, Urban Development, Rural Development and Environment and Forests etc. can be achieved through the preparation of a tourism component plan. Private Sector investment can be enhanced by removing the barriers to growth and expediting critical policies that are being evolved. Public and legislative support will be essential for the sustainable development of the sector.

The success of the New Tourism Policy 2002 will be largely determined by the success achieved on all these fronts.

11.6.1 A New Tourism Policy for Delhi

Delhi Tourism has recently outlined a new Tourism Policy. The approach is based on the spirit of "Bhagidari" and aims at "Tourism for All". One of the principal objectives is to make Delhi, which is also the national capital, into a World Class Heritage City. In order to give thrust to this objective, a multi pronged approach is to be adopted, incorporating all the key players such as the Department of Culture, MCD, NDMC, ASI, INTACH etc. The selected sites are to be developed with view to providing better visitor experience both to the heritage sites and its surrounds. The second component of the policy is that a Government led Private Sector driven community welfare approach should be adopted. The ways of effecting better private participation need to be better spelt out in order to attract the private sector.

The third component of the policy is to offer incentives so as to encourage heavy capital investment in the development of tourism infrastructure and provide increased employment opportunities.

The policy is to be supported by an aggressive marketing campaign and training programme for tourism personnel.

The areas identified for attention in development of the "Delhi Tourism" experience are:

1. Cultural/heritage aspects.
2. Business tourism.
3. Convention and conferences.
4. Ethnic appeal—handicrafts, cuisine etc.
5. Leisure—shopping, golf, adventure etc.
6. Medical Tourism.
7. Hub destination for North India.

An action plan for fulfilling the objectives of the policy has also been attempted which calls for the setting up of a high level Tourism Advisory Board with the requisite financial and regulatory capability to fulfill the task assigned to it.

11.7 Status of Department of Tourism Delhi Administration

The Department of Tourism, Delhi has been created with the following objectives assigned to it as per the allocation of business rules 1993:

1. Promotion of Domestic and International Tourism.
2. Development of Tourism related infrastructure.
3. Coordination with agencies involved in Tourism Industry.
4. Classification of Hotels.
5. Licensing the Tour Operators, Travel Agents etc.
6. To be the administrative department for
   a. Delhi Tourism and Transportation Corporation Ltd.
   b. Delhi Institute of Hotel Management and Catering Technology.

It also administers the Paying Guest Residential Accommodation Schemes

11.7.1 Financial Outlay of the Tourism Department

The approved outlay of Ninth Five Year Plan 1997-2002 and approved outlay of Tenth Five Plan to 2002-2007 and Annual Plan 2002-2003 are as under:

TABLE 11.6

Financial Outlay of the Tourism Department

(*Rs. in lakh*)

S. No.	Agency	9th Five Year Plan 1997-02	Exp. 1997-98 to 2000-01	Annual Plan 2001-02		10th Five Year Plan 2002-07 Approved Outlay	Annual Plan 2002-03 Approved Outlay
1	2	3	4	5	6	7	8
1.	Department of Tourism	1000.00	147.79	200. 00	110.00	3800.00	380.00
2.	Delhi Instt. Of Hotel Management & Catering Tech	1800.00	89.82	300.00	190.00	2000.00	145.00
3.	GIA to DTTDC	400.00	206.50	20.00	20.00	100.00	20.00
4.	Urban Development Department	—	—	25.00	5.00	100.00	5.00
	Total	3200.00	451.21	545.00	325.00	6000.00	550.00

Source: Plans & schemes of Tourism Department available at *www.delhiplanning.ni.in/write-up/2002-03/volume-I/tourism.pdf*

Brief description of the allocation of funds of projects and schemes of the Tourism Department, Delhi Administration are as follows:

11.7.2 Tourism Infrastructure (Rs. 2025 Lakh)

The Ongoing Schemes of the Ninth Five Year Plan under this head are

1. Establishment of wayside amenities.
2. Development of mini India heritage complex.
3. Development of Garden of Five Senses.
4. Development of Dilli Haat type projects.
5. Setting up of Coffee Home.
6. Upgradation of monuments to provide basic facilities (water, electricity and signage). Construction of souvenir shops, public convenience, cafeteria, illumination etc.

11.7.3 Indian Institute of Tourism and Travel Management (IITTM)—Tenth Five Plan Outlay Rs. 2025 lakh and Annual Plan Outlay Rs.200 lakh

The IITTM (Delhi Chapter) was set up by the Ministry of Tourism, Government of India in 1993 that the first Institution of its kind to provide professional manpower through a Diploma in Tourism and Management Development Program, Workshops, Seminars and Conferences, Foreign Language Training Programme and Practical Training for meeting the needs of Travel Industry.

It is proposed to acquire land and construct building with library, computer lab facilities for students with trained and experienced facility members.

The IITTM is an institution managed by Ministry of Tourism with its centre at Gwalior. It plays an important role in human resource development of tourism related services.

11.7.4 Promotion of Tourism of Delhi as a Destination (Tenth Five Year Plan Rs. 1750 lakh including Rs 175 lakh for Annual Plan 2002-03)

The following activities are included in the scheme

1. Production of tourist literature, CDs etc.
2. Publicity through hoardings, print, electronic media.
3. Information and facilitation of tourist.
4. Participation of national and International fairs, conference, exhibition etc.
5. Public relation campaign.
6. Production and distribution of films on Delhi and Delhi Tourism.

Apart from this the Department also proposed to provide facilitation such as tourism assuring and airports control room for help stock complain form tourist guide maps etc. and computer kiosks.

As part of promotion of Tourism the Department also holds Cultural Festivals and Events Festivals that includes 1. "Mango" 2. "Chrysanthemum" 3. "Winter Carnival" 4. "Roshanara" 5. "Shalimar" 6. "Qutub" 7. "Chandni Chowk" 8. "Deep Utsav" 9. "Baisakhi" 10. "Holi Milan" 11. "Basant" 12. "Teej" 13. "Nav Samvatsar" 14. "Ganesh Utsav" 15. "Amir Khusrau Utsav" 16. "Urs of Nizamuddin Oliya" 17. "Phool Walo ki Sair"

Adventure Tourism Activities such as Motor Rally, Ballooning, Camel Safari, Hand Gliding, Kayaking, Canoeing, Boating, Rock Climbing and Trekking are also taken up. As part of these activities the Tourism Department has taken up projects for development on Naina Lake, Bhalswa Lake, Sanjay Jheel, Roshanara Bagh Lake, Purana Quila Lake, etc.

11.7.5 Human Resource Development {(Outlay of Rs. 2000 lakh (Revenue Rs. 150 lakh + Capital

Rs. 1850 lakh is approved for Tenth Five Year Plan 2002-07) and amount Rs. 145 lakh (Revenue Rs. 40 lakh and Capital Rs. 105 lakh approved for Annual Plan 2002-03)}.

The Institute of Hotel Management and Catering Technology has launched an ambitious plan in the Ninth Five Year Plan. A building is under construction for institute on 5.06 acre land with a view to doubling the in take of 80 students by year for the Three Year Diploma Course. For this faculty would also have to be strengthened by creatiing new posts.

11.7.6 Grant in Aid to DTTDC for strengthing of tourist information center (outlay Rs. 100 lakh for Tenth Five Year Plan 2002-07, Rs, 20 lakh for Annual Plan 2002-03).

It is proposed to reduce of number of information center from 16 to 6 centers including information centers located outside Delhi.

11.7.7 Redevelopment of Historical Monuments/ Tourist Spots (outlay of Rs 100 lakh approve for the Tenth Five Year Plan out of which 5 lakh for Annual Plan to 2002-03).

The proposal is to improve the surroundings of location of such as Red Fort, Qutub Minar etc. This work to be implemented by the urban development department for providing sanitation services, beautification etc.

The following statement shows the plan outlay and the expenditure during the Tenth Five Year Plan:

11.8 Plan Outlay and Expenditure during 10th Five Year Plan

TABLE 11.7

Plan Outlay and Expenditure during 10th Five Year Plan

(Rs. in Lakhs)

S.No	Name	10th Plan Outlay	2002-03 R.E.	2002-03 Exp.	2003-04 R.E	2003-04 Exp.	2004-05 Approved Outlay	2004-05 Exp.	2005-06 Approved Outlay
1.	Department of Tourism	25	2	2	3	3	5	3	5
2.	DTTDC	4075	378	352	962	755	1015	700	695
3.	DIHM&CT	2050	260	125	210	185	300	400	500
	Total	6150	640	479	1175	943	1320	1123	1200

Source: Department of Tourism, Government of NCT of Delhi.

The DTTDC was set up in 1975 with an authorised capital of Rs. 10 crore and paid up capital of Rs.6.28 crore. It is the main implementing arm of Delhi Tourism Department The Role of the DTTDC is to:

1. Develop and promote Tourism in Delhi
2. Run the Tourist Information Bureau
3. Provide entertainment to tourists by cultural shows and festivals
4. Manage and run the tourist transport fleet
5. Manage the Travel Bureau
6. Deal in money exchange
7. Construct flyovers etc.
8. Retail trade of liquor.

The other main activities of the DTTDC Ltd. are running Coffee Homes, Dilli Haat and running the IITM for training of travel personnel.

Some of the new initiatives/projects of the DTTDC are:

Setting up of the Garden of Five Senses. The introduction of the new tours—Delhi-Amirtsar, Delhi-Anandpursahib, Kangra, Delhi-Vrindavan Gokul, Hop-on hop-off services. It is starting new activities such as boating at Sanjay Lake, Cultural Centre at Shahdra, Adventure Tourism etc.

In the last one year DTTDC has taken up project for development of Dilli Haat type project at Pitampura Geeta Colony etc. An eco-tourism project is to start at Chawala Kangenheri. 24 hours Coffee Home is to start at R.K. Puram. On the side of promotion and publicity DTTDC is

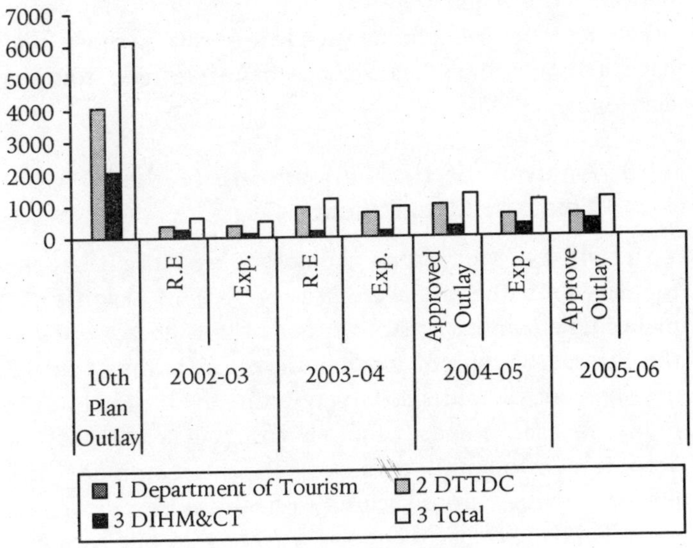

taking up a new film on tourism in Delhi, Yoga Classes at Sanjay Lake, Multilingual Website, etc. The DTTDC is taking up the following a civil work projects like Flyover at Lajpat Nagar (completed), Guru Teg Bahadur Memorial at Singhu, Bridge at Faizabad, Underpass at Prembari.

For the Commonwealth Games 2010 DTTDC proposes to take up special projects for providing better amenities at the monuments, provide better transport facility through AC Shuttle Bus Services, Evening Entertainment and Cultural programmes, multilingual Guides, and escorts. It also proposed to develop new locations such as Mehrauli Park, City Museum at Dara Shikoh, Library and Women Museum at Qudasia Park.

A sum of Rs. 200 crore has been set aside by Delhi Government for projects relating to the Commonwealth Games. This is to meet the preliminary works on selected projects planned for the Games. The details of the projects are yet to be outlined. The overall requirement of funds has been estimated at Rs. 1250 crores. The draft proposal includes two bridges over river Yamuna, 11 flyovers, improvement and beautification of roads, upgradation of airport, railway services and bus stations, setting up of five grid stations for the games village and a 50-bedded hospital inside the games village.

The Delhi Institute and Hotel Management and Catering Technology proposed to further strengthen its training programmes. It will introduce a Masters and a Doctorate Programme and also a training programme for working professionals. It will increase the total intake of students from the present level in coming years.

Some of the allied activities of the DTTDC, and which in fact have much larger revenue implications, are retail trade of liquor and developing infrastructure such as flyovers etc. While these are important activities many other activities remain unattended, specially those that have a more direct bearing on their role as a tourism development body.

11.9 Analysis of the Functioning of the Tourism Department

It will be seen from the foregoing note that the tourism department, Government of NCT of Delhi is the main implementing agency of tourism related activities in the State. Its scope of work however, in terms of actual development of tourism, is very limited. Considering the many faceted needs of a visitor that ranges from accommodation and transport to entertainment and leisure activities, from security to health requirement, the state Tourism Department has a large role but barely is able to address any of them to full satisfaction in keeping with its potential as a world class destination. The total manpower available with the department is 15 against the sanctioned strength of 33. It has very little role in motivating and guiding the activities of the other 'Players' and 'Stake - holders' in the state. Particularly, it needs to have links and close coordination with institution such as NDMC, MCD Department of Transport, Police, Health, Roads, etc. It must also have similar linkages with national level institutions such as Airport Authority, Railways, ASI, etc. It will be seen for the above statement that the main outlays relate to activities of the DTTDC and the DIHM & CT. This leaves very little opportunity for the Tourism Department of Delhi to play a more meaningful role in tourism development of the state.

11.10 Constraints Identified by Tourism Department

The tourism department of Delhi State is of the view that there are serious constraints in its ability to develop tourism in the state. These are:

1. Insufficient Budgetary Support from the state as well as Central government.
2. Lack of suitable organisation setup to fulfill the objective.
3. Lack of Laws and Regulations to support the tourism industry.
4. Lack of tourism infrastructure particularly accommodation, tourist transport etc., especially for middle budget tourist. It has also lack of coordination with civil agencies such as NDMC, MCD, DDA, and organisations such as ASI, Railways, Airport Authority for providing proper facilitation and convenience to tourist.

There is obvious need to enlarge the scope of activities of the Tourism Department with additional resource and to empower it to undertake the task.

It is significant to note in this regard that the overall tourism budget of Delhi for 2003-04 is only Rs. 9.65 crore. However, Department of Tourism, Government of NCT of Delhi has not felt the shortage of funds as a constraint.

This compares with Goa—Rs. 26 crore, Kerala—Rs. 74 crore, Maharashtra—Rs. 101 crore, Uttarakhand—Rs. 25 crore. There is obvious need to increase the budget of the Tourism Department substantially.

11.11 A Broad Picture of Tourism in Delhi

Delhi is the major entry point of tourists for India by air, that accounts for 30.8 per cent of the tourist, who enter India as compared to Mumbai which account for 30.9 per cent. So far as comparison of foreign and domestic is concerned the figures are as follows:

TABLE 11.8

A Broad Picture of Tourism in Delhi

State	*2001*		*2002*		*2003*	
	Domestic	*Foreign*	*Domestic*	*Foreign*	*Domestic*	*Foreign*
Delhi	1324636	830092	1228059	543036	1430546	693827

Source: Delhi Tourism Department.

Delhi

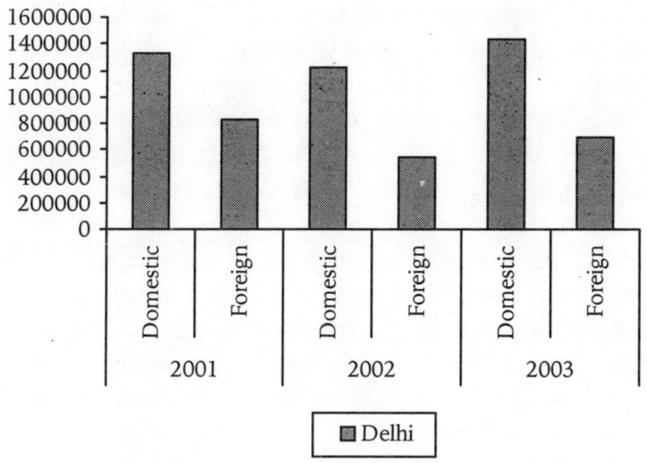

In comparison to the National figures the foreign tourists comprise 10.3 per cent of the total and only 0.5 per cent domestic of the tourists. It will be seen therefore, that Delhi is more significant for as a destination for foreign tourists rather than domestic tourists in the National scene.

As per the estimate of the Delhi Tourism Department the total number of foreign tourists who visit Delhi is 1.35 million per annum at present. This includes those who enter the country from Delhi or another spot. However, it is showing a downward trend, going down from 62 per cent to 51 per cent of the total arrivals in India. The average length of stay of foreign tourists in Delhi is two days. This is considered to be very short in comparison with capital cities of other major international destinations. There is scope for developing Delhi as a major tourist hub with an increased share of the national tourist arrivals and to reverse the downward trend.

11.12 Tourism Data Relating to Tourist Facilities in Delhi

The most important tourist facility is tourist accommodation. The total number of classified Hotel Rooms is 9,841. The following statement shows the break up:

Of these 14 are Five Star Deluxe (4,819 rooms), 13 Five Star (2,280 Rooms), 9 Four Star (925 Rooms), 14 Three Star (899 Room), 18 Two Star (524 Rooms), 12 One Star (284 Rooms), (One Hotel unclassified 110 Rooms), Total number of Hotels 81. In addition there are 82 Paying Guest accommodations of approved category with 270 rooms. In addition it is estimated that there are another 10,000 rooms in the unclassified category, many of these in the well-known Pahargunj area of Delhi. Therefore there is need to bring the unorganised sector in to the organised category.

With the rapid increase in tourism activities it has become clear that there is a serious shortage of hotel rooms at present. It is imperative therefore, that the number of hotel rooms be increased in every category. Suitable land for hotels would have to be made available by authorities to meet this shortage. It is estimated that an additional 30,000 room should be added in the next five years in Delhi and the contiguous areas of Gurgaon and Noida to meet the demand.

DTDC has indicated that as of July 2006, 22 new hotel sites have been identified in Delhi. Of these 'options' 8 sites have been accepted.

Tourism Transport is another very important area that requires attention. The following is a broad picture of the Road transport facility, which is available in Delhi at present.

1. DTC etc. Buses-4,000
2. Black Yellow Bus Taxi-6,000
3. Three Wheelers-55,000
4. DLY Tourist Cars-20,000
5. Charter Buses-5,000
6. Inter State Buses-3,000
7. All India Permit Coaches-800
8. Radio Taxies-150

The association of Tourist Transport Operators is of the view that Radio Taxies services need to be very substantially increased in order to fulfil the need felt by the tourists and in order to meet the international standards for tourist transport. It is felt that it can be achieved only by the early replacement of three-wheelers by cheap and efficient Radio Taxies.

In addition, the recently introduced Metro Mass Transit has started operating in Delhi and is being rapidly expanded. This is expected to provide much better transport facility to both the general public and the tourists and will help to reduced the pressure very substantially and make it both more comfortable and less expensive.

11.13 Tourism Services Providers

Travel Agents Tour Operators and Tourist Transport Operators are very important services provided to the tourist. Delhi is particularly provided by such services in comparison to the other states and destinations. The total number of travel agents in Delhi is 85. The number of tour operators is 238 and number of tourist transport operators is 64. This is against the national total of 186 travel agents, 340-tour operators and 154 tourist transport operators. In comparison, Maharashtra, which is the next largest, has 40 travel agents, 30 tours operators and 11 tourist transport operators. It will be seen therefore, that the tourism services sector is reasonably well developed and the emphasis must be on upgrading and improving of the quality of the services.

11.14 Opportunities in Delhi Tourism Sector

Delhi should be positioned as a global destination and "bench marked" with other global capital cities. Delhi as the National Capital has very high potential for tourism development. Being the capital city of the country it has a natural advantage in terms of infrastructure, in terms of roads, rails, etc., and also tourism related services such as hotels, transport services, travel and guide related services etc. Delhi has a strong and historic culture and tradition with as many as 1317 historically important monuments including world heritage sites. It has also institutions such as national museum, handicraft museum, cultural centers and art galleries. There are year round events ranging from the Republic Day Parade to international festivals of dance, drama, music and crafts, and industry exhibition and conferences. It is a hub for both business and government related activities, which attract professionals from India and abroad in large numbers. The growth of Delhi as a tourist destination is to be seen in the perspective of the development of the national capital region. This includes Gurgaon, Noida, Greater Noida etc., all of which are also growing rapidly as important commercial centres with international links and superior infrastructure. The most recent development of significance which will have an impact on the growth of Delhi has a tourism destination is the forthcoming Commonwealth Games 2010 to be held at Delhi.

While the tourism development of Delhi has broadly been in line with the National policy it has admittedly been on a small scale as is reflected in the very low budgetary support. The Tenth Five Year Plan and more significantly the Commonwealth Games preparation will provide a substantial increase in funds in areas that will directly impact on the Tourism Sector in and around Delhi.

11.15 The Tourism Product that Need to be Developed for Achieving Growth in the Tourism Industry in Delhi

11.15.1 Heritage Tourism/Culture/Museums

Visit to monuments and places of historic interest is the most important tourism product in the state, along with the visit to Museums, Art Galleries, Culture centre etc. Delhi is dotted with historically important monuments. There are 1317 listed monuments of which many are would heritage sites. There are 477 heritage buildings listed by INTACH. Although Delhi has a large number of historical monuments it is desirable that a selective approach is adopted for tourism development. The selected location should be well integrated and connected so that special attention can be paid from the tourism point of view. It is suggested that the following locations should be taken up for development as 'integrated tourism zones'.

1. Red Fort, Chandni Chowk area.
2. Purana Quila – Paragati Maidan, Humayun's Tomb.
3. Rajiv Gandhi Chowk, Parliament, Rashtrapati Bhavan area.
4. Qutub Minar, Garden of Five Senses, Mehrauli heritage area.
5. Airport, and
6. Railway Station areas to be developed as tourism reception zones.

Each of these zones have a unique characteristic with tourism potential. A Tourism product/experience must be created at each of these locations. These must be made easily accessible with transport and other support facilities and amenities. These 'products' must then be marketed by the private industry with the support of a publicity campaign supported by government.

The six locations zones should be developed in an integrated manner, with all tourist related facilities of an international standard. These locations should in turn be linked to all the important hotels and transports hubs namely railway stations, airport, hotels, bus stations etc., so as to facilitate easy access and better tourism 'packages'. These zones should be developed not only from the point of view of their historic importance but also serve as the focus for a 'theme' and provide a wider experience of the which should include unique food, fashion, craft, culture, music, art etc., associated with these locations. This will be more attractive to the tourists who will, therefore, spend more time and money, which will lead to growth in tourism earning and activities. Another new opportunity, which has yet to be explored, and which can yield very good results is 'night tourism'. Some important monuments, shopping areas and places of interest should be kept open till late hours of the night to tap the latent market for such tourism.

There are several cultural centres including Indira Gandhi Centre for the Arts. They have year round event of music, drama, art etc., which can attract tourists in good members. There is an untapped potential here. Most significantly Delhi lacks a National Theatre like that of London, New York, Beijing, Tokyo, Sydney, Singapore. There is a need for such a centre for Performing Arts to attract visitors round the year.

11.15.2 Business Tourism and International Conferences and Conventions

Meetings, Incentives, Conventions, and Events—the so-called MICE segment—is one of the fastest growing segments in the travel and tourism sector. No Indian city features in the top 50 destination of a list prepared by International Convention and Conference Association (IICA). ICCA's listing of top Asian cities for MICE tourism is as follows:

TABLE 11.9

Business Tourism and International Conferences and Conventions

Rank	*City*
11	Singapore
17	Hong Kong
23	Bangkok
27	Beijing
39	Shanghai
41	Manila
43	Taipei
46	Tokyo

Delhi does not feature in the list. This is in spite of the fact that Asia Pacific region is the second most popular destination after Europe for conference/convention tourism.

In Delhi convention facility are presently available at the Vigyan Bhawan. It is however, mostly reserved for government meetings and facilities are inadequate for very large convention. The Paragati Maidan as a venue is very big but with no suitable infrastructure for conferences. It has 54,648 sq.m. of covered space spread over 160 acres. Delegates have to walk a long stretch between halls. The shuttle service of ITPO is not of international standard and cannot transport a large number. The Ashoka Hotel in Delhi can accommodate 2,500 delegates in the convention hall and has 10 meeting halls with capacity ranging from sixty to four hundred. The hotel has 550 rooms. The convention hall has 8 channel translation facilities. It has support services such as business centre, bank, 24 hours money change travel agency, airline counter, shopping arcade, post office etc. but it has no exhibition space. This limits its usefulness as a venue for large conventions.

In order to meet international standards a convention centre should have 4 lakh sq ft. space with the following facilities:

- General Convention hall that can accommodated 5,000 delegates.
- "15-20 break out" area of different sizes, total about 15,000sq.ft.
- Restaurant, other services, banking, facility etc. 100000sq. ft.
- Exhibition area 150000sq.ft.
- Parking and circulation area.

It should also have easy connectivity to the major hotels of the city.

Indian Trade Promotion Organisation (under the Ministry of Commerce, Government of India) is engaged in promoting International Trade events at the 'Pragati Maidan' Complex in Delhi.

The I.T.P.O holds regular Trade Fairs and National Fairs which attract a large number of professional visitors as well as the general public and are immensely popular and attract lakhs of domestic visitors.

The ITPO is presently engaged in improving its infrastructure, which can give a big boost to MICE and leisure related tourism.

As per the estimates of the Indian Convention Promotion Bureau (ICPB) conference tourism in Delhi accounts for almost 40 per cent of the total conference tourism activity in the country. According to UIA there were 101 international conferences held in India in 2003. Of these it was estimated that 40 per cent were held in Delhi with approximately 15,000 international participants. Similarly ITPO estimates that about 10,000 international participants per annum attend international exhibition at Delhi. In addition, a large number of government sponsored conferences are held in Delhi. The exact figure is not readily available. The full potential of conference tourism in Delhi remains unrealised owing to serious inadequacy of conference facilities. Central Government has decided to earmark Rs. 1000 crore for developing such facilities. Proposals are also under consideration for developing consideration but are to be finalised. There will be considerable expansion of conference tourism related activity once these facilities become available.

Countries such as Malaysia, Singapore, and Thailand have benefited greatly by setting up purpose built Convention Centres for International Conventions. Delhi needs at least one such Convention centre.

11.15.3 Medical Tourism

This is a subject that has recently attracted the attention of the tourism industry. It is estimated that 1.5 lakh foreigners come to India annually for medical reasons. At present these are mainly NRIs, West Asians and Africans. Recently India has been attracting patients from UK and US also. This is in recognition of the quality of medical services that India can provide which is also both affordable and easily accessible. For instance heart surgery in the US costs USD 30,000 and costs USD 6000 in India. Similarly a bone marrow transplant in US costs USD 250,000 while in India it is USD 26,000 according to Harpal Singh, President, Indian Health Care Federation.

A study done by Mckinsey Consultants has estimated in a report for the CII that medical tourism can generate Rs 10,000 crore additional revenue by 2012. It is estimated that each medical tourist brings is a revenue of USD 600 as compared to USD 230 from ordinary tourist. Delhi is well served with world-class health facility to take advantage of this opportunity. However, it needs to be more organised and standardised in accordance with international standards.

The Ministry of Health is now actively engaged in developing medical tourism for which a committee has been setup for promoting India as a health care destination and is preparing a strategy document for which a Task Force has been set up. The highlights of the deliberation so far are as follows:

1. India can provide medical and health care of international standard at a comparatively low cost.
2. About one million people are awaiting treatment under the National Health Scheme in UK alone. There is waiting time, as adequate facilities and specialist staff/doctors are not available to meet the demand. This opportunity can be tapped.
3. Thailand has made significant progress in medical and health tourism. It is necessary to establish standards of medical services, price bands for services, quality assurances, hospital accreditation norms, and meet medico-legal requirements so as to make the services internationally acceptable. This is especially required as a pre requisite for those covered by medical insurance.
4. It would be necessary to coordinate the medical facilities with other related service in to comprehensive packages to cover not only the cost of treatment but also the cost of accommodation, travel, post operative care etc. Support services of the patient and the family members' companion would also need to be addressed.
5. Ministry of Health has agreed to draw up a list of "Centres of Excellence" along with details relating to facilities available on a format devised by Indian Health Care Foundation. Ministry of Tourism would print the list of institution and coordinate with the tourism industry to promote health tourism packages. A strategy paper is being prepared for developing India as a health care destination.
6. The latest thinking in the Ministry of Health is that the Government should not directly engage itself in the approval process of internationally recognised hospitals and that this may be better left to the professional body of the medical industry.

Apart from western medicine it is felt that traditional medicine, particularly Ayurvedic system would also be promoted in a similar manner. The department of alternative medicine (Ayush) are also undertaking a similar exercise and have drawn up a list of Ayurvedic institutions of excellence.

A significant development is the setting up or a world class Research cum Treatment Centre at Gurgaon. This will be a 2000 bed institution of Integrated Medical Sciences and Holistic Therapy. The Director of this institution Dr. Naresh Trehan has been Director, Escorts Hearts Institution in Delhi, which is already a recognised centre attracting foreign patient for the last 20 years.

11.15.4 Leisure, Adventure and Sports Tourism

Delhi has a large variety of tourism attractions for tourism. The tourism department, DTTDC have developed a location such as Dilli Haat which provides ethnic experience of food and handicraft. Several more such locations are proposed to be developed in North, East and West Delhi. The Garden of Five Senses has provided an experience of nature. Events highlighting the scene of unique cultural traditions are held regularly. The Bhalswa Lake has been developed with facilities such as public toilets, parking spaces, etc. The location has now been handed over to DDA for developing a golf course. The Sanjay Lake and the Purana Quila Lake have been developed with facilities for boating etc. It is proposed to develop Chawla-kanganhari Lake as a nature sport and water sports activities.

The DDA has already developed a golf course at Saket and is developing another one at Bhalswa Lake. The DDA also has developed infrastructure facilities such as public toilets, parking spaces, etc. which help to improve civic amenities for the visitors. While these golf courses meet local requirements they need upgradation to meet the international standards. Another important development is improvement in shopping facilities being developed at Rajiv Gandhi Chowk, Vasant Kunj etc., where the large shopping arcades and malls are coming up. These will greatly increase facilities for shopping tourism. The development of shopping malls in Gurgaon will also have an impact on the shopping experience of visitors to the national capital region.

Apart from the shopping experience the newly setup malls etc. have all given rise to large number of restaurant and food malls, eating places etc. The will also be attractive to tourists who will the able to experience a wide variety of national and international cuisine. More liberal policy regarding licence for serving alcoholic drink will also increase restaurant and pub activities.

The Commonwealth Games 2010 will be a major event which will have impact on tourism development in Delhi. The selected venue for the event will be the river area of the Yamuna in East Delhi. However, many of the events will be spread throughout Delhi such as the Nehru Stadium, Indira Gandhi Stadium, and Talkatora Garden etc. World class facilities are to be provided for the participants and spectators who are expected to visit Delhi in large number. In order to coordinate the development of infra and the facilities for the event a Commonwealth Games secretariat has been setup. The full details of the infrastructure and services for the Commonwealth Games are be prepared and will be ready shortly. Particulars and details are been consented from the Commonwealth games secretariat.

The MCD and the NDMC are the two statutory bodies responsible for providing civic amenities in the state. Many of the projects and the schemes of the MCD and the NDMC have a direct bearing on the entire a tourism sector. Details regarding these are to be collected and will be included in the report.

11.16 The Way Forward

The rapid economic upturn in India has impacted the tourism sector significantly. There has been 25 per cent increase in tourism activities in 2004-05. The lack of tourism related infrastructure in now being seriously felt. In Delhi and National Capital Region rapid changes are taking place and these will improve the infrastructure. The Transport sector will be considerably strengthened by the expansion of the Metro services. The roads and flyovers have been upgraded and new improved bus and taxi services have been introduced. The liberalisation of the investment policy in Real Estate sector and in the hotel sector will also impact the quality of the tourist accommodation, shopping and other civic amenities. The privatisation of the Airport and liberalised air services policy will improve the quality of the connectivity of Delhi for tourists. The forthcoming Commonwealth Games will provide a new opportunity for the convergence of the major stake holders for improving the quality of services. The Commonwealth Games Committee set-up could play a major role in achieving this.

In order to effectively achieve these objectives it is necessary to make some basic changes in the organisation and the structure of the Tourism Department and setup of Delhi also. Some policy decisions affecting the tourism sector will have to be taken at the State Government level.

11.16.1 The following is a brief outline of the issue that needs to be addressed:

(i) Tourism is the "industry of industries". It is built on the base of a reasonable level of socio-cultural and economic development of the host community. It must also have an acceptable level of tourism related infrastructure.

(ii) Delhi is set to get huge 'face lift' and upgradation of its infrastructure that will impact tourism in terms of new facilities and better visitor experience.

(iii) The Delhi Tourism must therefore, leverage the emerging scenario of economic upturn of India and the upgradation of urban infrastructure in and around Delhi.

To affect a quantum jump in the tourism industry the following course of action is recommended:

(a) Enhanced budgetary support for the tourism support would be necessary as the existing funds are inadequate for meeting the enhanced level of the services facilities which needs to be provided to the Tourism sector.

(b) The administrative infrastructure would have to be strengthened and enlarged.

It is necessary to consider the setting up of a statutory Tourism Board on the lines of some other countries such as UK and Singapore. The Tourism Board setup in some states such as Uttaranchal has given more effective powers to the Tourism administration of the State.

In the case of Delhi such a Board would require a wider role as it would have to include bodies that are strictly outside the purview of the State government such as NDMC, MCD, DDA, ASI etc. It is therefore, suggested that the tourist board with statutory power with setup under the Chief Minister of the State with representation of the principal stake holders organisation.

Officials from the Board could be placed on deputation with the other stakeholder organisations so as to provide better linkage and coordination in respect of tourism related activities of each of these organisations. The statutory board should have the power to effectively regulate and guide all such tourism related activities in these organisations.

(c) Rules, regulations and statutes relating to the tourism sector would have to be revised and streamlined so as to empower the authorities to effectively run the tourism related services and achieve an international level of quality in services.

(d) Tourist accommodation is one of the most important areas that need attention. For this land for setting up hotels of different category, according to projected demand would have to be made available. At present there is disproportionately low number of budget hotels. This need will have to be arrested. Similarly the paying guest accommodation sector needs to be enlarged for which the bye-laws will require changes.

(e) Delhi's growth as a tourist destination must go hand in hand with the NCR region of the neigbouring areas, particularly Noida and Gurgaon.

The tourism policy and plan of the entire NCR area therefore, needs to be taken up in a comprehensive manner along with that of Delhi.

In fact such an integrated approach could adopted for nearby destinations such as Agra, Jaipur, etc. Delhi would be the hub of this tourist region. Such a coordinated approach will greatly benefit the tourism sector of the region as a whole and will enlarge both the volume and quality of tourist arrivals and substantially increase the earnings from tourism activities.

(f) Private investment and private enterprise is to be a major partner in the development of tourism in Delhi. At present almost all the major hotel groups/chains have a presence in Delhi. The Taj, Maurya ITC group, Oberoi-Hiltons, Hayatt, Raddison all have a major presence in Delhi. New international hotel-chains have also made an entry in the hotel sector. The large international and national Travel and Tour companies such as Kounis, Cox and Kings, Travel House, Sita are active in Delhi. Even so the new liberalised investment policy is expected attract many new international players who are now making their presence felt in India. Private investment in new tourism sectors such as "convention " tourism, incentive tourism etc., which are yet to have a meaningful impact on the tourism market can be expected grow rapidly with the entry of the se international 'players'. All this investment can happen provided an investment friendly environment is created by the state and Central government. Also, the infrastructure and support facilities to support the growth must be put in place in a time bound manner. The challenge therefore in to harmonise and synergies the initiatives taken by the main players and which will enable the industry to move forward by making a cohesive, creative and positive effort that will lead to growth in the Tourism sector in keeping with the objectives of the Tenth Five Year Plan.

11.17 The Vision for Delhi Tourism

11.17.1 Delhi must Position itself as a Major Tourism Destination like Paris, London, Rome

As the capital city of a vast country like India with its rich history and diverse culture, Delhi must position itself as a tourist destination like other great capital cities of the world. At present it is sadly lacking in tourism infrastructure and quality and content of a world class tourism experience. While the present approach and initiatives have all yielded varying degrees of success, what is needed is a quantum shift in approach and programme of activities.

In order to achieve this it must have the following.

1. The Airport needs to be upgraded with world-class facilities. This exercise is already underway by the 'privatisation' route for which action has already been initiated by Ministry of Civil Aviation. The new liberal air service policy has also increased the number of available 'air seats' in both domestic and international flights. This will result in increased tourist arrivals and higher level of tourist satisfaction.

2. Urban transport system in the city must be modernised. The "metro" system in the city is being rapidly extended and will greatly increase the transport capacity and speed and comfort of movement within the city. The bus services are also due to be upgraded by induction of an additional 1000 air-conditioned buses in time for the Commonwealth Games.

3. The Road transport system in the city needs to be upgraded by widening and improving the existing roads and building additional flyovers and also improving the traffic system in the city. Parking spaces must be increased and improved to handle the rapidly increasing number of cars and other vehicles (present number of cars in Delhi - 44 lakhs.)

4. Delhi Municipal Corporation must upgrade the general upkeep of civic amenities in the city. The overall hygiene and civic amenities such as public toilets, drainage and sewage, water supply etc., need to be addressed urgently. Public areas and roads need to be well maintained. All this is particularly important in places of tourist interest. DMC is taking up special tourism related projects such as the 'heritage walk' in Chandni Chowk area.

5. The New Delhi Municipal Corporation must upgrade the level of civic amenities in its control. The Lutyens' Delhi, Rajiv Chowk, Pragati Maidan are all important tourism related assets that will have to be developed to match the expectation of the international and domestic tourists. Parking facilities and public toilets are the two most important facilities that need attention, as well as the upkeep of the Roads and public areas, parks, walkways etc.

6. Convention Tourism and Conference Tourism are the areas that are seriously in need of attention. This cannot be developed without the requisite infrastructure. The best way to do this is to develop the existing Pragati Maidan complex into a purpose built International Convention Centre, incorporating if possible the National Stadium complex to provide an integrated convention facility. Other suitable locations that my be considered are Safdarjung Airport area and Dwarka near the International Airport.

7. Heritage Tourism is already the mainstay of Delhi Tourism experience with more than 1317 historical sites. This needs to be improved and enriched by upgrading the monuments and providing better tourist facilities and conveniences. This heritage experience can be enhanced by providing a more integrated approach to the monuments by treating them as Heritage Zones with the active participation (bhagidari) of the stakeholders in the vicinity. This is especially relevant for locations such as Chandni Chowk, Mehrauli, Nizamuudin, Rajiv Chowk etc. Facility for "night tourism" in these areas will be especially attractive.

8. Culture Tourism, though a major attraction of Delhi, is inadequate. Events such as 26 January Parade and the many cultural events make Delhi a great attraction. But it has nothing like the Broadway of New York, The Theatre districts of London, the Bolshoi of Moscow. At present the Indira Gandhi National Centre for the Arts is functioning at a very low key. With its 25 acre prime location in the center of Delhi it could be built up on the lines of, say the Barbican centre of London to provide a cultural hub for the city which will provide a year round and varied cultural experience of international standard.

9. Eco-Tourism, river front, lakes, nature: With the rapid urbanisation of Delhi there is grave danger of losing the natural assets of the State. Efforts being made to improve the Yamuna river front for the Commonwealth Games and creating nature parks at Kanganheri-Chhawla, Sanjay Lake etc., will have to be given special attention to provide relief to the city dweller and attract the visitors from outside the State to experience the natural beauty of the State, its flora and fauna. Projects like the Garden of Five Senses would be another way of creating this experience.

10. Medical Tourism can allure an entirely new segment of visitors attracted by the quality and cost of medical treatment offered by the high level medical facility that is now becoming available in and around Delhi. Such tourism can also be linked to other forms of tourism, particularly 'wellness' tourism. This has already been done very successfully by some countries such as Thailand.

11. A New Organisation structure is necessary to implement this vision. Delhi Administration and Delhi Tourism are not equipped to deliver the ambitious vision in its present state of organisation and manpower. It needs an entirely new setup and organisation possibly a 'Tourism Board' headed by the Chief Minister, Delhi. Such an organisation must be able to integrate the many different 'players' under a single decision making and implementing body with the requisite statutory powers. This setup will have to play a much greater role, which must certainly go far beyond the marginal–player that the 'Delhi Tourism' is today.

Chapter 12

Employment and Integrated Rural Development

12.1 Introduction

The generation of employment has been an explicit objective of Indian Five Year Plans for a long time at the National level. At the State level too, the Five Year Plans have emphasised the creation of sufficient employment opportunities to take care of not only the backlog of unemployment and severe underemployment from the past but also additions to labour force. However, it is also accepted that measurement of employment/ unemployment is not easy in an agrarian economy with seasonal operations. Therefore, at the National level the measurements have been based on time utilisation (by individuals) concept, as estimated by various Rounds of the National Sample Survey Organisation (NSSO). This organisation utilises three concepts for estimates of unemployment, namely, usual status (US), current weekly status (CWS) and current daily status (CDS), all based on time utilisation only, ignoring the quality of work or income generated through that work. While these approaches have been accepted at the National level and implemented by NSSO and Planning Commission for the entire country, the underlying concepts are not necessarily relevant for the almost non-agrarian National Capital Territory of Delhi (NCT of Delhi or shortly, NCTD). However, reliable estimates of employment and unemployment even in the NCT of Delhi are obtained from NSSO rounds through its nationally accepted sampling procedures.

In the case of Delhi with an estimated population close to 1.6 crores, the most recent estimates are those from the 61st Round of the NSSO (2004-05) as also from the last census of March 2001. However, Delhi Government has taken care to analyse not only the data thrown up by the Central Sample of NSSO of Delhi but also the State Sample which is more than three times larger than the Central Sample in terms of households canvassed. It also has a large network of employment exchanges spread over the entire territory and therefore, more representative of the situation of job seekers than in other parts of the country where the rural population constitutes almost three-fourth of the total but is hardly served by them. In Delhi, the population of rural areas has fluctuated from census to census and is currently estimated to be around 10 per cent, the rest being urban whether living in the planned city or in the unplanned *jhuggi jhopri* (JJ) clusters, slums, re-settlement colonies and unauthorised colonies etc. Therefore, if a comparison of unemployment or under-employment situation of Delhi has to be made, it should rather be with the urban areas of the country or the constituent states rather than the entire national population. Further, it would be useful to look at the gender dimensions of employment/unemployment since the sex ratio for Delhi is rather low mainly because a very large section of Delhi's population migrated from different parts of the country and as is natural, the initial migration of a family is more by the males. In fact, the importance of migrant population and their employment status cannot be over-emphasised. In this respect, Delhi is almost unique in the country.

It may be useful to point out here that detailed picture of employment/unemployment for the entire country can not be presented without taking note of the special cases of states like Goa and Delhi. The picture of smaller states including Delhi, cannot reliably obtained in sufficient details from the national level picture, if based on the central sample only, which is why the Delhi Government in its Directorate of Economics and Statistics did a more detailed analysis based on the larger state sample. However, there are macro variables like employment elasticities, sectoral break up of employment and broad strategies of generating employment, which should be examined not from the State level data alone but also from National level picture. This is being attempted in the next few paragraphs.

12.2 Employment Generation Strategy and Employment Elasticity

The NSSO data convincingly shows that rate of growth of employment in the country's economy went down during the period 1993-94 to 1999-2000 as compared to previous five or six years blocks or even the longer period 1983 to 1993-94. For example the workforce growth declined from a high of 2.7 per cent per annum (239.57 million in 1983 to 315.84 million in 1993-94) during the earlier 10 years period to as low as 1.07 per cent (315.84 million in 1993-94 to 336.75 million in 1999-2000) during the 6-year period, 1993-94 to 1999-2000 on 'current daily status' (CDS) concept.* The Planning Commission also examined the corresponding rate of growth of workforce (male workers) to find an annual growth rate of even lower figure of 0.81 per cent during the inter-censal period 1991-2001. Thus the census gives a more pessimistic picture of the employment situation than even the NSSO. However, a clear picture of employment elasticities is available only from the NSSO data. The Planning Commission has given this data in its Annexure 5.6 on Employment Elasticities, for the years 1993-94 and 1999-2000. These figures are the following:

TABLE 12.1

Sector wise Employment Elasticities

i	Agriculture	0.01
ii	Mining/Quarrying etc.	-0.41
iii	Manufacturing	0.33
iv	Electricity, Gas etc.	-0.52
v	Construction	0.82
vi	Trade, Hotel etc.	0.62
vii	Transport, Communication etc.	0.63
viii	Financing, Real Estate etc.	0.64
ix	Community, Social & Personal Services	-0.25

Source: Planning Commission, Government of India, New Delhi.

The overall elasticity based on years 1993-94 and 1999-2000, thus works out to a low of 0.16 i.e., the GDP growth has to be over 6 per cent to ensure that the overall employment on CDS basis grows at the rate of 1 per cent a year. The growth of economy after 1993-94 has been averaging below 6 per cent recently and if the value of elasticities remains as worked out through NSSO rounds, the rate of growth of employment is likely to remain below one per cent which is rather low for the country with the population growth of approximately 1.9 per cent.

As for the Labour Force Participation Rates (LFPRs), the national picture indicates decline both on the basis of the NSSO Rounds and the censuses. Taking the growth rate of labour force from the NSSO Rounds as more relevant, based on the CDS concept, the annual rate of 1.31 per cent, needs to be contrasted with relevant work force growth rate of 1.07 per cent. This shows that even though the labour force is not growing as fast as before or as fast as the population as a whole, the decline in the workforce growth rate being sharper, the workforce is now growing slower than the labour force. This can only lead to increase in the backlog of unemployment/severe under-employment, as evident from the substantial rise in the unemployment rate in 1999-2000 at 7.2 per cent and further increased to 8.3 per cent in 2004-05. Looking at it in another way, the proportion of the organised sector employment has been declining within overall employment. Based on the same NSSO Rounds, the annual growth rate of organised sector employment over this 6-year period has been just above 0.5 per cent. In terms of public *vs.* private components, it is now well established that the organised sector employment in public sector has been declining while the private sector employment growth has picked up substantially. However, since the share of public sector employment in the total organised sector has been around 70 per cent, the substantial annual increase from the private sector is not able to make any real change in the organised sector employment growth. On the other hand, figures put out by the DGE&T, Ministry of Labour indicate that there has been a small decline in the total organised sector employment in the recent 3 years, which is rather disturbing.

The Planning Commission had devised a strategy for substantial growth in employment over the 11th Five-year Plan period during 2007 to 2012. The approach paper of 11th Five Year Plan devised broad strategies of employment generation as follows:

- Additional employment opportunities in the future will be generated mainly in the services and manufacturing sectors.

* Quoted from chapter 5 on Employment Perspective, *Tenth Five Year Plan*, Vol.1, Dimensions and Stategies, Planning Commission, Government of India (Annexure 5.1).

- Emphasis will be given to labour absorbing manufacturing sectors such as food processing, leather products, footwear and textiles; and services sectors such as tourism and construction.
- Accelerated agricultural growth should be viewed not much as source of direct employment but as necessary condition for reducing under employment and promoting employment.
- Education, health, PRI sectors and agricultural extension will be thrust areas for employment generation. These sectors faces shortage of staff.
- Village and small scale enterprises (VSE) will have to provide most of the new employment during the 11th Plan, atleast half of which will have to be created in rural areas.
- About 50 million new workers to be absorbed in unorganised non-agricultural sector employment during the Eleventh Five Year Plan.
- National rural employment guarantee programme assures every small household at least 100 days of manual work at minimum wages initially in 200 districts of country.

The special group set up by Planning Commission on "Targeting Ten Million Employment Opportunities per year over the 10th plan period", had recommended possible generation of 49 million jobs over 10th plan period. The 10th Plan document has accepted this and has recommended minimum annual growth rate of 8 per cent of GDP during the 10th Plan and around 9 per cent during 11th plan period.

The Approach Paper for the 11th Plan had focused on providing gainful high quality employment to the additional labour force and had listed the growth of such gainful high quality employment as one of the monitorable objectives of the 11th Plan and beyond. Some of the objectives of the 11th Plan, as approved by the National Development Council for the period 2007-2012 are:

- Accelerate growth rate of GDP from 8 per cent to 10 per cent and then maintain at 10 per cent in the 12th Plan in order to double per capita income by 2016-17.
- Increase agricultural GDP growth rate to 4 per cent per year to ensure a broader spread of benefits.
- Reduce educated unemployment to below 5 per cent.
- Increase real wage rate of unskilled workers by 20 per cent.
- Reduce the headcount ratio of consumption poverty by 10 percentage points.
- Reduce dropout rates of children from elementary school from 52.2 per cent in 2003-04 to 20 per cent by 2011-12.
- Increase literacy rate for persons of age 7 years or more to 85 per cent.
- Increase the percentage of each cohort going to higher education from the present 10 per cent to 15 per cent by the end of 11th plan.
- Reduce infant mortality rate (IMR) to 28 and maternal mortality ratio (MMR) to 1 per 1000 live births.
- Provide clean drinking water for all by 2009 and ensure that there are no slip backs by the end of the 11th plan.
- Ensure that atleast 33 per cent of the direct and indirect beneficiaries of all government schemes are women and girl children.

12.3 Specific Employment/Labour Force Situation of Delhi

While the overall work force participation rate in the country, as per the census 2001, was 30.5 per cent for main workers and 39.2 per cent for main and marginal workers, the corresponding participation rate for Delhi, based on the State sample of the NSSO 2004-05 was found to be 33.5 per cent. The participation rate was much higher for urban areas than for rural. Similarly, it was found that the participation rate for males was much higher compared to the females. In both cases, Delhi seems to be different from the rest of the country. The

TABLE 12.2

Labour Force Participation Rate (LFPR)

Sector	*Year*	*Labour Force Participation Rate (Per 1000 Population)*			
		Male	*Female*	*Persons*	*Sex ratio*
Rural	2004-2005	505	108	328	173
	1999-2000	488	35	286	58
	1993-1994	586	75	398	-
Urban	2004-2005	547	77	336	115
	1999-2000	535	106	340	165
	1993-1994	543	98	350	-
Delhi	2004-2005	544	79	335	118
	1999-2000	530	99	335	155

Source: Directorate of Economics and Statistics, Government of NCT of Delhi, NSS 61st Round.

following Table 12.2 indicates the labour force participation rates by sex and residential status.

Taking into consideration Delhi's current population, the males account for overall 89.6 per cent while the female constitute only 10.4 per cent of labour force. The rural areas of Delhi differ from the country significantly since the population living there is small and the percentage of the small population participating in labour force is even smaller. It also appears that (like in the country as well) the LFPR in Delhi fell during 1999-2000 and 2004-05 compared to earlier years. Similarly, though even in the country the number of females in the workforce was much smaller than males, the proportions were even lower in Delhi. The distribution of workforce by type of activity in Delhi is also different from the rest of the country as can be seen in Table 12.3.

TABLE 12.3

Distribution of Work Force by Type of Activity

Sl. No.	Activity	Work Force	
		Number	Per cent
1.	Agriculture	42898	1.24
2.	Manufacturing	721563	20.92
3.	Electricity, Gas, Water etc.	41998	1.22
4.	Construction	261792	7.59
5.	Trade, Hotel & Restaurants	953622	27.65
6.	Transport, Communication etc.	294517	8.54
7.	Services	886266	25.70
8.	Non-Economic Activities	234263	7.14
	Total	3258667	100.00

Source: Directorate of Economics and Statistics, Govt. of NCT of Delhi, NSS 61st Round 2004-05.

From the Table 12.3, it is clear that unlike at the country level, agriculture sector holds an insignificant proportion of Delhi's workforce while mining accounts for zero. The bulk of workforce of Delhi is in the sectors of trade, hotels, etc. (27.65 per cent) followed by services (25.70 per cent), and manufacturing (20.92 per cent). Even though construction activity in Delhi always remains high, its share in the total workforce is not high. It should also be noted that Electricity etc., accounts for a very small number even though Delhi's consumption of water, electricity and gas etc. may be higher than the rest of the country in per capita terms.

Another significant finding from the employment picture is that the proportion of people in regular wages/ salaries is very high as can be seen in the Table 12.4.

The above Table 12.4 shows that proportion of regular workforce is higher in the urban areas than rural in Delhi. It is also significant that the proportion of females in regular jobs is lower than that of males namely, 63.15 per cent. Unfortunately, the overall significance of this high proportion is marginal since female participation rates in Delhi are rather low. Correspondingly, the proportion of self-employed females is much lower compared to males but even this should not be considered very significant for the same reasons. Finally, reading of various tables from the state sample do raise a doubt that the participation of females might have been underestimated since casual observations indicate that a very large number of housewives do undertake household economic activities even in the urban areas from time to time, including wives of regular government servants. In the absence of any better sources of data however, this observation may be treated as a possibility only.

TABLE 12.4

Status-wise Distribution of Work Force in Delhi

Sl.No.	Description	Rural		Urban		Total		Grand Total
		Male	Female	Male	Female	Male	Female	
1.	Self Employed	96235 (39.95)	17,846 (45.56)	1768307 (41.24)	163148 (33.45)	1864542 (41.17)	180994 (34.35)	2045536 (40.46)
2.	Regular wage/salaried	112510 (46.71)	15732 (40.16)	2220815 (51.80)	316977 (65.0)	23333 (65.0)	332709 (63.15)	2666034 (52.74)
3.	Casual Labourers	32126 (13.34)	5594 (14.28)	298423 (6.96)	7562 (1.55)	330549 (7.30)	13156 (2.50)	343705 (6.80)
	Total	240871 (100.00)	39172 (100.00)	4287545 (100.00)	487687 (100.00)	4528416 (100.00)	526859 (100.00)	5055275 (100.00)

Note: Figures in brackets represent percentages under each category in a column.

Source: Directorate of Economics & Statistics, Government of NCT, Delhi, NSS 61st Round.

It has already been noted that the overall labour force participation rate in Delhi is rather low and has been falling for some years now. However, LFPRs of the population in the 15⁺ age groups is the most appropriate and meaningful indicator, especially in the urbanised and literate metropolis of Delhi. Therefore, the following table 12.5 is important as it gives the LFPRs, classified by age and both sex and residential status. The overall participation rate for this age group 15⁺ is only 46.9 per cent as against 48.3 per cent in the same age group during the previous Round conducted in 1999-2000. While these figures do not make any major difference to the position analysed earlier, it is worth noting that LFPR of urban females in the 15⁺ age group decreased sharply from the previous Round (it was 15.2 per cent against only 10.7 per cent now).

The labour force participation rate of females is much lower as compared to male in rural as well as in the urban areas. The low participation of women in economic activities is attributed to large number of factors such as; social, economic, modernisation of work processes, type of economic activities and also due to inappropriate statistical system of accounting of the labour force participation rates. Women have to bear larger domestic responsibilities. Their working outside home is not appreciated and more so if there are no economic compulsions.

The upgradation in skill requirements due to modernisation of work processes had reduced participation of women in such activities. The contribution of women in economic activities in agriculture sector as well as the unorganised sector is often under estimated. The national accounting system do not consider and evaluate the economic value of the household work primarily taken care of by female community.

TABLE 12.5

Labour Force Participation Rates of Age Group 15 years and above by Sex and Residential Status

Sl. No.	Location	*Labour Force Participation Rate (Percentage to Total)*		
		Male	*Female*	*Total*
1.	Rural	73.35	15.87	47.84
2.	Urban	77.12	10.68	46.82
3.	Total	76.90	10.97	46.87

Source: Directorate of Economics Statistics, Govt. of NCT, Delhi, NSS 61st Round

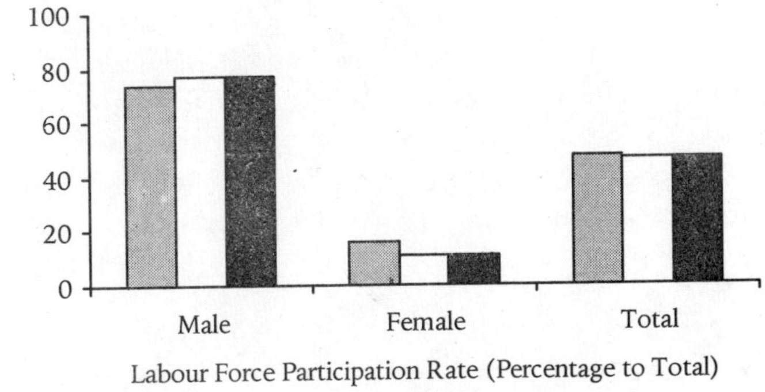

As regards further de-composition of LFPRs in terms of age groups, cross classified by urban-rural, the picture of Delhi is not very different from that of the country as a whole. The highest LFPR in Delhi was found to be in the age group 30-44 followed by the age group 45-59. It is, however, significant to note that the participation rate in the age group 0-14 is well about one per cent.

TABLE 12.6

Distribution of Labour Force Participation by Age group, Sex and Residential status

Age Group	*Rural*		*Urban*		*Total*	
	Male	*Female*	*Male*	*Female*	*Male*	*Female*
0-14	0.00	0.0	1.60	0.00	1.50	0.0
15-29	68.55	7.42	63.65	10.95	63.93	10.76
30-44	94.71	29.72	99.33	11.62	99.05	12.75
45-59	86.47	12.97	93.08	13.05	92.83	13.04
>=59	21.59	0.00	29.81	3.08	29.09	2.95
Total	50.45	10.80	54.69	7.72	54.44	7.90

Source: Directorate of Economics & Statistics, Government of NCT, Delhi, NSS 61st Round.

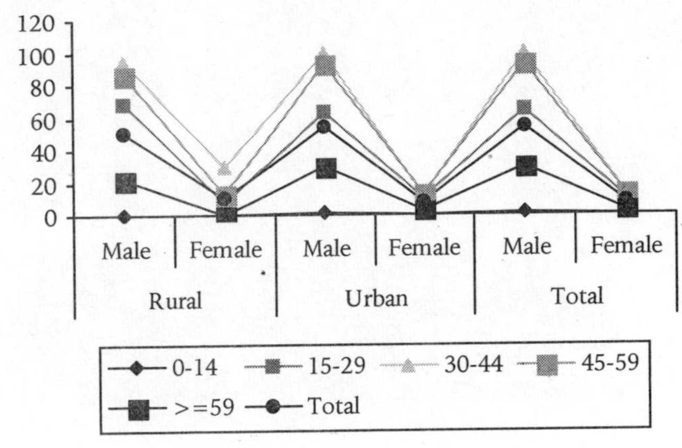

The Delhi Government documents have also cross-classified the LFPRs by sex as well and it was found that (as different from males), the LFPR for females was the highest in the age group of 45-59 years whereas it was much higher for males in the earlier age group of 30-44 years. This may be seen in Table 12.7.

TABLE 12.7

Rates of LFPRs by Age Groups and Sex

Age Group	*Male*	*Female*
0-14	1.50	0.00
15-29	63.93	10.76
30-44	99.05	12.75
45-59	92.83	13.04
>=59	29.09	2.95
Total	54.44	7.90

Source: Directorate of Economics and Statistics, Govt. of NCTD – NSS 61st Round

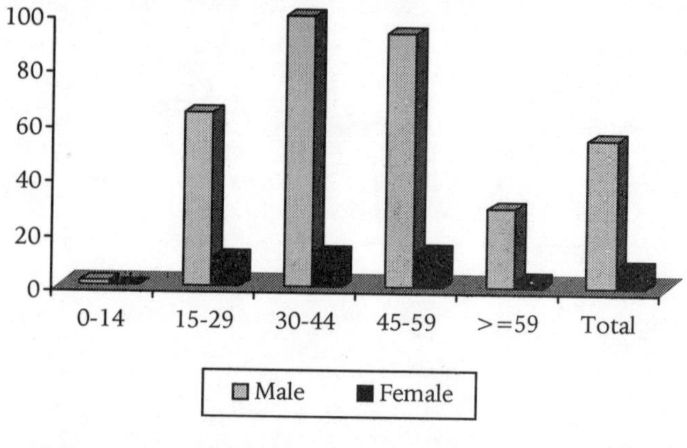

The All India picture of LFPRs for the entire population can be seen in Table 12.8.

TABLE 12.8

State/UT-wise Labour Force Participation Rates

S.No.	*State/UT*	*Rural*	*Urban*
1.	Andhra Pradesh	548	406
2.	Arunachal Pradesh	462	323
3.	Assam	401	362
4.	Bihar	320	290
5.	Goa	385	398
6.	Gujarat	516	387
7.	Haryana	434	353
8.	Himachal Pradesh	540	474
9.	J&K	422	348
10.	Karnataka	546	397
11.	Kerala	448	440
12.	Madhya Pradesh	461	357
13.	Maharashtra	527	399
14.	Manipur	445	358
15.	Meghalaya	527	387
16.	Mizoram	523	390
17.	Nagaland	537	385
18.	Orissa	476	386
19.	Punjab	458	385
20.	Rajasthan	463	359
21.	Sikkim	453	383
22.	Tamil Nadu	534	434
23.	Tripura	373	414
24.	Uttar Pradesh	373	342
25.	West Bengal	389	410
26.	A&N Islands	471	416
27.	Chandigarh	399	358
28.	D&N Haveli	533	466
29.	Daman & Diu	403	428
30.	Delhi	317	351
31.	Lakshadweep	408	363
32.	Pondicherry	495	373
	All India	446	382

Source: Directorate of Economics and Statistics, Govt. of NCTD, NSS 61st Round

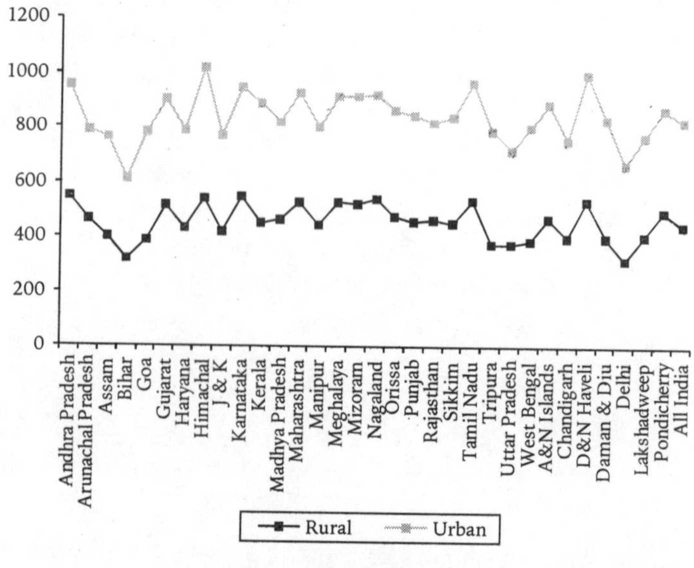

As mentioned earlier, Delhi had rather low LFPRs (61st Round) but in the case of females, there are some States/UTs which have even lower LFPR in urban areas. However, it must also be stated that most of these states (with lower LFPR for urban areas) are more rural in character and therefore, comparison with them is not very relevant.

12.4 Unemployment

The Delhi Government documents provide detailed workforce participation rates cross-classified by sex, residential status and even age groups. In this chapter the focus is on *unemployment* which can be derived by subtracting workforce participation rates from the corresponding LFPRs. As indicated earlier, these rates are rather high for Delhi, for both sexes, particularly females. Since the population estimates used by various Delhi Government documents differ from each other, the following Table 12.9 indicates the overall unemployment rates by sex and residential status, as proportions of the corresponding estimates of population.

TABLE 12.9

Unemployment Rates as Percentage of Population Estimates

S.No.	Item	Estimated Percentage		
		Rural	Urban	Delhi
(a)	Male	4.70	2.79	2.89
(b)	Female	10.26	4.12	4.61
	Total	**5.52**	**2.93**	**3.07**

Source: Directorate of Economics and Statistics, Govt. of NCT of Delhi, NSS 61st Round.

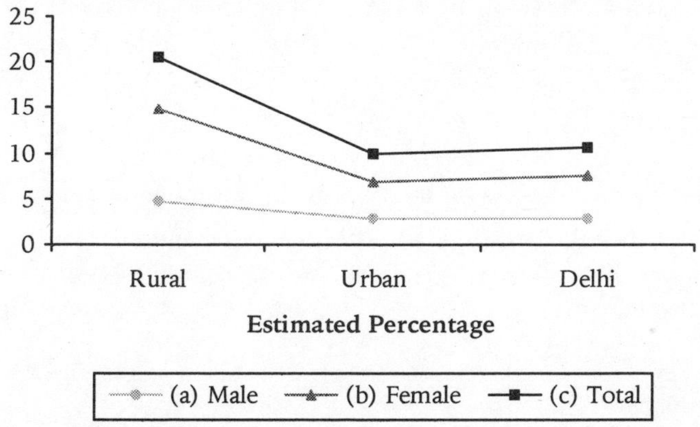

However, a better measure and the one used by Planning Commission defines the rate of unemployment as the proportion of estimated number of persons unemployed to the number of persons in the labour force, not in the population. Taking this definition, estimates of unemployment, cross-classified by sex and residential status are shown in Table 12.10.

Table 12.9 at macro-level is not good enough for manpower planning purposes and therefore, Table 12.10 has been prepared, giving the rates of unemployment by age group and sex-wise.

TABLE 12.10

Proportion of Unemployment by Age Groups and Sex

Age Group	Estimated Rates of Unemployment		
	Male	Female	All
0-14	3.68	0.00	3.11
15-29	87.30	100.00	89.27
30-44	8.29	0.00	7.00
45-59	0.73	0.00	0.62
60 & above	0.00	0.00	0.00
All	100.00	100.00	100.00

Source: Directorate of Economics & Statistics, Govt. of NCTD, NSS 61st Round

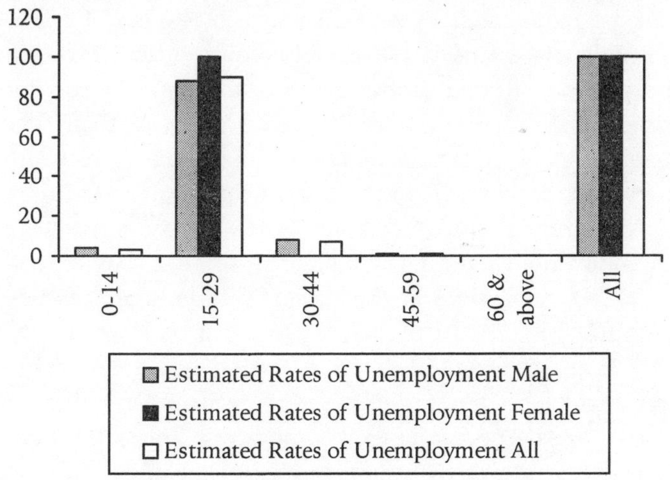

Table 12.11 has been prepared by cross-classifying the same rates by age groups and residential status.

TABLE 12.11

Proportion of Unemployment by Age Groups and Residential Status

Age Group	Estimated Rates of Unemployment		
	Rural	Urban	All
0-14	0.00	3.43	3.11
15-29	66.95	91.73	89.27
30-44	33.05	4.12	7.00
45-59	0.00	0.68	0.62
60 & above	0.00	0.00	0.00
All	100.00	100.00	100.00

Source: Directorate of Economics and Statistics, Govt. of NCTD-NSS 61st Round

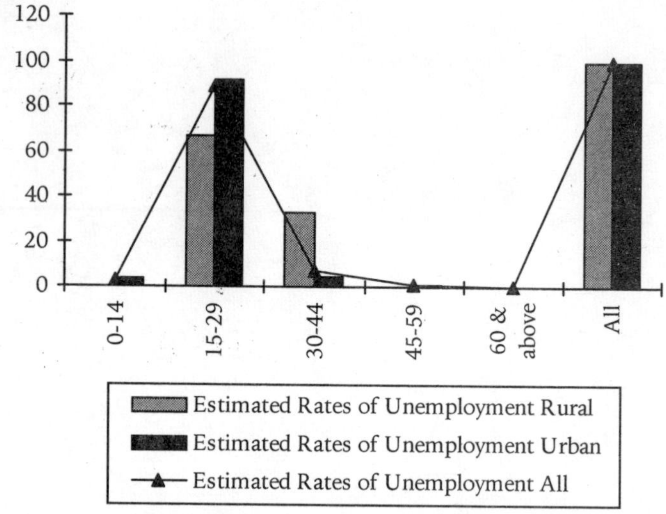

Some special features of unemployment in Delhi can now be mentioned. Firstly, the rates in respect of males are higher from the latest Round compared with those in the previous Round, both in urban and rural areas. For some 'categories, they have increased by more than four times. This is also true in respect of females which are higher in both rural and urban Delhi. It is even more significant to note that in some age groups, the unemployment rate for young males (15-29) exceeded 87.30 per cent while in the case of females they reached over 100 per cent in the same age group (age group 15-29). These are not tolerable in any well-ordered society and could be a pointer to severe youth unrest unless of course, female population gets withdrawn from the labour force (persuade them to join full time education!). To an extent, this has already been happening in the entire country and is one of the explanations for reduction in the LFPRs noticed in the latest Round. Alternatively, the recent migrants from outside Delhi could give up on Delhi (Discouraged!) and return to their native places.

The state sample obtained by the educational attainments of the unemployed persons, in the expectation that comparison of unemployment rates for different qualifications will indicate what type of education helps in getting employment or otherwise. However, the data analysed indicates eight levels of education, from illiterates to post-graduates etc. For example, the highest number of the unemployed is in the primary education level. The next number is that of those who have at least middle level education while the category of illiterates has relatively lower number of persons. These figures need to be compared with the number of persons in the labour force in the relevant categories.

The Directorate of Economics and Statistics document based on the 61st Round analysis has also given data on the number of persons by educational attainments for the entire population. If a similar table on Labour force were made available, it would have been possible to get real Rates of Unemployment, as per Planning Commission definition.

12.5 Alternative Estimates of Educated Unemployment

The Employment Exchanges in Delhi register local job-seekers approaching them for assistance in locating employment. As mentioned earlier, Delhi Territory is almost fully covered by a various Employment Exchanges, approachable by the rural people also, unlike in the country as a whole. Even more, there is evidence to indicate that the rural people do actually use the Employment Exchanges and register themselves there. Therefore, it is useful to look at the number of persons registered in Delhi's Employment Exchanges, cross-classified by levels of education attainment and other variables. Table 12.13 gives the number of persons

TABLE 12.12

Distribution of Unemployed Persons by Levels of Education Attained

Educational Level	*Rural*			*Urban*			*Total*		
	Male	*Female*	*Total*	*Male*	*Female*	*Total*	*Male*	*Female*	*Total*
Illiterate	2705	-	2705	7632	957	8589	10337	956	11293
Primary	3984	2202	6186	48761	5780	54541	52745	7982	60727
Middle	136	75	211	28690	3443	32133	28826	3518	32344
Secondary	2716	-	2716	10554	333	10887	13270	333	13603
Higher Secondary	2344	2202	4546	15431	1977	17408	17775	4179	21954
Diploma Certificate	-	-	-	3582	2622	6204	3582	2622	6204
Graduates	-	-	-	12123	3020	15143	12123	3020	15143
Postgraduates	-	-	-	384	2846	3230	384	2846	3230
Total	**11885**	**4479**	**16364**	**127157**	**20977**	**148135**	**139042**	**25456**	**164498**

Source: Directorate of Economics and Statistics, Govt. of NCTD- NSS 61st Round.

registered with Delhi Government Exchanges from the year 1990 onwards.

TABLE 12.13

Employment Exchange Registrants by Levels of Education

Year	*Below Matric*	*Matriculates & Under-Graduates*	*Graduates & Post-Graduates*	*Other Diploma Holders*	*Total Applicants*	*Annual Growth Rate*
1	*2*	*3*	*4*	*5*	*6*	*7*
1990	211920	399522	215166	16717	843325	—
1991	226267	426948	218666	19005	890886	5.64
1992	238243	429027	221568	18154	906992	1.81
1993	232306	432871	223382	19476	908035	0.11
1994	227948	482905	239024	20237	970114	6.84
1995	243905	522291	245919	21705	1033820	6.57
1996	255457	545221	258337	22085	1081300	4.59
1997	251514	562633	261433	21873	1097453	1.49
1998	273364	559068	273476	22280	1128188	2.80
1999	253606	496918	194908	20689	966121	(-)14.37
2000	238386	528554	203081	20646	990667	2.54
2001	230695	562781	193941	18825	1006242	1.57
2002	233695	594999	210548	19763	1059005	5.24
2003	226663	535623	216917	19774	1098977	3.77
2004	160434	294928	164815	16023	636200	-42.11
2005	186662	296527	196537	14126	673852	5.92

Note: Overall increase in respect of registered unemployed persons during the 12 years (1990-2002) was 25.57 per cent

Source: Directorate of Employment, Govt. of NCTD

Table 12.13 indicates that the educated categories (Matric or 10⁺) account for a very large proportion of the total registrants in Employment Exchanges. In some Exchanges they constitute more than 80 per cent of the total. It also shows that the number of registrants in Delhi has been going up over the last decade and the figure of 6.7 lakhs in 2005 represents a very high proportion of the labour force of Delhi. It is no more as easy to register in Delhi's Employment exchanges as it was earlier and people from outside Delhi have to give evidence of their stay in Delhi before they get registered. Despite these precautions, it is likely that there would be some registrants who do not really live in Delhi but have given Delhi's address and shown evidence of their stay here. During the year 2004, there was sharp decline in total number of registrants in the employment exchanges. This was due to scrutiny of lapsed registrations. Lapsed registrations were weeded out from employment exchange during this particular year.

The number of registrants in Delhi has been basically swelling on account of the fact that a large proportion of them are not exactly unemployed but are seeking change in their current employment i.e., being dissatisfied with their current occupational status they want to rise higher which is perfectly legitimate for every person. The number in the Employment Exchange Live Register also tends to go up because several persons succeed in registering themselves in several Employment Exchanges despite steps taken by the Directorate of Employment of Delhi to stop it (lack of full computerisation!). There is another category of registrants who are full-time students who could be treated as out-of-labour-force but even in this categorisation there are problems since many students are not serious—they join various courses of study but continue searching jobs. This again should be considered a legitimate activity by job-seekers but it is very difficult to separate such non-serious students and cull them out from the list of job-seekers (live register). In any case, they have to be treated as under-employed, if not totally unemployed.

At the National level, the DGE&T, Ministry of Labour had got a survey conducted to throw light on activity status of job-seekers/registrants. Though the report is rather old, the field work having been done in 1988 at all-India level, it still gives some interesting and useful facts, as may be seen below:

(i) The Live Register showed increased preponderance of those without professional/ technical training or previous experience—increase being from 74.1 per cent in 1973 to 82.3 per cent in 1988. The proportion of female registrants inched up in the country, being 21.4 per cent in urban and 14.1 per cent in rural. The proportion of educated job-seekers (Matric & above) also increased during the 15 years period from 52.1 per cent to 62.5 per cent.

(ii) The percentage of registrants on the Live Register for three years or more, increased from 15.3 to 45.1 during the 15 years and about 3.5 per cent registrants had multiple registration. 32.2 per cent of job-seekers were found employed under "usual status" classification while 11.9 per cent were pursuing further studies. The corresponding proportions on the "current weekly status" were not very different.

(iii) The percentage of employed (usual status) registrants ranged between 40 and 50 in Delhi alongside Goa, Gujarat, Haryana etc. The percentage of employed (usual status) literates but-below-Matric was 55.3. Amongst the professional graduates/postgraduates, this percentage ranged well above 50 for doctors, dentists and engineers. The percentages of technically qualified but-below-degree were 42.2 for engineering diploma, 39.5 for ITI pass-outs and 38.7 for apprentices. On the other hand, agriculture and animal husbandry graduates had much lower rates. About half the employed registrants had salaried/regular wage jobs while one-fifth were self-employed. Only 10 per cent students indicated that they would not give up study if offered jobs from Employment Exchanges.

While some highlights of the National level picture can be relevant to Delhi, no similar detailed survey of Employment Exchange registrants has been conducted in Delhi recently. In its absence, it is not safe to extrapolate the proportions obtained from the National level survey conducted by the Ministry of Labour in 1988 wholesale, to the Delhi NCT.

The Delhi Government documents have used the Principal usual status concept i.e., basis of major time spent during the reference period of the previous 365 days in their tables indicating absolute number of persons in the labour force and actual persons unemployed. However, the Planning Commission preferred to use the concept of "current daily status" in the 10th Five Year Plan, as different from earlier Plans where the basic measures of employment and labour force etc., were based on Principal usual status concept. Therefore, there is a difficulty in comparing Delhi figures with the earlier Plan documents. In this Chapter however, there has not been too much comparison of Delhi's data based on the state sample and that of the country and various states, based on the central sample. As the situation of Delhi is different from the rest of the country, use of the state sample data for Delhi is relevant and useful.

12.6 Rural/Urban Development Plan

12.6.1 Integrated Rural Development of Villages (IRDV)

Rural development implies economic betterment of people as well as social transformation. In order to ensure economic development for rural poor, greater participation of community in developmental process, decentralisation of planning, enforcement of land reforms and greater access to credit are envisaged by the Government of NCTD. This was manifested through a number of programmes originally initiated by the Ministry of Rural Development, GOI and expected to reach out to the poorest and the most disadvantaged sections of society. These programmes are meant to support the rural poor to improve their socio-economic conditions to a level where they could sustain themselves without depending further on government schemes. Based on programme evaluation and experience of implementation, there have been continuous changes in these rural development schemes. Although the programmes target the population below poverty line, special emphasis has been placed on the depressed sections of society.

Rural area of Delhi is thinly populated comprising 53.81 per cent of geographical area but having 6.99 per cent population as per 2001 census. This rural population is relatively well off in terms of income compared to neighbouring states of Haryana, Uttar Pradesh and Rajasthan. The land price in these areas has shot up due to unabated growth and expansion of urban areas. While DDA is active in acquiring land for upcoming urban population in future, the demand for urban amenities and infrastructural development is rising among the rural masses who have adopted more or less, urban ways of living. These rural areas are in outer Delhi, in five Community Development Blocks namely, Alipur, Kanjhawala, Najafgarh, Mehrauli and Shahdara. They have enough space to accommodate large number of industries, institutions and people. Therefore, this region can meet the twin objectives of meeting the growing needs of infrastructure and growing aspirations of the people for employment, entrepreneurship and urban amenities.

Rural Development Department deals and three plan schemes:

1. Delhi Rural Development Board Schemes
2. MMP Schemes and
3. Grants-in-Aid to MCD Schemes

The main scheme of the Rural Development is Integrated Development of Rural Villages (IDRV). The provision of funds in IDRV for the last two years and projected for the next 5 years given in the Table 12.14.

TABLE 12.14

Provision of Funds in IDRV

Year	*IDRV/DRDP(Rs.Crore)*
2004-05	27.00
2005-06	27.50
2006-07	30.00
2007-08	35.00
2008-09	40.00
2009-10	45.00
2010-11	**50.00**

Source: Department of Rural Development, Delhi.

The information given in the table reveals that there has been net increase of about 85 per cent during 2004-05 to 2010-11 in IDRF Scheme in the State. Under the plan schemes the following works are undertaken:

A. IDRV envisages:

1. Construction of approach roads
2. Construction of link roads
3. Development of ponds in rural villages
4. Development of parks, *Vyagan Shalas* in rural villages
5. Development of cremation grounds
6. Development of play grounds
7. Fencing of *Gram sabha* land
8. Construction of drainage mainly to protect rural areas from flooding.

B. Mini Master Plan (MMP) envisages:

Repair and maintenance of MPCCS

C. Grants in Aid to MCD

Grants in Aid to MCD is provided for Development of Rural Villages and Construction of Rural roads:

1. Construction of approach roads
2. Construction of link roads
3. Construction of internal gullies (street in rural villages)

12.6.2 Urban Development

The urban population dwells in a small geographical area of 46.19 per cent but constitute 93.01 per cent of the total population of Delhi. The growth rate and density of this part is exceptionally high due to natural growth rate plus inward migration, thus hampering the city development. The problems so created include shortage of dwelling units, mushrooming growth of *jhuggis*, encroachment of public land, expansion of unauthorised colonies and creation/expansion of slums etc. They have put pressure on limited civic services and created major bottlenecks in orderly development of Delhi, like in other mega-cities. Another important dimension of such unplanned human settlements is availability of cheap labour, especially for informal industries, construction, domestic services, transport, trade etc. Their productive role in city development needs to be recognised. They are the poor who are leading life, often below the poverty line. The rapid in-migration and the consequent development of unplanned human settlements in Delhi have been accepted as a spontaneous process of urbanisation and urban geographers, planners and thinkers alike have accepted them as an inalienable part of the city. Therefore, there is a need to adopt a balanced approach to meet the growing needs and aspirations of all the residents of Delhi.

Keeping in view the peculiar and gigantic problems of Delhi, several measures had been initiated including environmental improvement of urban slums, provision of various facilities in urbanised villages, additional facilities in resettlement colonies, development of regularised unauthorised colonies etc. On the environment front, a number of steps had been taken like mechanisation of conservancy and sanitation services, environmental improvement through horticulture works, construction of public and community centers of mass scale in different substandard localities of this territory etc.

In order to wipe out poverty from Delhi, a number of centrally sponsored and state schemes have been launched in Delhi. They can be grouped under two heads:

a) Self-Employment Programme; and

b) Wage Employment Programme.

a) Self-Employment Programmes

The Self-employment programmes were initiated by a number of departments i.e., Industries, Urban Development and Department for the Welfare of SC/ST/OBC etc. Assistance was offered to all segments of people including educated-unemployed youth, women, urban poor living below the poverty line etc. Some of these programmes are:

i) Society for Promotion of Self-Employment

This Society for self-employment was set up in 1986 by the Industries Department, Government of Delhi and became functional with effect from 1 April 1987. The main objective of the society was to provide short term training in technical trades to the educated unemployed youth of NCT of Delhi to enable them set up their own ventures or get gainful employment after completing the training. The Society has two training centres and the following courses are offered:

TABLE 12.15

The Courses Conducted by Society for Promotion of Self-Employment

S.No.	Name of the Trade	Duration of Training in Months	Intake Capacity (Yearly)	Eligibility	No. of Persons Trained
1.	Repair of Radio & TV	6	100	10th Pass	835
2.	Repair & Maintenance of Household Electric Appliances/Fittings	6	50	10th Pass	838
3.	Refrigeration & Air Conditioning	4	150	10th Pass	1419
4.	Plumbing	4	75	8th Pass	483
5.	Fashion Designing (for girls only)	12	75	12th Pass	1153
6.	Carpentary*	-	-	-	9*
	Total		**450**	-	**4737**

Note: * Trade discontinued w.e.f. Oct.31, 1999.
Source: Society for Promotion of Self Employment, Delhi.

The Society trained 4,737 persons up to March 31, 2001. So far till February 2006 society has trained 6033 candidates in different courses. Society has a target of giving training to 300 more candidates in 2007-08.

(ii) Assistance to Women Entrepreneurs

This programme provides financial assistance/ incentives to fresh women entrepreneurs for setting up tiny industries in Delhi. Women in the age group 18-35 years with minimum qualification of matriculation are eligible to avail its benefits with preference to those who have acquired skills by way of inheritance or developed skills by way of education, professional qualifications etc. There are reservations for SC/ST, weaker sections, widows (especially war widows) etc.

Financial assistance upto Rs.50,000 is given for fixed and working capitals. In case of general category, the grant component has been 15 per cent the rest to be provided in the form of loan while, in the case of disadvantaged categories the grant has been 25 per cent. Repayment of loan has to be completed within 5 years with a grace period of 1 year. In the 10th Five Year Plan (2002-2007), 90 women entrepreneurs were given such assistance. During the first year of 11th Five Year Plan i.e., 2007-08, Rs.10 lakh has been approved for the purpose.

(iii) Apart from aid, assistance and awards some useful training and capacity building is also being made by the Government of NCTD for productive employment. For providing quality training, collaborative steps have been taken e.g., foreign collaboration from Denmark and Italy i.e., Tool Room Training Centre (TRTC), High-Tech Vocational Training Centre (HTVTC) etc. It was proposed to train 3000 candidates by TRTC and 1800 candidates by the HTVTC during the period 2002-2007. An amount of Rs.400 lakh is earmarked for TRTC and Rs.200 lakh for HTVTC during the year 2007-08.

(iv) Prime Minister's Rozgar Yojana (PMRY) launched on 2 October 1993 is one of the major self-employment programmes of the Ministry of Industry, GOI for providing self-employment to educated youth. During 1994-95, the earlier scheme of Self-Employment for the Educated Unemployed Youth (SEEUY) was merged. The main objective of PMRY is to provide financial and technical support to educated unemployed youth setting up self employment micro enterprises in industry or business or service sector and now covers the whole of the country. Banking support for PMRY is being coordinated through a State level Bankers Committee chaired by the SBI and mainly the nationalised banks that provide loans.

The eligibility for PMRY is 18-35 years in general with a 10 years relaxation for SC/STs, ex-servicemen, physically handicapped and women. The Minimum educational qualification is 8th passed. However, preference is given to those who have skills for any trade. The income of the beneficiaries should not exceed Rs.40,000 per annum. The project cost has been fixed at Rs.1 lakh for business sector, Rs. 2 lakh for other activities and the loan is of composite nature. The subsidy is fixed at the rate of 15 per cent of the project cost, subject to ceiling of Rs.7,500 per entrepreneur. The training and other operational expenditure has to be covered within a ceiling of Rs.2,000 per case. There is also a provision to give preference to weaker sections including women. The scheme has 22.5 per cent reservation for SC/ST and 27 per cent for other backward classes.

This important scheme has been evaluated twice at National level but Delhi was not included in either sample survey and the peculiar problems of Delhi unemployed educated youth have not been addressed so far. For example, the beneficiary-family income ceiling of Rs.40,000 p.a. is too low to be useful to unemployed educated youth.

(v) The SJSRY scheme is being implemented in Delhi through urban local bodies and community organisations. A ratio of 75:25 funding has been adopted between the Centre and states for the scheme. Rs.95 lakh has been approved for Annual Plan 2007-08 for this scheme. Training will be given to 2000 beneficiaries during the year 2007-08.

(vi) The Urban Self-Employment Programme is being made on whole town basis with special emphasis on urban poor clusters living below the poverty line in which a provision of 30 per cent for poor women and 3 per cent for disabled poor is made whereas the percentage reservation for SCs and STs is as per their population in local population.

USEP in Delhi has three parts *viz.*:

a) Assistance to the urban poor beneficiaries for setting up gainful self-employment like auto servicing, petty business and manufacturing;

b) Assistance to group of urban poor for setting up gainful self employment ventures, also called the Development of Women and Children in Urban Areas (DWCUA) and,

c) Training of beneficiaries/potential beneficiaries and other persons associated with the Urban Employment Programme for updating/acquisition of vocational and entrepreneurial skills. Persons educated only upto class IX are considered under this programme.

Under DWCUA, a group society consisting of at least 10 urban women, is entitled to a subsidy of Rs.1.25 lakh or 50 per cent the cost of the project, whichever is less, for thrift entrepreneurial activities. Appropriate training for upgrading/acquiring vocational and entrepreneurial skills of the beneficiaries is also part of this programme. The unit cost allowed for training is Rs.2000 per trainee and the training period varies from two to six months, subject to a maximum of 300 hours. During 2006-07, 475 beneficiaries were given training under DWCUA Scheme. Two DWCUA groups and three Thrift and Credit Societies were formed during 2006-07.

(vii) Loans in Collaboration with Banks/NSFDC:

The main objective of this centrally sponsored scheme is all-round economic uplift and development of SC/STs population living below the poverty line by providing them loan and subsidy. It has several components:

Training for self-employment of SC/STs includes training in computers as well as other trades for all those educated upto class XII. This scheme proved successful and productive in creating employment opportunities to SC/ST youths. A new dimension has been included in the training to upgrade the skills and tradition of shoe artisans i.e., computerised Footwear Designing.

Loans and subsidy are being provided to the better off sections of SC & ST youths of Delhi to purchase light commercial vehicles to help them become self-employed. Similarly, provision has been made for purchasing CNG three-wheelers/scooters.

Under the Centrally sponsored programme to liberate and rehabilitate the scavengers and their dependents from their existing hereditary obnoxious and inhumane occupation and engage them in alternative dignified occupations, the scheme is being implemented by DSCFDC and the 10th Plan target proposed is to benefit 600 scavengers, mostly through financial assistance but some also through training.

During first year of 11th Plan i.e., 2007-08, Rs.900 lakh has been earmarked for financial assistance to SC/ST/ OBC/Minority/*Safai Karamchari*/Handicapped for self-employment training through DSCFDC.

b) Wage Employment Programme

Urban Development Department of the GOI had started an Urban Wage Employment Programme to provide wage employment to beneficiaries living below the poverty line by utilising their labour for construction of socially and economically useful public assets. This programme applies to such urban local bodies whose population is less than 5 lakh and is not applicable to Delhi.

The cosmopolitan character of Delhi has put it into a unique situation where orthodox wage employment programmes do not work. Moreover, ample scope for regular or part-time employment is available in Delhi in almost all sectors. It does not mean that the aspiration for regular jobs is irrelevant—rather aspirations for white collar jobs are rising continuously, which are very difficult to meet by any Government.

12.6.3 Expenditure on Rural Development Programme

In the 10th Five Year Plan (2002-2007), the following action plan was proposed by the NCTD and approved by the Planning Commission:

1. Optimum utilisation of assets already created in rural villages in the form of multi-purpose community centre.

2. Construction of a network of approach road/link road to facilitate better movement of people of rural areas and transportation of goods and services in rural areas.

3. Prioritisation of development work of growth centres/points in already identified areas.

4. Expeditious acquisition of land for growth centers at Alipur and Chhawala.

5. Development of ponds in rural areas with a view to provide better civic and hygienic conditions.

In the 9th Five Year Plan the acquisition of land for several growth centers was completed and land handed over to the implementing agency. Similarly, financial provisions were made for the construction of Bawana Sports Complex, many Multi purpose community centers and development of Trunk infrastructure.

During first year of 11th Five Year Plan, i.e., the year 2007-2008, a provision of Rs.250 lakh was made for implementing the Mini-master plan. Further, provision of Rs.4750 lakh has been made for the integrated development of rural villages. This scheme mainly covered the construction of link roads, approach roads, developments of cremation grounds and some other basic amenities. Another provision of Rs.500 lakh has been made for the protection of *Gaon Sabha* facilities and infrastructure relating to Panchayati Raj institutions, including construction and repair of *chaupals, panchayat ghars*, wells, *phirni*/inner roads, drainage, street lights, ponds and other essential public utilities. An outlay of Rs.7500 lakh has been made for developmental work within rural villages for making *katcha* roads *pucca* and metalling them with pavements. The metalled and premixed roads in certain cases require to be raised further due to high berms and high plinth level of the houses constructed later on. Many small drains are to be made bigger. Some *phirnies* requires to be strengthened. Since sewerage system is not available in villages, it is proposed to construct *Sulabh shouchalayas* in about 50 per cent of the villages in the first phase so as to make the village environment healthier.

A noteworthy provision of Rs.7500 lakh has been made for rural roads in the Annual Plan 2007-2008, including improvement and widening of rural roads. Another provision of Rs.10 lakh has been made for safe energy (through DEDA) in rural areas—the main objective of the Integrated Rural Energy Programme being to meet cooking and lighting needs of the villages.

TABLE 12.16

Outlays in the 10th Five Year Plan and Annual Plan 2007–2008 of Select Employment Oriented Programmes

(in Rs. Lakh)

S.No	*Programmes on Rural Development*	*10th Five Year Plan*	*Annual Plan 2007–2008*
1.	The Mini Master Plan	5000.0	250.0
2.	Integrated Development of Rural Villages (IDRV)	11000.0	4750.0
3.	Strengthening and modernisation of the Panchayat Unit and its function.	4000.0	500.0
4.	Rural Roads	26000.0	7500.0
5.	Consolidation of land Holdings	25.0	5.0
6.	Grant-in-Aid to DEDA	100.0	10.0
7.	Others	200.0	120.0

Source: Annual Plan 2007-08 (Volume-I) Govt. of NCTD, 2007.

References

Directorate of Economics & Statistics, NCTD (2002). *Employment and Unemployment Situation in Delhi.*

———. (2007). *Employment and Unemployment Situation in Delhi.*

Institute of Applied Manpower Research, Delhi (2001). *Impact Assessment of Rural Development Programmes in Baharaich District of Uttar Pradesh.*

———. (2002). *Manpower Profile.*

———. (2005). *Manpower Profile.*

Govt. of India (2003). *Annual Report 2002-2003*, Ministry of Labour, New Delhi.

———. (1990). *Survey on Activity Status of Jobseekers Registered with the Employment Exchanges*, Ministry of Labour, New Delhi.

———. *National Sample Survey Organisation 61st Round (2004-05)*, "Employment and Unemployment Situation in India", New Delhi.

———. *National Sample Survey Organisation 61st Round* (1999-2000), "Employment and Unemployment Situation in India", New Delhi.

———. *Tenth Five-year Plan* (2002-07). New Delhi: Planning Commission.

———. *Eleventh Five-year Plan Approach Paper* (2007-2012). New Delhi: Planning Commission.

Govt. of NCTD, *Annual Plan 2003-04*, Volumes I&II. Planning Department.

———. *Annual Plan 2007-08*, Volumes I&II. Planning Department.

———. *Economic Survey of Delhi, 2005-06*, Planning Department.

Craftsmen Training and Employment (2003). Resource Development Centre, New Delhi,

Aggarwal, Garima (2003). "Relocation of Industries in NCR" (Unpublished); Thesis presented for fulfilling Post Graduate Diploma in SPA, New Delhi.

Kumar, Barun (2003). "Political Dialectics of Slums in NCT Delhi" (unpublished), a paper presented in National Association of Geographers India in December 28, 2003.

This chapter has been prepared by Institute of Applied Manpower Research, team associated with the preparation of the chapter includes Shri M.C. Verma, Consultant, Smt. Madhu Srivastava, Head (E&U Studies Unit), Shri U.S. Bhandari, SRO, Shri S.K. Yadav, SRO, Shri J.S. Chauhan, RA and Shri Barun Kumar, RA. Study team members were highly benefited from the comments and suggestions of Professor Ajeet Narain Mathur, Director, IAMR in preparation of the chapter.

Chapter 13

Science & Technology—IT and Biotechnology

13.1 Framework

In the context of development policy, planning and programmes, it is preferable to categorise Science and Technology-IT& Biotechnology (S&T-IT & BT) activities in the National Capital Territory of Delhi (indeed in any region) under the following three categories, each category of activity has a distinct purpose and related policy, planning and implementation mechanism.

Category 1

S&T-IT&BT Education including technical training. The purpose of this activity is to generate adequately trained human resource. This is a legitimate S&T activity but is usually subsumed under education.

Category 2

Research and Development in S&T-IT&BT; the purpose of this activity is to generate new knowledge. Knowledge that can potentially feed into a variety of socio-economy sectors as well as into the education sector (often this alone is narrowly taken to represent the totality of S&T)

Category 3

Use of S&T-IT&BT in socio-economic sectors for example in health and other services and industry. This is essentially adaptive S&T-IT&BT; this is S&T-IT&BT activity targeted to immediate applications to enhance the efficacy and efficiency of services and products or leverage commercial activity by utilising relevant results of S&T-IT&BT.

Category 3 activities (adaptive S&T-IT&BT) undertaken by socio-economic development agencies contribute directly to development of a region but are often ignored in accounting for S&T activities.

Each of the three categories of activities is important for overall development of a region and although the three are interlinked, the institutional and agency channels for each are different.

For example, educational and technical agencies have no mandate of providing products and services or engage in industrial policy and planning or in R&D (for example schools or poly-techniques) nor do they have the mandate of providing health and social services, but they provide S&T trained human resource that gets utilised by those engaged in Category 2 and 3 activities.

Similarly agencies in Category 3 have the prime responsibility for development of industry, trade and commerce or for providing health, transportation and other services or engage in governance; they use S&T without necessarily engaging in teaching and education and the research carried out by them is essentially for adaptation of new knowledge. These agencies are quite competent at understanding and applying S&T-IT&BT. Such competences are of prime importance and can not be overlooked in development plans.

The reason for treating R&D as a separate Category under 2 is because many R&D institutions and agencies do not engage directly in either education or in socio-economic activity, but they feed into both.

From the perspective of policy, planning, and implementation of S&T-IT&BT that can contribute to socio-economic development, it is critical to strengthen inter-linkages between the three categories of activities.

13.2 Organisation of S&T Activities

Organisationally and institutionally, activities in all the three categories are channelled in Delhi through three types of agencies:

- The Central government.
- Government of the National Capital Territory of Delhi (GNCTD), MCD and NDMC.
- Private sector including NGOs.

Major thrust of GNCTD is on Category 3 activities that is science and technology programmes that form part of plans of industry and other socio-economic sectors. It is however important to note that the region has vibrant S&T-IT&BT activities in all the three categories.

An examination of status of totality of S&T-IT&BT activities in Delhi and of 10th Five Year Plan and programmes of the GNCTD brings out a clearer picture of who is doing what; that is which agency channel is taking initiative for what type of S&T-IT&BT activity in Delhi.

13.2.1 An organisational overview

Table 13.1 is a summary overview of the channel-wise S&T-IT&BT activities in Delhi under the three categories.

TABLE 13.1

An Organisational Overview

Channel and its main Programme Emphasis/ Thrust	*S&T-IT&BT Education & Training*	*R&D*	*S&T-IT&BT Applications in Social & Economic Sectors*
	Category 1	*Category 2*	*Category 3*
GNCTD	1. School level Science including IT. 2. Technical and vocational training in high technology including IT related CAD/CAM. 3. Popularisation of IT. 4. Lately also in higher science, IT and Biotechnology education.	Lately R&D in Energy, Environment, Biotechnology and IT.	1. Applications of S&T-IT&BT in rural development, energy, small scale, industry, environment, health, and other services. 2. IT and Biotechnology based enterprises.
Central Government	Higher Education in Science, Technology, IT and Biotechnology.	All areas of R&D covered by laboratores in Delhi belonging to CSIR, ICMR, ICAR, DRDO in addition to strong R&D groups in IIT and Universities in Delhi.	Supporting role through testing centres, prototype centres and dealing with specific issues as and when required.
Private sector & NGO	1. Private sector in School Level science education. 2. NGOs in ITand school science education especially for under-privileged.	Marginal	NGOs: S&T for development of rural areas, in environment and for women enterprise. Private Sector in IT marketing and consultancy.

13.3 Description of S&T-IT&BT Programmes in Delhi

13.3.1 S&T in Education

- **Schools**

Initiatives include, strengthening of science education in schools, introduction of computer as an elective subject and making teaching of science compulsory up to secondary level.

The Centre for Science Education and Communication of the University of Delhi and the State Council for Educational Research and Training have collaborated in preparing science text books.

A number of NGOs are also active in school science teaching through programmes such as 'Joy of Learning'. National Council for Educational Research and Training headquartered in Delhi is another resource for school science education.

- **Higher Education**

Delhi has a strong conglomeration of undergraduate and post graduate science and engineering education (including Biotechnology and IT) supported by the Centre comprising the departments in the University of Delhi, Jawaharlal Nehru University, Jamia Millia Islamia University, Hamdard University, Indian Institute of Technology and Delhi College of Engineering.

New initiatives of GNCTD include Netaji Subhash Institute of Technology and Guru Gobind Singh Indra Prastha University and plans for Cyber Asia Networking University.

Taken together, Delhi has a substantial and growing infrastructure for higher science, engineering and technology education.

- **Technical Education**

GNCTD accords a high priority in the State plans to training of technicians in vocations ranging from computer, electronics to civil and mechanical engineering.

In addition to Polytechnics, Industrial Training Institutes, training in Footwear and Garment Technology mention should be made of High Technology Vocational Training Centre for reverse engineering and CAD/CAM and the Centre of Art in Tool Engineering/Computer Aided Tool.

As parts of Delhi are classified as rural, training in handloom technology, handicrafts, innovative agricultural technologies, and in the use of non conventional energy devices also come under the category of technical training programmes.

13.3.2 Science Popularisation

Nehru Planetarium at Teen Murty and the National Science Centre, Pragati Maidan are two excellent locations for popularisation of science, especially amongst children in addition to Railway Museum.

Periodic events by some NGOs also add to science popularisation activities. Occasional lectures at the India International Centre and lectures in halls and conference venues by eminent scientists also add to this activity, though catering to a limited audience.

Setting up of a science park is a new initiative of GNCTD in addition to mass awareness campaigns for popularising of IT.

13.3.3 Research & Development

The National Laboratories of CSIR (6), Indian Agricultural Research Institute of Indian Council of Agricultural Research, Solid State Physics Laboratory of Defence Research and Development Organisation, Institute of Immunology of Department of Biotechnology carry out front line R&D.

Specifically in Information Technology, mention should be made of IBM Research Centre at IIT and in Biotechnology of the International Centre for Genetic Engineering. Strong R&D laboratories in these areas also exist in Universities and IIT located in Delhi.

R&D initiatives taken by GNCTD include setting up of Biotechnology R&D Centre, promotion of research in IT, research in rural energy systems by Mahatma Gandhi Institute for Integrated Rural Energy Planning and Development, R&D Centre in Pollution Monitoring and Setting-up of Remote Sensing and GIS Centre.

13.3.4 S&T-IT&BT in Socio-Economic Sectors

One of the major initiatives by GNCTD is in the applications and utilisation of IT; computerisation of the functioning of *Gaon Sabha*, functioning of all the departments, Agriculture Market Information Network, IT in all branches of transport services, modernisation of MCD, IT in Survey, Statistics and Planning functions.

In terms of IT based industry, High Technology City for IT and Software Multimedia Park are the two major initiatives. Strengthening of infrastructure for IT related industry in the Industrial Estates and Flatted Factory Complexes is also part of promotion of IT industry in Delhi.

(It is to be noted that in IT, the majority of private sector in Delhi is essentially to promote the business of their parent IT industries located outside Delhi).

Biotech Based industrial development is reflected in the setting up of Biotechnology R&D Centre in partnership with Industry and in the strengthening of infrastructure for Biotech industry in the Industrial estates and in Flatted Factory Complexes.

Other science and technology intensive socio-economic programmes are:

- Agriculture Plant Protection, Integrated horticulture and Vegetable development, Seed Testing Laboratory and Floriculture development
- Programmes for Non-conventional sources of energy
- Development of manufacturing and small scale industry (for example introduction of computer aided design and manufacturing)

It is seen that programmes of almost all the sectors of Delhi development have inbuilt component of S&T in them, comprehensive understanding of S&T-IT&BT in Delhi's development can not emerge by treating Science and Technology- IT& Biotechnology (S&T-IT & BT) as a separate sector of development or group of activities.

Financial resources that go into this totality of S&T have been collated from the different chapters of Plan documents are given in the next section.

13.4 Financial Resources

13.4.1 S&T &Environment Sector

The Annual Plan 2003-04 of National Capital Territory of Delhi has a separate chapter on S&T including Environment with the following budgetary allocations:

Main Budget Head	*9th FY Plan outlay (Lakh) % of Total Plan*	*9th FY Plan Expenditure (Lakh) % of Total Plan*	*10th FY Plan outlay (Lakh) % of Total Plan*
Science Technology & Environment	11200.00 (0.7%)	1906.74 (0.14%)	5500.00 (0.2%)

The above table would give the impression that in so far as financial allocations are concerned, GNCTD accords a low priority to S&T. This may be a misleading conclusion. As the major thrust of GNCTD is on IT and Biotechnology programmes that are embedded in the development programmes of various socio-economic sectors, it was necessary to examine programmes under each of the development sectors and delineate in them the S&T-IT&BT component and allocations thereof.

13.4.2 Comprehensive S&T Outlays Culled out from all the Developmental Sectors

Table 13.2 is based on culling out from the Tenth Five Year Plan document of GNCTD, allocations to S&T-IT& Biotechnology related activities mentioned under the programmes of various sectors.

TABLE 13.2

Tenth Plan Allocations for S&T-IT&BT

Programme 2003-04	*Tenth Plan Outlay Source: NCTD-Annual Plan 2003(Rs. in Lakh)*
Information Technology Computerisation of: *Panchayat* (Gaon Sabha Land Records), Registrar Cooperative societies, Transport Dept., Urban development, MCD Records of Industry Dept, Secretariat LAN, Directorate of Consumer Affairs Agricultural marketing network Soft Ware Multimedia Park (high-tech City for IT Infrastructure for IT industry in Industrial Cyber Asia Networking University Internet Information Kiosks (spreading IT awareness) & Mass awareness of IT, R&D in IT (encouraging research by teaching community)	6082
Biotechnology Biotechnology R&D Centre Infrastructure for Biotech Industry in Industrial Estates and Complexes (estimated)	310
Applied S&T related components Science Park, Technical know how for Plant protection (Agriculture), Technology for horticulture & vegetable development, Seed Testing Laboratory, Popularising Innovative agriculture, New technology in floriculture, M.G Inst. for integrated rural energy (R&D), Delhi Energy Development Agency (Biogas, Solar, Smokeless *Chullahs*, Integrated Rural Energy Programme)	1841
Science & Technology Entrepreneurship Park	200
Technical Education High-Tech Vocational training, (Reverse engineering, CAD/CAM), Tool room Training Centre(Centre for Computer Aided Tool design),Other technical education /training programmes	11200
Higher S&T & Research Creation of Centres of Advanced Studies, Research & Extension ServicesPolymer Science, Environment Eng., Manufacturing & automaton, Research in IT, Energy Sciences, Fibre Optics.	300
Total 10th Plan Outlay for S&T	19933 (0.72%)

13.5 Assessment

13.5.1 Focus and Thrust of GNCTD

The planned thrust of GNCTD is rightly on S&T-IT&BT programmes that contribute directly to social and economic development namely on application oriented activities. Allocated funds are a good 0.72 per cent of total plan outlay.

R&D programmes of GNCTD not directly linked to the immediate socio-economic returns however need better and stronger linkages with R&D institutions of central agencies.

13.5.2 Planned Impact of S&T-IT& Biotechnology

These are summarised below along with brief assessment comments in italics.

- Creating technically trained human resource

The objective is to provide trained workforce to industrial complexes and flatted factory complexes. Training in modern techniques such as CAD/CAM and IT, in addition to the conventional techniques implies modernisation of existing or setting up of new units.

Manufacturing units being private ventures, there is a need to match the technical training facilities with the demand profile. Joint assessment with private ventures would be useful

- Improvement of rural parts of Delhi

Another development goal is to apply and adapt technologies for development of rural areas.

Human resource and intuitional strategies for adaptation and diffusion these technologies need attention. Combination of formal S&T institutions, Management Schools and NGOs appears necessary.

- IT and Biotechnology industrial units

Being highly competitive sectors, market niche of these units will have to be carefully examined. Government has to play a proactive role to form consortia of different stake holders.

- Introduction of IT in schools.

Extensive programme of providing hardware and soft ware is being taken up.

Maintenance and upgradation of the systems need attention. Often procurement of hard ware and software programmes and setting-up of web sites receive attention but in the absence of a well thought out plan and strategy for the updating of content and for the utilisation of network, returns on investments are not realised.

- E-Governance

Computerisation of government records and hosting the information on websites is an extensive programme.

While outsourcing of jobs by line departments facilitates creation of distributed data bases, their coordination for single window delivery to citizens requires a strong core unit within the government.

From the citizen's point of view, convenient access to Kiosks by public and the user-friendlyness of these sites needs continued assessment for feed back and improvement. In addition, model strategies need to be in place for the continued financial sustainability of 'kiosks'.

13.6 Suggested Vision and Initiatives

13.6.1 Delhi as IT Integrated Region : Technology Mission Approach

Technology Missions are planned and implemented as end to end programmes from R&D to actual delivery to achieve a desired development goal

A Technology Mission towards making Delhi an IT Integrated Region could start by integrating several IT supported services at present being planned and executed as separate programmes by individual agencies into a single major mission.

Difficulties in inter-departmental/agency coordination are often cited as a major hurdle in planning and execution of integrated programmes.

The experience of Technology Missions at National Level however confirms that once a major target is commonly shared between different agencies, coordination and integration problems get resolved.

Following example illustrates the point:

Goal is to set up an integrated computerised transport system for the region

This would mean integration of several components like registration of vehicles, testing and issue of driving licence, movement of vehicles, traffic control, ticketing and other passenger services into one major programme. Experience of using IT effectively in each and every component is available in the country, budgetary allocations are also available; these individual elements can be converted into a single Technology Mission programme.

The region has the requisite capability from R&D to actual delivery; the R&D strength of central institutions, adaptive capabilities of GNCTD institutions and the implementation strengths of line departments.

13.5.2 Missions for Rural Areas

Effective Technological interventions specific to the rural region can be sourced from Central government and GNCTD R&D and technical institutions. Targeted and integrated region specific intervention Plans are required.

Competent private and government aided management and business schools as also NGOs in Delhi are assets that can be utilised to implement these interventions. Business and management schools located in and around rural areas can become effective intuitional nodal points for integrated planning and managing the execution of S&T interventions in neighbourhood rural area jointly with concerned departments/agencies of GNCTD. Sustained and accountable NGO input can then be obtained by attaching NGOs to a local established institution for the purpose of specific Mission programmes.

Chapter 14

Labour Management and Manpower Planning

14.1 Literacy

Delhi is a member of a select group of States/Union Territories, where literacy rate crossed 80 per cent in 2001. Rank-wise, Delhi stands at fifth position in literacy –seventh in male literacy and fifth position in female literacy. In the last 20 years, there has been an appreciable rise in literacy at all levels. The overall literacy rate in 1981 was 71.93 per cent, which improved to 81.82 per cent in 2001, while for males rate went up from 79.28 per cent in 1981 to 87.37 per cent in 2001. In case of females, the improvement was even greater, from 62.57 per cent in 1981 to 75 per cent in 2001. Considering the cosmopolitan character of Delhi, the literacy rate is however, below expected lines—it was lower than Kerala (90.92 per cent) and Mizoram (88.49 per cent). These changes are clear from Table 14.1.

Efforts are continuing to involve the communities to achieve total literacy. Special stress has been laid on the education of the deprived groups such as women, rural people and socially/economically backward sections of the society. Besides economic support to students from poor families, welfare schemes are intended to encourage retention and check dropouts in schools e.g., Mid-day meals and stipends. The Government of Delhi has also started implementing the Central sponsored "Sarva Shiksha Abhiyan" from Tenth Five Year Plan.

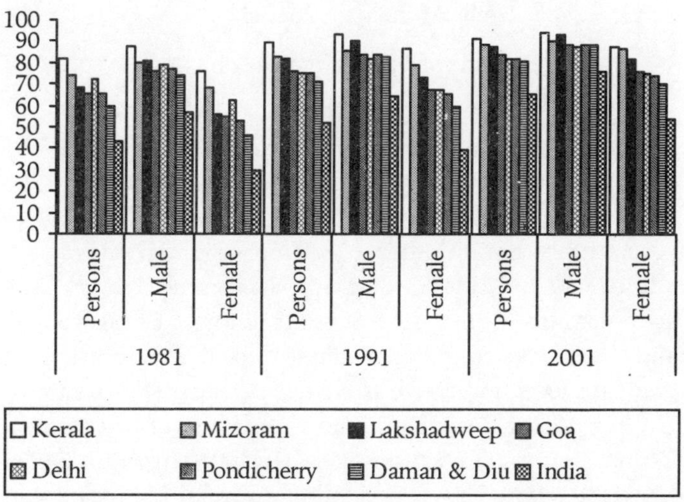

TABLE 14.1

Literacy Rates in Select High-performing States/Union Territories

	States/UTs	*1981*			*1991*			*2001*		
		Persons	*Male*	*Female*	*Persons*	*Male*	*Female*	*Persons*	*Male*	*Female*
1.	Kerala	81.56	87.74	75.65	89.81	93.62	86.13	90.92	94.20	87.86
2.	Mizoram	74.26	79.37	68.60	82.87	85.61	78.60	88.49	90.69	86.13
3.	Lakshadweep	68.42	81.24	55.32	81.78	90.18	72.89	87.52	93.15	81.56
4.	Goa	65.71	76.01	55.17	75.51	83.64	67.09	83.32	88.88	75.51
5.	**Delhi**	**71.93**	**79.28**	**62.57**	**75.29**	**82.01**	**66.99**	**81.82**	**87.37**	**75.00**
6.	Pondicherry	65.14	77.09	53.03	74.74	83.68	65.63	81.49	88.89	74.13
7.	Daman & Diu	59.91	74.45	46.51	71.20	82.66	59.40	81.09	88.40	70.37
	India	43.56	56.37	29.75	52.20	64.13	39.29	65.38	75.85	54.16

Source: Register General of India, *Census of India* for relevant years.

14.1.1 Education

A long but sequential study in which student acquires wide knowledge about the discipline and academic competence is known as General Education. In Technical Education/Training, a person acquires skills to apply theoretical knowledge into practical terms. Both kinds of education have importance of their own. General education up to Class XII is essential for entry into professional courses like Medical/Engineering and up to Class X for joining ITIs and equivalent courses.

14.1.2 General Education

General education has various stages i.e., Pre-primary, Primary, Middle, Secondary, Senior-secondary, Graduate and Postgraduate levels and above. There are four Government agencies, which have the responsibility of General Education in Delhi, namely;

1. Directorate of Education, Govt. of NCT of Delhi
2. Municipal Corporation of Delhi
3. New Delhi Municipal Council
4. Directorate of Higher Education, Govt. of NCT of Delhi.

Pre-primary and primary education is basically the responsibility of local bodies i.e., MCD and NDMC. The Directorate of Education, Delhi, primarily looks after education from middle to senior secondary level. In addition, Government of Delhi has converted its 343 schools into Composite Schools known as Sarvodaya Vidyalayas, starting from class I to XII. Education at graduate level and above is shared between Directorate of Higher Education, Delhi and the University Grants Commission, Government of India (through Delhi University/JLN University, other universities located in Delhi and the new GGSIP University).

MCD has a wide network of Primary schools (more than 1800) where 9 lakh students are enrolled. Besides Primary schools, NDMC also runs 6 middle, 11 Secondary and 6 Senior Secondary Schools in its area. Apart from this, a large number of autonomous bodies and private organisations are engaged in imparting education at elementary and secondary level.

The enrollment in Government, Government-aided and Unaided Schools are given below under Table 14.2.

For promoting education at Graduate level and above, the responsibility is shared between several Universities located in Delhi and the Directorate of Higher Education,

TABLE 14.2

Enrollment in Govt., Govt.-Aided and Unaided Schools

(In Lakh)

School	2000	2001	2002
A. Government	8.40	8.57	8.74
B. Aided	1.55	1.60	1.68
C. Unaided	10.02	10.72	11.47
Total	19.97	20.89	21.89

Source: Directorate of Education, Govt. of NCT of Delhi.

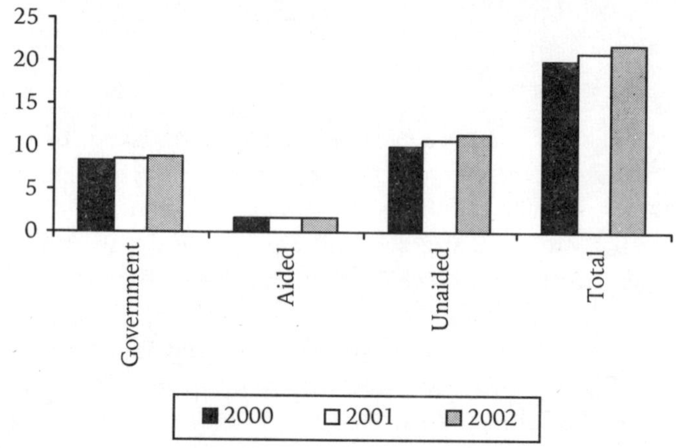

Delhi. At present, there are 28 Delhi Government sponsored colleges affiliated to Delhi University, 16 of which are being funded by UGC and Delhi Government on sharing basis and the remaining 12 colleges funded by Delhi Government on 100 per cent basis. Due to pressing demands to open more colleges including the private sector, a Delhi State Guru Gobind Singh Indraprastha University was established in 1998. This University, in its role of acting as a nucleus for dissemination of knowledge and as a facilitator, introduced new programmes of studies at Graduate and Post-graduate level in engineering, medicine, management and law etc. It has affiliated 47 self-financing institutions (privately managed) and eight Government managed institutions including the Mahila Institute of Technology.

The total enrolment in General Education in Delhi was 19.79 lakh persons which was 1.01 per cent of the total enrolment in general education in India as on 30 September 2000. The enrolment in Delhi was quite high compared to the national level in percentage terms at all levels (except primary level), especially at graduation and above. The same pattern was noticed in enrolment of boys and girls, as can be seen in the three tables presented below:

TABLE 14.3

Total Enrolment in General Education by Levels, in Delhi and India, 2000-01*

(In thousands)

State	*Pre-primary*	*Primary*	*Middle*	*Secondary*	*Senior Secondary*	*Graduate & Above*	*Total*
Delhi	52 (2.63)	996 (50.33)	475 (24.0)	200 (10.11)	107 (5.41)	149 (7.53)	1,979 (100)
India	2,658 (1.34)	113,827 (58.06)	42,810 (21.84)	18,993 (9.69)	9,851 (5.02)	7,937 (4.05)	196,045 (100)

Note: * As on Sept. 30, 2000

Figures shown in the parenthesis are percentages of the row totals.

Source: Ministry of Human Resource Development, Govt. of India.

TABLE 14.4

Total Enrolment of Boys in General Education by Level in Delhi and India, 2000-01*

(In thousands)

State	*Pre-primary*	*Primary*	*Middle*	*Secondary*	*Senior Secondary*	*Graduate & Above*	*Total*
Delhi	27 (2.67)	501 (49.50)	250 (24.70)	104 (10.28)	51 (5.04)	79 (7.81)	1,012 (100.00)
India	1441 (1.27)	64,006 (56.44)	25,289 (22.30)	11,623 (10.27)	6,077 (5.36)	4,961 (4.37)	113,405 (100.00)

Note: * As on Sept. 30, 2000

Figures shown in the parenthesis are percentages of the row totals.

Source: Ministry of Human Resource Development, Govt. of India.

TABLE 14.5

Total Enrolment of Girls in General Education by Level in Delhi and India, 2000-01*

(In thousands)

State	*Pre-primary*	*Primary*	*Middle*	*Secondary*	*Senior Secondary*	*Graduate & Above*	*Total*
Delhi	26 (2.68)	495 (51.08)	226 (23.32)	96 (9.91)	56 (5.78)	70 (7.22)	969 (100.00)
India	1,177 (1.42)	49,821 (60.29)	17,521 (21.92)	7,370 (8.92)	3,775 (4.57)	2,976 (3.60)	82,640 (100.00)

Note: Figures shown in the parenthesis are percentages of the row totals.

Source: Ministry of Human Resource Development, Govt. of India.

Directorate of Education, Delhi has made a comprehensive plan to revamp general education, including improvement in quality of education, encouragement of education among weaker sections of society, economic support to students from poor families, efforts to achieve total literacy etc. Delhi Government has planned to cover all government schools under computer education programme. In order to nurture talented students from Government Schools, 10 Model Schools i.e., Pratibha Vikas Vidyalayas have been opened where students from Government schools are admitted through competitive examinations. Apart from awards and incentives to students as well as teachers, special attention is being paid to weaker sections of society.

In the MCD schools, free textbooks and uniforms are supplied to all students in primary classes. To encourage education among girls, free transport and stipends are paid to girls in rural areas and unauthorised colonies. Besides economic support to students from poor families, welfare schemes are intended to encourage retention and check dropouts in schools. Mid-day meals and stipends are direct incentives to promote attendance in the schools.

As regards the scheme '*Sarva Siksha Abhiyan*', a Mission Director has been appointed in Directorate of Education and a Society registered to implement it specifically. The Mission has prepared a Plan of action and strategy to ensure that all children in the age group 6-14 years are brought into mainstream education. The strategy includes institutional reforms, sustainable financing, institutional capacity building, community-based monitoring, and priority in education for girls, focus on special groups etc. Delhi Government's Bhagidari scheme, which envisages Government and community partnership in governance, will be used for this programme. Delhi Government has also decided to constitute Vidyalaya Kalyan Samitis (VKS) for schools representing local RWAs, PTAs, and NGOs etc. to bring academic, administrative and infrastructural improvements in the schools.

14.1.2 Technical Education/Training

There is a need to translate the imperatives of modern manufacturing processes, state-of-the-art technology, diversified technological changes and complex training requirements resulting from these changes into the planning process. Therefore, objectives of the technical education system in Delhi are to produce manpower needed to meet diversified requirements of the economy. There are four major Government agencies, which provide various types of technical education/training in Delhi. These are as follows:

1. Directorate of Training and Technical Education.
2. Delhi College of Engineering.
3. Netaji Subhash Institute of Technology and,
4. College of Pharmacy/Institute of Pharmaceutical Sciences Directorate of Training and Technical Education has the responsibility of imparting education/training at diploma and certificate levels. This Directorate, apart from seven

Polytechnics, is also running eight ITIs. For imparting technical education at under-graduate and postgraduate levels, there are 4 high-level institutions under the Delhi Government. In addition, there are many others run by private sector and affiliated to the IP University.

In the 10th Five Year Plan, the Government of NCTD had taken steps to strengthen the technical infrastructure, programmes related to Continuing Education and Entrepreneurship Development, strengthening of Community Polytechnics, interaction between institutes and industry, new courses in emerging technologies, short-term computer-based and other courses in existing institutions etc. The Community Polytechnics seek to provide non-formal training in basic skills, knowledge and correct attitudes to adopt any occupational activity leading to self-employment.

Continuing Education & Entrepreneurship Development Programme aims at extending evening diploma courses in a number of Polytechnics/ITIs and encourage entrepreneurship development. Similarly, technical personnel from industry can acquire short-term training in the institutions to improve career prospects.

14.1.4 Vocational Education and Training

Vocational education is provided in General Education institutions after the secondary stage, with duration ranging from 1 to 3 years. The target of Delhi Government is to diversify 30 per cent students at +2 stage towards vocational courses. At school level, both formal as well as non-formal vocational education is provided. The formal vocational education aims firstly, at linking education with productivity; secondly, to make students more employment-worthy and capable of seeking self/wage employment; thirdly to provide essential technical knowledge and to imbibe skills; fourthly, to attract sizeable number of students to various vocational courses as to reduce the rush for higher General Education; and finally, to meet the middle level manpower needs for the growing economy.

Non-formal vocational education programme is also conducted by the Directorate of Education, which aims at catering to the educational needs of the unemployed, dropouts and neo-literates who cannot attend classes regularly. The principals of the schools coordinate the programme with the help of regular school teachers who maintain the accounts of raw materials etc. and have the responsibility for day-to-day functioning of the programme.

14.2 Financial Provisions for Education Sector

14.2.1 General Education

There are four agencies namely; MCD, NDMC, Directorate of Education and Directorate of Higher Education through which educational schemes/ programmes are carried out.

TABLE 14.6

Financial outlays for Tenth Five-Year Plan and Annual Plan 2007-08

(In Lakh)

Sl. No.	*Agency/Department*	*Tenth Five-year Plan (in Lakhs)*	*Annual Plan (2007-08)*
1.	MCD	70,000.0	15,300.00
2.	NDMC	1,400.0	200.00
3.	Directorate of Education	88,600.0	28,000.00
4.	Directorate of Higher Education	24,000.0	10,500.00
	Total	184,000.0	53,915.00

Source: Annual Plan of NCTD, 2007-08.

These agencies have prepared comprehensive plans to revamp education in Delhi. A number of Schemes/ Programmes have been made by them to provide quality education to all sections of people as detailed below:

14.2.1.1 Directorate of Education

In the Tenth Five Year Plan, some new programmes were added and a sum of Rs.88,600 lakh was approved. A sum of Rs.28,000 lakh was approved for Annual Plan 2007-08.

14.2.1.2 Directorate of Higher Education

Directorate of Higher Education has a number of programmes to give impetus to higher education in Delhi. The allocation of funds for annual plan 2007-08 was approved of Rs.10,500 lakh.

14.2.1.3 Municipal Corporation of Delhi

The Municipal Corporation of Delhi has the responsibility to nurture education upto primary level. The allocation of funds for annual plan 2007-08 was approved at Rs.15,300.0 lakh which includes approx. Rs.8,400 lakh for capital works.

14.2.1.4 New Delhi Municipal Council

NDMC is engaged mainly in primary education but it has some schools at higher levels also. The schemes adopted by the NDMC deal with universalisation of education, expansion and improvement in quality of education etc. The allocation of funds for Annual Plan 2007-08 was approved at Rs.200 lakh.

14.2.1.5 Netaji Subhash Chandra Institute of Technology

A financial provision of Rs.6500 lakh for the 10th Five Year Plan and Rs.3800 lakh for Annual Plan 2007-08 has been made for this Institute.

14.2.1.6 College of Art

A financial outlay of Rs.700 lakh has been made for 10th Five Year Plan and Rs.250 lakh for the Annual Plan 2007-08.

14.2.1.7 Directorate of Technical Education

Directorate of Technical Education has approved a number of schemes and the outlays on these schemes allocated about 6015 lakh for the year 2007-08.

14.2.1.8 Delhi College of Engineering

An allocation of 2900 lakh has been made to Delhi College of Engineering for Annual Plan 2007-08.

14.2.1.9 Growth of Private Institutions

Apart from Government and Government-aided Schools, many autonomous bodies and private organisations are engaged in imparting education at elementary, secondary and senior secondary levels and are monitored under the provisions of the Delhi School Education Act 1973 and Rules. The number of public-private institutions was quite high in 1998-1999 and 1999-2000, involving 39.81 per cent and 43.76 per cent schools respectively. (This came down to 23.13 per cent in 2000-01 due to addition of Primary/Nursery MCD and NDMC schools).

As regards enrolment, the share of such institutions was 50.18 per cent of the total enrolment in 1999, which improved to 52.40 per cent in 2001.

Public-private institutions in primary education covered 73.68 per cent of Primary schools in 2001-02 the proportion of these institutions was lower at secondary levels, namely 46 per cent in 2001-02. At the Senior Secondary level, the proportion of such institutions was only 28 per cent in 2001-02.

The rate of growth in such Middle schools was 16.96 per cent during 1999-2000 over the previous year. This declined to 0.64 per cent during the next year but picked up to 3.18 per cent during 2000-01 to 2001-02. The growth rate at Secondary levels was 19.18 per cent during 1999-2000 over the previous year. This became negative (-1.15 per cent) during the next year 2000-01 but improved appreciably to 8.14 per cent during 2001-02. In case of Senior Secondary level, the number of private institutions shot up by 22.8 per cent during 1998-99/1999-2000 but the growth rate came down to 2.61 per cent during 1999-2000/2000-01. The growth remained at smaller level (2.22 per cent) during 2000-01/2001-02.

14.2.1.10 Management of Education

There are four major agencies/departments through which general education is provided in Delhi. Pre-primary and Primary education is mainly the responsibility of the local bodies i.e., MCD and NDMC. The Directorate of Education, Government of Delhi, primarily looks after middle, secondary and senior secondary education. Finally, the Directorate of Higher Education and other Universities of Delhi provide education at university level. Similarly, there are five major agencies, which provide various types of technical education. Directorate of Training and Technical Education provides training at diploma and certificate levels. The other four agencies, namely Delhi College of Engineering, Netaji Subhash Institute of Technology, College of Art and College of Pharmacy provide technical education at under-graduate and postgraduate levels.

To raise the enrolment and effective management of schools, Delhi Government's Bhagidari scheme, which envisages Government and community partnership in the governance, carried out activities to ensure primary education for all children in age group of 6 to 14 years. Government has also decided to constitute Vidyalaya Kalyan Samiti (VKS) for schools, representing local RWAs, PTAs, NGOs, etc. with a view to bring improvements in academic administration and infrastructure under the Bhagidari Scheme.

The scheme of Sarvodaya Schools was implemented to provide quality education to children for I to XII classes under one roof, as is often done in the public-private schools. Primary classes were also introduced in existing schools, wherever necessary. In order to bring the dropouts back into the mainstream, Delhi government also provided educational facilities to the children of age group 11-14 and 14-17 years.

Correspondence courses at school level was another programme to cater to the needs of schools drop-outs, housewives, personnel of armed or para-military forces who are posted in far-flung areas. The experiment was found successful for all those who were not able to study and adjust themselves at the pace of regular classes in schools.

In order to improve results in Government schools, the management of academic and other resources of public-private schools was used in Government Schools as well. The exposure to the public-private school atmosphere was provided to the teachers of Government schools. Some public schools have offered to exchange their faculty with Government schools to use their materials, library etc. Assistance of NGOs is also proposed to be taken by the Government wherever it is felt that NGOs could provide additional inputs to school education.

14.3 Manpower Planning

Delhi has fairly literate population and the total literacy rate has increased considerably over the years. The progress has been even more for females. The enrolment in schools has also been very good though the Government figures do not always show how much better Delhi is compared to the entire country. Part of the explanation for this could be the existence of large number of schools outside the Government, many of which are unrecognised for quite a few years. The existence of private institutions both in general education and technical training/education has been quite significant, but all of it does not get reflected in official figures immediately. In fact, the number of unrecognised technical training institutes providing courses of various durations, for different educated groups and of different levels of quality is quite large but most of them are not visible in Government records. There have been hardly any surveys to locate such institutions to understand their contribution to the development of manpower in the city. Very often, it is the institute, which approaches the Government and makes itself visible before any Government functionary comes to inspect it. Unlike Delhi School Education Act, 1973 that covers all types of schools imparting general education; there is no similar law for technical training institutions.

The provision of schools, technical institutes and even higher education colleges/polytechnics is driven more by social demand from the students and families rather than from the industry or service sector organisations. Such demand has been steadily going up, not necessarily for satisfaction of demands generated by various types of employers in the city. In fact, the Government employment is controlled more and more by recruitment boards and commissions rather than through employment exchanges network, which at one time was supposed to provide names for all middle and lower level vacancies (e.g. group C and group D posts) where they could favour local candidates. On the other hand, the recruitment boards almost always have to advertise in the national dailies and therefore, the applicants can come from far and wide. Since Delhi does not have a domicile of its own, it cannot stop people from outside the city to apply for all levels of jobs, whether in public or private sector.

In these circumstances of a very open economy, it is not practical to follow the classical methods of manpower planning in the city. Rather the evolution of labour markets within the city have followed the normal dictates of a liberal economy where demands for manpower vary from time to time and the qualifications/experience required for filling in such positions also change quite often. Therefore, it appears that the educational system has to be much more flexible after the minimum number of years in school, say 8 in the country but more or less 10 years in Delhi. Beyond these minimum years of schooling, flexible methods of training and education should be available in the city, as has been happening without Government backing over the last two decades. The flexible system would also include open schooling at various levels as for example, the National Open School. At a higher level, the Indira Gandhi National Open University also provides flexibility to the types of courses liked or required in the city. Correspondence course are the other means of providing flexible education to those who need it at various levels for various groups of people. The Delhi Government departments however, find it difficult to keep up with such changes in the demands for different types of courses and they are not even able to collect full information about such institutions, the variety of courses, the levels of competence provided and the problems which individual seekers of education/training run into when what they hoped for from a particular institutions is not delivered. Therefore, there is always a demand to regulate these components of the education/training system, outside the reach of Delhi School Education Act, 1973. It is difficult to see how the Government could regulate such a complex web of educational and training institutions, which do provide something useful to the local people even though they may not be fully satisfied with the quality provided or fees charged from them.

14.4 General Remarks

While the growth of employment in the organised sector has gone down all over the country in recent years, the story in Delhi is slightly better. Because of the entry of new types of services included IT-related services, the job opportunities have continued to grow in Delhi side by side with rise in the rates of unemployment of several age-sex-educational categories. The explanation for this discrepancy lies in the fact of continued in-migration into Delhi with migrants having practically all levels of education. In fact, it can be stated without any contradiction that more and more educated persons from relatively less developed states of Uttar Pradesh, Bihar, Jharkhand, Madhya Pradesh, Rajhasthan, Chhattisgarh, and Uttaranchal look forward to getting a job in Delhi. It is also true that due to changes in the employee complexion due to influx of people of neighbouring States, it has also changed the character of various occupations in Delhi and perhaps increased their skill or technology contents. Unfortunately, no hard data on these matters is readily available but it is likely that individual researchers have done research on related issues in limited areas. A lot of changes are visible even to the naked eye and the same have been confirmed in discussions with senior officers of various departments, especially those of labour and employment.

Since Delhi's economy is becoming more and more service oriented and since unionisation is traditionally low in the services sub-sectors, especially the high-end modern services, it has also been noticed that there are not many demonstrations of discontent among employees in Delhi. The latest one-day strike of employees of public sector banking and insurance companies had little to do with the conditions in Delhi and practically everything to do with points of ideology or policy at the national level. In any case, there has been a shift out of large number of older industries; especially textiles and many of them have been closed for good. A recent study by Ms. Garima Aggarwal on the impact of the Industrial Relocation in NCR on the workers so displaced gives a range of figures about closure of major industries and makes an assessment of about one lakh workers displaced in the period 1996 onwards. It also gives a figure of about 7,000 units/ industries closed during the same period due to relocation of industries as a result of intervention of higher Courts. The study in fact, goes on to paint a grim picture for the future by indicating that workers likely to be displaced by relocation of industries could amount to as much as 10 lakh. However, not much supporting data is available from discussions or observations to validate this large figure of 10 lakh workers. It is also to be noted that despite the loss of jobs by about one lakh workers over the last 7 years or so, there has not been much of discontent, strikes and violent demonstrations in Delhi. Perhaps, the main reason for this lies in the fact that most of such workers belong to other states in the country and their incompetence to formally plant their roots in Delhi.

It is well known that most of the casual workers in Delhi Small Scale Industries are still "outsiders" and therefore, they are under pressure to return to their places of origin in the neighbouring states in case a downturn occurs in industry. Even otherwise, there has been a general decline in labour militancy and workers are more worried about losing employment rather than to fight for increase in remuneration or better working conditions through the trade unions. Since the new jobs in the 'sun-rise' industries are hardly unionised and since area level concentrations of workers are not required in the new industries or services, trade unions are not able to organise workers in the same way as in the past. The low level of discontent among Delhi labour, including regular employees is, therefore, not much of surprise.

One of the significant features of Delhi's economy is rather high rate of unemployment of the educated (10+), most of whom are now residents of the city even though no domicile policy can be prepared for the National Capital. It is difficult to say, however, what percentage of the educated unemployed are from areas outside Delhi. In the absence of a formal domicile policy, it is perhaps, possible to use the location of the schools from which a person passed out as proxy variable. A study of this kind (unpublished) was conducted for the Government of NCTD in the year 2000-01 to find out the proportion of people in the Employment exchange registers who had passed out from non-Delhi schools. This study was made in the context of preparation of a new scheme for promoting self-employment to the educated unemployed youth. It was to be an improvement over the PMRY but has not yet seen the light of the day.

According to the study, the proportion of educated job-seekers from outside Delhi's school in the year 1999-2000 was as high as 50 per cent. Therefore, taking a parochial view of Delhi's problem, it is possible to reduce the rates of unemployment of the educated youth in Delhi by somewhere around 50 per cent. Even so, the fact remains that Delhi being a highly educated city, the unemployed persons of Delhi are most likely to have been educated upto Class X and therefore, would still have to suffer relatively high rate of unemployment.

The Delhi Government has a department devoted to the problems of employment and manpower planning but even in the 10th Five Year Plan no exercise was done to work out balances of manpower in different categories, especially high and middle level manpower categories. It is unlikely that any outsider agency can do this kind of exercise of developing balances say, for engineers, doctors, veterinary and other professionals with different levels of competence and skills. What the private sector in Delhi knows is clear—if there are no local candidates available to fill up such vacancies, they can always draw upon the manpower surpluses elsewhere in the country since Delhi is such a good place to work and has never pushed out migrants from outside. However, there could be problems of getting sufficient number of candidates for some middle level technical categories, including stenographers, various kinds of mechanics etc. Even these vacancies in the private sector get filled up by less educated but skilled persons i.e., those who may not have undergone formal courses in ITIs or any other technical institution but who have learned on-the-job or have acquired competencies from their extended families.

Again, there are differences in approach with the public sector where there could be vacancies for such categories, which remain unfilled for sometime. As already stated, no firm figures on any of these categories are available but it can be said without any hesitation that manpower demand does not create any serious problems for public or private or the NGO sector in Delhi. On the other hand, there are surpluses of various categories as evident from the employment exchanges data, which could be either in nature of "waiting period" or inability to get some kind of employment opportunity. It is this type of persons who need to be targeted by any new scheme as an improvement over the PMRY because of its low income ceiling (Rs.40,000 per annum for the family), it has been noticed that not much benefit is being derived by unemployed educated persons of Delhi from this scheme so far.

The growth of private sector enterprises in Delhi is sizeable and character of such enterprises goes on changing all the time in tune with the changes in the economy and technology in use. This is all good for an economy without any borders like Delhi. However, not enough information is available or even collected on the changing nature of enterprises or employment since the employment exchanges network, especially its EMI set-up has failed to collect information on such new areas. There is very little information of direct relevance available from the EMI for various reasons, including lack of computerisation, lack of transportation facilities dependence on postal type questionnaires, late information (sometimes 3-4 years) and non-availbility of motivated personnel for the employment exchanges as a whole. Even though the organised sector employment in the country has shrunk to as little as 7-8 per cent of total employment, the situation in Delhi is different and with a little effort the coverage of employment of the organised sector can be increased manifold. The policymakers outside labour and employment departments have more or less given up on the employment exchanges but this should not be so. On the other hand, there is an evidence of proliferation of small and sometimes irresponsible job placement agencies in the city.

There is a need to regularise the entry of private sector in collection of information and placement activities since private sector is now the dominant driver of manpower growth. The Government needs to regulate them but allow them to function for the benefit of employment seekers, better than what has been happening so far. Gujarat has already regularised the entry of private sector into this area and allowed such agencies to charge reasonable fees etc. Even the private sector would like to use the analyses based on revamped EMI data. For the employment/manpower planners such data are constantly needed to track the changes in the manpower profile, the enterprises and the education-skill *vs.* occupational mix, which is constantly evolving in Delhi.

Management of labour, especially skilled labour, is not a real problem in the city mainly because of the flexibility of enterprises in Delhi and the influx of educated/skilled migrants and new technologies in the city e.g. various types of IT-enabled services like call centers or BPO outfits. Side by side, it is also a fact that trade unions are neither as powerful nor disruptive and in any case, the highly skilled personnel tend not to join trade unions. These characteristics do have a negative fall out as a whole since unscrupulous enterprises or seekers for quick profits can more easily exploit unorganised labour. The ready availability of workers at practically all the levels of education or skills from outside the city also makes it difficult to organise the unorganised sector workers to ensure that they are not exploited and do get the benefits of social security laws.

The Government of India has just started a scheme for providing basic social security benefits to the workers of the unorganised sector in the nature of a pilot scheme, but Delhi is getting covered under it with a target of approximately 1 lakh workers to be enrolled under the scheme. Hopefully, the pilot scheme would lead to large scale provision of minimal social security benefits to many others scattered all over the city and the rural areas in the next few years. Practically, all these workers are in the private sector though some of them also exist with the education and training servie providers, regulated or otherwise in Delhi. In fact, an undocumented number of persons, both below adulthood and above, are roped in by a variety of such service providers though all of them may not really get the right level of education/training from them. Therefore, Government of India has been thinking of a Training Fund for the benefit of such consumers of education/training as well as providers of the same. Like the proposed new scheme of promoting self-employment for the unemployed educated youth, this idea has also not gone very far and the set up for the Training Fund has not yet materialised despite the existence of "*Bharat Shiksha Kosh*" under the auspices of Ministry of HRD, Government of India. It is very clear, therefore, that a lot of work remains to be done to bring together the potential employers, the service providers and jobseekers to encourage productive employment in Delhi's economy and accelerate its growth.

References

Directorate of Economics & Statistics, NCTD (2002). *Employment and Unemployment Situation in Delhi.*

——. (2007). *Employment and Unemployment Situation in Delhi.*

Institute of Applied Manpower Research, Delhi (2001). *Impact Assessment of Rural Development Programmes in Baharaich District of Uttar Pradesh*

——. (2002). *Manpower Profile.*

——. (2005). *Manpower Profile*

Govt of India, *Annual Report 2002-2003,* Ministry of Labour, New Delhi.

——. (1990). *Survey on Activity Status of Jobseekers Registered with the Employment Exchanges,* Ministry of Labour, New Delhi.

——. *National Sample Survey Organisation 61st Round (2004-05),* "Employment and Unemployment Situation in India", New Delhi.

——. *National Sample Survey Organisation 61st Round (1999-2000),* "Employment and Unemployment Situation in India", New Delhi.

——. *Tenth Five-year Plan (2002-07),* Planning Commission, New Delhi.

——. *Eleventh Five-year Plan Approach Paper (2007-2012),* Planning Commission, New Delhi.

——. *Annual Plan 2003-04,* Planning Department, Volumes I&II

——. *Annual Plan 2007-08,* Planning Department, Volumes I&II

——. *Economic Survey of Delhi,* 2005-06, Planning Department.

Craftsmen Training and Employment (2003). Resource Development Centre, New Delhi.

Aggarwal, Garima (2003). "Relocation of Industries in NCR" (Unpublished); Thesis presented for fulfilling Post Graduate Diploma in SPA, New Delhi.

Kumar, Barun (2003). "Political Dialectics of Slums in NCT Delhi" (unpublished), a paper presented in National Association of Geographers India in December 28, 2003.

This chapter has been prepared by Institute of Applied Manpower Research, team associated with the preparation of the chapter includes Shri M.C. Verma, Consultant, Smt. Madhu Srivastava, Head (E&U Studies Unit), Shri U.S. Bhandari, SRO, Shri S.K. Yadav, SRO, Shri J.S. Chauhan, RA and Shri Barun Kumar, RA. Study team members were highly benefited from the comments and suggestions of Professor Ajeet Narain Mathur, Director, IAMR in preparation of the chapter.

Chapter 15

Women and Vulnerable Groups

15.0 Introduction

The development of the metropolitan-city, capital-state of Delhi brings into focus a host of social concerns, which are partly structural, partly institutional, and in some ways associated with the very process of development. The concept of vulnerable groups derives from a certain notion of well-being, human rights and role of the state towards its citizens, following principles of equality and justice. The word 'vulnerable' connotes weakness, susceptibility, defenselessness, helplessness, exclusion and refers to persons exposed to danger or at risk due to their location in a weak, subordinate position. It refers to a state of being that calls for recognition, protection and security measures. Structural and institutional factors leading to deficiencies, vulnerabilities and insecurities, as opposed to certain kinds of personal choice or individual characteristic, legitimise positive discrimination practices and invite state interventions as corrective or supportive measures.

Vulnerable groups as relevant in the current context refers to all such persons who are weak and helpless due to social, physical, economic, educational, financial, infrastructural, health, legal, political or institutional dimensions that intensify across caste, religion, class, gender and community connotations. Powerlessness, income and structural poverty, and social exclusion are the characteristics that are associated with vulnerabilities. The conventional meaning flowing from the Constitutional provisions refers to linguistic and religious minorities, and right to equality in various spheres. Alternatively, it extends to the socially deprived and disadvantaged groups of scheduled castes and tribes; the physically disabled and mentally challenged, the destitutes; and survival livelihood seeking unorganised workers and migrants from the economically vulnerable sections who are also education wise poor and low in marketable skills; the social caste-class dimensions accentuate the vulnerability of the politically disempowered by rendering them voiceless and without citizenship based human rights; even the lack of infrastructural availability or access to facilities; the risk arising of natural or human calamities; health related vulnerabilities; inadequate legal protection and persons who do not fit the accepted dominant social behaviour such as single women, divorcées, children who run away from home and so on.

Consider any aspect such as growing urbanisation for instance and a wide range of issues concerning the livelihoods, shelter and basic human rights of the poor and vulnerable groups stand to be addressed. The capital, metropolitan state of Delhi attracts a variety of persons for the better opportunities it offers, but the situation for certain sections, whether recognised or not as vulnerable groups, remains wanting in various ways. This chapter focuses on some of the prominently vulnerable groups and addresses aspects that generate or perpetuate their vulnerabilities with a view to improve their situation. The question often posed is whether the status of vulnerable sections of the populations improve or worsen due to their location in the relatively privileged state of Delhi? Such a comparison in the context of measuring or assessing social development levels in the state is of poor significance if not insignificant, since the very fact that there are hungry, destitute, shelterless persons in any state calls for improving their situation and intervening so as to eliminate these dimensions that generate vulnerability. In other words, it is immaterial whether Delhi has more or less disabled, destitutes or migrants than any other place, however, what is important is the attention and addressal of the issues of concern pertinent to persons vulnerable due to any of these factors.

The employment potential of the state attracts migrants. These migrant workers are contributing significantly to the economy of the city by offering their labour services. Yet, they are viewed as a burden, with the State trying to shun its responsibility towards them. The growth of slums and squatters are a source of grave distress to the administrators who strategise and plan for their resettlement and displacement in an effort to beautify and clean up the metropolitan city. Social discrimination in its worst form manifests itself in the manner State approaches the concerns of the vulnerable groups. While the professional and upper strata of society among the migrants are warmly assimilated into the social and political fabric; the poor, working masses are viewed with disdain, not to be trusted and all efforts are being made to dissuade migration for these segments.

The utter lack of social security for segments of the population in the context of a modern, developed or developing state worsens the plight of historically, socio-economically poor and backward sections of the population. The SC/STs, the OBCs are the sections excluded from development and in spite of the positive intervention policies adopted by the state to move towards a more egalitarian society, the institutional structures delimit benefits accruing to them.

Women are another category by themselves who are viewed as vulnerable, albeit for slightly different reasons. The fundamental element that weakens or disempowers women is the power and authority equations stemming from patriarchal structures which locate them at the lower rungs of the hierarchies prevalent in society, economy and polity. In the context of Delhi, the simultaneous presence of progressive and retrogressive forces seems to be in operation.

Women in Delhi (as in rest of the country and in fact even the globe) also face discrimination and gender biases that affect them adversely in their daily conduct of life and living. This is in spite of the few other dimensions where positive, progressive opportunities are noted for the female gender as in the case of better employment avenues in the organised sector for the educated women for instance. The chance to undertake jobs in the non-traditional, unconventional spheres is another noteworthy aspect, with women in the technical spheres, in the police force, as detectives, as drivers and so on. Many of these alterations are a reflection of changing mindsets and social support from parents and other agents who assist women in breaking gender stereotypes and help them to be in better control of their lives. Apart from these spheres changes were occurring; in most others women remain marginalised and vulnerable. What is most distressing is the resilience in social perceptions of gender roles and inflexibilities noted in the stereotypical norms prevalent that serve as hurdles to overcome the inequalities and discriminations against women.

The need for addressing or focusing on vulnerable groups arises also due to the predominant approach of state provision and intervention that is not always individual based. In case of a bulk of these provisions, the male head of the household is considered to be the beneficiary representing the household. This perpetuates the dependent status of women and children. It is as if they have no citizenship based rights of their own as individuals. This is of tremendous significance in the context of changing kinship structures, increasing nuclearisation, declining support institutions, rising urbanisation, its association with development that is based on individual oriented growth, as all these factors work towards diminishing the protection offered by the traditional social fabric and exposing persons to heightened vulnerabilities.

Apart from the structural and institutional vulnerabilities as in the case of socially disadvantaged SC/STs and OBCs, and women and children; the other segments which may be affected by one or more dimensions of exclusion and deprivation are the differently abled—physically and mentally challenged; those who work in spheres not protected by legal provisions or not recognised—such as unorganised workers, child labourer, street-vendors, domestic workers, rag/waste pickers, sex workers and so on; those who suffer from health related disability – malaria, TB, cancer, HIV/AIDs, other chronic ailments, aged; also individuals who do not fit the accepted dominant normative behaviour and therefore face difficulties in social assimilation or due to treatment meted out to them, such as single women (including divorced women) children who run away from their homes, and so on.

Among the vulnerable groups there are also persons affected due to natural or human calamity such as death of main earners leading to dependents vulnerability, as widows, orphans and other dependents; development related displacement caused by land acquisition for construction of say dams, roads, hospitals, factories and so on. In Delhi, the agenda of cleaning up the city for beautification and demolition of illegal settlements has occurred, that is slightly distinct from the development project led displacement. The illegal settlements and habitations that involve the rich and powerful remain unaffected while the slum dwellers and poor migrants are removed even from their temporary shelters. Other factors that generate vulnerability are accidents; gutting by fire or flooding that slum dwellers and persons living in temporary shelters are at risk of; the precarious living on pavements, under bridges and flyovers; exposure to violence, abuse and hazardous living.

The socially disadvantaged groups, poor, women, children, physically challenged, aged, and sections of the working masses that have almost no legal recognition or protective rights are affected by these vulnerabilities in a more intensified manner. This is true for the capital-city-state of Delhi as well. The capital-city is better in terms of the job avenues it makes available and in many cases also the earnings and consumption patterns, however, in as much as the inequalities are concerned the poor and vulnerable sections of Delhi are in certain aspects worse-off. The conditions of living environment (shelter, water, sanitation, etc.) and work relations are an affront to their human dignity. Any citizen of this democratic country is legitimately due for a life with dignity and it is the responsibility of the governance structures along with the partnership of other social agents to ensure at least a basic level of well being to all its citizens.

15.1 Women's Issues

Women as a category of vulnerable groups constitute the largest segment, by virtue of being almost one-half of the population. Except for a minuscule among them, most women are affected by the gender biases and discrimination against them in various spheres—social, legal, economic, political, educational, health related, violence and so on. Despite the heterogeneities of caste, class, region, religion and location within Delhi, women are affected in very similar ways that are an affront to their dignity, self-respect, individual identity and equality. While it is true that overlaps exist between other vulnerable categories, each segment deserves specific attention. The women inhabiting the posh colonies of Delhi as well as those living in the slums are afflicted as a result of the pervasiveness of gender ideologies that assign a lower status to women. The additional dimension of income poverty and deprivation worsens the situation of the slum dwellers, while the prosperity at the other extreme stifles the cries of the conflicts women face. Violence emanating from the notion that women need protection and have to be controlled by the men in their lives affects the dignity of all women irrespective of the class they belong to.

The women among the poor and socially disadvantaged sections of the population are doubly vulnerable, however women *per se*, also suffer from the overall lower status ascribed by the dominant social perceptions and these are reflected via media a range of indicators (some of which will be discussed here). Even the rich and prosperous segments treat women unequally as compared to the men and in fact, in certain spheres they are noted to be far worse than even their poorer counterparts, as in sex ratios, which link to the girl children's survival, nutrition, mortality and neglect. The plotting of sex ratios especially child sex ratios for 0-6 years age cohorts across different locations in Delhi highlights the lower or declining sex ratios in the relatively prosperous parts of the city (Table 15.1).

TABLE 15.1

Some Gender Development Indicators for the Districts of Delhi: Total (Rural+Urban)

Indicator/ District	*North West*	*North*	*North East*	*East*	*New Delhi*	*Central*	*West*	*South West*	*South*
Sex Ratio (0-6 years)	857	886	875	865	898	903	859	846	888
Sex Ratio among population of 7 years and above	814	817	844	840	778	834	826	774	785
Female Literacy Rate	73	75	69	79	76	76	78	76	74
Gender Gap in Literacy	14	10	16	10	12	7	10	14	14

Source: *Census of India, 2001*.

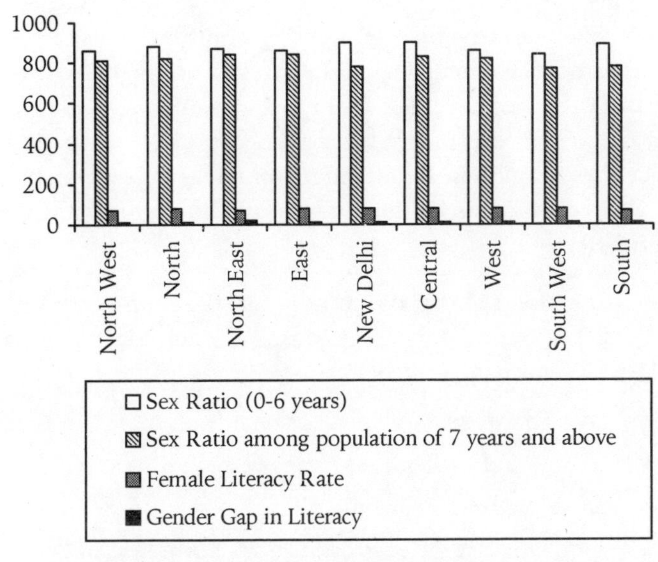

The age specific death rates for Delhi reveal that in the younger age cohort up to 4 years, females experience a higher death rate than males. For the years 1998-2000, the death rate among girls from one to four years is 2.3, while the male counterparts it is 1.1 only (Registrar

General, *Vital Rates of Delhi at a Glance*). The death rate for children before attaining the age of one year is strikingly high for both girls and boys, with girl infants death rate being 42, while that for boys was 36. The differentiation in nutrition, nurture and care given to boys and girls due to the lower significance attributed to the female gender that are viewed as a burden explains this indifferent attitude of guardians and family towards them.

The practice of using modern scientific technologies such as ultrasonography and amniocentesis to detect the sex of the foetus and eliminate female fetuses are being reported even in Delhi. This is occurring in spite of the legislative strictures against such practices. The desire for male progeny creates the demand for illegal usage of such medical services with the connivance of medical professionals who offer to undertake the unethical sex determination foetal tests.

Neglect of female health reflected in the higher female mortality rates among children and adults, especially during their reproductive years is noted. The body mass index (BMI) for women in Delhi is 24 (NFHS-II). Chronic energy deficiency is usually indicated by a BMI of less than 18.5. Twelve per cent of women in Delhi have a BMI below 18.5. The mean BMI for women in India is 20.3. At the all India level, 36 per cent of women have a BMI below 18.5. Though the percentage of women in Delhi falling below the required BMI is lower than the all India level, there is no reason for complacency for the percentage is still high.

A similar health situation is brought out by the rate of anemia among women. The all India rates are higher than that of Delhi, but again the Delhi rates are high enough to be a cause of concern. For the age cohort 15-19 years, 47 per cent of women in Delhi suffer from anaemia, while all India percentage is 56 per cent for the same group, (NFHS-II).

A study by the ICMR noted that the number of women suffering from breast cancer is increasing in Delhi. Reasons specified in the report are

- late marriages and pregnancy
- social and professional stress
- changing eating habits
- rampant use of oestrogen laced hormonal pills

Among the reasons for lower access by women for health care over and above the economic cost factor, relative insignificance associated with their health needs and inadequate health infrastructure (including women health personnel); there is also the less noted factor of insecurity and discomfort faced by women and girls (especially adolescents) due to the undue attention and physical handling by male health attendants and doctors. The vulnerability of women seeking health care is further accentuated under such circumstances. The poor security and protection levels of health institutions have come to light with recent cases of sexual assault, molestation and even rape of nurses, with newly born infants being stolen from their mothers and so on. The vulnerability of a patient who is under the direction and care of health providers can be very high unless certain stringent measures for their protection are put in place.

Lack of awareness among young adolescent girls about their bodies, its functions, health needs and related symptoms, acts as a further deterrent in their access to health care. The process of socialisation intensifies at adolescence stage when girls are made to accede to patriarchal, male authority and superiority; to the extent of being taught to be docile, not to retaliate and even learn to live with sexual harassment and victimisation very often. The lessons learnt prevent girls from raising their voices in protest against being assaulted and sexually harassed. Education and sensitisation around these dimensions of socialisation can go a long way in developing self-esteem and confidence in women.

The universality of marriage, especially for girls, the context of posing professional careers in juxtaposition to performing household responsibilities and the significance laid on the latter lead to lower importance given to girls education, employment and individual development. Even in the capital-city of Delhi, 18 per cent of the females in the ages of 15-19 years are married (NFHS-Delhi; Census of India, 1991). The incidence of child marriages relate directly to education among girls, with the illiterate women displaying a lower average age at marriage.

The presence of single women, divorcees, widows in Delhi and other metros raises the concern regarding their vulnerability due to the gender biases prevalent in our society. Women living without a family (to be precise, a male protector) are often viewed in suspicion. This has an impact on the women in terms of their access to shelter (when they are in search of rented accommodation), their daily existence and interaction in the social environment they inhabit, and in terms of their security and safety. This is apart from the concerns in their professional spheres at work, with regard to inter-personal relations and work performance evaluation.

The increasing numbers of women working in non-traditional jobs, especially those which keep them at work or out on the roads at odd hours, such as in case of call centre workers, news reporters, nurse and doctors, round-the-clock service providers and so on necessitates the change in the perceptions of society regarding their roles in society as well as the notions about such women. The change in the law which earlier prohibited night work for women is likely to bring more women into the workforce at so-called 'abnormal' working hours. This alteration has to accompany change in attitudes around such work and women involved in these employments.

Many women who come from other states to study or work and are unable to accommodate themselves in the government run or institutionally provided hostels have to seek alternative accommodation. This is a difficult and cumbersome task due to the societal mindsets regarding single women. Working women accommodations in the form of hostels run by government and various other organisations fall short of the demand for them. A large number of women have to exercise alternative private options of accommodation. They negotiate to live with the socially governed expectations and work out methods for safeguarding themselves. Where and when lapses in these occur, there is very little hope they can lay upon the existing institutional mechanisms to protect them, as was reflected in the recent case of the south Delhi college student's rape. The common voices raise doubts regarding the purpose for women to be out at certain hours, about how they finance themselves, their inter-personal relations, attire, behaviour, etc., casting aspersions on them and insinuating immoral behaviour. The fact that these are matters of personal choice, on which no other being can exercise control and the issue of concern is the violence meted out that needs to be outraged, is often lost in the din raised by irrelevant matters.

Crimes against women form a kind of insecurity that instills fear in girls and women that affects their participation in all spheres of life and living. Delhi reports more than 50000 crime cases every year. Of these, more than 2000 cases are that of crimes against women, a majority of them cases of kidnapping and abduction of women and girls (Tables 15.2 and 15.3). The frequent occurrence of molestation and rape cases in the capital-city has earned it the dubious distinction of being called the rape capital.

Among the new category of cyber crimes, Delhi police investigations have revealed that in 40 per cent of all cases, women are at the receiving end of malice in cyberland (NCRB, 2001). Innocent women victims are targets of various forms of image tarnishing, such as faces morphed on pornographic websites or posted on message boards.

TABLE 15.2

Crime Incidence for Districts of Delhi, 2001

District	*Crimes against Women*	*Total Crimes*	*(%) CAW*
North-west	568	10001	5.68
North	126	3998	3.15
North-east	222	3449	6.44
East	168	4447	3.78
New Delhi	56	2660	2.11
Central	113	3750	3.01
West	251	7690	3.26
South-west	277	5389	5.14
South	392	10745	3.65
Delhi	2188	54384	4.02

Source: Calculated from NCRB, 2001 and Census 2001.

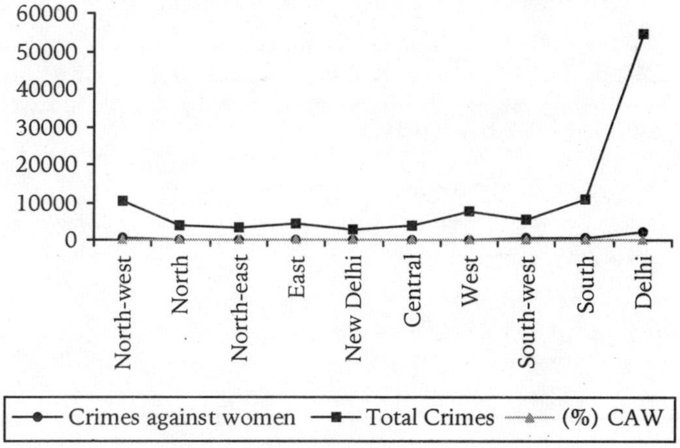

TABLE 15.3

Categories of Crimes against Women: Districts of Delhi (2001)

(Number of cases)

Districts of Delhi	*Rape*	*Kid-napping Abduction of Women & Girls*	*Dowry Deaths*	*Mole-station*	*Sexual Harass-ment*	*Cruelty at Home*	*CAW*
Central	28	42	4	30	7	2	113
East	24	39	11	56	11	27	168
New Delhi	9	19	0	20	6	2	56
North	28	53	4	26	6	9	126
North East	36	123	20	34	1	8	222
North West	103	298	25	102	18	22	568
South	65	170	15	96	24	22	392
South West	42	113	16	69	13	24	277
West	45	99	18	65	2	22	251
Delhi	381	964	113	502	90	138	2188

Source: NCRB, 2001.

The statistics on crime are a poor reflection of the exact extent of the crimes committed since only some forms are recognised and even fewer instances of them are reported to the police or other designated authorities. This is especially so in the case of women, due to the socially imposed constraints on reporting or seeking action against the accused. The greatest deterrent to crime reportage, especially in cases of crimes against women, stems from the slack process of justice delivery, delays in police and court proceedings and low conviction rates. In comparison, police disposal of cases are relatively better than that of the courts in Delhi. While the pendency rate for disposal of cases by police is 46 per cent and conviction rate 54 per cent, the respective rates for disposal by courts are 81 per cent pendency rate and 50 per cent conviction rate (Tables 15.4 and 15.5).

TABLE 15.4

Disposal of IPC Cases by Police during 2001 (Delhi)

Total No. of cases for investigation (including pending cases)	106761
Charge found false/ mistake of fact etc.	899
Among cases where investigation was completed: Total	57836
- Final report true submitted	26494
- Charge sheets were submitted	30443
No. of cases pending investigation	48925
Pendency percentage	**45.8**
Conviction Rate	**53.5**

TABLE 15.5

Disposal of IPC Cases by Court during 2001 (Delhi)

Total No. of cases for Trials including Pending cases	174634
No. of cases in which trials were completed	32422
Of which Convicted cases	16353
Acquitted or Discharged	16069
Pending Trial	142212
Pendency Percentage	**81.4**
Conviction Rate	**50.4**

Source: NCRB, 2001.

The conviction rate for rape cases is the lowest among all the six categories of crimes against women. The chances of rapists going unpunished and victims further being victimised in the course of the justice proceedings deter women from reporting cases of crimes against them. A large number of cases therefore go in for reconciliation or out of court settlement, which is not necessarily in the direction of meting out justice.

15.2 Socially Disadvantaged Groups

Women, scheduled castes/tribes and the other backward castes (OBCs) are the prominent sections of population which may be classified as constituents of the socially disadvantaged and vulnerable groups. The gender stereotype based norms define women's roles and their subservience to patriarchal authority place them at the lower end of social hierarchies. The Scheduled Castes and OBCs also find themselves located at the low end of hierarchical ladders. Their poverty and assetlessness is further debilitated by low access to education and skill development which intensifies the vulnerability levels. Women within the SC/OBC groups are doubly vulnerable due to the social disadvantage and due to their weaker position in gender relations.

The lack of adequate information on OBCs limits the analysis on this segment. Scheduled Tribes (STs) are not enumerated for Delhi and hence although there are a few STs living in the capital-city, the Census does not provide any information on them. Only the NSS provides some data on the OBCs and STs in terms of their population shares, education and employment profiles. The Scheduled Castes are covered by both the sources of data.

The Scheduled Caste population in Delhi as per the Census 2001 enumeration total to 23.4 lakh persons, which is nearly 17 per cent of the entire population of the state (Tables 15.6 and 15.7). The share of rural SC concentration as compared to non-SC population of Delhi

TABLE 15.6

Scheduled Castes in Delhi, 2001

	Persons	*Males*	*Females*
Total	2343255	1265182	1078073
Rural	188378	101500	86878
Urban	2154877	1163682	991195

Source: Census of India, 2001.

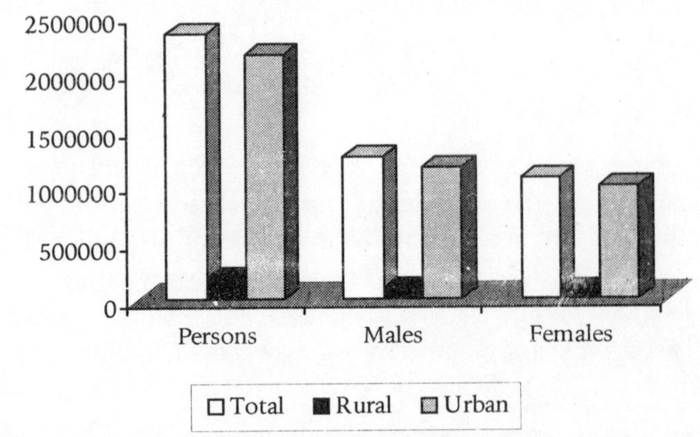

TABLE 15.7

Percentage of Scheduled Castes in Total Population

	Persons	*Males*	*Females*
Total	16.92	16.63	17.27
Rural	19.94	19.44	20.56
Urban	16.70	16.42	17.03

Source: Census of India, 2001.

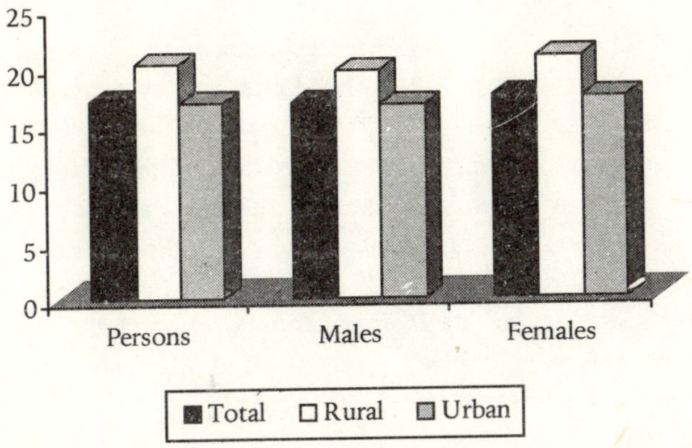

is higher with nearly 20 per cent of the rural population being SCs. The sex ratio among the SCs who are relatively poorer with far lower endowments shows a more balanced picture than for the rest of the population. The sex ratio among SCs stood at 852, while for the rural areas it was slightly higher at 856, as opposed to the total population sex ratio figures which are 821 for Delhi as a whole (Table 15.8).

TABLE 15.8

Comparative Sex Ratios for Delhi - 2001

	Sex Ratio – Total Population	*Sex Ratio – Scheduled Castes*
Total	821	852
Rural	806	856
Urban	822	852

Source: Census of India, 2001.

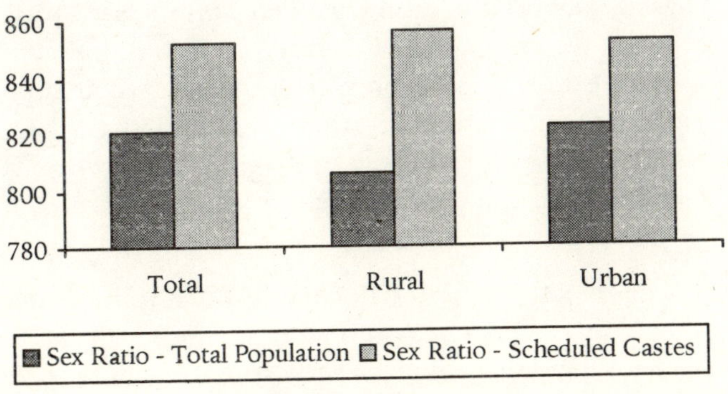

Most studies based on surveys highlight the lower access to education and health care by the socially disadvantaged groups and this aspect remains similar even in the context of Delhi. While it is true that Delhi offers better opportunities for the scheduled castes and OBCs when compared to other states, the social disparity among them and the non-backward classes continues to remain prominent. Educational levels remain lower even if literacy rates are better; retention rates display higher dropout rates among the SCs/OBCs.

The Census provides information for SC/STs, but not for the other backward castes. Scheduled Tribes are not enumerated for Delhi since the Census following the President's order specified under Article 342 of the Constitution, does not enlist any domicile tribes for Delhi. There is a small proportion of STs living in Delhi, which the NSS reports to be around 2 per cent of the population in the 55th round. In addition to this, the NSS also provides data for the OBCs. Nearly 22 per cent of the population in Delhi belongs to the OBCs (Table 15.9). The proportion of SCs as calculated by the NSS and the Census display a wide discrepancy for rural Delhi. This is probably due to the small sample for rural Delhi that the NSS figures are based on. As opposed to the concentration of SCs and non-backward castes in urban areas of Delhi, the STs and OBCs are located in rural counterparts (Table 15.9).

TABLE 15.9

Percentage Distribution of Social Categories in Delhi's Population

Social Category	*Total Population*	*Percentage Shares in Population*		
		Rural	*Urban*	*Total*
Scheduled Tribes	200091	4	2	2
Scheduled Castes	1378540	11	17	15
Other Backward Castes	1962651	46	14	22
Other	5529556	39	68	61
Total	9070837	100	100	100

Source: NSS, 55th round.

A very small minuscule of the SCs/STs is employed in the organised sector jobs with the government. Among those who work for Delhi government, there are 22 per cent SCs and 5 per cent STs. fifty per cent of the scheduled castes who constitute a sizeable number are employed as class IV employees (Table 15.10). This is a clear reflection of their lower educational and human capital attributes as well as of the discrimination they face.

TABLE 15.10

Class-wise Distribution of Employment in Delhi Government: Shares of SC and ST

	2001				
	Total Employees	Scheduled Castes		Scheduled Tribes	
		Employees	(%)	Employees	(%)
Class I	3465	444	12.8	135	3.9
Class II	34078	5136	15.1	2364	6.9
Class III	26625	3963	14.9	906	3.4
Class IV	16190	8026	49.6	543	3.4
Total	80358	17570	21.9	3948	4.9
	2002				
	Total Employees	Scheduled Castes		Scheduled Tribes	
		Employees	(%)	Employees	(%)
Class I	3791	448	11.8	138	3.6
Class II	32798	4932	15.0	2366	7.2
Class III	27193	4066	15.0	931	3.4
Class IV	15723	7876	50.1	505	3.2
Total	79505	17322	21.8	3940	5.0

Source: DES, GNCTD.

15.3 Child Labour

Estimates of child labour are often considered unreliable from the standard secondary sources, which have an in built bias against most of the unorganised categories of work. Among the poor, slum dwellers and shelterless, most children are involved in activities to supplement their household incomes. From rag picking, begging, peddling drugs to working in tea shops/eateries, various shops, repairing and domestic services, children are visible in large numbers around the city.

Organisations working with child labour estimate more than 6 lakh working children for the city of Delhi. As stated in the framework for this chapter, the actual numbers are of less significance as compared to the issues concerning working children, such as, the impact on their growth—physical and mental, the health hazards, and denial of access to basic amenities.

There are different kinds of child labour. Those children who help their parents or families as part of household labour often get camouflaged under domestic work. Distinction is drawn between child work and child labour based on payment, hours of work, full-time or too many hours at work preventing children from attending school, excessive strain, unhealthy and dangerous conditions, too much responsibility (due to incapacity of breadearners) to earn and factors that deter overall child's development.

A study in Delhi capturing facets of childwork was undertaken by Delhi FORCES which documented the time spent by older children on sibling care thus interfering with their own education and often leading to dropout from school. According to the study, there is a clear paucity of child care services for women workers in the unorganised sector, the Delhi Government having only 239 creches for a total of 19,23,995 children in the age group of 0-6 years.

The burden of child care therefore comes on to the older children of the families. More often than not it is the elder daughter who shoulders the responsibility of sibling care. These girls are themselves young which has an impaired impact on the development of both younger and older children. Women in the study clearly had in built patriarchal bias against their daughters. Eighty per cent women desired that their daughter get minimal education but for their sons, they wished them to study up to 10th or 12th class. They wanted their sons to learn vocational and technical skills but for their daughters they felt that education should be designed so as to help them in their married and familial lives.

The study held 14 group discussions with 249 children who were entrusted with sibling care. In 90 per cent of the cases, girls were looking after their younger siblings either along with their studies or after dropping out of school. Sibling care was an important reason stated for older girls dropping out of school.

There is no particular location where child labour is prevalent in Delhi. It is visible to the discerning eye throughout the length and breadth of the NCT of Delhi. Employers prefer child labour for the lower cost, and to avoid any labour unrest in factories and workshops. In the local markets and residential areas of the capital city, children are observed working as domestic servants, vegetable sellers, milk carriers, car cleaners, cloth pressers, errand and delivery boys, petty vendors, mechanics, and so on. The girl child workers are a majority (nearly 90 per cent) among the child domestic workers. Apart from the exploitation as a result of their physical labour at a young age and other abuses they are exposed to, the adolescent years of girl children when they undertake these chores, often without adult support, exposes them to abuse in the form of molestation, sexual assault and rape. The conditions under which they work, and the social compulsions, very often prevent them from reporting these cases of violence.

The reasons for children working stem from the overall poverty and adult unemployment. This is especially so in the rural places of origin, from where a majority of them have migrated. The increasingly contractual nature of jobs that are highly insecure, indebtedness, ill-health of breadearner or sheer compulsion for additional earnings pushes children into employment. The desire to be independent and escape ill treatment of guardians can also result in children running away from home and having to fend for themselves.

15.3.1 Street Children

A subset of these vulnerable sections of child labour constitutes street children. They are identified on the basis of the shelter available to them and levels of family contact. While some of the street children are a part of their families who are shelterless and live on the pavement themselves, others may be living on the street with or without contact of their families. The latter group of street children who are on their own may be that of orphans or run-away children. Almost all of these street children who are on their own have to work for survival or resort to beggary, stealing and so on.

It is estimated that there are nearly 100,000 street children in Delhi (Panicker and Nangia, 1988). Children engaged in rag picking, vending, coolie work and a range of street trades who work and live on the streets are included among street children. They are often harassed and live in near-distress circumstances. These children are helpless without a home, as they often have deserted their guardians due to mistreatment, abuse, cruelty or indifference.

The search for freedom and a chance to survive brings them to cities, where very often they are subject to abuse of all kinds—verbal, mental, physical, psychological and sexual. The plight of girl child is even more susceptible to maltreatment, violence and misguidance. Estimates of sex workers reveal that a large proportion of the girls in brothels are minors below the age of 18 years. The routes through which these girls land up in the red light areas of the city are complex and involve layers of deception, fraud, false information and temptation luring them on various pretexts such as marriage, employment and other similar promises.

There are various organisations that work with street children and some of them run shelter homes, while others provide non-formal education, vocational training, recreation avenues and assist them to benefit from saving schemes. Some of the prominent ones are Salaam Balak Trust, Butterflies, Prayas, Deepalaya and so on.

The government has enacted laws regarding child labour (abolition of child labour in hazardous occupations), juvenile justice and has ratified the UN Convention on the Rights of the Child in order to prevent exploitation of children and for the protection of their rights. However, experience on the ground highlights that these are inadequate to tackle the root of this problem. Introduction of further restrictions and prohibitions make it harder for children to earn a living, rendering their pursuits illegal and easily prone to harassment. In this respect the working child merges with the vast mass of unorganised labourforce that faces similar challenges in pursuing their livelihood in a dignified and respectful manner.

15.4 Vulnerabilities Stemming from Disability

The challenges posed by disability, both physical and mental, manifest in rendering vulnerable the persons affected by it, not only in the absolute sense but also in terms of the neglect, exclusion and non-recognition associated with it. The common perception of disability is limited to the physically challenged persons who are affected due to locomotor, visual, hearing or speech disability. The understanding of what constitutes mental disability is very poor. Until recently, there were almost no reliable secondary data based estimates for mental disability. The NSS included mental disability (both mental retardation and mental illness) for the first time in their 2002 survey. Most mental disability is congenital, although there can be number of other reasons, some known, while many are still undiscovered/unknown due to medical limitations (Addlakha, 2005). Malnutrition and micronutrient deficiencies may also result in disabling conditions for children by stunting their physical and mental growth. The loss of limb due to an accident may debilitate a person that can be categorised as a static form of disability. Alternatively, injuries from a mishap may over time assume some form of episodic outburst of symptoms resulting in degeneration in the condition of the affected person. There are difficulties in recognising certain forms of disability, such as diabetes, epilepsy, schizophrenia, and so on which may be considered relatively invisible due to the medical limitation, social prejudices and levels of awareness among the public.

In addition to the vulnerability stemming from the form of disability, the approach of the society at large and the State deprive and disempower the disabled from their due rights as citizens of the country. Women among the disabled remain further marginalised and neglected and have to face worse conditions than the non-disabled women and even the disabled men due to the prevalent notions of her inability to perform the normative roles expected of women and of the associated social dishonour and shame that propels families to keep them hidden (Addlakha, 2005).

The NSS (over three quinquennial rounds) and Census of India (for the first time in 2001) enumerated the disabled population. The data relates to both physical and mental disabilities, namely, (i) mental disability, (ii) visual disability, (iii) hearing disability, (iv) speech disability, and (v) locomotor disability. The NSS defines disability as "A person with restrictions or lack of abilities to perform an activity in the manner or within the range considered normal for a human being. It excluded illness/injury of recent origin (morbidity) resulting into temporary loss of ability to see, hear, speak or move".

Mental disability is defined as "Persons who had difficulty in understanding routine instructions, who could not carry out their activities like others of similar age or exhibited behaviours like talking to self, laughing/crying, staring, violence, fear and suspicion without reason were considered as mentally disabled for the purpose of the survey. The "activities like others of similar age" included activities of communication (speech), self-care (cleaning of teeth, wearing clothes, taking bath, taking food, personal hygiene, etc.), home living (doing some household chores) and social skills". In the capital city of Delhi itself 12970 persons are enumerated as mentally disabled. Two-third of them is affected with mental retardation, while one-third has reported mental illness (Table 15.11).

TABLE 15.11

Estimated Disabled Persons in Delhi

Type of Disability	*Male*	*Female*	*Total*
A. Mental			
i) Retardation	5121	3456	8577
ii) Illness	3153	1240	4393
Total	8274	4696	12970
B. Visual			
i) Blindness	4958	1661	6619
ii) Low Vision	457	232	689
Total	5415	1893	7308
C. Communication			
i) Hearing	1265	1374	2639
ii) Speech	1716	971	2687
Total	2981	2345	5326
D. Locomotor	44480	25546	70026
E. Multiple	4201	2596	6797
Total	65351	37076	102427

Source: Provisional Estimates based on NSS 58th Round (State Sample).

Visual disability is defined as "loss or lack of ability to execute tasks requiring adequate visual acuity". For the survey, visually disabled included (a) those who did not have any light perception—both eyes taken together and (b) those who had light perception but could not correctly count fingers of hand (with spectacles/contact lenses if he/she used spectacles/contact lenses) from a distance of 3 metres (or 10 feet) in good day light with both eyes open. Night blindness was not considered as visual disability. A total of 7309 persons are reported under this category as being vulnerable due to visual disability in Delhi.

Hearing disability refers to "persons' inability to hear properly. Hearing disability was judged taking into consideration the disability of the better ear. In other words, if one ear of a person was normal and the other ear had total hearing loss, then the person was judged as normal in hearing for the purpose of the survey. Hearing disability was judged without taking into consideration the use of hearing aids (i.e., the position for the person when hearing aid was not used). Persons with hearing disability might be having different degrees of disability, such as profound, severe or moderate. A person was treated as having 'profound' hearing disability if he/she could not hear at all or could only hear loud sounds, such as, thunder or understands only gestures. A person was treated as having 'severe' hearing disability if he/she could hear only shouted words or could hear only if the speaker was sitting in the front. A person was treated as having 'moderate' hearing disability if his/her disability was neither profound nor severe. Such a person would usually ask to repeat the words spoken by the speaker or would like to see the face of the speaker while he/she spoke or would feel difficulty in conducting conversations".

Speech disability refers to "persons' inability to speak properly. Speech of a person was judged to be disordered if the person's speech was not understood by the listener. Persons with speech disability included those who could not speak, spoke only with limited words or those with loss of voice. It also included those whose speech was not understood due to defects in speech, such as stammering, nasal voice, hoarse voice and discordant voice and articulation defects, etc." The NSS estimates communication disability as including both hearing and speech disability. Delhi has a total of estimated 5326 persons vulnerable due to communication disability (NSS, 58th round).

A person affected by locomotor disability is one with— "(a) loss or lack of normal ability to execute distinctive activities associated with the movement of self and objects from place to place and (b) physical deformities, other than those involving the hand or leg or both, regardless of whether the same caused loss or lack of normal movement of body—was considered as disabled with locomotor disability. Thus, persons having locomotor disability included those with (a) loss or absence or inactivity of whole or part of hand or leg or both due to amputation, paralysis, deformity or dysfunction of joints which affected his/her "normal ability to move self or objects" and (b) those with physical deformities in the body (other than limbs), such as, hunch back, deformed spine, etc. Dwarfs and persons with stiff neck of permanent nature who generally did not have difficulty in the normal movement of body and limbs was also treated as disabled". Persons with locomotor disability estimated for Delhi were 70026, of which males constitute 44480, while women were 25546 in number. The large numbers of persons affected from locomotor disability is an offshoot of the increasing numbers of industrial and road accidents that result in permanent loss or deformity of some kind.

The incidences of multiple disabilities are reported in 6.6 per cent of the total number estimated by the disability survey for Delhi. The absence of sensitivity to the needs of the disabled in negotiating any public space is being taken note of only now. However, even today, very few places are really structured so as to make it easily accessible for the disabled. Inadequacy and poor conditions of institutional structures for the disabled leave little other option than to live with family.

It is heartening to note however that nearly one-fourth of all disabled in Delhi are employed. Among the employed disabled population in Delhi, 9.9 per cent are disabled women (Table 15.12). The fresh impetus derived from the disability rights movement in raising awareness and emphasising the provisions of the Act as well as the reservations in the public sector employment avenues may hopefully lead to further improvements in future.

TABLE 15.12

Number of Physically or Mentally Challenged Persons of age 5 years and above by usual Activity Status

	Male	*Female*	*Persons*
Employed	22106	2440	24546
Unemployed	3323	579	3902
Labourforce	25429	3019	28448
Not in Labourforce	38178	32836	71014
Total (5+ years)	63607	35855	99462
Total (All ages)	65351	37076	102427
Total Population	7607234	6243273	13850507

Source: Provisional Estimates based on NSS 58th Round (State Sample).

The inadequate attention and recognition given to disability in the country is reflected from the fact that it was as late as in the 1990s that the disability rights movement began and it was in 1995 that the Persons with Disabilities (Equal Opportunities, Protection of Rights and Full Participation) Act was passed by parliament.

TABLE 15.13

Number of Institutions and Beneficiaries in Delhi

Physically & Mentally Challenged	*Population Estimates*	*No. of Institutions (Schools)*	*Beneficiaries as on 31-03-2003 (Students)*
Mental Retardation	8577	1	40
Blind	6619	2	150
Deaf	2639	4	933

Source: Provisional Estimates based on NSS 58th Round (State Sample).

15.5 Migrants

The Census of India figures may not be able to capture the exact extent of migration, however, the share of in-migrants in NCT of Delhi's population has been falling. This is direct contradiction to what is visible and noted by the authorities who find it extremely difficult to cater to the needs of the migrants who are moving into the capital every year. The exact composition by 1991 among migrants and those living in Delhi as per the Census based calculations shows that the proportion of persons born in Delhi has been rising over the years reaching 61 per cent in 1991, while in-migrants have reduced (as per the secondary sources) to 39.4 per cent (Table 15.14).

TABLE 15.14

Composition of Delhi's Population and Immigrants: 1951-1991

Year	*Born in Delhi*	*In-migrants*
1951	41.1	58.9
1961	43.6	56.4
1971	51.8	48.2
1981	54.6	45.4
1991	60.6	39.4

Source: Calculated from Census, different years.

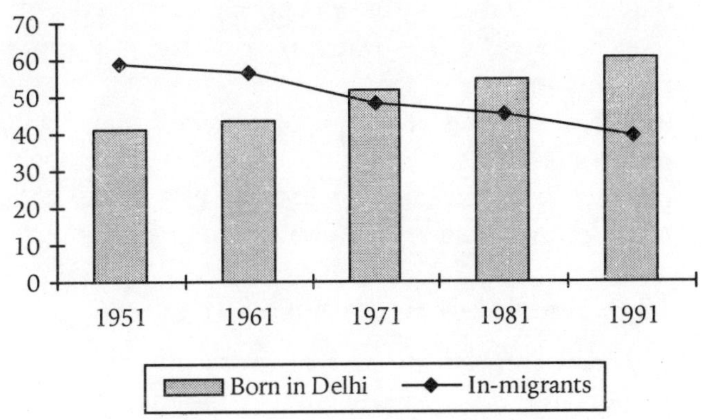

As per Singh's calculation based on census data, nearly 80 per cent of in-migrants to Delhi come from the north Indian neighbouring states. Uttar Pradesh contributes a large share of 46 per cent while Haryana and Bihar record 12 and 7 per cent respectively (Table 15.15).

TABLE 15.15

Distribution of In-migrants from different Regions/States to Delhi, 1991

Region/State	*In-migrants Population*	*Percentage*
North	29,69,315	80.0
Bihar	2,67,567	7.2
U.P.	17,04,197	45.9
Punjab	2,35,142	6.3
Haryana	4,40,275	11.9
Rajasthan	2,31,856	6.3
West	1,31,636	3.5
East and North-east	1,06,491	2.9
South	1,25,719	3.4

Source: Same as Table 15.14.

The assimilation of certain class categories of migrants who are entering Delhi to work in organised sector jobs is a characteristic that gives the capital-state its socio-cultural heterogeneous profile. On the other hand, the labouring masses who migrate into Delhi in search of a livelihood seen to never belong to the city. Even if they are second and third generation migrants, having established steady, relatively stable entrepreneurial ventures, the caste-class and social status seems to classify them into the divisions of acceptable and unacceptable groups. The poor and vulnerable migrants who live in slums, JJ clusters, and similar conditions akin to substandard housing remain the unacceptable populations in public image as well as in state policymakers perceptions. The pavement dwellers and shelterless, destitute persons are worse off in the hierarchy of vulnerabilities. Women among these groups are affected the most due to exposure to insecurities stemming from a range of factors like water to violence. The inflow of migrants, even the temporary ones who try to save on cost of financing for an accommodation by living on pavements and so on add to the numbers of shelterless persons. The shortage of housing for these segments becomes more acute as a result of such migrants.

15.6 Housing Vulnerability/Shelterless

Large numbers of persons living in the capital city (especially the socially and economically backward population groups) live in substandard housing, in slums and *jhuggi jhopri* clusters. The Planning Commission calculated nearly 12 lakh people in the capital as living below the poverty line—this accounts for 8 per cent of Delhi's population. Most of it is urban poverty. The Census of India 2001 estimates Delhi's slum population to be above 20 lakhs, of which nearly 9 lakhs are women. Only 4.3 lakhs of women inhabiting the slums in Delhi are literate. The JJ clusters numbering 1160, houses 32 lakhs of people, which is nearly 24 per cent (Table 15.16). Ali (2004) mentions that nearly 50-55 per cent of Delhi's population lives in substandard housing akin to slum like conditions (Women's Link, Jan.-March, 2004).

TABLE 15.16

Urban Settlement Pattern in 1999-2000

Category	*No. of Settlements*	*Population (in Lakhs)*	*Percentage to Total Population*	*Population as per DUEIIP*
Jhuggi Jhopri Clusters	1160	32.0	23.84	20.72
Resettlement Colonies	52	20.0	14.90	17.76
Unauthorised Colonies	1500	35.0	26.08	25.16
Urban Villages	216	6.0	4.47	8.88
Notified Slum Areas	-	9.5	7.08	26.64
Shelterless	-	0.6	0.44	-
Planned Colonies	-	29.2	23.18	33.08
Total	-	132.3	100.00	132.34

Source: Hazards Centre, 2003;

i) Reports on Slums in Delhi, Slum & JJ Deptt, MCD, 1994.
ii) Evaluation of Slum upgradation strategies in Delhi, (2001), Parvesh Siroha, Unpublished Thesis, SPA, New Delhi
iii) Economic Survey of Delhi 2001-2002
iv) DUEIP, Status Report for Delhi 21, GOI & MoE&F, January 2001, page 1, chapter 7.

The reasons for people to migrate to Delhi relate to the higher per capita investment by the Central and state government, the higher income earning levels and better employment avenues it offers. A comparison of the State Government Plan and non-plan expenditure between Delhi and the neighbouring States (Table 15.17) show that Delhi invests about 3 times more per capita excluding the Union Government spending under Central projects in Delhi. As expected this is going to provide much greater opportunities for employment than what is available in Uttar Pradesh, Rajasthan, Madhya Pradesh, Bihar and even Haryana.

The increasing population in Delhi puts undue pressure on the city's administration for provision of infrastructure and urban utilities such as water, roads, electricity, shelter, sanitation, health, education and so on.

Non-availability of safe water for drinking purposes causes health problems which can be of very severe nature. Inadequate provision of basic facilities such as water, sanitation, health and so on, impact women more adversely, adding on to their vulnerabilities. Women have to often resort to open defecation for lack of any other alternative options. The social shame associated with it compels them to opt for darker hours of the day during dawn or dusk that exposes them to violence and abuse.

TABLE 15.17

Per Capita Investment in Delhi and Neighbouring States

Year 2001-2002	*State Government Expenditure (Rs. in crores)*	*Population*	*Rupees per Capita*
Central Government	4,10,309	1,027,015,247	3995
Bihar	15,599	82,878,796	1879
Haryana	10,832	21,082,989	5158
Madhya Pradesh	16,794	60,385,118	2799
Rajasthan	19,561	56,443,122	3493
Uttar Pradesh	43,247	166,052,859	2605
Delhi	7,575	13,782,976	5410

Source: Hazards Centre, 2003; Public Finance, Centre for Monitoring, Indian Economy Pvt. Ltd., Mumbai, March 2002.

The pursuit to beautify the city has been undertaken at the cost of some sections of the city's population—the poor and labouring masses. Extensive demolitions and relocation of slums to the outskirts are underway by way of resettling these slums and JJ clusters. In 1999-2001, nearly 23,000 families were relocated while another 80,000 families were targeted for 2002.

According to MCD, the migrant population of Delhi is about 5 to 6 lakhs per annum. Census decadal figures reveal an overall growth of 4.4 lakhs per year. During 1991-2001, the *Jhuggi Jhopri* cluster population grew from 1.3 million to 3.2 million—approximately 2 lakh per year.

In 2001, of the 13.8 million populations in Delhi: about 8 million live in subhuman conditions. There are 3.5 million people in the estimated 1500 unauthorised colonies, which are not entitled to any civic services. Another 3 million live in 1200 jhuggi clusters (slums) where the municipality is supposed to provide communal facilities. And more than 1.5 million live in resettlement colonies that are entitled to household sites and services (Sagar, to be published; Roy, 2000).

Many concerned groups have lamented the absence of infrastructural facilities and basic amenities in the place where these households have been relocated. Alpana Sagar (based on her work in the Gautam Nagar slums where the families have been relocated to Badarpur border) reveals how this resettlement ruptures the fabric of people's existence. Apart from the physical disruption, many people face economic disruption, especially the women, as they lose out on the livelihood opportunities offered by the surrounding areas. Even for the children, the existing links for schooling established in the original place are disturbed and often the place of relocation may not be adequately equipped to replace their needs. The added burden due to shifts in the livelihood profile of the households also affects the children who are no longer in a position to pursue education due to financial constraints. Thus, while women find it difficult to manage the domestic duties with the paid work as servants, helpers that they earlier undertook, children have been deprived of the social support structures in the new location due to the nature of the resettling undertaken by lottery. The need for transportation from the relocated areas to their workplaces adds to the costs incurred by the displaced persons.

A study by the Hazards Centre (2003) stated that under the environmental improvement strategy, basic amenities such as water, toilets, bathrooms, drainage, pavements, *dhalaos*, *Basti Vikas Kendras*, community spaces, etc. are extended to the JJ clusters within a norm of Rs.800 per capita. Delhi Government provides necessary funds to the tune of Rs.20 crores for this purpose. The facilities provided since 1990 and up to March 2000 are as follows:

- 19,049 toilets at 657 locations
- 18,00,340 sq. m. of pavements and 8,49,000 m. of drains in most locations.
- 2692 water hydrants, 892 deep hand pumps, 4 tubewells up to 1991-92. DJB has been providing water supply after that.
- 284 Shishu Vatikas.

Based on these figures it may be surmised that less than half the JJ clusters have been provided with even the basic urban amenities of water and sanitation. The facilities that are lacking reflect the deprivations and vulnerabilities faced by all those inhabiting these locations and they are primary schools; dispensaries; street lights; peripheral infrastructural services like roads, transport, parks, workplaces, and hospitals (Hazards Centre, 2003).

As per government policy the relocation is necessitated on the basis of certain priorities as follows:

1. where the lands is required for specific projects;

2. because the existing JJ clusters are a cause of social tension in the area;
3. from areas where they are continuously exposed to the vagaries of nature such as 'Yamuna Bandh'.
4. from along the railway tracks for both environmental and human safety.

The people's housing policy document drafted by the Hazards Centre pointed out that the relocation scheme of the government is based on two assumptions: (1) all the squatters occupying public land would be given alternative sites (on the basis of cut-off dates, beyond which *jhuggies* would not be eligible for relocation); and (2) no new *jhuggies* would be allowed to come up on public land in Delhi after the cut-off date. The National Alliance of People's Movements has pointed out that the government has failed on both these grounds.

15.7 Public Transportation

The availability of adequate means for public transportation is an essential element to reduce vulnerability of the commuting public in Delhi. The major source of public commutation is traveling by buses, DTC, Blue line or chartered services. In spite of possessing the largest fleet of buses, Delhi still falls short of the demand for transportation services. This may be due to the outreach and routes followed, timing of services, capacity of vehicle and so on. The public perception survey conducted by DRS for Delhi found that public dependence on bus transport services is quite significant. The cost of traveling is also fairly reasonable, although the absence of bus pass facility for poor, unorganised workers who earn small sums and have to travel long distances within the capital-city is a matter of grave concern and worthy of attention. There is also a need to re-examine the demand pattern for bus routes after resettlement and relocation of large numbers of slums and squatters, as well as industrial complexes subsequent to the order for closure of polluting industries located within Delhi.

The increasing numbers of private vehicles in the city, especially cars and other four wheelers have resulted in clogging the roads of Delhi. Even the operation of flyovers and widening of roads have not been able to ebb the pressure put by these ever-growing numbers of vehicles. The effort of Delhi Government to check for the in flow from other states by putting some restrictions on timings of goods carrying vehicles can only address a minor part of the problem.

The operation of DMRC and its widening scope will have some impact on easing the burden. At the moment, 1.5 lakh persons use the Delhi metro every day. Reliable and comfortable public transportation can assist in reducing the usage of privately owned vehicles. This may help in preventing the accidents on roads, curb the rising rage levels of drivers and the fear of common persons being killed/hurt as a result of the high number of accidents. More than 10,000 traffic accidents are reported by the NCRB during 2001 in Delhi. Nearly 115 cases of accidents involve private cars.

The other modes of private transport such as cycles, two wheelers are also at risk of accidents. A substantial number of pedestrians (557) are killed due to road accidents, which accounts for nearly one-third of all pedestrian deaths in the country (NCRB, 2001).

The new flyovers and high speed roads built with a view to bring Delhi at par with international standards of metropolitan cities, have limited concern for the walking pedestrian. The manually driven handcarts, cycle rickshaws, bicycles and so on also have to exert more physical strain to negotiate these roads.

The control exercised on the number of cycle-*rickshaws* by the Municipal Authorities of Delhi and the area designated for their plying puts the operators through tremendous insecurity and exposes them to harassment. The city administration declared that it would not allow more than 90,000 licenses for the entire city (Kishwar, 2003). There is no such ceiling imposed on the plying of any other motorised vehicles. The imposition of such a restrictive policy gives space for a flourishing extortion racket for issuing and renewing licences as well as periodical bribes for plying cycle-*rickshaws*. The vehicles are arbitrarily seized in the name of decongestion of the city with the city authorities proudly claiming destruction of 50,000 rickshaws every year (Kishwar, 2003). The harried rickshaw puller, often not even the owner but a mere tenant operating the vehicle, is already under tremendous pressure and has to face economic assault, humiliation, physical beating for the service that is being rendered to the population of Delhi.

The authorities expend quite a lot of energy trying to restrict the movement of such slow/manually operated modes of transportation, such as bullock-cart, *tonga, thela, rickshaw* and so on especially in certain parts of the city which they desire to make into the main travel corridors. The need to plan for these sections of the population who depend on these modes of transport for commuting or livelihood is completely lost on them. It is highly desirable that the authorities exert some of their energies towards legitimately legalising these operations and providing the space to work and live with dignity. These concerns are shared by the vast range of the unorganised workers in Delhi who are providing their labour services for various tasks.

15.8 Unorganised Workers

The capital state offers better opportunities for employment, attracting migrants, who involve themselves in a host of unorganised sector activities that are inherently vulnerable. The vulnerability stems from the ambiguity in their legal status as no overt recognition of their work/activity exists. A whole range of petty transport activities (public and goods carriers), street vendors as well as the contractual workers (who are not on the rolls and therefore cannot claim any of the worker's rights) and service providers fall under the vast group of working population, who are in no way illegal or indulging in unlawful practices, but in absence of mechanisms within state governance structures to acknowledge or register them, they are vulnerable and exposed to harassment.

TABLE 15.18

Status-wise Distribution of Workforce – DELHI

Status	*Male*	*Female*	*Total*
Self-Employed	1254706 (34.97)	50285 (16.43)	1304991 (33.51)
Regular Wage/Salaried	2054453 (57.25)	237222 (77.52)	2291675 (58.84)
Others	279245 (7.78)	18523 (6.05)	297768 (7.65)
Total Workforce	3588404 (100)	306030 (100)	3894434 (100)

Source: DES, NSS State Sample 55th Round.

A number of auto, cycle-*rickshaw* drivers of the city are not themselves owners of the vehicle, but operate on hired vehicles (often on a daily basis). Similarly, contractors who hire labour groups by sub-contracting work orders to them are technically neither the employers nor do they owe any worker protection to the workers under such arrangements. Women who undertake homebased contractual jobs are also in a similar situation.

Entire mass of agricultural labourers, construction workers, manufacturing and repairing, personal service providers as well as those who work within the trading sector (from large shops to petty traders) fall under the category of unorganised workers, who have no protection, are working under insecure conditions, are paid low wages and are extremely vulnerable.

The self-employed entrepreneurs who are involved in petty vending activities and similar other sectors of work, especially the street vendors and those who sell on foot at crossroads or on pavements are vulnerable to the persistent harassment of police and municipal authorities. A mechanism to issue licences or identity cards to such operators needs to be worked out to avoid such humiliation and insecurity so that they can work with dignity and not be in constant fear of the authorities.

15.8.1 Street Vending

In a rare gesture by the government municipal authorities MCD filed a petition to the Supreme Court raising concerns over the government policy for street vending and hawking. There have been proposals to designate certain areas in localities for the street vendors and hawkers, who are catering to the local needs of inhabitants. It has been emphasised that these hawker zones be created where there is a natural market (as it occurs among the unorganised operators), rather than designating artificial zones for hawking that are likely to have few takers. Manushi began work on the pilot project for hawkers by building the infrastructure for the model market for street vendors at Sewa Nagar after crossing numerous hurdles and obstacles. The MCD is committed to replicate this model all over the city if the pilot endeavour proves to be successful.

15.8.2 Sex Workers

This constitutes a category of work that is not entirely recognised despite its presence and growth. Persons involved in sex work are still not enumerated as workers, since the prevailing morality does not permit acceptance of explicit sexual services for monetary compensation as economic work. The result of this non-recognition is that sex workers who are very often extremely poor, belong to socially backward populations, and thus already vulnerable are deprived of any workers' rights or protection. The social stigma associated with the work affects their children too.

The health issues by far have been one of the critical areas that have brought the focus directly upon sex work, especially in the context of HIV/AIDS. Protection from sexually transmitted diseases and fatal infections such as HIV/AIDS have been the basis for government and social groups to address the issues concerning sex workers and the legalisation of their work.

The sex worker as a person involved in illegal activities is further victimised, while the demander of their services who is actually paying for it often goes unnoticed or unmarked.

TABLE 15.19

Classification of Workers by Major Activity Group

S. No.	Major Activity Group	Workers ('000) 1980	1990	1998
1.	Agricultural activities (other than crop production and plantation)	17 (1.15)	21 (1.01)	22 (0.64)
2.	Mining and Quarrying	12 (0.82)	9 (0.43)	0 (0.00)
3.	Manufacturing & repair services	463 (31.45)	636 (30.52)	1440 (41.13)
4.	Electricity, Gas & Water Supply	20 (1.36)	21 (1.01)	115 (3.29)
5.	Construction	8 (0.54)	11 (0.53)	22 (0.63)
6.	Wholesale Trade	256 (17.39)	105 (5.04)	158 (4.52)
7.	Retail Trade	-	340 (16.31)	535 (15.30)
8.	Hotels & Restaurants	59 (4.01)	80 (3.84)	115 (3.30)
9.	Transport	49 (3.33)	62 (2.97)	136 (3.90)
10.	Storage & Warehousing	20 (1.36)	33 (1.58)	27 (0.77)
11.	Communications	21 (1.43)	51 (2.45)	97 (2.79)
12.	Financing, Insurance, Real Estate and Business Services	112 (7.61)	194 (9.31)	207 (5.43)
13.	Community, Social & Personal Services	435 (29.55)	521 (25.00)	622 (17.78)
	Total	1472((100)	2084 100)	3500 (100)

Note: Figure in the brackets denotes the percentage to the total.

Source: *Socio-Economic Profile of Delhi—2001-02*, Planning Department, GNCTD, New Delhi, page 13.

15.8.3 Domestic Workers

This is one of the employment avenues that involves a large number of persons and has been growing over the years. As household incomes go up and/or women begin to undertake paid work outside their homes and are unable to carry out these domestic chores of washing and cleaning utensils, clothes, and the house, many domestic help providers are hired. Among some households this has come to be accepted as a status symbol and therefore the need for a servant is created. The availability of these services at a low cost due to the cheap and abundant labour facilitates easy access.

Many households who offer some space for the domestic help to stay with them, have full time access to the services and can seek assistance in a number of tasks from household maintenance to child care, cooking and shopping and so on. There are no securities or protection of worker's rights for these workers. Few organisations have tried to formalise the structures through which hiring of domestic helps occur so that they can negotiate slightly better terms of work. The stress on police verification of these workers especially due to the rising incidence of crimes committed by them has resulted in suspicion on the workers. The absence of a universal registration system for all beings is required, so that the basic information for every individual is available with the state authorities. The partisan approach of only verification for some sections is as if to say that all other segments cannot ever be involved with any criminal activity. Quite the contrary is true in the case of Delhi as also elsewhere in the country.

15.9 Old Age and Other Health Vulnerabilities

The increasing life expectancies have resulted in a larger number of the population surviving beyond the age of 65 years. A larger number of the old persons are women. The shift in family size and structure to small nuclear families with children moving away from parents to pursue greener pastures has the consequence of old

TABLE 15.20

Old Age Population in Delhi

		Male 1981	Male 1991	Female 1981	Female 1991	Persons 1981	Persons 1991
Percentage of Population above 60 years	Urban	4.33	4.67	4.55	4.84	4.43	4.75
	Rural	5.39	3.96	4.94	3.95	5.19	3.96
	Total	4.40	4.60	4.58	4.75	4.48	4.67
Old Age Dependency	Urban	6.69	7.53	7.82	8.20	7.32	7.82
	Rural	9.92	6.95	9.55	7.35	9.75	7.13
	Total	7.15	7.48	7.94	8.12	7.48	7.76

Source: Census of India, 1991.

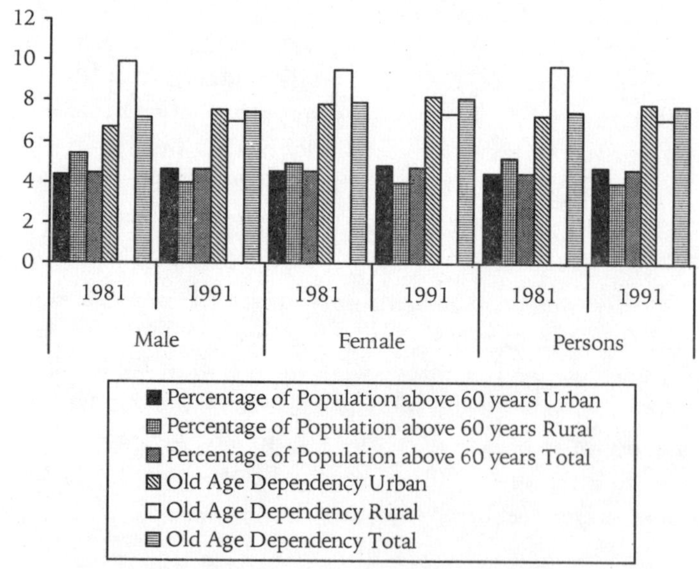

parents being left behind alone to fend for themselves. This is the age of failing health and physical strength. Among those who are relatively resourceful, the risk of being robbed, killed and cheated is stronger. The increasing pressure on the unemployed in the city for survival often pushes them to resort to such crimes.

15.10 Child Abuse and Violence against Children

The compulsion to work itself may be seen as child abuse in the form of economic exploitation of children by different agents involved—the employers, the parents and the government—for their inability to provide for and safeguard them against such a need. Children within society as part of it and as a result of their vulnerability are exposed to various crimes. The Indian Penal Code (IPC) lists the crimes against children and for the prominent categories data is collated annually from the cases registered with the police.

Crimes Against Children (CAC) under the IPC sections are: Murder (302 IPC); Foeticides (Crime against being born) (Section 315 & 316 IPC); Infanticides (Crime against Unborn Child) (Section 315 IPC); Abetment of Suicide (Section 305 IPC); Exposure and Abandonment (Crime against Children by Parents or Others to Expose or to Leave them with the Intention of Abandonment) (Section 317 IPC); Kidnapping and Abduction for Several Reasons: for exporting (Section 360 IPC); from lawful guardianship (Section 361 IPC); for ransom (Section 363 to be read along with 384 IPC); for camel racing (Section 363); for begging (Section 363 A; to compel for marriage (Section 366); for slavery (Section 367); for stealing from its person (under 10 years of age only) (Section 369 IPC); Procuration of Minor Girls for Inducement to force or seduce to illicit intercourse (Section 366 A); Selling of Girls for Prostitution (Section 372 IPC); Buying of Girls for Prostitution (Section 373 IPC); Rape and Unnatural Offences.

The Special and Local Laws (SLL) sections are: Immoral Trafficking (Prevention) Act (ITPA) (minors abused in prostitution); Child Marriage Restraint Act; and Child Labour (Prevention) Act.

As per the NCRB, a total of 697 cases of crimes against children were registered in the UT of Delhi during the year 2002. Nearly two-thirds of these involve cases of kidnapping and abduction (426) for various reasons. Other crimes against children involve rape (38 cases), murder (29 cases), exposure and abandonment (29 cases) and foeticide (20 cases).

Even a quick look at the newspaper reports highlighting the growing malaise in our society show that where even institutions of education are unsafe from violence and the educators themselves are perpetrators of crimes. This acts as a severe deterrent in achieving the goal of universal elementary education and improving school enrollments, especially of girls. It is horrific that this should be occurring in the capital city of Delhi.

- O.P. Sharma, Principal of Government Middle School in Raghubir Nagar and Ved Prakash Sharma, Vice Principal of Sarvodaya Bal Vidyalaya, West Patel Nagar and their two friends were arrested for allegedly raping a 16 year old girl – a correspondence student. They threatened to kill her if she disclosed the matter.
- A government school teacher, Naeem Ahmed Siddiqui of Sarvodaya Bal Vidyalaya, Rouse Avenue, was sent to judicial custody for allegedly sodomising a 10-year old student.
- November, 2004 – Teacher of a Mehrauli Government School, held on charges of raping an 8-year old student in the school's toilet. He had threatened to kill the girl if she talked about it.
- Summer 2004 – A Jehangiri Government School teacher raped a 10-year old student, the daughter of a daily wage labour. Later arrested by police.
- September 2003 – A class VII student was raped inside a Government School at Saket no arrests yet.
- June 2003 – Samaipur Badli School teacher raped a 10-year old student inside school; later arrested;
- February 2004 – a 14 year old girl was allegedly molested by an unidentified man in a government school at R.K. Puram. No trace of the accused.

Within Delhi, in terms of districts, Northwest stands out to be the worst with 263 of the 697 cases being registered are from this district (Table 15.21). In cases of crimes against children, the guardians have a critical role in generating awareness, identification and assisting in the process of justice delivery along with the police and judiciary. In 2002, the total number of cases pending with the police for investigation was 949. Only in 28 cases, investigation was refused, whereas in 203 cases the charge was found false or a mistake of fact or law. Chargesheets were submitted in 342 cases, with another 115 cases remaining pending during the year. As compared to the all India scenario, the chargesheeting rate for Delhi is lower and the pendancy rate slightly higher in cases of crimes committed against children.

In comparison, the performance of courts with respect to disposal of persons arrested for committing crimes against children has been very poor. Of the 967 cases under trial at the beginning of the year 2002, in only 111 cases the trial could be completed. A large number of the

TABLE 15.21

District-wise Incidence of Crimes Committed Against Children during 2002

District/ Division	*Incidence (total number of cases)*
Central	26
G.R.P (Rly)	2
East	27
IGI Airport	0
New Delhi	22
North	62
North East	89
North West	263
South	63
South West	59
Special Cell	0
S.T.F	0
West	84
Total	**697**

Source: NCRB, 2002.

cases remained pending and only 22 persons were convicted among the cases in which trial was completed. Speeding up the process of justice delivery and ensuring an improvement in the conviction rate is essential for building trust among the public for reposing confidence on the systems of justice that are in place.

15.11 Some Recommendations

- Improve educational levels for women, especially belonging to SCs, OBCs and poor households.
- Assess the shortfall of special schools and institutions in terms of both their provision and performance levels through thorough evaluation and assessment studies, so that concrete recommendations can be made regarding the needs pertaining to different segments of the population.
- Mechanisms to evolve better health care infrastructure and access for the vulnerable sections of Delhi's population.
- Evolve measures for checking the decline in sex ratios, especially among the children.
- Improve family planning outreach and coverage.
- Enhance the proportion of women having institutional deliveries.
- Provision of hostels for students, working women, differently abled and challenged populations, paying specific attention to their requirements.
- Elimination of child labour especially from the hazardous occupations, together with efforts to provide education and vocational skills to them.
- Measures to address the street children's problems and examine ways to provide institutional support to them.
- Assimilation of the migrant populations and provision for their basic needs.
- Low cost shelter/housing to be provided for the shelterless and slum dwellers.
- Involve local governance structures in innovative ways learning from the experiences of other states to minimise exploitation and harassment of the unorganised workers, especially street vendors, sex workers and domestic workers.
- Strategise for inclusion of the vulnerable segments for social security mechanisms.
- Evolve security measures for the aged populations, especially women who have a higher life expectancy and lower access to property and resources.
- Safety of children against abuse of all forms to be ensured.

References

Addlakha, R. (2008). "Disability, Gender and Society", *Indian Journal of Gender Studies* 15(2): 191-207.

Ali, Sabir (2004). "Women's Participation in Improvement of Environment and Urban Utilities in Slums", *Women's Link* 10(1): 2-5, January-March.

Hazards Centre (2003). *A People's Housing Policy: A Case Study of Delhi*. New Delhi.

Kishwar, Madhu (2003). "Denial of Constitutional Equality: Government's War on Cycle Rickshaw Pullers", *Manushi* 134.

National Crime Records Bureau (Various Years). *Crime in India*. Ministry of Home Affairs, Government of India.

National Sample Survey (2002). "Mentally and Physically Challenged Persons in Delhi", *National Sample Survey 58th Round*. Delhi: Directorate of Economics and Statistics.

Panicker, R. and P. Nangia (1988). *Working and Street Children of Delhi*. Study conducted by United Nations Children's Fund, Middle and North India Office and V.V.G. National Labour Institute.

Roy, Dunu (2000). *http://www.india-seminar.com/2004/533/533%20dunu%20roy.htm*

Sagar, Alpana (unpublished). "Who Pays the Cost of Resettlement? A Tale of the Gautam Nagar Slum Dwellers". (*mimeo*).

Chapter 16

Industrial Development, Village & Small Industries

Industrial Development in Delhi

This chapter is divided into two Section—Section A and Section B. Part A focuses on organised sector in Delhi while, Part B is about unorganised sector in Delhi.

SECTION—A

16.1 Introduction

With the role of agriculture being extremely restricted in expanding the magnitude of economic activity and generating higher levels of income and employment, the task of secondary and tertiary sectors becomes critically important in Delhi. With the Master Plan for the region ruling out large and heavy industries, Delhi's industry (factory sector) accounted for less than 3 per cent of factories at the national level and less than 2 per cent of industrial output, manufacturing net value added and employment and barely 1 per cent of fixed capital in manufacturing in 2002-03 (Table 16.1). Compared to the fourteen major states, Delhi ranked third from the bottom in terms of the number of factories in 2002-03, second from the bottom in terms of employment and fixed capital (preceding only Orissa) and at the bottom ranked in terms of manufacturing output and net value added. It has to be noted, however, that Delhi is a small state in terms of absolute size as compared to the others.

TABLE 16.1

Contribution by Delhi to Indian Industry (Factory Sector)

	Percentage Share in National Industrial				
	Number of Factories	*Output*	*Net Value Added*	*Employment*	*Fixed Capital*
1970-71	2.61 (12)	1.88 (15)	1.66 (14)	1.93 (15)	1.19 (14)
1980-81	3.33 (11)	2.21 (15)	1.59 (14)	1.81 (15)	1.59 (14)
1990-91	3.13 (12)	2.09 (15)	1.97 (14)	1.77 (14)	0.66 (14)
2000-01	2.66 (13)	1.54 (15)	1.40 (14)	1.51 (14)	0.55 (14)
2002-03	2.68 (13)	1.62 (15)	1.95 (15)	1.70 (14)	1.05 (14)

Note: Figures in the parenthesis represent rank when compared to the 14 major states (see Table 16.2 for the names of the states).

Source: Annual Survey of Industries 1973-74 to 1997-98: A Data Base on the Industrial Sector in India, EPW Research Foundation and Annual Survey of Industries Quick Estimates for 2002-03.

A comparison of inter-regional levels of industrialisation in terms of the share of states in net value added in factory sector is presented in Table 16.2. Maharashtra accounted for more than a quarter of industrial value added in 1970-71 and 1980-81 and though its share came down to about one-fifth by 2002-2003, the state maintained its top rank throughout. Gujarat ranked second in 2002-03 followed by Tamil Nadu, undivided Uttar Pradesh and Karnataka. Five states—Maharashtra, West Bengal, Tamil Nadu, Gujarat, and Uttar Pradesh—had a dominant share in manufacturing value added throughout the period, accounting for over three-fifths in the first two reference years and over one-half in the remaining three. The share of Delhi remained below 2 per cent throughout reaching a peak of 1.97 per cent in 1990-91 and the state was ranked at the bottom except in 2002-03 when Orissa in that position displaced it. The share in net value added, however, was larger than Delhi's share in Indian population of 1.37 per cent in 2002-03. The same year, value added per person in Delhi was Rs.2294 as compared to the national figure of Rs.1618.

TABLE 16.2

Inter-Regional Disparity in Levels of Industrialisation: 1970-71 to 2002-03

	Percentage Share in National Net Value Added (Factory Sector)									
	1970-71		*1980-81*		*1990-91*		*2000-01*		*2002-03*	
	Share	*Rank*	*Share*	*Rank*	*Share*	*Rank*	*Share*	*Rank*	*Share*	*Rank*
Andhra Pradesh	3.97	8	4.89	8	5.79	7	6.18	5	6.51	6
Bihar[1]	5.53	7	4.20	9	5.04	9	3.32	11	4.09	10
Delhi	1.66	15	1.59	15	1.97	15	1.40	15	1.95	14
Gujarat	9.14	4	9.55	4	8.67	4	11.74	2	12.61	2
Haryana	2.21	12	2.90	12	3.18	11	3.88	9	4.46	8
Karnataka	5.75	6	5.06	6	5.38	8	5.78	7	6.95	5
Kerala	2.87	10	3.28	10	2.37	13	2.47	13	2.19	13
Maharashtra	26.79	1	25.04	1	23.30	1	21.77	1	20.43	1
Madhya Pradesh[2]	3.55	9	5.05	7	5.84	6	6.06	6	4.86	7
Orissa	1.89	14	1.66	14	2.24	14	1.64	14	1.34	15
Punjab	2.26	11	3.24	11	3.61	10	2.99	12	3.00	11
Rajasthan	2.10	13	2.80	13	3.02	12	3.66	10	2.89	12
Tamil Nadu	9.82	3	10.31	3	11.25	2	11.51	3	9.07	3
Uttar Pradesh[3]	6.61	5	6.28	5	8.98	3	7.34	4	7.70	4
West Bengal	13.64	2	11.53	2	6.21	5	3.97	8	4.11	9

Notes: (1) includes Jharkhand (2) includes Chhattisgarh (3) includes Uttarakhand.

Source: Annual Survey of Industries 1973-74 to 1997-98: A Data Base on the Industrial Sector in India EPW Research Foundation and Annual Survey of Industries: Quick Estimates for 2002-03 Central Statistical Organisation.

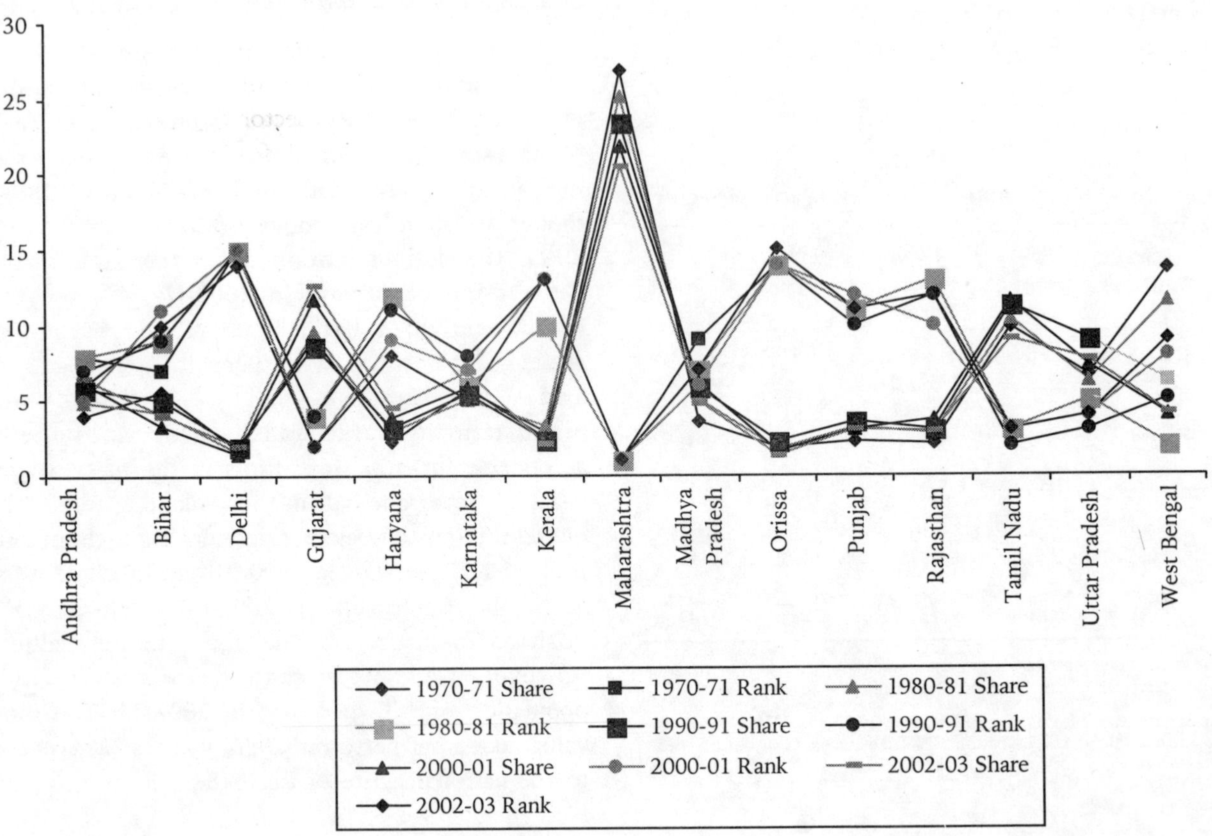

Manufacturing accounted for about one-fifth of Delhi's Gross State Domestic Product in the 80s and the first half of the 90s (Figure 16.1). From then on its share dropped to hover around 12 per cent for the remainder of the period. This share was well below that of the industrialised states of Maharashtra, West Bengal, and Tamil Nadu though the three states experienced a decline similar to that of Delhi (Table 16.3). Gujarat, in contrast, experienced an increase over the two decades. In 2002-03, Delhi's share of 12 per cent for manufacturing was well below the national figure of 15.6 per cent.

TABLE 16.3

Contribution of Manufacturing to GSDP

Year	*Manufacturing as % of GSDP*					*Regd Manufacturing as % of Manufacturing*				
	Delhi	*GUJ*	*MAH*	*TN*	*WB*	*Delhi*	*GUJ*	*MAH*	*TN*	*WB*
1980-81	18.4	22.0	27.4	27.4	21.7	40.2	74.7	69.9	54.5	59.5
1985-86	19.9	27.7	27.3	26.0	19.5	41.8	76.6	71.6	60.5	58.6
1990-91	21.3	29.6	28.2	24.2	18.8	44.5	76.7	75.5	67.1	59.0
1995-96	14.9	31.3	26.6	28.7	17.3	42.5	71.6	68.6	64.8	50.2
2000-01	12.0	34.3	27.1	23.7	16.0	47.1	69.1	66.9	62.9	50.0
2002-03	12.0	29.8	21.1	23.6	15.3	39.8	65.6	63.4	63.2	49.0

Source: *Domestic Product of States of India: 1960-61 to 2000-01*, EPW Research Foundation, and *SDP State Series (1993-94)*, Central Statistical Organisation.

Unregistered manufacturing was clearly the dominant sub sector of manufacturing in Delhi, with the registered component accounting for only about two-fifths of total manufacturing. This share remained fairly stable over the entire period (Figure 16.1).

FIGURE 16.1

Relative Importance of Manufacturing in the Gross State Domestic Produt of Delhi

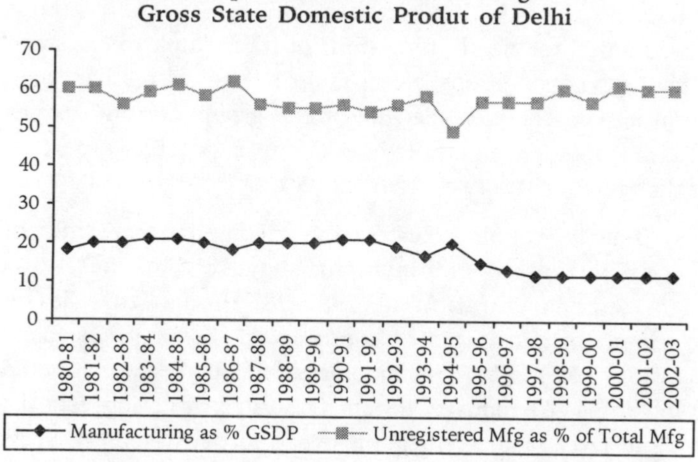

Source: *Domestic Product of States of India: 1960-61 to 2000-01*, EPW Research Foundation, and *SDP State Series (1993-94)*, Central Statistical Organisation.

This is in contrast to the states of Maharashtra, Gujarat and Tamil Nadu, where it is the registered component that accounted for well over three-fifth of the manufacturing sector (Table 16.3). For Delhi, the share of registered sub-sector (39.8 per cent) in total manufacturing in 2002-03 was well below its share for the nation as a whole at 66.1 per cent.

16.2 Industrial Base and Structure

Composition

The composition of the industrial base of Delhi is examined in terms of the relative shares of different industry groups (at 2-digit level of NIC) in Net Value Added and Employment (Table 16.4). In 1980-81 five industry groups accounted for more than half of net value added originating in the factory sector of Delhi. These groups were Machinery and Equipment (17.6 per cent), Paper and Paper products (9.3 per cent), Textile Products (9.2 per cent), Cotton Textiles (8.5 per cent), and Basic Chemicals and Chemical Products (9.1 per cent). In 1997-1998 the share of the top five sectors had come down to less than half. The sectors, with the exception of Cotton Textiles, which was replaced by Food Products, remained the same though their ranking in order of relative contribution had changed. The highest contributor to net value added was Textile Products (17.5 per cent) followed by Machinery and Equipment (11.0 per cent), Paper and Paper Products (6.7), Food Products (6.4), and Basic Chemicals (4.4 per cent). An interesting aspect of this change over the two reference years is the drastic decline of the industry group Cotton Textiles (NIC code 23).

The concentration ratios derived in respect of both the top 3 and 5 industry groups suggest a greater diversification between the two reference years (Table 16.5). These ratios, however, do not include the industry category 'Others'. In 1997-98, this category contributed 36.6 per cent to net value added with the industry group Electricity, Gas, Steam, and Hot Water Supply (NIC code 40) alone contributing 33.6 per cent. If this group is included for both years, then there was clearly an increase in concentration, with the top two industry groups alone (Electricity etc., and Textile Products) contributing more than one-half to net value added in 1997-98. The Hirschman-Herfindahl indices derived for both the reference years, with and without inclusion of the industry group 'Others' clearly indicate greater concentration (Table 16.5). For sustained industrial growth and development in the long run, a desirable prerequisite is that the industrial base broadens and becomes more diversified. This does not seem to have occurred as far as Delhi is concerned. For the nation as a whole, the Hirschman-Herfindahl index suggests a minor increase in levels of concentration over the two reference years though the increase was clearly less marked than in Delhi.

TABLE 16.4

Changing Industrial Base of Delhi: 1980-81 and 1997-98 (All Figures as Percentages to Respective All-Industries Totals)

NIC 1987 Code	*Industry*	*Share in NVA*		*Share in Employment*	
		1980-81	*1997-98*	*1980-81*	*1997-98*
20-21	Food Products	7.7	6.4	5.1	7.1
22	Beverages, Tobacco & Related Products	1.6	1.4	1.4	2.0
23	Cotton Textiles	8.5	0.0	12.5	0.2
24	Wool, Silk & Man-made Fibre Textiles	0.6	0.2	1.2	0.4
25	Jute, other Vegetable Fibre Textiles except Cotton	0.0	0.0	0.0	0.0
26	Textile Products (incl. Wearing Apparel)	9.2	17.5	8.7	20.0
27	Wood and Wood Products: Furnitures and Fixtures	0.3	0.2	0.5	0.5
28	Paper and Paper Products, Printing, Publishing and Allied Industries	9.3	6.7	8.8	8.7
29	Leather and Leather Products, Fur and Leather Substitutes	0.4	0.7	0.2	0.7
30	Basic Chemicals and Chemical Products (except Petroleum and Coal Products)	9.1	4.4	4.9	6.5
31	Rubber, Plastic, Petroleum & Coal Products	2.5	2.0	3.3	5.9
32	Non-Metallic Mineral Products	1.6	0.3	2.4	1.2
33	Basic Metals and Alloys	3.5	2.9	3.5	3.0
34	Metal Products and Parts (except Machinery and Equipment)	4.5	4.1	5.2	6.1
35-36	Machinery and Equipment (other than Transport, Scientific, Photographic/ Cinematographic Equipment etc.)	17.6	11.0	14.7	16.6
37	Transport Equipment and Parts	7.1	2.2	5.9	7.1
38	Other Manufacturing Industries	2.0	2.2	2.3	2.8
39	Repair of Capital Goods	0.0	1.3	0.0	4.5
	Others	14.7	36.6	19.3	6.8
	All Industries	100	100	100.0	100.0

Source: Estimated from data presented in *Annual Survey of Industries 1973-74 to 1997-98: A Data Base on the Industrial Sector in India*, EPW Research Foundation.

The composition of the industrial base of Delhi, evaluated in terms of share in employment suggests a similar pattern of greater concentration. In 1980-81 the sector contributing the most to employment was Machinery and Equipment (14.7 per cent), followed by Cotton Textiles (12.5 per cent), Paper and Paper Products (8.8 per cent), Textile Products (8.7 per cent), and Transport Equipment and Parts (5.9 per cent). These five industry groups accounted for a little more than one-half of total industrial employment in the factory sector.

TABLE 16.5

Industrial Concentration in Delhi

Measure	*Delhi*			
	Share in NVA		*Share in Employment*	
	1980-81	*1997-98*	*1980-81*	*1997-98*
CR_3	36.1*	35.2*	36.0*	45.3*
CR_5	53.7*	46.0*	50.6*	59.5*
HH index	0.104	0.199	0.108	0.108
	0.112*	0.148*	0.106*	0.120*
	All India			
HH index	0.096	0.107	0.095	0.077
	0.103*	0.108*	0.104	0.081

Note: * indicates that the industry category 'Others' is excluded.

Source: Estimated from data presented in *Annual Survey of Industries 1973-74 to 1997-98: A Data Base on the Industrial Sector in India*, EPW Research Foundation.

By 1997-78 Textile Products had emerged as the single largest contributor replacing Machinery and Equipment and accounting, by itself, for one-fifth of total employment. The latter group was second-placed at 16.6 per cent followed by Paper and Paper Products (8.7 per cent), Transport Equipment and Parts (7.1 per cent), and Food Products (7.1 per cent). These five industry groups accounted for nearly three-fifth of total employment, with the first two groups alone contributing more than one-third. The complete decline of the group Cotton Textiles as a provider of employment was a notable aspect of change over the two reference years.

The concentration ratios derived in terms of contribution to employment suggest that there was greater concentration in 1997-98, though to a lesser degree than in terms of contribution to net value added (Table 16.5). The Hirschman-Herfindahl index, computed including the industry group 'Others', in fact suggests the same level of diversification over the two reference years though the index calculated excluding this group indicates a small increase in concentration levels. For the nation as a whole, however, the index reveals a clear increase in levels of diversification in terms of contribution to employment.

Regional theory suggests that, in the absence of perfect competition, industries would locate either to minimise costs or to maximise revenues and profits. In case of mobile factors of production, factors affecting location would include technical coefficients and the weights of inputs, the distance the inputs have to be transported, the nature of inputs (weight losing etc.), fragility or other factors affecting transport costs of inputs. In case of immobile factors, location decisions would involve determination of 'low-cost areas', choice between low-cost and transport cost minimising locations, potential benefits from agglomeration and so on. Decisions to locate near markets would be dependent again on comparison of transport costs of inputs *vis-à-vis* that of finished products, price elasticity of demand for the product and, finally, the trade off between production cost advantages of low-cost location in a situation of high locational variation in production costs and benefits from market segment proximity.[1]

A comparison of the industrial base of Delhi with that of the nation as a whole will be useful at this point to determine: (a) what industries the state has and, equally importantly, does not have, (b) the extent to which industry groups are under- or over-represented in Delhi as compared to the nation, that is, the extent to which the state has less than its 'fair' share and in which industries, more than its 'fair' share. The results of this exercise, done for the year 2002-03, have been presented in table 16.6 in terms of both relative shares of different industry groups (at 2-digit level of NIC 1998) within the state *vis-à-vis* that of all-India and Location Quotients (LQ). Location quotients have been derived as proportion of a region's total industrial employment in activity '*i*' compared to the same proportion derived for the same activity for the nation.[2] A value greater than unity is indicative of over-representation while a value less than unity indicates that the region has less than its 'fair' share in that activity.

TABLE 16.6

Comparison of the Industrial Base of Delhi with All-India: 2002-03 (All Figures as Percentages to Respective All-Industries Totals)

NIC 1998 Code	Industry	Share in Employment			Share in NVA	
		Delhi	All India	Location Quotient	Delhi	All India
15	Food Products & Beverages	7.2	16.4	0.4	12	9.6
16	Tobacco Products	0.4	5.7	0.1	0.9	3.2
17	Textiles	2.1	15.4	0.1	1.2	7.1
18	Wearing Apparel; Dressing & Dyeing of Fur	27.2	4.4	6.2	30.8	2.3
19	Leather & Leather Products	3.7	1.9	1.9	2.1	0.8
20	Wood & Wood Products except furniture etc.	0.2	0.7	0.3	0	0.2
21	Paper & Paper Products	1	2.3	0.4	0.2	1.5
22	Publishing, Printing etc.	10.5	1.6	6.5	13.3	1.7
23	Coke, Refined Petroleum Products etc.	0	0.9	0	0	10.7
24	Chemicals & Chemical Products	6.9	9.5	0.7	7.5	19
25	Rubber & Plastic Products	3.6	3.5	1	1.6	3.7
26	Other Non-Metallic Mineral Products	0.6	6.5	0.1	0.2	4
27	Basic Metals	1.5	7.1	0.2	1	9.2
28	Fabricated Metal Products except Machinery & Equipment	6.2	3.6	1.7	3.3	2.6
29	Machinery & Equipment n.e.c.	6.4	5	1.3	4.2	6
30	Office, Accounting & Computing Machinery	0.1	0.2	0.4	0	0.7
31	Electrical Machinery & Apparatus n.e.c.	4.4	2.8	1.6	3	3.4
32	Radio, Television & Communication Equipment etc.	3.4	1.4	2.5	8.8	2.2
33	Medical, Precision & Optical Instruments etc.	1.1	0.9	1.3	1.9	0.9
34	Motor Vehicles, Trailers & Semi-Trailers	4.1	3.4	1.2	1.9	4.4
35	Other Transport Equipment	2.1	2.2	0.9	1.3	3.2
36	Furniture, Manufacturing n.e.c.	3.6	1.7	2.1	1.7	1.5
	Other Industries	3.8	2.9	1.3	3.1	2
	All Industries	100	100		100	100

Source: Estimated from data presented in Annual Survey of Industries: Quick Estimates for 2002-03, Central Statistical Organisation.

---

1. Among others Isard *et al.* (1998), Kumar (2005), and Richardson (1973).
2. The Location Quotient serves as a tool for making comparisons essentially as a measure of an activity's relative concentration, and for any sector *i* in region $R(LQ_i^R)$ it may be defined as

$$LQ_i^R = \frac{E_i^R / E_i^N}{E^R / E^N}$$

or

$$LQ_i^R = \frac{E_i^R / E^R}{E_i^N / E^N}$$

In 2002-03, Delhi was heavily over-represented in Publishing, Printing, etc (NIC code 22- LQ 6.5), Wearing Apparel (NIC code 18- LQ 6.2), Radio, Television, Communication Equipment etc. (NIC code 32- LQ 2.5), and Furniture and Manufacturing n.e.c (NIC code 36- LQ 2.1). Not surprisingly, the first two were the top ranked industry groups in terms of their contribution to employment and value added. From Table 16.6 it is clear that the other industries with lower levels of over-representation were NIC codes 19, 28, 31, 33, 29, and 34. Industry groups that are gravely under-represented include Coke, Refined Petroleum Products etc. (NIC code 23- LQ 0.0), Tobacco Products (NIC code 16- LQ 0.1), Other Non-Metallic Mineral Products (NIC code 26-LQ 0.1), Textile Products (NIC code 17-LQ 0.1), Basic Metals (NIC code 27-LQ 0.2), and Wood and Wood Products except Furniture (NIC code 20-LQ 0.3). Other under-represented industries include NIC codes 21, 30, 15, 24, and 35. The industry group Rubber and Plastic Products (NIC code 25) was exactly represented with a LQ value of 1.0.

TABLE 16.7

Regional Specialisation in Industry: 2002-03

	Specialisation Index for 2002-03 (NIC 1998)		
State	*Value*	*State*	*Value*
Andhra Pradesh	0.238	Madhya Pradesh[2]	0.425
Bihar[1]	0.548	Orissa	0.495
Delhi	0.552	Punjab	0.345
Gujarat	0.370	Rajasthan	0.308
Haryana	0.394	Tamil Nadu	0.319
Karnataka	0.286	Uttar Pradesh[3]	0.220
Kerala	0.372	West Bengal	0.242
Maharashtra	0.213		

Specialisation Index for Delhi (NIC 1987)	
Year	Value
1980-81	0.255
1990-91	0.351
1997-98	0.388

Notes: (1) includes Jharkhand
(2) includes Chhattisgarh
(3) includes Uttarakhand.

Source: Estimated from data presented in Annual Survey of Industries Quick Estimates for 2002-03, Central Statistical Organisation and Annual Survey of Industries 1973-74 to 1997-98: A Data Base on the Industrial Sector in India, EPW Research Foundation.

The specialisation index measures the degree of divergence between the regional economic structures. Where the relative importance of any of the industry groups (2-digit) is exactly the same in all regions, the index takes the value of zero indicating the absence of any degree of specialisation. At the other extreme if any industry group is specific to one region only then the index takes the value of unity indicating that the level of specialisation is at its maximum.[3] In 2002-03, Delhi had the most specialised industrial structure as compared with the fourteen major states, closely followed by undivided Bihar and Orissa (Table 16.7). The specialisation index estimated for Delhi over three earlier reference years (1980-81, 1990-91, and 1997-98) suggests an increasing degree of specialisation.

The degree to which a region's activities are diversified is important in determining the extent to which its economy will be resilient. Narrow specialisation could result in short-term collapse in certain conditions while diversification will ensure that it is highly unlikely that a major proportion of total activity will suffer at any one point in time. Diversity also enables the development of a wide variety of skills and interests as also an extensive network of regional institutions and services. This growing lack of diversification of the industrial base of Delhi may be indicative of weakening inter-regional and inter-industry linkages. There is clearly a need for policy intervention to ensure greater diversification of Delhi's industrial base.

16.2.1 Decomposition of Industrial Growth

Variations in industrial employment in Delhi over the period 1980-81 to 1997-98 have been decomposed using shift-share analysis to identify the elements of that change with the purpose of identifying that component of regional growth that was region-specific

3. The Specialisation Index (*SI*) for any region *R* in a system with '*n*' industries and '*m*' regions is derived as $SI^R = 1/2\sum_i^n \left|S_i^R - \overline{S}_i\right|$

where SI^R denotes the share of industry '*i*' in the gross value added of region *R* and $\overline{S}_i$ the mean of the shares of industry '*i*' in the gross value added of all other (*m*-1) regions. The difference $\left(S_i^R - \overline{S}_i\right)$ measures the level of over- or under-representation of industry '*i*' in region *R*. The aggregate of absolute values of these differences indicates the extent of specialisation of region *R*. For details on this aspect see Batisse and Poncet (2003) and Bai *et al.* (2003).

and assessing the relative performance of Delhi in a specific industry.[4]

A positive shift is linked with relative locational advantage of a specific region for that specific industry and a negative shift with comparative locational disadvantages.

The results of shift-share analysis of NIC 2-digit industry groups over two sub-periods 1980-81 to 1990-91 and 1990-91 to 1997-98 have been presented in Table 16.8.

TABLE 16.8

Decomposition of Industrial Growth: 1980-81 to 1997-98

NIC 1987	*Growth Attributed to*				*Growth Attributed to*			
	NGE	*IMX*	*CET*	*LQ Change*	*NGE*	*IMX*	*CET*	*LQ Change*
20-21	+	-	+	+	+	-	-	-
22	+	+	+	+	+	-	-	-
23	+	-	-	-	+	-	-	-
24	+	+	-	-	+	+	-	-
25	+	-	+	+	+	-	-	-
26	+	+	+	+	+	+	+	-
27	+	-	-	+	+	-	-	-
28	+	-	-	+	+	-	-	-
29	+	+	+	+	+	-	-	-
30	+	+	+	+	+	+	-	-
31	+	+	+	+	+	+	-	-
32	+	+	-	-	+	-	-	-
33	+	-	+	+	+	-	-	-
34	+	+	-	-	+	+	-	-
35-36	+	+	+	+	+	-	-	-
37	+	-	+	+	+	-	-	+
38	+	+	-	-	+	+	-	-
39	+	+	+	+	+	+	-	-
40	+	+	-	-	+	-	+	+
41-42-43	+	+	+	+	+	+	+	+
74	+	+	+	+	+	+	-	-
97	+	-	-	+	+	-	-	+

Note: Growth rates of employment were estimated from 3-year averages for the base and terminal years of the sub-period.

Source: Estimated from data presented in Annual Survey of Industries 1973-74 to 1997-98: A Data Base on the Industrial Sector in India, EPW Research Foundation.

The national growth effect (NGE) is the extent to which the region would have expanded or contracted if it had altered at the same rate as the national economy. The industry mix effect (IMX) is the degree of change attributable to divergence in the sectoral composition of the region *vis-à-vis* that of the nation. If the effect is positive, then the region is specialising in industries that are growing faster than the overall national average and if negative, in industries that are growing at rates lower than the national average. The competitive effect (CET) measures the degree to which the region has shifted away from a path defined purely as a function of national growth and its specific sectoral composition. Each of the three effects can be determined for each industry within a region and summed over all industries to derive estimates for the entire region.

For the 80s, the national growth effect was positive for all industry groups indicating increasing employment in industry for the nation at large. In addition, the industry-mix effect was positive for 14 out of the 22 industry groups (NIC 2-digit codes 22, 24, 26, 29, 30, 31, 32, 34, 35-36, 38, 39, 40, 41-43, and 74) suggesting that the composition of industries was favourable to Delhi, with many of the 'high growth'

Industry groups being located within the region. The competitive effect was also positive for 13 industry groups within Delhi—20-21, 22, 25, 26, 29, 30, 31, 33, 35-36, 37, 39, 41-43, and 74—indicating that these grew at rates faster than the national average.

---

4. The Shift-Share model is as

$$^{R}E_i^t - E_i^{t-1} = NGE_i^R + IMX_i^R + CET_i^R$$

where $^{R}E_i^t$ is the employment in the ith sector of any region R at time t, NGE_i^R is the National Growth Effect, IMX_i^R the Industry Mix Effect, and CET_i^R the Competitive Effect. The three effects are in turn determined as

$$NGE_i^R = g_{ALL}^N \cdot {}^{R}E_i^{t-1},$$

$$IMX_i^R = {}^{R}E_i^{t-1} \cdot (g_i^N - g_{ALL}^N)$$

$$CET_i^R = {}^{R}E_i^{t-1} \cdot (g_i^R - g_i^N)$$

where g_{ALL}^N is per cent change in nationwide all-industries employment relative to the base period (t-1), g_i^N the per cent change in the ith industry national employment, and g_i^R the per cent change in i^{th} industry employment in region R. For different variations of the shift-share models see Kumar (2005), Loveridge and Selting (1998).

Nine industry groups experienced industry-mix and competitive effects that were both positive. These were Beverages, Tobacco and Related Products (NIC code 22), Textile Products (26), Leather and Leather Products (29), Basic Chemicals and Chemical Products (30), Rubber and Plastic Products (31), Machinery and Equipment (35-36), Repair of Capital Goods (39), Generation and Distribution of Gas, Steam etc. (41-43), and Storage and Warehousing Services (74). Not surprisingly, all these nine industry groups witnessed higher levels of concentration within Delhi with their location quotients increasing in value at the end of the sub-period (Table 16.8).

The national growth effect was similar for the second sub-period with all the industry groups experiencing a positive impact. However, the other two effects operated very differently in the nineties. Out of the 22 industry groups only nine—NIC codes 24, 26, 30, 31, 34, 38, 39, 41-43, and 74—had a positive industry mix effect and even more significantly, only 3 groups—NIC codes 26, 40, and 41-43—experienced a positive competitive effect (Table 16.8). Only two groups—Textile Products (NIC code 26), and Generation and Distribution of Gas, Steam etc. (41-43)—had both effects as positive. Not surprisingly, the value of location quotients decreased for 18 out of the 22 industry groups. Even out of the two groups that had both industry mix and competitive effects as positive, only industry group 41-43 experienced an increase in location quotient values.

Delhi's industrial development is not only dependent on locational and other external stimuli but also the activity-mix of industries it possesses. A region's economic structure influences its ability to retain (or expand) its share of prevailing activities or draw in new ones. Industrial growth is dependent on both the overall national growth rates and the region's competitive position. In addition, growth disadvantage may occur due to specialisation in industries that are not doing well either due to lack of technological progress or demand shift to other competing products that are being produced by industries in other regions or factors such as location, resources both human and material, and work culture. Policy intervention is required to ensure that Delhi (a) does not become structurally disadvantaged in that its industries loose out in competition with other similar industries in other states, (b) specialises in 'growth' industries that will result in higher overall growth, (c) does not specialise in cyclically sensitive industries that are particularly sensitive to cyclical swings, and (d) ensure, to the extent possible, that the prevalent terms of trade do not become detrimental to its current exports and imports.

16.2.2 Cost, Profitability, and Productivity

It is necessary at this point to analyse the cost structure and return to factors associated with Delhi's industrial sector. Examination of some of the ratios and technical coefficients underlying the overall industrial (factory) structure indicates that the region does not seem to be suffering from locational disadvantages (relative to the country at large) associated with high levels capital use. Figure 16.2 represents capital intensity (as reflected in fixed capital per employee—FK/E), capital productivity (measured as fixed capital per unit of value of output- FK/O), and capital-output ratio (fixed capital per unit of value added-FK/NVA) values for Delhi's industrial (factory) sector computed as a ratio to corresponding all-India values for the period 1980-81 to 2002-03. A value of unity for the ratio indicates similar levels of capital use while a value greater than unity is indicative of higher levels of capital use within the region relative to the nation. As may be seen from Figure 16.2, the values were continuously below unity throughout the period.

In 2002-03, the capital intensity for the region (average for all industries factory sector) was lower than the national average (Table 16.9). A mere six sectors (NIC codes 15, 16, 17, 18, 19, and 28) had capital intensity higher than that for the nation. Of these, only three—15, 18 and 28—were among the larger industry groups in Delhi. Again, capital productivity was higher for Delhi's industrial sector with the ratio for the region much lower-

FIGURE 16.2

Capital Intensity and Productivity-Comparison between Delhi and All-India

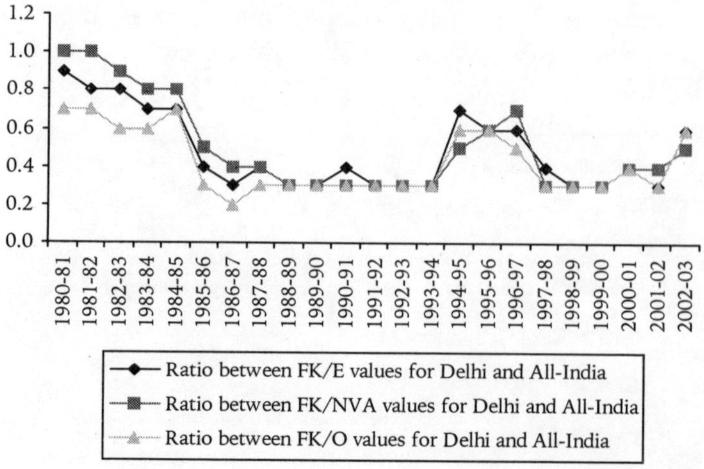

Source: Estimated from data presented in *Annual Survey of Industries 1973-74 to 1997-98: A Data Base on the Industrial Sector in India*, EPW Research Foundation and *Annual Survey of Industries* (various issues), Central Statistical Organisation.

TABLE 16.9

Structural Ratios and Co-efficient: 2002-03

NIC 1998 Code	*FK/E (Rs.000)*		*NVA/E (Rs.000)*		*FK/NVA Ratio*		*FK/O Ratio*		*NVA/O Ratio*		*TI/O Ratio*	
	Delhi	*India*	*Delhi*	*India*	*Delhi*	*India*	*Delhi*	*India*	*Delhi*	*India*	*Delhi*	*India*
15	65.4	43.6	413	127	0.16	0.34	0.02	0.03	0.12	0.10	0.86	0.88
16	37.1	6.7	567	120	0.07	0.06	0.02	0.02	0.30	0.35	0.69	0.64
17	77.7	43.3	144	99	0.54	0.44	0.08	0.06	0.15	0.14	0.80	0.80
18	46.5	23.3	280	113	0.17	0.21	0.03	0.04	0.19	0.20	0.79	0.77
19	66.3	28.5	144	92	0.46	0.31	0.07	0.04	0.15	0.14	0.81	0.84
20	2.2	21.3	39	68	0.06	0.31	0.01	0.04	0.14	0.14	0.84	0.82
21	22.0	138.2	60	139	0.37	0.997	0.02	0.13	0.07	0.13	0.89	0.82
22	73.8	78.7	315	224	0.23	0.35	0.06	0.09	0.24	0.25	0.71	0.70
23	62.1	692.8	390	2528	0.16	0.27	0.09	0.03	0.57	0.12	0.41	0.85
24	43.3	115.6	270	431	0.16	0.27	0.04	0.05	0.24	0.20	0.75	0.75
25	26.5	82.1	110	230	0.24	0.36	0.03	0.06	0.14	0.17	0.82	0.78
26	6.4	74.7	71	135	0.09	0.56	0.02	0.11	0.22	0.19	0.75	0.73
27	14.2	142.5	168	282	0.08	0.51	0.01	0.07	0.08	0.13	0.91	0.81
28	41.0	34.7	131	155	0.31	0.22	0.03	0.04	0.11	0.18	0.87	0.78
29	38.7	56.3	163	259	0.24	0.22	0.06	0.05	0.23	0.21	0.74	0.75
30	30.9	660.7	-81	679	-0.38	0.97	0.04	0.27	-0.10	0.28	1.07	0.68
31	19.8	45.4	166	262	0.12	0.17	0.02	0.03	0.17	0.19	0.82	0.78
32	59.9	194.3	650	359	0.09	0.54	0.04	0.08	0.40	0.15	0.59	0.81
33	38.7	44.6	405	235	0.10	0.19	0.02	0.04	0.24	0.22	0.75	0.75
34	37.8	127.0	113	278	0.33	0.46	0.07	0.06	0.20	0.13	0.78	0.82
35	21.6	77.4	153	323	0.14	0.24	0.03	0.05	0.20	0.20	0.77	0.78
36	25.0	42.3	120	191	0.21	0.22	0.03	0.03	0.17	0.15	0.80	0.83
Others	21.3	77.2	200	146	0.11	0.53	0.03	0.11	0.29	0.21	0.69	0.71
All	45.8	74.4	248	216	0.18	0.34	0.03	0.05	0.19	0.16	0.79	0.80

Source: Estimated from data presented in Annual Survey of Industries: Quick Estimates for 2002-03, Central Statistical Organisation.

about three-fifth of the national average (Table 16.9). Only six industry groups had a ratio higher than their all-India counterparts—NIC codes 17, 19, 29, 34, 36, and 16. Of these, the last two groups exceeded the national average only marginally and, in addition, only industry group 29 was in the top-ranked six industries in Delhi. The capital-output ratio was also lower within the region, being only slightly above half of the national ratio (Table 16.9). Not more than five industry groups—NIC codes 16, 17, 19, 28, and 29—had capital-output ratios higher than the respective groups at the national level and of these only the last two were among the major groups within the region.

To assess the competitiveness and locational advantages/disadvantages it is necessary examine the different aspects of the cost structure associated with the overall industrial system of the region. The average wage rate of labour (measured as money wages per worker) went up in absolute terms over the period 1980-81 to 2001-02, this increase being commensurated with that for the entire industrial system (factory sector) of the country at large (Figure 16.3 and Table 16.10).

TABLE 16.10

Wage Rate, Labour Productivity, and Efficiency Wage: 1980-81 to 2001-02

Year	*Delhi*			*All-India*		
	Wage Rate (Rs. '0000)	*Labour Productivity (Rs. '0000)*	*Efficiency Wage Coefficient*	*Wage Rate (Rs. '0000)*	*Labour Productivity (Rs. '0000)*	*Efficiency Wage Coefficient*
1980-81	0.71	0.18	1.00	0.65	0.20	1.00
1985-86	1.06	0.37	0.71	1.22	0.40	0.92
1990-91	1.98	0.99	0.52	2.09	0.82	0.84
1995-96	3.63	1.89	0.58	3.66	2.06	0.71
2000-01	4.57	2.44	0.39	4.78	2.34	0.65
2001-02	5.06	2.71	0.37	4.87	2.42	0.62

Compound Annual Growth Rate of Efficiency Wages (per cent)

Period	*Delhi*	*All-India*
1980-81 to 1990-91	-5.7	-2.0
1990-91 to 2000-01	-4.7	-2.6
1980-81 to 2000-01	-5.2	-2.3

Note: CARG estimated from 3-year averages.

Source: Estimated from data presented in *Annual Survey of Industries 1973-74 to 1997-98: A Data Base on the Industrial Sector in India, EPW Research Foundation and Annual Survey of Industries* (various issues).

FIGURE 16.3

Wage Rates, Labour Productivity and Efficiency Wages 1980-81 to 2001-02

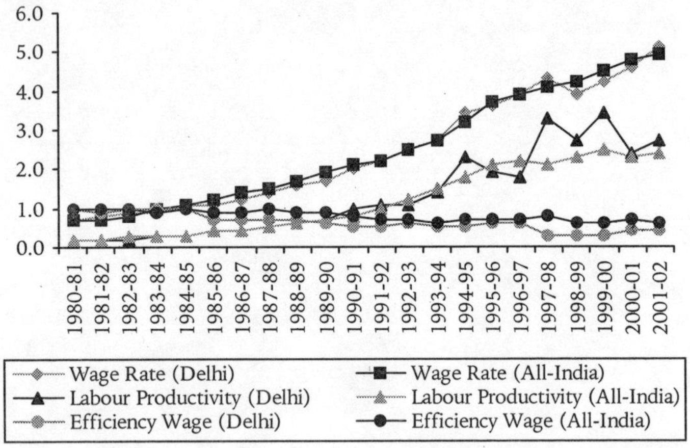

Source: Estimated from data presented in *Annual Survey of Industries 1973-74 to 1997-98: A Data Base on the Industrial Sector in India*, EPW Research Foundation and *Annual Survey of Industries* (various issues), Central Statistical Organisation.

Labour productivity (measured as value added per worker) also increased for Delhi during this period as it did at the all-India level. An important determinant of the investment location decision process is the wage-productivity relationship. To evaluate the competitiveness of Delhi's industrial system *vis-à-vis* that of the nation at large, the relative movement of wage rate and labour productivity has been integrated in the concept of efficiency wage—a coefficient that is derived by dividing the index of money wage rate (base 3-year average for 1980-1981) by the index of labour productivity (base 3-year average for 1980-1981). A fall in the efficiency wage coefficient denotes an increase in labour productivity relative to the wage rate and, therefore, an advantage in terms of comparative cost for the region. Though efficiency wages fell both for Delhi and All India, the decrease was clearly more marked for the region (Figure 16.3 and Table 16.10). The estimated compound annual growth rates of efficiency wages for Delhi (with 3-year averages for both the base and terminal years) were negative for the overall period 1980-81 to 2000-01 as well as for both sub-periods 1980-81 to 1990-91 and 1990-91 to 2000-01 (Table 16.10). More significantly, the rate of decrease was higher for the region than for the country as a whole indicating that, in terms of labour costs, Delhi has enhanced its competitive advantage for industrial location over the last two decades.

Figure 16.4 represents total input per unit of output (TI/O), value added per unit of output (NVA/O), and value added per employee (NVA/E) values for Delhi's industrial (factory) sector computed as a ratio to corresponding all-India values for the period 1980-81 to 2002-03. A value of unity for the ratio indicates similar relationships between the aggregates within the region relative to the nation. With the TI/O line lying above unity throughout the period (except for 2002-03), Delhi's industries utilised a greater amount of input per unit of output relative to the industries at the all India level. In 2002-03, industry groups NIC code 15, 19, 23, 29, 32, 34, 35, 36, and 'Others' all had input use levels lower than their counter parts at the national level (Table 16.10). Of these, industry groups 15 (Food Products and Beverages), and 29 (Machinery and Equipment n.e.c.) were among the more important in Delhi's industrial sector.

FIGURE 16.4

Input Cost and Value Added-Comparison between Delhi and All-India

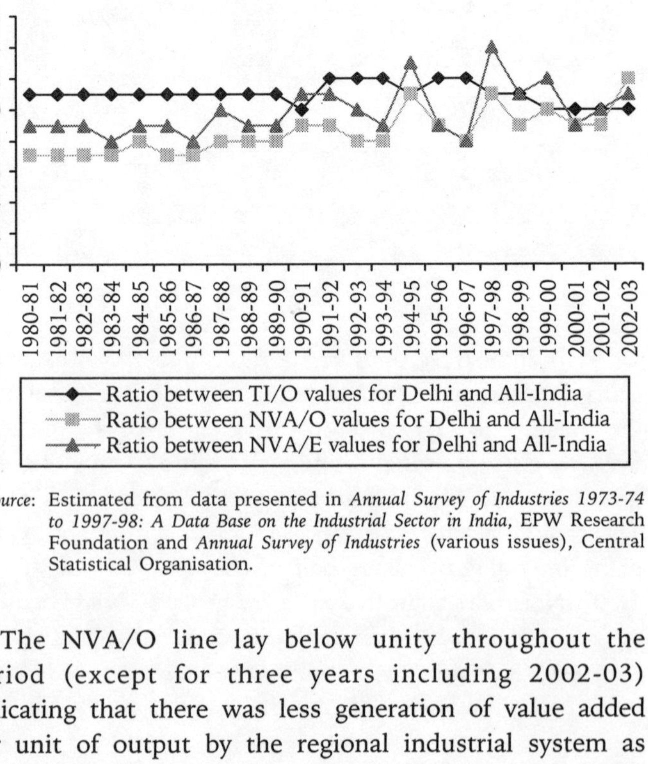

Source: Estimated from data presented in *Annual Survey of Industries 1973-74 to 1997-98: A Data Base on the Industrial Sector in India*, EPW Research Foundation and *Annual Survey of Industries* (various issues), Central Statistical Organisation.

The NVA/O line lay below unity throughout the period (except for three years including 2002-03) indicating that there was less generation of value added per unit of output by the regional industrial system as compared to the nation. In 2002-03, industry groups NIC code 17, 19, 23, 24, 26, 29, 32, 33, 34, 36, and 'Others' had higher NVA/O values than that for all-India. Of these, Chemicals and Chemical Products (code 24), and Machinery and Equipment n.e.c. (Code 29) were the fourth and fifth ranked groups in terms of contribution to employment within the region. Net value added was actually negative for industry group Office, Accounting, and Computing Machinery (code 30) for 2002-03. Value added per employee was lower for the region relative to the nation for much of the eighties and improved from thereon (Figure 16.4). In 2002-03, industry groups NIC code 15, 16, 17, 18, 19, 22, 32, 33, and 'Others' exhibited higher levels of value added per employee as compared to corresponding groups at the national level. Of these, the first three—NIC code 15 (Food Products and Beverages), 18 (Wearing Apparel, Dressing and Dyeing of Fur), and 22 (Publishing, Printing etc.)—were the largest industry groups in the region's factory sector.

The profitability of Delhi's industrial system, measured as profits per unit of value of output (PRO/K ratio), was below that of the three industrialised states—Maharashtra, Gujarat, and Tamil Nadu—for most of the 80s and then, though fluctuating, became comparable with them (Figure 16.5). The profit ratio for Delhi was actually the highest for about half of the remaining period. Again, the profitability of Delhi's industrial (factory) sector was below that of the nation for much of the decade of the eighties but moved up above all-India levels for the remainder of the period, except for 1995-96 and 1996-97.

FIGURE 16.5

Profitability-Comparison between Delhi, Industrialised States, and All-India

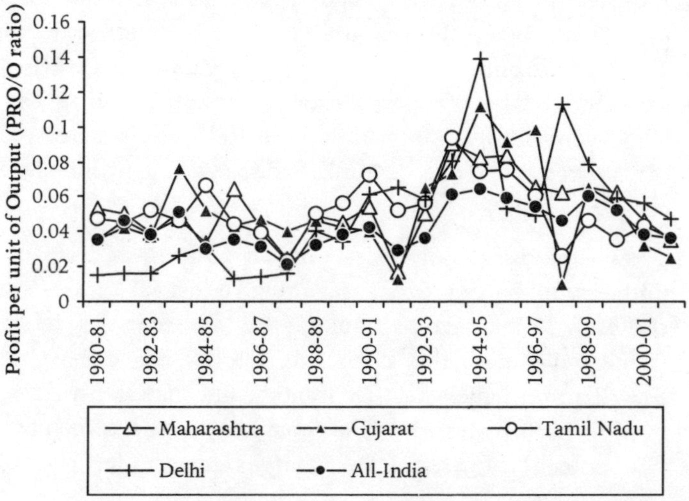

Source: Estimated from data presented in *Annual Survey of Industries 1973-74 to 1997-98: A Data Base on the Industrial Sector in India*, EPW Research Foundation and *Annual Survey of Industries* (various issues), Central Statistical Organisation.

FIGURE 16.6

TFP Growth—Comparison between Delhi, Industrialised States and All-India

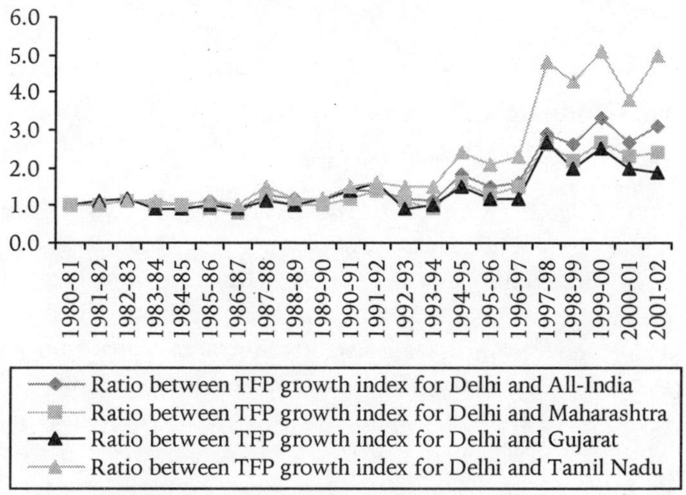

Source: Estimated from data presented in *Annual Survey of Industries 1973-74 to 1997-98: A Data Base on the Industrial Sector in India*, EPW Research Foundation and *Annual Survey of Industries* (various issues), Central Statistical Organisation.

Finally, the relative efficiency of Delhi's industries are evaluated *vis-à-vis* that for the nation and the three industrialised states. Efficiency indices were constructed based on a modified version of Kendrick's index of total factor productivity (TFP) for the case of gross value added as output.[5] The index measures average productivity of an arithmetic combination of the different inputs with base year (1980-81=100) period factor prices. The measure assumes constant returns to scale and factor neutral technical progress as well as a linear and homogeneous production function of degree one. Figure 16.6 represents the index of growth of TFP for Delhi expressed as a ration of TFP growth index for All-India and the three states. While a value of unity for the ratio indicates similar rate of growth of TFP within Delhi relative to the nation and the three states, a value greater than unity is indicative of a faster growth of TFP in the industrial (factory) sector of Delhi. As may be seen from Figure 16.6, TFP growth among the four states and the nation at large, was broadly similar over the decade of the 80s but became differentiated from the beginning of the 90s. From the mid-nineties, total factor productivity of Delhi's industries

5. Kendrick's index of total factor productivity for the case of value added as output, and two inputs can be denoted as

$A_t = V_t / (r_0 K_t + w_0 L_t)$

where A_t is the value of the index in a given year '*t*', V_t is the value of gross output in the year '*t*', and w_0 and r_0 denote the factor rewards of labour and capital respectively in the base year.

grew at rates faster than that of the nation and even that experienced by the three developed industrial states. Delhi's industrial system seems to be becoming relatively more efficient than the rest of the country in terms of factor use.

16.3 Industrial Support System

16.3.1 Delhi Finance Corporation

The Delhi Finance Corporation (DFC) was set-up under State Financial Corporation's Act, 1951 and has been in existence since 1967 with the objective of promoting, developing and financing industries in the small and medium scale sectors in Union Territories of Delhi & Chandigarh. DFC has an authorised capital of Rs.50 crore and share capital of Rs.25.64 crore and as on 31 March 2003, DFC had Rs.27.93 crore as reserves and surplus. Financial assistance in the form of long-term credit is provided to new industrial units as well as existing ones for expansion, modernisation, diversification, as well as for up gradation of technology to increase productivity and promote pollution control. Assistance can be availed for projects having fixed assets such as land, building, plant and machinery for working capital. Concessional loans are also provided for relocation and rehabilitation of industrial units.

DFC provides maximum financial assistance up to Rs.500 lakh in case of companies/cooperative societies where paid up capital and free reserves do not exceed Rs.10 crore, and up to Rs.200 lakh in case of partnership/proprietorship concerns. The industrial loans are released in phases in proportion to the investment brought in by the promoter in the project while in case of transport loans, the loan is released after the entire equity has been arranged/invested by the promoter. Loans are given to the industrial as well as service sectors units like medical & health care centres, hotels, as well as to small road transport operators for commercial vehicles and tourism related facilities, software/hardware services, and hi-tech agro industries. DFC also offers different loan schemes to virtually all categories of entrepreneurs who may be from weaker sections of society or a borrower under special category or a general category. Its special schemes for different sections of the society include: (a) Scheme for women entrepreneurs under MUN, (b) Special scheme for household industries, (c) Scheme for scheduled castes/ scheduled tribes, (d) Scheme for physically challenged, (e) Scheme for acquisition of ISO 9000 series certification by SSI units, and (f) Scheme for marketing support to SSI/Cottage & Village Industries. The corporation sanctioned loans worth Rs. 77.47 crore during 2002-03.

16.3.2 The Delhi State Industrial Development Corporation

The Delhi State Industrial Development Corporation (DSIDC) was established in February 1971 with the objective of assisting, financing, and promoting the interests of small-scale industries (SSIs) in the NCT of Delhi. Its primary purpose is to create an industrial environment where a wide variety of high-value and high technology products are produced by the region's SSIs. The Corporation has an authorised capital of Rs. 30 crore and paid-up capital of Rs.21.86 crore.

The Corporation has developed some major industrial complexes in the past. Recently, it has acquired 1903 acres of land in Bawana (West Delhi) where world-class infrastructure has been created in a record time of 18 months to facilitate the shifting of units from the city. The specifications used to lay the services are very stringent and match the best in the world including for road construction, water supply etc. In Bawana, more than 16,400 plots have been developed and allotted to the eligible units. Other allied facilities like wholesale market, commercial complex etc. are being added in the near future. Another 450 acres of land has been recently acquired in Bhorgarh village, Delhi, where about 5000 plots have been allotted under the Relocation Scheme. The development work in this industrial estate is expected to be completed soon. Industrial units have also been allotted plots under the Relocation Scheme at other sites in Narela, Jhilmil, Badli, Patparganj industrial estates.

One of the major constraints in shifting of industrial units from the city to the far-flung industrial estates was the lack of affordable housing for the workers in the vicinity. To meet this challenge, DSIDC has constructed 3164 flats in which new technology and material has been used to keep prices low. The price here is said to be about 70 per cent of what DDA charges for similar housing units.

DSIDC was mandated by the Honourable Supreme Court of India to construct 15 CETPs to treat the industrial effluents in order to reduce pollution in the city. Twelve CETPs have already been constructed, eight of which have been handed over to the respective societies for operation and maintenance, two are in the process of being handed over and the remaining two are nearing completion.

DSIDC has also provided quick, effective, and cheaper technology solutions to provide accommodation to government schools by constructing pre-fabricated porta cabins in 43 such schools at very competitive prices and handed over in record time, enabling the Corporation to get further orders from the Department of Education under the *Sarva Shiksha Abhiyan*.

The Corporation provides marketing assistance to the small scale cottage handicrafts, and handlooms industries, especially for sales to the government and its various agencies. It also facilitates their participation in Trade Fairs and Exhibitions both at national and international level.

Recently, DSIDC took the initiative to boost Gem and Jewellery trade infrastructure in Delhi which is hitherto, confined in Surat, Mumbai, Jaipur and Coimbatore, by starting The National Institute of Jewellery Design and Technology at Okhla, to impart training in different aspects of Gem and Jewellery trade.

16.3.3 The Delhi Khadi and Village Industries Board

The Delhi Khadi and Village Industries Board (DKVIB) was established on 1 May 1983 by extending the Himachal Pradesh Khadi and Village Industries Act 1966 to the NCT of Delhi in order to plan, programme and promote Khadi and Village Industries and to generate employment especially in the rural areas. Though earlier there were only about 26 Village Industries, apart from Khadi, Government of India has enhanced them to more than 100 village industries depending upon the local conditions, rules and regulations of the respective states. In order to achieve its various objective and functions, the Board has been receiving financial assistance from two sources (a) the Government of Delhi provides 100 per cent Grant-in-aid (under plan scheme) to meet its administrative and establishment expenditure, through the Industries Department and (b) the Khadi and Village Industries Commission (KVIC). The Ministry of Industry, Government of India has provided a State Guarantee to KVIC on behalf of the Board.

There are six developmental schemes on the panel of the Board; (a) KVIC pattern based, (b) Block Loan, (c) Consortium Bank Credit Scheme, (d) Rural Employment Generation Programme (REGP), (e) Rajiv Gandhi Swavlamban Rozgar Yojna, and (f) Self Employment for Educated Unemployed Youth. Funds disbursement under the first three schemes has been discontinued and only recoveries are being made from the beneficiaries, who have already availed financial assistance under these schemes. The fourth scheme i.e., Rural Employment Generation Programme (REGP) is being implemented in the rural areas of Delhi with the help of the nationalised banks. Under this scheme the funds for margin money component is to be received through KVIC, Government of India. The schemes of Rajiv Gandhi Swavlamban Rozgar Yojna, and Self Employment for Educated Unemployed Youth are being implemented in the entire vicinity of Delhi with the view to generate employment opportunities in Delhi. These two schemes are implemented from 2004-05. The funds for implementation of these schemes are received from GNCT of Delhi. The goals of the present schemes are (a) to generate employment opportunities in the rural as well as urban areas of Delhi, (b) to develop entrepreneur skills among the unemployed youth, and (to achieve the goal of rural industrialisation only through REGP.

The financial assistance under the above mentioned schemes are made subject to the local conditions indicated in the Delhi Master Plan 2001 and other notifications issued by the civic bodies from time to time regarding what type of industries are to be set up and the places where the industries are to be set up. By the end of 2004-05, the Board had disbursed 6815 units involving an amount of Rs.968.71 lakhs in the various schemes of KVIC, Government of India, and 588 units involving an amount of Rs.112.71 lakhs in the schemes financed and supported by the GNCT of Delhi. The GNCT of Delhi reconstituted the Board on 8 February 2002 with a full time Chairman and a Managing Director-cum-Member Secretary.

16.3.4 Haryana Delhi Industrial Consultants Limited

Haryana Delhi Industrial Consultants Limited (HARDICON) is a consultancy body set up by All India Financial Institutions such as IFCI, IDBI, ICICI in association with the DFC and Nationalised Banks and with the objective of providing Technical and Financial Consultancy Services to the medium, small and tiny industrial units of Delhi.

16.3.5 Hi-Tech Vocational Training Centre

This Centre has been set up in the Okhla Industrial area by the Government of Delhi in 1993, in collaboration with the Government of Italy with the basic objectives of (a) providing training in various fields of industrial automation in the hi-tech areas by the way of conducting various training programmes for the industrial workers and fresh pass outs from engineering colleges and polytechnics and (b) providing consultancy for the benefit of small and medium industries. The Italian government has provided some of the most advanced industrial machinery and equipment for this purpose. The centre has been conducting nine different courses on widely diverse areas ranging from Programmable Logic Controllers, Digital Electronics to CNC programming and Operation, CAD/CAM and Reverse Engineering techniques. The centre has been undertaking major steps towards facility upgradation in its various training labs in order to remain in the forefront of technology for providing competitive edge to the industrial workers, students and small and medium industrial units.

16.3.6 Tool Room Training Centre

This Centre has been functioning from 1978 in the Wazirpur Industrial Area with Danish collaboration for training young persons as toolmakers and designers and also for providing technical consultancy in tool making. The Centre is equipped with modern high-tech computerised numerically controlled machines so as to manufacture high-tech high-precision tools, jigs, fixtures and moulds for small scale and other industries. A new Centre for Information Technology in Tool Engineering and Computer Applications providing technical know-how in the field of CAD/CAM has also been set up in the campus.

16.3.7 Society for Self-Employment

The Society for Self-Employment established by Government of NCT of Delhi, became functional from 1 April 1987 with the objective of providing short-term training to economically deprived persons in the age group of 18-25 in different technical trades to enable them to establish their own ventures or to obtain employment in private sector. Professional training is being provided in trades like Repair of Radio & T.V., Household Electrical Appliances, Refrigeration and Air-conditioning and Plumbing. A course in Fashion Designing is also being conducted exclusively for female candidates. There are two such training centres at present functioning from Jhandewalan and Nand Nagri.

16.3.8 Other Facilities

In addition to these, other facilities for industries include a Carpet Weaving and Training Centre as well as a Paper Craft and Paper Mache Centre at Bharat Nagar, the Indian Institute of Packaging operating from Patparganj Industrial Area, Common Facilities Centre for leather goods at the Flatted Factories Complex at Wazirpur and Jhandewalan. Financial assistance is provided to Scheduled Caste families to set up their own enterprises by the Delhi Scheduled Caste Financial & Development Corporation.

16.4 Industrial Policy

The Draft Industrial Policy for Delhi has already been finalised. A Draft Cabinet note for seeking approval of the Council of Ministers in respect of industrial policy was circulated to all the concerned departments. The Finance Minister, GNCT of Delhi has observed that industrial policy should be finalised only after the 'White Paper' on industries in Delhi is ready. The committee constituted for the preparation of the 'White Paper' on industries in Delhi has already finalised its report. The Draft Cabinet note, after interdepartmental consultations, has also been finalised and the same is likely to be placed before the Cabinet. However, the industrial policy of Delhi could not be earlier finalised because of the matter relating to closure/shifting of industries from residential/nonconforming areas being subjudice.

Since the draft Master Plan 2021 is likely to be notified soon, the industrial policy for Delhi can only be suitably modified and declared after the said Master Plan is notified.

The salient features of the Draft Industrial Policy include; (a) Promotion of sophisticated industries which could achieve optimum level of production with less space, power, water etc., (b) generation of employment avenues through non-polluting industries, (c) emphasis on encouraging non-polluting industries, (d) emphasis on promotion of computer software, I.T. and I.T. enabled services, electronics and high-tech industries irrespective of investment limits, (e) no new industrial unit shall be permitted in residential areas except household industries, (f) a single unified agency for development and maintenance of industrial areas in Delhi. The involvement of industrial association of the area in the maintenance of industrial areas shall be encouraged, (g) Low-tech industries to be encouraged to recycle into high-tech industries in industrial areas, (h) hazardous/obnoxious industries as well as large/heavy industries shall not be permitted in Delhi, and (i) small-scale industries graduating to the medium sector as a result of modernisation, technical upgradation shall be permitted provided there is no substantial expansion and where growth is in the same line or allied line, and where industry is operating in an approved industrial area.

A different policy exercise with a 20 year perspective relates to formulating policies and projects for creating a more environmental friendly and better governed region is the 'Delhi Urban Environment and Infrastructure Improvement Project (DUEIIP)- 2021'. This study was sponsored by the Government of Delhi and the Ministry of Environment, Government of India and funded by Japan through the World Bank. A specific report prepared under the DUEIIP-21 was a policy framework and guidelines for Industrial Area Upgradation.

The strategic plan for twenty years for the NCT of Delhi incorporated in DUEIIP-21 suggests that industrial location policies should include: (a) compulsory registration of all industrial units, (b) permitting new units or expansion of existing ones only after environmental clearance, (c) promotion of high tech, high skill industrial units, (d) no hazardous units be allowed, (e) one window approach for cases relating to industrial development, and (f) special efforts for promoting industrial units. In preparing the Tenth Five-Year Plan for Delhi, all departments/agencies were directed to take into account the recommendations of DUEIIP-21.

16.4.1 Industrial Pollution and Relocation

An important development in the last decade has been environmental concerns arising out of industrial operations within Delhi. The major sources of industrial pollution in Delhi were identified as thermal power plants, brick kilns, hot mix plants and industrial units. In 1996, the Supreme Court ordered the closure of 168 hazardous units, 46 hot-mix plants, 243 brick kilns, and 21 arc/induction furnaces in addition to 513 other industries. A high powered Committee headed by Principal Secretary-cum-Commissioner of Industries had been constituted in accordance with directives of the Supreme Court for ensuring that the provisions of the Master Plan are complied with and to examine the permissibility of functioning of units in the residential/non-conforming areas in terms of provisions contained in MPD-2001.

According to a survey by the Government of Delhi, there are 98,000 industries, out of a total of 1,25,000 industries, in non-conforming areas as per the Master Plan of Delhi. The Supreme Court has agreed to the Delhi Government's proposal to rehabilitate such industries and relocate them in the conforming use zones and the latter has identified 102 acres of developed land in the existing industrial estates and seven other locations with an area of approximately 4,800 acres for relocation of the industries. A mega industrial estate on about 1865 acres of land in North-West Delhi (Bawana and surrounding areas) is being developed through DSIDC for relocation of industries operating in residential and non-conforming areas of Delhi along with a flatted factory complex with 370 factories in the Jhilmil Industrial Area. The DDA and the Union Ministry of Urban Development as well as the Delhi Urban Arts Commission have approved the change from agricultural to industrial land use as also the lay out plans in respect of the land in Bawana. Approximately 27,055 applicants out of a total of over 51,000 applicants have been found eligible to be relocated from residential/non-conforming areas under the Relocation Scheme for industries operating on a self-financing basis and costing approximately Rs.100,000 lakh.

Another intervention by the Supreme Court in the industrial operations in Delhi relate to the setting up of 15 Common Effluent Treatment Plants (CETPs) for the 28 industrial areas of Delhi in order to control pollution. The funding pattern is based on a World Bank scheme and the Delhi Government and the Ministry of Environment and Forests have each deposited 25 per cent of the total cost of Rs.90 crores of the CETPs. The DSIDC is the executing agency in collaboration with the National Environmental Research Institute (NEERI) and the Delhi Pollution Control Committee (DPCC).

The construction of the following ten CETPs have been completed and after their successful trial runs handed over to the respective CETPs for their operation and maintenance. Of the remaining five, two CETPs at Naraina and Najafgarh are under construction at a very slow pace because of paucity of funds as reported by the DSIDC. The construction of three other CETPs at Anand Parbat, Mohan cooperative societies, and Okhla Industrial Estate have been kept in abeyance as per the direction of EPCA. An issue that had come up in the costing aspect of the CETPs was the non-inclusion of three components *viz.*, land, conveyance system and HT lines and also the cost of other essential items required as per detailed engineering. This has increased the total financial liability of the Delhi Government to Rs.116.15 crores which is finally to be approved by EPCA. The Delhi Government has already paid an amount of Rs. 87.77 crores to DSIDC and balance amount to the tune of Rs. 28.38 crores is pending till its final decision by EPCA. The costing adpect of the 15 CETPs and the pending amount not paid by the society towards their cost apportionment and the amount to be paid by the Government of India of their share contribution etc., has now been entrusted to EPCA vide the Supreme Court order dated 2 February 2006. The concerned department has, however, kept a provision in the Plan scheme during the current financial year 2006-07 of a token amount of Rs. 1 lakh.

16.5 Prospects and Potential for Industry

Though manufacturing accounts for about 12 per cent of Delhi's GSDP and about 40 per cent of the total work force, the priority given to the industrial sector in the Five Year Plans is extremely low. During the Ninth Plan (1997-2002), expenditure on industry accounted for Rs.134 crore (0.98 per cent) out of total Plan expenditure of Rs.13660 crore. The industrial sector ranked twelfth out of a total of 31 sectors in terms of share in total outlays. Industry has been given even lower priority during the Tenth Plan (2002-2007) with budgeted absolute expenditure on the industrial sector dropping to Rs.100 crore out of the total proposed expenditure of Rs.23,000 crore. The share of industry decreased by nearly half to a mere 0.43 per cent of total outlays as compared to its expenditure share in the Ninth Plan. Five sectors—Transport (23.7 per cent), Water Supply (16.4 per cent), Energy (15.0 per cent), Urban Development (12.8 per cent), and Medical (9.7 per cent)—accounted for more than three-fourth of total outlays. In terms of expenditure priorities, industry dropped to rank nineteenth out a total of thirty-one sectors.

The industrial sector of Delhi has to play an important role in generating higher levels of income and employment since the role of the primary sector can only be extremely limited in the region. With manufacturing accounting for the employment of about two-fifths of total workers and there is clearly a need to assign a greater role for this sector in terms of a higher priority in the State's Plan. Many of the fastest growing and highly industrialised states have assigned a larger proportion of Tenth Plan (2002-2007) outlays to industry—Andhra Pradesh (3.2 per cent), Gujarat (3.5 per cent), Karnataka (3.3 per cent), Maharashtra (2.5 per cent), and Tamil Nadu (4.1 per cent). The all-states average outlay on industry for the Tenth Plan is 3.2 per cent—nearly eight times that for Delhi.

The closure of many polluting and hazardous industrial units and the Relocation Scheme for non-conforming units, though reducing environmental pollution levels, may be expected to have had an adverse impact on industrial growth and employment within Delhi. The contribution of industrial sources of pollution (including Thermal Power Plants) to ambient air has come down from 56 per cent in 1970-71 to 20 per cent in 2000-01, and with the coming into operation of all the 15 CETPs the contribution of this sector to both air and water pollution levels would be heavily reduced. Under these circumstances there is some justification for the ongoing effort for regularisation of other industries situated in residential/non-conforming areas. The DUEIIP-21 has suggested the regularisation of about 54,000 industrial units if they are non-polluting and satisfy revised norms and broader parameters of environmental management and industrial/economic planning. The Government of NCT of Delhi has identified 24 industrial concentration areas where more than 70 per cent residential premises have already been converted to industrial use and has requested for relevant amendments to the Master Plan to agencies like DDA, DUAC and the Ministry of Urban Development, Government of India for *in situ* regularisation, as well as for broadening parameters governing household and service industries which cater to the day to day needs of the residents. As long as they are non-polluting and non-hazardous, regularisation would avoid loss of output, employment, underutilisation of capacity, entrepreneurial confidence and productivity. Corrective measures incorporating a system of suitable incentives and disincentives are required in relation to such industries in order to ensure shifting and relocation of industries failing to meet the broadened parameters in terms of environmental and other norms.

As mentioned before, a desirable prerequisite for sustained industrial growth and development in the long run is that the industrial base broadens and becomes more diversified thus ensuring a higher level of resilience of the regional economy. Analysis indicates an increasing degree of specialisation in Delhi over time, which may be suggestive of weakening inter-regional and inter-industry linkages. In 2002-03, Delhi had the most specialised industrial structure as compared with the fourteen major states. There is clearly a need for policy intervention to ensure greater diversification of Delhi's industrial base in terms of development of new industries that are hi-tech and high value added in nature. Ad hoc licensing of industrial units should be avoided and policy measures introduced to ensure dispersal of existing industries as well as their modernisation and technological up gradation.

The project of setting of Hi-Tech city, Science Park and Bio-Tech Park has been taken up together and they have been renamed now as Knowledge Park. The requirement of land for setting up the Knowledge Park is assessed around 90-100 acres. The matter of identification of land which may be ideally suitable for this project is being pursued with Land and Building Department and Divisional Commissioner of GNCT of Delhi as well the DDA. This project will be a joint venture of the Delhi Government with the private sector for facilitating growth of software driven IT/ITES units and in establishing linkages between academics and the business sector/ industry in HRD sector. The Delhi Government's contribution will be limited to providing land as its share of equity capital. A budget provision of Rs. 55 lakhs for acquisition of land under capital head has been provided in 2006-07 for this project.

Another joint venture being planned by the GNCT of Delhi is the setting up of a World Trade Center (WTC) in order to facilitate the nation's (and the region's) trade and commerce by becoming a nodal point for international flows of information, funds and technologies. This will complement the other seven Centres (Mumbai, Bangalore, Kolkata, Kochi, Coimbatore, Hyderabad, and Chennai) as it will be in capital city and the first in the North Indian region. The WTC will provide space for the offices of international institutions, trade promotion services, international trade community, trade missions, as well as conference and seminar facilities, business and corporate meetings, information services, arrange for international exhibitions and expositions and so on. The Delhi Government's contribution will be limited to providing land as its share of equity capital. An amount of Rs. 5.5 lakh is earmarked in the financial year 2006-07 for the WTC. The matter of land allotment is being pursued with the DDA for this project.

SECTION—B

16.6 Unorganised Sector and Khadi and Village Industries in Delhi

The Industrial Policy statement issued in 1982 put special emphasis on promoting sophisticated industries, which could achieve optimum levels of production with less space, power and generate employment avenues for skilled persons. The statement also postulated that industrial growth should be in the small scale sector. The small scale sector or village and small scale industries comprises two sectors (i) Modern small sector (ii) Traditional Sector. Modern small scale Industries includes small scale industries (both factory and non-factory sector) and power loom units. The traditional sector comprises Khadi and Village Industries, handlooms, sericulture, handicrafts, coir sector, etc. The first part of this chapter was mainly focused on the organised sector comprising mainly factory sector (inclusive of modern small scale sector) and the second part i.e., the following section addresses the nature and extent of unorganised sector and the village industries. The Khadi and Village industry is part of unorganised sector also because of their nature of activity and employment size since they also fall out of purview of the factory sector definition which is defined on the basis of number of workers and use of power. In the following section first part will discuss the unorganised sector in Delhi and subsequent section will discuss the Khadi and village industries sector including handicrafts in Delhi.

16.6.1 Unorganised Sector in Delhi

There are 2.30 lakh (NSSO 56 round) enterprises engaged in activities pertaining to unorganised manufacturing and 2.2 lakh enterprises in unorganised service sector together making 4.5 lakh enterprises in unorganised manufacturing and service sector in Delhi.

1.34 per cent of total population of all India lives in Delhi. The share of Delhi in terms of unorganised sector enterprises is 1.52 per cent, 4.51 per cent of fixed capital is invested here, production share is 5.41 per cent, employment share is 2.51 per cent and share in GVA is 6.37 per cent. Table 16.11 above gives the percentage of employment, number of enterprises and gross value added by the manufacturing and service sectors of all states to the all-India value of these variables. It may be seen that in terms of employment and the number of MSE, Delhi's position is at the 13 and 16 respectively. In terms of gross value added, it has jumped to position no. 7.

However, the absolute value of any state variable does not convey a correct idea about the relative significance of any variable for the state's economy since the absolute magnitude of any variable is dependent upon the relative size of the state concerned. Delhi's relative size may be judged in terms of its population size. In order to neutralise the effect of size on any of the three variables which we are considering, one may estimate location quotient of Delhi in terms of the three variables, namely, employment, number of enterprises and gross value added, with regard to population by using the location quotient formula given below:

$$Lq^{j}i = \frac{V^{j}i / V^{j}i}{P^{j} / P^{j}} X\,100$$

Where Lq^j_i denotes location quotient of state j in respect of segment i; V^j_i is value of variable i for state j; Vi^J is value variable i for the country, i.e, $Vi^J=Vi^1=Vi^2=Vi^3=...+Vi^n$;P^j is population of jth state ; P^J is population of the country, i.e., $PJ=P^1+P^2+P^3+...+P^n$; i= L, E, VA, i.e., Labour, Enterprises and Gross Value Added; j= 1,2, 3 ....n; n= Total number of states in India including the three new and very small states (=35).

The ratio in the numerator of Lq^j_i gives the proportion of variable i for state j to the all-India magnitude of variable i. Similarly, the ratio in the denominator gives the proportion of population of jth state to population of the country. The ratio P^j/P^J thus plays the role of neutralising the ratio in the numerator with regard to population.

The value of location quotients or the year 2000-01 of different states in respect of employment, enterprises and gross value added are given in Table 16.12. As may be observed, , once these ratios are neutralised with regard to the effect of size in terms of population, the location quotient values for Delhi emerge to be at top not only in terms of employment but also in terms of GVA. In spite of the fact, that with respect to number of enterprises Delhi's position is 18th, in terms of relative significance of the unorganised sector enterprises, the position of Delhi turns to be as of a leader.

If one considers the relative position of Delhi for manufacturing and services separately, the position is by and large similar as portrayed in Table 16.13. But there is one difference. In case of service enterprises the rank of Delhi's LQ for enterprises, employment, and value added is 5th, 3rd and 1st. But when we look at rank in terms of these variables, in the same sequence, for the small unorganised manufacturing enterprises, the ranks of Delhi emerge to be 9th, 2ndand 1st. Thus in terms of the number of manufacturing enterprises relative position of Delhi is 4 ranks lower compared to service enterprises. However, there is no change in the position of GVA across the sectors and it is on top in both the cases.

TABLE 16.11

Share of Different States in the Total Unorganised Enterprises, Employment and Value Added (2001)

States/UT	*% Share of Enterprise*	*Rank*	*% Share of Workers*	*Rank*	*% Share of GVA*	*Rank*
Andhra Pradesh	4.32	8	9.18	3	6.31	8
Arunachal Pradesh	0.00	34	0.01	34	0.02	33
Assam	2.13	15	1.65	16	1.55	16
Bihar	6.32	5	5.16	8	4.27	10
Goa	0.12	25	0.15	26	0.23	24
Gujarat	3.62	11	4.41	9	7.34	5
Haryana	1.33	17	1.37	17	2.01	14
Himachal	0.57	21	0.46	21	0.63	21
J&K	1.01	19	1.04	19	1.23	18
Karnataka	5.43	6	5.37	6	6.52	6
Kerala	3.54	12	3.59	11	4.69	9
MP	3.81	9	3.77	10	2.82	13
Maharashtra	7.71	4	8.76	4	14.00	1
Manipur	0.25	23	0.20	23	0.18	26
Meghalaya	0.18	24	0.17	24	0.20	25
Mizoram	0.04	29	0.04	29	0.07	29
Nagaland	0.06	28	0.06	28	0.09	28
Orissa	5.08	7	5.27	7	1.94	15
Punjab	2.22	14	2.21	14	3.33	12
Rajasthan	3.77	10	3.42	12	3.73	11
Sikkim	0.03	30	0.03	30	0.06	30
Tamil Nadu	8.08	3	8.76	5	8.67	4
Tripura	0.25	22	0.21	22	0.15	27
Uttar Pradesh	15.17	1	15.03	1	10.91	2
West Bengal	13.75	2	12.87	2	9.23	3
A&N island	0.02	31	0.02	31	0.03	32
Chandigarh	0.08	27	0.11	27	0.24	23
D&N Haveli	0.01	32	0.01	33	0.02	34
Daman& Diu	0.01	33	0.02	32	0.03	31
Delhi	1.52	16	2.40	13	6.37	7
Lakshadweep	0.00	35	0.00	35	0.01	35
Pondichery	0.10	26	0.16	25	0.25	22
Jharkhand	2.31	13	2.10	15	1.38	17
Chattisgarh	1.26	18	1.24	18	0.77	20
Uttarakhand	0.87	20	0.76	20	0.81	19
All India	100.00		100.00		100.00	
Total (in lakhs)	299		636		13497765	

Source: IHD estimates based on NSSO data 'Unorganised Manufacturing Sector in India 2000-01, NSS 56th Round, Unorganised Service Sector in India 2001-02, NSS 57th Round.

TABLE 16.12

State-wise Location Quotients of Overall MSE, i.e., Combined Manufacturing and Service Enterprises

States/UT	*% Share of pop*	*Rank*	*LQ ent*	*Rank*	*LQ wf*	*Rank*	*LQ gva*	*Rank*
Andhra Pradesh	7.37	5	0.59	29	1.24	6	0.86	21
Arunachal Pradesh	0.11	27	0.04	35	0.08	35	0.16	35
Assam	2.59	14	0.82	17	0.64	27	0.60	27
Bihar	8.07	3	0.78	21	0.64	26	0.53	29
Goa	0.13	26	0.94	12	1.16	9	1.76	5
Gujarat	4.93	10	0.74	22	0.89	17	1.49	7
Haryana	2.05	16	0.65	24	0.67	23	0.98	17
Himachal Pradesh	0.59	21	0.96	11	0.79	20	1.07	14
J&K	0.98	19	1.03	10	1.06	10	1.26	12
Karnataka	5.13	9	1.06	8	1.05	11	1.27	11
Kerala	3.10	12	1.14	4	1.16	8	1.51	6
MP	5.88	7	0.65	25	0.64	25	0.48	32
Maharashtra	9.42	2	0.82	18	0.93	14	1.49	8
Manipur	0.23	23	1.08	6	0.86	18	0.77	23
Meghalaya	0.22	24	0.79	20	0.78	21	0.90	19
Mizoram	0.09	30	0.41	33	0.41	33	0.85	22
Nagaland	0.19	25	0.31	34	0.29	34	0.48	31
Orissa	3.57	11	1.42	2	1.47	4	0.54	28
Punjab	2.37	15	0.94	13	0.93	13	1.41	10
Rajasthan	5.50	8	0.69	23	0.62	28	0.68	25
Sikkim	0.05	31	0.52	30	0.66	24	1.05	15
Tamil Nadu	6.05	6	1.34	3	1.45	5	1.43	9
Tripura	0.31	22	0.81	19	0.68	22	0.48	33
Uttar Pradesh	16.17	1	0.94	14	0.93	15	0.67	26
West Bengal	7.81	4	1.76	1	1.65	3	1.18	13
A & N island	0.03	32	0.44	32	0.59	31	0.94	18
Chandigarh	0.09	29	0.87	16	1.20	7	2.77	2
D & N Haveli	0.02	33	0.49	31	0.50	32	0.72	24
Daman & Diu	0.02	34	0.62	28	0.98	12	2.18	4
Delhi	1.34	18	1.13	5	1.79	1	4.74	1
Lakshadweep	0.01	35	0.65	26	0.61	29	0.86	20
Pondichery	0.09	28	1.06	7	1.70	2	2.64	3
Jharkhand	2.62	13	0.88	15	0.80	19	0.52	30
Chattisgarh	2.02	17	0.62	27	0.61	30	0.38	34
Uttarakhand	0.83	20	1.05	9	0.92	16	0.98	16

Note: LQ ent- Location Quotient of enterprises, LQ wf- Location Quotient of workforce/employment, and LQ gva- Location Quotient of Gross Value Added.

Source: IHD estimates based on NSSO data.

Unorganised Manuf. Sector in India 2000-01, NSS 56th Round, Report no. 477.

Unorganised Service Sector in India 2001-02, NSS 57th Round, Report no 482.

TABLE 16.13

State-wise Location Quotients of Unorganised anufacturing and Service Sub-Sectors

State/UT	*Unorganized Manufacturing Sector*						*Unorg.Service Sector*					
	LQ ent	*Rank*	*LQ wf*	*Rank*	*LQ gva*	*Rank*	*LQ ent*	*Rank*	*LQ wf*	*Rank*	*LQ gva*	*Rank*
Andhra Pradesh	1.28	5	1.21	7	0.88	17	1.26	6	1.30	8	0.83	22
Arunachal Pradesh	0.02	35	0.03	35	0.08	35	0.07	36	0.14	35	0.22	35
Assam	0.63	24	0.52	28	0.52	28	1.04	13	0.80	23	0.65	27
Bihar	0.59	25	0.50	29	0.43	31	1.01	14	0.83	21	0.61	28
Goa	1.12	8	1.24	6	1.62	7	0.74	25	1.04	15	1.87	5
Gujarat	0.65	23	0.81	16	1.41	10	0.84	22	1.01	17	1.56	7
Hariyana	0.55	26	0.55	26	0.91	16	0.76	24	0.83	22	1.03	14
Himachal Prasdesh	0.97	11	0.71	18	0.92	15	0.93	16	0.90	20	1.19	13
J & K	1.25	6	1.30	5	1.66	4	0.77	23	0.73	26	0.93	16
Karnataka	1.18	7	1.07	9	0.95	13	0.91	18	1.01	16	1.53	7
Kerala	0.96	12	0.93	11	1.09	12	1.35	4	1.47	4	1.85	5
Madhya Pradesh	0.74	18	0.66	21	0.46	30	0.54	30	0.61	30	0.50	22
Maharashtra	0.77	17	0.85	14	1.34	11	0.87	20	1.04	14	1.60	5
Manipur	1.36	4	0.91	12	0.74	20	0.74	26	0.78	24	0.78	15
Meghalaya	0.73	19	0.66	20	0.82	18	0.86	21	0.94	19	0.96	11
Mizoram	0.43	28	0.37	30	0.78	19	0.40	35	0.48	34	0.89	12
Nagalasnd	0.17	34	0.14	33	0.18	34	0.46	32	0.51	33	0.73	14
Orissa	1.62	2	1.66	3	0.56	26	1.19	8	1.22	10	0.53	16
Punjab	0.85	14	0.85	15	1.56	8	1.05	12	1.05	13	1.28	6
Rajasthan	0.67	22	0.56	25	0.71	22	0.71	28	0.71	27	0.65	13
Sakkim	0.18	33	0.15	32	0.53	27	0.92	17	1.36	6	1.48	5
Tamil Nadu	1.48	3	1.54	4	1.66	6	1.16	10	1.33	7	1.25	7
Tripura	0.67	21	0.63	24	0.50	29	0.98	15	0.74	25	0.46	12
UP	0.83	15	0.90	13	0.72	21	1.06	11	0.97	18	0.64	11
West Bengal	2.08	1	2.03	1	1.56	9	1.38	2	1.12	12	0.88	9
A & N Island	0.47	27	0.55	27	0.94	14	0.40	34	0.65	29	0.95	8
Chandigarh	0.40	29	0.70	19	2.57	2	1.42	1	1.89	2	2.92	3
D&N Haveli	0.36	31	0.35	31	0.68	23	0.64	29	0.70	28	0.76	7
Daman & Diu	0.38	30	0.63	23	2.33	3	0.90	19	1.47	5	2.06	3
Delhi	1.01	9	1.85	2	4.88	1	1.27	5	1.70	3	4.62	1
Lakshadweep	0.20	32	0.14	34	0.36	33	1.17	9	1.28	9	1.26	2
Pondichery	0.79	16	1.15	8	1.66	5	1.38	3	2.46	1	3.43	1
Jharkhand	1.01	10	0.95	10	0.61	25	0.73	27	0.60	31	0.46	3
Chattishgarh	0.71	20	0.66	22	0.37	32	0.51	31	0.55	32	0.39	3
Uttarakhand	0.87	13	0.72	17	0.65	24	1.26	7	1.21	11	1.25	1

Note: LQ ent- Location Quotient of enterprises, LQ wf- Location Quotient of workforce, and LQ gva- Location Quotient of Gross Value Added.

Source: IHD estimates based on NSSO data, Unorganised Manufacturing Sector in India 2000-01, NSS 56th Round, Report no. 477 Unorganised Service Sector in India 2001-02, NSS 57th Round, Report no 482.

16.7 Characteristics of Unorganised Enterprises in Delhi

16.7.1 Manufacturing Enterprises

Most of the enterprises engaged in activities pertaining to manufacturing in unorganised sector in Delhi are unregistered that's why there is a lot of variation in the estimates from different sources. In unorganised manufacturing more than 90 per cent enterprises in rural areas are not registered with any of the agency leaving only 10 per cent in the registered category. However, in urban Delhi the percentage of registration is higher (20.7 per cent) as compared to OAME (1.0 per cent) and NDME (6.9 per cent). (Table 16.14)

TABLE 16.14

Enterprises by Status of Registration and Sector

	Rural			Urban		
Un. Manufacturing	*OAME*	*NDME*	*DME*	*OAME*	*NDME*	*DME*
Registered	9.9	3.6	17.9	1.0	6.9	20.7
Not Registered	90.1	96.4	82.1	99.0	93.1	79.3

Source: Unorganised Manufacturing Sector in India, 2000-01, NSS 56th Round, NSSO, GoI.

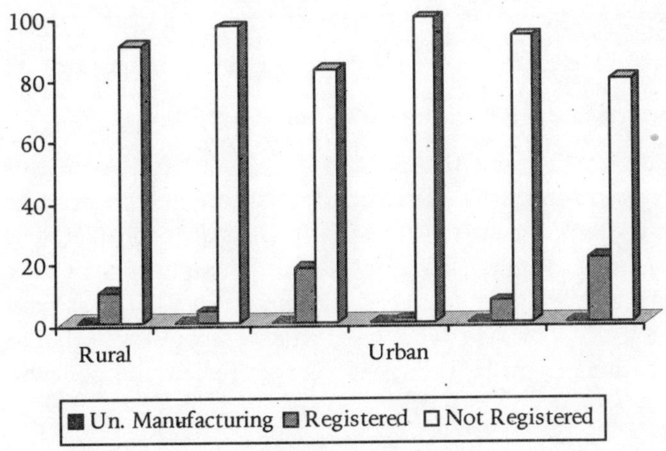

16.7.2 Activities of Enterprises

91.7 per cent of Enterprises in this sector works more than 9 months in the Year. However 48.6 per cent enterprises perceived that their growth was stagnant during the three years prior to the survey period i.e., year 2000-2001. Only 13 per cent perceived that they expanded during the above-mentioned period.

TABLE 16.15

Percentage Distribution of Manufacturing Enterprises By Growth Status (Over a Period of Last 3 Years)

	Expanding	*Stagnant*	*Contracting*	*Not Applicable**	*Total*
Delhi	13.0	48.6	16.8	21.6	100
All India	15.6	63.4	12.3	8.7	100

Note: * Enterprises operating for less than three years.

Source: Unorganised Manufacturing Sector in India, 2000-01, NSS 56th Round, NSSO, GoI.

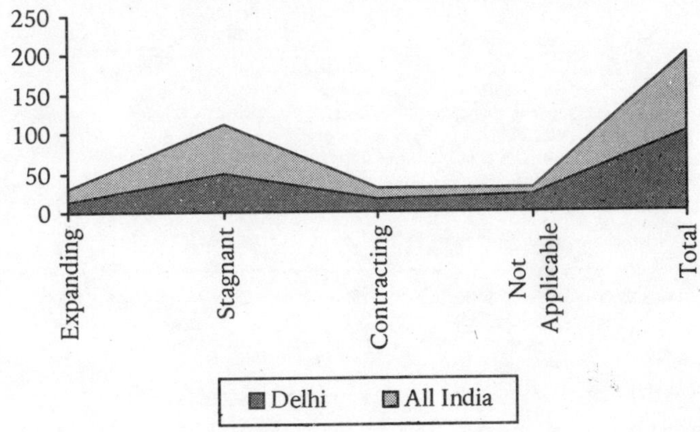

16.7.3 Economic Activities in a Year

Most of the enterprises that is 971 out of 1000 in Delhi are engaged in only one economic activity (Table 16.16)

TABLE 16.16

Per Thousand of Enterprises Engaged in Other Economic Activities Undertaken During Last 365 Days

	Zero	*One*	*Two*	** Three or more*	*Total*
Delhi	971	27	20	0	1000
All India	563	364	70	3	1000

Note: *Addition may not add 1000 because enterprises are engaged in multi activities

Source: Unorganised Manufacturing Sector in India, 2000-01, NSS 56th Round, NSSO, GoI

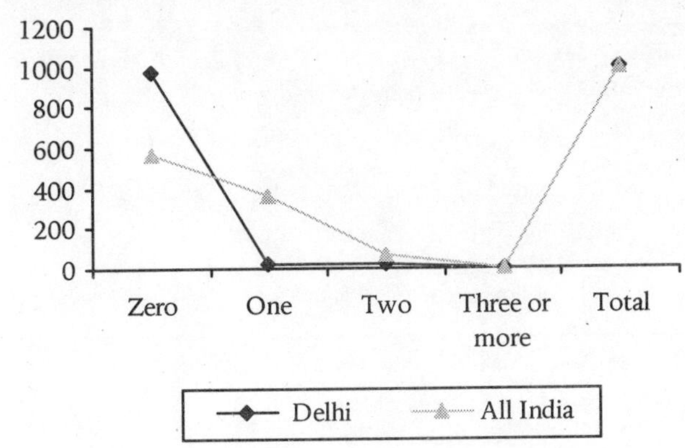

16.7.4 Nature of Activities

In Delhi about 60 per cent enterprises are working on contract. Out of theses 67.4 per cent (Table 16.17) are working solely for master entrepreneurs/contractor. This suggests that there are organised linkages among the enterprises.

TABLE 16.17

Per Thousand Distribution of Manufacturing Enterprises by Type of Contract Separately by State

	Number (Per Thousand) of Enterprises Not Working on contract	No. (Per Thousand) of Enterprises Working on Contract			
		Solely For Master Enterprise/ Contractor	Mainly on Contract	Mainly/ Solely for Customer	All
Delhi	406	674	193	119	1000
All India	69	796	89	108	1000

Source: Unorganised Manufacturing Sector in India, 2000-01, NSS 56th Round, NSSO, GOI

And majority of them are located outside the household in permanent structures (67.1 per cent) implying that nature of this sector is not household industry but probably an organised market economy.

Problems

The major problem faced by enterprises in Delhi is Power Cut, and Shortage of Capital. This emerges to be more important (56.9 per cent) than at the all India. A large percentage also reported some 'other problems' that are given in Table 16.18. As per this the major threat under other problems is perceived competition from larger units.

TABLE 16.18

Percentage Distribution of Enterprises by Type of Location – Unorganised Manufacturing

		Delhi	All India
Within hh Premises		30.1	70.0
Outside hh	with permanent structure	67.2	22.6
	with temporary structure	2.2	1.3
	without any structure	0.2	1.4
Without Fixed Premises	mobile market	0	1.3
	street vendors	0.3	3.4
		100	100

Source: Unorganised Manufacturing Sector in India, 2000-01, NSS 56th Round, NSSO, GoI.

TABLE 16.19

Problems Faced by Enterprises

	Percentage Distribution of Manufacturing Enterprises Reporting Problems						
	% of Enterprises Not Reporting Any Problem	Non Availability of Electricity Connection	Power Cut	Shortage of Capital	Non Availability of Raw Materials	Marketing of Products	Any Other Problem
Delhi	13.9	6.0	56.9	57.3	9.9	9.2	33.8
India	26.7	10.8	15.5	49.2	15.1	18.9	34.7

Note: Total may not add up to 100 because of multiple problems reported by Entrepreneurs.

Source: Unorganised Manufacturing Sector in India, 2000-01, NSS 56th Round, NSSO, GoI.

TABLE 16.20

Percentage Distribution of Manufacturing Enterprises Reporting Problems other than the Common

	Percentage Distribution of Enterprises by Other Problems Faced Number of Enterprises Nature of other Problem Faced						
	Lack of Infrastructure Facility	Local Problems	Harassment	Competition from Larger Units	Non Availability of Labo	Labour Problem	Fuel Not Availability/ Very Costly
Delhi	2.5	7.4	0.3	52.8	1.7	4.6	1.6
India	6.9	17.8	3.8	29.3	1.4	2.5	3.4

Source: Unorganised Manuf. Sector in India, 2000-01, NSS 56th Round, NSSO, GoI.

Enterprising Receiving Assistance by State

In Delhi more than 98.8 per cent enterprises in this sector do not seek assistance from the government. And on the other hand shortage of capital is also considered as a major problem. This implies that government assistance policies are either not very enterprise friendly or are not reaching to those who need them most. In both the situations there is an urgent need to review the policies.

TABLE 16.21

Percentage Distribution Enterprises Receiving Assistance

	Proportion (Per Thousand) of enterprises Reporting no Assistance	Loan	Subsidy	Machinery/ Equipment	Training		Procurement Raw Material	Others	
Delhi	98.8	0.8	0.4	0	0	0.1	0	0.1	100
All India	94.7	3.6	0.6	0.8	0.3	0.4	0.4	0.3	100

Source: Unorganised Manuf. Sector in India, 2000-01, NSS 56th Round, NSSO, GoI.

Service Sector

In case of service sector, the rural enterprises especially OAE showed a high percentage (44.9 per cent) of registration as compared to their urban counterpart (26.2 per cent). However, a large percentage is again not registered under any authority.

TABLE 16.22

Status of Registration in Service Sector Enterprises

	Rural		Urban	
Service	*OAE*	*Establishment*	*OAE*	*Establishment*
Registered	44.9	40.6	26.2	36.0
Not Registered	55.1	59.4	73.8	64.0

Source: Unorganised Service Sector in India, 2000-01, NSS 57th Round, NSSO, GoI.

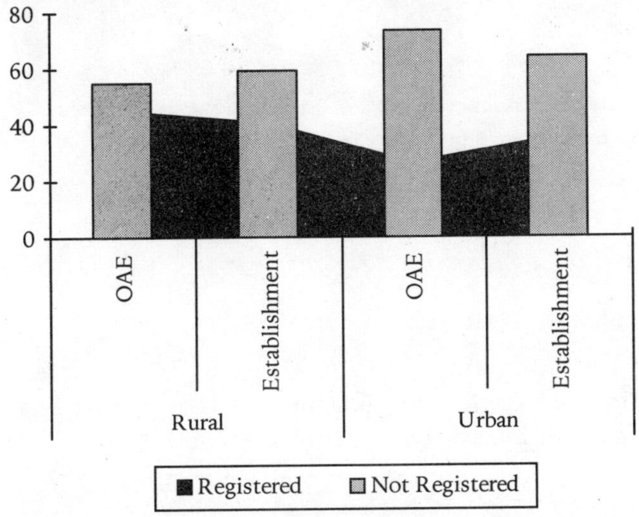

Nature of Activity

In Delhi data suggests that all the enterprises in service sector are engaged in economic activities throughout the year (Table 16.22)

TABLE 16.23

Percentage Distribution of Enterprises by Nature of Operation

	Perennial	*Seasonal*	*Casual*	*Total*
Delhi	100	0	0	100
All India	98.3	1.3	0.4	100

Source: Unorganised Service Sector in India, 2000-01, NSS 57th Round, NSSO, GoI.

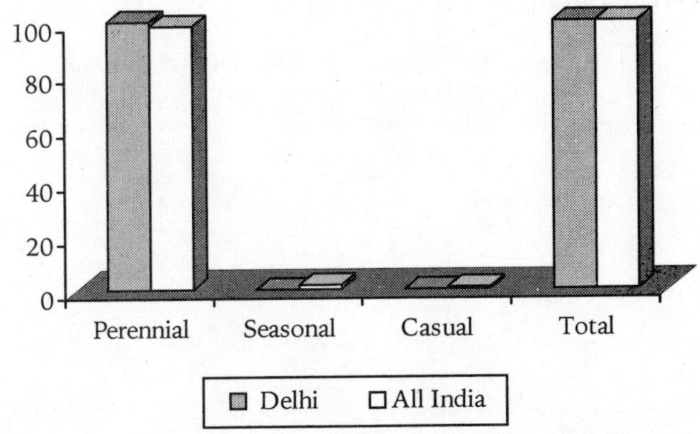

Enterprises by Type of Location

In service sector again a majority of entrepreneurs (45.5 per cent) are having enterprises outside the household and in permanent structures. Unlike manufacturing, this sector has more than 18 per cent entrepreneurs who are without fixed premises. Among these majority is of street vendors (11.0 per cent) and others are part of mobile market (4.1 per cent) (Table 16.24)

TABLE 16.24

Percentage Distribution of Enterprises by Type of Location Unorganised Service

		Delhi	*All India*
Within hh premises		29.9	27.3
Outside hh	with permanent structure	45.5	34.5
	with temporary structure	2.4	2.5
	without any structure	4.1	3.3
Without fixed premises	Mobile market	7.1	7.6
	street vendors	11.0	24.7
	n.r	0	0.1
Total		100	100

Source: Unorganised Service Sector in India, 2000-01, NSS 57th Round, NSSO, GoI.

Enterprising Receiving Assistance by State

As far as assistance is concerned despite the fact that entrepreneurs perceive capital shortage as a problem hardly 3 per cent of them received any assistance from the State.

TABLE 16.25

Percentage Distribution of Enterprises Receiving Assistance from State

	Proportion (Per Thousand) of Enterprises Reporting No Assistance	*Loan*	*Sub-sidy*	*Machi-nery/ Equip-ment*	*Training*	*Marke-ting*	*Procure-ment Raw Material*	*Others*	
Delhi	97.0	1.4	0.4	0	0	0	0	12	100
All India	87.1	8.3	0.5	0.5	0.1	0	0.1	3.8	100

Source: Unorganised Service Sector in India, 2000-01, NSS 57th Round, NSSO, GoI.

Number of Activities

The majority of enterprises (92.6 per cent) are engaged in no extra economic activity implies that enterprises are engaged in one economic activity only showing the stability of that service in the market.

TABLE 16.26

Per Thousand of Enterprises Engaged in Other Economic Activities Undertaken During Last 365 Days

	Zero	*One*	*Two*	*Three or More*	*Total**
Delhi	926	43	31	0	1000
All India	572	384	41	3	1000

Note: *Addition may not add 1000 because enterprises are engaged in multi activities

Source: Unorganised Service Sector in India, 2000-01, NSS 57th Round, NSSO, GoI

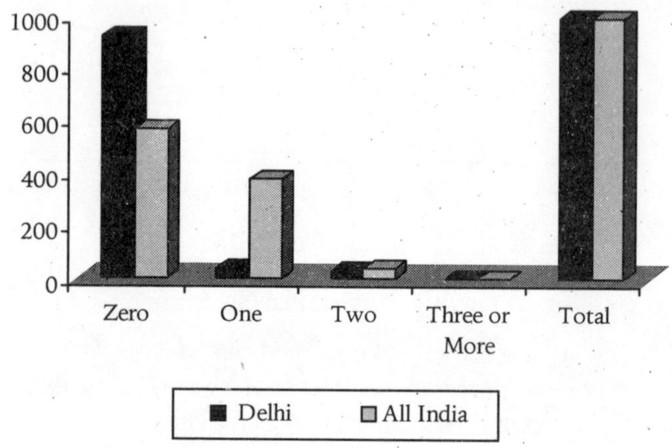

Growth Status

The majority of entrepreneurs perceive stagnation during the last three years. Only 17 per cent units perceive that they are expanding.

TABLE 16.27

Percentage Distribution of Manufacturing Enterprises by Growth Status (Over A Period of Last 3 Years 1999-2000 To 2001-2002)

	Expanding	*Stagnant*	*Contracting*	*Not Applicable**	*Total*
Delhi	10.1	48.8	16.6	24.5	100
All India	17.0	53.7	12.7	16.6	100

Note: *enterprises operating for less than three years.

Source: Unorganised Service Sector in India, 2000-01, NSS 57th Round, NSSO, GoI

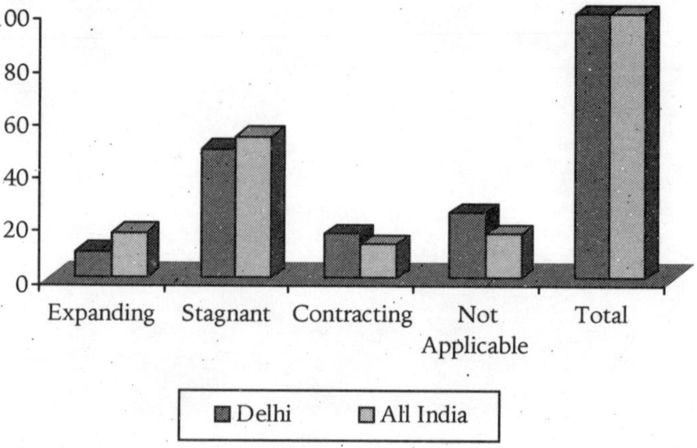

Problems

The major problem in this sector is also perceived competition from large units and shortage of capital as in the case of manufacturing.

TABLE 16.28

Per thousand Distribution of Enterprises by Problems Faced and Type of Enterprise in Unorganised Sector in All-India and Delhi

Combined (Rural + Urban)	*Delhi*	*All India*
No Specific Problem	513	326
Non Availability of Electricity Connection	1	7
Power Cut	9	16
Shortage of Capital	172	234
Marketing of Products/Services	83	100
Lack of Infrastructure	5	40
Local Problems	19	76
Harassment	11	27
Competition from Large Units	326	331
Non Availability of Labour	14	3
Labour Problem	2	3
Fuel not Available/Costly	4	8
Non Recovery of Service Charges fee/credit	60	74
Other	26	32

Source: Unorganised Service Sector in India, 2000-01, NSS 57th Round, NSSO, GoI.

Village Industries

In the N.C.T. of Delhi, the implementation of the Khadi and Village Industries (KVI) scheme is undertaken by the Delhi Khadi & Village Industries Board, which was established on 1.5.83. This Board has been reconstituted from time to time; the last one on 29.2.2000. At present the Board is implementing Rural Employment Generation Programme scheme in Delhi. The scheme is owned by Khadi and Village Industries Commission, Government of India and implemented by this board in the rural areas of NCT Delhi through KVIC.

Products and Services

Under KVI Sector products are of two types one is related to manufacturing and other is with services. The following products are manufactured and services are offered under this sector

Products

There is no sector, which remains untouched under the Village Industries in Delhi besides Khadi. The range includes products such as jewellery, various pottery products, items of stone cutting like statues, toys, chalk, bangles, *gulal* and *rangoli* used by ladies, paints, polishes and distemper used in house furnishing, forest based industries such as handmade products stationery, fancy articles, bamboo, cane work like furniture, *agarbatti* and matches used in every house, jute products of various varieties, manufacture of exercise book, register and envelope used by commoner.

Products of different type of spices/masala, cereals such as *dalia*, *papads*, jams and jelly, pickles, *ghani* oil that are used in every household. Under polymer and chemical based industry, there are products likes soap either for toilet soap, washing soap, various types of rubber products, candles, *mehandi*, shampoos, hair oil, detergents and washing powders.

Engineering & non-conventional energy group of village industries covers any item manufactured under Carpentry industry, Blacksmith industry and various household aluminum utensils and also utensils made of brass copper and bimetal. It also covers electronics and computer items of different varieties. Textile industry covers hosiery items, readymade garments, toys and dolls, embroidery and even manufacturing of surgical bandages. However, the exact numbers of these units are not available. (The only available estimates are of NSSO, which to a great extent covers this sector.)

Service:

Another group is of service industry which covers laundry, barber, plumbing servicing of electric wiring, electronics appliances, equipment, art board painting, cycle repair, repairs of diesel engine and pump set, *dhabas*, and tea stall etc. The Delhi Khadi and Village Industries Board is presently implementing Rural employment Generation Programme Scheme in Delhi which is owned by Khadi and Village Industries Commission , Government of India. From year 1999 onwards Board also started limited marketing activities. It procures items from the certified KVIC units and sells them at its sales outlet.

The data regarding the sector are available only for those units that are financed under REGP and again for current years the data are not available. Under Village Industries also data are a big deficiency.

Handicraft Sector in Delhi

The handicraft sector of Delhi comes under the Northern Regional Handicraft Commissioner. The main crafts of Delhi are Paper Mache, Embroidery, Metal Craft, *Madhubani* Painting, Jewellery, Bone Craft, and Metal jewellery, Block Printing etc. The artisans involved in these are mainly the migrated artisans from other parts of the country to the state. The Handicraft Commissioner provides these artisans the direct opportunity to sell their products in places like Dilli Haat.

Summary and Conclusion

The unorganised sector largely covers both the small and village industries. There are around 4.5 lakh enterprises in Delhi, which are engaged in activities pertaining to manufacturing and service. The share of Delhi's population in All India is 1.34 per cent whereas the share of Delhi in terms of unorganised sector enterprises is 1.52 per cent, 4.51 per cent of fixed capital invested here, production share is 5.41 per cent, employment share is 2.51 per cent and share in GVA is 6.37 which gives Delhi a position of leader among all the states of India. It is difficult to segregate the data of KVIC from the unorganised sector. This is mainly because there is as such no compulsion for units to get registered under any act or authority if they fall out of the purview of definition of enterprise under Factories Act. This is also reflected in the NSSO latest data, which do not show any entries under KVIC sector.

Regarding the nature of activities, majority of them work throughout the year from the permanent structures out of their household premises. In service sector however there are almost 18 per cent of enterprises which work as mobile market or street vendors.

The major problems faced by enterprises in this sector are competition from the larger units and shortage of capital. On the other hand, the data suggest that in manufacturing less than 0.8 per cent enterprises and in services only 1.4 per cent enterprises availed the loan facility. The majority of them more than 96 per cent do not take any assistance from the state. This refers to a serious drawback in the policies related to small scale units that too in the unorganised sector. This sector is the largest employment provider and contributing in the GVA also therefore steps should be initiated so that more and more units can come forward. The other problem that is competition from larger units implies that somewhere small-scale units are lacking in technology and as a result are finding themselves unable to compete with the larger units. Thus, it is required that Government should also look into this matter and some facilitation centres providing technology up gradation facilities should be set up and widely publicised.

The increasing concept of Retail Marketing giants is increasing in NCR that gives the opportunity to the small manufacturers to link with them. The information dissemination among the small manufacturers regarding this type of upcoming opportunities may prove beneficial for them.

Policy Issues

- The government should recognise the importance of unorganised sector in small scale industry so that proper policies as per their need could be designed.
- There is an urgent need to review the credit policies for small scale units falling into the unorganised sector.
- There is an urgent need to resolve the issue of power cuts.
- There is an urgent need to save the small scale sector from competition from larger units by providing them facilities for technical up gradation and marketing.

Notes

Concentration Ratios (*C*) were derived as proportion of industry value added accounted for by the 'r' largest industry groups, where 'r' is an arbitrary number. That is,

$$C_r = \sum_{i=1}^{r} x_i / \sum_{i=1}^{n} x_i$$

where 'n' is the total number of industry groups, and '*i*' (*i* = 1,2,3,...., *n*) any industry group.

The Hirschman-Herfindahl Index (*HH*) was derived as

$$HH = (C^2 + 1) / n$$

where '*c*' is the coefficient of variation of industry group size measured by share in value added and '*n*' the number of industry groups.

Among others Isard *et al.* (1998), Kumar (2005), and Richardson (1973).

The Location Quotient serves as a tool for making comparisons essentially as a measure of an activity's relative concentration, and for any sector *i* in region *R* (LQ_i^R) it may be defined as

$$LQ_i^R = \frac{E_i^R / E_i^N}{E^R / E^N} \quad \text{or} \quad LQ_i^R = \frac{E_i^R / E^R}{E_i^N / E^N}$$

The Specialisation Index (*SI*) for any region *R* in a system with '*n*' industries and '*m*' regions is derived as

$$SI^R = 1/2 \sum_{i}^{n} \left| S_t^R - \overline{S} \right|$$

where S_i^R denotes the share of industry '*i*' in the gross value added of region *R* and $\overline{S}_i$ the mean of the shares of industry '*i*' in the gross value added of all other (*m*-1) regions. The difference $(S_i^R - \overline{S}_i)$ measures the level of over- or under-representation of industry '*i*' in region *R*. The aggregate of absolute values of these differences indicates the extent of specialisation of region *R*. For details on this aspect see Batisse and Poncet (2003), and Bai *et al.* (2003).

The Shift-Share model is as

$$^{R}E_i^t - {}^{R}E_i^{t-1} = NGE_i^R + IMX_i^R + CET_i^R,$$

where $^{R}E_i^t$ is the employment in the ith sector of any region *R* at time *t*, NGE_i^R is the National Growth Effect, IMX_i^R the Industry Mix Effect, and CET_i^R the Competitive Effect. The three effects are in turn determined as

$$NGE_i^R = g_{ALL}^N \cdot {}^{R}E_i^{t-1}$$

$$IMX_i^R = {}^{R}E_i^{t-1} . (g_i^N - g_{ALL}^N)$$

$$CET_i^R = {}^{R}E_i^{t-1} . (g_i^R - g_i^N)$$

where g_{ALL}^N is per cent change in nationwide all-industries employment relative to the base period (*t*-1), g_i^N the per cent change in the ith industry national employment, and g_i^R the per cent change in i^{th} industry employment in region *R*. For different variations of the shift-share models see Kumar (200), Loveridge and Selting (1998)

Kendrick's index of total factor

$$A_t = V_t / (r_o K_t + w_o L_t)$$

Where A_t is the value of the index in a given year 't', V_t is the value of gross output in the year 't', and w_o and r_o denote the factor rewards of labour and capital respectively in the base year.

References

Bai, Chong-En, Ying Juan Du, Zhigang Tao, and Sarah Y. Tong (2003). "Local Protectionism and Regional Specialization: Evidence from China's Industries", *WP No.* 565, William Davidson Institute.

Batisse Cecile and Sandra Poncet (2003). "Protectionism and Industry Localization in Chinese Provinces", *ERSA Conference Papers*, No. ersa03.

EPW Research Foundation (2002). *Annual Survey of Industries 1973-74 to 1997-98: A Data Base on the Industrial Sector in India.*

———. (2003). *Domestic Product of States of India 1960-61 to 2000-01.*

Government of India (2002). *Tenth Five-Year Plan, 2002-2007*, 3 Volumes. Planning Commission.

Government of India (various years). *Annual Survey of Industries*, Central Statistical Organisation, various issues.

———. *Estimates of State Domestic Product*, Central Statistical Organisation, various issues.

Government of the National Capital Territory of Delhi (various years). *Annual Plans* (various years).

———. *Economic Survey* (various issues).

———. *Tenth Five-Year Plan 2002-2007.*

Isard, Walter, Iwan J. Azis, Matthew P. Drennan, Ronald E. Miller, Sidney Saltzman, and Erik Thorbecke (1998). *Methods of Interregional and Regional Analysis*, Aldershot: Ashgate.

Kendrick, J.W. and B.N. Vaccara, (eds) (1980). *New Developments in Productivity Measurement and Analysis*, University of Chicago Press.

Krishna, K.L. (1987). "Industrial Growth and Productivity in India" in P.R. Brahmananda and V.R. Panchmukhi (eds.) *The Development Process of the Indian Economy*. Mumbai: Himalaya Publishing Home.

Kumar, T. Ravi (2002). "The Impact of Regional Infrastructure Investment in India", *Regional Studies* 36 (2): 194-200, Journal of the International Regional Studies Association.

———. (2005). *Industry and the Region*. Hyderabad: Orient Longman (forthcoming).

Loveridge, Scott, and Anne C. Selting (1998). *"A Review and Comparison of Shift-Share Identities", International Regional Science Review* 21 (1): 37-58.

Richardson, Harry W. (1973). *Regional Growth Theory*. London: Macmillan.

Chapter 17

Institutional Reforms and Governance

17.1 Concept

> "The goal of governance initiatives should be to develop capacities that are needed to realise development that gives priority to the poor, advances women, sustains the environment and creates needed opportunities for employment and other livelihoods."
>
> *UNDP 1994 Initiatives for Change*

> "Democracy and transparent and accountable governance and administration in all sectors of society are indispensable foundations for the realisation of social and people-centred sustainable development."
>
> *Declaration of the World Summit for Social Development, 1995*

The concept of "governance" is as old as human civilisation. It is used in several contexts including those of national or local governance. Governance is inextricably linked to development but it is understood to have many meanings; the implication being that for 'sustainable development' good governance is a necessary condition. Two of the definitions are given here.

Governance may be defined as the process of decision-making and the process by which decisions are implemented.

According to the 10th Plan Document of the Planning Commission, "Governance relates to the management of all such processes that, in any society, define the environment which permits and enables individuals to raise their capability levels, on the one hand, and provide opportunities to realise their potential and enlarge the set of available choices, on the other."

17.2 Link between Governance and Development

Even though the notions of good governance and the link between governance and sustainable human development vary, good governance and sustainable human development are indivisible. According to UNDP 1994 Initiatives for Change, the goal of governance initiatives should be to develop capacities that are needed to realise development that gives priority to the disadvantaged, advances women, sustains the environment and creates needed opportunities for employment and other livelihoods. Good governance can be—and should be—the primary way to eliminate poverty. The view is widely held that good governance assures that corruption is minimised, the views of minorities are taken into account, that the voices of the most vulnerable in society are heard in decision-making and that it is responsive to the present and future needs of society. Experience shows that while good governance can help secure human well being and sustained development, it is equally important to recognise that poor governance could well erode the individual capabilities, as well as institutional and community capacities to meet the needs of sustenance. Experience also shows that good governance is an ideal which is difficult to achieve in its totality and very few countries and societies have come close to achieving good governance in its totality. However, to ensure sustainable human development, actions must be taken to work towards this ideal with the aim of making it a reality.

These processes, covering the political, social and economic aspects of life impact every level of human enterprise, be it the individual, the household, the village, the region or the national level. It covers the State, civil society and the market, each of which is critical for sustaining human development. The State is responsible for creating a conducive political, legal and economic environment for building individual capabilities and encouraging private initiative. The market is expected to create opportunities for people. Civil society facilitates the mobilisation of public opinion and peoples' participation in economic, social and political activities.

17.3 Actors in Governance

Since governance is the process of decision-making and the process by which decisions are implemented, an analysis of governance focuses on the formal and informal actors involved in decision-making and implementing the decisions made and the formal and informal structures that have been set in place to arrive at and implement the decision.

Government including Union, State and Local, is one of the main actors in governance. Governance includes the state, but transcends it by taking in the private sector and civil society. All three are critical for sustaining human development. The state creates a conducive political and legal environment. The private sector generates jobs and income. And civil society facilitates political and social interaction—mobilising groups to participate in economic, social and political activities. Because each has weaknesses and strengths, a major objective of our support for good governance is to promote constructive interaction among all three.

Actors involved in governance are included in the term "Civil Society". All actors other than government and the military are grouped together as part of the "civil society." In urban areas, for example, other actors may include those belonging to and representing industry and commerce, professions including medicine, law, accounts and finance, academic, cooperatives, NGOs, research institutes, religious leaders, groups based on social stratification, political parties etc. The situation in urban areas is very complex.

Analysis of governance focuses on the formal and informal actors involved in decision-making and implementing the decisions made and the formal and informal structures that have been set in place to arrive at and implement the decision. In urban areas an example of informal actors is organised crime syndicates such as the "land Mafia" that may try to influence decision-making. Such, influence is often the result of corrupt practices or leads to corrupt practices.

17.4 Characteristics of Good Governance

Good governance has 8 major characteristics. It

a) is participatory

b) follows rule of law

c) is consensus oriented

d) is accountable

e) is transparent

f) is responsive

g) is effective and efficient

h) is equitable and inclusive.

17.5 Improving Governance

The social and political stability associated with good governance are fundamental to sustainable human development. Good governance is by nature preventive. By valuing development assets and building social cohesion and consensus, it can help reduce vulnerability to—and even the likelihood of—disasters and conflicts. During crises, systems and institutions that protect the vulnerable are the first things to be destroyed and must be restored.

Good governance includes both procedural and substantive elements; so too does the management of economic and financial matters. There is need to establish relationships between the state, the private sector and civil society and develop frameworks that provide incentives for broadly based and sustainable growth.

17.6 Governance in NCTD

Having discussed the theoretical aspects of the concept of governance and its relationship with development, we can move on to governance in the context of NCTD.

17.7 Evolution of Governance in NCTD

Till 1956, Delhi was a 'state'. On the recommendation of State Reorganisation Commission, Delhi was declared a Union Territory in 1956. Delhi Municipal Corporation Act 1957 created a Municipal Corporation with jurisdiction covering the entire Union Territory of Delhi but excluding New Delhi Municipal Committee and Delhi Cantonment. In this the MCD took over the functions previously entrusted to 10 local bodies—municipalities, notified area committees, Delhi District Board and three statutory bodies, *viz*. Delhi State Electricity Board, Delhi Road Transport Authority and Delhi Joint Water and Sewerage Board. The Municipal Corporation became the premier body for provision and maintenance of urban services, sanitation and certain community facilities in Delhi. It lacked power in regard to the planning, development and disposal of urban land.

The Government of India, in November 1955, set up "Delhi Development (Provisional) Authority", which became Delhi Development Authority with the passing of its Act by the Parliament in December 1957.

The Delhi Development Authority is the apex agency for planning and development of the city, is empowered to prepare a master plan, zonal plans, to implement and enforce the plans and to develop, manage and dispose of lands in Delhi. It also discharges the functions of developing housing, commercial centres, parks, playgrounds, etc. Master Plan for Delhi provides a basic policy frame for guiding Delhi's development.

In 1966, the Delhi Administration Act was passed by the Parliament, as a result of which the Metropolitan Council, a representative body consisting of 56 elected and 5 nominated members was created. Simultaneously an Executive Council consisting of 4 members of whom one as Chief Executive Councilor was created. But this body had very limited powers, since the Administrator (Lt. Governor) continued to enjoy vast decision making and discretionary powers.

In January 1992, the Government of NCT of Delhi Act, 1991 was enacted by Parliament,. A Legislative Assembly with a Council of Ministers under Articles 239 AA and 239 AB was created.

As Union Territory with an Assembly and a Council of Ministers, NTDC has very many features of a State such as Government, Assembly and Municipal bodies. Yet Delhi is different from a State. As will be seen from the constitutional provisions relating to NCTD, its powers are seriously curtailed as mentioned below:

a) Although Legislative Assembly has the power to make laws with respect to any of the matters enumerated in the State List or in the Concurrent List, it has no such power relating to public order, police and offences relating to the subjects.

b) Even in respect of other subjects the Parliament has overriding powers to make laws.

c) The advice of the Council of Ministers to the Lieutenant Governor is not binding for in the case of difference of opinion between the Lieutenant Governor and his Council of Ministers on any matter, the Lieutenant Governor can refer it to the President for decision and act according to the decision given thereon. Pending such decision the Lieutenant Governor may take such action or give such direction in the matter as he deems necessary.

d) Law and order and land are within the jurisdiction of the Government of India.

e) A Bill of Amendment relating to financial matters shall not be introduced in the Assembly except on the recommendations of the Lt. Governor in relation to State taxes, financial expenditure charged on consolidated fund of the Capital etc.

f) The annual budget is to be laid before the Legislative Assembly by the Lt. Governor with the previous sanction of the President as this is mandatory under Article 239 (1) of the Constitution according to which the President is responsible for the Administration of every Union Territory. Additional demand for expenditure upon the consolidated fund of the Capital shall be made on the recommendation of the Lt. Governor.

g) Delhi is a city state in that most of its geographical area is included within the Municipal Corporation of Delhi (MCD), a very powerful elected body. The remaining area is covered by New Delhi Municipal Committee (NDMC), a body under the Government of India and a small portion under the Cantonment Board. Delhi is divided into nine districts. The Municipal Corporation of Delhi has created eleven divisions of its jurisdiction to provide decentralised services to the people. The civic services, elementary education, health services, engineering services many others are provided by these bodies.

h) Independent of Delhi Government and MCD, NDMC performs municipal functions and supplies electricity and water to the core area in New Delhi, where the Government of India's main functionaries work and reside. NDMC functions more as an administrative set-up under the Ministry of Home Affairs through the Lt. Governor, Delhi. Delhi Government has hardly any role in its functioning.

i) The present relationship between the MCD and the Delhi government is rather nebulous. The DMC Act, 1957 was enacted without provision for a Legislative Assembly in Delhi, which was constituted only in 1992-93. Delhi Government's functions *vis-à-vis* MCD are limited to those of paramount nature, which are reserved for the Central government for exercise through the Lt. Governor. The MCD, as a potent third force is itself a centre of power in the affairs of Delhi.

The following table gives the evolution of governance since Independence in 1947.

TABLE 17.1

Evolution of Governance

Period	*Governing Institutions*
1947-1952	Government of India
1952-1956	Self Governing part C State with the Legislative Assembly of 48 members
1956	Delhi Legislative Assembly abolished
1956-1966	Directly Administered Union Territory and the Birth of the Delhi Administration
1957	Delhi Municipal Corporation & Delhi Development Authority created
1966	Metropolitan Council set up under the Delhi Administration Act
1980-1983	No Metropolitan Council as it was dissolved by the Central Government
1990	Central Government dissolved Metropolitan Council
1992 onwards	Elected Government of the National Capital Territory of Delhi with a Council of Ministers led by the Chief Minister.

17.8 Urban Process: Organisations and Functions

Delhi has a complex administrative set-up with a multiplicity of authorities dealing with a subject as has been compiled by A.K.Jain in his book Delhi—*Governance, Planning and Development* reproduced below:

TABLE 17.2

Major Organisations Providing Various Services in the NCT of Delhi (2000)

Service	*Organisation providing the service*
Urban Planning and Development	Delhi Development Authority (Also NCRPB) (Ministry of Urban Development)
Land	Central Govt. , DDA, MCD, PWD, Delhi Govt., DSIDC, Cooperatives/Private, etc.
Water & Sewerage	Delhi Jal Board, (Delhi Govt.), MCD, NDMC (Autonomous elected body under GoI,)
Electricity	Delhi Vidyut Board (Delhi Government)
Transport	Delhi Transport Corporation, State Transport Corpn., Private Operators
Milk	Delhi Milk Scheme, Mother Dairy (Delhi Govt./Central government)
Law and Order	Delhi Police (Home Ministry)
Enforcement of Planning Controls	Special Task Force (Home Ministry) DDA, MCD, NDMC
Urban Form and Aesthetics	Delhi Urban Art Commission
Slum/*Jhuggi Jhopri* rehabilitation	Delhi Slum Improvement Board (Delhi Government) Slum & JJ Deptt. (MCD)
Finance for Industry and Business	Delhi Finance and Development Corporation (Delhi Government)
Education	Central Govt./State Govt., Universities, Colleges, MCD, NDMC, Govt. of National Capital Territory of Delhi (GNCTD), Private
Health	MCD, NDMC, GNCTD, Private
Recreation	DDA, MCD, NDMC, TFAI, Private Sector
Lands, Residential & Industrial	DDA, CPWD, DSIDC Govt. of Delhi, MCD
Horticulture	DDA, MCD, NDMC, CPWD
Utilities	DDA, MCD, NDMC, Delhi Govt., etc.
Commercial	DDA, NDMC, MCD, DAMB, L & DO, Govt. of India
Security & Emergency Services	Delhi Police, Delhi Fire Service
Fuel Distribution	Oil Companies, Gas Authority of India
Heritage Conservation	Archaeological Survey of India, GNCTD, DDA, INTACH, etc.
Roads	Central Govt. (N.H.), PWD (Ring Road), MCD, NDMC, Cantt. Bd., DDA (Inner city Roads)
Building Plan Approval	MCD, DDA, NDMC, DUAC, AAI, DPCC, DFS, etc.
Pollution Control	Conservator of Forests, Delhi Govt., Env. Pollution Control Authority, DOE, Delhi Pollution Control Committee, CPCB, MCD,
Drainage & Flood Control	I&F Deptt., GNCTD, DDA, MCD
Safety	Fire Department, Boiler Inspector, MCD, DOI, Central Government (Deptt. of Explosives) etc.
Telephones, Cellular, Internet	MTNL, Private companies, VSNL, etc.
Sales Tax Registration	Govt. of Delhi
Factory Licence	MCD, DOI, CIF, Labour Deptt., Delhi Govt.

Source: Delhi - Governance, Planning And Development by A.K. Jain.

17.9 Unique Features of NCT Delhi

The governance in Delhi is very complex. The constitutional provisions have maintained the status of NCTD as a Union Territory with a legislature and Council of Ministers and given it more powers than other Union Territories but considerably less than those enjoyed by a State. The allocation of work is among a plethora of agencies. The result is that there is a multiplicity of public bodies dealing with the same subject. Unlike other states law & order, police and land are under the areas of responsibility of the Government of India and even in other matters, the Government of India and the parliament have overriding powers.

17.9.1 Relevance of Characteristics of Good Governance in NCTD

The relevance of any specific characteristic or area needing attention is a function of the stage of political, economic and social development of the country. Some of the characteristics/areas may seem not to have relevance in the context of our country which is governed in the framework of our constitution and a comprehensive set of laws.

In theory and law, the governance is participatory as elected bodies are in position. They are accountable to people and have the authority to make laws, rules and procedures, as the case may be, and to take decisions and have them implemented. Moreover, every organ of the State must follow law and principles of natural justice and if it does not do so, it faces the risk of being called to account in the High Court and the Supreme Court. The consensus has to be achieved because minorities too have a decisive voice and the majority cannot bulldoze its decisions. There is accountability—financial and administrative.

The accounts of government and bodies receiving public funds are subject to audit by statutory authorities and administrative actions have to be explained in the appropriate elected body. The actions are again required to be equitable and inclusive because there cannot be discrimination against any body as guaranteed by the constitution which enshrines the Fundamental Rights, the principle of equality before the law and rights of minorities. Thus it may appear on superficial examination that there is no need for action relating to these characteristics.

However, it is well known that theoretical provisions do not conform to the ground reality and there is a big gap between 'precept and practice'. The governance is weak institutions, though consisting of very bright people, are subject to various kinds of pressure/influences, and the procedures are cumbersome and time consuming and so on. The result is that the public image of governance is not very complimentary. It is perceived to have a tendency to be inefficient, ineffective, corrupt and dilatory. The unscrupulous among the citizens, in turn, tend to dodge the law and appropriate public resources at the cost of other fellow citizens. Thus there is need to take action to strengthen all the eight characteristics identified in paragraph 1.4.

17.9.2 Relevance of Areas Needing Attention

In the case of our country and NCTD, there is written constitution and legislative and judicial institutions enjoy autonomy. Any initiative for reforms, if any, will have to come from these institutions. Any discussion of these institutions and the processes followed by them are irrelevant for the purposes of this report. However, other areas mentioned in paragraph 17.5 are relevant.

The characteristics of Good Governance and areas needing attention are equally applicable to all sectors—education, health, transport or any other sector. Hence these need to be discussed not sector wise but in a general way cutting across all sectors and pertaining to each of the principal organisations in the NCTD *viz.*, the Government of NCTD, Municipal Corporation of Delhi, NDMC and the DDA.

17.10 Measures Initiated to Improve Governance in NCTD

The Government of NCT of Delhi through its Department of Administrative Reforms has been taking measures that cut across other departments of the Government of NCTD, agencies and institutions and monitoring the progress made by them.

17.10.1 Vision

The Government of Delhi in its Administrative Reforms Department has adopted a vision to facilitate the pursuit of excellence in governance through improvements in Government structures and processes to achieve:

- economy in Government expenditure;
- citizen-friendly initiatives including redressal of public grievances;
- dissemination of best practices;
- simplification of procedures; and

- implementation of Delhi Right to Information Act.

17.10.2 Organisations Selected

The organisations where these improvements are sought to be achieved are:-

- Delhi Government Departments.
- Autonomous Bodies/Public Sector Undertakings of Delhi Government.
- MCD/NDMC/Delhi Cantonment Board.

17.10.3 Means Used

The means used to achieve the improvements consist of

- Promote Role of civil society, People's participation and decentralisation. This has been sought to be achieved through the introduction of Bhagidari Scheme.
- e-Governance for the citizens of Delhi.
- To set up a dynamic website leading to e-governance for departments/agencies.
- Mechanism to redress public grievances of which establishment of Public Grievances Commission is the main element.
- Civil Service Reforms.
- Procedural Reform.
- Synergy and Coordination.
- Empowerment of the weak.
- Social Audit.
- Implementation of the Right to Information Act.
- Introducing the Tender Information System under which all notices for tenders are placed on the Website of the Government of NCTD.
- Introducing a Unified Call Centre to register grievances as a Listening Post of Lt. Governor.

To promote the role of civil society, people's participation and decentralisation in governance, the scheme of Bhagidari has been introduced within the government departments and its agencies including those under the Union government.

17.11 Bhagidari

a) Concept

In line with the ideological heritage of involving the common man in governance, initially propounded by Mahatma Gandhi, and given expression to by Rajiv Gandhi by giving constitutional status to *Panchayats* and Municipal Bodies through 73rd and 74th amendments of the Constitution, in December 1998 the Government of NCTD outlined a philosophy for governance—responsive to and participative with the citizen—known as Bhagidari. This has specifically stemmed from the belief that Government must work in partnership with the people and that the citizens must feel that successful and meaningful governance cannot be achieved without their involvement and without their role.

To evolve a mechanism for putting the concept of Bhagidari into practice, wide consultations were initiated with various citizen groups—the Resident Welfare Associations (RWAs), the Market and Traders Associations (MTAs) and other NGOs. Discussions were also held with Municipal Corporation of Delhi, Delhi Development Authority, New Delhi Municipal Committee, Delhi Vidyut Board, Delhi Jal Board and Delhi Police and the Department of Environment and Forest. These departments subsequently became the participating Departments in the Bhagidari Programme.

Launched in January 2000, Bhagidari, the Citizen's Partnership in Governance is conceived to:

- be a means for facilitating citywide changes in Delhi;
- utilise processes and principles of multi-stakeholders (citizen groups, NGOs, the Government...) collaboration;
- apply the method of Large Group Interactive Events;
- aim to develop 'joint ownership' by the citizens and government of the change process; and
- to facilitate people's participation in governance.

b) Issues Taken up under Bhagidari Scheme

The issues that have been taken up are simple and common and have impact on a citizen's everyday life and are amenable to simple solutions. The idea is to build up on these first successes and to take the movement forward to addressing more complex matters. The participating organisations and the number of activities under the Bhagidari Scheme are given in the table below. The details of the Scheme, organisation-wise, are given in the annexure 17.1.

TABLE 17.3

Issues Taken Up under Bhagidari Scheme

Name of Organisation	*No of Activities Covered under Bhagidari*
Delhi Jal Board (DJB)	8
Delhi Vidyut Board (DVB)*	8
Municipal Corporation of Delhi (MCD)	9
Department of Environment and Forests (E&F)	3
Delhi Police (DP)	6
Delhi Development Authority (DDA)	5
Weights and Measures	5
Sales Tax	5
Industries Department	15

Note: * BSES and Tata Power, the successor distribution companies are also now participating in Bhagidari Scheme.

Source: Abstracted from the information in the website of NCTD (*delhigovt.nic.in/bhagi.asp#6*) under the title "BHAGIDARI".

c) "Large Group Interactive Events" (LGIE) Discussion of Common Problems

In consultation with the Asian Centre for Organisation Research and Development, (ACORD), a professional body, the "Large Group Interactive Events' (LGIE) was devised as an appropriate model to train citizen-groups and government officials (of all levels) to sit together, to discuss their viewpoints on common problems and build up consensus for solutions and their implementation. This model envisages the following steps:

1. Workshops with citizen groups be held where representatives of citizen groups discuss the selected issues with officials of Public Utility Departments, *viz.*, Municipal Corporation of Delhi, Delhi Development Authority, Delhi Vidyut Board, Delhi Jal Board, Delhi Police, Sales Tax Department and the Department of Environment and Forests.
2. Each workshop of three days duration will have the participants seated in a tablewise arrangement. Each table has 4 citizens (2 each from 2 citizen groups, *viz.*, Residents Welfare Association or Market Traders Association) and 5-6 officials of Public Utility Departments. Care is taken to seat area officials of Public Utility Departments at the table where representatives from citizen groups of their area are sitting. In a workshop around 30-35 such table arrangements are made.
3. Each table group works on issues selected by the Design Team. The group discusses and builds consensus on solution of issue-based problems. Each stake holder's (including the citizen's) role and responsibilities are identified and committed.
4. After the workshop, the RWA/MTA-wise list of solutions is sent to concerned departments and Deputy Commissioner (Revenue) offices. They hold regular meetings to implement and monitor solutions.
5. The Area Officers ensure a fortnightly meeting with their area RWAs. The District Officers of the public utilities monitor and coordinate the working of these Area Officers.
6. Monthly reviews are taken by the Heads of Departments and the Deputy Commissioners.
7. Quarterly reviews are taken by the Chief Secretary and the Steering Committee headed by Chief Minister.
8. Mid Term Impact Assessment through consultant firm, i.e., ACORD has indicated that people have by and large appreciated the programme but the Government officials are required to be sensitised further.

d) Financial and Administrative Sustainability

The Bhagidari Programme envisages voluntary participation of the citizens. Efforts have been made to make it well structured and sustainable. A 'Bhagidari Cell' has been created in the Chief Minister's office and the General Administration Department has been designated as the Nodal Department to provide financial and administrative support. The 'Bhagidari Cell' has been coordinating the activities covered under Bhagidari as well as in conducting workshops.

To make it a sustainable programme, the Government has come up with a detailed plan scheme of 'Citizen-Government Interface'. This covers Bhagidari Workshops, various activities with citizen groups, documentation of the process, printing of monthly newsletter and award scheme for best citizen groups including MTAs & RWAs.

e) Decentralisation of Bhagidari

Initially, the entire interaction with citizen groups, resource mobilisation, etc., was being done centrally by the Bhagidari Cell in the Chief Minister's office. To ensure a spatial spread the programme was decentralised at the Revenue District level with the Deputy Commissioner (Revenue) as the district coordinator. This has helped to involve more than 1100 citizen groups in the programme. According to the Government, requests keep coming in from new associations and NGOs to join the movement.

After decentralisation Bhagidari has been spread to Social Welfare Department where Stree-Shakti Programme and Stree-Kosh have been launched. In Education Department, the School Welfare Committees have been appointed in more than 600 schools. Industrial Associations have also been made *Bhagidars* after conducting special Bhagidari workshop with them through the Industries department.

f) Major Initiatives

The programme has become popular, leading to Major initiatives under 'Bhagidari' by the Government since January, 2002:

- Water Conservation and Water Harvesting by Delhi Jal Board & Urban Development Department.
- Anti Plastic and Anti-littering campaign by Environment and Forest Department.
- Programmes for the welfare of Senior Citizens.
- Reforms in Hospital Management & Quality Control by Health & Family Welfare Department. 'Janhit Society' in each major hospital has been set up ith representation from RWAs of the area and other citizen groups.
- Students Welfare Committee for Government.
- In addition to the above programmes, Bhagidari has taken in its span the Industrial Associations. In Conforming Industrial Areas of Delhi have been made *Bhagidars* through their Industrial Associations. A high power apex level committee of senior officers and representatives of industries is to prepare the policy frame work for growth and development of Industries in Delhi.

g) Results of Bhagidari

More than 1100 citizen groups have become *Bhagidars* after having participated in various Bhagidari workshops. The *Bhagidars* have not only been successful in solving their day-to-day problems, but have also been providing help to public utility departments in maintenance and up gradation of services. Some examples are:

1. Successful implementation of "Clean Yamuna", "Say no to plastic bags" & "No crackers on Diwali" campaigns.
2. Switching on/off of streetlights by RWAs.
3. Meter reading by RWAs in their residential colony.
4. Traffic regulation in the colonies.
5. Clean Delhi: "Green Delhi" campaign.
6. Tenant verification in the colonies.
7. Rain-water Harvesting.
8. Conservation of water by checking misuse of water.
9. Water Bill collection and payment by RWAs.
10. Desilting of sewers.
11. Coordinating with DVB for handling load shedding and power breakdown.
12. Prevention of power-theft.
13. Door to door collection of garbage.
14. Maintenance of community parks and halls.
15. Crime prevention and successful implementation of neighbourhood watch scheme.
16. Prevention of encroachment.

h) Challenges

First, bringing together a large number of citizen groups and government officials on a common platform was not an easy task. It required detailed planning and coordinated action holding preliminary meetings, interactions and a whole gamut of logistical arrangements. It required managing a change process—a change in perceptions of both the citizens and government officials.

There was initially resistance from the field-level government officers who were not willing to step out of their bureaucratic shell and embrace the direct interaction with citizen groups. They felt it was erosion of their authority and in many instances it also stemmed corruption at the field-level. So far the citizen-groups have been registered associations, the challenge is now step out with the programme into the slum clusters, resettlement colonies and the unauthorised regularised areas.

Reaching out to rural areas, women groups and non-governmental organisations work out changes in policies and legislation, which would enable the citizen groups to statutorily interact with Government.

17.12 Vigilance

The Central Vigilance Commissioner has jurisdiction over personnel of the NCTD. The Delhi Lokayukta & Upalokayukta Act, 1995 provides a forum for attending to complaints against public functionaries to eradicate the vice of corruption, favouritism, abuse of position and power and present cleaner image. The Act takes within its ambit the Ministers including the Chief Minister, Members of Legislative Assembly, Members of Municipal Corporation, etc.

17.13 Improve Governance, Bring Openness and Transparency

In pursuance of the objective to improve governance, bring openness and transparency in providing citizen-friendly services the Government of NCT of Delhi has initiated the following actions with emphasis on "preventive vigilance". It is expected that adoption of such measures would, in the long run, help Governments in curbing the menace of corruption and minimise it to a large extent.

17.13.1 e-Governance for the Citizens of Delhi

To reduce citizens' visit to offices and provide information electronically rather than over the counter and making Delhi a cyber city the government has set up a dynamic website leading to e-governance for departments/agencies to provide on line services including services on e-applications. The Government has instituted a system of making on line complaint. The citizen can also check the status of the complaint, send a reminder and send suggestions.

17.13.2 Right to Information

The Delhi Government has enacted the Delhi Right to Information Act, 2001. It makes provision for securing information as a matter of right, barring some exemptions. The citizens can file an application with the competent authority of the concerned Department along with fee and get information within 30 days. In case the information cannot be given, then a rejection letter with reasons has to be issued. It provides for right to appeal in Public Grievances Commission. The Act provides for a unique provision for punitive action against the officials in the form of fine at the rate of Rs.50 per day for delay and Rs.1000 for tendering wrong information.

The Government has appointed State Public Information Officers/Assistant State Public Information Officers/First appellate Authority in all the departments of the Government of NCTD, PSUs and Local Bodies. Training programmes have been organised to sensitise the officials of the officials of these bodies.

This measure is being widely used by the citizens and as on 12 July 2007, 36390 applications were received out of which 34090 were disposed of.

17.13.3 Tender Information System

In order to bring openness and transparency in the tender inviting system the publication of all tenders on a newly developed powerful website capable of handling tenders of 356 tender issuing authorities has been made obligatory.

17.13.4 Listening Post of Lt. Governor

A number of call centres have been providing information to the citizens for different departments. To do away with multiplicity of these call centres, the Government of NCTD has decided to set up a unified Call Centre which will also be used for registering complaints/ grievances. The Call Centre is equipped with a Grievance Redressal Mechanism that has a computer network loaded with software with time bound escalation matrix for prompt redressal of the complaint.

17.13.5 Public Grievances Commission

The Government of Delhi has set up a Public Grievance Commission through a Resolution for effective redressal of grievances. It is an autonomous body which attends to complaints received against the departments of Government of Delhi, its local bodies, undertakings, autonomous institutions/undertakings, etc. The commission is an independent body responsible for speedy redressal of complaints relating to acts of omission or of commission. It can also take up *suomoto* action, where required.

17.13.6 Citizen's Charter

The innovation of citizen's charter was made by the British Government. Its objective is to address some of the problems of interface between the Government and citizens and to continuously improve the quality of public services and to make them responsive to their needs and wishes by empowering the citizens in relation to public service delivery. It is expected to lead to accountability of organisations and their staff with total transparency about the rules, regulations and the processes and procedures. It also aims to provide a mechanism for redressal of citizens' grievances.

The citizens' charter programme has been adopted in the NCTD. Coupled with the enactment of the Right to Information and putting in to place the mechanism of dealing with public grievances, the framework of providing the basic information to the public and to open the vistas of transparency and accountability in the systems has been created. These charters are required to spell out the standards of services and time limits within which the public can reasonably expect the disposal of the requests made by them to the government. Delhi Government has brought out 73 such citizens charters. These charters are available with the concerned departments and can be obtained free of cost. The organisations in the NCTD that have prepared the citizens' charters are given in Annexure No. 17.2 (List is not complete.)

17.13.7 Decentralisation

a) Administrative Decentralisation

D.C., Delhi use to be the Head of the District Administration, responsible for law and order, excise, issue of arms and explosive licenses, and citizenship certificates, apart from revenue and criminal judicial work. In the mid-70s, the DC office was reorganised with four administrative districts – New, Central, North and South, looked after by three ADMs, amongst whom the various other powers and functions, such as treasuries, excise, entertainment etc., were divided. Revenue and Land Acquisition work was supervised by ADM (Revenue) and ADM (LA) respectively. There were 12 Sub-Divisions, each headed by SDM, which was later reduced to seven.

Two major changes greatly diluted the role of DC Office. The first was the separation of the executive and the judiciary in 1969, after which heinous crimes were dealt with by Sessions Courts and other offences including IPC offences were dealt with by Judicial Magistrates. The Executive Magistrates were to look after executive and administrative matters such as licensing, sanction of prosecution, and preventive sections of the Cr.P.C. such as Section 107,109,110,133,144 and 145.

In 1978, the Delhi Police Act was promulgated, by which Delhi came under the Commissioner of Police system. Almost all powers of the District Magistrates as per the Cr.P.C. were vested in the Police Commissioner. Section 107 and Section 144 Cr.P.C., which are very important for maintaining law and order, since then have been directly dealt with by the Police. Furthermore, powers of licensing and entertainment, which earlier vested in the D.C., were also given to the Police.

This was the situation in 1996 when the exercise of decentralising the DC office by setting up 27 SDM offices and 9 DC offices was started. While the SDMs were put in place in mid-1996, the DCs began functioning from 1.1.97.

b) Social Audit

Outside professional agencies were engaged to get social audit done of agencies providing public services as below:

TABLE 17.4

Social Audit

S. No.	*Departments/Organisations*	*Audit Done For*
1.	Delhi Jal board	Supply of water through tankers
2.	Hospitals of Delhi Government/ MCD	OPD & IPD Services
3.	Education (Delhi Govt. Schools and Primary Schools of MCD.	Education provided in the respective schools
4.	Food and Supplies	Services provided by ration shops and kerosene oil dealers
5.	Transport	Services provided by licensing offices
6.	DTC	Public Transport Services
7.	Divisional Commissioner's Office	Issue of caste and income certificate and registration of documents by Sub-Registrar Offices.

Source: Report of Independent Social Audit carried out by the Public Affairs Foundation, released by Chief Minister Sheila Dikshit on September 4, 2006 and available on the website *http://www.pafglobal.org/publications/Social_Audit_Draft_Press_Release.pdf*

A committee headed by the Chief Secretary has suggested remedial measures to the concerned departments and monitor the progress of Reforms Measures.

17.14 Municipal Corporation of Delhi

The Municipal Corporation of Delhi (MCD) came into existence on the 7 April 1958 under an Act of Parliament. The Amendment of 1993 in the Act brought about fundamental changes in composition, functions, governance and administration of the Corporation.

The entire MCD area is divided into 12 zones to make access easier. The Citizens' representatives in the corporation, namely councilors are always approachable for removal of grievances.

It provides civic services to some of the most densely populated areas in the world covering both rural and urban areas, Resettlement Colonies, regularised unauthorised colonies, *Jhuggi Jhopri* squatter settlements, slum *basties*, private *katras*, etc.

17.14.1 Citizen Service Bureau

MCD has started a unique and path breaking IT initiative with the objective to deliver electronically its services to citizens of Delhi through a Citizen Service Bureau set-up, one in each Zone and one at Town Hall. These Bureaus are run by a consortium of IT companies namely ECIL & Sark Systems Ltd. Further MCD plans to open 134 ICSBs(one in each ward).

The concept behind establishing Citizen Service Bureau is to provide all municipal services under one roof in air-conditioned comfort on payment of a very small transaction fee. The transaction fee that is charged for all municipal services, other than payment of property tax, depends on the value of transaction.

17.15 New Delhi Municipal Council (NDMC)

17.15.1 Establishment

In 1911 the seat of the Government of India was transferred from Calcutta to Delhi. Raisina Hill was selected as the site for the Viceregal Palace and the area East, North and South of it was chosen for the new capital. Edwin Lutyens and his compatriot Herbert Baker built the new capital of India to be known as New Delhi.

The 'Raisina Municipal Committee' was established in 1916 to cater to the municipal needs of the labour engaged in the construction of new capital. In 1925, it was upgraded and around this time, it was designated as 'Imperial Delhi Municipal Committee". It was named 'New Delhi Municipal Committee" and in 1932, it became a "First Class" municipality.

In May 1994, the NDMC Act replaced the Punjab Municipal Act, 1911 under which the 'Raisina Municipal Committee' was established, and the committee was renamed as "New Delhi Municipal Council". The act has been passed by the Parliament. An eleven member Council headed by a Chairperson governs the NDMC. Five of them are officials, three are elected members of the legislature representing the constituencies in the NDMC area, two are drawn from among eminent personalities. The MP of New Delhi parliamentary constituency is an invitee to council's meetings.

The area of NDMC includes the seat of Central Government, Rashtrapati Bhawan, the Prime Minister's office and residence, Central Government office, Foreign Missions, residences of Ministers, Members of Parliament, Diplomats and Central Government employees.

17.15.2 Main Functions

In addition to providing basic civic amenities to its residents, the Municipal Council also ensures various social, cultural, educational and medical facilities, especially to the government/municipal employees and other weaker sections of society. Actually, the NDMC is a municipality with a difference. The Act enjoins upon it a role of a mini-government, with all facets of city management except that of policing and transportation.

It is perhaps the only municipality in the country that supplies electricity and water and its discretionary functions encompass promotion of sports, art, music and culture, maintenance of libraries, and care for the old, mentally and hearing impaired. It takes care of working women, housing problems and social facilities like *barat ghars* and community centres. It always aims to achieve it by eliciting peoples' cooperation and public participation.

17.15.3 Citizens' Charter

The NDMC had issued the first charter in 1997 and has issued the new one in February 2005. It is a simplified and yet a very comprehensive Charter giving all the details of citizens' entitlement to municipal services, quality of services, access to information, stages in decision-making, time bound schedule of services, sanctions and approvals. It is a measure towards transparency and efficient and timely provision of services. Its Vision and Mission are reproduced below:

Vision: "NDMC resolves to intensify its efforts in providing better civic services to the citizens and a multitude of visiting patrons from all over the country and overseas. Other objectives before the NDMC are to improve quality of life providing social and community welfare amenities with public, private participation—with special emphasis on promotion of art and culture, environmental improvement, cleaning and greening campaigns to serve as a show window of "A Model Well Planned Metropolitan City".

17.15.4 Mission

"NDMC is committed to providing efficient, qualitative, responsive and accountable services to all the citizens and visitors of its area with instant access to information to bring transparency."

17.15.5 Grievance Redressal System

NDMC has set up an Information and Facilitation Centre and opened two Palika Suvidha Kendras where citizens can pay their taxes, fees, etc., obtain birth/death certificates, book *Barat Ghars* and register their complaints relating to civic services. Very detailed information has been provided in the Citizens' Charter about the main sectors of activity of the NDMC separately such as electricity, water, felling of trees, sewers, unauthorised construction, education, health, etc., as to who is responsible, contact points, telephone numbers and the complaint centres.

17.15.6 Annual Administrative Report

The NDMC publishes an Annual Administrative Report enabling those interested in getting to know the work done in the year gone by and the programme for the coming year.

17.15.7 Delhi Development Authority

17.15.7.1 Establishment and Functions

India's Independence in 1947 and resultant migration increased Delhi's population from 7 lakhs to 17 lakhs by 1951. Delhi Improvement Trust and Municipal Body, the two local bodies at that time, were not adequately equipped to cope up with the changing scenario.

The Central government appointed a Committee under the chairmanship of Sh. G D. Birla in 1950. This Committee recommended a Single Planning and Controlling Authority for all the urban areas of Delhi.

Consequently, the Delhi Development (Provisional) Authority - DDPA - was constituted by promulgating the Delhi (Control of Building Operations) Ordinance, 1955 followed by the Delhi Development Act, 1957 with the primary objective of ensuring the development of Delhi in accordance with a plan. On 30th December, 1957, Delhi Development Authority acquired its present name and its role as the 9th builder of the grand city of Delhi.

- Planned development of Delhi is the main function of DDA under Sections 7-11A of the DD Act of 1957.
- DDA prepares plans, policies and proposals for guiding Delhi's planned development through the process of Master Plan, Zonal Plans, Action Area Plans and Urban Extension Projects etc.
- Some of the major achievements of Planning Department towards planned development of Delhi are as follows:
    - *Master Plan for Delhi-2021* (under preparation)
    - Preparation of
        - *Master Plan for Delhi-2001*
        - *Master Plan for Delhi-1962*
        - *Zonal Plans*
        - *Urban Extension Projects*
        - *Special Projects*
        - *Other Projects*
        - *Policy Modifications*: Mixed Land Use, Housing, Transport, and Infrastructure in respect of Urban Development, Development Areas, Buildings by-laws Development etc.
- DDA commenced its housing activities in 1967 and has played a crucial role in providing more than a million houses to the people of Delhi, housing about half the population of the national capital.
- DDA has been constructing houses in Delhi according to the requirements and purchasing capacity of different strata of society.
- DDA, from time to time, has been announcing schemes through newspapers and advertisements for various categories of flats.
- Till March 2003, DDA has allotted a total of 333306 flats (including the re-allotment of surrendered and cancelled flats). About half the allotments are to weaker sections of society and to those belonging to low income groups.
- Flats allotted by the DDA are provided with essential services like electricity, water and sewage disposal, besides other infrastructural facilities required to make them habitable.
- Till March 2003, DDA has announced 35 housing registration schemes for the benefit of the people and allotment of houses has been made to registrants of all 33 schemes.

Delhi Development Authority acquires land for the planned development of Delhi. It develops these lands and properties in implementation of the Master Plan and Zonal Plans. DDA also disposes land and properties for residential, commercial, industrial and institutional uses.

Despite very impressive achievements of DDA, it has an image of being an organisation that needs to improve its sensitivity to the needs of its clients, efficiency and public perception about incidence of corruption in the organisation. The 'Systems and Training Department' has adopted the following measures in this behalf.

17.15.7.2 Transparency and Automaticity in DDA

To minimise downtime, it has introduced systemic automation in the following departments:

- Land Disposal
- Housing

Launching of a Website which is dynamic and provides information on various aspects like housing, land, master plan, environment etc. The results of housing and land and tender notices are displayed. Senior officers are reachable through e-mail. Different forms are available on the website which can be down loaded.

- Land Record

This department has normal administrative functions such as payroll, receipt and dispatch, legal cases monitoring system etc. A training programme for computer literacy seeks to train the staff in the use of computers.

Apart from increasing transparency and automaticity in the functions of its various departments concerned with public dealings, through computerisation and automation as above, there is a vigilance department to take action to see that there are no unwarranted irregularities and also handle complaints that could tarnish the image of the DDA. The vigilance department is active as can be seen from the record of complaints received, processed and action taken on them.

17.16 Conclusion

17.16.1 Multiplicity of Institutions and Divided Responsibility and Authority

National Capital Territory of Delhi, being the capital of fast developing India, is a Global City and has to serve a large variety of purposes. As such it has been retained as a Union Territory. Yet in order to satisfy the aspirations of the people, it has been given a legislature and a Council of Ministers headed by the Chief Minister. The areas of responsibility of the Government of NCTD are restricted and so also its powers. While land, police and law and order are specifically outside its jurisdiction, in other matters too, the powers are not absolute with the Lt. Governor having the power to intervene in any matter and refer the matter to the Government of India. The MCD is an elected body. It is a very powerful body and performs all civic functions. Then the area where the Government of India is housed is covered by the NDMC. Delhi Development Authority is responsible for the planned development of Delhi and exercises influential voice in land use and development of housing. Then there are a number of other bodies whose concurrence is needed in specified matters. There is duplication in the performance of functions and the same function is performed by a number of bodies. The plethora of bodies results in confusion and the citizen is totally confused about the agency that should be approached for a particular service or grievance. It also enables the agencies to pass the buck to other agencies. All agencies operating in the NCTD find themselves seriously constrained in implementing their decisions as consultation with and concurrence of a large number of bodies becomes unavoidable.

17.16.2 Migration Resulting in Rapid Increase of Population Causing Intense Pressure on Physical and Administrative Infrastructure

In view of very good infrastructure of Delhi, excellent educational facilities and the very fast growth of Delhi's economy, there is huge migration of population from other states. Although this migration meets the growing manpower needs for workers, there is tremendous pressure on Delhi's physical infrastructure and there is a growing gap between demand and supply. Ambitious schemes have been drawn and are being implemented such as better and new roads, housing, air and surface transport, communication. But the increased demand as a result of economic development and immigration, soon out-paces the expanded facilities. The administrative system also is under severe pressure and there could be a growing gap between expectation and delivery of services.

Delhi, has a very sound body of laws and regulations, but suffers from ineffective implementation for a variety of reasons, although, as described in this chapter, every effort is being made to improve governance.

The changes taking place in Delhi are tending to place it in the category of capitals of developed countries and so its requirements of human, physical and financial capitals are changing in a fundamental manner. The educational system, does not place enough emphasis on vocational and training component and so is not designed to produce a work force in the required numbers, which is equipped with the required skills, in the organised, formal and informal sectors. It is much easier to raise finances for projects and investment; but much more difficult and time-consuming to produce manpower equipped with the right attitude and skills to perform numerous kinds of tasks in services, industry and agriculture. This requires a coordinated approach by the executive, legislature, judiciary, the political parties, the bureaucracy and above all the citizen.

Despite the unique character of Delhi and limitations as mentioned above in this chapter, Delhi has been developing into one of the finest cities in the country. However, problems arise between state government and Government of India and its agencies. State government and MCD. The Lt. Governor is a powerful institution and ensures that the governance runs smoothly.

17.16.3 Issues Needing Urgent Consideration

The following issues are complex involving the Government of India and the Government of NCTD and need to be considered at the highest level of the Government and resolved:

a) Divided responsibility and authority between the Government of India and the Government of NCTD.

b) Multiplicity of organisations resulting in overlapping functions, time consuming consultations among them before a decision can be taken and the absence of an effective over-arching institutional authority.

c) Migration into Delhi.

d) Measures to provide marketable skills and opportunities for employment to sections of population prone to migration in the areas which are known to be sources of migrants need to be considered by the Government of India.

e) The manpower required to satisfy increasing demand for the various socio-economic activities requires a very well thought out plan for imparting vocational education and training to the entrants to the job market and to the workers who are already employed but are ill equipped in terms of skills to do their job well.

f) Enforcement of laws and regulations needs to be effective to deter people from violating them. Adequate numbers of well trained enforcement staff and magistrates to punish the violators need to be provided.

g) Outsourcing of the maintenance functions of those infrastructure facilities as may be amenable to being outsourced with efficient supervisory and regulatory machinery may be considered.

h) Necessary resources may be provided to expand and upgrade the physical and administrative infrastructure to meet the growing needs.

i) The principle of payment of compensation for damage or loss suffered by the citizens because of substandard public service provided should be accepted and suitable provision in law be made.

j) Good quality public infrastructure is dependent on the involvement of the people implying that the population needs to be aware of their duties and rights and willing to respectively discharge and demand them. A suitably designed programme of public awareness and participation needs to be developed and implemented for a length of time.

k) Use of Information Technology is proving to be helpful in NCTD. A crash programme to re-engineer processes related to the public services and make them computer and network enabled needs to be introduced.

l) The areas included in the National Capital Region need to be integrated in the matters of transport, state-taxation, standards of infrastructure and law and order.

The vision of a World Class City for Delhi is achievable provided a concerted effort is made to deal with deficiencies and improve efficiencies and effectiveness of systems is made.

ANNEXURE 17.1

Organisations Participating in Bhagidari Scheme

a) For Delhi Jal Board (DJB):

- RWAs to be made aware of water saving/waste conservation
- Payment and collection of water bills to be done by RWAs
- Distribution of water through water-tankers
- Replacing old/leaking pipelines
- Water Harvesting—involving RWAs
- RWAs role in internal colony sewage system
- Desilting of sewers
- Awareness against using water from handpumps for drinking purposes.

b) For Delhi Vidyut Board (DVB):

- Load shedding information will be given to RWAs/MTAs
- DVB will establish Complaint Cell specially for *Bhagidars*.
- Information will be provided to RWAs by DVB staff posted in their respective areas
- Electricity meter reading will be done by RWAs and officials of DVB
- Load enhancement to be made easy
- Meter name change in cooperation with RWAs
- Revenue enhancement and its re-investment involving the RWAs
- Replacement of 'low tension wires" and "faulty meters".
- Delhi Vidyut Board has now been unbundled into five companies as a part of power sector reforms. The Generation Company and the Transmission Company are Government owned whereas the three Distribution Companies are in private hands (two owned by BSES and one by Tata Power). The private distribution companies are also now participating in Bhagidari.

c) For Municipal Corporation of Delhi (MCD):

- House tax collection by interested RWAs
- Maintenance of community parks through RWAs
- Management of community hall through RWAs
- Sanitation services to be supervised by RWAs
- Information on Sanitary staff to be given to RWAs
- Imposition of fine on littering in co-operation with RWAs
- Desilting of *nallahs*
- Removal of stray and dead animals from colony
- Maintenance of Roads and Back Lanes on regular basis

d) Sanitation:

- Solutions on community bins
- RWAs role in internal colony sewage system
- Overseeing the work of sanitary staff by RWAs
- Door to Door collection of Waste/Garbage
- Generation of public awareness on sanitation

e) For Department of Environment and Forests (E&F):

- Plantation and maintenance of saplings
- Greening of the colony
- To discourage use of plastic bags

f) For Delhi Police (DP):

- Crime prevention through involvement of RWAs
- Neighbourhood watch scheme
- Verification of antecedents of domestic help
- Prevention of encroachments
- Regulation of traffic through colonies
- Prevention of illegal sale of liquor

g) For Delhi Development Authority (DDA)

- Solutions to prevent encroachment
- Maintenance of community parks
- Prevention of encroachment
- Maintenance of common areas
- Parking inside the colony

h) Issues exclusively for MTAs

A) Weights and Measures

- Weights and measurements used for commercial purposes
- Indigenous and imported package commodities
- Sale of beverages, ice creams, mineral water bottles at MRP
- Registration of packers and importers
- Inspections and challans

B) Sales Tax

- Strengthening communication channels for disseminating Sales Tax information.
- Better communication channels for reviewing feedback on Sales Tax from dealers.
- Joint detection of bogus and unregistered dealers.
- Interface between sales tax field officers.
- Grievance handling.

C) Industries Department

- Handing over of the estate/maintenance services to MCD in a time-bound manner—procedural aspects only.
- Uninterrupted Power supply metering, billing and changes in rules/regulations.
- Adequate and potable water supply "No Supply, No Billing" principle.
- CETP – a) Costing of Plants, b) escalation and govt. to bear escalation, c) Responsibility of maintenance, d) Cost of maintenance.
- Clearance of encroachments in parks, and on roadsides and pavements within industrial area/estates.
- Provision of streetlights in the Industrial Estates.
- Removal of Slums/JJ clusters, encroachments on approach roads and pavements, etc.
- Rain Water Harvesting.
- MCD factory license—one time fee—no renewal-permission for industries on floors (as flatted factories).
- One-window service concept.
- Inspection methods and procedures.
- Conversion to freehold plots and shed—procedures/modalities.
- Allotment of land to associations for administration of estate and provision of P.O., Bank, Fire Station (on TOP priority where land already allocated), R&D centre, tool room, etc.
- Categorisation of units by DPCC (Green Orange, Issue of consent in time-bound manner).
- Industrial waste/solid-waste disposal.

ANNEXURE 17.2

Details of the Bhagidari Scheme

Delhi Jal Board

- Water is an essential civic commodity. Delhi has limited water resources. We are mainly dependent on neighbouring states for supply of raw water to quench the thirst of our vast population (1.25 crore) and also the migratory population, i.e., people visiting Delhi everyday for business/job.
- As against present demand of 800 MGD ONLY 650 MGD potable water is available. So we sought intensive involvement of people/citizen groups in water conservation and water harvesting programme.
- Delhi Jal Board (DJB), an autonomous body under Urban Development Department has been identified as Nodal Agency for this purpose. It has taken following steps :-
    i. Nominating 500 Water Wardens and 1500 Assistant Water Wardens from amongst citizen groups. They will be imparted specialised training to check and rectify water leakage through supply lines.
    ii. Intensive advertisement campaign to create awareness about need and means of water conservation.
    iii. To provide technical and financial assistance to Group Housing Societies and individuals taking up rain water harvesting projects in their buildings. This would help to recharge ground water table. 150 such work have been completed and 35 are in progress at present.

Anti Plastic and Anti-littering campaign by Environment and Forest Department

Use of plastic bags has become a big menace largely due to its non-biodegradable nature. These bags choke our sewerage system, damage the soil and kill our cows. The problem is further aggravated by unchecked habit of people who litter at any spot convenient to them. We felt that involvement of citizen groups is a must to desist people from using plastic bags and littering at public places. Our approach to this has been persuasion and not coercion. Environmlent & Forest Department has taken up 'Anti-Plastic' & 'Anti-Littering' campaigns with the active cooperation of *Bhagidar* RWAs, MTAs and Eco-Clubs constituted in schools. Important steps taken :-

i. The 'Delhi Plastic Bag (Manufacture, Sale & Usage) and Non-Biodegradable Garbage (Control) Act 2000' has been made effective from 02.10.2001 in the NCT of Delhi. The act bans the manufacture and sale of plastic bags of thickness less than 20 microns. The offence is punishable. The first offence is compounded at the rate of Rs.10,000/-.

ii. A plastic bag collection drive-cum-competition was launched under which 5000 kgs. Of used plastic bags of less than 20 micron thickness were collected. For public awareness, the huge pile of collected plastic bags was given the shape of a Dinosaur and kept at Nehru Park.

iii. In 125 colonies programme on waste management has been initiated as a pilot project for segregation of waste at source level itself into biodegradable & non-biodegradable and its further recycling.

Senior Citizens

Our Government recognises its responsibility towards our senior citizens. We have launched certain programmes as a token of respect to them :-

i. Opening of special clinics in 9 hospitals of Delhi Govt. where they can get all types of required medical services on Sundays from 10.00 a.m. to 12.00 noon.

ii. Separate queues in OPD on working days for the senior citizens and giving them preferential treatment.

iii. Concessional travel passes in DTC buses.

iv. Special protection scheme for senior citizens has been launched by Delhi Police. SHO of the area conducts survey of elderly people living alone.

v. At present 2 old age homes are functioning and we are considering more such homes where not only recreational facilities but also the health care facilities be provided to the senior citizens.

vi. Old age pension scheme has been started. Eligible senior citizens are given Rs.200 per month on the recommendation of area MLA which is paid to them on quarterly basis through banks and post offices.

vii. Smart Card Scheme—the 'Ayush Patra'—for senior citizens of Delhi will be issued a Smart Card free of cost. The card will digitally contain the vital profiles of the holder including his blood group and preferential access to various civic services.

Reforms in Hospital Management & Quality Control by Health & Family Welfare Department:

- To improve the management of Hospitals of Delhi Government and to make it responsible towards patients, we have decided to constitute 'Janhit Society' in each major hospital. The society will have representation from RWAs of the area and other citizen groups. The expert studies are being conducted for improving the quality of services offered by Hospitals and reducing delays in imparting medical help.
- Students Welfare Committee for Government Schools
- Although improvements have been made in the standards of Govt. schools of Delhi since my Govt. came to power but still a lot needs to be done and at a faster pace. With the existing administrative structure the progress has been slow. Therefore, my Government decided to take help of local RWAs and NGOs in school administration. As a pilot project School Welfare Committees – 'Vidhyalaya Kalyan Samitis' – have been appointed in nearly 600 Govt. schools. These committees will advise in matters of school administration, cleanliness, petty repairs, etc. for which they have been given required administrative and financial powers. These Committees have been given powers to recommend expenditure up to Rs.10,000 per month for proper upkeep of school infrastructure.

Development of Industries

In addition to the above programmes, Bhagidari has taken in its span the Industrial Associations. In association with the Industries Department confirming Industrial Areas of Delhi have been made *Bhagidars* through their Industrial Associations. A High power Apex level Committee of Senior officers and representatives of Industries to prepare the policy frame work for growth and development of Industries in Delhi in the right earnest.

Results Achieved

The initiative launched in January 2000 has firmed up and become a movement in two years. More than 1100 citizen groups have become our *Bhagidars* after having participated in various Bhagidari workshops. The "Bhagidars" have not only been successful in solving their day-to-day problems, but have also been providing help to public utility departments in maintenance and up gradation of services. Some examples are:-

1. Successful implementation of 'Clean Yamuna", 'Say no to plastic bags' & 'No crackers on Diwali' campaigns.
2. Switching on/off of streetlights by RWAs.
3. Meter reading by RWAs in their residential colony.
4. Traffic regulation in the colonies.
5. Clean Delhi: "Green Delhi" campaign.
6. Tenant verification in the colonies.
7. Rain-water Harvesting.
8. Conservation of water by checking misuse of water.
9. Water Bill collection and payment by RWAs.
10. Desilting of sewers
11. Coordinating with DVB for handling load shedding and power breakdown.
12. Prevention of power-theft.
13. Door to door collection of garbage.
14. Maintenance of community parks and halls

15. Crime prevention and successful implementation of neighbourhood watch scheme.
16. Prevention of encroachment.

Some Success Stories

- RWAs and MTAs have started taking up the collective payment of water bills by cheque on fixed date and time.
- 267 RWAs and 5 MTAs are actively participating in observing water leakage and noting them down in a special register kept by DJB.
- RWAs and MTAs in most of the colonies are participating in the distribution of water through tankers.
- 140 RWAs have taken up Rain-water harvesting measures.
- 143 RWAs and 5 MTAs have voluntarily taken up participation in the replacement of old/leaking service pipes in their area.
- Delhi Vidyut Board had organised 16 camps under the Bhagidari scheme for load enhancement. The department received and processed 5279 applications generating revenue of Rs.2.64 crore.
- Federation of I.P. Extension II Housing Societies (Regd.) Kiran Vihar, Delhi having 35 housing and Group Housing Societies as its members covering a population of more than 50,000 people, in association with the Delhi Police conducts verification of tenants, security guards and domestic servants in the Society itself and residents are regularly educated about use of safety devices for vehicles and internal security has been tightened through issue of identity cards to hawkers, kabaries.
    i. Active cooperation with Delhi Jal Board resulted in desilting of sewer lines in scheduled manner and the complaints are attended to without delay or harassment.
    ii. Water bills are distributed through member societies. Bill collections are being done through collection boxes and the Jal Board has agreed to accept any amount from the consumer and arrears, if any, being carried forward.
- The Federation of Group Housing Societies, I.P. Extension started the meter reading scheme in the member RWAs with active co-operation of the concerned Zonal Officers of the Delhi Vidyut Board. This federation is one such Bhagidar which have implemented the meter reading scheme by the RWAs themselves. Under this programme, presently meter reading of around 23000 electric meters belonging to 22 RWAs is being done. The Delhi Vidyut Board paid the federation at the rate of 2.00 per meter for the electric meter reading. The federation gives this money to the participating RWAs.
- Mayur Vihar Phase-I, Pocket-III Apartment Owners Association has been successful in solving the following problems under 'Bhagidari':-
    i. The old and obsolete panels of two sub-stations, which were causing frequent break downs of power supply, were got replaced by the Chairman, DVB, within two days. Now, there is no disruption of power supply from these sub stations.
    ii. Transformer of one of the sub-stations, which got burnt, was replaced by DVB within a matter of 4 to 5 hours.
    iii. One electric pole, which was uprooted by a heavy vehicle was replaced the same day.
    iv. The street lighting of the area has greatly improved with the help of the member RWAs.
    v. The water and power supply in the area has improved tremendously.
    vi. The cash counter centre in Mayur Vihar Phase-I has been included in the list of authorised cash counter centres of DVB for accepting electricity bills in bulk from RWAs. Similarly, DJB cash counter centre also accepts payment of water bills by cheques in bulk. A new cash counter is being opened by DJB in the area shortly.
    vii. Camps for collection of property tax bills are being organised by MCD.
    viii. The standard of sanitation and hygiene is very satisfactory. The Sanitary Supervisor meets them regularly in this regard.
- The Vasant Vihar Welfare Association is one of our founder *Bhagidars*. With the active efforts of its President, Ms. Deepa Kapoor, the association has successfully undertaken Rainwater harvesting project and recycling of used water. The association creates awareness among its residents through printing of posters, organising cultural programmes and seminars. Their successful implementation of the Rainwater harvesting project especially in the A-Block Nursery has become a model for the other RWAs to follow.
- After participating in the workshop for Market & Traders Association in July 2001, Prithviraj Market & Traders Association came forward to voluntarily take up the Anti-Plastic bags campaign in their market. The association printed the posters to create awareness among its member shops and offices and has been successful. The market no longer does give carry bags made of plastic to their customers.
- The Gaffar Market and Traders Association, Karol Bagh has undertaken the replacements of the generators in the shops in their markets as a step towards making the environment clean.
- The Govt. colonies of Timarpur & Gulabi Bagh with active cooperation of the Delhi Police officials have successfully carried out the tenant verification in their respective colonies.
- Kalkaji Bhagidari Coordination Committee is successfully coordinating the Bhagidari activities of its 25 Residents Welfare Associations.
- Harijan Basti Sudhar Samiti, East Loni Road, Ashok Nagar has created awareness against use of plastic bags, AIDS and waste of drinking water by organising camps. The association has issued identity cards to the hawkers in their colony.
- Rainwater harvesting projects are increasingly being taken up by our RWAs. Some notable initiatives in this direction have been by our *Bhagidars* of Maharani Bagh Cooperative Housing Society, S-Block, Greater Kailash-II, RWA, Som Vihar RWA, Punch Shila Co-operative House Building Society Ltd. and Sector-3, Rohini, RWA
- Tree plantation projects have been very popular with our *Bhagidars*. Extensive plantation measures within the colonies have been taken up by the RWAs of Greater Kailash-II, Niti Bagh, Chand Nagar, Tilak Nagar, Federation of Group Housing Society, Patparganj, Delhi, Chetra Vikas Sangthan, Palam and Dilshad Garden Pocket-E.
- The Bhagidari programme was sent by Govt. of India as one of the official entries to the Commonwealth Association for Public Administration and Management (CAPAM) International Awards. The programme has been selected as one of the 30 semi-finalist out of a total of 150 international entries from all over the world. The CAPAM has recognised the programme as being truly Innovative and worthy of the recognition that accompanies achievements such as this in the Public Sector.
- Our government has also issued instructions that in the Annual Confidential Reports (ACR) of officers who have a role in implementing the Bhagidari scheme, a special mention will be made by the Reporting and Reviewing officers about the involvement and ability of the officer in implementing the Bhagidari in improving the provision of services to the public. In particular, mention will be made of significant innovations introduced, which have made a difference to people's life.

Challenges

1. First, bringing together a large number of citizen groups and government officials on a common platform was not an easy task. It required detailed planning and coordinated action holding preliminary meetings, interactions and a whole gamut of logistical arrangements. As the concept emphasised the voluntary nature of all activities, we wanted to reply on the existing resources and manpower.
2. It required managing a change process—a change in perceptions of both the citizens and government officials. The first reaction of citizens was to view this programme as another avenue for redressal of public grievances. It took some time to convince them that what we were talking of was a partnership—a two way process—in which the citizens had to contribute as much as the government officials. Not only this, they had to acknowledge the 'ownership' of the programme—acknowledge that they were the stakeholders in the development of this city.
3. We faced resistance from the field-level government officers who were not willing to step out of their bureaucratic shell and embrace the direct interaction with citizen groups. They felt it was erosion of their authority and in many instances it also stemmed corruption at the field-level.

4. So far the citizen-groups interacting with us have been registered associations. The challenge is now step out with the programme into the slum clusters, resettlement colonies and the unauthorised regularised areas.
5. We have also broad based the movement by including industrial associations. Shortly we will reach out to rural areas, women groups and non-governmental organisations.
6. Our intent would be to gradually work out changes in policies and legislation, which would enable the citizen groups to statutorily interact with Government.

Conclusion

- With pride one can say that the Bhagidari initiative has attracted the attention of the government of India, which is documenting the entire process for replication in the country. The documentation of Phase-I of Bhagidari (January 2000–June 2001) has been completed with the cooperation of the Department of Administrative Reforms, Ministry of Personnel, Pension & Public Grievances, Government of India. The documentation of Phase-II (July 2001–October 2002) is ongoing and is scheduled to be published by end of November, 2002.
- In order to build up a regular interaction with the *Bhagidars* and to keep them apprised of the new activities under Bhagidari a monthly newsletter under the title *'Bhagidari Masik Patrika'* is being published since December 2001.
- From a movement beginning with 20 Residents Welfare Associations we are now in active partnership with more than 1100 citizen groups.
- Our efforts have been recognised by the government of India, and they recommended our initiative for CAPAM International Innovations Award, 2002. The scheme has been chosen as one of the 30 semi-finalists out of the total 150 international entries from all over the world. Our initiative was also recommended by Human Settlement Management Institute (HSMI), New Delhi for Dubai International Award for Best Practices, 2002. [The HSMI has been designated by Govt. of India as the National Level Nodal Agency for identification and documentation of Best practices as well as for submission of these Best Practice Entries for the awards of excellence instituted by Dubai Municipality, in associations with the United Nations Conference of Human Settlements (UNCHS).]
- The success of Bhagidari process is real. The reason of its success lies in the application of democratic processes of problem solving by dialogue and consensus, where every stake-holder shares both responsibility and authority, and takes 'ownership' for finding and implementing solutions together. This non-partisan and democratic method of problem solving has been able to touch the right chord in the citizens' hearts and they believe that 'Bhagidari' can really give them a more meaningful role in governance.

List of Departments that have prepared the Citizens' Charter:

Administrative Reforms, Archaeology, Central Jail, Chit Fund, D.F.C., DDU Hospital, Delhi Commission for Women, Delhi Institute of Hotel, Management, Delhi Jal Board(DJB), Delhi Khadi Village Industries, Board(DKVIB), Delhi Minority Commission, Delhi SC/ST/OBC Minorities Fin. & Dev. Corp. Ltd. Development, Directorate of Health Services(DHS), Drug Control, DSIDC, DTC, Dte Agrl. Mktg., Dte. of Eco. And Stat. & O/o Chief Reg. Births & Deaths, DTT & DC, Election (Chief Electoral Office), Environment, Excise, Food and Supplies, G. B. Pant Hospital, GTB Hospital, Guru Nanak Eye Center, IBHAS, Industries, Information and Publicity, Irrigation and Flood Control(I&FC), Labour, Land and Building, Law and Justice and Legislative Affairs, LN Hospital, NCC, NDMC, Nehru Homeopathy Medical College, Netaji Subhash Institute of Tech., OBC Commission, Prevention of Food Adultration (PFA), Prosecution, Public Grievances Commission, PWD, Registrar Cooperative, Society, Sales Tax, Sanjay Gandhi Memorial Hospital, Social Welfare, Rehabilitation Services, Training & Technical Education, Urban Development, Vigilance, Weights & Measures.

DELHI LOKAYUKTA AND UPLOKAYUKTA ACT, 1995 (Delhi Act No.1 of 1996)

AN ACT To make provision for the establishment and functioning of the Institution of Lokayukta to inquire into the allegations against public functionaries in the National Capital Territory of Delhi and for matters connected therewith.

"public functionary" means a person who is or has been at any time-

(i) the Chief Minister or a Minister;

(ii) a Member of Legislative Assembly;

(iii) a person having the rank of a Minister but shall not include Speaker and Deputy Speaker of the Legislative Assembly;

(iv) a Chairman, Vice-Chairman or Managing Director or a Member of a Board of Directors (by Whatever name they be called) in respect of –

(1). an Apex Cooperative Society or any Cooperative Society constituted or registered under the Delhi Cooperative Societies Act, 1972, which is subject to the control of the Government;

(2) a Government Company within the meaning of section 617 of the Companies Act, 1956, engaged in connection with the affairs, and is under the control of the Government;

(3) a Local Authority established under any law in relation to Delhi; provided that the provisions of this Act shall not be applicable to any authority of a Local Authority constituted under an enactment relatable to Entry No.18 of the State List of the Seventh Schedule of the Constitution;

(4) a Corporation engaged in connection with the affairs, and under the control, of the Government;

(5) any Commission or body set up by the Government which is owned and controlled by it;

(v) a Member of the Municipal Corporation of Delhi as defined in clause 2(27) of the Municipal Corporation Act, 1957 (as amended in 1993);

AR Departments activities:

- Policy support to all Departments of Delhi Government and coordination relating to issues of :
- Simplification of procedures and improvement of organisational structure;
- Matters relating to organisation and method.
- Conducting work measurement study of various departments of Delhi government;
- Re-organisation of departments.
- Office inspections.
- Enforcement of Delhi right to information act & rules, 2001.
- Lokayukta.
- Formulation and implementation of Citizen's Charters.

Civil Service Reform/Procedural Reform

The officers and staff members of Government of Delhi and its Autonomous Bodies are encouraged to contribute to decision making through the suggestion scheme and can get even cash awards up to Rs.5,000. The citizen's and Non-Government Organisations are welcome to extend their cooperation in bringing reforms in different fields.

a) Contextual Characteristics:

- Socio-economic indicators including education, access to basic needs and the role of women.
- The economy: its base, growth and type; financial dependence on external resources, including aid and debt; and degree of integration with the global economy.
- Human capacities and sustainability.
- Natural resource base and trends in the environment.
- Cultural, religious and ethnic diversity and structures, conflict or polarisation and internal means of resolving conflict.
- Indigenous values, networks and knowledge.

The efforts made by them as well as the measures taken by the MCD; NDMC and the DDA are reviewed. The main organs of governance in NCTD are the Government, MCD, NDMC and the DDA.

Chapter 18

Conclusions and Recommendations

On the basis of the discussions in the previous chapters it is easy to draw conclusions about the subjects discussed and make recommendations. This is done in two parts. First some general conclusions are drawn and then the conclusions and recommendations are made sector-wise.

18.0 General

a) Delhi, located in an area, which is agriculturally very fertile, has developed, in the northern part of the country, as the biggest market for agricultural as well as other goods. It is a historical city and has numerous architectural monuments of ages down its history. Its service sector has grown very fast. It is the capital of the largest democracy of the world. People from all parts of the country reside here and it has an international community in the foreign missions. It is thus a very cosmopolitan place where people may feel comfortable irrespective of their background—religious, social, cultural and economic. Therefore, Delhi attracts people for work, trade and commerce, tourism etc., from all over the country, especially from the neighbouring states. Delhi has become the most densely populated city with a population density of 9224 per sq.km. Compared to an average all-India density of 324.

b) Because of its unique position and the requirement of the various roles that it has to perform, Delhi has been given the status of a Union Territory. In order to satisfy the democratic aspiration of self-governance, striking a balance, it has been provided with an elected legislature and a government headed by a Chief Minister. However, the powers with the NCTD are considerably less than that of a normal State of the Indian Union but they are much wider than those of a Union Territory.

c) The MCD covers a very large proportion of the area of Delhi. It is an elected and a very powerful body and performs all civic functions. The area where the Government of India is housed is covered by the NDMC. Cantonment Board is responsible for the remainder. Delhi Development Authority is responsible for the planned development of Delhi and exercises influential voice in land use and development of housing. Apart from DDA, Central government departments too perform a number of functions.

d) Thus there are many bodies for performing a function and this creates confusion and results in waste of resources and the need for coordinating their activities. The citizen is confused about the agency that should be approached for a particular service or grievance. It also enables the agencies to pass the buck to other agencies. All agencies operating in the NCTD find themselves seriously constrained in implementing their decisions as consultation with and concurrence of a large number of bodies becomes unavoidable.

e) Despite the unique character of Delhi and limitations as mentioned above in this chapter, Delhi has been developing into one of the finest cities in the country. The parameters briefly discussed below corroborate this view.

- It is a cosmopolitan city and provides equality of opportunity to people irrespective of social, regional and religious differences.
- It attracts people from all over the country because of the opportunities that this city offers in the field of education, health, employment and enterprise etc. The growth of population is so rapid that despite availability of land, which appeared plentiful soon after Independence when the expansion phase began looks too inadequate now and the city's infrastructure is unable to keep pace with its expanding population.

- Delhi has a developed economy with services sector being dominant, the secondary sector way behind and agricultural being negligible. It had the second highest per capita NSDP at Rs. 48974 in 2001-02 and a very low poverty ratio. However, wide disparities are reflected in the social and economic status of the population with many layers having differential access to various facilities.
- In the sphere of education it has a high literacy rate and the standards of higher education are believed by many to be the best in the country. It ranks not higher than fourth among the states in the matter of literacy mainly because of continuous migration of the poor in search of employment from all parts of the country.
- Of the metropolitan towns, Delhi has the least percentage of its population living in slums.
- Delhi has initiated measures to deal with the problem of transport and the Metro Rail project has started making its impact felt.
- The over all birth rate in Delhi is substantially lower than the national average and the Life Expectancy at birth is 68.6 years against the national average of 60.7 years.
- It is a green city having 12.5 trees per ha, as against the national average of 12.
- Being a service industry centric city, the labour relations in Delhi are harmonious.

f) Despite the rosy picture which emerges from the impressive statistics mentioned above in relation to some sectors in the NTDC, it is found that wide disparities are reflected in the social and economic status of the population with many layers having differential access to facilities in the areas of health, education, housing, transport etc. There is scope for improvement in almost every sector.

18.1 SECTOR-WISE CONCLUSIONS AND RECOMMENDATIONS

18.2 Fiscal and Financial Management

a) Delhi gives the picture of a developed economy, with a dwindling primary sector, and a declining secondary sector. Future development has to concentrate on creation of more and more of employment opportunities for the growing local and migrant population.

b) Areas of concern are the rising debt burden and the consequent fiscal deficit. Tax-GSDP ratio has to be improved. For this, mounting tax arrears have to be reduced, and it has to be ensured that there is no further addition to these arrears in future.

c) Despite the Union Government and local bodies taking the responsibilities of activities on which other states are required to spend their resources, the revenue expenditure of NCT has been steadily increasing in recent years.

d) The NCT of Delhi has been consistently having surplus on revenue account. But, its fiscal deficit has also been consistently going up, being 2.91 per cent of GSDP in 2003-04 against a low of 1.39 per cent in 1997-98.

e) Public debt of the NCT has been growing—from 2.42 per cent at the end of March 1995 to 17.08 per cent of the GSDP at the end of March 2004. The NCT borrows from the Central government and gives loans to its own public sector undertakings and other bodies. It is a net creditor, unlike many states.

f) The various bodies getting funds are defaulting on repayment. Since some of these are providing essential social and economic services, these cannot be closed down but have to be supported until some viable alternative is found. This is a matter of concern.

18.3 Urban Development Housing and Utilisation of URIF, Slums etc.

a) A number of features of the National Capital Territory of Delhi are unique in that it is almost entirely urbanised, substantial population lives in the unplanned clusters, and unauthorised colonies, majority of Delhi population is immigrant and employment in the primary sector including agriculture and mining has dwindled to negligible levels.

b) In 2004 only 23.6 per cent of the population was living in planned colonies, 64.5 per cent in *Jhuggi Jhopri* (JJ) clusters, slum designated areas and unauthorised colonies and the remaining 11.9 per cent in rural and urban villages indicating the need of massive effort in the housing sector.

c) The contribution to housing stock through institutional agencies was only 53 per cent (this excludes squatter housing) in 1991. DDA, the nodal agency for providing housing units, till March 2003, had allotted a total of 0.33 million flats. The component of housing through non institutional sources *viz.*, unauthorised colonies, squatter/JJ clusters, etc. is significant.

d) Slums/Informal Sector Housing

- The slum population in Delhi was about 26.0 per cent in 2001, least of the metropolitan cities. Greater Mumbai (34.3 per cent) was followed by Kolkata (32.90 per cent) and Chennai (28.1 per cent). In JJ clusters/squatter settlements about 6 lakh house holds with a population of 30 lakh was living (1997).
- Relocation of Slum Population

  The Municipal Corporation of Delhi (MCD) initiated the process of relocating the slum dwellers in early 1991. The relocation sites are generally located at the peripheries of Delhi. These sites have been selected with a vision of having a density of 200 dwelling units per acre with a plot size of 18 sq.m for each eligible family and 12.5 sq.m for each ineligible family.

e) *Type of Houses:* The National Sample Survey (NSS) 50th Round (1993-94) data for Delhi indicates that 35.40 per cent of dwellings were independent houses, 24.90 per cent are flats and 15.4 per cent are *chawl/Basti*. About 24.3 per cent of the dwellings fall under "others" category.

f) *Ownership of Houses:* An analysis of housing data for 1991 indicates that in Delhi 68.1 per cent of houses are owned by the residents and 28.61 are rented. Status of 3.29 per cent of the houses was not known

g) *Size of Houses:* About 44 per cent of the dwelling units have only one room, 27 per cent two rooms and 15.5 per cent three rooms each. Larger accommodation accounts for only 12.4 per cent of the total dwelling units.

h) *Shortage of Housing:* In 2001 Delhi's backlog of dwelling units stood at 4 lakh comprising of one lakh net shortage and the rest by way of dilapidated and *kutcha* structures requiring replacement.

i) *Living Conditions:* An analysis of data on housing indicates that 58 per cent of the houses are in good condition, 36.65 per cent are livable and 5.35 per cent are in dilapidated condition.

j) *Land Availability:* According to the draft NCR Plan 2021 the land that can be urbanised in the NCT Delhi is 97190.90 ha. or 65.54 per cent of its total geographical area of 148,300 ha. The population holding capacity of the existing urban areas of Delhi is 122 lakh, which is adequate to accommodate the existing (2001) population of 109 lakh. However, further urban extension in about 27,000 ha. will be required to accommodate the population in the future.

k) *Water Supply And Waste Water Treatment and Disposal:* The total water supply capacity of Delhi Jal Board (DJB) as on 31 March 2002, was 675 MGD. There are large areas where the position of water supply is unsatisfactory. Yamuna river being the only source of water, the matter has to be pursued with the concerned states and the Government of India so that the water supply needs can be satisfied. There is need for conservation of water and prevention of waste and recycling.

The actual quantity of wastewater treated is much below the installed capacity of the 16 sewage treatment plants (STP) of about 497.4 MGD. The low level of capacity utilisation at the STPs is due to missing links in sewer connectivity and choking/silting of sewer lines. These must be remedied on priority.

l) *Garbage Management:* Generation of garbage was estimated to be 9384 tons/day at the rate of 0.68 kg/capita/day. The total handling capacity of MCD, NDMC and cantonment Board is about 5543 tons.

m) *Housing Policy:* The long term goal of the NHP is to eradicate houselessness, improve the housing conditions of the inadequately housed and provide a minimum level of basic services and amenities to all; for this purpose provide land and legal and infrastructure support to enable the private sector to make heavy investments. No fresh encroachments are to be permitted on public land and past encroachments which had been in existence prior to 31 January 1990 will not be removed without providing alternatives.

n) *Data Base Development and Management:* Data on housing in Delhi by agencies involved remains uncoordinated. The process of data collection is not within any regulatory framework. Such a framework needs to be developed for India and, until it is developed, the broad guidelines provided by the United Nations Human Settlements Programme may be adopted.

o) *National Capital Region:* The concept of a national capital region covering an area of 30,242 sq. kms spread over the states of Haryana, Rajasthan and the U.P. has taken some shape. Action has been taken for preparation of regional, and functional plans for transport, power, telecommunication and industrial sector. However, the population in Delhi continues to grow at a very rapid rate much faster than the rate at which its infrastructure has grown. Already a large proportion of its population lives in slums. Essential institutions such as schools cannot be provided for want of land in areas where the poor live for want of land. Water and electricity are in short supply and drainage is inadequate for even small quantity of rain leading to flooding of roads. Let alone parking of vehicles, pedestrians and cyclists have a very tough time; congestion and shrinking road space will continue to pose huge traffic problems. Unless migration is checked, very soon a stage is likely to be reached when there would be no land for its further expansion. There is no single administrative structure contemplated for this area. This would have problems of governance in the area of maintenance of public order, policing and judicial administration.

p) *Suggestion for Future Plans:* The Draft Delhi Master Plan 2021 suggests general strategy for future development to meet the housing needs and for improvements in other physical infrastructure. After it has been finalised, the recommendations may be implemented with sincerity.

18.4 Infrastructure

A) Transport

Roads

The main limitations relating to roads include inadequate design, absence of clearly defined road hierarchy and lack of access control, inadequate provision of land to take care of, haphazard growth, poor maintenance, encroachments and hawking on carriage way, poor traffic management, inadequate integration of rail and road services and the environmental degradation resulting from the same, lack of road user discipline, huge amount of traffic using Delhi road system for passing through and absence of bypasses, satellite towns have instead of easing pressure added to it and poor project implementation.

The main features of road improvement plan include:

- Providing an institutional framework for development, management and operation of an integrated multi-modal transport system,
- Measures to deal with identified deficiencies.
- Using improvements in technology for road surfaces such as improved wearing coats and plastic roads, fibre reinforced concrete surface and concrete roads depending on the circumstances.
- A separate Road Maintenance Corporation is to be set-up generating its own resources.
- Road safety education should be provided in schools.
- Preparation and implementation of strategic action plans for special areas.
- Implementation of urban transport information system which will proivde updated inputs of actual traffic flows to enable proper planning.
- Providing special attention to slow green modes of transport namely, cycles and pedestrians.

Railways

The Railway services to Delhi primarily consist of national network services to all major cities of India, commuter services to surrounding towns and local services for the citizens of Delhi. All these services are unable to cope with the traffic offered and extensive capacity generation and inputs are essential. The upgradation and expansion plans of the railways include additional passenger terminals, Upgradation of stations at New Delhi Delhi main and Hazarat Nizamuddin, construction of separate freight corridors from Delhi to Kolkata/Mumbai, strengthening of rail corridors to neighbouring towns, revitalisation of Ring Railway is an essential component of Delhi's transport scenario by augmenting capacity, increasing EMU services to suit commuter timings and coordinating feeder bus linkages at ring railway stations

Vision of Transport Facilities

The vision for the State recommended in its Master Plan is that Delhi should be a well-managed, clean and dynamic model capital city. The mission is to provide safe, eco-friendly, cost-effective and efficient modes of transportation through a well-integrated multi-modal transport system. The policy action required would include, among other measures, up gradation and strengthening of road system, provision of metro system to cater for demand up to 2021, an integrated rail bus transit to neighbouring towns, augmentation of bus system, high capacity bus system on selected corridors (100 kms), introduction of electric trolley bus, provision of LRT in walled city.

B) Power

DERC should complete its exercise of finalising a multi-year tariff expeditiously. The consumer mix data provided by Discoms after unbundling seems to require further regulatory scrutiny. It should also focus effectively on consumer satisfaction, and impose and monitor objective performance criteria like SAIDI and SAIFI. Steps to promote local generation should be expedited.

- The Discoms have accepted the risk that DERC may not take decisions favourable to them in matters not covered by the Policy Directions; they may pursue the appellate and judicial remedies available, but should not seek remedies against the Government for grievances against DERC's decisions.
- As long as the Discoms make investments in the system which DERC deems appropriate and achieve the loss reduction targets agreed upon, it should be ensured that they actually earn the prescribed return.
- To achieve the above, the switchover from concealed subsidies (including the 'regulatory asset' idea) to transparent subsidies as envisaged in the Electricity Act, 2003 (and, indeed, earlier in DERA) should be made complete as soon as possible.
- The Government should address the necessary further unbundling of Transco. The issue of creating local generating capacity, preferably without further large-scale public investment, should be addressed. DERC should complete its exercise of finalising a multi-year tariff expeditiously. The consumer mix data provided by Discoms after unbundling seems to require further regulatory scrutiny. It should also focus effectively on consumer satisfaction, and impose and monitor objective performance criteria like SAIDI and SAIFI. Steps to promote local generation should be expedited.

a) Strengths, Weaknesses and Areas for Intervention

Strengths

The greatest strength of Delhi's power sector is the background of successful restructuring, freeing the successor companies from DVB's financial burden and providing an opportunity to modernise and change the organisational culture.

Secondly, the restructuring has created scope for private sector investment not only in the distribution sector itself but also in generation. There is every prospect of the sector becoming substantially self-sustaining.

Weaknesses

The two main weaknesses are the high degree of dissatisfaction with the power situation in Delhi and with the management of the distribution system by the distribution companies. The distribution loss continues to be disconcertingly high that makes the honest consumers bear the burden of theft. There is an impression that the meters run fast by design and coupled with the raise in tariff, the situation is aggravated further. If the situation is not corrected soon it may become very difficult to provide consumer satisfaction, which is so important for the sustainability of the new distribution arrangement evolved after strenuous effort. The tariff issue is another area major area that needs to be addressed.

Suggestions

For the remaining duration of the transitional period, i.e., until the end of FY, 07, the apportionment of regulatory, investment, management and commercial risks as envisaged in the reform package should be strictly adhered to. It is also time to begin reflecting on the issues that will arise after the transitional period is over. The Government should address the necessary further unbundling of Transco. The issue of creating local generating capacity, preferably without further large-scale public investment, should be addressed.

Drinking Water

The main features in this sector are given below:

- Nearly 31 per cent of the population living in JJ clusters, unauthorised colonies and villages of various categories and does not have access to the piped water supply and sewerage system.
- The Delhi Jal Board (DJB) has adopted the norm of water supply as 275 lpcd at the source of production.
- South and Southwest zones suffer on account of water shortage.
- A significant portion of the water supply network of 9000 kms 40-50 years old and the total distribution losses are about 40 per cent of the total water supplied. DJB has the target to bring down the leakage losses to 20 per cent.
- There are about 1 million connections where the supply is to be metered. DJB proposes to involve consumers as well as private players to ensure that the work of installation of all the 0.53 million meters is completed by May 2006.
- The water tariff, which was heavily subsidised, has been revised, still it continues to be subsidised.
- Rapid urbanisation of Delhi has put tremendous pressure on the groundwater table. DJB has

initiated a scheme of rainwater harvesting in Delhi under which DJB provides financial assistance up to 50 per cent of the total cost of structures.

- Under Bhagidari Scheme in the water sector, RWAs and various associations are actively participating with DJB in a number of activities.
- DJB is planning to switchover to 24 hours supply system in phases through private firms and utility operators.
- DJB has adopted universally proven state-of-art technologies at its WTPs. It is one of the few public utilities to undertake extensive work of GIS mapping of its various utilities. DJB has also initiated action to obtain ISO-9002 certification.

Policy Interventions and Recommendations (Drinking Water)

- Measures including water conservation, loss reduction, dual plumbing, water recycling need to be taken.
- There is significant variation in river flows during the lean periods. The proposals for construction of the reservoirs on Yamuna river need to be implemented.
- The Ministry of Water Resources should intervene and resolve the matter of availability of raw water for Sonia Vihar Water Treatment Plant.
- The withdrawal of ground water should be regulated. Central Ground Water Authority may consider delegating necessary powers to bring the management and development of groundwater under DJB.
- A decentralised approach for treating sewage may be more economic. The treated water from such STPs may be used for horticulture, parks and greening of Delhi.
- All the works and other measures in hand to augment and conserve water should be completed on priority.
- On the lines of Mumbai, wastewater from the high rise building should be treated *in-situ* to desirable standards and re-used for air conditioning and other industrial applications.
- Public awareness and education through the Bhagidari Scheme should be encouraged for conserving and managing potable water optimally.
- Delhi may have to depend on Yamuna only to meet the demand projected in the Master Plan Document-2021. An additional quantity of 350 cusec needs to be made available by the UYRB during the lean period.
- There is need to construct dams to minimise the shortfall during the lean periods. UYRB should be persuaded to treat the allocation of Yamuna water for consumptive use only.

Telecommunication

- Telecommunication has made commendable progress in all services. The number of Telephone subscribers (Fixed + Mobile) has increased from 3.17 million in March 2002 to 7.98 million in March 2005 in Delhi representing a growth rate of more than 35 per cent. This leads to a Telephone Density of more than 50 per 100 populations. The major growth has come from mobile telephones. There is a good competition with 6 service providers for mobile telephones in Delhi. There are about 100,000 PCOs (Public Call Office or Payphone) in Delhi. Internet service is also quite popular with a number of service providers giving this service.
- Broadband service is a recent phenomenon in India and Delhi. Government has recently announced a Broadband Policy. Broadband service provides "Triple Play" i.e., voice (telephony), data, and video which may include TV and video-on-demand. Broadband service will lead to great opportunity in tele-education, e-health, e-governance, entertainment, tele-working (home working) etc. A tele-working lead to less strain on transport system and is eco-friendly.
- Telecom technology is fast changing and it is difficult to assess resource requirement on long term basis. There is likely to be no problem on this score since the capital required (a few thousand crore Rupees per year) are arranged by service providers out of their revenue earnings and market borrowings.
- Introduction of private sector has led to good competition in telecom sector. This has led to a) faster growth b) lower tariff c) improved quality of service and d) new types of applications and service. TRAI (Telecom Regulatory Authority of India) and TDSAT (Telecom Dispute Settlement and Appellate Tribunal) have been set up under the TRAI Act 1997 to fix tariff, regulate the

telecom sector and provide for dispute settlement mechanism.

- Vision should include broadband to all households and mobile phone to all who need it.
- Central government is the main policy making authority for telecom but state government must make policies to facilitate proper and fast growth of telecom infrastructure.

18.5 Environment

a) The unprecedented growth of Delhi has an adverse impact on the environment. Motor vehicles are the biggest source of air pollution. The number of registered working factories has doubled between 1981 and 2000; so has the industrial production. The industrial census of 1988 gives a figure of 76559 industrial units in Delhi—many in residential or non-conforming areas. The problem of toxic gases and discharge of liquid wastes has been a problem leading to air and water pollution. The standards prescribed by the regulatory agencies have not always been enforced. Recent interventions by the Supreme Court have led to some improvement but these would continue to be problem areas.

b) The flora and fauna of Delhi have depleted to a very great extent. The ridge, which used to be the habitat of many species of plant and animal life, has had unprecedented human intrusions in the last century. The technological changes as also the exposure to foreign countries have brought tremendous changes in the life styles of people, working to the degradation of the environment.

18.6 Public Distribution System

PDS emerged as a social safety system making food grains available at a fair-price and to keep a check on the speculative tendencies in the market. Department of Food Supplies and Consumer Affairs, Delhi is responsible for the Public Distribution System. The Government of NCT of Delhi has a marked categorisation of the household consumers on the following basis:

- Wheat or rice eater
- LPG or kerosene user
- *Jhuggi* Ration card holder (JRC) & Permanent Ration Card holder (PRC)

In spite of various steps taken from time to time to streamline PDS it still has its weaknesses. Some of the measures taken by Department of Food Supplies and Consumer Affairs, Delhi for improving the efficiency of the system are as under:

- Area vigilance committees have been set up.
- There is a periodical checking of FPSs and mechanism of issuance of ration cards to identify and eliminate bogus rations cards.
- A system of 'Public Audit' has been introduced.
- Stern action against persons found guilty of misusing the TPDS benefit.
- Audio-Video cameras have been set up at the FPSs.
- Penalties are imposed for violation.
- Citizen Charter has been formulated.

It is recommended to implement the following in order to further improve the system:

- Reward for the meritorious and honest officers who are vigilant and care for people's needs.
- Recognition or annual award for the FSPs.
- There can be a provision for the supply of other essential items like tea, soap, matchbox etc. be made available through FPS.
- A timely arrival of food grains at FPS can ensure timely distribution of essential commodities. It is interesting to note that most of the people get their wages/salaries in first seven days of the month so the system should be such that it ensures the supply of food grains during that period. Failing which people will buy from the commercial outfits leading to non-lifting of the quota and diversion of supply to blank marketers.

18.7 Forest, Tree Crop Management, Greening, etc.

a) Current Status

NCT of Delhi has three main physiographical segments, *viz.*, Flood Plains of Yamuna, about the Ridge and the Plains. Agriculture is practiced extensively along the stretch of river. Most of the native vegetation has been cleared for the purpose of farming and the areas, which are not fit for agriculture, are used as grazing grounds when the floodwater recedes. The riverine ecosystem is under major threat.

On Delhi Ridge, planting was confined initially to indigenous species and *Prosopis juliflora* was introduced later, which showed good drought resistance and gradually the ridge has been covered with this species.

Although the capital has 12.5 trees per ha. as against the national average of 12, tree cover is unevenly distributed and is progressively declining. Delhi has 121 sq. km of forest cover and 40 sq. km of tree cover, which constitutes only 10.2 per cent of geographical area under green cover much less than 33 per cent as envisaged by National Forest Policy, 1988. More than 70 per cent of the forest cover is in south and southwest Delhi alone. The rest of Delhi has very little green cover and enormous biodiversity has been lost.

b) Management Initiatives and Past Afforestation

Various initiatives have been taken in the past to manage hotspots impacting Delhi's dwindling flora.

- A large portion of the ridge was declared a protected zone. Subsequently, large chunks of land on the ridge have also been notified Reserve Forest. Another development was the establishment of Asola Wildlife Sanctury in 1991 to enhance the protection and conservation of the city's floral and faunal diversity.
- Delhi Tree Preservation Act 1994 laid down heavy penalties on individuals, institutions and organisations for tree felling.
- Greening Delhi Action Plan is launched every year to undertake additional plantation. A task force under the chairmanship of the Conservator of Forests, Government of NCT, Delhi was constituted. The plantation scales in the recent past have increased from around one-lakh seedlings per year in mid-90s to about eleven lakhs presently.

c) Impediments

- Forests and tree cover in Delhi have always remained vulnerable to developmental activities.
- Inadequate coordination among agencies like forest department, CPWD, DDA and MCD further aggravates the existing threats.

d) Agencies their Role in Plantation

- An area of 8,422 hectares, marked as green, is managed by a large number of government and non-government agencies.
- The Forest Department is carrying out a number of activities for the development of forests including enrichment planting in ridge area to augment the natural regeneration. It has identified about 1,400 acres in different zones to develop into mini forests in addition to the ridge.
- DDA has a greening project. It is working in collaboration with the Department of Botany, Delhi University to develop a Bio-Diversity park along the Yamuna river-bed in North Delhi. It has fixed a target of planting 1.68 lakh trees during 2004-05
- The Municipal Corporation of Delhi (MCD) undertakes plantation in various areas such as schools, parks, bus stands and along roadsides. It has also set a target of planting 1.6 lakhs saplings in the current year.
- The New Delhi Municipal Committee (NDMC) undertakes tree plantation along the wide roads, residential areas, parks etc. It has proposed to plant 10,000 trees during 2004-05.
- Other agencies also are involved in plantation work. Residents Welfare Associations (RWAs), Market traders Associations (MTAs), non-governmental organisations and schools have planted 90 lakh seedlings in the last four years. Apart from this, 1500 Eco-clubs have been established in various schools/ colleges of Delhi.

e) Greening of Delhi—Vision 2015

In the next ten years Delhi should be one of the green and clean capitals of the world with high aesthetic value, providing its people a safe and healthy environment and setting up an example of a modern metropolis. The following strategic actions should be taken up in this regard:

- To expand green area the afforestation of all available areas should be undertaken. The feasibility of acquiring a 2 km wide area on both sides of Yamuna and a 2 km wide strip of available land along the border of the state of Haryana for developing it into a green belt should be examined. It would serve the dual purpose of protecting the flood plains from further encroachment and degradation as well as help in recharge of ground water.
- To protect Delhi from desertification from southwest direction, massive afforestation on private and public lands needs to be undertaken.

- The existing tree cover should be protected and maintained by strictly enforcing the provisions of The Delhi Preservation of Tree Act, 1994.
- Delhi Ridge should be preserved by adopting suitable combinations in which trees, shrubs and herbs co-exist as multi-layered vegetation. Assisted natural regeneration cum enrichment planting can be useful in conserving and protecting the biodiversity of this region.
- Information of green cover and forests should be maintained in Geographical Information System format for a which a suitably equipped Cell may be set up.

18.8 Wildlife Management

The fast pace of urbanisation leaves very little scope for wild life to thrive and it has been dwindling rapidly. However, efforts must be made to conserve whatever is possible under the circumstances. Efforts at increasing awareness about the importance of wild life conservation need to be made. Delhi is being used as a transit point for the illegal trade in wildlife products. There is need for increased vigil and action on part of the concerned authorities. A multi-pronged approach is required to manage the problematic species *Macaca mulatta* and captive elephants.

18.9 Education

Delhi is one of the few states in the county where literacy rate is above 80 per cent, but there are four other states/UTs with a higher literacy rates, and this is mainly attributable to continuous inward migration from relatively poor and underdeveloped states. The problem of out-of-school and school drop out children is prevalent in Delhi as in other states.

The MCD (Municipal Corporation) and NDMC (New Delhi Municipal Council) have responsibility for elementary education in their respective areas. The State Directorate of Education also looks after middle education and has converted 350 schools into composite, Sarvodaya Vidyalayas, covering classes from I to XII. The MCD has a network of 1,800 primary schools with 900,000 students. In addition, large numbers of private unaided or aided schools have come up in Delhi. About 20 lakh students study at any point of time in the government, aided or unaided schools in Delhi. However, there are uncovered areas and irregular settlements, especially of migrants, without a neighborhood school.

Delhi government in its 10th Plan has provided for economic support for students from the poor families and the weaker section to encourage the retention and check dropouts in schools at the elementary stage. It has also started taking measures under the new scheme of 'Sarva Shiksha Abhiyan' (SSA).

Other programmes include covering all government schools with computer education, setting up special schools for the talented children. In the MCD schools, free text books and uniforms are available to all children but girls also get free transport and stipends if they come from rural areas, JJ colonies or unauthorised colonies. Mid-day meals and stipends are the other direct incentives to encourage school attendance. The SSA has already prepared a plan of action and strategy to ensure that every child in 6-14 years age group gets main stream education. There is a special focus on weaker sections of the society and 'Bhagidari schemes' envisage government and community participation for the purpose. It is interesting to note that though the labour force participation rates of females is rather low in Delhi, the difference in enrolments between boys and girls is rather small.

The private (non-government) schools play a major role in providing school education; their share had already crossed 50 per cent in 1999, which may be closer to 53 per cent now.

There are also correspondence courses at school level and special programmes for the benefit of the school drop-outs, house wives, etc. Many government schools have also got assistance from private schools in management of academic and other programmes. Some private schools have offered to exchange their faculty with the government schools.

The 10th Five Year Plan of Delhi provides for Rs. 1,840 crore for general education. In addition, there are comparable allocations of funds for higher education institutions run under the Directorate of Higher Education of the Delhi government. The MCD and the NDMC also have a large allocation of funds under the 10th plan amounting.

At the post senior-secondary level, there are several technical institutions providing degree or diploma or even shorter courses with a certificate. Three more polytechnics are coming up during the 10th Plan while a number of community polytechnics are being strengthened with new courses in emerging technologies, computer education, etc. The community polytechnics, in particular, assist weaker sections of the society through non-formal training in basic skills, knowledge and correct attitudes leading to worthwhile self-employment.

The private sector contribution in various forms of training and skill development is not fully documented. Many private institutions are run by fly-by-night operators, which give a bad name to all others. In any case, there is no law like the Delhi School Education Act for full reporting of new technical training institutions, either for short or medium term courses. Long-term courses (Degree/Diploma) are regulated by the AICTE but not others.

There is need for a comprehensive survey of training providers. The training providers need some regulatory framework which has legal backing so as to ensure high standards of training and protect the trainees from exploitation.

18.10 Health

A) Current Status

- Delhi has done well in family welfare with birth rate being 18.1 against the national average of 25.4.
- Sex ratio at birth i.e., 820 females birth/1000 male births suggests the prevalence of sex selective abortion. This needs to be probed.
- Communicable diseases are still a major cause of morbidity. However, this trend is rapidly changing and is expected to reverse within the new next few years.
- Delhi represents a widely varying populace and correspondingly a widely varying disease pattern ranging from life style diseases on the one hand to the infective and malnutrition related diseases.
- Many urbanised villages lack basic infrastructure and proper planning of the residential areas leading to unhealthy overcrowding with unhealthy surroundings.
- The Life Expectancy at birth for Delhi's population is 68.6 years compared to an all India average of 60.7 years.
- Delhi has the best medical facilities available in the country, but most of them are beyond the reach of the common man. The per capita public expenditure at Rs. 436 in 2001-02 is more than double of the all-India average of 180. But this is inadequate since most people depend on the government hospitals and dispensaries.

B) Recommendations

- There are multiple agencies operating the health care outlets leading to/duplication of services, wastage of efforts and resources and deficient services. Exercise to optimise the use of available resources needs to be taken.
- Qualified hospital administrators need to be posted in government hospitals to improve their services.
- Integration of the local area family practitioners with the government hospitals and dispensaries in the area for two-way referrals needs to be promoted.
- Development of high-class healthcare infrastructure in NCR towns should be encouraged.
- In the localities deficient in potable water supply system, sewerage/sanitation system and electric supply infrastructure their improvement will minimise incidence of morbidity and mortality.
- Greater attention needs to be given to health education of public with emphasis on preventive aspects.
- Health related topics should be included in school and college curricula.
- Strict enforcement of laws for control of food/ water borne infections and adulterations is necessary.
- Health Insurance sector base and corporate support to their employees for medical check ups and treatments need to be widened.
- Well-equipped and dedicated trauma centres along the main highways entering Delhi need to be set up.
- Industries need to be shifted to outskirts to reduce health hazards, accidents, pollution and traffic congestion.
- The hazard caused by stray dogs and animals needs to be addressed to minimise traffic hazards/accidents and need for Anti Rabies vaccine.
- The values for various parameters like the gender, educational levels, residence type, region, religion, caste, community, socio-economic status, occupation, etc are not available and studies need to be undertaken accordingly.
- Policies and programmes should be oriented to the realisation of the 'Vision' of the Chief Minister to make Delhi as a 'role model' for healthcare infrastructure.

18.11 Tourism

18.11.1 National and State Policy

(a) The National priority for Tourism is low as reflected in the Five year Plans.

(b) This low priority is also reflected in state government policy.

(c) The Tenth Five year Plan provides a significant shift in policy:

(i) An increased importance has been given to Tourism and Tourism related infrastructure eg. Airports, Roads etc.

(ii) Provides increased opportunity for private investiment and participation in tourism development.

(iii) Furthering socio-economic objectives such as Employment generation, people's participation ('Bhagidari').

(d) The Policy and growth of tourism in the State of Delhi reflects the National trend.

18.11.2 Market Trends and Prospects

(a) Global trends indicate an annual growth of 4.5 per cent for international tourism in the 2002-2012 periods.

(b) In India the growth trend is higher at 9.7 per cent in the next ten years.

(c) Growth in domestic tourism is likely to be at a higher rate and will impact future growth.

(d) In Delhi the Commonwealth Games 2010 provides a special opportunity to development as a destination.

18.11.3 The New Tourism Policy of Delhi

(a) The Policy is based on "Tourism for All" and is covered under 'Bhagidari'.

(b) It is a Government led, private sector driven community welfare approach.

(c) Delhi should become a World Class Heritage City.

(d) Special imitiative will be taken in developing Tourism in the following areas:

(i) Cultural/Heritage tourism.

(ii) Business Tourism

(iii) Convention and Conference Tourism (MICE)

(iv) Increase ethnic appeal—handicrafts, fashion, cuisine.

(v) Leisure Tourism—shopping, golf, adventure

(vi) Medical/Health Tourism

(vii) Develop Delhi as a hub for Tourism in North India.

(e) Increased funds for projects and promotion activity

(f) Enlarged Training facility and Human Resource Development and create job opportunities.

18.11.4 An Evaluation of the Present Role and Status of Department of Tourism, DTTDC etc

(a) Delhi Tourism Department has a very limited role in creating an impact in Tourism in the State.

(b) Funds and resources disproportionately low for the objectives identified.

(c) DTTDC role as an implementing agency is diluted by other activities e.g. liquor trade, flyover construction.

18.11.5 A Broad Picture of the Delhi Tourism Scene

(a) Tourist traffic trends:

(i) Delhi accounts for 30.8 per cent of international arrivals.

(ii) It accounts for 51 per cent (1.35 million) of total arrivals of international tourists. This has been showing a downward trend (it was 62 per cent earlier).

(iii) It accounts for only 0.5 per cent of domestic tourists (most of them are pilgrim tourists).

(b) Hotel Room:

(i) Delhi has 9841 classified rooms—nearly half in the five star category.

(ii) Almost an equal number are in the unclassified category.

(iii) There is an obvious imbalance in the categories and classification spread in the tourist accommodation.

(iv) Growth in demand has led to recent scarcity of hotel rooms to the tune of 3,000 rooms.

(c) Tourist transport:

(i) Tourist transport needs to be strengthened by improving tourist transport facilities.

(ii) Existing infrastructure can be improved by better traffic movement, flyover, etc.

(iii) Improved services—Radio taxis, Volvo buses, easier inter state movement.

(iv) Metro will improve overall connectivity but have limited impact on tourist movement.

(d) Tourist traffic providers—Travel agents, tour operators, guides, need to improve this quality of service and reliability.

18.11.6 Suggestions—Way Forward for Delhi Tourism

(a) A new mindset for Tourism Development is needed. It means that—

(i) Tourism must be seen as "the industry of industries" to fully realise the socio-economic benefits.

(ii) A statutory Tourism Board will make for more effective implementation and management of Tourism in the state.

(iii) An empowered body such as a Tourism Board can effect better "Convergence" with important state agencies such as NDMC, DMC, DDA, Police, Transport etc.

(iv) It can also coordinate more effectively with Airport Authority, Railway, ASI etc.

(b) Delhi can become a world class Heritage City by developing "integrated tourism zones"—keeping tourism needs in mind and creating a unique tourism experience at each location as identified:

(i) Red Fort/Chandni Chowk

(ii) Purana Quila/Pragati Maidan/Humayun's Tomb

(iii) Rajiv Chowk, India Gate, Rashtrapati Bhawan.

(iv) Qutub Minar, Mehrauli heritage area, Garden of Five Senses.

(v) Create tourism friendly transport and other services linking them to Airport, Hotels, Railway station, and Road transport.

(c) Create a world class Convention facility with all related infrastructure and systems including administrative and manpower support.

(d) Develop Delhi as a destination for Medical Tourism—Task force recommendations or "Chemical Establishment Act", medical visa, health insurance and linkages with tourism marketing need to be acted on.

(e) Develop leisure and entertainment facilities at selected locations:

(i) Shopping—handicrafts, fashion goods, jewellery

(ii) Parks, gardens, water bodies, golf courses

(iii) Food and ethnic cuisine

(iv) Festivals and special events

(f) Create effective linkages with NCR and nearby destinations particularly Agra so as to prolong stay by tourists.

18.12 Employment, Rural Development and Poverty Alleviation:

(a) The main features of the employment situation and points on which action is required are

- The employment base in Delhi is almost entirely composed of services of various kinds and manufacturing
- It has a low workforce participation rate of 33.5 per cent as against 39.2 per cent at the national level.
- Males account for 86 per cent of labour force as a whole with urban areas indicating as high as 91 per cent share of the males. Majority workforce is in the regular/wage-employed category for females the figure is over 77 per cent.
- The largest sector of activity on the basis of workforce numbers is the service group trade and hotels etc., followed by public administration. Services are followed by manufacturing.
- The construction sector accounts for less than 6 per cent of total workforce.
- Delhi has an overall unemployment rate of 12.5 per cent, higher than the national level with very high unemployment rates for females in the age group 20-24 and 25-29 years.
- The male unemployment rates are very high for the age groups 15-19 and 20-24 years. These are much higher than the countrywide picture.
- In Delhi, the phenomenon of 'discouraged workers' could possibly reduce the workforce

participation rate and ultimately the rate of migration into Delhi itself.

- Educated unemployed form a large proportion of the unemployed.
- The simple rate of growth of the registered unemployed persons has been 2.5 per cent a year —majority of them is increasingly from the educated category.

(b) Suggestions

The above deficiencies in the employment situation need to be carefully examined and a plan prepared to take effective remedial measures. The employment situation reflects the state of health of the economy of the area and if the aspiration is to have Delhi as a capital which may be counted among the best capitals in the world, the situation will have to be addressed on priority.

18.13 Science & Technology

18.13.1 Categories of Activities

The activities in this sector can be divided into three categories:

(a) Category 1: S&T-IT&BT Education including technical training.

It includes school level science (including IT), vocational training in high technology (including IT related CAD/ CAM), popularisation of IT and lately also higher education in Science, IT and Biotechnology.

(b) Category 2: Research and Development in S&T-IT&BT.

(c) Category 3: Use of S&T-IT&BT in socio-economic sectors

It includes use of Information Technology (IT) in governance and health delivery, software industry and promotion of IT and Biotechnology related enterprise. S&T component is also reflected in programmes for development of rural areas, in energy supply, small-scale industry development and environmental protection.

18.13.2 Channels of Activities

Activities are channeled through three main agencies; the departments and institutions under the GNCTD (Government of Delhi), Laboratories of Central government agencies including Universities and IIT and Private sector including NGO.

- Government of the National Capital Territory of Delhi (GNCTD), MCD and NDMC are active in Category 1 and Category 3 programmes. Category 2, namely R&D is mainly performed by the laboratories of the Central Government and Universities and IIT located in the NCTD. The thrust of S&T activities supported by the State Government is on IT and science education in schools, IT in governance, IT and BT embedded in its industrial and rural development programmes.
- Private sector is active in IT and Biotechnology marketing and consultancy as also lately in. software industry through the IT Park being set up by the Delhi Metro Rail Corporation and in Biotechnology R&D Centre at South Campus of the University of Delhi.
- NGO participation is in science education, environment awareness, and water conservation and in rural development through Bhagidari is also note worthy.

18.13.3 Recommendations

(a) The vision from the point of Science and Technology should be to make the economy of National Capital Region of Delhi a knowledge intensive economy.

(b) One of the areas of thrust is to upgrade the technical competence of human resource in the use of modern techniques such as CAD/CAM and IT enabling them to work in industrial complexes.

(c) Manufacturing units being private sector ventures, the technical training and facilities need to be matched with the demand profiles of the manufacturing units. It would be appropriate to associate the companies with the training programmes.

(d) Improvement of rural parts of Delhi by applying so called rural technologies developed in laboratories is another development goal receiving attention in the development plans of Delhi.

(e) The maximum concentration of villages is in the Mehrauli sub-division of Delhi (28 villages). Linking technology suppliers/sources and the rural populations is critical for such programmes. Some business and management schools are located in and around rural areas and can become effective link institutions. Business and management schools need to be utilised for coordinated implementation including the activities of NGOs.

(f) It is recognised that knowledge industries are highly competitive and market niche of these units will have to be carefully developed. Exercise in this direction through industry involvement is necessary.

(g) Substantive investment is envisaged for introduction of IT in government departments. There is a desire in the plan to strengthen government-citizen interface. The Delhi Government has made progress towards computerisation of its administration.

(h) The next critical issue is the easy accessibility of information to the citizens. It is necessary to establish effective and sustainable network of access centres. These can be set up as micro enterprises. The example of the entrepreneurial model of AISECT (All India Society for Electronics and Computer Technology) that has already spread all over the country with maximum concentration in semi urban and rural areas of Madhya Pradesh and Chhattisgarh is worth emulating. AISECT model has been recognised by the Indian Innovation Award as the largest network with potential of wider applicability. This model can be effectively used in the National Capital Region.

(i) Setting up of IT and Biotechnology industrial units in Delhi are important new initiatives towards knowledge based industries. These are best established through industry-academic linkages making full use of Delhi's strong conglomeration of post graduate science and engineering education (including Biotechnology and IT) and of R&D laboratories supported by the State and the Centre.

18.14 Labour

18.14.1 Labour Situation

The main features of the labour situation in Delhi are:

(a) The proportion of employment in the organised sector is much higher than the national average.

(b) Most activities are still in the unorganised sector without proper reporting.

(c) The employment exchanges have failed to satisfy both the employers and potential employees. The organised sector has its own recruitment mechanisms.

(d) Both the employees and the training providers are more and more in the private sector.

(e) The job opportunities in Delhi have not only continued to grow, they have also changed and become more complex.

(f) Requirement of any skill or education level is met by outsiders coming to Delhi in search of employment.

(g) The casual workers in Delhi's small industries/ enterprises came from outside without much of skills and learned the crafts on-the-job.

18.14.2 Skill Development and Training

(a) In an open economy like Delhi, the classical methods of manpower balancing as part of manpower planning are not practical. It is also not practical to decide the length of the course, subject matter, the skill sets and the teachers at the government level in a centralised fashion.

(b) Delhi's economy lies mainly in the service sector whose needs are not known in advance. The government institutes have found it difficult to change courses/curricula to meet such short-term needs of potential employers.

(c) In the case of Information Technology enabled services private training providers did the job under some kind of supervision of the Ministry of IT and the government accepted a variety of courses with different lengths, different quality/ levels and different subject matters in the private unorganised sector. Likewise, there is enormous scope for innovation and participation by private sector to develop and organise a variety of courses.

(d) The providers of the training in the private sector are in a position to develop some skills of use to the employers; they need to be encouraged.

(e) In this regard ideas like Skill Development Fund have been mooted but none has come into existence so far.

(f) However, government must ensure proper supervision over such training providers so that fresh migrants or weaker sections of society are protected against potential exploitation.

18.14.3 Labour management

(a) Labour management especially that of skilled/educated labour force or those engaged in services outside the Government has not been a problem in the city.

(b) The behaviour of trade unions in large manufacturing enterprises, i.e. blue-collar workers has been always different from that in the service sector and educated people. Formal trade unions have not had much impact on workers in Delhi after a large number of manufacturing enterprises, especially the bigger ones shifted out of Delhi.

(c) The unorganised sector manufacturing, by definition, is not unionised; but such workers face potential exploitation such as low wages and long hours of work.

(d) The scheme of the NDA government for providing social security to unorganised sector workers became a non-starter.

(e) The government needs to provide some form of social security to such workers.

18.15 Social Development and Vulnerable Groups

18.15.1 Categories of Vulnerable Groups

Ten different segments are categorised as vulnerable groups that include women, socially disadvantaged groups, child labour and street children, the disabled and challenged, migrants, shelterless, those affected by the inadequacy of public transportation, unorganised workers (such as street vendors, sex and domestic workers), the elderly, and children facing violence and abuse.

18.15.2 Sources of Vulnerability

Vulnerabilities are derived from a host of parameters including social, physical, gender related, economic, financial, infrastructural, health-related, legal, political or institutional. Powerlessness, income and structural poverty, and social exclusion are the characteristics associated with vulnerabilities.

18.15.3 Women's Issues

The issues pertaining to women in Delhi in the context of vulnerability go beyond the poor and the needy and cover even the prosperous and better-off populations. There are various indicators to establish women's vulnerability. Declining sex ratio highlights the lower significance given to the girl child.

18.15.4 Socially Deprived Sections

The socially deprived sections belonging to Scheduled Castes and Other Backward Castes face social discrimination and educational differentiation in terms of access and retention. There are a number of socio-economic reasons. The initial unequal resource position perpetuates imbalance and disparity in their access to other infrastructure. In the labour market, they tend to find place in the lower echelons of the job hierarchies.

18.15.5 Children

(a) Substantial numbers of children in the capital work as service providers, helpers, assistants, vendors and so on.

(b) The poor, slum dwellers, pavement dwellers, shelterless, orphans, and street children are all vulnerable, easily exploitable and voiceless.

(c) The concerns of many of these workers are akin to the plight of the unorganised workers who are unprotected by legal provisions and have no security as workers.

(d) These children are deprived of childhood and avenues to develop themselves.

(e) The girl child is often left in charge of the younger siblings in order to relieve her mother for labour market participation at the cost of her own all round growth.

(f) The street children are exposed to and unprotected from abuse of various kinds, with the girls susceptible to finding themselves as part of trafficking and sex worker chains.

18.15.6 The Disabled

(a) The challenges posed by disability, both physical and mental render persons vulnerable.

(b) The lack of understanding regarding these adds to the difficulties of the challenged in negotiating the institutional and infrastructural constraints present.

(c) The incorporation of the disabled in the 2001 Census was a landmark that provided one crucial tool to make their presence and needs visible.

18.15.7 Migrants

(a) Migration into the capital-state from various parts has assumed a problem of tremendous magnitude.

(b) The migrants are able to find some paid employment, howsoever low paying and insecure.

(c) There are however, no provisions for them by the state administrative authorities in terms of housing, water, toilets, electricity and so on, leave alone the needs of their families.

(d) Commonly housed in some slum squatter settlement, these families have to face many difficulties.

(e) The attempt to clean the city and remove the slums by relocation and rehabilitation without adequate transportation facilities curtails the workers from negotiating between their residences and workplaces.

(f) There is need to re-examine the demand pattern for bus routes after resettlement of large slums as well as industrial complexes subsequent to closure of polluting industries.

18.15.8 Unorganised Sector Workers

(a) The vulnerability of the unorganised sector workers arises out of the ambiguity in their legal status as no overt recognition of their work/activity exists.

(b) These workers go through undue suffering.

(c) The lack of recognition as sex workers and the taboo attached to the service provider while the demander is often unaffected, makes the women sex worker vulnerable. The recognition of the sex worker to some extent has occurred in the context of the drive for protection against HIV/AIDS.

18.15.9 Vulnerable Groups Not Covered Above

(a) The elderly and the aged who are left alone in the city after children have gone for greener pastures or due to the death of the other family members, are vulnerable on account of the insecurity stemming from their loneliness and their health needs.

(b) Abuse and violence forms another deplorable dimension of vulnerability faced by children in the capital. From heinous crimes like rape and murder to kidnapping and abduction, there seems to be a growing incidence of crimes against children.

(c) The pedestrian in the wake of the flyovers and high speed roads that have come up faces great difficulty and feels unsafe while wanting to cross the road.

(d) In the context of transportation, the shrinking spaces for the manually driven handcarts, cycle rickshaws and bicycles make things difficult for the class.

18.16 Industrial Development

18.16.1 Contribution of Primary, Secondary and Tertiary Sectors in Economy of NCTD

(a) The contribution of the primary sector has rapidly declined and has become negligible. The share of manufacturing in the 80s and the first half of the 90s has declined from about 20 per cent to about 12 per cent. However, the contribution of the Tertiary Sector has been rapidly rising and dominant in the economy of the NCTD.

(b) The share of registered sub-sector (39.8 per cent) in total manufacturing in 2002-03 was well below its share for the nation as a whole at 66.1 per cent.

18.16.2 Contribution of Industry Groups

(a) The highest contributor to net value added was Textile Products (17.5 per cent) followed by Machinery and Equipment (12.0), Paper and Paper Products (6.7), Food Products (6.4), and Basic Chemicals (4.4).

(b) The concentration ratios derived in respect of both the top 3 and 5 industry groups suggest that there was clearly an increase in concentration, with the top two industry groups alone (Electricity etc., and Textile Products) contributing more than one-half to net value added.

(c) The Hirschman-Herfindahl indices derived for both the reference years also clearly indicate greater concentration in terms of share in NVA.

(d) In 2002-03, Delhi was heavily over-represented in Publishing, Printing, etc., Wearing Apparel, Radio, Television, Communication Equipment etc., and Furniture and Manufacturing.

(e) Industry groups that are gravely under-represented include Coke, Refined Petroleum Products etc., Tobacco Products, Other Non-Metallic Mineral Products, Textile Products, Basic Metals, and Wood and Wood Products except Furniture.

18.16.3 *Industrial Structure*

(a) In 2002-03, Delhi had the most specialised industrial structure as compared with the 14 major states.

(b) Decomposing employment growth indicates that in the 1980s nine industry groups experienced industry-mix and competitive effects that were both positive. These were Beverages, Tobacco and Related Products, Textile Products, Leather and Leather Products, Basic Chemicals and Chemical Products, Rubber and Plastic Products, Machinery and Equipment, Repair of Capital Goods, Generation and Distribution of Gas, Steam etc., and Storage and Warehousing Services.

(c) The industry-mix and competitive effects operated very differently in the 90s. Out of the 22 industry groups only nine had a positive industry mix effect and even more significantly, only 3 groups experienced a positive competitive effect.

(d) Examination of some of the ratios and technical coefficients underlying the overall industrial (factory) structure indicates that the region does not seem to be suffering from locational disadvantages (relative to the country at large) associated with high levels capital use.

(e) In 2002-03, the capital intensity for the region (average for all industries factory sector) was lower than the national average.

18.16.4 *Productivity and Other Indicators*

(a) The capital-output ratio was also lower within the region, being only slightly above half of the national ratio. Not more than five industry groups had capital-output ratios higher than the respective groups at the national level and of these only the last two were among the major groups within the region.

(b) The average wage rate of labour went up in absolute terms over the period 1980-81 to 2001-2002, this increase being commensurate with that for the entire industrial system (factory sector) of the country at large.

(c) Labour productivity also increased for Delhi during this period as it did at the all-India level.

(d) Delhi's industries utilised a greater amount of input per unit of output relative to the industries at the all India level. In 2002-03, only 8 industry groups had input use levels lower than their counter parts at the national level. Of these, industry groups Food Products and Beverages, and Machinery and Equipment were among the more important groups in Delhi's industrial sector.

(e) There was less generation of value added per unit of output by the regional industrial system as compared to the nation. In 2002-03, 10 industry groups had higher value added per unit of output values than that for all-India.

(f) The profitability of Delhi's industrial system, measured as profits per unit of value of output, was below that of the three industrialised states-Maharashtra, Gujarat, and Tamil Nadu for most of the 80s and then, though fluctuating, became comparable with them. The profit ratio for Delhi was actually the highest for about half of the remaining period.

(g) The profitability of Delhi's industrial (factory) sector was below that of the nation for much of the decade of the 80s but moved up above all-India levels for the remainder of the period, except for 1995-96 and 1996-97.

(h) From the mid-90s, total factor productivity of Delhi's industries grew at rates faster than that of the nation and even that experienced by the three developed industrial states. Delhi's industrial system seems to be becoming relatively more efficient than the rest of the country in terms of factor use.

18.16.5 *Priorities*

(a) Though manufacturing accounts for about 12 per cent of Delhi's GSDP and about 40 per cent of the total work force, the priority given to the industrial sector in the Five Year Plans is extremely low. In the Tenth Plan, the share of industry in the outlay decreased by nearly half to a mere 0.43 per cent of total outlays as compared to its expenditure share in the Ninth Plan.

(b) In terms of expenditure priorities, industry dropped to rank nineteenth out of a total of 31 sectors. The all-States average outlay on industry for the Tenth Plan is 3.2 per cent—nearly eight times that for Delhi.

18.16.6 *Environmental Factors Impact on Industry*

(a) The closure of many polluting and hazardous industrial units and the Relocation Scheme for non-conforming units, though reducing environmental pollution levels, may be expected to have had an adverse impact on industrial growth and employment within Delhi.

(b) The contribution of industrial sources of pollution (including Thermal Power Plants) to ambient air has come down from 56 per cent in 1970-71 to 20 percent in 2000-01, and with the coming into operation of all the 15 CETPs the contribution of this sector to both air and water pollution levels would be heavily reduced.

(c) Under these circumstances there is some justification for the ongoing effort for regularisation of other industries situated in residential/non-conforming areas.

(d) Corrective measures incorporating a system of suitable incentives and disincentives are required in relation to such industries in order to ensure shifting and relocation of industries failing to meet the broadened parameters in terms of environmental and other norms.

18.16.7 Need of Diversification, Dispersal and Technological Upgradation

There is clearly a need for policy intervention to ensure greater diversification of Delhi's industrial base in terms of development of new industries that are hi-tech and high value added in nature. Ad hoc licensing of industrial units should be avoided and policy measures introduced to ensure dispersal of existing industries as well as their modernisation and technological upgradation.

18.17 Agriculture and Allied Activities

The National Capital Region is witnessing a surge of physical and economic growth of Delhi and under development of the area outside. The process of globalisation relies primarily on private sector initiative, aided by the evolution of the global information network. There is constant influx of population into Delhi. Central government has a very important supportive or facilitating role in this connection to check this influx of population from villages to the cities and Metros. Strategies should focus upon retaining the farming population to villages through creating better opportunities at farm.

Initiatives as mentioned in NCR Plan (2001) need to be translated into following concrete action at grass root level:

- Training programmes in micro-entrepreneurship, processing of local produce, vocational skill up gradation etc. Allied agro-economic activities such as poultry, dairy, pottery, handlooms, handicrafts and rural tourism may be encouraged.
- Financial incentives and loan schemes for starting micro-enterprises.
- Rural settlements may be planned to have the very best technological input in various aspects of its development including rural sanitation, water supply, communications and information system.
- Cultivating non-conventional crops such as mushrooms, broccoli, babycorn, bamboo shoot, poultry, fish etc. as well as floriculture. The state government should provide necessary infrastructure in terms of technical know-how, finance and marketing support facilities, etc. to the farmers to promote the non-conventional high value commercial farming in the NCR.
- Promotion of strategic partnership between government agencies, private sector, NGOs and cooperatives in the area of marketing, research & development and development of rural infrastructure.
- Dissemination of relevant information on regular basis to apprise rural people about the new opportunities on-going programmes, sources of micro-credit, market potentials, etc.

Resource Constraints like improper information network, transport system, packing houses and modernised market places result in farmers fetching low price for their produce. But Delhi has a number of premier institutions of agricultural research, and like IARI and these can be looked for all sorts of technical guidance.

It is recommended to implement the following schemes:

- Unemployed but educated rural youth and women are available to be trained in vegetable cultivation for gainful employment and increased production. This potential needs to be tapped.
- A fresh vegetable export zone (VEZ) can be established comprising of a group of villages involved in custom production conforming to norms of export in certain low volume-high value vegetables.
- Protected cultivation of off-season vegetables of high quality.
- Organic farms can be established and recycled wastes from city and APMC *Mandis* (fresh vegetables sale points) consumed as organic

manure. This will also reduce environmental pollution and health hazards.

- Arrangement/production of sufficient planting material/seed including F1 seed. And establishment of commercial nursery seed production units.
- Establishment of protected crop cultivation demonstration units.
- Establishment of model production farms for fresh vegetable export.
- Promotion of IPM, IPNM and micro–irrigation (drip, sprinkler) systems.
- Development/improvement of infrastructural facilities for post harvest management of the produce, including cool chain, cold storage, etc.
- Reclamation and conversion of un-utilised cultivable land, wasteland, fallow land, and riverbed and Diara land area into scientific vegetable cultivation.
- Promotion of organic farming, mushroom cultivation and bee keeping.
- Promotion of cultivation and marketing of medicinal and aromatic plants. Development of market information system to regulate supply, price, and efficient sale of the produce.

18.18 Institutional Reforms and Governance

18.18.1 Evolution of Institutions of Governance:

(a) Having gone through various phases, the present status of Delhi has evolved with the enactment in January 1992, of the Government of National Capital Territory of Delhi. As Union Territory with an Assembly and a Council of Ministers, NCTD has very many features of a State. Yet Delhi is not a State as its powers are seriously curtailed as mentioned below:

(i) It has no power to make laws relating to public order, police and offences relating to the subjects and law and order and land are within the jurisdiction of the Government of India.

(ii) Even in respect of other subjects the Parliament has overriding powers to make laws.

(iii) The Lt. Governor is a powerful institution and ensures that the governance runs smoothly.

(iv) The advice of the Council of Ministers to the Lieutenant Governor is not binding.

(v) A Bill of Amendment relating to financial matters shall not be introduced in the Assembly except on the recommendations of the Lt. Governor.

(vi) The annual budget is to be laid before the Legislative Assembly by the Lt. Governor with the previous sanction of the President.

(vii) Delhi is a city state in that most of its geographical area is included within the Municipal Corporation of Delhi (MCD), New Delhi Municipal Committee (NDMC), and the Cantonment Board, bodies which are very powerful providing civic and other services. These are legal bodies and are very powerful, specially the MCD.

(b) The Delhi Development Authority, set up in December 1957 is the apex agency for planning and development of the city, is empowered to prepare plans, to implement and enforce them and to develop, manage and dispose of lands in Delhi. It also discharges the functions of developing housing, commercial centres, parks, playgrounds, etc.

(c) The multifarious factors have led to the evolution of institutions that are required to satisfy, in some matters, seemingly irreconcilable interests and objectives. This has resulted in a complex system of governance with a multiplicity of organisations and institutions and, quite often, duplication of functions.

(d) Problems arise between state government and Government of India and its agencies; state government and MCD. The Lt. Governor is a powerful institution and ensures that the governance runs smoothly.

18.18.2 Measures Initiated to Improve Governance in the Government of NCTD

Although the issues of governance needing attention are large and many are under multiple authorities, all organisations are conscious of the fact that there is considerable scope for improvement of governance. The media is playing an important role in raising awareness among all sections of population and though rather slowly, one finds improvements taking place in systems that result in improving efficiency and movement to a more citizen friendly and law enforcing governance.

(a) Vision

The Government of Delhi has adopted a vision to facilitate the pursuit of excellence in governance through improvements in Government structures and processes.

(b) Means Used

The means used to achieve the improvements consist of:

- Promote role of civil society, People's participation and decentralisation through the introduction of Bhagidari Scheme within the government departments and its agencies including those under the Union Government.
- Institute Preventive Vigilance.
- Introduction of:
  - e-Governance for the citizens of Delhi and creation of a dynamic websites of Departments/Agencies.
  - Right of the citizen to information.
  - Mechanism to redress public grievances of which establishment of Public Grievances Commission are the main elements.
  - Civil Service Reforms.
  - Procedural Reform.
  - Synergy and Coordination.
  - Empowerment of the weak.

(c) Bhagidari Scheme

The Bhagidari Programme envisages voluntary participation of the citizens. Efforts have been made to make it well structured and sustainable. Nine organisations and 64 of their activities have been covered. A 'Bhagidari Cell' has been created in the Chief Minister's office. A detailed plan of 'Citizen-Government Interface' has been prepared. It has been decentralised at the Revenue District level.

In consultation with the Asian Centre for Organisation Research and Development, (ACORD), the "Large Group Interactive Events' (LGIE) a model was developed to train citizen-groups and government officials to agree on solutions and their implementation.

The programme has shown encouraging results leading to the formation of more than 1200 citizen groups that have not only been successful in addressing their day-to-day problems, but have also been providing help to public utility departments in maintenance and upgradation of services.

(d) Decentralisation

Administrative Decentralisation:

With a view to making the access of the citizen to the government easier, in 1996 the exercise of decentralising the DC office was done by setting up 27 SDM offices and 9 DC offices.

(e) Vigilance

- The Central Vigilance Commissioner has jurisdiction over personnel of the NCTD.
- The Delhi Lokayukta & Upalokayukta Act, 1995 provides a forum for attending to complaints against public functionaries to eradicate the vice of corruption, favouritism, abuse of position and power and present cleaner image. The Act takes within its ambit the Ministers including the Chief Minister, Members of Legislative Assembly, Members of Municipal Corporation etc.

(f) Preventive Vigilance–Openness and Transparency

The Government of NCT of Delhi has initiated the following actions with emphasis on "preventive vigilance".

- *e-Governance for the Citizens of Delhi:* The government has set up a dynamic website of Departments/Agencies to provide online services including services on e-applications and making online complaint. The citizen can also check the status of the complaint, send a reminder and send suggestions.
- *Right to Information:* The Delhi Right to Information Act, 2001 makes provision for securing information as a matter of right. It provides for right to appeal in Public Grievances Commission.
- *Public Grievances Commission:* The Government has set up a Public Grievance Commission, which attends to complaints received against the departments of Government of Delhi, its local bodies, undertakings, autonomous institutions/ undertakings etc.
- *Citizens' Charter:* The citizens' charter programme has been adopted in the NCTD. These charters are required to spell out the standards of services and time limits within which the public can reasonably expect the disposal of the requests made by them to the government. Delhi Government has brought out 73 such citizens

charters. Coupled with the enactment of the Right to Information and putting in to place the mechanism of dealing with public grievances, the framework of providing the basic information to the public and to open the vistas of transparency and accountability in the systems has been created.

18.18.3 Measures to Improve Governance in Municipal Corporation of Delhi

(a) The Municipal Corporation of Delhi provides civic services to some of the most densely populated areas in the world covering both rural and urban areas. The measures initiated are briefly mentioned below:

(b) The entire MCD area is divided into 12 zones to make access easier.

(c) Citizen Service Bureau:

The concept behind establishing Citizen Service Bureau is to provide all municipal services under one roof. MCD has started a unique and path breaking IT initiative with the objective to deliver electronically its services to citizens of Delhi through a Citizen Service Bureau set-up, one in each Zone and one at Town Hall.

18.18.4 Measures to Improve Governance in New Delhi Municipal Council (NDMC)

(a) NDMC is a municipality with a difference and also performs the role of a mini-government. It is perhaps the only municipality in the country that supplies electricity and water and its discretionary functions encompass promotion of sports, art, music and culture, maintenance of libraries, and care for the old, mentally and hearing impaired.

The area of NDMC includes the seat of Central Government, Rashtrapati Bhawan, the Prime Minister's office and residence, Central government office, Foreign Missions, residences of Ministers, Members of Parliament, Diplomats and Central government employees.

(b) Measures taken to improve governance include:

- *Citizens' Charter*

The NDMC had issued the first charter in 1997 and has issued the new one in February 2005. It is a measure towards transparency and efficient and timely provision of services. Grievance Redressal System:

- *Information and Facilitation Centre*

NDMC has set up an Information and Facilitation Centre and opened two Palika Suvidha Kendras where citizens can pay their taxes, fees etc., obtain birth/death certificates, book *Barat Ghars* and register their complaints relating to civic services.

- *Annual Administrative Report*

The NDMC publishes an Annual Administrative Report enabling those interested in getting to know the work done in the year gone by and the programme for the coming year.

18.18.5 Delhi Development Authority

(a) Delhi Development Authority was constituted by promulgating the Delhi Development Act, 1957 with the primary objective of ensuring the development of Delhi in accordance with a plan. Planned development of Delhi is the main function of DDA. Presently the *Master Plan for Delhi-2021* is under preparation.

(b) Despite very impressive achievements of DDA, it has an image of being an organisation that needs to improve its sensitivity to the needs of its clients, efficiency and public perception about integrity of the organisation. The organisation is actively engaged in taking a host of measures among which transparency and automation are basic which if successful can make a qualitative impact.

Transparency and Automation in DDA

To minimise downtime, it has introduced systemic automation in the following departments:

- Land Disposal.
- Housing.
- Launching of a Website, which is dynamic and provides information on various aspects like housing, land, master plan, environment etc. The results of housing and land and tender notices are displayed. Senior officers are reachable through e-mail. Different forms are available on the website which can be down loaded.
- Land Record.
- Normal administrative functions such as payroll, receipt and dispatch, legal cases monitoring system etc. A training programme for computer literacy seeks to train the staffing in the use of computers.
- Vigilance department takes action to see that there are no unwarranted irregularities and also handle complaints that could tarnish the image of the DDA.